THE GOOD BOOK

THE GOOD BOOK

THE GOOD BOOK

A HUMANIST BIBLE

CONCEIVED SELECTED REDACTED ARRANGED WORKED
AND IN PART WRITTEN BY

A. C. GRAYLING

Walker & Co.
New York

Published by Walker Publishing Company, Inc., New York

All papers used by Walker & Company are natural, recyclable products made from wood grown in well-managed forests. The manufacturing processes conform to the environmental regulations of the country of origin.

LIBRARY OF CONGRESS CATALOGING-IN-PUBLICATION DATA HAS BEEN APPLIED FOR.

ISBN: 978-0-8027-1737-5 (hardcover)

Visit Walker & Company's Web site at www.walkerbooks.com

First U.S. edition 2011

1 3 5 7 9 10 8 6 4 2

Typeset by Hewer Text UK Ltd, Edinburgh
Printed in the U.S.A. by Quad/Graphics, Fairfield, Pennsylvania

EPISTLE TO THE READER

Dear reader:

It might be thought vain to offer a work such as this to humankind in the hope that it will be useful, because the diversity of principles, ideas and tastes among people is very great, as is the fixity of our notions and our reluctance to change. But in truth it would be a greater vanity to offer a work for any other reason. Let the sincerity of the intention, then, be this book's main commendation. No work of this or any kind can please everyone, whatever its ambition; but this one at least gives satisfaction to its maker, of having aimed sincerely at truth and usefulness, and having done so by following in the paths of the wise. Throughout history the commonwealth of humankind has had master-thinkers whose mighty works are monuments to posterity; it is aspiration enough to be a guide among them, and to take from them resources to promote what is true and good.

All who read this book, therefore, if they read with care, may come to be more than they were before. This is not praise of the work itself, but of its attentive readers, for the worth to be found in it will come from their minds. If there is anyone who learns nothing from this book, that will not be attributable to faults in it, but to that reader's excellence. If readers judge candidly, none among them can be harmed or offended by what it asks them to consider. Yet all who come hungry to these granaries of the harvest made by their fellows and forebears, will find nourishment here.

Every art and inquiry, and similarly every action and pursuit, aims at some good; therefore the ultimate good has rightly been described as that at which all things aim. If there is a goal of what we do that we desire for its own sake, everything else being desired for the sake of this, that goal must constitute our chief and highest good. Seeking knowledge of that good cannot fail to have a great influence on life. When archers choose a target to aim at, they are more likely to aim true; shall we not do likewise by having as our target the discovery and doing of what is right? To determine what the good is, and of the best ways to know it, is the most important of all our endeavours, and is truly the master art of living.

Here in your hands is just such an endeavour, consisting in distillations of the wisdom and experience of humankind, to the end that reflecting on them might bring profit and comfort. It has been remarked that a person who fishes a stream might find something of advantage to himself there, but he who takes his nets to the ocean might expect greater catches, and from greater depths. In what follows these great catches are brought before us by fishers of wisdom, returned from the storms as well as the calms of their voyages, and from both near and distant shores.

Anyone who rises above his daily concerns in hope of finding and following truth, will discover it here. Every moment of the pursuit of truth rewards the pursuer's pains, when seeking it alongside the great company of those who have trodden the paths of life before us. These are gifts which they have passed back to us; they have freely given the best of themselves, and their gifts have been freely accepted here. Other such books have been similarly made: writings of many hands, ancient and otherwise, taken, wrought, arranged, edited, supplemented and changed, and offered with a familiar purpose in view. Here the procedure has been the same, but the purpose is different: not to demand acceptance of beliefs or obedience to commands, not to impose obligations and threaten with punishments, but to aid and guide, to suggest, inform, warn and console; and above all to hold up the light of the human mind and heart against the shadows of life.

For we live in deeds, not years; in thoughts, not breaths; and our time should be counted in the throbs of our hearts as we love and help, learn and strive, and make from our own talents whatever can increase the stock of the world's good.

To let light in upon ignorance and falsehood is a service to human understanding; a yet greater service is to show the way to an upland where the view of life is clearer. It is certain, therefore, that most readers will find profit in the following pages, if they read with the attention that those pages merit. How can it be otherwise? All times are seasonable to the increase of wisdom, and no time is lost when spent in the kind of company that inhabits here.

For this is a good book as well as a book of the good, its words from mighty pens, its thoughts from votaries of the right and true. It is a text made from all times for all times, its aspiration and aim the good for humanity and the good of the world.

CONTENTS

GENESIS

Chapter 1

1. In the garden stands a tree. In springtime it bears flowers; in the autumn, fruit.
2. Its fruit is knowledge, teaching the good gardener how to understand the world.
3. From it he learns how the tree grows from seed to sapling, from sapling to maturity, at last ready to offer more life;
4. And from maturity to age and sleep, whence it returns to the elements of things.
5. The elements in turn feed new births; such is nature's method, and its parallel with the course of humankind.
6. It was from the fall of a fruit from such a tree that new inspiration came for inquiry into the nature of things,
7. When Newton sat in his garden, and saw what no one had seen before: that an apple draws the earth to itself, and the earth the apple,
8. Through a mutual force of nature that holds all things, from the planets to the stars, in unifying embrace.
9. So all things are gathered into one thing: the universe of nature, in which there are many worlds: the orbs of light in an immensity of space and time,
10. And among them their satellites, on one of which is a part of nature that mirrors nature in itself,
11. And can ponder its beauty and significance, and seek to understand it: this is humankind.
12. All other things, in their cycles and rhythms, exist in and of themselves;
13. But in humankind there is experience also, which is what makes good and its opposite,
14. In both of which humankind seeks to grasp the meaning of things.

Chapter 2

1. Those who first set themselves to discover nature's secrets and designs, fearlessly opposing mankind's early ignorance, deserve our praise;
2. For they began the quest to measure what once was unmeasurable, to discern its laws, and conquer time itself by understanding.
3. New eyes were needed to see what lay hidden in ignorance, new language to express the unknown,
4. New hope that the world would reveal itself to inquiry and investigation.
5. They sought to unfold the world's primordial sources, asking how nature yields its abundance and fosters it,

6. And where in its course everything goes when it ends, either to change or cease.

7. The first inquirers named nature's elements atoms, matter, seeds, primal bodies, and understood that they are coeval with the world;

8. They saw that nothing comes from nothing, so that discovering the elements reveals how the things of nature exist and evolve.

9. Fear holds dominion over people when they understand little, and need simple stories and legends to comfort and explain;

10. But legends and the ignorance that give them birth are a house of limitations and darkness.

11. Knowledge is freedom, freedom from ignorance and its offspring fear; knowledge is light and liberation,

12. Knowledge that the world contains itself, and its origins, and the mind of man,

13. From which comes more know-ledge, and hope of knowledge again.

14. Dare to know: that is the motto of enlightenment.

Chapter 3

1. All things take their origin from earlier kinds:

2. Ancestors of most creatures rose from the sea, some inhabitants of the sea evolved from land-dwelling forefathers;

3. Birds descend from creatures that once ran flightless on the ground;

4. Horned cattle, the herds and all the wild creatures of nature, that graze

both the wasteland and the sown, are the progeny of earlier kinds.

5. Nor do fruits for ever keep their ancient forms, but grow new forms through time and nature's changing course.

6. Could such be the outcome of an anarchy in things, arbitrarily arising from nothing? No:

7. For nature is orderly, and works by measure; all things arise from the elements in their generations,

8. Each kind exists by its own nature, formed from the primal bodies that are their source, and descended by steps through life's rhythms.

9. We see lavished over the lands at spring the rose, at summer heat the corn,

10. The vines that mellow when autumn brings them to ripeness, because the seeds of things at their own season stream together,

11. And new forms and births are revealed when their due times arrive, and pregnant earth safely gives her offspring to the shores of light.

12. But if they came from nothing, without order and natural law, they might suddenly appear, unforeseen, in alien months, without parent;

13. Nor would they grow from living seeds, if life were an arbitrary product of emptiness or chaos:

14. Then the newborn infant would suddenly walk a man, and from the turf would leap a full-branched tree;

15. Rather, by nature each thing increases in order from its seed,

and through its increase conserves its kind.

Chapter 4

1. From this comes the proof that nature's bounty has proper origins in all its forms.
2. The fruitful earth, without its seasons of rains and sun, could not bear the produce that makes us glad,
3. And everything that lives, if deprived of nourishment, could neither survive nor further its kind.
4. We see that all things have elements in common, as we see letters common to many words.
5. Why should nature not make men large enough to ford the seas afoot, or tear mountains with their hands,
6. Or conquer time with great length of days, if it were not that all things are subject to proportion?
7. We see how far the tilled fields surpass the untilled, returning to the labour of our hands their more abounding crops;
8. Would we see, without toil of ours, the straight furrow and the tended orchard, fairer forms than ours coming from spontaneous generation? Yes;
9. For nature likewise is a husbandman, whose ploughshare turns the fertile soil and kneads the mould, quickening life to birth;
10. Nothing comes from nothing; all things have their origins in nature's laws, and by their edicts reach the shores of light.

Chapter 5

1. When things fall and decay they return to primal bodies again; nothing perishes to annihilation.
2. For if time, that wastes with age the works of all the world, destroyed things entirely, how would nature's generations replenish themselves, kind by kind?
3. How might the water-springs of the mountain, and the far-flowing inland rivers, keep the oceans full?
4. And what feeds the stars? Time and ages must otherwise eat all things away, except that nature's laws infallibly rule that nothing returns to nothing.
5. Behold, the rains, streamed down from the sky, sink into the earth; then springs up the shining grain,
6. And boughs are green amid the trees, and trees themselves are heavy with fruit.
7. By these gifts of nature mankind and all creatures are fed; so joyful cities thrive with children, and woodlands echo with birdsong;
8. Cattle, fat and drowsy, lay their bulk in the pastures while their milk flows, and sheep grow their wool on lush hillsides;
9. Nature offers its bounties; the kind earth gives up its stores; then what is given returns to its source, to prepare bounties anew;
10. Nothing perishes utterly, nor does anything come to birth but through some other thing's death,
11. For death is nothing but the origin

of life, as life is the compensation of death.

Chapter 6

1. And now, since nature teaches that things cannot be born from nothing,
2. Nor the same, when born, be recalled to nothingness, do not doubt this truth because our eyes cannot see the minute parts of things.
3. For mark those bodies which, though known and felt, yet are invisible:
4. The winds lash our face and frame, unseen, and swamp ships at sea when the waves rage, and rend the clouds,
5. Or, eddying wildly down, strew the plains with broken branches, or scour the mountaintops with forest-rending blasts.
6. The winds are invisible, yet they sweep sea, lands, the clouds along the sky, vexing and whirling all amain;
7. Invisible, yet mighty as the river flood that dashes houses and trees headlong down its raging course,
8. So that even a solid bridge cannot bide the shock when floods over-whelm: the turbulent stream,
9. Strong with a hundred rains, beats round the piers, crashes with havoc, and rolls beneath its waves down-toppled masonry and ponderous stone,
10. Hurling away whatever opposes it. Even so the blasts of the hurricane, like a mighty flood hither or thither driving all before,

11. Or sometimes in their circling vortex seizing and bearing helpless objects in whirlwinds down the world:
12. Yet these invisible winds are real, both in works and ways rivalling mighty rivers whose waters we can see.

Chapter 7

1. Consider, too, we know the varied perfumes of things, yet never see the scent touch our nostrils;
2. With eyes we do not see heat, nor cold, yet we feel them; nor do we see men's voices, yet we hear them: everything is corporeal,
3. All things are body or arise from it; the real is the corporeal, visible and invisible alike.
4. Raiment, hung by the surf-beaten shore, grows moist; the same, spread before the sun, then dries;
5. No one saw how the moisture sank in, nor how it was lifted by heat. Thus we know that moisture is dispersed in parts too small to see.
6. A ring upon the finger thins away along the under side, with the passing of the years;
7. Raindrops dripping from our roof's eaves will scoop the stone;
8. The hooked ploughshare, though of iron, wastes insidiously amid the furrows of the fields.
9. We see the rock-paved highways worn by many feet, and the gates' bronze statues show right hands leaner from the greeting touch of wayfarers.

10. We see how wearing-down diminishes these, but what tiny parts depart, the envious nature of vision bars from our sight.
11. Lastly whatever days and nature add little by little, constraining things to grow in due proportion,
12. No unaided gaze, however keen, sees. No more can we observe what time steals, when things wane with age and decay,
13. Or when salt seas eat away the beetling cliffs. Thus nature by unseen bodies and forces works;
14. Thus the elements and seeds of nature lie far beneath the ordinary gaze of eyes,
15. Needing instead the mind's gaze, the eye of science and reason's eye, to penetrate and understand;
16. And at last the instruments that man's ingenuity has devised, to see and record the minute parts of things,
17. And nature's ultimates, from which its infinite variety is built.

Chapter 8

1. Bodies are unions of the primal atoms. And these no power can quench; they live by their own powers, and endure.
2. Though it is hard to think that anything is solid; for lightnings pass, like sound, through walls,
3. And iron liquefies in fire, and rocks burn with fierce exhalations in the volcano's heart, and burst asunder;
4. Rigid gold dissolves in heat; cold bronze melts, conquered by the flame;
5. Warmth and the piercing cold seep through silver, since, with cup in hand, we often feel either, when liquid pours in;
6. It seems that nothing truly solid can be found, other than the world's foundation of elements.
7. But if nature had given scope for things to be dissolved for ever, no more rejoined or renewed in being,
8. By now all bodies that once existed would be reduced to ultimate parts alone, nothing returned or built from them again.
9. For each thing is quicker marred than made; whatever the long infinitude of days and all fore-passed time dissolved,
10. That same could never refurnish the world, no matter how much time remained.
11. Yet we see things renewed, in their seasons and after their kind: renewed or new made, by nature's laws and necessities;
12. We see how things endure, great crags of basalt and bars of strong iron, demonstrating the foundations of nature's frame.
13. The entities and forces underlying everything are powerful in their ancient simplicity, knitting and tying all objects.
14. By this they show their strength, binding each other by bonds which our senses do not perceive:
15. A bonding that exists within all

parts, in the minima of nature,
each thing itself a parcel of another,

16. From which other parts and others
similar in order lie, packed in
phalanx: the plenitude of body.

17. Whatever has parts, its parts have
their bonds, connections and
motions, whereby things have
being, and continue, decay, and
renew.

18. What is less than atoms make
atoms; and atoms, molecules; and
these in the animate and inanimate
make the solid, liquid and gaseous
varieties that in their systems and
relationships are nature,

19. Forming everything from the
animalcule to the host of stars that
figure the night with brilliance, vast
in time and space.

Chapter 9

1. The generations of the world and
life in the world evolve, one from
another, through the vastness of
time.

2. Earths from each sun burst, and
second planets issued from the first;

3. Then the sea at their coeval birth,
surge over surge, involved the
shoreless earth;

4. Nursed by warm sunlight in the
primeval caves, organic life arose
beneath the waves.

5. First, heat from chemical changes
springs, and gives to matter its
elliptic wings;

6. With strong repulsion parts the
exploding mass, melts into solids,
or kindles into gas.

7. Attraction next, as earth or air
subside, the heavy atoms from the
light divide,

8. Approaching parts with quick
embrace combine, swell into
spheres, and lengthen to a line.

9. Last, as fine goads the matter-
threads excite, cords grapple cords,
and webs with webs unite,

10. And quick contraction with
ethereal flame lights into life the
atom-woven frame.

11. Hence in biochemical spontaneous
birth rose the first specks of
animated earth;

12. From nature's womb the plant or
insect swims, and buds or breathes,
with microscopic limbs.

13. In earth, sea, air, around, below,
above, life's subtle weft in nature's
loom is wove;

14. Points joined to points a living line
extends, and touched by light
approach the bending ends.

15. Rings join to rings; and outreach-
ing tubes clasp with young lips the
nutrient globes or cubes,

16. And urged by new appetencies
select, imbibe, retain, digest,
secrete, eject.

17. In branching cones the living web
expands, organs grow, and life-
giving glands;

18. Arterial tubes carry nascent blood,
and lengthening veins return the
crimson flood;

19. Leaves, lungs and gills the vital
ether breathe, on earth's green
surface, or in the waves beneath.

20. So life's first powers arrest the winds

and floods, to bones convert them, or to shells, or woods;

21. Stretch the vast beds of argil, lime and sand, and from diminished oceans form the land.

Chapter 10

1. Next, nerves unite their long synaptic train, and new sensations wake the early brain;
2. Through each new sense the keen emotions dart, flush the cheek, and swell the throbbing heart.
3. From pain and pleasure quick volitions rise, command the limbs and guide enquiring eyes;
4. With reason's light new-woken man direct, and right and wrong with balance nice detect.
5. Last, multiple associations spring, thoughts join to thoughts, feelings to emotions cling;
6. Whence in long trains of linkage quickly flow imagined joy and voluntary woe.
7. Organic life beneath the shoreless waves was born and nursed in ocean's pearly caves;
8. First forms minute, unseen by microscope, swim the sea, or climb the muddy slope;
9. These, as successive generations bloom, new powers acquire, and larger forms assume;
10. Whence countless forms of vegetation spring, and breathing realms of fin, and feet, and wing.
11. Thus came our world and life, a natural realm, from nature born, with nature at the helm:

12. By evolution, in the aeons vast, since life first rose, to complex life at last.

Chapter 11

1. In all species, nature works to renew itself as it works to nourish itself, and to protect itself from danger,
2. Each by its kind and for its kind, in the great work of continuation that is evolution.
3. In humankind the work of renewal lies in the work of affection, the bond of one to another made by desire;
4. Among the objects that nature everywhere offers desire, there is little more worthy of pursuit, little that makes people happier,
5. Than the enjoyment of another who thinks and feels as oneself,
6. Who has the same ideas, experiences the same sensations, the same ecstasies,
7. Who brings affectionate and sensitive arms towards one's own,
8. Whose embraces and caresses are followed with the existence of a new being who resembles its progenitors,
9. And looks for them in the first movements of life to embrace them,
10. Who will be brought up by their side to be loved together, whose happy birth already strengthens the ties that bind its parents together.
11. If there is anyone who could take offence at the praise given to the most noble and universal of

passions, let us evoke nature before him, and make it speak.

12. For nature would say: 'Why do you blush to hear the praise of pleasure, when you do not blush to indulge its temptations under cover of night?

13. 'Are you ignorant of its purpose and of what you owe to it?

14. 'Do you believe that your own mother would have imperilled her life to give you yours if there were not inexpressible charms in the embrace of her husband?

15. 'Be quiet, unhappy man, and consider that it was this pleasure that pulled you out of nothingness, and gave you life.

16. 'The propagation of beings is the greatest object of nature. It imperiously solicits both sexes as soon as they have gained their share of strength and beauty.

17. 'A vague and brooding restlessness warns them of the moment; their condition is mixed with pain and pleasure.

18. 'At that time they listen to their senses and turn their attention to themselves.

19. 'But if an individual should be presented to another of the same species and of a different sex,

20. 'Then the feeling of all other needs is suspended: the heart palpitates, the limbs tremble;

21. 'Voluptuous images wander through the mind; a flood of sensations runs through the nerves, excites them,

22. 'And proceeds to the seat of a new sense that reveals itself and torments the body.

23. 'Sight is troubled, delirium is born; reason, the slave of instinct, limits itself to serving the latter, and nature is satisfied.

24. 'This is the way things took place at the beginning of the world,

25. 'And the way they still take place among the silks of the wealthy boudoir, just as in the shadows of the savage's cave.'

26. Such is the great command of nature, that in a hundred thousand ways and forms, seeds flood in abundance and super-abundance,

27. Sea and air in season float myriads of possible lives; man and animals in season turn to their mates, obedient to desire;

28. Spring sees newborns emerge into light, or call from the nest for sustenance; and at the mother's breast the suckling lies,

29. Proof that no human law or folly can change the river of life, that must flow in its power from the beginning always onwards,

30. And seek every path to its future, accepting no obstacle or hindrance.

31. For its one monarch is nature, its one guide nature's hand, its one aim fulfilment of nature's great imperatives.

Chapter 12

1. I wander afield, thriving in studious thought, through unpathed groves of woods trodden by none before.

2. I delight to come on undefiled fountains there, to drink their cool waters deep,

3. To pluck new flowers, and the leaves of laurel and green myrtle,

4. To make a crown for my head from regions where inquiry never yet garlanded the brow of man.

5. For, since I teach concerning mighty things, and seek to loose man's mind from coils of blinding ignorance;

6. Since I vouchsafe themes so large, of smallest and greatest, of origin and end, in nature's broad empire,

7. I choose a path without brambles, and frame a lucid song, touching all throughout with charm,

8. As when physicians, needing to give infants the bitter wormwood, first spread the cup's brim with juice and honey,

9. That the unheeding child might be cajoled as far as the lips, and meanwhile swallow a healthsome draught;

10. So now I too expound in song, soft-speaking, to touch with honey the rim of truth.

11. If one thereby might teach the world, its multitudes would cease the strife that ignorances bring,

12. Knowing truth at last, and the nature of things.

Chapter 13

1. Let us admit no more causes of natural things than are both true and sufficient to explain what we see.

2. For it is observed that nature does nothing in vain, and more is vain where less will serve.

3. Nature is pleased with simplicity, and does not need the pomp of superfluous causes.

4. Always assign the same effects to the same causes, as respiration in a man and in a beast;

5. As the geological formations of mountains in Europe and in America;

6. As the heat of our cooking fire and the heat of the sun;

7. As the reflection of light on the earth and by the planets.

8. For the same laws apply everywhere, and the phenomena of nature are the same, whether here at hand or in a distant galaxy.

9. Those qualities of bodies, which admit neither intension nor remission of degrees,

10. And which are found to belong to all bodies within the reach of our investigations,

11. Are to be esteemed the universal qualities of bodies everywhere.

12. For since the qualities of bodies are only known to us by experiment, we are to hold for universal all such as universally agree with experiment.

13. We are not to ignore the evidence of experiments for the sake of dreams and fictions of our own devising;

14. Nor are we to part from the analogy of nature, which is simple, and always consonant to itself.

15. We know the extension of bodies only by means of our senses, and our senses do not reach into all the parts of bodies;

16. But because we perceive extension in everything that we can sense, therefore we ascribe it universally to what we cannot directly sense.

17. This is the order and discipline of science.

18. We are to look upon propositions collected by general induction from phenomena as accurately or nearly true, notwithstanding any contrary hypotheses that may be imagined,

19. Till such time as other phenomena occur, by which they may either be refuted, or made more accurate.

20. This rule we must follow, that the argument of induction may not be evaded by hypotheses.

Chapter 14

1. I am convinced that the human intellect makes its own difficulties, not using the true, sober and judicious methods of inquiry at our disposal,

2. From which comes the manifold ignorance of things which causes innumerable mischiefs in the world.

3. Therefore let us try to see whether that commerce between the human mind and the nature of things,

4. A commerce more precious than anything on earth, for it is nothing less than the search for truth,

5. Can be perfected; or if not, yet improved to a better condition than it now displays.

6. We cannot hope that the errors which have hitherto prevailed, and which will prevail for ever if inquiry is left uninstructed and uncorrected, will correct themselves;

7. Because the early notions of things, which our minds in childhood or without education so readily and passively imbibe,

8. Are false, confused, and overhastily abstracted from the facts; nor are the secondary and subsequent notions we form from them less arbitrary and inconstant.

9. It follows that the entire fabric of human reason employed in the inquisition of nature, is badly built up, like a great structure lacking foundations.

10. For while people are occupied in admiring and applauding the false powers of the mind, they pass by and throw away its true powers,

11. Which, if supplied with proper aids, and if content to wait upon nature instead of vainly affecting to overrule her, are within its reach.

12. Such is the way to truth and the advancement of understanding.

Chapter 15

1. There was but one course left, at the dawn of true science:

2. To try the whole anew on a better plan, and to commence a reconstruction of human knowledge on proper foundations.

3. And this, though in the project and undertaking it may seem a thing

infinite and beyond the powers of man,

4. Yet when it came to be dealt with was found sound and sober, vastly more so than what had been done before.

5. For from this there have been great advances; whereas earlier speculations, unscientific and fanciful,

6. Produced only a whirling and perpetual agitation, ending where it began.

7. And although the first encouragers of enquiry were aware how solitary an enterprise it would at first be,

8. To encourage science where there had been only ignorance drawn from the dreams of mankind's infancy,

9. And how hard a thing to win credit for, nevertheless they were resolved not to abandon the attempt,

10. Nor to be deterred from trying and entering upon the great path of truth open to human inquiry.

11. For it is better to make a beginning in that which may lead to something,

12. Than to engage in perpetual struggle and pursuit in courses which have no exit.

13. And certainly the two ways of contemplation are much like those two ways of action, so much celebrated, in this:

14. That the one, arduous and difficult in the beginning, leads out at last into open country;

15. While the other, seeming at first sight easy and free from obstruction, leads to pathless and precipitous places.

16. Moreover, because people did not know how long it might be before these things would occur to others,

17. Judging especially from this, that they had found no one who had hitherto applied thought to the like,

18. They resolved at once to say as much as they were able. The cause of which was not ambition for themselves, but solicitude for true knowledge;

19. That there might remain some outline and project of what could be achieved for the benefit of humanity.

20. Many other ambitions of the human breast seem poor compared with such work,

21. Seeing that the task is a thing so great that it can be content with its own merit, requiring no further reward:

22. For it is nothing less than seeking to understand the world, and mankind within it:

23. It is nothing less than science, mankind's greatest endeavour, greatest achievement, and greatest promise:

24. If only humanity will be wise in its use.

WISDOM

Chapter 1

1. Give your ears to hear what is said, and your heart to understand what is meant.

2. Let what is wise rest in the casket of your mind, to be a key to your heart.

3. He whose works exceed his wisdom, his wisdom will endure.

4. But he whose wisdom exceeds his works, his wisdom will not endure.

5. The mighty man is he who conquers himself;

6. The rich man is he who is satisfied with what he has;

7. The honourable man is he who honours others;

8. But the wise man is he who learns from all men.

9. The wise do not speak before the face of one who is wiser.

10. The wise do not interrupt, but open the gates of their eyes and ears to learn.

11. The wise do not hasten into speech, nor to reply.

12. The wise ask what is relevant, and speak to the point.

13. The wise speak of first things first, and last things last.

14. The wise say of things they have not heard, 'I have not heard',

15. And of things they have not seen, 'I have not seen'.

16. The wise acknowledge truth.

17. The wise are hard to anger and easy to appease.

18. The wise study to practise, not only to teach.

19. The wise know that according to the painstaking is the reward.

20. The wise know to say little, do much, and face the world with cheerful countenance.

21. The question to be asked at the end of each day is, 'How long will you delay to be wise?'

Chapter 2

1. Let your house be a meeting-place for sages. Sit at their feet, and drink in their words thirstily.

2. Silence is a safeguard around wisdom, and attentiveness is its gateway.

3. Those who say they know everything and do not wish to learn more, are not wise;

4. But those who wish to learn more, even if they know nothing, they are wise.

5. The best have said: much I learned from my teacher, more from my colleagues, most from my pupils.

6. The wise judge everyone with scales weighted in their favour.

7. The wise see others with a liberal eye, not begrudging their good, neither wishing them ill.

8. The wise are as quick to carry out small duties as great ones.

9. The wise would rather be least among the best than first among the worst:

10. As they have said, be rather a tail to a lion than a head to a jackal.

11. The wise know that the right course is whatever a man deems praiseworthy,

12. Among whatever is deemed praiseworthy by well-judging persons.

13. Hope is the armour of the wise, kindness their weapon, courage their mount;

14. And the destination of all their journeys is understanding.

15. The question to be asked at the end of each day is, 'How long will you delay to be wise?'

Chapter 3

1. A human life is less than a thousand months long. The wise are those who multiply their months by endeavour, living many lives in the fullness of one life.

2. For we are everywhere under sentence, but with an indefinite reprieve: we have an interval, and then our place knows us no more.

3. Some spend this interval in listlessness, some in high passions, the wisest in art and song.

4. The wise see that our great chance lies in expanding that interval, in getting as much as possible into the given time.

5. Passion may offer a quickened sense of life, may give the ecstasy and the sorrow of love:

6. The wise say, let us only be sure that it yields the fruit of a true and multiplied consciousness.

7. Of such wisdom the poetic passion, the desire of beauty, the love of art,

8. The desire of knowledge for its own sake and the sake of the human good, has most.

9. To burn always with this hard, gemlike flame, to maintain this ecstasy, is success in life.

10. The wise say that our failure is to form habits: for habit is the mark of a stereotyped world,

11. And it is only the roughness of the eye that makes any two things seem alike.

12. And the wise say: while all melts away under our feet, let us grasp at the exquisite passion,

13. Let us use the knowledge that by a lifted horizon sets the heart free;

14. Or that does so by the stirring of the senses, by colours, perfumes, the work of the artist's hand, the face of a friend;

15. Not to recognise, every moment, some passionate attitude in those about us, and in the brilliancy of their gifts some tragic dividing of their ways,

16. Is, in life's short day of frost and sun, to sleep before evening.

17. With this sense of the splendour of experience and its awful brevity,

18. Gathering all we are into one profound effort to see, to love, to

achieve, to understand, we shall have time enough to live.

19. Let us ever curiously test new ideas and court new impressions, never acquiescing in a facile orthodoxy.

20. Philosophy may help us gather up what might otherwise pass unregarded, for philosophy is the microscope of thought;

21. But theory which requires the sacrifice of any part of this experience, in consideration of some interest we cannot enter, has no claim upon us.

22. It is life itself that has the first and last claim, and it is the fresh light and clear air that wisdom brings to life that answers it,

23. For to love and to strive, to seek to know, to attend to the best that has been thought, said and done in the world, and to learn from it, is wisdom:

24. And wisdom is life.

25. The question to be asked at the end of each day is, 'How long will you delay to be wise?'

Chapter 4

1. Who or what is the best counsellor, to counsel us to be wise? Nothing less than life itself.

2. The beginning of wisdom is the question, the end of wisdom is acceptance;

3. But in the interval, it is not enough to be wise only with the wisdom of one's day, for wisdom is of all time.

4. To be wise is to know when to act, and when to leave alone.

5. To be wise is to know when to speak, and when to be silent.

6. To be wise is to know that amity and peace do not come from nothing, nor do they sustain themselves without help, but require wisdom for their birth and continuance.

7. The gaining of knowledge is accumulation; the acquisition of wisdom is simplification.

8. Wisdom is the recognition of consequences, a respect for causality and the profit in foresight.

9. Wisdom lies in bringing the past to serve the future, and in opening one's ears to hear the voices of the past.

10. Learning may be had without wisdom, and wisdom without learning; but nothing can overthrow their combination.

11. No one came to be wise who did not sometimes fail;

12. No one came to be wise who did not know how to revise an opinion.

13. The wise change their minds when facts and experience so demand. The fool either does not hear or does not heed.

14. But the wise man knows that even a fool can speak truth.

15. Wisdom belongs to everyone, and is possible everywhere: none need lack it who will only allow experience to teach them.

16. Happy are those who encounter someone wise: he reveals treasure when he reproves and guides.

17. He will teach that as a rock is not shaken by the wind, so the wise are

steadfast through both blame and praise.

18. As a deep lake remains peaceful in all seasons, so are the wise when they reflect on good teaching.

19. The question to be asked at the end of each day is, 'How long will you delay to be wise?'

Chapter 5

1. Told of someone who had made a vast fortune, the wise man asked whether he had also made time to spend it.

2. Told of someone who had conceived a great love for another, the wise man said, 'It is better to love than to desire.'

3. Told of someone who had children, the wise man said, 'Let him treat his children as he would cook a small fish.'

4. The wise do not expect always to be healthy, or never to suffer hardship or grief. Instead they prepare.

5. The wise do not expect to master anything worthwhile without effort. Instead they make the effort.

6. The wise do not expect never to have adversaries or to meet disagreement. Instead they contemplate beforehand the best way of making difficulties useful.

7. From an enemy, a difficulty, an illness or a failure, the wise learn much, and grow wiser therefore.

8. The wise know the value of friendship, and that it is wisdom to be a friend to oneself too.

9. For who would harm a friend, instead of seeking the best for him, in advice and deed?

10. As a friend to oneself, can wisdom allow one to do less?

11. The question to be asked at the end of each day is, 'How long will you delay to be wise?'

Chapter 6

1. The meditation of the wise man is a meditation on life, not on death.

2. The wise see the necessity of things, and by this they free themselves from distress:

3. For the pain arising from loss is mitigated as soon as its inevitability is perceived;

4. And likewise no one pities a newborn baby for being unable to speak or walk, because this is natural to its state.

5. Thus the recognition of necessities is a liberation, and the wise are those who distinguish between necessity and contingency.

6. Emotion is bad if it hinders the mind from thinking. An emotion that opens the mind to contemplate several aspects of things at once is better than one that fixes thought to an obsession.

7. By framing a system of right conduct and practical precepts, one better bears adversity and resists evil.

8. The wise thus remember what is to their true advantage, and the good that follows from friendship, and the fact that men act by the necessity of their nature.

9. The wise thus moderate anger and resentment by understanding the causes of others' actions;

10. The wise thus reflect on the value of courage, and on the good that can be found even in negative things.

11. The wise ask themselves what they truly seek in wealth, or position, in love, or honour, in victory, or retirement from life;

12. For only clear and distinct ideas of these things guard against false objects of ambition.

13. He who would govern his emotions and appetites by the love of freedom strives, as far as he can, to gain knowledge of the virtues and their causes;

14. He will not wish to dwell on men's faults, or carp at his fellows, but by diligently observing and practising precepts he will direct his actions by the commandments of reason.

15. The wise know that the good and the bad can be absolute, and can be relative:

16. Absolute, when the demand is to seek good and act upon it;

17. Relative, when one recognises that the same thing can be good, bad or indifferent according to circumstance,

18. As when music is good to one who is melancholy, bad to one who mourns, indifferent to the deaf.

19. The wise call things good when they enhance the activity of life and bring benefit;

20. The wise call things bad when they hinder activity, and bring malignity, discord and pain.

21. But the wise recognise too that misperception of things, and inadequacy of ideas, can make things seem bad that have good in them, or are inevitable and must be borne;

22. For the grace of bearing life's inevitable evils is itself a good, and makes goodness arise even from evils by opposing them or enduring them with courage.

23. The mind has power over the emotions, and can be free. Whence it appears how potent are the wise, and how much they surpass the ignorant, who are driven by appetites and fears.

24. For the ignorant are distracted by external causes which never gain the true acquiescence of their minds, so that they live unwitting of themselves and of things.

25. Whereas the wise are less disturbed because they are more aware of themselves and of things, and understand necessities, and are capable of true acquiescence of mind.

26. The question to be asked at the end of each day is, 'How long will you delay to be wise?'

Chapter 7

1. Some things lie under our control and others not. Things we may control are opinion, pursuit, desire, aversion, and, in a word, whatever are our own actions.

2. Things far less in our control are body, property, reputation, command, and, in one word, whatever are not our own actions.

3. What we can ourselves control are by nature free, unrestrained, unhindered; but those not in our control are weak, slavish, limited, and belong to others.

4. Remember, then, that if you wrongly suppose that things which are slavish by nature are also free, and that what belongs to others is your own, you will be hindered.

5. You will lament, you will be disturbed, you will find fault both with the people about you and with the tools you use.

6. But if you rightly suppose those things are your own which are truly your own, and what belongs to others is not your own, then no one will be able to compel or hinder you.

7. And you will find fault with no one or accuse no one. To the extent possible in a world of conflicts, you will do nothing against your will, no one will hurt you, you will have no enemies, you will not be harmed.

8. Aiming therefore at such great things, remember that you must not allow yourself to be carried, even with a slight tendency, towards the attainment of lesser things.

9. Instead, entirely quit what is bad, and postpone what is doubtful. But if you would have these great

things, and also desire power and riches, consider:

10. How can he gain the latter with honour and peace, if he aims at the former too?

11. Only the former guarantees happiness and freedom, while the latter are always uncertain.

12. Work, therefore, to be able to say to every harsh appearance, 'You are but an appearance, and not absolutely the thing you appear to be.'

13. Examine appearances by the rules of reason, first and chiefly by this: whether it concerns the things which are in our own control, or those which are not;

14. And, if it concerns anything not in our control, be prepared to say that it is nothing to you.

15. The question to be asked at the end of each day is, 'How long will you delay to be wise?'

Chapter 8

1. It has been said, that to learn how to philosophise is to learn how to die.

2. The wise die less than the unwise; the wise die fewer times than the unwise; for the unwise die in their imaginations and fears as often as they think of death.

3. But the evil of our own death is not death itself; it is the fear of death that is evil. To be free of the fear of one's own death is to be free indeed.

4. The death of others is the true

sorrow of death; and the remedies of
sorrow are love, courage and time.

5. To learn how to philosophise is to
learn how to bear the inevitability
of loss. We desire life and are averse
to death: this is the root of fearing
death.

6. Remember that following desire
promises the attainment of what
you desire; and aversion promises
the avoiding of that to which you
are averse.

7. But he who fails to obtain what he
desires, is disappointed; and he
who suffers what he is averse to, is
wretched.

8. If you are averse to sickness, or
death, or poverty, you will be
wretched: for death must come, and
sickness and poverty may come too.

9. Remove aversion, then, from all
things that are not in our control,
and transfer it to things contrary to
the nature of what is in our control.

10. Have regard to desire: for, if you
desire any of the things which are
not under your control, you must
necessarily be disappointed;

11. And of those which are, and which
it would be laudable to desire, do
not desire them only, but pursue
them.

12. Use only the appropriate actions of
pursuit and avoidance; and even
these lightly, and with gentleness
and reservation.

13. The question to be asked at the end
of each day is, 'How long will you
delay to be wise?'

Chapter 9

1. With regard to the things that give
you delight, are useful, or which
you deeply love,

2. Remember to tell yourself of what
general nature they are, beginning
from the most insignificant things.

3. If, for example, you are fond of a
specific cup, remind yourself that it
is only a cup. Then, if it breaks, you
will not be disturbed.

4. If you kiss your child, or your wife,
say that you kiss what is human, and
prepare to bear the grief that is the
cost of loving, should you lose them.

5. When you are going about any
action, remind yourself what nature
the action is:

6. People are disturbed, not by things,
but by the principles and notions
which they form concerning things.

7. Death, for instance, is not terrible,
otherwise it would have appeared
so to Socrates. Rather, the terror
consists in our belief that death is
terrible.

8. When therefore we are hindered, or
disturbed, or grieved, let us never
attribute the cause to others, but to
ourselves; that is, to our own
principles.

9. An uninstructed person will lay the
fault of his own bad condition
upon others.

10. Someone just starting instruction
will lay the fault on himself.

11. Someone who is perfectly
instructed will place blame neither
on others nor on himself if it is
something from outside his control,

12. But he will say: this is in the nature of things.
13. The question to be asked at the end of each day is, 'How long will you delay to be wise?'

Chapter 10

1. Do not be proud of any excellence that is not your own. If a horse should be proud and say, 'I am handsome', it would be supportable.
2. But when you are proud and say, 'I have a handsome horse', know that you are proud of something that belongs not to you but to the horse.
3. What, then, is your own? Only your reaction to the appearances of things.
4. Thus, when you react to how things appear in true accordance with their nature, you will be proud with reason; for you will take pride in some good of your own.
5. Consider when, on a voyage, your ship is anchored; if you go on shore to get water you may amuse yourself along the way with picking up a shellfish.
6. However, your attention must also be towards the ship, waiting for the captain to call you on board;
7. For when he does so, you must immediately leave all these things, otherwise you will miss the ship as it sails.
8. So it is with life. Whatever you find while, so to say, wandering on the beach, is fine.
9. But if necessity calls, you must run to the ship, leaving these things, and regarding none of them.
10. For there is a proper time for all things, including a proper time to grieve, and to prepare to die.
11. The question to be asked at the end of each day is, 'How long will you delay to be wise?'

Chapter 11

1. Do not demand that things should happen as you wish, but wish that they happen as they do happen, and you will go on well.
2. Sickness is a hindrance to the body, but not to your ability to choose, unless that is your choice. Lameness is a hindrance to the leg, but not to your ability to choose.
3. Say this to yourself with regard to everything that happens, then you will see such obstacles as hindrances to something else, but not to yourself.
4. With every accident, ask yourself what abilities you have for making a proper use of it.
5. If you see an attractive person, you will find that self-restraint is the ability you have against your desire.
6. If you are in pain, you will find fortitude. If you hear unpleasant language, you will find patience. And thus habituated, the appearances of things will not hurry you away along with them.
7. Never say of anything, 'I have lost it'; but, 'I have returned it'. For things come, even when we labour for them, as if it were a gift; and in the end all things are returned.

8. Be content to be thought uncon-
ventional with regard to external
things.

9. Do not wish to be thought to know
anything; and even if you appear to
be somebody important to others,
distrust yourself.

10. If you do not wish your desires to
be frustrated, this is in your own
control. Exercise, therefore, what is
in your control.

11. He is the master of every other
person who is able to confer or
remove whatever that person wishes
either to have or to avoid.

12. Whoever, then, would be free, let
him not wish too earnestly for
anything that depends on others.

13. Behave in life as at a dinner party.
Is anything brought around to you?
Put out your hand and take your
share with moderation.

14. Does it pass by you? Do not stop it.

15. Is it not yet come? Do not stretch
your desire towards it, but wait till
it reaches you.

16. Do this with regard to children, to
a spouse, to public posts, to riches,
and you will eventually be a worthy
guest at the feast of life.

17. And if you do not even take all the
things that are set before you, but
are able willingly to reject them,
then you will not only be a partner
at the feasts of life, but one of its
princes.

18. The question to be asked at the end
of each day is, 'How long will you
delay to be wise?'

Chapter 12

1. When you see anyone weeping in
grief because his loved one has gone
abroad, or is dead, or because he
has suffered in his affairs, be careful
that the appearance may not
misdirect you.

2. Instead, distinguish within your
own mind, and be prepared to say,
'It's not the accident that distresses
this person, because it does not
distress another person; it is the
judgement he makes about it.'

3. It is our attitudes to things that give
them their value, whether good or
bad, or indifferent. Strengthen your
mind to right attitudes, and you
will live with fortitude and just
measure.

4. You are an actor in a drama, of
which the author is jointly you and
matters beyond your control.

5. Thus say to yourself, 'Whatever
happens, it is in my control to
derive advantage from it, even if
only to learn how to bear
misfortune.'

6. You will be unconquerable, if
you enter only into combat you
can win.

7. When, therefore, you see anyone
eminent in honours, or power, or
in high esteem on any other
account, take heed not to be
hurried away with the appearance,
and to pronounce him happy;

8. For, if the essence of good consists
in our own choices, there will be no
room for envy or emulation.

9. But, for your part, do not wish to

be a general, or a senator, or a consul, but rather: wish to be free;

10. And the only way to be completely free is the right attitude to things not in your own control.

11. Remember that insult does not come from the one who gives ill language or a blow, but from the principle which represents these things as insulting.

12. When, therefore, anyone provokes you, be assured that it is your own opinion which provokes you.

13. Try, therefore, in the first place, not to be hurried away with the appearance. For if you once gain time and respite, you will more easily command yourself.

14. The question to be asked at the end of each day is, 'How long will you delay to be wise?'

Chapter 13

1. Let death, illness, failure and loss, and any other thing which appears terrible, be frankly gazed upon, to be seen for what it is;

2. And chiefly death, which is no more than dreamless sleep, and rest from strife;

3. And you will cease to entertain abject thoughts; nor will you too eagerly covet anything, since all must be left behind one day.

4. If you have an earnest desire of attaining wisdom, prepare yourself from the first to be laughed at by the multitude,

5. To hear them say, 'He does not covet what we covet, or seek what we hasten after and pursue, but he stands apart.'

6. Do not mind such rejection, but keep steadily to those things which appear best to you.

7. For if you adhere to your principles, those very persons who at first ridiculed will afterwards admire you.

8. But if you are conquered by them, you will incur a double ridicule.

9. If you turn your attention to externals, so as to wish to please anyone, be assured that you will hinder your scheme of life.

10. Be contented, then, in everything devoted to living wisely, and it will suffice you.

11. The question to be asked at the end of each day is, 'How long will you delay to be wise?'

Chapter 14

1. Do not allow such a consideration as this to distress you: 'I will be nobody anywhere.' Is it the meaning of life to get power, or to be admitted to the first rank?

2. And how is it true that you will be nobody anywhere, when you will be somebody in those things which lie under your own control, where you yourself matter most?

3. 'But my friends will be unassisted.' What do you mean by unassisted? Who told you that these are among the things in your own control, and not the affair of others? Who can give to another things that he himself does not have?

4. 'Well, but if I get them, then my friends too may have a share.' If I can get them with the preservation of my own honour and fidelity of mind, show me the way and I will get them, and willingly share them;

5. But if you require me to lose the proper good so that another may gain what is not good, let me decline.

6. Besides, which would you rather have, a sum of money, or a faithful friend? Rather assist me, then, to gain this character than require me to do those things by which I may lose it.

7. 'Well, but my country, as far as it depends on me, will be unassisted.' Here again, what assistance do you mean?

8. If I may serve my country with honour and fidelity of mind, let me serve it to the uttermost;

9. And most by supplying it with another citizen of honour and fidelity, which is of greater use to it.

10. 'What place, then, say you, will I hold in the state?' Whatever you can hold with the preservation of your fidelity and honour.

11. But if, by desiring to be useful to that, you lose these, of what use can you be to your country should you become faithless and void of shame?

12. The question to be asked at the end of each day is, 'How long will you delay to be wise?'

Chapter 15

1. Is anyone raised above you at a meeting, or given a greater compliment, or admitted to the counsels of the rulers where you are not invited?

2. If such things are good, you ought to be glad that the other has them; and if they are evil, do not be grieved that you do not have them.

3. Remember that you cannot, without using the same means as others do, acquire things not in your own control, or expect to be thought worthy of an equal share of them.

4. For how can he who does not frequent the door of some influential person, and serve him with flattery, have an equal share with him who does?

5. You are unjust, then, and insatiable, if you are unwilling to pay the price for which these things are sold, and wish to get them for nothing.

6. For how much is lettuce sold? Fifty pence, for instance. If another pays fifty pence and takes the lettuce, and you, not paying it, go without a lettuce, do not imagine that he has gained any advantage over you.

7. For as he has the lettuce, so you have the fifty pence which you did not spend. Likewise in the present case, you have not been invited to such a person's entertainment, because you have not paid him the price for which a supper is sold.

8. It is sold for praise; it is sold for

attendance. Give him then the value, if it is for your advantage.

9. But if you would, at the same time, not pay the one and yet receive the other, you are insatiable, and a blockhead.

10. Have you nothing, then, instead of the supper? Yes, indeed, you have: your honour, and self-sufficiency.

11. The right attitude may be learned from small things. For example, when our neighbour's boy breaks a cup, or the like, we say, 'These things will happen.'

12. Be assured, then, that when your own cup likewise is broken, you ought to be affected just as when another's cup is broken.

13. Apply this in like manner to greater things, seeing illness and death, and grief for others, as what will happen because it must.

14. The question to be asked at the end of each day is, 'How long will you delay to be wise?'

Chapter 16

1. As a mark is not set up for the sake of missing the aim, so neither does the nature of evil exist in the world.

2. If a person gave your body to any stranger he met on his way, you would be angry.

3. Why then do you feel no shame in handing over your mind to be confused and mystified by anyone who tries to persuade you for his own advantage?

4. In every affair consider what precedes and follows, and then undertake it.

5. Otherwise you will begin with enthusiasm; but not having thought of the consequences, when some of them appear you will shamefully desist.

6. 'I would conquer at the Games.' But consider what precedes and follows, and then, if it is for your advantage, engage in the affair:

7. You must conform to rules, submit to a diet, refrain from dainties; exercise your body, whether you choose it or not, at a stated hour, in heat and cold; you must drink no cold water, nor sometimes even wine.

8. In a word, you must give yourself up to your master, as to a physician. Then, in the combat, you may be thrown into a ditch, dislocate your arm, turn your ankle, swallow dust, be whipped, and, after all, not gain the victory.

9. When you have evaluated all this, if your inclination still holds, then do it, and with a will, with all your might; and for the sake of the good that comes of it, even if you do not win.

10. Otherwise you will behave like children who play at wrestling, or at gladiators, sometimes blow a trumpet, and sometimes act a tragedy when they have seen and admired it.

11. Thus you too will be at one time a wrestler, at another a gladiator, now a philosopher, then an orator; but

unless you do it with your whole will, you will be nothing at all.

12. Like an ape, you will mimic all you see, and one thing after another is sure to please you, but will fall out of favour as soon as it becomes familiar.

13. For unless you enter upon things with forethought and resolution to do your best, but instead rashly and with a cold inclination only, you will be a mimic and a playing child merely in all you do.

14. Consider first, then, what the matter is, and to what your own nature is suited.

15. If you would be a wrestler, consider your shoulders, your back, your thighs; for different persons are made for different things.

16. Do you think that you can act the fool, and be a philosopher? You must watch, you must labour, you must get the better of certain appetites,

17. You must set at their true value the honours and blandishments of the world.

18. When you have considered all these things round, approach, if you please; if, by parting with them, you have a mind to purchase freedom and strength of mind.

19. If not, do not come here; do not, like children, be for a while a philosopher, then a publican, then an orator, then an officer.

20. You must cultivate either your own ruling faculty or externals, and apply yourself either to things

within or without you; that is, be either wise, or one who is led by others to do their will.

21. The question to be asked at the end of each day is, 'How long will you delay to be wise?'

Chapter 17

1. Prescribe a character and form of conduct to yourself, which you can keep both when alone and in company.

2. Be a listener, speak what is necessary, remember few words are better than many.

3. Enter into discourse when occasion calls for it, but not on vulgar and fruitless subjects, and principally not of men, so as either to blame, or praise, or make comparisons.

4. If you are able by your own conversation, bring over that of your company to proper subjects; if you happen to be among strangers, be for the most part silent.

5. Do not allow your laughter to be too much, nor on many occasions, nor profuse.

6. Avoid swearing, if possible, altogether; if not, as far as you are able.

7. Avoid vulgar entertainments; but, if occasion calls you to them, keep alert, that you may not imperceptibly slide into vulgar manners.

8. For be assured that however sound a person is himself, yet, if his companion is infected, he who converses with him will be infected likewise.

9. Do not be troublesome and full of

reproofs to those who use liberties, nor frequently boast that you yourself do not: people are various, and merit sympathy.

10. If anyone tells you that such a person speaks ill of you, do not make excuses about what is said of you, but answer: 'He does not know my other faults, else he would not have mentioned only these.'

11. Abstain from declamations and derision and violent emotions. When you are going to confer with anyone, and particularly with those in a superior station, represent to yourself how Socrates or Zeno would behave in such a case.

12. When you are going to anyone in power, represent to yourself that you will not find him at home; that you will not be admitted; that the doors will not be opened to you; that he will take no notice of your petition.

13. If, with all this, it is your duty to go, bear what happens, and never say, 'It was not worth so much.'

14. For if you went with a reason that was right, the disdain of the powerful will not make it wrong.

15. In parties of conversation, avoid a frequent and excessive mention of your own actions and dangers.

16. For, however agreeable it may be to yourself to mention the risks you have run, it is not equally agreeable to others to hear your adventures.

17. If you are struck by the appearance of any promised pleasure, guard yourself against being hurried

away by it; but let the affair wait your leisure, and procure yourself some delay.

18. Then bring to your mind both points of time: that in which you will enjoy the pleasure, and that in which you might have to repent and reproach yourself after you have enjoyed it;

19. And set before yourself, in opposition to these, how you will be glad and applaud yourself if you abstain.

20. And even though it should appear to you a seasonable gratification, take heed that its enticing, and agreeable and attractive force may not subdue you;

21. But set in opposition to this how much better it is to be conscious of gaining a victory over what leads you astray.

22. The question to be asked at the end of each day is, 'How long will you delay to be wise?'

Chapter 18

1. When you do anything from a clear judgement that it ought to be done, never delay to do it, even though the world should make a wrong supposition about it.

2. When eating with others, to choose the largest share is suitable to the bodily appetite, but inconsistent with the social nature of the occasion.

3. When you eat with another, then, remember not only the value to the body of those things which are set before you,

4. But also the value of that behaviour which ought to be observed towards the person who gives the entertainment.

5. If you have assumed a character above your strength, you have both made an ill figure in that and quitted one which you might have supported.

6. When walking, you are careful not to step on a nail or turn your foot; so likewise be careful not to hurt the ruling faculty of your mind.

7. The body is to everyone the measure of the possessions proper for it, just as the foot is of the shoe.

8. If, therefore, you stop at this, you will keep the measure; but if you move beyond it, you must necessarily be carried forward, as down a cliff;

9. As in the case of a shoe, if you go beyond its fitness to the foot, it comes first to be gilded, then purple, and then studded with jewels.

10. For to that which once exceeds a due measure, there is no bound.

11. Though it is good to take thought for our exercises, for eating and drinking proportionately, and discharging the animal functions,

12. These should be done in due measure, for most of our attention should be engaged in the care of the understanding.

13. When any person harms you, or speaks badly of you, remember that he acts or speaks from a supposition of its being his right.

14. Now, it is not possible that he should follow what appears right to you, but what appears so to himself.

15. Therefore, if he judges from a wrong appearance, he is the person hurt, since he is the person deceived.

16. For if anyone should suppose a true proposition to be false, the proposition is not hurt, but he who is deceived about it.

17. Setting out, then, from these principles, you will bear with fortitude a person who reviles you, for you will say upon every occasion, 'It seemed so to him.'

18. Everything has two handles, the one by which it may be carried, the other by which it cannot.

19. If your brother acts unjustly, do not lay hold on the action by the handle of his injustice, for by that it cannot be carried;

20. But by the opposite, that he is your brother, that he was brought up with you; and thus you will lay hold on it, as it is to be carried.

21. The question to be asked at the end of each day is, 'How long will you delay to be wise?'

Chapter 19

1. When you have brought yourself to supply the necessities of your body at a small price, don't pique yourself upon it;

2. Nor, if you drink only water, say on every occasion, 'I drink only water.'

3. But first consider how much the poor are more sparing and patient

of hardship than those who have a sufficiency, or are rich.

4. But if at any time you would inure yourself by exercise to labour, and bearing hard trials, do it for your own sake, and not for the world.

5. These reasonings are unconnected, though foolish people think them:

6. 'I am richer than you, therefore I am better'; 'I am more eloquent than you, therefore I am better'.

7. The true connection is this: 'I am richer than you, therefore my property is greater than yours'; 'I am more eloquent than you, therefore my style is better than yours'.

8. But a human being, after all, is neither property nor style.

9. Does anyone bathe in a very short time? Do not say that he does it ill, but in a short time.

10. Does anyone drink a great quantity of wine? Do not say that he does ill, but that he drinks a great quantity.

11. For, unless you perfectly understand the principle from which anyone acts, how should you know if he acts ill?

12. Thus you will not run the hazard of assenting to any appearances but such as you fully comprehend.

13. Never call yourself wise, nor talk a great deal among the unlearned about wisdom, but act conformably to it.

14. Thus, when taking food in company, do not talk about how persons ought to eat, but eat as you ought.

15. If ever any talk should happen among the unlearned concerning learned things, be you, for the most part, silent.

16. For there is great danger in immediately throwing out what you have not digested.

17. And if anyone tells you that you know nothing, and you are not angered by what he says, you may be sure that you have begun to be wise.

18. For sheep do not regurgitate the grass to show the shepherds how much they have eaten; but, inwardly digesting their food, they outwardly produce wool and milk.

19. Thus, therefore, do you likewise not show off knowledge to the unlearned, but the actions produced by them after they have been digested.

20. The question to be asked at the end of each day is, 'How long will you delay to be wise?'

Chapter 20

1. The first and most necessary topic in the search for wisdom is the use of moral imjunctions, such as, 'We ought not to lie';

2. The second is that of demonstrations, such as, 'What is the origin of our obligation not to lie?'

3. The third gives strength and articulation to the other two, such as, 'What is the logical basis of this demonstration?'

4. For what is demonstration? What is consequence? What is

contradiction? What is truth? What is falsehood?

5. The third topic, then, is necessary on the account of the second, and the second on the account of the first.

6. But the most necessary, and that whereon we ought to act, is the first.

7. Yet we act just on the contrary: we spend all our time on the third topic, and employ all our diligence about that, and entirely neglect the first.

8. Therefore, at the same time that we lie, let us already be prepared to show how it is demonstrated that lying is not right;

9. And let us live by what reason and the right teach, without delay.

10. The question to be asked at the end of each day is, 'How long will you delay to be wise?'

Chapter 21

1. The characteristic of the unwise is, that they never expect either benefit or hurt from themselves, but from externals.

2. The condition and characteristic of the wise is that they expect all hurt and benefit from themselves.

3. The marks of the wise are, that they censure no one, praise where it is due, blame no one, accuse no one, say nothing concerning themselves as being anybody, or knowing anything:

4. When they are, in any instance, hindered or limited, they blame only themselves; if they are praised, they take it with modesty and proportion; if censured, they make no defence.

5. But they go about with the caution of sick or injured people, careful not to move anything that is set right, intent on putting right what is wrong.

6. When anyone shows himself overly confident in ability to understand and interpret the teachings of the sages, say,

7. 'Unless the sages taught obscurely, this person would have had no subject for his vanity.

8. 'But what do I desire? To understand nature and follow her. I ask, then, who interprets her, and, finding someone who does, I have recourse to his teaching.

9. 'If I do not understand his writings, I seek one to explain them.' So far there is nothing to value myself upon.

10. And when I find a teacher, what remains is to make use of his instructions. This alone is the valuable thing.

11. But, if I admire nothing but merely the teaching, what do I become more than a grammarian instead of a philosopher?

12. I blush when I cannot show my actions agreeable and consonant to the teachings of the good.

13. The question to be asked at the end of each day is, 'How long will you delay to be wise?'

Chapter 22

1. Whatever moral rules you have proposed to yourself after careful thought, abide by them as if they were laws.

2. Do not regard what anyone says of you, for this, after all, is no concern of yours, unless it is to your benefit to learn from it.

3. How long, then, will you put off thinking yourself worthy of the highest improvements and follow the distinctions of reason?

4. What other master, then, do you wait for, to throw upon that the delay of reforming yourself? You are no longer a child, but an adult.

5. If, therefore, you will be negligent and slothful, and always add procrastination to procrastination, purpose to purpose, and delay day after day until you will attend to yourself,

6. You will insensibly continue without proficiency, and, living and dying, persevere in being one of the thoughtless.

7. This instant, then, think yourself worthy of living as a grown-up. Let whatever is the best be your law.

8. And if any instance of pain or pleasure, of glory or disgrace, is set before you, remember that now is the combat, now the struggle, nor can it be put off.

9. And though you are not yet a Socrates, you ought to live as one desirous of becoming a Socrates, who said, 'The life most worth living is the life considered and chosen.'

10. The question to be asked at the end of each day is, 'How long will you delay to be wise?'

11. And the great lesson that the end of each day teaches is that wisdom and the freedom it brings must daily be won anew.

PARABLES

Chapter 1

1. A rich king named Plousios had planted a forest for his sport, and made an edict forbidding anyone to trespass in it.

2. Out hunting one day he came across a hut that a beggar named Penicros had built there, in violation of the edict.

3. In anger Plousios ordered Penicros to be hanged, and his hut destroyed; but Penicros said, 'If you hang me before you hear my wisdom, you will always regret it.'

4. 'What makes you think you are wise?' asked Plousios, and Penicros answered, 'Because I have built my lodging in Plousios' forest,

5. 'And in consequence have met him; which I wished to do, as having counsel to offer him.'

6. Amused by the temerity of this answer, Plousios ordered Penicros to be placed on a donkey and brought back with them to the city; and on the way questioned him.

7. 'Tell me the difference between a good man and a bad man,' said Plousios.

8. Penicros answered, 'A bad man quarrelled with a good man, saying "For every word of abuse I hear from you, I will retort ten."

9. 'The good man replied, "For every ten words of abuse I hear from you, I will not retort one."

10. 'That is the difference between a bad man and a good; and between a foolish man and a wise.'

11. Impressed by this answer, Plousios asked, 'Is it true that in both man and nature all things grow with time?'

12. And Penicros answered, 'There is one thing that does not; and that is grief.'

13. Plousios said, 'We are told to take care who we send with our messages. Why is that so?'

14. Penicros answered, 'Because the character of the sent tells the character of the sender.'

15. Plousios asked, 'Each animal has its colour, its spots or stripes, to conceal itself in the forest. What is the best method of concealment for man?' Penicros answered, 'Speech.'

16. Plousios asked, 'What kind of man is the worst among men?' Penicros answered, 'He who is good in his own esteem.'

17. Plousios asked, 'Would it not be sweet if a king's reign lasted for ever?' Penicros answered, 'If that had been the lot of your father, where would you be now?'

18. Plousios said, 'Levellers say there is

no difference between nobles and commoners. Is that true?'

19. And Penicros answered, 'There was once a nobleman who spoke contemptuously to a poor scholar, who replied in courteous terms.

20. 'After this had continued for some time, the scholar at last remarked, "It seems that your noble line ends with you, while mine might be beginning with me."

21. 'And again: a man of high birth spoke abusively to a wise man of lowly birth. "You say that my lineage is a blot on me," said the sage, "but you are a blot on yours."'

22. And Penicros said, 'Death is the dread of the rich and the hope of the poor. A story shows us a deeper truth about the difference between noble and commoner, rich and poor:

23. 'One like Plousios and one like Penicros were once travelling together, and were set upon by thieves.

24. '"Woe is me," said he who was like Plousios, "if they recognise me." "Woe is me," said he who was like Penicros, "if they do not recognise me."

25. 'And again: the heir of a wealthy man squandered his money, and a poor sage saw him eating bread and salted olives.

26. 'He said to the impoverished heir, "Had you thought that this might be your food, this would not be your food."

27. 'Such are the differences. As man

and man, woman and woman, there is not – neither ought there to be – any difference between any two people in the eyes of a king or judge, for there is no difference between them in nature.'

28. Plousios asked, 'Why do we die?' And Penicros answered, 'Because we live.'

29. Plousios asked Penicros about enemies and friends, and Penicros answered, 'Rather a wise enemy than a foolish friend.'

30. Plousios asked, 'Is it ever right to tell a lie?' And Penicros answered, 'In three cases lying is permissible: in war, in reconciling man to man, and in appeasing one's spouse.

31. 'And more generally, it has been well said that it does an injury to tell an untimely truth.'

32. Plousios said, 'You are not a beggar but a wise man.' And Penicros answered, 'Indeed; for it is you who have been the beggar, asking wisdom from me.

33. 'In life reason is the pilot, law is the light it steers by, wisdom is knowing that the law comes from nature; and reason is nature's gift to man.

34. 'Man has neither claws to fight with nor a furred pelt to abide the winter, but may rule the clawed and furred if he will.'

35. Plousios said, 'For what you have taught me today, tell me what you would have as a reward.'

36. To which Penicros replied, 'It is said of Diogenes the philosopher that when Emperor Alexander

spoke to him as he lay in his barrel, offering him rewards, he answered, "Yes, you may reward me, by standing out of my sunlight."

37. 'But I will indeed accept a reward from you: allow me to build a hut in your forest, and to live there in peace.'

38. And Plousios, who that same day had ordered Penicros to be hanged for building a hut in his forest, granted him permission to live there ever afterwards.

39. Such is the recompense of wisdom.

Chapter 2

1. A man called Charicles, a scholar who lived in former times in the city of five gates and ten towers, told of a dream he once had,

2. In which he was woken from his afternoon sleep by a stranger carrying a basket of food,

3. Containing a round crusted loaf of bread, the white cheese of goat's milk, bunches of sweet grapes, and a flask of wine, red as rubies.

4. The stranger invited him saying, 'Come eat my bread and cheese, and drink the ruby-red wine with me, as if we were sons of the same mother.'

5. And the stranger carried a lit lamp, even though it was daylight and the sun cast its beams into every corner of the house.

6. Charicles pointed at the basket and asked the stranger, 'What are these things, and why are you offering them to me?'

7. The stranger replied, 'They are my wine, my bread and cheese, and my sweet grapes; come, eat with me, and drink, and we will be as if sons of the same mother.'

8. But Charicles said, 'I cannot eat until I have washed my face and hands, because sleep still hangs heavily on me in this afternoon heat.'

9. 'Wash,' said the stranger, 'if you will; then come eat my bread and grapes with me, and drink the ruby-red wine.'

10. So Charicles washed, and set himself down with the stranger, and began to eat;

11. And he ate some of the bread and cheese, and the grapes, but he declined to drink the wine.

12. 'Why will you not taste my wine?' asked the stranger. 'It is from my own vineyard, and the grapes were crushed by my own feet.'

13. 'I could not drink your wine,' said Charicles, 'or any wine. It blinds the eyes, robs the mind of wisdom and the body of strength, reveals the secrets of friends, and raises dissension between brothers.'

14. At this the stranger smiled. 'Why do you blaspheme against wine,' he said, 'and believe these falsehoods about it?

15. 'Wine brings joy; it chases away sorrow, strengthens the sentiments, makes hearts generous, prolongs pleasure, defers old age, and brings a shine to the face and brightness to the senses.

16. 'Wine is life, and has the sweetness in it of the best of life; it takes the veils of everyday concerns from the eyes so that one can see life's promises.'

17. 'Well,' Charicles said, 'perhaps you are right; and after I have finished eating, and taken some water, I will try a little of your wine.'

18. So after Charicles finished eating, and had taken some water, he accepted a goblet from the stranger in which the ruby-red wine gleamed, and round the rim of which the small bubbles gathered.

19. But he did not put the goblet to his lips; he held it in his hand as if to drink, and asked the stranger, 'Where are you from?'

20. The stranger said, 'I come from a distant land, from pleasant and fruitful hills. Its knowledge and wisdom is greater than in your country, and so are its laws.

21. 'Come with me to my land and I will show you its happy environs and teach you its lore, for here your acquaintances and neighbours do not appreciate worth, nor know wisdom.

22. 'My country is like a pleasant garden, full of loving people, wise beyond all other people.

23. 'You are a scholar, and would learn much from what I could show you; it would be for you to bring that wisdom back again, to teach it to your fellows.'

24. But Charicles said, still holding the undrunk wine in his hand, 'I cannot accompany you there; here my neighbours are good, and bear me on the wings of their love; when I die, they will make my death sweet and bury me with songs.

25. 'I fear you, truly I do; you are a stranger, and one who has come unbidden; I am afraid to trust you.

26. 'If this seems unfriendly of me, forgive me; but it is explained by the tale of the fox and the leopard. Do you know it? Then I will tell it to you.'

27. And Charicles told the following tale.

Chapter 3

1. A fox once lived near a leopard in a land of such plenty that the leopard always had as much as he needed to eat, as well for himself as for his wife the leopardess, and their young; and therefore the fox felt safe.

2. But although the fox and leopard were friends and good neighbours, the fox knew that if dearth came, and the plenty ceased, he might end as prey for the leopard himself; for hunger ends friendships, and necessity brings great changes.

3. So the fox counselled himself, saying, 'The sages teach that if one comes to slay you, slay him first.' And he resolved to remove the leopard, leading him into the ways of death to be rid of him.

4. Next day the fox went to the leopard and said, 'I have seen a place of gardens and lilies, where

deer disport themselves in innocence, unwitting of danger;

5. 'Fawn and doe, and buck alike;
handsome and well-grazed with
fat flanks and shining coats; easy
prey and good eating for such as
you.'

6. The leopard was delighted by this
picture, and accompanied the fox
to the place that the latter had
described, smiling with anticipa-
tion. The fox said to himself, 'Ah,
how many a smile ends in tears!'

7. When the leopard had seen the
paradise, he said to the fox, 'I must
go and tell my wife, and bring her
here; how happy she will be to
know of it.'

8. But the fox was dismayed by this,
for he knew that the leopard's wife
had much wisdom, and would
suspect the design that lay behind
all he had planned.

9. So he said to the leopard, 'Do not
trust your wife's judgement in this.
Having once built their homes
wives do not like to leave them,
even if there are better places to
live,

10. 'For they are attached by emotion,
not reason, to the den where they
raised their young. Hear what she
says, but do the opposite.'

11. And indeed when the leopard told
his wife, she did not want to move
to the garden of lilies with its
unsuspecting herds of deer, all the
less so because her husband had
been shown the garden by the fox.

12. 'Beware of the fox,' she told her

husband. 'There are two creatures
one cannot trust, because they are
crafty: the serpent and the fox. Did
you not hear how the fox tricked
the lion and killed him with
cunning?'

13. 'How could a fox dare to do such a
thing,' asked the leopard, 'and kill a
lion, so much more powerful than
he?'

14. So the leopard's wife told him the
following tale.

Chapter 4

1. The lion loved the fox, but the fox
mistrusted the lion because he
feared that if famine came into the
land, the lion would not hesitate to
eat him.

2. One day therefore the fox went to
the lion complaining of a terrible
headache and asking for his help;

3. And when the lion asked what he
could do to help, the fox said,
'There is a sovereign remedy that
the physicians prescribe, and I
know what it is.'

4. 'Tell me,' said the lion, 'for I do not
like to see you suffer; and if you can
teach me to administer the remedy,
then I beg you to do so.'

5. The fox replied, 'The treatment
involves tying the patient hand and
foot, and binding him tightly so
that for a time he cannot move.
Here is a cord; please do this to
me.'

6. 'Then I shall do it, my friend,' cried
the lion, 'to relieve you from this
affliction.' And he bound the fox,

who after a few moments said, 'Ah! The pain has gone! You have cured me!'

7. The lion released him, and rejoiced to see him better; and the two continued as friends for a time after.

8. But then the lion fell victim to the headache, and suffered grievously; and went to the fox to ask for his help.

9. 'Remember how I cured your headache,' the lion asked, nursing his head, 'by tying you up? I ask you to do the same to me, for I suffer now as you did then.'

10. So the fox took bonds, and cast them round the feet of the lion, and tied him up tightly; and when he was bound, he went and fetched great stones, and hurled them on the lion's head to kill him; and by this trick and treachery ended the lion's life.

11. 'I urge you', said the leopardess, 'to think of this, and take warning of the fox's craftiness; for you should ask yourself, "Why has he shown me so sovereign a place, where he himself might take profit in your place?"'

12. The leopard did not wish to take his wife's advice, but at the same time her words had stirred a doubt in him. He told the fox that his wife did not wish to accompany him, and that his own feelings misgave him;

13. Whereupon the fox said, 'If you are guided by your wife in this, your fate will be like that of the silver-smith. Do you know that story?'

14. And so he told the following story to the leopard.

Chapter 5

1. In ancient times, said the fox, there lived a very skilful silversmith, who made beautiful settings for gemstones,

2. But he worked very slowly, so that although his reputation was great, his wealth was small.

3. One day his wife said to him, 'We have not grown rich even though you are so good at your craft.

4. 'But I have a plan; and if you will listen to me I will make us the wealthiest residents of this city.'

5. So the silversmith put down his tools to listen to his wife, who spoke as follows.

6. 'Our lord the king has a new wife, very young and beautiful, and he dotes on her. Make a silver image of her, and I will take it to the palace as a gift.

7. 'We will be rewarded with far more than the value of the silver, and your fame will bring people from far away, who will pay twice for what you make.'

8. But the wife had not reckoned with the jealousy of the king, who could not abide the thought that another would dwell on his wife's beauty, and make an image of it;

9. So that when the silversmith's wife presented the silver statuette at the palace, he was enraged, and ordered the silversmith's arrest;

10. And when the silversmith was brought before him, the king ordered his right hand to be cut off, so that he could no longer work at his trade.

11. Every day thereafter the silversmith wept, until he and his wife at last died of hunger.

12. 'This tale', said the fox, 'teaches us never to listen to our wives' advice in matters of livelihood.'

13. The leopard shuddered to hear this tale; but the fox continued to press home the advantage he saw that he was gaining.

14. 'Have you not heard,' he asked, 'what the great Socrates said when asked why he had married a wife so short and thin? "In order to have of evil the least amount," he replied.

15. 'Have you heard what he said on seeing a woman hanging from a tree? "Would that all trees bore such fruit."

16. 'Have you heard what he replied when one said to him, "Your enemy is dead"? He replied, "I would rather hear that he was married."

17. With these ill tales and false reports the fox steeled the leopard against his wife,

18. And the leopard commanded his wife with anger to bring the cubs to the paradise of fatted deer and green meadows; and there they camped by the water.

19. The fox bade them farewell, his head laughing at his tail.

20. Seven days passed, and in the deep night of the eighth day the waters rose in a customary flood of the place, and engulfed the leopard family where they lay.

21. Even as the leopard struggled under the water of the flood he lamented, 'Woe is me that I did not listen to my wife,' and he and all his family died before their time.

Chapter 6

1. After hearing Charicles tell these stories the stranger said, 'I have shared my bread and cheese and ruby-red wine with you, that I grew in my own vineyard;

2. 'From these tokens of friendship you can see I am no fox who seeks to do you harm. I understand your reluctance;

3. 'But if you wish to learn something new, and to profit from opportunity, you must have courage, and take a risk.'

4. So with reluctance, but persuaded by the stranger's words, Charicles agreed to accompany him, and they started out together, riding on asses.

5. The stranger said to Charicles, 'Carry me, or I will carry you.' Charicles said, 'What do you mean? We are both riding on an ass. Why should either of us carry the other? Explain your words.'

6. The stranger replied, 'The explanation is given in the story of the peasant's daughter and the sage.' And he told Charicles the tale, as follows.

7. There was once a king with an extensive harem of wives and concubines. One night he dreamed that he saw a monkey among his women, and woke with a start.

8. He was very troubled, and thought, 'This is none other than a foreign king who will conquer my realm and take my harem for his prize.'

9. The king called one of his sages and asked him to find out what his ominous dream meant.

10. The sage set out on a mule, and rode into the countryside, where after a while he met an elderly peasant, also on a mule, travelling in the same direction.

11. He said to the peasant, 'Let us travel together,' and the peasant agreed. And as they set forward the sage said, 'Carry me, or I will carry you.'

12. 'But our mules carry us both,' said the peasant, amazed. 'What do you mean?'

13. 'You are a tiller of the earth, and you eat earth,' said the sage. 'And there is snow on the hills.'

14. Because it was the height of summer, the peasant laughed at this, and began to think the sage a madman.

15. They passed through the midst of a wheat field, with wheat growing on each side. 'A one-eyed horse has passed here,' said the sage, 'loaded with oil on one side and vinegar on the other.'

16. They saw a field rich in abounding corn, and the peasant praised it;

'Yes,' said the sage, 'such a field is to be praised until the corn is eaten.'

17. They went on a little further and saw a lofty tower. 'That tower is well fortified,' said the peasant. 'Yes,' said the sage, 'fortified without, if it is not ruined within.'

18. As they rode they passed a funeral. 'I cannot tell whether the man in the coffin is alive or dead,' said the sage.

19. The peasant was now convinced that the sage must be mad, to say such unintelligible things.

20. They arrived at the village where the peasant lived, and he invited the sage to pass the night with him and his family.

Chapter 7

1. In the dead of night the peasant told his wife and daughter of the foolish things the sage had said.

2. 'No,' said the daughter, 'they were not foolish things; you did not understand the depth of his meaning.

3. '"Carry me, or I will carry you" signifies that he who beguiles the way with stories, proverbs, riddles and songs, will make the journey light for his companion.

4. 'The tiller of the earth eats food grown from the earth. The snow on the hill is the white hairs on your head, father; you should have replied, "Time caused it."

5. 'He knew that a one-eyed horse had passed, because the wheat was eaten on one side of the path only.

6. 'And he knew what the horse carried, for the vinegar had parched the dust where it spilled, but the oil had not.

7. 'The corn of the field you passed would already have been eaten if its owner was poor. The lofty tower was not well fortified if there were division or argument among those within.

8. 'And as for the funeral: the dead man lived, if he had children; but was truly dead, if he left no progeny behind.'

9. At this the peasant and his wife marvelled, and understood; and unbeknown to them the sage, who was not sleeping as they thought, heard the daughter's words.

10. In the morning the daughter asked her father to give the sage some food she had prepared.

11. She gave her father thirty eggs, a dish of milk, and a whole loaf of bread, bade him eat and drink his fill, then take the remainder to the sage.

12. 'Ask him when you give him the remainder,' she said, 'how many days old the month is; ask him, is the moon new, and is the sun at its zenith?'

13. The peasant ate two eggs, a little of the loaf, and sipped some of the milk, then carried the rest to the sage and gave it to him.

14. When he returned to his daughter he laughed, and said, 'Surely the man is a fool; for it is the mid-month and the moon is full;

15. 'But when I gave him the remainder of the food, he said, "The sun is not full, neither is the moon, for the month is two days old."

16. 'Now I know for certain that the man is wise,' said the daughter, and she went to the sage and said, 'You are seeking something: tell me what it is and I will answer you.'

17. So the sage told her of the king's dream, and the daughter answered, 'I know the answer. But you must take me to the king himself so that I can tell him.'

18. When the sage and the peasant's daughter came before the king, she said, 'Search your harem; you will find among the women a man disguised as one of them,

19. 'For he is the lover of one of the women, and hides among them to be with her.'

20. The king's guards searched and found that it was true; and brought the offenders before the king. He said to the peasant's daughter,

21. 'Before I punish them, I wish to know what gift I can give you to express my thanks: ask what you will, and if it is agreeable to me, you shall have it.'

22. The peasant's daughter said, 'I ask two things. First, these two have transgressed because of love. I ask you to let them go, for can love ever be a crime that should be punished as other crimes?'

23. The king granted her request, sparing the erring couple's lives but

banishing them from the kingdom for ever.

24. Then the peasant's daughter gestured towards the sage and said, 'For my second request, I would have this man for my husband, if he will take me,

25. 'Because wisdom is the fountain of all good things, and is worthy of love itself; and this man is wise.'

26. Now because the sage had heard the peasant's daughter interpret all his sayings, he had loved her from that moment;

27. So he said to the king, 'And I would marry her for the same reason; for she is wise, and worthy of love in herself.'

28. So the peasant's daughter and the sage were married, and between them raised many wise children, and gave the king counsel whenever he asked.

Chapter 8

1. Charicles was pleased with this story, and thanked the stranger for telling it; and he began to think the stranger was good after all, to honour wisdom with a tale such as this.

2. 'You have carried me,' he said, 'with an instructive story, and made the journey light.' It was nightfall, and they were approaching a city, hoping to find an inn.

3. When Charicles recognised the city they were entering, he wept, and said, 'Here in this place lived one who was a dear friend of mine;

4. 'He died some years ago, but not so many years that my eyes can help filling when I think of him.

5. 'His name was Adasnes. He was a judge, and a good man. I will tell you a story to illustrate his cleverness.' And Charicles told the following tale.

6. A man once came to Adasnes in distress. His only daughter was betrothed to a young man, who with his father had visited the bride's house on the eve of the wedding to see her trousseau and the gifts that had been made ready there.

7. They had come accompanied by a musician who lived nearby, and who played his harp as they sat and enjoyed the rich things made ready for the wedding,

8. And other guests and visitors came too, who wished to salute the engaged couple, and wish them well for the next day.

9. The gathering made merry until midnight, and then departed, leaving the bride and her family to sleep.

10. When the bride and all the household rose the next morning, they found that the trousseau and all the gifts had been stolen.

11. The bride and her family were in despair, for every last penny of what they owned had been lavished on the trousseau and gifts.

12. When Judge Adasnes heard this report he went back with the bride's father to the house to inspect the scene of the robbery.

13. He saw that the walls of the garden in which the house stood were too high to scale.
14. He saw that there was only one possible place of entry, a crevice in the wall where an orange tree grew, covered with a thorny creeper that guarded the crevice like a fence.
15. Adasnes summoned the bridegroom, and the neighbours, and the servants in the neighbours' houses, and all who had been at the celebration that previous night;
16. All the menfolk who had been at the celebration he gathered, and instructed them to roll up the sleeves of their shirts to the elbow, and their trousers to the knee.
17. When they had all done so Adasnes pointed at the musician, and at his servant. 'Arrest these men,' he said, 'for they are the thieves.'
18. On the arms and legs of the musician and his servant were scratches from the thorny creeper round the orange tree, each like a message of guilt to the judge's eye.
19. Seeing that he was caught, the musician's servant fell to his knees and confessed to the crime that he and his master had committed.
20. Adasnes said, 'The greater crime is committed by he who leads another into crime. A mitigation of punishment is owed to him who confesses freely, and is repentant.'
21. They searched the musician's house and found all the stolen goods, which were safely restored to the bride in time for the wedding.

22. Adasnes exiled the musician's servant, but sent the musician to prison, without his harp so that he could not charm the guards with music to let him free.
23. 'Such was the wisdom of my friend Adasnes the judge,' said Charicles, and he brushed a tear from his eye.

Chapter 9

1. 'Tell me more of the judge's wisdom,' the stranger asked, 'because tales of wisdom, along with tales of courage and kindness, are among our best guides in life.'
2. 'Then I will tell you how Adasnes judged the case of the necklace and the nobleman,' Charicles replied, and recounted as follows.
3. There was once a broker of this city, a man of tried honesty, who was entrusted with the care of a beautiful and very valuable necklace,
4. Whose owner asked him to sell it for five hundred pieces of gold. A nobleman holding high office under the king came to the broker's shop,
5. Saw the necklace, admired it, and coveted it; and offered three hundred gold pieces for it.
6. The broker told him that the owner required five hundred gold pieces, and would accept nothing less.
7. 'Come with me to my house,' the nobleman said. 'Bring the necklace to show my wife, and I will consider the price.'
8. The broker went with the nobleman to his house, and waited at the

gate when the latter went indoors.

9. There he waited until dusk, and then long into the night; but no one came out to him, or answered his ringing on the bell.

10. After a sleepless and troubled night he went back to the nobleman's mansion and rang the bell.

11. This time he was admitted. 'Buy the necklace for the price asked,' he said to the nobleman, 'or return the necklace to me.'

12. 'What necklace?' asked the nobleman, feigning surprise before those who stood about them in the reception hall. 'I know of no necklace. You are trying to trick me; leave at once.'

13. So the broker went to Adasnes the judge, and laid the case before him. Adasnes sent for the nobleman, and when he had arrived, he instructed him to remove one of his shoes, and then to wait in another room.

14. Adasnes gave the shoe to the nobleman's servant, who had been standing outside, and said, 'Take this to your master's wife, and say, My master asks for the necklace he brought home to you yesterday, so that he can show off its beauty to his friends.'

15. The servant went, and the nobleman's wife, seeing the shoe and therefore confident that the message was from her husband, gave the necklace to the servant.

16. In this way the theft was proved, the necklace restored to the honest broker, and the nobleman punished for his crime.

Chapter 10

1. 'Worthy judge,' said the stranger, 'who makes the truth come to light. This comes about by understanding the nature of men.'

2. 'True,' Charicles said, 'and nothing shows this better than the story of how Judge Adasnes dealt with a certain servant and a rich man's son. The story is as follows.'

3. There was a very wealthy merchant of this city, who had an only son. The son said to his father one day, 'Father, send me on a voyage, that I might learn to trade, to see foreign lands, and to talk with men of wisdom, and learn from my experiences.'

4. Pleased with this request, the father bought a full-bottomed ship, filled it with quality goods, and sent his son abroad with steady companions and sound words of advice.

5. He himself remained at home with his servant, whom he trusted and who held the second place in his affection after his son.

6. Some years after the son had gone abroad, with only rare messages to tell of his wanderings, the merchant was seized at the heart, and died before he had directed how his property was to be divided.

7. The servant, by now passing himself off as the merchant's son,

took possession of everything, and lived thereafter as a wealthy man.

8. Ten years passed, and the real son returned, his ship freighted with wealth many times greater than his father had given him on departing.

9. But before the ship had weathered the treacherous cape beyond which the harbour's mouth lay, a sudden storm blew up,

10. And drove the ship onto the rocks, where it foundered, and everything was lost, goods and lives all, except for the son himself,

11. Who struggled ashore, with nothing but the wet rags in which he had escaped death.

12. He went to his father's house, and entered; but the servant drove him away with harsh words, denying his identity, and calling him a beggar and imposter;

13. Though in truth the servant knew who he was, but he had no intention to share the old merchant's wealth with anyone; and was determined to claim himself the merchant's son.

14. The real son went to Adasnes the judge to lay his case before him. Adasnes said, 'Bring the merchant's heir before me too, who also says he is the son,' and the servant was summoned.

15. Then Adasnes said, 'Go to the merchant's grave, and dig up the bones; and bring them here to be burnt, as a posthumous punishment for making no will, and

leaving his property to be a cause of strife.'

16. The servant immediately rose in obedience to go to the grave, there to dig up the bones for burning;

17. But the son also immediately rose and petitioned Adasnes, saying, 'Let this servant keep everything; I would not disturb my father's bones, or have him punished even in death.'

18. 'This proves that you are the true son,' said Adasnes the judge. 'Let all be restored to you, and take this man as your slave.'

Chapter 11

1. After their long journey, and these tales, Charicles and the stranger were weary, and slept; but they were woken early by the noise of the city, and decided to go on their way before the sun grew hot.

2. As they rode their asses along the main street, the stranger said, 'You can ask me anything, for I know the half of all knowledge.'

3. 'The half of all knowledge? I cannot believe that,' said Charicles with a laugh. 'Who can know the half of all knowledge?'

4. 'But I do know it,' insisted the stranger; 'I know the half of all knowledge in the world. Test me.'

5. So Charicles asked the stranger what he knew of medicine, and the stranger said, 'Nothing.'

6. And Charicles asked him what he knew of mathematics, and the stranger said, 'Nothing.'

7. And Charicles asked him what he knew of astronomy, and the stranger said, 'Nothing.'
8. And Charicles asked him what he knew of philosophy, and the stranger said, 'Nothing.'
9. And Charicles asked him what he knew of history, and the stranger said, 'Nothing.'
10. And Charicles asked him what he knew of literature, and the stranger said, 'Nothing.'
11. And Charicles asked him what he knew of this subject and that, and every time the stranger said, 'Nothing.'
12. Eventually Charicles said, 'How can you claim to know the half of all knowledge, which is something not even the wisest man would claim?
13. 'For it is clear that when I ask you on any subject we study in the schools, you know nothing at all.'
14. To which the stranger replied, 'Exactly so; for Aristotle says, "He who says, I do not know, has already attained the half of all knowledge."'

Chapter 12

1. 'And yet,' said the stranger, 'if only you will consider the questions you asked to test my knowledge, and what answers any man could give.
2. 'He could answer that he knows medicine, because he can say that if a man is buried, he was formerly ill or had an accident;
3. 'He knows astronomy, for he can tell that it is day when the sun shines, and night when he sees stars;
4. 'He knows arithmetic, because he can ask for a second pot of beer to follow the first;
5. 'He knows measurement, because he can tell whether his belly has grown bigger with feeding;
6. 'He knows music, for he can tell the difference between the barking of a dog and the braying of an ass.
7. 'What is the worth of mere words, if their true meanings make no difference to what a man does?
8. 'In my land, to which I am taking you, though you feared to come with me, every stone has a story to tell of times past, and in every garden the roses bloom.
9. 'The city sits on a hill, on whose slopes the vineyards flourish, and it overlooks a valley, where the vegetable plots are full of ripeness, and a river flows with clear waters.
10. 'On the walls of our city, so pleasant and in a land so fruitful, we have inscribed the teachings of our sages.
11. 'On the walls by the great gates we have placed the teachings of Tibon, who wrote to his son,
12. '"Plant your garden of flowers and herbs by the river; but let your bookshelves also be gardens and pleasure grounds;
13. '"Pluck the fruit that grows there, gather the spices and myrrh. If your heart grows weary, go from garden to garden of your bookshelves,

14. "'From flower bed to flower bed, scene to scene; and refresh yourself;

15. "'For how shall the heart not grow new when there are words of scholarship to teach it, and poetry to delight it,

16. "'And comedy to bring it laughter, and stories of love to make it yearn, and books of sorrows to unburden the tears of things that lie waiting within us all?

17. "'The greatest joy is when you pluck a flower from this garden of bookshelves, and carry it into the garden you have planted by the river,

18. "'There in the summer evening to read even while the music of the water flows quietly around you.

19. "'Then shall desire for the good renew itself in you, and your heart will be rich with manifold delight."

20. 'This is what our sage Tibon wrote to his son; and the words are carved on the walls so that everyone can learn them by heart.'

21. Charicles was impressed by this, and at last looked forward to seeing the stranger's homeland, which at first he had been so reluctant to visit.

Chapter 13

1. Charicles said, 'Now I am eager to visit your city on its hill, and its gardens, and to reading the wise words inscribed on its walls.

2. 'I was nervous to accompany you at first, a stranger; but you tell me good things; and the idea of gardens of flowers and books inspires me.'

3. The stranger said, 'In ancient Athens the philosophers thought out their best ideas walking up and down their groves; nature sobers us, and instructs us.

4. 'When we look up at the night sky we are giddied by its vastness, and the immense distance of the stars;

5. 'And when we look down the steeps of a mountain into the abyss below, we nearly fall;

6. 'And when the moon paints everything silver and white in the stillness of night, when all others sleep and only we ourselves wake, and are watchful and sad,

7. 'Then we hear the voice of thought, and come face to face with ourselves, with the brevity of life, with the lack of all we once had and have lost;

8. 'And yet, also, once we have been patient awhile and continued to listen, we come face to face with hope.

9. 'For we learn then, if we are brave, the power of mind, which is the greatest thing in man; of how, though man is small before nature, his mind can encompass all nature,

10. 'In thinking of it, and singing about it, searching it in science, and celebrating it in poetry.

11. 'So I think all the sages found both courage and modesty through the mind's contact with nature, and these two things are the begetters of hope.

12. 'Is there proof that they were right to hope? Well, only consider: it is many centuries since the first sages paced their groves, and their words and thoughts are with us today, and we speak of them;

13. 'Though nature conquered their bodies and their bodies are dispersed into the elements once more, the fruit of their minds is with us still.

14. 'I like to think of the philosophers walking in their groves. What a mistake it is to stop the child fidgeting (so they call it) over his book, for the body must be active as the mind learns.

15. 'It would be best to teach children while walking in a meadow. You see the scholars swaying as they recite their texts; mind is part of the dance; let the body be active when the mind is active too.

16. 'Though it is good to be in the kingdom of one's library, walking with the greatest of the past in thought, it is good to take the thoughts thus acquired into the air,

17. 'For though it is true that literature is the criticism of life, so is it also true that life is the criticism of learning.

18. 'Another of the sayings written on our city walls is this: let the door to the library of the world open from the library of one's books, and vice versa.'

Chapter 14

1. Charicles listened with great interest to these words, for as a scholar himself he enjoyed nothing more than talk of such things. He said,

2. 'You speak as if you know the text which says that books teach us without rods or stripes, unlike the lessons taught by impatient schoolmasters;

3. 'Without taunts or anger, without gifts or money. Books are not asleep when we approach them,

4. 'Nor do they deny us when we question them, or chide us when we err, or laugh at our ignorance.

5. 'No one is ever ashamed of turning to a book. We might blush to admit ignorance to a fellow human, but never to a dictionary.

6. 'Books are the golden pots of manna, which feed our hunger.

7. 'There is the story of a starving man who called out for food at the city gate, and a kind man gave him a scroll of words, which he ate: and it tasted of honey.

8. 'For this reason the wise man might say, "Eat the book, and be refreshed."

9. 'And he might further say, "Do not make your bookcase of acacia wood, covered with gold leaf, and doors of bevelled glass with mullions and a lock of brass;

10. '"But of plain wood, open to everyone who wishes to take down a volume and read."'

11. The stranger replied, 'These thoughts remind me of a story. There was a married couple in our city, who because they married

young were poor to begin with, while both studied before finding their first jobs.

12. 'They would go together to the bookstalls in the market every weekend, and look through the old torn books being sold cheaply,

13. 'And sometimes were able to afford one, but more often might not be able to resist one, even if it meant no supper that night;

14. 'But they did not feel hungry, because they had the book and could pore over it together, reading to each other by turns.

15. 'As their careers progressed and they became richer, it was easier to buy books; they bought them new, several at a time;

16. 'And many of the new books they bought lay unread, and were put on high shelves out of reach.

17. 'And then they could afford rare and beautiful old books, which they locked in a glass case and never touched, so delicate was the embossed gold leaf, and so fragile the ancient paper smelling of spices and history.

18. 'But one day the wife found one of the cheap old second-hand books they had bought with such excitement in their youthful days, and had read together with pleasure;

19. 'And she wept to think what had passed and been lost.'

Chapter 15

1. Charicles said, 'You remind us that reading profits most when, beside

the book, you have someone with whom to talk of it.

2. 'If it is the book's author, good; if your teacher, better; if a friend, best of all.

3. 'The teacher knows he has succeeded when the pupil no longer needs him. But discussion between friends can never exhaust itself.

4. 'There is a saying: if you would study, find a fellow-student.

5. 'Those are wise words. Friendship made over a book is enduring, and a great solace.'

6. The stranger said, 'I would rather read a good book than meet its author. The best of him is, or should be, in the book; in person he might disappoint us, and ruin the book therefore.

7. 'Someone once said, "Respect the book, or you disrespect its author";

8. 'But it is better to respect not the author but the best of his mind from which his book came.

9. 'In that way we respect an immortality, not a life; lives burden the earth, but a good book is the distillation of something excellent, captured and stored to a use beyond the daily and the passing.'

10. With these conversations and meditations the second day of journeying was passed as lightly as the first, and Charicles and the stranger came to another city, and sought out an inn.

Chapter 16

1. Because he had had travelled two days in the saddle, Charicles was sore, and wondered aloud to the stranger as they settled for the night, why anyone should travel.

2. The stranger said, 'Some travel because they must, some because they will.

3. 'Some feel a destiny, which is in fact curiosity and restlessness, and of their own accord take long and arduous journeys.

4. 'Some love to live in the whole world, and the whole world often responds by refusing to give them anywhere to call their own.

5. 'And so they wander still; the wood pigeon has a nest, the fox her den, but the wanderer's home is both nowhere and everywhere.

6. 'The wise of every culture have their views about how to travel. It is well said that they know nothing of their homelands who know only their homelands, which implies that to travel is to learn;

7. 'But there are those who travel, and who learn nothing. It is well said that at the farthest point of our journeyings what we meet is ourselves;

8. 'But there are those who leave themselves behind, and forget themselves enough to err in foreign places, because they believe they are nowhere that matters.

9. 'The wise say, do not travel with a fool. So the fool had better stay at home, because travel will increase his folly.

10. 'When the wise travel they take note of customs, of people, of the way things are done differently.

11. 'By the same token, to receive a traveller in one's home country is an opportunity to hear news and to learn of far places.

12. 'The ideal traveller is he who travels with no baggage but his thoughts, eager to learn, ready to speak of what he has seen,

13. 'But never to speak with exaggeration or falsehood, keeping due respect for all differences and strangeness he has encountered,

14. 'Knowing that he is himself strange to the stranger, and that he seems different to those who are different from himself.

15. 'Such a traveller is never more at home than when far from home. He sees with clearer eyes than the rest of mankind what ruins have been made by man,

16. 'And what works he can be praised for. When he crosses the mountains on his travels, he can see the coming dawn of peace, because he sees further than the rest.

17. 'The good traveller brings the time of peace nearer. He builds bridges across the seas, he draws nations closer together,

18. 'He shows men that there are many ways of living and loving. He teaches them tolerance,

19. 'He humanises them by being a

brother to them even though he is a
stranger in their midst.'

Chapter 17

1. As they set forward on the third
   day of their journey, the stranger
   said, 'Will you carry me, or shall I
   carry you?'

2. Charicles replied, 'I will carry you,
   with another story of a cunning
   animal;

3. 'Not the fox this time, but the
   monkey, whose tricks teach us
   more about men than men can
   teach us about monkeys.' The story
   went as follows.

4. A crocodile and a monkey were
   friends, and the monkey lived in a
   tree not far from the stream where
   the crocodile lived with his wife.

5. The monkey ate nuts that he picked
   from the treetops, and daily gave
   some to the crocodile; and the
   crocodile relished them greatly.

6. One day the crocodile took some of
   the nuts home to his wife, and she
   found them excellent.

7. She asked, 'Who gave these to
   you?' so he told her of the monkey.

8. She said, 'If the monkey feeds on
   such ambrosial nuts, his heart must
   be ambrosia itself, for there the
   essence of these nuts will be
   collected.

9. 'Bring him to me so that I can tear
   him and eat his heart; a dinner
   such as that would give me more
   pleasure than anything I have
   experienced in my life.'

10. The crocodile refused to bring his

friend the monkey to his wife, so
one day when he was away in
another part of the river, his wife
summoned the hyena, and
explained her desire to him, saying,

11. 'If you will catch the monkey who
    is my husband's friend, and bring
    him to me alive, I will give you
    anything you ask by way of reward.'

12. So the hyena went and lay in wait
    for the monkey, and after several
    days of patience succeeded in
    catching him in his powerful jaws.

13. At first the monkey thought he was
    going to be eaten by the hyena, but
    when he perceived that the hyena
    was carrying him along he asked,
    'Where are you taking me?'

14. In a muffled voice the hyena said,
    'The crocodile's wife wants you, for
    she wishes to eat your heart, which
    she thinks must be ambrosia
    because of the nuts you eat.'

15. At this the monkey began to laugh,
    to the hyena's annoyance; he said to
    the monkey, 'Why are you laugh-
    ing? You are just about to have your
    heart eaten by the crocodile's wife;
    how is that an amusing fate?'

16. The monkey said, 'The crocodile's
    wife is going to be very disap-
    pointed, and at the same time very
    angry with you;

17. 'For you forgot to make sure that I
    had my heart with me when you
    caught me.'

18. The hyena stopped in puzzlement
    at this. 'What do you mean?' he
    asked. 'Have you not got your heart
    with you?'

19. 'No,' said the monkey. 'We monkeys always leave our hearts at home, for otherwise we would be too afraid to go swinging in the trees, so high up from the ground. Did you not know that?'

20. 'Well,' said the hyena, disconsolate, 'what am I to do? You are right: she will be angry, and might eat me instead of you.'

21. 'I would not like that to happen to you,' said the monkey kindly. 'If you wait here I will hasten home and get my heart, and then I will have it with me when we reach the crocodile's wife.'

22. 'That's very kind,' said the hyena, most gratefully, and opened his jaws to let the monkey down.

23. The monkey leaped up into the trees, laughing again and even more loudly; and bade the hyena farewell.

24. 'There are many morals in this tale,' Charicles said, 'but one that always occurs to me is that the politician who takes your vote is like the monkey who promises to fetch his heart;

25. 'Once he has your vote and is in office, he is like the monkey who has tricked you and leaped into the tree;

26. 'But the one difference is, you discover that he has no heart at all.'

Chapter 18

1. With such stories the day's journey of Charicles and the stranger was beguiled. They rode through meadows of anemone, cyclamen, daffodil and iris,

2. Knee-deep in long sweet grass, and in the shade of woods thickly studded with oak and terebinth trees;

3. They rode by the side of streams, and their talk mingled with the sound of waters rushing over stones polished round and clean.

4. Just as the shadows were lengthening towards the east, and the starlings began to gather in the topmost branches of cedars, Charicles with astonishment noticed something:

5. That they had ridden out of a wood on a hillside overlooking his own home-town, where three days before the stranger had visited him.

6. He stopped his ass, and turned open-mouthed to the stranger to seek an explanation for how, all appearance to the contrary, they had ridden in a great circle, and arrived where they had begun.

7. And just as he did so he woke from the dream, but not before he heard the voice of the stranger say:

8. 'This is the country I told you of, when I said, "Come with me to my land and I will show you its happy environs and teach you its lore,"

9. 'For here your acquaintances and neighbours do not appreciate worth, nor know wisdom.

10. 'My country is like a pleasant garden, full of loving people, wise beyond all other people.

11. 'You are a scholar, and would learn

much from what I could show you;
it would be for you to bring that
wisdom back again, to teach it to
your fellows.

12. 'And now you have seen my
country; it exists in our talk; and it
exists here in what your own
country could be if it could be its
best;

13. 'For all countries are my country if
only they would make the effort to
be it;

14. 'And if more such men would
dream as you have dreamed today.'

15. At that Charicles came fully awake,
and wondered mightily at his
dream, which was as clear in his
mind as if he dreamed it still.

Chapter 19

1. The king of the City of Stones was
out riding one day when he saw an
old man planting a fig tree in a
garden.

2. The king stopped to ask him why
he took such pains to plant a tree
whose fruit he could in all probability not expect to eat, because of
his age.

3. Said the old man, 'King, if I do not
live long enough to taste the figs
from this tree, my sons and their
children will certainly do so.'

4. The king asked, 'How old are you?'
to which the other replied, 'Some
weeks short of ninety-one.'

5. The king said, 'If you live long
enough to enjoy the fruit from this
tree, be sure to let me know.'

6. Some years passed, and the king

had forgotten this incident, when a
page told him one day that an old
man wished to present a basket of
figs to him.

7. These words stirred the king's
memory, and he asked for the old
man to be brought before him.

8. Sure enough it was the ancient of
the fig tree, who had brought the
choicest specimens of the tree's
offering.

9. The king accepted the gift with
gracious words, and made the old
man sit beside him as he tasted the
figs,

10. Ordering his servants to put a fine
cloak on the old man, and to give
him a gold coin for every fig in the
basket.

11. When the old man had gone the
king's son asked, 'Father, why did
you show such honour to that old
man?'

12. And the king replied, 'He has
been honoured by nature twice
over: in preserving him to great
age, and in providing him with
abundance of fruits. Shall I
honour him less?'

13. At home in his village the old man
told the story of the king's kindness
and generosity. An envious neighbour decided to outdo him, by
filling a very large basket with figs
and other fruits, and taking them
to the king.

14. At the palace door he explained
that he had heard of the king's
bounty to the ancient, and wished
to have the same reward in

proportion, for here was a basket even more numerously filled with fruits.

15. When the king heard this he ordered the grasping man to be pelted with his own fruits, and driven from the palace grounds.

Chapter 20

1. The king of the City of Stones one day heard two beggars calling out for alms in the street. One cried, 'Take pity on one less fortunate than yourself!'

2. And the other cried, 'Give alms to bring luck to the king and his kingdom!'

3. Pleased by the second beggar's attention to his interests, the king told his servants to take a roast fowl down to the street, stuffed with gold coins, and give it to the second beggar.

4. Now the second beggar was not in want of food, having plenty at home; and was chiefly interested in money.

5. But the first beggar was truly hungry. The second beggar said to him, 'I do not want this fowl; you may have it for the coins you have begged today.'

6. The first beggar said, 'The coins here are not many, and nowhere near the price of a cooked chicken.'

7. But the second said, 'You can have it anyway.' So they exchanged, and the second beggar went home.

8. The first beggar was of course vastly the gainer, finding as he satisfied his hunger the money hidden inside the chicken's carcass.

9. The next day the same thing happened; and again the first beggar found that he was vastly the gainer,

10. Even though he tried to tell the second beggar what a mistake he was making in selling the king's gift so cheaply.

11. For the second beggar did not wish to listen to one whom he thought a fool for giving away all his begged coins for a mere chicken.

12. As a result of this good fortune the first beggar had enough money to open a little shop on the street corner.

13. But again the second beggar came, crying out, 'Give alms to bring luck to the king and his kingdom!'

14. When the king heard the beggar cry out in this way for the third time, he grew impatient. 'I have given that beggar enough to start a little business of his own,' he said. 'Why does he continue to beg outside my palace windows?'

15. So he sent his servants to bring the beggar in, that he might question him. 'After all I have given you, why do you still beg in the street outside my windows?' asked the king. 'Are you so greedy that you cannot be satisfied with what is sent to you?'

16. And the second beggar said, 'But all I have had is the fowls you gave me, which, not requiring food, I sold for a few pennies to the other

beggar who cried in the street with me.'

17. At this the king marvelled, and said, 'The person who gained was one who asked us to think of the less fortunate;

18. 'The one who sought only to flatter me did not understand his good fortune.

19. 'Thus, justice has been done in how matters have here worked out.'

Chapter 21

1. The king of the City of Stones once disputed with his chamberlain whether more kindness was to be found among poor people than among the rich.

2. The chamberlain maintained that only those who are well-to-do show kindness and charity, because only they can afford it.

3. The king, not persuaded by this, summoned a scribe to write down the arguments he and the chamberlain had put forward, and then to lay up the document in a box.

4. After the chamberlain had departed, the king asked the scribe to accompany him in disguise around the kingdom, to see for themselves which of the king or chamberlain was right.

5. They walked in the darkness for a long time before seeing a distant light, which they discovered came from a poor goatherd's hut. There they knocked on the door, and were welcomed by the goatherd

and his family, and offered bread and fruit.

6. The disguised king said, 'We are wayfarers who have taken a vow to eat only kidneys on our journey.'

7. Immediately the goatherd went and slaughtered all four of his goats, and removed their kidneys, so that he had something to offer his guests.

8. The disguised king said, 'Our vow also precludes us from eating before midnight; so we must travel on.'

9. So the goatherd lit them to their path with the only lantern in his hut, leaving his wife and daughters for a time in darkness.

10. The king and scribe then made their way to the mansion of the chamberlain, who had grown wealthy in the king's service;

11. And they found the chamberlain entertaining lavishly, with many guests and much food and wine burdening great tables in his hall.

12. The king and the scribe knocked at the door, and asked if they could have a little food and something to drink.

13. Hearing this the chamberlain strode to the door where they stood and said, 'Off with you beggars! If you do not leave my premises immediately I will have you whipped and beaten. How dare you trouble your betters!'

14. The next day the king sent his courtiers to bring the goatherd and his family to court, and likewise to summon the chamberlain.

15. He had the scribe take out and read the transcript of his discussion with the chamberlain; and then he and the scribe recounted the occurrences of the night before.

16. The king said to the chamberlain, 'You who have much were prepared to give nothing to someone who asked for little. The goatherd had very little, but gave it all to someone who asked.

17. 'This confirms what I argued in our debate: that those with little tend often to be kind because they know what it is to lack means, and they understand that kindness returns on itself in due time.

18. 'But those who have much grow selfish and inconsiderate, and wish to have nothing to do with people who do not equal them socially and in means.

19. 'So you yourself have refuted your own argument, and you will now learn not only what the truth is, but what it feels like.'

20. And the king ordered that the goatherd and his family be lodged in the chamberlain's palace, and the chamberlain in the goatherd's hut; and recommended the moral of this tale to all who heard it.

Chapter 22

1. On a day of fair weather and sunshine, Philologus saw his friend Toxophilus strolling in a meadow while intently reading a book, and went to him, saying,

2. 'You study too closely, Toxophilus.'

To which the other replied, 'I study without effort, for the matter pleases and instructs me, which is all delight.'

3. Said Philologus, 'We physicians say that it is neither good for the eyes to read in bright sunlight, nor wholesome for the digestion to read so soon after dinner.'

4. 'I will never follow physic either in eating or studying,' said Toxophilus, 'for if I did I am sure there would be less pleasure in the one, or profit in the other. But what news brings you here?'

5. 'No news,' replied Philologus, 'just that as I was walking I saw several of our friends go to archery, there to shoot at the butts; but you were not with them.

6. 'So I sought you, and found you looking on your book intently; and thought to come and talk with you, lest your book should run away with you.

7. 'For by your wavering pace and earnest look I perceived that your book was leading you, not you it.'

8. 'There you are right,' said Toxophilus, 'For truly my thoughts were going faster than my feet.

9. 'I am reading a treatise of the mind, which says how well-feathered minds fly true and high, while those with moulted and drooping feathers sink always to base things.'

10. Said Philologus, 'I remember the passage well; it is wonderfully expressed. And now I see it is no marvel that your feet failed you, for

your well-feathered thought was flying so fast.'

11. 'So it was. But perhaps I should go now and practise archery,' said Toxophilus, 'for you put me in mind of a different duty;

12. 'It is a fair day for exercise, and it is as necessary to mingle pastimes with study for the mind's health, as eating and sleeping are for the body's health.

13. 'Aristotle himself says that although it were a fond and childish thing to be always at play, yet play may be used for the sake of earnest matter too;

14. 'And as rest is the antidote of labour, so play is the relief of study and business.'

15. 'And I have heard it said,' Philologus replied, 'that study is like husbandry, in which we till the ground and sow with seed to reap thereafter;

16. 'For I heard myself a good husbandman at his book once say, that to rest from study some time of the day and some time of the year, made as much for the increase of learning as to let the land lie fallow for a season.'

17. Thus persuaded, Toxophilus went with his friend to the butts to shoot arrows as well-feathered as Plato's thoughts; and by that rest and diversion found refreshment for his mind.

Chapter 23

1. One evening, when the old woman's grandchildren demanded a story, she asked them,

2. 'Have you heard about the sisters who hunted deer in the clouds and caught the wind in a net?' They shook their heads.

3. So she pointed at the space under a tree which served as the village school, and said,

4. 'When I was a child there was no school here, and never had been.

5. 'One day a foreigner was brought to the village by some of our men.

6. 'They had found him lying injured in the forest, where he had fallen from a tree trying to catch butterflies.

7. 'My uncle was our medicine man, and he mended his bones and brought him back to health.

8. 'As he recovered he spent many hours talking to my uncle about the country he came from. And my mother's youngest sister sat listening from the next room.

9. 'There in that other country, the foreigner said, not only boys but girls go to school, and learn to read books, and thereby come to know many things,

10. 'And as a result they do many things, and some of them travel the world to learn even more, as he himself had done.

11. 'My mother's sister grew thoughtful. When it was time for the foreigner to leave, she told her family,

12. '"I want to go to this man's country to learn to read, if he will take me."

13. 'The family said that it would be easier to hunt deer among the clouds and catch the wind in a net

than to leave the village and travel far and learn to read.

14. 'But the foreigner said there were towns in the distant lowlands of our own country where she could do just such a thing.

15. 'Oh what discussion and argument there was about it! But my mother's youngest sister was determined, and at last the family agreed.

16. 'So when the foreigner left, accompanied by some of our men to show him to the edge of the forest, she went with him,

17. 'And her next eldest sister was sent with her as chaperone.

18. 'There was sorrow at their departure in the whole village, and some criticism that our family had let them go,

19. 'Not least for such a reason, which many were sceptical about; and no one thought to see either of the sisters again.

20. 'But they returned several years later, to the great excitement of all; and they were full of wonderful stories about what they had seen and done.

21. 'Moreover they could read, and they read marvels to us from books they had brought with them;

22. 'And the people of the village passed the books from one to another,

23. 'Looking in awe at the marks that covered every part of them, and wondering at the mystery they contained.

24. 'And the sisters said they would start a school, and teach anyone in the village who wished to read, and especially the children.

25. 'But the headman said they might as well sow cornseed in the treetops and build huts out of water,

26. 'For where would they get what was needed to build and furnish a school such as the women had seen during their travels?

27. 'So my mother's youngest sister opened one of the books at a certain page,

28. 'And read out a passage to the headman and the whole village, which was part of a story and went as follows:

29. '"A young woman rose from her seat in the middle of the crowded hall where everyone was discussing how this thing should be done,

30. '"And she addressed the men on the platform, saying,

31. '"'When a plan is laid, men always say, "Where shall we get the wherewithal?"

32. '"'But women say, "What have we already got available?"'"

33. 'And immediately the whole village saw that they had a school in any space under a tree, and stones to sit on,

34. 'And two teachers in my mother's sisters, and books in their hands that they had brought with them.

35. 'Now,' the old woman concluded, again pointing down the lane to the tree, 'You can see what their teaching has already done:

36. 'The space under that tree has become a school-house, and into it all the world comes through the pages of the books,

37. 'And the past and future gather round you when you and your teacher are sitting there.

38. 'So the sisters hunted deer in the clouds, and caught the wind in a net;

39. 'And they planted cornseeds in the treetops, and they have grown; and built huts out of water, stronger than huts of wood.'

CONCORD

Chapter 1

1. Fannius said to Laelius, 'Since you have mentioned the word friendship, and we are at leisure,

2. 'You would be doing us a great kindness, Laelius, if you would tell us what you mean by it, for you are famous for your friendships,

3. 'And before now have spoken so eloquently about their importance to us and to the possibility of good lives.'

4. Laelius replied: 'I should certainly have no objection if I felt confidence in myself, Fannius,

5. 'For the theme of friendship is a noble one, and we are indeed at leisure;

6. 'But who am I to speak of this? What ability do I have? What you propose is a task for philosophers;

7. 'For a set discourse on friendship, and an analysis of its meaning, you must go to them.'

8. To which Fannius said, 'But you have much practical experience in friendship, and are accounted the best of friends by your friends;

9. 'Surely this is the best qualification to speak of so important a relationship?

10. 'Not least, Laelius, is the fact that your great friendship with Scipio is the subject almost of legend; and

from its example we all wish to learn.'

11. 'Well,' replied Laelius, 'all I can do is to urge you to regard friendship as indeed the greatest thing in the world,

12. 'For there is nothing which so fits human nature, or is so exactly what we both desire and need, whether in prosperity or adversity.

13. 'But I must at the very beginning lay down this principle: that true friendship can only exist between good people.

14. 'I do not, however, press this too closely, like those who give their definitions a pedantic accuracy.

15. 'There is no practical use in doing that: we must concern ourselves with the facts of everyday life as we find it, not imaginary and ideal perfections.

16. 'Let us mean by "good people" those whose actions and lives leave no question as to their honour, sense of justice, and generosity both of hand and heart;

17. 'Who have the courage to stand by their principles, and who are free from greed, intemperance and violence.

18. 'Such people as these are generally accounted "good", so let us agree to call them that,

19. 'On the ground that to the best of their ability they take nature and human fellow-feeling as the true guides to an honourable and well-lived life.'

Chapter 2

1. 'Now this truth seems clear to me, that nature has so formed us that a certain tie unites us all, but that this tie becomes stronger with proximity.

2. 'So it is that we prefer our fellow-citizens to foreigners, relations to strangers;

3. 'For in their case nature herself has caused a kind of friendship to exist, though it is one which lacks some of the elements of permanence.

4. 'Friendship excels mere acquaint-anceship in this, that whereas you may eliminate affection from acquaintanceship,

5. 'You cannot do so from friendship. Without affection, acquaintance-ship still exists in name; but friendship does not.

6. 'You may best understand friend-ship by considering that, whereas merely social ties uniting people are indefinite,

7. 'Friendship is a tie concentrated into affection, which is the bond one shares most deeply only with a few.

8. 'And now we can try to define friendship, as: enjoyment of the other's company, accord on many things, mutual goodwill and liking.

9. 'With the exception of wisdom, I am inclined to think nothing better than this can be found in human experience.

10. 'There are people who give the palm to riches or to good health, or to power and office;

11. 'Many give the name of the best thing in life to sensual pleasures.

12. 'But all these we may say are frail and uncertain, and depend less on our own prudence than on the caprice of fortune.

13. 'Then there are those who find the "chief good" in virtue. And that is a noble doctrine.

14. 'But the very virtue they talk of is the parent and preserver of friend-ship, and without it friendship cannot exist.'

Chapter 3

1. 'I repeat: let us account as good the persons usually considered so; such as are good in the true sense of everyday life;

2. 'And we need not trouble ourselves about ideal characters who are nowhere to be met.

3. 'Between people like these, Fannius, the advantages of friend-ship are almost more than I can say.

4. 'To begin with, how can life be worth living, which lacks the repose to be found in the companionship and goodwill of a friend?

5. 'What can be more delightful than to have someone you can say anything to, with the same absolute confidence as to yourself?

6. 'Is not prosperity robbed of half its

value if you have no one to share your joy?

7. 'On the other hand, misfortunes would be hard to bear if there were no one to feel them even more acutely than yourself.

8. 'In a word, other objects of ambition serve for particular ends:

9. 'Thus, riches for use, power for securing homage, office for reputation,

10. 'Pleasure for enjoyment, health for freedom from pain and the full use of the functions of the body.

11. 'But friendship alone embraces all advantages. Turn which way you please, you will find it at hand;

12. 'It is everywhere; and yet never out of place, never unwelcome. Fire and water themselves are not of more universal value.

13. 'I am not now speaking of the common or modified form of friendship, Fannius, though even that is a source of pleasure and profit,

14. 'But of that true and complete friendship which enhances prosperity, and relieves adversity of its burden by halving and sharing it.

15. 'And great and numerous as are the blessings of friendship, this certainly is the sovereign one, that it gives us bright hopes for the future, supports our weakness, and banishes despair.

16. 'In the face of a true friend we see as it were a second self. So that where a man's friend is, he is; if his friend be rich, he is not poor;

17. 'Though he be weak, his friend's strength is his; and in his friend's life he enjoys a second life after his own is finished.

18. 'This last is perhaps the most difficult to understand. But such is the effect of the respect, the loving remembrance, and the regret of friends which follow us to the grave.

19. 'While they take the sting out of death, they add a glory to the life of the survivors.

20. 'And indeed: if you eliminate from nature the tie of affection, there will be an end of house and city, nor will so much as the cultivation of the soil be left.'

Chapter 4

1. 'Anyone who does not see the virtue of friendship for its own sake, Fannius, may learn it by observing the effects of quarrels and feuds.

2. 'Was any family ever so well established, any state so firmly settled, as to be beyond destruction by animosities and factions?

3. 'This may teach the immense advantage of friendship; a truth which everybody understands through experience.

4. 'For if any instance of loyal friendship in confronting or sharing danger becomes apparent, everyone applauds it greatly.

5. 'One can easily see what a natural feeling it is, when men who would not have the courage to help a friend, themselves show how right they think it when another does so.

6. 'And it often occurs to me, when thinking about friendship, to ask: is it weakness and want of means that make friendship desired?

7. 'Is its aim an exchange of services, so that each may give that in which he is strong, and receive that in which he is weak?

8. 'Or is it not rather true that, although mutual help is an advantage naturally belonging to friendship,

9. 'Yet its original cause is quite other, prior in time, more noble in character, and springing more directly from human nature itself?

10. 'The Latin word for friendship, "amicitia", is derived from the word for love, "amor", and affection is the prime mover in forming bonds.

11. 'For as to material advantages, it often happens that they are obtained by people merely pretending friendship, who treat others with respect only from self-interest.

12. 'But friendship by its nature admits of no feigning, no pretence: it is both genuine and spontaneous.

13. 'Therefore, Fannius, I say that friendship springs from a natural impulse rather than a wish for help:

14. 'From an inclination of the heart, combined with a feeling of affection, rather than from calculation of the material advantage.

15. 'The strength of this feeling you may notice in animals. They show such love to their offspring for a time, and are so beloved by them,

that they clearly display the bond of affection.

16. 'But this is even more evident in the case of humanity: first, in the affection between children and parents, an affection which only shocking wickedness can sunder;

17. 'Next, when the passion of love has attained mutual strength, on our finding someone with whose character and nature we are in full sympathy,

18. 'Because we think that we perceive in him the beacon-light of what we cherish or admire, respect or like.

19. 'For nothing inspires love, nothing conciliates affection, like the answering chord of what we see is good.

20. 'Why, in a certain sense we may be said to feel affection even for people we have never seen, owing to their reputation for honesty and virtue.

21. 'If the attraction of probity is so great that we can love it not only in those we have never seen,

22. 'But even in an enemy we respect, we need not be surprised if affections are roused when they meet goodness in those with whom intimacy is possible.'

Chapter 5

1. 'I do not deny that affection is strengthened by the receipt of benefits, Fannius, as well as by the perception of a wish to render service,

2. 'But when these are added to the original impulse of the heart, a great warmth of feeling springs up.

3. 'And if anyone thinks that this comes from a sense of weakness, based on a need for help or security,

4. 'All I can say is that he who thinks so gives friendship an origin very base, and an ignoble pedigree.

5. 'For if this were the case, a man's inclination to friendship would be exactly proportional to his low opinion of his own resources. Whereas the truth is quite the other way.

6. 'For when a man's confidence in himself is greatest, when he is so fortified by virtue and wisdom as to want nothing and to feel absolutely self-dependent,

7. 'It is then that he is most conspicuous for seeking out and keeping up friendships.

8. 'Did Scipio, for example, want anything of me? Not the least in the world! Neither did I of him.

9. 'In my case it was an admiration of his virtue, in his case it was perhaps the opinion he entertained of my character, that caused our affection.

10. 'Closer intimacy added to the warmth of our feelings. But though many great advantages ensued, they were not the source of our affection.

11. 'For as we are not beneficent and liberal with a view to receiving gratitude, and do not regard kindness as an investment, but follow a natural inclination to liberality;

12. 'So we looked on friendship as worth seeking, not for ulterior gain, but in the conviction that what it had to give was from first to last included in the feeling itself.

13. 'When once people have found a friend, their aim is to be on the same footing in regard to affection, and be more inclined to do a good service than to ask a return.'

Chapter 6

1. 'Scipio and I frequently discussed friendship. He used to say that the most difficult thing in the world was for a friendship to remain unimpaired to the end of life:

2. 'So many things might intervene, as for example conflicting interests, differences of opinion in politics,

3. 'Frequent changes in character, whether owing to misfortunes or to advancing years.

4. 'He used to illustrate these facts from the analogy of childhood, since the warmest affections between children are often laid aside with their toys;

5. 'And even if they managed to keep friendships into adolescence, they were sometimes broken by a rivalry in courtship,

6. 'Or for some other advantage to which their mutual claims were incompatible.

7. 'Even if the friendship was prolonged beyond that time, yet it frequently received a shock should the two happen to be competitors for office.

8. 'For while the most fatal blow to

friendship in the majority of cases was the lust of money,

9. 'In the case of the best people it was rivalry for office and reputation,

10. 'By which it had often happened that the most violent enmity had arisen between the closest friends.

11. 'Again, wide and justifiable breaches were caused by an immoral request made by one friend of another, to pander to someone's desire to assist him in doing wrong.

12. 'A refusal, though perfectly right, is attacked by the asker as a violation of the laws of friendship.

13. 'Now the people who have no scruples about the requests they make to their friends, thereby allow that they are ready to have no scruples about what they will do for their friends;

14. 'And it is the recriminations of such people which commonly not only quench friendships, but give rise to lasting enmities.

15. '"In fact," Cato used to say, "these fatalities overhang friendship in such numbers that it requires not only wisdom but good luck to escape them all."

16. 'With these premises, then, let us first, if you please Fannius, examine the question: how far ought personal feeling to go in friendship?

17. 'I think that the plea of having acted in the interests of a friend is not a valid excuse for a wrong action.

18. 'For, seeing that a belief in a person's virtue is the original cause of friendship, friendship can hardly remain if virtue is abandoned.

19. 'But if we decide it is right to grant our friends whatever they wish, and to ask them for whatever we wish,

20. 'Perfect wisdom must be assumed on both sides if no mischief is to follow.

21. 'But we cannot assume this perfect wisdom; for we are speaking only of such friends as are ordinarily met with,

22. 'Whether we have actually seen them or have been told about them: people, that is to say, of everyday life.

23. 'We may then lay down this rule of friendship: neither ask nor consent to do what is wrong.

24. 'For the plea "for friendship's sake" is a discreditable one, and not to be allowed.'

Chapter 7

1. 'Let this, then, be laid down as the first law of friendship, that we should ask from friends, and do for friends, only what is good.

2. 'But do not let us wait to be asked either: let there always be an eager readiness, and an absence of hesitation.

3. 'Let us have the courage to give advice with candour. In friendship, let the influence of friends who give good advice be paramount.

4. 'I offer you these rules, Fannius, because I believe that remarkable opinions are held by some, who say

we should avoid close friendships, for fear that one person should have to endure the anxieties of several.

5. 'Each person, they say, has enough and to spare on his own hands; it is too bad to be involved in the cares of other people.

6. 'The wisest course is to hold the reins of friendship as loose as possible; you can then tighten or slacken them at your will.

7. 'For the first condition of a happy life, they say, is freedom from care, which no one can enjoy if he has to worry for others as well as himself.

8. 'Another opinion is still less generous: that friendships should be sought solely for the sake of the profit they give, not from motives of feeling and affection;

9. 'And that therefore just in proportion as a man's power and means of support are lowest, he is most eager to gain friendships.

10. 'What ignoble philosophy! For let us examine these two doctrines.

11. 'What is the value of this "freedom from care"? It might seem tempting at first sight, but in practice it has often to be put on one side.

12. 'For there is no business and no course of action demanded from us by our honour which we can consistently avoid from a mere wish to escape anxiety.

13. 'No, if we wish to avoid anxiety we must avoid virtue itself, which necessarily involves some anxious

thoughts in abhorring qualities that are opposite to itself,

14. 'As for example kindness for ill-nature, self-control for licentiousness, courage for cowardice.

15. 'Thus you may notice that it is the just who are most pained by injustice,

16. 'The brave who are most pained by cowardly actions,

17. 'The temperate who are most pained by depravity.

18. 'It is then characteristic of a rightly ordered mind to be pleased at what is good and grieved at the reverse.'

Chapter 8

1. 'Seeing then that the wise are not exempt from heartache, why should we banish friendship from our lives, for fear of its involving us in some amount of distress?

2. 'If you take away emotion, what difference remains, I do not say between a man and a beast, but between a man and a stone or a log of wood?

3. 'So I say again, the clear indication of virtue, to which a mind of like character is naturally attracted, is the beginning of friendship.

4. 'When that is the case the rise of affection is a necessity.

5. 'For what can be more irrational than to take delight in objects incapable of response,

6. 'Such as office, fame, splendid buildings and personal decoration,

7. 'And yet to take little or no delight in a sentient being endowed with

virtue, who has the faculty of loving and returning love?

8. 'For nothing gives more pleasure than a return of affection, and the mutual interchange of kind feeling and good offices.

9. 'And if we add, as we may fairly do, that nothing so powerfully attracts one thing to itself as likeness does to friendship,

10. 'It will at once be recognised that the good love the good, and attach them to themselves as though they were united by blood and nature.

11. 'For nothing can be more eager for what is like itself than nature.

12. 'So, my dear Fannius, we may look upon this as an established fact, that between good people there is, as if of necessity, a kindly feeling, which is the true source of friendship.

13. 'Again, the believers in the "interest" theory appear to me to destroy the most attractive link in the chain of friendship.

14. 'For it is not so much what one gets from a friendship that gives one pleasure, as the warmth of the friend's feeling;

15. 'And we only care for a friend's service if it has been prompted by affection.

16. 'And so far from its being true that lack of means is a motive for seeking friendship, it is usually those who possess sufficient means,

17. 'And above all who possess virtue (which is a man's best support; so the virtuous are least in need of others), who are most open-handed and beneficent.

18. 'Indeed I am inclined to think that friends ought at times to be in want of something.

19. 'For instance, what scope would my affections have had if Scipio had never wanted my advice or co-operation at home or abroad?

20. 'It is not friendship, then, that follows material advantage, but material advantage follows friendship.'

Chapter 9

1. 'Who would choose a life of the greatest wealth and abundance on condition of neither loving nor being loved by any creature?

2. 'That is the sort of life tyrants endure. They can count on no fidelity, no affection, no security in the goodwill of anyone.

3. 'For them all is suspicion and anxiety; for them there is no possibility of friendship.

4. 'Who can love one whom he fears, or by whom he knows that he is feared?

5. 'Yet such men often have a show of friendship offered them, but it is only a fair-weather show.

6. 'If it ever happen that they fall, as it frequently does, they will at once understand how friendless they are.

7. 'It often happens in the case of men of unusually great means that their very wealth forbids genuine friendships.

8. 'For not only is fortune blind herself, but she generally makes

those blind also who enjoy her favours.

9. 'Now, can anything be more foolish than that men who have all the opportunities that wealth can bestow, should secure all else that money can buy: horses, servants, costly plate;

10. 'But do not secure friends, who are, if I may use the expression, the most valuable and beautiful furniture of life?

11. 'And yet, when the rich acquire the former, they know not who will enjoy them, nor for whom they may be taking all this trouble;

12. 'For such things will all eventually belong to the strongest: while each man has a stable and inalienable ownership in his friendships.

13. 'Scipio often said that no one ever said anything more opposed to the essence of friendship than this: "You should love your friend with the consciousness that you may one day hate him."

14. 'For how can a man be friends with another, if he thinks it possible that he may be his enemy?

15. 'Why, it will follow that he must wish and desire his friend to commit as many mistakes as possible, that he may have all the more handles against him;

16. 'And, conversely, that he must be annoyed and jealous at the right actions or good fortune of his friends.

17. 'This maxim, then, let it be whose it will, is the utter negation of friendship.

18. 'The true rule is to take such care in the selection of our friends as never to enter upon a friendship with anyone whom we could come to hate.

19. 'Scipio used to complain that there is nothing on which people bestow so little pains as friendship:

20. 'That everyone could tell exactly how many goats or sheep he had, but not how many friends;

21. 'And while they took pains in procuring the former, they were careless in selecting friends, and applied no thought to how they might judge of their suitability for friendship.'

Chapter 10

1. 'The qualities we ought to look for in choosing friends are firmness, stability and constancy.

2. 'Where shall we look for these in people who put friendship beneath office, civil or military promotions, and political power,

3. 'And who, when the choice lies between these things on the one side and the claims of friendship on the other, do not give a strong preference to the former?

4. 'It is not in human nature to be indifferent to power; and if the price men have to pay for it is the sacrifice of friendship,

5. 'They think their treason will be eclipsed by the magnitude of the reward.

6. 'This is why true friendship is so difficult to find among politicians and those who contest for office.

7. 'Where can you find the man to prefer his friend's advancement to his own?

8. 'And think how grievous and intolerable it is to most men to share political disaster. You will scarcely find anyone who can bring himself to do that.

9. 'And though it is true that the hour of need shows the friend indeed, yet it is in the following two ways that most people betray their untrustworthiness and inconstancy:

10. 'By disdaining friends when they are themselves prosperous, or by deserting them in their distress.

11. 'A person, then, who has shown a firm, unshaken and unvarying friendship in both these contingencies,

12. 'Must be reckoned as one of a class the rarest in the world, and all but superhuman.'

Chapter 11

1. 'What is the quality to look for as a promise of stability and permanence in friendship? Loyalty.

2. 'We should also look for simplicity, a sociable disposition, and a sympathetic nature, moved by what moves us.

3. 'You can never trust a character which is intricate and tortuous.

4. 'Nor is it possible for one to be trustworthy and firm who is unsympathetic by nature and unmoved by what affects others.

5. 'There are two characteristic features in his treatment of his friends that a good person will always display:

6. 'First, he will be entirely without make-believe or pretence of feeling;

7. 'For the open display even of dislike is more becoming to an ingenuous character than a studied concealment of sentiment.

8. 'Second, there should be a certain pleasantness in word and manner, for these add much flavour to friendship.

9. 'A gloomy temper and unvarying gravity may seem impressive; but friendship should be less unbending,

10. 'More indulgent and gracious, more inclined to all kinds of good-fellowship and good nature.

11. 'But here arises a question of some little difficulty. Are there any occasions on which, assuming their worthiness, we should prefer new to old friends, just as we prefer young to aged horses?

12. 'The answer is clear. There should be no satiety in friendship, as there is in other things. The older the sweeter, as in wines that keep well.

13. 'And the proverb is a true one, "You must eat many a peck of salt with a man to be thorough friends with him."'

Chapter 12

1. 'Have I yet said enough, Fannius, to show that in friendship, just as those who possess any superiority must put themselves on an equal

footing with those who are less fortunate,

2. 'So these latter must not be annoyed at being surpassed in genius, fortune, or rank.

3. 'People who are always mentioning their services to their friends are a nuisance. The recipient ought to remember them; the performer should never mention them.

4. 'In the case of friends, then, as the superior are bound to descend, so are they bound in a certain sense to raise those below them.

5. 'The measure of your benefits should be in the first place your own power to bestow,

6. 'And in the second place the capacity to bear them on the part of those on whom you bestow affection and help.

7. 'For, however great your personal prestige may be, you cannot raise all your friends to the highest state.

8. 'As a general rule, we must wait to make up our minds about friend-ships till men's characters and years have reached their full maturity.

9. 'People must not, for instance, regard as fast friends all whom in their youthful enthusiasm for hunting or football they liked because they shared the same tastes.

10. 'For difference of character leads to difference of aims, and the result of such diversity is to estrange friends.

11. 'Another good rule in friendship is this: do not let an excessive affec-tion hinder the highest interests of your friends. This often happens.

12. 'Our first aim should be to prevent a breach; our second, to secure that, if it does occur, our friendship should seem to have died a natural rather than a quarrelsome death.

13. 'Next, we should take care that friendship is not converted into hostility, from which flow personal quarrels, abusive language and angry recriminations.

14. 'By "worthy of friendship" I mean the friendship of those who have in themselves the qualities that attract affection.

15. 'Such people are rare; and indeed all excellent things are rare; and nothing in the world is so hard to find as a thing entirely and completely perfect of its kind.

16. 'But most people not only recog-nise nothing as good in our life unless it is profitable,

17. 'But they also look upon friends as so much stock, caring most for those who will bring them most profit.

18. 'Accordingly they never possess that most beautiful and most spontane-ous friendship which exists solely for itself, without any ulterior motive.'

Chapter 13

1. 'They fail also to learn about the nature and strength of friendship from their own feelings.

2. 'For everyone loves himself, not for any reward which such love may bring, but because he is dear to himself independently of anything else.

3. 'But unless this feeling is transferred to another, true friendship will never be understood; for a true friend is, as Aristotle says, a kind of second self.

4. 'Most people unreasonably want such a friend as they are unable to be themselves, and expect from their friends what they do not themselves give.

5. 'The fair course is first to be good yourself, and then to look out for another of like character.

6. 'It is between such that the stability in friendship we have been talking about can be secured;

7. 'When, that is to say, those who are united by affection learn, first of all, to rule those passions which enslave others,

8. 'And secondly to take delight in fair and equitable conduct, to bear each other's burdens,

9. 'Never to ask each other for anything inconsistent with virtue and rectitude, and not only to serve and love but also to respect each other.

10. 'I say "respect", Fannius; for if respect is gone, friendship has lost its brightest jewel.

11. 'And this shows the mistake of those who imagine that friendship gives a privilege to licentiousness and ill-behaviour.

12. 'Friendship is the handmaid of virtue, not a partner in guilt:

13. 'To the end that virtue, which is powerless to reach the highest objects when it is isolated, might succeed in doing so in partnership with another.

14. 'Those who enjoy, or have ever enjoyed, such a partnership as this, must be considered to have secured the most excellent and auspicious combination for reaching nature's highest good.'

Chapter 14

1. 'Friendship is the partnership which combines moral rectitude with the mutual gift of peace of mind,

2. 'And with all that men think desirable because with them life is happy but without them cannot be so.

3. 'This being our best and highest object, we must, if we wish for it, devote ourselves to virtue;

4. 'For without virtue we can obtain neither friendship nor anything else worthwhile.

5. 'In fact, if virtue be neglected, those who imagine they have friends will discover their mistake as soon as some disaster forces a test of their supposed friendship.

6. 'Therefore I must repeat, Fannius: satisfy your judgement before engaging your affections; do not love first and judge afterwards.

7. 'We suffer from carelessness in many of our undertakings: in none more than in choosing and cultivating friends.

8. 'All think alike about friendship, whether those who have devoted themselves to politics, or those who delight in science and philosophy,

9. 'Or those who follow a private way of life and care for nothing but their own business,

10. 'Or those lastly who have given themselves body and mind to sensuality;

11. 'They all think, I say, that without friendship life is no life – if they want some part of it, at any rate, to be noble.

12. 'For friendship, in one way or another, penetrates into the lives of us all, and suffers nothing to be entirely free from its influence.

13. 'Though a man be so unsociable as to shun the company of mankind, yet even he cannot refrain from seeking someone to whom he can complain when he suffers.

14. 'We should see this most clearly, if it were possible that we should be carried away to a place of perfect solitude, supplied with every abundance except companionship.

15. 'Who could endure such a life? Who would not lose the zest for all pleasures in his loneliness?

16. 'If a man could ascend the sky and get a clear view of the natural order of the universe, and the beauty of the stars,

17. 'Yet that wonderful spectacle would give him small pleasure, though nothing could be conceived more delightful if only he had someone to tell what he had seen.'

Chapter 15

1. 'Friendship is varied and complex, and it happens that causes of suspicion and offence occasionally arise,

2. 'Which a wise man will sometimes avoid, sometimes remove, and sometimes treat with indulgence.

3. 'A major possible cause of offence arises when the interests of your friend and your own sincerity are in conflict.

4. 'For instance, it often happens that friends need remonstrance and even reproof.

5. 'When these are administered in a kindly manner they ought to be taken in good part.

6. 'But alas, it is all too true that compliance gets us friends, but plain speaking gets us enemies.

7. 'Plain speaking is a cause of trouble, if the result is resentment, which is a poison to friendship;

8. 'But compliance is really the cause of much more trouble, because by indulging a friend's faults one lets him plunge into harm.

9. 'But the man who is most to blame is he who resents plain speaking and allows flattery to egg him on to his detriment.

10. 'On this point, then, from first to last there is need of deliberation and care. If we remonstrate, it should be without bitterness;

11. 'If we reprove, there should be no word of insult. In the matter of compliance, though there should be every courtesy,

12. 'Yet that base kind which assists a man in vice should be unacceptable

to us, for it is unworthy of a free-born man, to say nothing of a friend.

13. 'If a man's ears are so closed to plain speaking that he cannot bear to hear the truth from a friend, we may give him up in despair.

14. 'There are people who owe more to bitter enemies than to apparently pleasant friends: the former often speak the truth, the latter never.

15. 'It is a strange paradox that people are not at all vexed at having committed a fault, but very angry at being reproved for it.

16. 'For on the contrary, they ought to be grieved at the crime and glad of the correction.

17. 'If it is true that to give and receive advice – to give it with freedom and yet without bitterness, receive it with patience and without irritation – is peculiarly appropriate to friendship,

18. 'It is no less true that there can be nothing more subversive of friendship than flattery, adulation and base compliance.

19. 'I use as many terms as possible to brand this vice of light-minded, untrustworthy people, whose sole object is to please without regard to truth.

20. 'In everything false pretence is bad, for it negates our power of discerning the truth.

21. 'But to nothing is it so hostile as friendship; for it destroys that frankness without which friendship is an empty name.

22. 'For if the essence of friendship lies in the closeness of two minds, how can friendship exist if the two minds are in reality at variance?

23. 'Fannius, if we take reasonable care it is as easy to distinguish a genuine from a specious friend

24. 'As it is to distinguish what is coloured and artificial from what is sincere and genuine.

25. 'Fewer people are endowed with virtue than wish to be thought to be so. It is such people that take delight in flattery.

26. 'When they are flattered they take it as testimony to the truth of their own self-praises.

27. 'It is not then properly friendship at all when the one will not listen to the truth, and the other is prepared to lie.'

Chapter 16

1. 'And so I repeat: it is virtue, virtue, which both creates and preserves friendship.

2. 'On it depends harmony of interest, permanence, fidelity.

3. 'When virtue has shewn the light of her countenance, and recognised the same light in another,

4. 'She gravitates towards it, and in turn welcomes what the other has to show;

5. 'And from it springs up a flame which you may call either love or friendship. Both words are from the same root;

6. 'And love is just the cleaving to one whom you love without the

prompting of need or any view to
advantage,

7. 'Though advantage blossoms
   spontaneously in friendship, little
   as you may have looked for it.

8. 'It is with such warmth of feeling,
   Fannius, that I cherished my
   friends. For it was their virtue that I
   loved, and even death has not taken
   that love away.

9. 'I declare that of all the blessings
   which either fortune or nature has
   bestowed upon me, I know none to
   compare with friendship.

10. 'In it I found sympathy in public
    business, counsel in private business;
    in it too I found a means of spending
    my leisure with unalloyed delight.

11. 'Why speak of the eagerness with
    which I and my friends always
    sought to learn something new,

12. 'Spending our leisure hours in the
    quest for knowledge, far from the
    gaze of the world?

13. 'If the recollection and memory of
    these things had perished with my
    friends, I could not possibly endure
    the regret for those so closely
    united with me in life and
    affection.

14. 'But these things have not perished;
    they are rather fed and strength-
    ened by reflection and memory.

15. 'This is everything I have to say on
    friendship. One piece of advice on
    parting; make up your minds to
    this:

16. 'To seek the good is the first
    demand we should make upon
    ourselves;

17. 'But next to the good, and to it
    alone, the greatest of all things is
    friendship.'

LAMENTATIONS

Chapter 1

1. When I was without comfort, and sorrowing; when the grief of life was present to me, and afflictions common to man were upon me, then I lamented, and said:

2. We are born to suffer and die, and the days of our laughter are few in the land.

3. Every joy we foresee has its cost in the loss that must follow, for nothing survives its hour, and the first to fade is the season of pleasantness.

4. To love is to contract for sorrow, since one of two must depart first, and affections diminish and vanish.

5. To love what is made of nature is to love what changes and passes; and yet we must love, and so we must suffer.

6. Likewise to strive is to fail; even the taste of victory grows rank in the mouth, and success is fleeting;

7. And yet we must strive, for what is man if he does not strive; and so we must suffer.

8. To make and hold anything of value is to give hostages to the thieves of time, who owe us nothing in return but the promise to steal us too.

9. At the road's side lie possibilities of accident, disaster and disease;

10. At the road's end lie certainties of age and death; even from our first setting out we are beset.

11. What is the life of man and woman, but labour and vexation, and an ever-uncertain future?

12. What is the truth that accompanies life, other than that we must endure if we make no end before the end?

13. By hope we live, and by reliefs: best in the conversation of a friend, worst in a pot of liquor; but only the ultimate relief of death relieves all.

14. What is hope, but the illusion of possible good: for hope prolongs torments, yet offers itself as their only medicine.

15. No one would be sick, or captive, bereft or bereaved, unloved or a failure, a victim or a scapegoat, lonely or afraid:

16. Yet how rare is he who is not one or more of these at some time, passing as mankind must between the millstones of the months and years?

17. It is vain to comfort the grieving, for grief must have its fill;

18. Like the ashes of roses, or the roses' shadows, that alone remain when their petals have blown, and litter the path behind.

Chapter 2

1. All that seems new is nothing but what the past has forgotten.
2. All things have been tossed on the seas of time; some submerge, then are cast up again as novelty,
3. Some drown and are lost for ever that were for mankind's good, and some whose loss is for mankind's benefit.
4. So it is that envy and malice, and the cruelty and rapine of human to human, always seem of the times, but have been the coin of their exchange for ever.
5. Sects and factions, divisions and quarrels, unforgiving separations of brother and brother, appear as today's problems: but are older than amity.
6. What is it that troubles our sleep, but the pangs of bitterness for what happened yesterday, and the fear that tomorrow will bring the same.
7. It is the weight on the heart that presses out an acid lees, tainting all we drink for our burning thirst.
8. Nothing begins or ends without this: that life starts in another's pain, and ends in our own.
9. Nothing is understood for its worth, until stolen away; making us poor, and the world a wilderness.
10. The brief, effortful, confused span of existence between two nothings, burdened with care and trial, is a tale traced on water, a story written in dust.
11. It is a wild theme, rife with sorrow, an empty theme, deformed with grief,
12. A dark theme, full of falsehood, under a biting and bitter sky.
13. Why live? Why live on? What is there that tomorrow promises so faithfully that yesterday has not hurt us with already?
14. And they give answer who say: deceitful hope, that makes us continue into the narrowing corridor of the windowless future, as if it led to a garden.

Chapter 3

1. I have followed the bier to that opened oblong of earth, have heard the small rain fall on it, and felt my tears choking my throat and stinging my eyes,
2. Even in the cold and grey of the funeral day I have felt the tears coursing on my cheeks.
3. Why? Why? There are holes in the world, where she was, and where the unspoken words of kindness and love wait still to be said, but to the vacancy of the unretrievable past.
4. Now the anger and silences, the misunderstandings and missed opportunities, grow so large that they overshadow the larger seasons of happiness, and blight them;
5. At the last there was no time to undo the wrongs that were left, and with a final kiss to forgive, and establish the best parts of our love as its monument.
6. The threnody of all loves devoured

by ravenous time is 'I wish, I wish';
yet this inevitability makes no
difference to what we do
beforehand:

7. It is as if we say, in our folly and our
ignorance or forgetfulness, 'We have
eternity, therefore I will be angry.'

8. But there are no eternities other
than grief while it lasts, no certainties other than that grief must
come, no escape other than from
life itself and what it asks us to
endure.

9. I have followed the bier to opened
oblongs of earth more than once
now, as the years accumulate and
the tired travellers fall aside one by
one.

10. I see that rapacious death is a
respecter neither of age nor of
condition, though it best likes to
choose those the good loved, to
punish the goodness of the living.

11. For they, living on, alone or
deprived, with the thorn of
memory, the abyss of mourning,
the unfair demand to remake their
world out of ruins of sorrow: they
are death's chief victims.

12. At night, and in the still stretches
of day, at waking, at lying down to
wearying half-sleep, the black bat
of grief closes its wings over us and
stifles our breath;

13. How unbearable, how inextin-
guishable by silence or utterance, is
the weight of this stifling; how
unlimited the horizon of suffering
then, at its worst period.

14. To live is to wait for grief, or to be

the occasion for it, or to witness it,
or cause it, or be changed by it, or
die of it.

Chapter 4

1. My prime of youth is a frost of
cares, my feast of joy but a dish of
pain,

2. My crop of corn is a field of tares,
my wealth no more than dreams of
gain;

3. My day is fled, yet I saw no sun;
and though I live, my life is done.

4. My spring is past, but not yet
sprung; the fruit is dead, with
leaves still green;

5. My youth is past, though I still
young; I saw the world, myself
unseen.

6. My thread is cut, though not yet
spun; and though I live, my life is
done.

7. I sought for death, it was the womb;
I looked for life, it was a shade;

8. I tread the ground, which is my
tomb; and now I die, though just
new made.

9. The glass is full, yet my glass is run;
and though I live, my life is done.

Chapter 5

1. Is nature spiteful, that we live such
a brief span? Life hastens by, and
ends just as we learn how to live it.

2. Maybe the wise can make one
lifetime into many, but the many
make one lifetime into less;

3. For so much of it is wasted, and
wasted moreover on the trivial and
passing, the momentary and empty.

4. One person is possessed by an avarice that is insatiable, another by a toilsome devotion to tasks that are useless;

5. One person is besotted with wine, another is paralysed by sloth;

6. One person is exhausted by ambition that always hangs upon the decision of others,

7. Another, driven by the greed of the trader, hastens wearily over lands and seas in hope of gain;

8. Some are tormented by passion for war and are bent either on inflicting danger or preserving their own safety;

9. Some are worn out by servitude in thankless attendance upon the great;

10. Many are kept busy in pursuit of other men's fortunes or in complaining of their own;

11. Many again, following no fixed aim, shifting and inconstant and dissatisfied, are plunged by their fickleness into plans that are ever new;

12. Some have no fixed principle by which to direct their course, but events take them unawares while they laze and yawn.

13. So surely does all this happen that we cannot doubt the poet who says, 'The part of life we really live is small.'

14. For all the rest of existence is not life, but merely time, wasted time.

15. Vices beset us and surround us on every side, and do not permit us to rise anew and lift up our eyes for the discernment of truth;

16. Rather, they keep us low when once they have overwhelmed us and we are chained to lust for gain, reputation, position and indulgence.

17. Their victims are never allowed to return to their true selves; if ever they chance to find some release,

18. Like the waters of the deep sea which continue to heave even after the storm is past, they are tossed about, and there is no rest from the tumult.

Chapter 6

1. Do you think I speak only of the wretches whose evils are admitted? Look at those whose prosperity men flock to behold; they are smothered by their blessings.

2. To how many are riches a burden! From how many do eloquence and the daily straining to display their powers merely amount to suffering!

3. And likewise, how many are pale from constant pleasures! To how many does the throng of admirers and supplicants that crowd about them leave no freedom!

4. In short, run through the list of citizens from lowest to highest – this one desires an advocate, this one answers the call,

5. That one is on trial, that one defends him, that one gives sentence;

6. No one asserts his claim to himself;

everyone is wasted for the sake of another.

7. Ask about famous people whose names are known everywhere, and you will see that these are the marks that distinguish them:

8. One cultivates another, and this other cultivates yet another; no one is his own master.

9. And then certain people show the most senseless indignation – they complain of the insolence of their superiors, because they were too busy to see them when they wished an audience!

10. But can anyone have the hardihood to complain of another's pride when he has no time to attend to himself?

11. Folly, and folly again, all is folly; the ceaseless, restless pursuit of nothing or little, until night engulfs them, and their place knows them no more.

Chapter 7

1. Though all the sages of history were to concentrate upon this one theme, never could they adequately express their wonder at human folly.

2. We do not suffer anyone to seize our estates, and we rush to law or arms if there is the slightest dispute about the boundary of our property,

3. Yet we allow others to trespass upon our lives; indeed, we ourselves lead in those who will eventually possess it.

4. No one is to be found who is willing to distribute his money, yet among how many does each of us distribute his life!

5. In guarding their fortunes people are often close-fisted, yet, when it comes to wasting time, in the case of the one thing in which it is right to be miserly, they show themselves most prodigal.

6. I should like to question anyone from the company of older men and women and say: 'I see that you have reached the farthest limit of human life, you are pressing hard towards the term of your years;

7. 'Come now, recall your life and make a reckoning. Consider how much time you gave to moneylenders, visitors, lovers, patrons, clients;

8. 'How much time you gave to wrangling with your spouse, how much in hastening about on social duties.

9. 'Add the diseases caused by your own acts; add, too, the time that has lain idle and unused;

10. 'You will see that you have fewer years to your credit than you count.

11. 'Look back in memory and consider when you had a fixed plan, how few days have passed as you intended,

12. 'How few when you were at your own disposal, how few when your face wore its natural expression, how few when your mind was unperturbed.

13. 'Consider what little you have really achieved in so long a life,

14. 'Consider how many have robbed you of life when you were not aware of what you were losing,

15. 'How much was taken up in useless sorrow, in foolish joy, in greedy desire,

16. 'In the allurements of society; see how little of yourself was left to you;

17. 'And then you will perceive that you are dying before your season!

18. 'What is the reason of this? You live as if you were destined to live for ever; no thought of your frailty ever enters your head, of how much time has already gone by you take no heed.

19. 'You squander time as if you drew from a full and abundant supply,

20. 'Though all the while that day which you bestow on some person or thing is perhaps your last.

21. 'You have all the fears of mortals and all the desire as if you were not mortal.

22. 'You will hear many men saying: "After my fiftieth year I shall retire into leisure, my sixtieth year shall release me from public duties."

23. 'And what guarantee, pray, have you that your life will last longer? Who will suffer your course to be just as you plan it?

24. 'Are you not ashamed to reserve for yourself only the remnant of life, and to set apart for wisdom only that time which cannot be devoted to business?

25. 'How late it is to begin to live just when we must cease to live!

26. 'What foolish forgetfulness of mortality to postpone wholesome plans to the fiftieth and sixtieth year, and to intend to begin life at a point which many do not even attain!'

Chapter 8

1. Alas! it is vain to exist: all existence is vain.

2. This vanity finds expression in the whole way in which things exist;

3. In the infinite nature of time and space, contrasted to the finite nature of individuals;

4. In the ever-passing present moment; in the dependence and relativity of all things;

5. In continual becoming without ever being; in constant wishing and never being satisfied;

6. In the long battle which forms the history of life, where every effort is checked by difficulties.

7. Time is that in which all things pass away; it is merely the form in which we discover that effort is vain;

8. It is the agent by which everything in our hands every moment becomes as nothing.

9. That which has been exists no more; it exists as little as that which has never been.

10. Hence a thing of great importance now past is inferior to something of little importance now present, because the latter alone seems real.

11. A man finds himself, to his great astonishment, suddenly existing,

after millions of years of
non-existence:

12. He lives for a while, and then again
    comes an equally long period when
    he exists no more.

13. The heart rebels against this, and
    suffers at the thought.

14. Of every event in life we can say
    only for one moment that it is; for
    ever after, that it was.

15. Every evening we are poorer by a
    day. It makes us mad to see how
    rapidly our short span of time ebbs
    away;

16. This might lead us to believe that
    the greatest wisdom is to make the
    enjoyment of the present the
    supreme object of life,

17. Because that is the only reality, all
    else being merely the play of
    thought.

18. Yet such a course might as well be
    called the greatest folly:

19. For that which in the next moment
    exists no more, and vanishes utterly,
    like a dream, can never be worth
    serious consideration.

20. The whole foundation on which
    our existence rests is the ever-fleet-
    ing present.

21. It lies, then, in the very nature of
    our existence to take the form of
    constant motion,

22. And to offer no possibility of our
    ever attaining the rest for which we
    are always striving.

23. We are like people running down-
    hill, who cannot keep on their legs
    unless they run on, and will
    inevitably fall if they stop;

24. Or, again, like a pole balanced on
    the tip of one's finger; or like a
    planet, which would fall into its
    sun the moment it ceased to hurry
    on its way.

25. Unrest is the mark of existence.

26. In a world where all is unstable,
    and nothing can endure, but is
    swept onwards at once in the
    hurrying whirlpool of change,

27. Where a man, if he is to keep erect
    at all, must always be advancing
    and moving, like an acrobat on a
    rope;

28. In such a world, happiness is
    inconceivable.

Chapter 9

1. The scenes of our life are like
   pictures in rough mosaic: looked at
   closely, they produce no effect.

2. There is nothing beautiful to be
   found in them, unless you stand
   some distance away.

3. So, to gain anything we have
   longed for is only to discover how
   vain and empty it is;

4. And even though we are always
   living in expectation of better
   things,

5. At the same time we often repent
   and long to have the past back
   again.

6. We look upon the present as something to be endured while it lasts.

7. Hence most people, if they glance
   back when they come to the end of
   life, will find that all along they
   have not been living, but merely
   waiting to live;

8. They will be surprised to find that the very thing they disregarded and allowed to pass them by unenjoyed, was the life they were expecting.

9. Of how many people may it not be said that hope made fools of them until they danced into the arms of death!

10. Then again, how insatiable a creature is a human being! Every satisfaction attained sows the seeds of some new desire,

11. So that there is no end to the wishes of each individual will.

12. And why? Because no single thing can ever give satisfaction, but only the whole, which is endless.

13. Life presents itself as a task – the task of surviving, of maintaining life and a precarious equilibrium.

14. Thus life is a burden, and then there comes the second task of fending off despair,

15. Which, like a bird of prey, hovers over us, ready to fall wherever it sees a life secure from need.

16. The first task is to win something; the second, to banish the feeling that it has been won; otherwise it is a burden.

17. Surely, human life is a mistake. Man is a compound of needs and necessities which are hard to satisfy,

18. And even when they are satisfied, all he obtains is a state of painlessness, where nothing remains to him but the danger of boredom.

19. This is proof that existence has no value in itself; for what is boredom but the feeling of the emptiness of life?

20. If life – the craving for which is the very essence of our being – had intrinsic value, there would be no such thing as boredom:

21. Existence would satisfy us in itself, and we should want for nothing.

22. But as it is, we take no delight in existence except when we are struggling for something;

23. And then distance and difficulties to be overcome make our goal look as though it would satisfy us: an illusion which vanishes when we reach it.

24. When we are not occupied by thought or striving, when we cast upon existence itself,

25. Its vain and worthless nature is brought home to us; and this is the essence of nullity.

26. If we turn from contemplating the world as a whole,

27. And the generations of people as they live their little hour of mock-existence and then are swept away in rapid succession;

28. If we turn from this, and look at life in its small details, how ridiculous it seems!

29. It is like a drop of water under a microscope, a single drop teeming with small things; or a speck of cheese full of mites invisible to the naked eye.

30. How we laugh as they bustle about so eagerly, and struggle with one another in so tiny a space!

31. And whether here, or in the little

span of human life, this terrible activity is merely comic.

32. It is only in the microscope that our life looks so big. It is an indivisible point, drawn out and magnified by the powerful lenses of time and space.

Chapter 10

1. Unless suffering is the object of life, our existence must entirely fail in its aim.

2. It is absurd to look upon the pain that abounds everywhere in the world, and originates in needs and necessities inseparable from life itself, as serving no purpose at all.

3. Each separate misfortune, as it comes, seems something exceptional; but misfortune in general is the rule.

4. We find pleasure not nearly so pleasant as we expected, and we find pain much more painful.

5. We are like lambs in a field, disporting themselves under the eye of the butcher, who chooses out first one and then another for his prey.

6. So it is that in our good days we are all unconscious of the evil that might presently be in store for us – sickness, poverty, mutilation, loss of sight or reason.

7. No little part of the torment of existence lies in this, that time is continually pressing upon us, never letting us take breath,

8. But always coming after us, a taskmaster with a whip.

9. If at any moment time stays its hand, it is only when we are delivered over to misery.

10. But misfortune has its uses; for, as our bodily frame would burst if the pressure of the atmosphere was removed,

11. So, if people were relieved of all need and adversity, if everything they undertook were successful, they would go mad.

12. Something of pain and trouble is necessary for everyone at all times: a ship without ballast is unstable and will not sail straight in the sea.

13. Work, worry, labour and trouble form the lot of almost all men all their lives.

14. But if all wishes were fulfilled as soon as they arose, how would men occupy their lives? What would they do with the time that would then oppress?

15. In youth, as we contemplate our coming life, we are like children in a theatre before the curtain is raised,

16. Eagerly waiting for the play to begin. It is fortunate that we do not know what is going to happen.

17. Could we foresee it, there are times when children might seem like innocent prisoners,

18. Condemned, not to death, but to life, and as yet all unconscious of what their sentence means.

19. Yet everyone desires to reach old age; a state of life of which it may be said: 'It is bad today, and it will be worse tomorrow; and so on till the worst of all.'

20. If two men who were friends in their youth meet again when old, the chief feeling they will have at sight of each other will be disappointment at life as a whole;

21. For their thoughts will go back to that earlier time when life seemed so promising,

22. As it lay spread out before them in the rosy light of dawn: only to end in so many failures and sufferings.

23. This feeling will so predominate that they will not consider it necessary to speak of it;

24. But on either side it will be silently assumed, and form the ground of all they talk about.

25. He who lives to see two or three generations is like a man who sits some time in the conjurer's booth at a fair, and witnesses the performance twice or thrice in succession.

26. The tricks were meant to be seen only once, and when they are no longer a novelty they cease to deceive; their effect is gone.

27. Life is a task to be done. It is a fine thing to say, 'He is dead'; it means he has done his task.

28. If children were brought into the world by an act of pure reason alone, would the human race continue?

29. Would not a man rather have so much sympathy with the coming generation as to spare it the burden of existence?

30. I shall be told philosophy is comfortless, because it speaks the truth; and people prefer illusions.

31. Go to the illusionists, then, and leave philosophers in peace! At any rate, do not ask us to accommodate our doctrines to your hopes.

32. That is what those rascals of illusion will do for you. Ask them for any doctrine you please, and you will get it.

Chapter II

1. Every state of well-being, every feeling of satisfaction, is negative;

2. It merely consists in freedom from pain, which is the positive element of existence.

3. It follows that the happiness of any given life is to be measured not by its joys and pleasures,

4. But by the extent to which it has been free from suffering.

5. If this is the true standpoint, the lower animals appear to enjoy a happier destiny than man.

6. However varied the forms taken by human happiness and misery,

7. Leading a man to seek the one and shun the other, the basis of it all is bodily pleasure or pain.

8. The chief source of all passion is thought for what is absent or lies in the future; these are what exercise such a powerful influence on all we do.

9. This is the origin of our cares, hopes and fears – emotions unknown to the brutes.

10. In his powers of reflection, memory and foresight, man possesses an instrument for condensing and storing up his pleasures and sorrows.

11. But the brute has nothing of the kind; whenever it is in pain, it is as though it were suffering for the first time,

12. Even though the same thing should have previously happened to it times out of number.

13. It has no power of summing up its feelings. Hence its careless and placid temper: how much one envies it!

14. But in man reflection enters, with all the emotions to which it gives rise;

15. And it develops his susceptibility to happiness and misery to so great a degree,

16. That at one moment he is delighted, at another he is in the depths of suicidal despair.

17. In order to increase his pleasures, man adds to the number and pressure of his needs,

18. Which in their original state were not much more difficult to satisfy than those of the brute.

19. Hence luxury in all its forms: rich food, tobacco and opium, alcohol, fine clothes, a thousand other things he considers necessary for existence.

20. And above and beyond all this, there is a yet greater source of pleasure and pain:

21. Ambition and the feeling of honour and shame; and with it anxiety about the opinion others have of him.

22. It is true that besides the sources of pleasure he shares with the brutes,

23. man has the pleasures of the mind as well.

24. These vary from the most trifling to the highest intellectual achievements; but there is anguish to be set against them on the side of suffering,

25. Anguish that only intellect can know, and reason, reflecting on the sorrow of things.

26. Anguish is a form of suffering unknown to brutes in their natural state.

Chapter 12

1. The crowd of miserable wretches whose one aim in life is to fill their purses,

2. But never their heads! offers a singular instance of self-inflicted suffering.

3. Their wealth becomes a punishment by being an end in itself and a substitute for life.

4. They hasten about, travelling restlessly. No sooner do they arrive somewhere than they anxiously seek to know what amusements it offers, just like beggars asking where they can receive a dole!

5. But all this only increases the measure of suffering in human life, out of all proportion to its pleasures;

6. And the pains of life are made worse for man by the fact that death is something real to him.

7. The brute flies from death instinctively without knowing what it is,

8. And therefore without ever

contemplating it as man does, who has the prospect of it always before him.

9. The brute is more content with mere existence than is a human; the plant is wholly so; and humans find satisfaction in life just in proportion as they are dull and obtuse.

10. Accordingly, the life of the brute has far less sorrow in it, but also less joy, when compared with a human life;

11. And while this may be traced to the brute's freedom from the torments of care and anxiety, it is also because the illusion of hope is unknown to it.

12. There is thus one respect in which brutes show greater wisdom than humans: their quiet, placid enjoyment of the present moment.

13. This contributes to the delight we take in our domestic pets. They are the present moment personified, and make us feel the value of every hour that is free from troubles,

14. A fact which we, with our thoughts and preoccupations, always ignore.

15. But humans, those selfish and heartless creatures, misuse this quality of the brute,

16. And work it to such an extent that they allow the brute absolutely nothing more than mere, bare life.

17. The bird which can wander over half of the world, they shut in a cage, there to die a slow death in longing and crying for freedom;

18. For in a cage it does not sing from pleasure, but despair.

19. And when I see how humans misuse their dogs, their most loyal friends; how they tie up these intelligent animals with chains,

20. I feel acute sympathy with the brute, and indignation against their owners.

21. Yet even the brutes suffer in nature, from disease or accident, and from the ravages of the beasts of prey.

22. We are forced to ask, Why does all this torment and agony exist, among brutes and among humankind?

23. Alas: the truth is that we suffer, and carry the burden of existence, and there is no remedy other than illusion.

24. The conviction that the world and humanity had better not have been,

25. Is of a kind to fill us with indulgence towards one another.

26. From this point of view, we might well consider that the proper way to address each other is, 'my fellow-sufferer, my companion in miseries'.

27. This may sound strange, but it is in keeping with the facts; it puts others in a right light;

28. And it reminds us of that which is after all the most necessary thing in life:

29. Tolerance, patience, regard, and love of neighbour, of which everyone stands in need, and which, therefore, we each owe to our fellows.

Chapter 13

1. Wife! Yes, I do write to you less often than I ought, because, though I am always wretched,

2. Yet when I write to you or read a letter from you, I am in such floods of tears that I cannot endure it.

3. Oh, that I had clung less to life! I should at least never have known real sorrow, or not so much of it.

4. Yet if I have any hope of recovering any position ever again, I was not utterly wrong to do so:

5. If these miseries are to be permanent, I only wish, my dear, to see you as soon as possible and to die in your arms,

6. For the good we have striven to do has been thankless and goes unrecompensed.

7. I have been thirteen days at Brundisium in the house of Laenius, an excellent man, who has despised the risk to his own safety to keep me safe,

8. Nor has he been induced by the penalty of a most iniquitous law to refuse me the rights and good offices of hospitality and friendship.

9. May I sometime have the opportunity of repaying him! Feel gratitude I always shall.

10. What a fall! What a disaster! What can I say? Should I ask you to come – a woman of weak health and broken heart? Should I refrain from asking you? Am I to be without you, then?

11. I think the best course is this: if there is any hope of my restoration, stay to promote it and push the thing on:

12. But if, as I fear, it proves hopeless, pray come to me by any means in your power.

13. Be sure of this, that if I have you I shall not think myself wholly lost. But what is to become of our beloved daughter Tullia?

14. You must see to that now: I can think of nothing. But certainly, however things turn out, we must do everything to promote that poor girl's happiness and reputation.

15. Again, what is my son to do? Let him, at any rate, be ever in my bosom and in my arms.

16. I cannot write more. A fit of weeping hinders me. I do not know how you have got on; whether you are left in possession of anything, or have been, as I fear, entirely plundered.

17. To your advice that I should keep up my courage and not give up hope of recovering my position, I say that I only wish there were any grounds for such a hope.

18. As it is, when, alas! shall I get a letter from you? Who will bring it me? I would have waited for it at Brundisium, but the sailors would not allow it, being unwilling to lose a favourable wind.

19. For the rest, put as dignified a face on the matter as you can, my dear Terentia.

20. Our life is over: we have had our day: it is not any fault of ours that has ruined us, but our virtue.

21. I have made no false step, except in not losing my life when I lost my honours.

22. But since our children asked me to keep living, let us bear everything else, however intolerable.

23. And yet I, who encourage you, cannot encourage myself.

24. Take the greatest care of your health, and believe me that I am more affected by your distress than my own.

25. My dear Terentia, most faithful and best of wives, and my darling daughter, and that last hope of my race, young Cicero, goodbye!

Chapter 14

1. Brother! My brother! Did you really fear that I had been induced by anger not to write to you? Or even that I did not wish to see you?

2. I to be angry with you! Is it possible for me to be angry with you? Why, one would think that it was you that brought me low!

3. Your enemies, your unpopularity, that miserably ruined me, and not I that unhappily ruined you!

4. The fact is, the much-praised consulate of mine has deprived me of you, of children, country, fortune; from you I should hope it will have taken nothing but myself.

5. From you I have experienced nothing but what was honourable and gratifying: from me you have grief for my fall and fear for yourself, and regret, mourning, desertion.

6. I not wish to see you? The truth is rather that I was unwilling to be seen by you.

7. For you would not have seen your brother – not the brother you had left, not the brother you knew,

8. Not him to whom you had with mutual tears bidden farewell as he followed you on your departure for your province:

9. Not a trace even or faint image of him, but rather what I may call the likeness of a living corpse.

10. And oh! that you had sooner seen me or heard of me as a corpse!

11. Oh that I could have left you to survive, not my life merely, but my undiminished rank!

12. But I call everyone to witness that the one argument which recalled me from death was, that all declared that to some extent your life depended upon mine.

13. In which matter I made an error and acted culpably. For if I had taken my life, my death would have given clear evidence of my fidelity and love to you.

14. As it is, I have allowed you to be deprived of my aid, though I am alive, and with me still living to need the help of others;

15. And my voice, of all others, to fail when dangers threatened my family, which had so often been successfully used in the defence of strangers.

16. For as to my not writing, it was

because of a numbness of my faculties, and a seemingly endless deluge of tears and sorrows.

17. How many tears do you suppose these very words have cost me?

18. As many as I know they will cost you to read them! Can I ever refrain from thinking of you or ever think of you without tears?

19. For when I miss you, is it only a brother that I miss?

20. Rather it is almost a twin brother in the charm of his companionship, a son in his consideration for my wishes, a father in the wisdom of his advice!

21. What pleasure did I ever have without you, or you without me? And what must my case be when at the same time I miss a daughter:

22. How affectionate! how modest! how clever! The express image of my face, of my speech, of my very heart! Or again a son, the prettiest boy, the very joy of my heart?

23. Cruel inhuman monster that I am, I dismissed him from my arms better schooled in the world than I could have wished: for the poor child began to understand what was going on.

24. So, too, your own son, your own image, whom my little boy loved as a companion, and was beginning to respect as an elder brother!

25. Need I mention also how I refused to allow my unhappy wife – the truest of helpmates – to accompany me,

26. That there might be someone to protect the wrecks of the calamity which had fallen on us both, and guard our common children?

27. I dreaded the renewed lamentation which our meeting would cause: while I could not have borne your departure,

28. And was afraid of the very thing you mention in your letter – that you would be unable to tear yourself away.

29. For these reasons the supreme pain of not seeing you – and nothing more painful or more wretched could, I think, have happened to the most affectionate and united of brothers –

30. Was a lesser misery than would have been such a meeting followed by such a parting.

Chapter 15

1. Now, if you can, though I, whom you always regarded as a brave man, cannot do so, rouse yourself and collect your energies in view of any challenge you may have to confront.

2. I hope, if my hope has anything to go upon, that your own spotless character and the love of your fellow citizens, and even remorse for my treatment, may prove a protection to you.

3. But if it turns out that you are free from personal danger, you will doubtless do whatever you think can be done for me.

4. In that matter, indeed, many write

to me at great length and declare they have hopes;

5. But I personally cannot see what hope there is, since my enemies have the greatest influence,

6. While my friends have in some cases deserted, in others even betrayed me.

7. I shall continue to live as long as you shall need me, in view of any danger you may have to undergo:

8. Longer than that I cannot go in this kind of life. For there is neither wisdom nor philosophy with sufficient strength to sustain such a weight of grief.

9. I know that there has been a time for dying, more honourable and more advantageous; and this is not the only one of my many omissions;

10. Which, if I should choose to bewail, I should merely be increasing your sorrow and emphasising my own stupidity.

11. But one thing I am not bound to do, and it is in fact impossible:

12. Remain in a life so wretched and so dishonoured any longer than your necessities, or some well-grounded hope, shall demand.

13. For I, who was lately supremely blessed in brother, children, wife, wealth, and in the very nature of that wealth,

14. While in position, influence, reputation, and popularity, I was inferior to none, however, distinguished –

15. I cannot, I repeat, go on longer lamenting over myself and those dear to me in a life of such humiliation as this, and in a state of such utter ruin.

16. I see and feel, to my misery, of what a culpable act I have been guilty in squandering to no purpose the money which I received from the treasury in your name,

17. I hope beyond hope that our enemies may be content with these endless miseries of ours; among which, after all, there is no discredit for any wrong thing done;

18. Sorrow is the beginning and end, sorrow that punishment is most severe when our conduct has been most unexceptionable.

19. As to my daughter and yours and my young son, why should I recommend them to you, my dear brother?

20. Rather I grieve that their orphan state will cause you no less sorrow than it does me.

21. Yet as long as you are uncondemned they will not be fatherless.

22. The rest, by my hopes of restoration and the privilege of dying in my fatherland, my tears will not allow me to write!

23. Terentia also I would ask you to protect, and to write me word on every subject.

24. Be as brave as the nature of the case admits, and I will endeavour to be likewise.

Chapter 16

1. Yes indeed, my dear Servius, I would have wished that you had been by my side at the time of my grievous loss.

2. How much help your presence might have given me, both by consolation and by your taking an almost equal share in my sorrow,

3. I know from the fact that after reading your letter I experienced a great feeling of relief.

4. For not only was what you wrote calculated to soothe a mourner, but in offering me consolation you manifested no slight sorrow of heart yourself.

5. Yet, after all, your son Servius by all the kindness of which such a time admitted made it evident, both how much he personally valued me,

6. And how gratifying to you he thought such affection for me would be. His kind offices have often been pleasanter to me, yet never more acceptable.

7. For myself again, it is not only your words and your partnership in my sorrow that consoles me, it is your character also.

8. For I think it a disgrace that I should not bear my loss as you – a man of such wisdom – think it should be borne.

9. But at times I am taken by surprise and scarcely offer any resistance to my grief,

10. Because those consolations fail me, which were not wanting in a similar misfortune to those others, whose examples I put before my eyes.

11. After losing the honours which I had gained by the greatest possible exertions, there was only that one solace left which has now been torn away.

12. My sad musings were not interrupted by the business of my friends, nor by the management of public affairs:

13. There was nothing I cared to do in the forum; I could not bear the sight of the senate-house;

14. I thought – as was the fact – that I had lost all the fruits both of my industry and of fortune.

15. But while I thought that I shared these losses with you and certain others, and while I was conquering my feelings and forcing myself to bear them with patience,

16. I had a refuge, one bosom where I could find repose, one in whose conversation and sweetness I could lay aside all anxieties and sorrows.

17. But now, after such a crushing blow as this, the wounds which seemed to have healed break out afresh.

18. For there is no republic now to offer me a refuge and a consolation by its good fortunes when I leave my home in sorrow,

19. As there once was a home to receive me when I returned saddened by the state of public affairs.

20. Hence I absent myself from both home and forum, because home can no longer console the sorrow which public affairs cause me, nor

public affairs that which I suffer at home.

21. All the more I look forward to your coming, and long to see you as soon as possible.

22. No reasoning can give me greater solace than a renewal of our friendship and conversation.

23. In our sadness and sorrow we need our friends, and I cannot imagine how life can be borne without them.

24. Where should we be if there were no love? Unhappy, most unhappy, all who are forsaken in their times of trouble,

25. All who lament, and feel the weariness and burden of the world in their suffering.

CONSOLATIONS

Chapter 1: Of grief: Laelius on the death of Scipio

1. How are we to bear the loss of those we loved? Is there wisdom that can save us from the worst grief, and give us strength to bear what all of us must learn, one inevitable day, to bear?

2. Consider what Laelius said when asked about the death of his friend Scipio, with whom he had passed all his life in work, in war, in office and in affection.

3. A friend said to Laelius, 'You are accounted wise not only for your natural ability and character, but also for your learning.

4. 'In this sense we hear of no one called wise save that one man at Athens, Socrates, who desired to know the good.

5. 'Your wisdom consists in this, that you look upon yourself as self-sufficing, and regard the accidents of life as powerless to affect your virtue.

6. 'How then do you respond to the death of your dear friend Scipio: for such grief is both a test of character, and a mark of the nature of friendship.

7. 'For you did not come to our regular meeting at our college, and it was asked: how fares Laelius in the death of Scipio?

8. 'What does a man reputed for wisdom think and feel in this heavy case?

9. 'I see that you bear your grief in a reasoned manner, even though you have lost one who was at the same time your dearest friend and a man of illustrious character;

10. 'So of course you could not but be affected; nothing else would have been natural in a man of your gentleness;

11. 'But yet I think that the cause of your absence from our college was illness, not melancholy; I do not think grief has defeated you.'

12. To which Laelius replied: 'My thanks, friend! What you say is correct; I would have no right, if in health, to withdraw from duties, not even for personal misfortune;

13. 'For I do not think that anything that can happen will cause a man of principle to intermit a duty.

14. 'As for the honourable appellation of wisdom you give me, I make no claim: you doubtless say this from affection;

15. 'But if anyone was ever truly wise, which I yet doubt, the great Cato most certainly was.

16. 'Putting aside everything else,

consider how he bore his son's death!
I have not forgotten those who lost
their sons when mere children; but
Cato lost his when full-grown with
an assured reputation.

17. 'Do not therefore be in a hurry to
reckon as Cato's superior even
Socrates, for remember that the
former's reputation rests on deeds,
the latter's on words.

18. 'But if I were to claim not to be
affected by grief for Scipio, I should
lie, for so I am:

19. 'Affected by the loss of a friend as I
think there will never be again,
such as I can fearlessly say there
never was before.

20. 'Yet I stand in no need of medicine.
I can find my own consolation, and
it consists chiefly in being free from
the mistaken notions that generally
cause pain at the death of friends.

21. 'To Scipio I am convinced no evil has
befallen. Mine is the disaster, if
disaster there be; and to be prostrated
by distress at one's own misfortunes
does not show that you love your
friend, but that you love yourself.

22. 'As for him, who can say that all is
not more than well? He rests for ever
now; and this after attainments in
life which any man would wish for.

23. 'He achieved great things by his
unswerving dedication in the work
that the world and our community
asked of him.

24. 'What need even to mention the
grace of his manners, his devotion
to those he loved, the integrity of
his conduct to everyone?

25. 'All this is known. What could such
a man have gained by the addition
of a few years?

26. 'Though age need not be a burden,
yet it cannot but take away a
measure of vigour and freshness;

27. 'And with little more to add, there
is nothing that is lost when so
much stands already gained.

28. 'Wherefore, as I said before, all is as
well as possible with him: he sleeps,
after much achievement.'

Chapter 2

1. 'Not so with me; for as I entered life
before him, it would have been fairer
for me to leave it also before him.

2. 'Yet such is the pleasure I take in
recalling our friendship, that I look
upon my life as having been a
happy one because I have spent it
with Scipio.

3. 'With him I was associated in public
and private business; with him I
lived at home and served abroad;

4. 'Between us there was harmony in
our tastes, our pursuits and our
sentiments, which is the true secret
of friendship.

5. 'It is not therefore in that reputation for wisdom you mentioned
just now, especially as it happens to
be groundless, that I find my
happiness so much,

6. 'As in the assurance that the memory
of our friendship will be lasting.

7. 'What makes me care about this is
the fact that in all history there are
scarcely three or four pairs of
friends on record;

8. 'And it is classed with them that I cherish a hope of the friendship of Scipio and Laelius being known to posterity.

9. 'Therefore though I grieve for Scipio, I take comfort and strength in what our friendship was like, and both he and our friendship survive this mere change;

10. 'We walked the earth together, and learned and shared much together; none of this can be taken away.

11. 'I think what he would wish for me, could he wish it now: that I would not allow my missing him to make me fail in my duties to myself, to others, and to his memory.

12. 'I dwell with pleasure on the good of the past, and summon courage to bear his absence now, and turn outward to others who likewise grieve, to comfort them in their affliction;

13. 'For there is comfort in what we share, and in the knowledge that others understand how we feel.

14. 'Nothing can replace Scipio, as nothing can replace any of those we love. We do not cease to grieve, but we learn to live with grief;

15. 'These are our consolations, if we face the inevitabilities of life bravely,

16. 'Nobly enduring, accepting the sincere condolences of our living friends,

17. 'Again and again calling upon ourselves for the courage to live on as those who loved us would wish us to live.

18. 'In this knowledge of our duty to ourselves and the dead we find the strength to perform that duty; and in that performance is our consolation.'

Chapter 3: Of grief: to Apollonius

1. Even before this time, Apollonius, I felt for you in your sorrow and trouble, when I heard of the untimely passing from life of your son, who was so dear to us all.

2. In those days, close upon the time of his death, to visit you and urge you to bear your suffering would have been unsuitable,

3. For you were prostrated by the unexpected calamity; and I could not help sharing in your feeling, and would have added to the weeping around you.

4. Now since time, which assuages all things, has intervened since the calamity, and your present condition demands the aid of your friends,

5. I send you some words of comfort, for the mitigation of grief and the pain of your lamentations.

6. Though there are many emotions that affect the mind, yet grief, from its nature, is the most cruel of all.

7. The pain felt at the death of one we love so dearly is a great cause to awaken grief, and over it we have no control.

8. Yet think of what we say about the right attitude to prosperity and good fortune:

9. We counsel ourselves to treat them rationally, and to maintain a becoming attitude towards them;

10. To put them in proportion, and understand that they are part of the possibilities of life that come and go, and are never certain.

11. If this is how we must view the good that might visit us, it is likewise how we must view the suffering that life brings.

12. For it is a rational safeguard, when pain of mind comes, to provide oneself with a noble patience to endure it.

13. Just as plants are at one time in a season of fruitage and at another time in a season of unfruitfulness,

14. And animals are at one time in fecundity and at another time in barrenness,

15. And on the sea and over the mountains there is both fair weather and storm,

16. So also in life many diverse circumstances occur which bring their changes and reversals in human fortunes;

17. This everyone knows who lives. Yet to try to find constancy in what is inconstant is a trait of people who do not rightly reason about the circumstances of life.

18. Why do I turn your thoughts in this direction? It is to remind you that misfortune is nothing novel for humankind,

19. But that we all have had the same experience of it, and share it with you; and we wish to remind you

that though we never forget, yet the scars heal.

20. Come then and rest on a seat with me in the garden; let us suffer our sorrows to slumber quietly now in our bosoms, in spite of our afflictions;

21. Nothing is ever accomplished by yielding too far to grief and painful lamentation.

22. Now is the time for courage and endurance, now is the time to turn our thoughts to the living who are dear to us too,

23. And not to take ourselves from them, but to help them with our own patience and strength to bear what must be borne; for they bear it too.

Chapter 4: Of grief: to a friend

1. I am grieved to hear that he is dead whom you loved, but I would not have you sorrow more than is fitting.

2. That you should not mourn at all I shall hardly dare insist; and yet I know that it is the better way; for he is at peace, safe from any further harms,

3. And you and his other friends will cherish the best memories of him, and speak of him, thus making him part of life still.

4. But what man will ever be so endowed with that ideal steadfastness of mind, unless he has already risen far above the reach of chance, not to mourn?

5. Even the most stoical would be

stung by an event like this, though for him it were only a sting.

6. We, however, may be forgiven our tears, if only our tears have not flowed to excess.

7. We may weep, but we must not wail. Do you think that this advice is harsh?

8. Well: only consider the reason for lamentations and weeping. It is because we mourn for ourselves as well as for he who has left us; we are sad because we are bereft.

9. But what would your friend say to you, if he could? That he welcomes the love for him you thus show, but that he does not wish you to suffer too much or too long.

10. He will say, let the time not be distant that you put off the soothing of every regret, the quieting of even the bitterest grief.

11. As soon as you cease to observe yourself, the picture of sorrow which you have contemplated will fade away;

12. At present you are keeping watch over your own suffering, and that prolongs it.

13. Let us see to it that the recollection of those whom we loved and have lost becomes a pleasant memory to us.

14. No man reverts with pleasure to any subject which he cannot reflect upon without pain.

15. So too it must be that the names of those whom we have lost come back to us with a grievous pang;

16. But when we recall the best and dearest things about them, and what they added to our own lives by their lives, we can even say, 'The remembrance of lost friends is a good;

17. 'It honours them and consoles us, and keeps them with us in our hearts.'

18. To think of friends who are alive and well is like enjoying a meal of cakes and honey; the recollection of friends who have passed away gives a pleasure that is not without a touch of bitterness.

19. Yet to me, the thought of my dead friends is a consolation nevertheless. For I have had them as if I should one day lose them; I have lost them as if I have them still.

20. Therefore act as befits your own serenity of mind, and cease to put a wrong interpretation on the chances of life and death.

21. Death has taken away, but life has given. Let us greedily enjoy our friends, because we do not know how long this privilege will be ours.

22. Let us think how often we shall leave them when we go on distant journeys, and how often we shall fail to see them even when we are in the same town;

23. We shall thus understand that we have lost too much of their time while they were alive.

24. But will you tolerate men who are most careless of their friends, and then mourn them most abjectly, and do not love anyone unless they have lost him?

25. If we have other friends, we surely

deserve ill at their hands and think ill of them, if they are of so little account that they fail to console us for the loss of one friend.

26. You have buried one whom you loved; look to the others you love and cherish them the more; now is the time for the living to comfort one another.

27. A man ends his grief by the mere passing of time, even if he has not ended it of his own accord.

28. But the most shameful cure for sorrow, in the case of a sensible man, is to grow weary of sorrowing.

29. I should prefer you to move on from grief by choice, rather than have grief abandon you; and you should stop grieving as soon as possible,

30. And honour the dead with loving remembrance that is positive and enhances your life, not hinders it: just as they would wish.

31. He who writes these words to you is no other than I, who wept so excessively for my own dear friend,

32. So that, in spite of my wishes, I must be included among the examples of men who have been overcome by grief.

33. Today, however, I regret this act of mine, and understand that the reason why I lamented so greatly was that I had never imagined it possible for his death to precede mine.

34. The only thought which occurred to me was that he was the younger, and much younger, too – as if

nature kept to the order of our ages!

35. Therefore let us continually think as much about our own mortality as about that of all those we love.

36. In former days I ought to have said: 'My friend is younger than I; but what does that matter? He would naturally die after me, but he may precede me.'

37. It was just because I did not do this that I was unprepared when fortune dealt me the sudden blow.

38. Now is the time for you to reflect, not only that all things are mortal, but also that their mortality is subject to no fixed law.

39. Whatever can happen at any time can happen today.

40. Let us therefore reflect that we shall soon come to the goal which this beloved friend, to our own sorrow, has reached.

Chapter 5: To Marcia

1. If I did not know, Marcia, that you are as far removed from weakness of mind as from all other vices,

2. I should not dare to assail your grief – the grief that we are all prone to nurse and brood upon;

3. Nor should I have hoped to be able to comfort you with philosophy in this trial.

4. But your strength of mind has been already so tested, and your courage, after such a tragic loss, so approved,

5. That this gives me confidence to try. How you bore yourself in

relation to your father is common knowledge;

6. For you loved him as dearly as you love your children, save only that you did not wish him to outlive you.

7. And yet I am not sure that you did not wish even that; for great affection sometimes ventures to break the natural law.

8. You dissuaded your father from taking his own life as long as you could;

9. After it became clear that, surrounded as he was by his enemies sent by Sejanus, he had no other way of escape from servitude,

10. So though you did not favour his plan, you acknowledged defeat, and you routed your tears in public and choked down your sobs,

11. Yet in spite of your composed face you did not conceal them – and these things in an age when the supremely filial was simply not to be unfilial!

12. When, however, changed times gave you an opportunity, you recovered for the benefit of men that genius of your father which had brought him to his end,

13. And thus saved him from the only real death, which is oblivion;

14. And the books which that brave hero had written with his own blood you restored to their place among the memorials of the nation.

15. You have done a great service to scholarship, for a large part of his writings had been burned;

16. You have done a great service to posterity, for history will come to them as an uncorrupted record whose honesty cost its author dear;

17. And you have done a great service to the man himself, whose memory now lives and will ever live so long as it shall be worthwhile to learn the facts of Roman history,

18. So long as there shall be anyone who will wish to know what it is to be unconquered when all necks are bowed and forced to bear the yoke of a tyrant:

19. What it is to be free in thought, in purpose and in act.

20. A great loss, in very truth, would the world have suffered, if you had not rescued this man who was made to suffer for the sake of two of the noblest things: eloquence and freedom.

21. But his books are now read, so he lives, and is held in the hands and hearts of men; thus he fears no passing of the years;

22. But his enemies, and even their crimes by which alone they deserved to be remembered, will soon be heard of no more.

Chapter 6

1. See! I have recalled to your memory old misfortunes, and, that you may know that even this deep wound will surely heal, I have shown you the scar of an old wound that was not less severe.

2. And so let others deal with you gently and ply soft words. I myself

have determined to battle with your grief, and your eyes that are wearied and worn with weeping;

3. Which shall be checked by measures that, if so it may be, you welcome;

4. If not, even against your will, even though you hug and embrace the sorrow that you have kept alive in place of this newly lost one.

5. Otherwise what end will your grief have? Every means has been tried in vain:

6. The consolations of your friends, the persuasions of great men who were your relatives, have been exhausted;

7. Books, your love for which was a gift from your father, are now void of comfort and scarcely serve for brief distraction, and make their appeal to your unheeding eyes in vain.

8. Even time, nature's great healer, that heals even our most grievous sorrows, in your case has lost its power.

9. Three whole years have now passed, and yet the first violence of your sorrow has in no way abated.

10. Your grief is renewed and grows stronger every day – by lingering it has established its right to stay, and has now reached the point that it is ashamed to make an end,

11. Just as all vices become deep-rooted unless they are crushed when they spring up, so, too, such a state of sadness and wretchedness,

12. With its self-afflicted torture, feeds at last upon its own bitterness, and the grief of an unhappy mind becomes a morbid pleasure.

13. And so I should have liked to approach your cure in the first stages of your sorrow;

14. While it was still young a gentler remedy might have been used to check its violence; but against inveterate evils the fight must be more vehement.

15. This is likewise true of wounds – they are easy to heal while they are still fresh and bloody,

16. But when they have festered and turned into a wicked sore, then they must be cauterised and, opened up to the very bottom, must submit to probing fingers.

17. As it is, I cannot possibly be a match for such hardened grief by being considerate and gentle; it must be challenged.

Chapter 7

1. I am aware that all those who wish to give admonition commonly begin with precepts, and end with examples.

2. But it is desirable at times to alter this practice; for different people must be dealt with differently.

3. Some are guided by reason, some must be confronted with famous names and an authority that does not leave a man's mind free, dazzled as he is by famous deeds.

4. I shall place before your eyes only two examples – the greatest of your sex and century:

5. One, a woman who allowed herself

to be swept away by grief; the other, a woman who, though she suffered a like misfortune and even greater loss,

6. Yet did not permit her ills to master her for long, but quickly restored her mind to its accustomed state.

7. They are Octavia and Livia, the first the sister of the Emperor Augustus, the other his wife.

8. They had both lost their sons, young men with the well-assured hope of becoming emperor.

9. Octavia lost Marcellus, upon whom Augustus, at once his uncle and his father-in-law, had begun to lean, upon whom he had begun to rest the burden of empire;

10. A young man of keen mind, of commanding ability, yet marked by a frugality and self-restraint that, for one of his years and wealth, commanded the highest admiration;

11. Patient under hardships, averse to pleasures, and ready to bear whatever his uncle might wish to place upon him.

12. Well had Augustus chosen a foundation that would not sink beneath any weight.

13. Through all the rest of her life Octavia set no bounds to her tears and sighs, and closed her ears to all words that offered wholesome advice;

14. With her whole mind fixed and centred upon one single thing, she did not allow herself even to relax.

15. Such she remained during her whole life as she was at the funeral;

I do not say lacking the courage to rise,

16. But refusing to be uplifted, counting any loss of tears a second bereavement.

17. Not a single portrait would she have of her darling son, not one mention of his name in her hearing.

18. She hated all mothers, and was inflamed most of all against Livia,

19. Because it seemed that the happiness which had once been held out to herself had passed to the other woman's son.

20. Companioned ever by darkness and solitude, giving no thought even to her brother,

21. She spurned the poems that were written to glorify the memory of Marcellus and all other literary honours, and closed her ears to every form of consolation.

22. Withdrawing from all her accustomed duties and hating even the good fortune that her brother's greatness shed around her, she buried herself in seclusion.

23. Surrounded by children and grandchildren, she would not lay aside her garb of mourning, and, putting a slight on all her nearest, accounted herself utterly bereft though they still lived.

Chapter 8

1. And now reflect on Livia. She lost her son Drusus, who would have made a great emperor, and had already shown himself a great leader.

2. For he had penetrated far into Germany, and had planted the Roman standards in a region where it was scarcely known that any Romans existed.

3. He had died on the campaign, and his very foes had reverently honoured his sickbed by maintaining peace along with us.

4. His death received the unbounded sorrow of his fellow-citizens, of the provinces, and of all Italy,

5. Through the length of which crowds poured forth from the towns and colonies, and, escorting the funeral train all the way to the city, made it seem more like a triumph.

6. His mother had not been permitted to receive her son's last kisses and drink in the fond words of his dying lips.

7. On the long journey through which she accompanied the remains of her dear Drusus, her heart was harrowed by the countless pyres that flamed throughout all Italy,

8. For on each she seemed to be losing her son afresh; yet as soon as she had placed him in the tomb, along with her son she laid away her sorrow,

9. And grieved no more than was respectful to the rest of her family, seeing, that they were alive.

10. And lastly, she never ceased from proclaiming the name of her dear Drusus.

11. She had him pictured everywhere, in private and in public places, and it was her greatest pleasure to talk about him and to listen to the talk of others; she lived with his memory.

12. But no one can cherish and cling to a memory that has become an affliction to himself. Livia conquered grief by keeping Drusus alive in her heart.

13. Choose, therefore, which of these two examples to follow.

14. If you prefer Octavia's example, you will remove yourself from the number of the living;

15. You will turn away your eyes both from other people's children and from your own, even from him whom you mourn;

16. Mothers will regard you as an unhappy example; honourable and permissible pleasures you will renounce as ill-becoming to your plight;

17. Hating the light of day, you will linger in it, and your deepest offence will be your age, because the years do not hurry you on and make an end of you as soon as possible;

18. You will show that you are unwilling to live and unable to die.

19. If, on the other hand, you follow the example of Livia, showing thus a more restrained and more gentle spirit, you will not dwell in sorrow, nor rack yourself with anguish.

20. For what madness it is – how monstrous! – to punish oneself for misfortune and add new ills to present ills!

21. That correctness of character and self-restraint which you have maintained all your life, you should exhibit in this matter also;

22. For there is such a thing as moderation even in grieving.

23. And as to he whom you have lost, who so richly deserved that mention of him should always bring you joy,

24. He will occupy a more fitting place, if he comes before his mother as the same merry and joyous son that he used to be when he was alive.

25. Nor shall I direct your mind to precepts of the sterner sort, so as to bid you bear a human fortune in inhuman fashion, so as to dry a mother's eyes on the very day of burial.

26. But I shall come with you before an arbiter, and this will be the question at issue between us – whether grief ought to be deep or never-ending.

Chapter 9

1. I do not doubt that the example of Livia, your intimate friend, will be a good one for you; she summons you to follow her.

2. She, during the first passion of grief, when its sufferers are most unsubmissive and most passionate, made herself accessible to the philosopher Areus, the friend of her husband,

3. And later confessed that she had gained much help from that source – more than from the Roman people, whom she was unwilling to sadden with this sadness of her own;

4. More than from Augustus, who was staggering under the loss of one of his main supports, and was in no condition to be further burdened by the grief of his dear ones;

5. More than from her son Tiberius, whose devotion at that untimely funeral, that made the nations weep,

6. Kept her from feeling that she had suffered any loss except in the number of her sons.

7. It was thus that Areus approached her, it was thus he commenced to address one who clung most tenaciously to her own opinion:

8. 'Up to this day, Livia, you have taken pains that no one should find anything at all in you to criticise; and not only in large matters, but in the smallest trifles,

9. 'You have been on your guard not to do anything that you could wish public opinion, that most unforgiving of judges, to excuse.

10. 'And nothing, I think, is more admirable than the rule that those who have been placed in high position should bestow pardon for many things, should seek pardon for none.

11. 'And so in this matter also you must still hold to your practice of doing nothing that you could wish undone, or done otherwise.

12. 'Furthermore I beg you, do not make yourself unapproachable and difficult to your friends.

13. 'For surely you must be aware that none of them know how to conduct themselves – whether they should speak of Drusus in your presence or not,

14. 'Wishing neither to wrong so distinguished a youth by forgetting him, nor to hurt you by mentioning him.

15. 'When we have withdrawn from your company and are gathered together, we extol his deeds and words with all the veneration he deserved;

16. 'In your presence there is deep silence about him. And so you are missing a very great pleasure in not hearing the praises of your son,

17. 'Which I doubt not, you would be glad, if you should be given the opportunity, to prolong to all times even at the cost of your life.

18. 'Therefore submit to conversation about your son; indeed, encourage it, and let your ears be open to his name and memory;

19. 'And do not consider this burdensome, after the fashion of some others, who in a calamity of this sort count it an added misfortune to listen to words of comfort.

20. 'As it is, you have tended wholly to the other extreme, and, forgetting the better aspects of your fortune, you gaze only on its worse side.

21. 'You do not turn your thought to the happy times you had with your son, nor to his fond and boyish caresses, nor to the progress of his studies;

22. 'You dwell only on that last appearance of fortune, and just as if it were not horrible enough in itself, you add to it all the horror you can.

23. 'Do not, I entreat you, covet that most perverse distinction – that of being considered the most unhappy of women!

24. 'Reflect, too, that it is no great thing to show oneself brave in the midst of prosperity, when life glides on in a tranquil course;

25. 'A quiet sea and a favouring wind do not show the skill of a pilot either; some hardship must be encountered that will test his ability.

26. 'Accordingly, do not be bowed down; on the contrary, plant your feet firmly, and, upset only at first by the din, support whatever burden may fall.

27. 'Nothing endures the chances and changes of life as a firm resolve.'

28. After this he directed her to the son who was still alive, he directed her to the children of the son she had lost.

29. It was your trouble, Marcia, that was dealt with there, it was at your side that Areus sat; change the role: it was you that he sought to comfort.

Chapter 10

1. But suppose, Marcia, more was snatched from you than any mother has ever lost – I am not trying to soothe you or to minimise your calamity.

2. If tears can bring back the past, let us summon tears;

3. Let every day be passed in grief, let every night be sleepless and consumed with sorrow;

4. Let hands rain blows on a bleeding breast, nor spare even the face from their assault;

5. If sorrow will help, let us vent it in every kind of cruelty on ourselves.

6. But if no wailing can recall the dead, if no distress can alter what is immutable and fixed for ever,

7. And if death holds fast whatever it has once carried off, then let grief, which is futile, cease.

8. Therefore let us steer our own ship, and not allow this power to sweep us from the course!

9. He is a sorry steersman who lets the waves tear the helm from his hands, who has left the sails to the mercy of the winds, and abandoned the ship to the storm;

10. But he deserves praise, even amid shipwreck, whom the sea over-whelms while still gripping the rudder, unyielding and firm.

11. 'But,' you say, 'nature bids us grieve for our dear ones.' Who denies it, so long as grief is tempered?

12. For not only the loss of those who are dearest to us, but a mere parting, brings an inevitable pang and wrings even the stoutest heart.

13. But false opinion has added something more to our grief than nature has prescribed.

14. Observe how passionate and yet how brief is the sorrow of dumb animals. The lowing of cows is heard, for one or two days only,

15. And that wild and frantic running about of mares lasts no longer;

16. Wild beasts, after following the tracks of their stolen cubs, after wandering through the forests and returning over and over to their plundered lairs,

17. Within a short space of time quench their agony;

18. Birds, making a great outcry, rage about their empty nests, yet in a trice become quiet and resume their ordinary flight;

19. Nor does any creature sorrow long for its offspring except mankind.

20. He nurses his grief, and the meas-ure of his affliction is not what he feels, but what he wills to feel.

21. Moreover, in order that you may know that it is not by nature that we are crushed by sorrow,

22. First, observe that poverty, grief and ambition are felt differently by different people according as their minds are predisposed,

23. And a false presumption, which arouses a fear of things that are not to be feared, makes a man weak and unresisting.

24. In the second place, note that whatever proceeds from nature is not diminished by its continuance.

25. But grief is effaced by the passing of time. However stubborn it may be, mounting higher every day and bursting forth in spite of efforts to allay it,

26. Yet the most powerful agent to

calm its fierceness is time; time will weaken it.

Chapter 11

1. There remains with you even now, Marcia, an immense sorrow; it seems already to have grown obdurate – no longer the passionate sorrow it was at first, but still persistent and stubborn;

2. Yet this also, little by little, time will remove. Whenever you engage in something else, your mind will be relieved.

3. As it is now, you keep watch on yourself; but there is a wide difference between permitting and commanding yourself to mourn.

4. How much better would it accord with the distinction of your character to form, and not merely to foresee, an end to your grief,

5. And not to wait for that distant day on which, even against your will, your distress will cease. Renounce it of your own will!

6. 'Why then,' you ask, 'do we all so persist in lamenting what was ours, if it is not nature's will that we should?'

7. Because we never anticipate any evil before it arrives, but, imagining that we ourselves are exempt and are travelling a less exposed path,

8. We refuse to be taught by the mishaps of others that such is the lot of all. So many funerals pass our doors, yet we never think of death!

9. So many deaths are untimely, yet we make plans for our own infants

– how they will don the toga, serve in the army, and succeed to their father's property!

10. So many rich men are stricken before our eyes with sudden poverty, yet it never occurs to us that our own wealth also rests on just as slippery a footing!

11. Of necessity, therefore, we are more prone to collapse; we are struck, as it were, off our guard; blows that are long foreseen fall less violently.

12. And you wish to be told that you stand exposed to blows of every sort, and that the darts that have transfixed others have quivered around you!

13. Just as if you were assaulting some city wall, or were mounting, only half-armed, against some lofty position manned by the enemy,

14. Expect to be wounded, and be sure that the missiles that whirl above your head, the stones and the arrows and the javelins, were all aimed at your own person.

15. Whenever anyone falls at your side or behind you, cry out: 'Life, you will not deceive me, you will not find me unprepared and heedless.

16. 'I know what you are planning; it is true you struck someone else, but you aimed at me.'

17. Who of us ever looked upon his possessions with the thought that he would die?

18. Who of us ever ventured to think upon exile, upon want, upon grief?

19. Who, if he were urged to reflect

upon these things, would not reject the idea as too uncomfortable?

20. You say: 'I did not think it would happen.' Do you think there is anything that will not happen, when you know that it is possible to happen, when you see that it has already happened to many?

21. Whatever can befall one man can befall all men.

22. That man lost his children; you also may lose yours.

23. That man was condemned to death; your innocence also is in peril.

24. Such is the delusion that deceives and weakens us while we suffer misfortunes which we never foresaw that we ourselves could possibly suffer.

Chapter 12

1. He robs present ills of their power who has perceived their coming beforehand.

2. All these fortuitous things, Marcia, that glitter about us – children, honours, wealth, spacious halls and vestibules packed with a throng of unadmitted clients,

3. A famous name, a high-born or beautiful wife, and all else that depends upon uncertain and fickle chance – these are not our own but borrowed trappings;

4. Not one of them belongs to us outright. The properties that adorn life's stage have been lent, and must go back to their owners;

5. Some of them will be returned on the first day, others on the second,

only a few will endure until the end.

6. We have, therefore, no reason to be prideful as if we were surrounded with things that belong to us; we have received them merely as a loan from time.

7. On our part we ought always to keep in readiness the gifts that have been granted for a time not fixed, and, when called upon, to restore them without complaint.

8. And so we should love all our dear ones, both those whom, by the condition of birth, we hope will survive us, and those whose own most just hope is to pass away before us,

9. But always with the thought that we have no promise that we may keep them for ever;

10. Nay, no promise even that we may keep them for long.

11. Often must the heart be reminded of this; it must remember that loved objects will surely leave, indeed, are already leaving.

12. Take whatever life gives, remembering that it has no promise to endure.

13. Snatch the pleasures your children bring, let your children in turn find delight in you, and drain joy to the dregs without delay;

14. No promise has been given you even for this night – nay, I have offered too long a respite! no promise has been given even for this hour.

15. We must hurry, the enemy presses

upon our rear. Soon these companions will all be scattered, soon the battle cry will be raised, and these comrade ties sundered.

16. Nothing escapes the pillage of time; men, poor wretches, scarcely know, amid the rout and tumult of time, that they live!

Chapter 13

1. If you grieve for the death of your son, the blame must go back to the time when he was born;

2. For his death was proclaimed at his birth; into this condition was he begotten, this promise attended him from the womb.

3. We have come into the realm of change and chance, and their power is harsh and invincible.

4. We must expect things deserved and undeserved. We will experience the kindness of chance, and its cruelty;

5. Some will burn with fire, applied, it may be, to punish, or it may be to heal;

6. Some will be bound in chains, in the power now of an enemy, now of a fellow-countryman;

7. Some will toss naked on the fickle sea, and, when their struggle with the waves is over, will not be cast up on the shore, but will be swallowed by some monster;

8. Others will be worn down with divers diseases, long suspended between life and death.

9. Time and chance are capricious. What need is there to weep over the different parts of life, one by one? The whole of it calls for tears.

10. New ills will press on before you have done with the old. Therefore we must observe moderation; against our many sorrows the power of the human mind must be arrayed.

11. Again, why this forgetfulness of what is the individual and the general lot? Mortal were you born, to mortals have you given birth.

12. You, who are a crumbling and perishable body and often assailed by the agents of disease,

13. Can you have hoped that from such frail matter you gave birth to anything imperishable?

14. Your son is dead; he has finished his course and reached that goal towards which all those whom you count more fortunate than your child are even now hastening.

15. Towards this, at different paces, moves all this throng that now quarrels in the forum, that looks on at the theatres, that buys in the markets;

16. Both those whom you love and revere and those whom you despise will be made equal as one heap of ashes.

17. Accept this: return now to the thought of Livia who conquered grief by love and remembrance; remember the living, who need you still;

18. Accept the mortality of ourselves and those we love, and see that to

give life is to prepare to lose it, to love is to prepare to grieve,

19. And yet: love, and give life, and be full of courage and honour, for this is our human lot, and we must make it as fine as our powers allow.

Chapter 14: Of old age

1. Wherever I turn, I see evidence of my advancing years. I visited the farm where I grew up, and protested against the money that the bailiff had spent on the tumble-down building.

2. He maintained that the flaws were not due to his own carelessness: 'I am doing everything possible,' he said, 'but the house is old.'

3. And this is the house I saw being built when I was a child! What has the future in store for me, if stones of my own age are already crumbling?

4. I was upset, and took the first opportunity to express my annoy-ance in the bailiff's presence. 'It is clear,' I cried, 'that these plane trees are neglected; they have no leaves.

5. 'Their branches are so gnarled and shrivelled, the boles so rough and unkempt! This would not happen, if someone loosened the earth at their feet, and watered them.'

6. The bailiff protested again that he was doing everything possible, and never relaxed his efforts, 'But,' he said, 'those trees are old.'

7. Now, I had planted those trees myself, I had seen them in their

first leaf. I owe it to the farm that my old age became apparent whichever way I turned.

8. And to it I also owed the realisation that one should cherish and love old age; for it is full of pleasure if one knows how to use it.

9. Just as the farm was serene and mature, with full-grown trees and the patina of use and familiarity making it mellow, so a human being reaches a point of beauty when time has done its work.

10. Fruits are most welcome when almost over; youth is most charm-ing at its close; the quiet conversation after dinner, when the candles burn low, is best.

11. Each pleasure reserves to the end its best things. Life is most delightful when it is on the downward slope, but has not yet reached the abrupt decline.

12. And I myself believe that even the period which stands, so to speak, on the edge of the roof, possesses pleasures of its own.

13. Or else the very fact of our not wanting pleasures has taken the place of the pleasures them-selves. How comforting it is to have tired out one's appetites, and to have done with them!

14. 'But,' you say, 'it is a nuisance to be looking death in the face!' Death, however, should be looked in the face by young and old alike. We are not summoned according to our birth dates.

15. Moreover, no one is so old that it

would be improper for him to hope for another day of existence. And one day, mind you, is a stage on life's journey.

16. Our span of life is divided into parts; it consists of large circles enclosing smaller. One circle embraces and bounds the rest; it reaches from birth to the last day of existence.

17. The next circle limits the period of our young manhood. The third confines all of childhood in its circumference.

18. Again, there is, in a class by itself, the year; it contains within itself all the divisions of time by multiplying which we get the total of life.

19. The month is bounded by a narrower ring. The smallest circle of all is the day; but even a day has its beginning and its ending, its sunrise and its sunset.

20. One day is equal to every day: hence, every day ought to be regarded as if it closed the series, as if it rounded out and completed our existence.

21. But if we add another day, we should welcome it with glad hearts.

22. Those people are happiest, and most secure in their possession of themselves, who can await the morrow without apprehension.

23. When a person has said: 'I have lived!' every morning he arises he receives a bonus. It is wrong to live under constraint; but no man is constrained to live under constraint,

24. Least of all the one that fills him with apprehension about whether this day or the next will be his last. Welcome all equally.

25. All truths are our own property; what any wise individual has said becomes the property of all the wise.

Chapter 15

1. How shall we live when we have lived long, and the years have come to weigh on our heads, and bowed our bodies to the necessities of age and the passing of our prime?

2. I know how well ordered and equable your mind is, my friend, and how rich in culture and good sense.

3. And yet I have an idea that you are at times stirred to the heart by the same circumstances as myself.

4. I have resolved therefore to ask your opinion of some thoughts about the burden of advancing age, common to us both.

5. I am fully aware that you will support old age, as you do everything else, with philosophic calm.

6. So no sooner had I resolved to meditate on the common destiny of all to whom the years gather,

7. But you at once occurred to me as the person best endowed to comment on my thoughts, and help me improve them.

8. To myself, indeed, thinking of this matter has been so helpful, that it has not only wiped away all the disagreeableness of old age, which I

now experience in full, but has even made it luxurious and delightful too.

9. Never, therefore, can philosophy be praised as highly as it deserves, considering that its faithful disciple is able to spend every period of life with fortitude and profit, by attending to its lessons and applying them.

10. People who have no resources in themselves for securing a good and happy life find every age burdensome.

11. But those who look for happiness from within can never think anything bad which nature makes inevitable.

12. In that category before anything else comes old age, which all wish to attain, and which all grumble about when attained. Such is folly's inconsistency and unreasonableness!

13. They say that age is stealing upon them faster than they expected. In the first place, who compelled them to cling to an illusion?

14. For in what respect did old age steal upon manhood faster than manhood stole upon childhood?

15. In what way would old age have been less disagreeable to them if they were in their eight-hundredth year than in their eightieth?

16. All wisdom begins in first following nature, the best of guides.

17. If nature has written the narrative of our lives like a play, she will not be least careless about the last act as if she were an idle poet.

18. For the last act is inevitable, just as to the berries of a tree and the fruits of the earth there comes in the fullness of time a period of ripeness and eventual fall.

19. A wise man will not make a grievance of this. To rebel against nature is folly, but to follow her course brings all the benefits of doing what is wise.

Chapter 16

1. It is typical of some to complain, when they have grown old, that they have lost the pleasures of the senses, without which they do not regard life as life at all;

2. And, secondly, that they are neglected by those from whom they were used to receive attentions.

3. Such men lay the blame on the wrong thing. For if these things had been the fault of old age, then these same misfortunes would have been felt by all others of advanced years.

4. Yet many have never said a word of complaint against old age; for they were only too glad to be freed from the bondage of passion, and were not at all disregarded by their friends.

5. The fact is that blame for complaints of that kind is to be charged to character, not to a particular time of life.

6. For the old who are reasonable and neither cross-grained nor churlish find age tolerable enough: whereas unreason and churlishness cause uneasiness at every time of life.

7. Some might reply to this that it is wealth and high position that make old age tolerable: whereas such good fortune only falls to few. There is something in this, but by no means all.

8. For the philosopher himself could not find old age easy to bear in the depths of poverty, nor the fool feel it anything but a burden though he were a millionaire.

9. You may be sure that the weapons best adapted to old age are culture and the active exercise of the virtues.

10. For if they have been maintained at every period – if one has lived much as well as long – the harvest they produce is wonderful,

11. Not only because they never fail us even in our last days, though that in itself is supremely important,

12. But also because the consciousness of a well-spent life and the recollection of many virtuous actions are exceedingly delightful.

13. There is a quiet, pure and cultivated life which produces a calm and gentle old age, such as we have been told Plato's was, who died at his writing desk in his eighty-first year;

14. Or like that of Isocrates, who says that he wrote the book called *The Panegyric* in his ninety-fourth year, and who lived for five years afterwards;

15. While his master Gorgias of Leontini lived a hundred and seven years without ever relaxing his diligence or giving up work.

16. When someone asked Gorgias why he consented to remain alive so long, he replied, 'I have no fault to find with old age.'

17. That was a noble answer, and worthy of a scholar. But fools impute their own frailties and guilt to old age, instead of to themselves.

Chapter 17

1. There are four reasons for old age being thought unhappy: first, that it withdraws us from active employments;

2. Second, that it enfeebles the body; third, that it deprives us of nearly all physical pleasures;

3. Fourth, that it is the next step to death. Let us examine each separately.

4. From which active employments does age withdraw us? Do you mean from those carried on by youth and bodily strength?

5. Are there then no old men's employments to be conducted by the intellect, even when bodies are weak?

6. The great affairs of life are not performed by physical strength, or activity, or nimbleness of body, but by deliberation, character, expression of opinion.

7. Of these old age is not only not deprived, but, as a rule, has them in a greater degree.

8. Those who say that old age takes no part in public business are like men who would say that a steersman does nothing in sailing a ship,

9. Because, while some of the crew are climbing the masts, others hurrying along the gangways, others pumping out the bilge water, he sits quietly in the stern holding the tiller.

10. He does not do what young men do; nevertheless he does what is much more important and better.

11. For rashness is the note of youth, prudence of old age.

Chapter 18

1. But it is said that memory dwindles. For some it does, but we can seek to retain it by practice and use.

2. Old men might retain their intellects well enough, if they will keep their minds active and employed.

3. Nor is that the case only with men of high position and great office; it applies equally to private life and peaceful pursuits.

4. Sophocles composed tragedies to extreme old age; and being believed to neglect the care of his property owing to his devotion to his art,

5. His sons brought him into court to get a judicial decision depriving him of the management of his estate on the ground of weak intellect.

6. Thereupon the old poet is said to have read to the judges the play he had just composed – the *Oedipus at Colonnus* – and was acquitted by the jury.

7. Did old age then compel this man to become silent in his particular art, or Homer, Hesiod, Simonides, or Isocrates and Gorgias whom I mentioned before,

8. Or the founders of schools of philosophy, Pythagoras, Democritus, Plato, Xenocrates, or later Zeno and Cleanthus, or Diogenes the Stoic?

9. Is it not rather the case with all these that the active pursuit of study only ended with life?

10. Nor need one regret the loss of youth's bodily strength, any more than, when young, we regretted not having the strength of a bull or elephant.

11. We must use what we have, and whatever we may chance to be doing, do it with all our might.

12. What could be weaker than Milo of Croton's exclamation? When in his old age this famous wrestler was watching some athletes practising,

13. And he is said to have looked at his arms and to have exclaimed with tears in his eyes: 'Ah well! these are now as good as dead.'

14. To this one might say: 'Yes, in your case, Milo, for at no time were you made famous by your mind or real self, but by your chest and biceps alone.'

15. Shall we not allow old age the strength to teach the young, to train and equip them for all the duties of life? And what can be a nobler employment?

16. Nor should we think any teachers of the fine arts otherwise than happy, however much their bodily forces may have decayed and failed.

17. And yet that same failure of the bodily forces is more often brought about by the vices of youth than of old age;

18. For a dissolute and intemperate youth bequeaths a body to old age in a worn-out state.

19. Xenophon's Cyrus, for instance, in the discourse he delivered on his death-bed at a very advanced age,

20. Says that he never perceived his old age to have become weaker than his youth had been.

Chapter 19

1. To reminisce and speak of himself is often an old man's way, but it is generally allowed at that time of life.

2. We see in Homer how frequently old Nestor talked of his own good qualities. He was living through a third generation;

3. Nor had he any reason to fear that upon saying what was true about himself he should appear either over-vain or talkative.

4. For, as Homer says, 'From his lips flowed discourse sweeter than honey,' for which sweet breath he wanted no bodily strength.

5. And yet, after all, the famous leader of the Greeks nowhere wishes to have ten men like that giant of strength Ajax, but rather like Nestor:

6. If he could get one Nestor, he feels no doubt of Troy shortly falling.

7. Would one not rather be an old man a somewhat shorter time than an old man before one's time?

8. Accordingly, let there be only a proper husbanding of strength, and let each man proportion his efforts to his powers.

9. Such a one will assuredly not have any great regret for his loss of strength.

10. At Olympia the famous strongman Milo is said to have stepped into the course carrying a live ox on his shoulders. Which of the two would you prefer to have given to you – bodily strength like that of Milo, or intellectual strength like that of Pythagoras?

11. In fine, enjoy the blessing of physical strength when you have it; when it is gone, don't wish it back, unless we are to think that young men should wish their childhood back.

12. The course of life has its bounds, and nature admits of being run but in one way, and only once; and to each part of our life there is something specially seasonable;

13. So that the dependence of children, the joyous feelings of youth, the soberness of maturer years, and the ripe wisdom of old age, all have a certain natural advantage which should be secured in its proper season.

14. Active exercise and temperance can preserve health in old age. Bodily strength may be diminished; but neither is bodily strength demanded from the old.

15. Both by law and custom, the elderly are exempt from duties

which cannot be supported without bodily strength.

16. But, it will be said, many old people are so feeble that they cannot perform any duty in life of any sort or kind.

17. That is not a weakness to be set down as peculiar to old age: it is one shared by ill health.

18. How must we stand up against old age and make up for its drawbacks? By taking pains; we must fight it as we should an illness.

19. We must look after our health, use moderate exercise, take just enough food and drink to recruit, but not to overload, our strength.

20. Nor is it the body alone that must be supported, but the intellect and reason much more.

21. For they are like lamps: unless you feed them with oil, they too go out from old age.

22. Again, the body is apt to become gross either from over-exercise or over-eating;

23. But the intellect becomes nimbler by exercising itself.

24. For what Caecilius means by 'old dotards of the comic stage' are the credulous, the forgetful and the slipshod.

25. These are faults that do not attach to old age as such, but to a sluggish, dull and sleepy old age.

Chapter 20

1. We may remember the words of Cato, when as an old man he was asked about age.

2. 'As I admire a young man who has something of an old man in him,' he said, 'so do I an old man who has something of a young man in him.'

3. The man who aims at this may possibly become old in body, but in mind he never will.

4. 'I am now engaged,' Cato continued, 'in composing the seventh book of my "Origins", for I collect records of antiquity.

5. 'The speeches delivered in all the celebrated cases in which I have acted I am now readying for publication.

6. 'I am writing treatises on law. I am, besides, studying hard at Greek, and after the manner of the Pythagoreans – to keep my memory in working order – I repeat in the evening whatever I have said, heard or done in the course of each day.

7. 'These are the exercises of the intellect, these the training grounds of the mind: while I sweat and labour on these I don't much feel the loss of bodily strength.

8. 'I appear in court for my friends; I frequently attend the senate and bring motions before it on my own responsibility, prepared after deep and long reflection. And these I support by my intellectual, not my bodily forces.

9. 'And if I were not strong enough to do these things, yet I should enjoy my ease, imagining the very activities which I was now unable to perform.

10. 'And what makes me capable of doing this is my past life. For a man who is always living in the midst of these studies and labours does not perceive when old age creeps upon him.

11. 'Thus, by slow and imperceptible degrees, life draws to its end.'

12. The third charge against age is that it reduces capacity for indulgence of the appetites, such as drinking and feasting.

13. But what is the point of this complaint? It is to show that, if we were unable to scorn over-indulgence or drunkenness by the aid of reason,

14. We ought to be very grateful to old age for depriving us of an inclination for that which it is harmful to do.

15. For excessive indulgences hinder thought, are a foe to reason, and blind the eyes of the mind.

16. Although old age has to abstain from extravagant banquets, it is still capable of enjoying modest festivities.

17. It was a good idea of our ancestors to view the presence of guests at a dinner table as a community of enjoyment, which they called 'convivial', meaning 'living together'.

18. And there are many pleasures besides the pleasures of the feast and the inn. We have already spoken of study;

19. Think also of the countryside, and the garden; and remember the story of Lysander's visit to Cyrus, the great Persian king:

20. When Lysander took Cyrus gifts from his allies, the king treated him with courteous familiarity and kindness, and among other things took him to see a carefully planted park near his palace.

21. Lysander expressed admiration of the trees and their arrangement, the careful cultivation of the soil free from weeds,

22. The sweet odours of the flowers planted there; and he asked who had planned and planted this garden.

23. 'It was I,' said Cyrus, 'many of the trees were placed in the earth by my own hands.'

24. Then Lysander, looking at the king's purple robe, the brilliance of his person, and his adornment in the Persian fashion with gold and many jewels, said:

25. 'People are quite right, Cyrus, to call you happy, since the advantages of high fortune have been joined to an excellence like yours.'

Chapter 21

1. The foregoing applies to an old age that has been well established on foundations laid by youth. It is a wretched old age that has to defend itself by speech.

2. Neither white hairs nor wrinkles can at once claim influence in themselves: it is the honourable conduct of earlier days that is rewarded by possessing influence at the last.

3. They say that Sparta was the most dignified home for old age; for nowhere was more respect paid to years, nowhere was old age held in higher honour.

4. Indeed, the story is told of how, when a man of advanced years came into the theatre at Athens, no place was given him anywhere in that large assembly by his own countrymen;

5. But when he came near the Spartans, who as ambassadors had a fixed place assigned to them, they rose as one man out of respect for him, and gave the veteran a seat.

6. When they were greeted with rounds of applause from the whole audience, one of them remarked: 'The Athenians know what is right, but will not do it.'

7. But, it will be said, old men are fretful, fidgety, ill-tempered and disagreeable. But these are faults of character, not of the time of life.

8. And, after all, fretfulness and the other faults I mentioned admit of some excuse – not, indeed, a complete one, but one that may possibly pass:

9. For with some justification the elderly think themselves neglected, looked down upon, mocked.

10. Besides, with bodily weakness every rub is a source of pain. Yet all these faults are softened both by good character and good education.

11. There remains the fourth reason, which more than anything else appears to torment some older people,

12. And to make the approach of age seem disagreeable to those who are younger: namely, the increasing nearness of death.

13. But what a poor dotard must he be who has not learnt in the course of so long a life that death is not a thing to be feared?

14. Death is no different from being unborn. It is sleep without dreams, it is rest, the final escape from all ills and passions.

15. It is immunity from wrong, from calumny, error and spite. Who would not welcome this, who can think clearly and without fear?

16. And in any case death is common to every time of life, and in many cases has a nearer approach to infancy and to youth, with its accidents and its own diseases.

17. What sort of charge against old age is the nearness of death, when this is shared by youth?

18. Yes, you will say; but a young man expects to live long; an old man cannot expect to do so.

19. Well, the young man is a fool to expect it. For what can be more foolish than to regard the uncertain as certain, the false as true?

20. 'An old man has nothing even to hope.' Ah, but it is just there that he is in a better position than the young man, since what the latter only hopes he has obtained:

21. The one wishes to live long; the other has lived long.

22. And yet! what is 'long' in a man's life? For grant the utmost limit: let us expect an age like that of the king of the Tartessi, who reigned eighty years and lived a hundred and twenty.

23. Nothing seems long in which there is any 'last', for when that arrives, then all the past has slipped away – only that remains which you have earned by virtue and righteous actions.

24. Hours indeed, and days and months and years depart, nor does past time ever return, nor can the future be known.

25. Whatever time each is granted for life, with that he is bound to be content.

26. An actor, to win approval, is not bound to perform the whole play; let him only satisfy the audience in whatever act he appears.

27. Nor need a wise man go on to the concluding applause. For a short term of life is long enough for living well and honourably.

28. But if you go farther, you have no more right to grumble than farmers do because the charm of the spring season is past and the summer and autumn have come.

29. The word 'spring' suggests youth, and points to the harvest to be: the other seasons are suited for the reaping and storing of the crops.

30. And the harvest of old age is the memory and rich store of achievements laid up in earlier life.

31. Again, all things that accord with nature are to be counted good. What can be more in accordance with nature than for old people at last to die?

32. A thing, indeed, which also befalls the young, though nature revolts and fights against it.

33. Just as apples when unripe are torn from trees, but when ripe and mellow drop down, so it is violence that takes life from the young, ripeness from the old.

34. This ripeness is so delightful to those who are wise in their old age, that as they approach nearer to death,

35. They seem as it were to be sighting land, and to be coming to port at last after a long voyage.

36. Again, there is no fixed borderline for old age, and you are making a good and proper use of it as long as you can satisfy the call of duty and disregard death.

37. The result of this is, that old age is even more confident and courageous than youth.

Chapter 22

1. That end of life is the best, when, without the intellect or senses being impaired, nature herself takes to pieces her own handiwork which she also put together.

2. Just as the builder of a ship or a house can break them up more easily than anyone else, so nature, which knitted together the human frame, can also best unfasten it.

3. Moreover, a thing freshly glued

together is always difficult to pull asunder; if old, this is easily done.

4. There may possibly be some sensation of dying and that only for a short time, especially in the case of an old man: after death, sensation disappears altogether.

5. But to disregard death is a lesson which must be studied from our youth up; for unless that is learnt, no one can have a quiet mind.

6. For die we certainly must, and that too without being certain whether it may not be this very day.

7. As a general truth, it is weariness of all pursuits that creates weariness of life.

8. There are certain pursuits adapted to childhood: do young men miss them?

9. There are others suited to early manhood: does that settled time of life called 'middle age' ask for them?

10. There are others, again, suited to that age, but not looked for in old age.

11. There are, finally, some which belong to old age.

12. Therefore, as the pursuits of the earlier ages have their time for disappearing, so also have those of old age.

13. And when that takes place, a satiety of life brings on the ripe time for death.

14. When man's natural frame is resolved into its elements by death, it is clearly seen whither each of the other elements departs:

15. For they all go to the place from which they came.

16. As to the personality and intelligence which the living frame supports, and which vanishes when it returns to nature among the trees and stars whence all natural things come,

17. All that need be said is that nothing is so like death as sleep.

18. Do not regret having lived, but while yet living live in a way that allows you to think that you were not born in vain.

19. And do not regret that you must die: it is what all who are wise must wish, to have life end at its proper time.

20. For nature puts a limit to living as to everything else,

21. And we are the sons and daughters of nature, and for us therefore the sleep of nature is nature's final kindness.

Chapter 23: Of poverty

1. There are those who fear poverty even worse than death,

2. Even though it has been well said that poverty, brought into conformity with the law of nature, is great wealth.

3. The minimum that the law of nature ordains for us is to avert hunger, thirst and cold.

4. In order to banish hunger and thirst, it is not necessary to pay court at the doors of the purse-proud,

5. Or to submit to the stern frown, or to the kindness that humiliates;

6. Nor is it necessary for us to scour the seas, or go campaigning; nature's needs are easily satisfied in anyone of temperate mind and habit.

7. It is the superfluous things for which men sweat, the superfluous things that weary our days,

8. That force us to labour for uncertain rewards, that make us risk our happiness.

9. There is a noble ambition which is not aimed at having superfluity,

10. There is a noble ambition not aimed at emulation of those we think richer and therefore happier than ourselves.

11. This is the ambition to do something genuinely worthwhile,

12. To foster those abilities we have both for the joy of exercising them to the utmost, and for offering their fruits to our fellows.

13. Thus the musician, painter, poet and statesman, the scientist and the inquirer,

14. Work with pleasure because they work at what they must and what they love;

15. For them the weariness at the day's end is sweet,

16. And whether or not they have the acclaim of others, they themselves know if they have done well.

17. To work with what one has, to make and to do, to fulfil what is within,

18. To tend the orchard of one's capacities, is to make one's life a good thing to live.

19. And if the harvest benefits others, adding to the store of good,

20. The justification for one's hour on earth is complete.

Chapter 24: On the consolation of wisdom regarding death

1. Hasten to be wise, for then you can enjoy for longer the pleasures of an improved mind which is at peace with itself.

2. You remember the joy you felt when you laid aside the garments of childhood and donned adult clothing, and took your place among adults;

3. Now you may look for an even greater joy when you have laid aside the mind of youth, and wisdom has enrolled you among those who are mature.

4. For it is not childhood that stays with us, but something worse: childishness.

5. And this condition is the more serious because we possess the authority of adulthood, yet we still have some of the follies of youth, even the follies of infancy.

6. Infants fear trifles, children fear shadows, many adults fear both.

7. Yet all you need do is to advance; you will thus understand that some things are less to be dreaded, precisely because they inspire us with great fear.

8. No evil is great which is the last evil of all. Death arrives; it would be a

thing to dread, if it could remain with you.

9. But death must either not come at all, or else must come and immediately pass away to nothingness.

10. 'It is difficult,' you say, 'to bring the mind to a point where it can scorn death.' But do you not see what trifling reasons sometimes impel people to scorn life instead?

11. One hangs himself because he has been rejected by a lover; another hurls himself from the house-top to escape the disgrace of debt;

12. A third, to be saved from arrest after running away, cuts his veins with a knife.

13. Do you not agree that virtue can be as efficacious as excessive fear?

14. No person will have a peaceful life who thinks too much about lengthening it, or believes that gaining higher office or making more money is a great blessing.

15. Repeat this thought to yourself every day, so that you may be able to depart from life contentedly;

16. For many people clutch and cling to life, even as those who are carried down a rushing stream clutch and cling to briars and sharp rocks.

17. Most people are jostled in wretchedness between the fear of death and the hardships of life; they are unwilling to live, and yet they do not know how to die.

18. For this reason, make life as a whole agreeable to yourself by banishing all worry about death;

19. It will come, and so long as the process of dying is itself easy, it has no more terror than dreamless sleep.

20. No good thing renders its possessor happy, unless his mind is reconciled to the possibility of its loss;

21. Nothing, however, is lost with less discomfort than that which, when lost, cannot be missed.

22. Therefore, encourage and toughen your mind against the mishaps that afflict even the most powerful and the most successful,

23. For accident and illness can in a moment take away all that was built over many years.

24. So I declare to you: he is lord of your life that scorns his own. Be the lord of your own life therefore, by not fearing to lose it.

25. Since the day we were born we are being led towards the day we die: in the interim let us be courageous, and do good things.

Chapter 25

1. You write to tell me that you are anxious about the outcome of a lawsuit, which an angry opponent is threatening you with;

2. And you ask me to advise you to picture to yourself a happier outcome, and to rest in the allurements of hope.

3. Why, indeed, is it necessary to summon trouble, which must be endured soon enough when it arrives;

4. Or to anticipate trouble, and ruin the present through fear of the future?

5. It is foolish to be unhappy now because you may be unhappy at some future time.

6. Think of how much keener a brave man is to lay hold of danger than a cruel man is to inflict it.

7. 'Oh,' you will say, 'spare me any lectures "On Despising Death" and the like; you will soon be repeating the story of Cato.'

8. But why should I not repeat the story of Cato, how he read Plato on that last glorious night, with a sword laid at his pillow?

9. He had provided these two requisites for his last moments: the first, that he might have the will to die, and the second, that he might have the means.

10. So he put his affairs in order, as well as one could put in order that which was ruined and near its end,

11. And thought that he ought to see to it that no one should have the power to slay Cato, or the good fortune to save him.

12. Drawing the sword, which he had kept unstained from all bloodshed against the final day, he cried: 'I have fought, till now, for my country's freedom, and not for my own;

13. 'I did not strive so doggedly to be free, but only to live among the free.

14. 'Now, since the affairs of mankind are beyond hope, let Cato be withdrawn to safety.' So saying, he inflicted a mortal wound upon his body.

15. I am reminding you of this for the purpose of encouraging you to face anything that might happen,

16. By knowing how to face that which is thought to be the most terrible thing that can happen: which fools think is death.

17. By which I mean that death is so little to be feared that through its good offices nothing is to be feared.

18. Therefore, when problems threaten, listen unconcernedly. Meet them with the best of your life; or end them by overcoming life.

19. Remember to strip things of all that disturbs and confuses, and to see what each is at bottom;

20. You will then comprehend that they contain nothing fearful except the actual fear.

21. We should strip the mask, not only from men, but from things, and restore to each object its own aspect.

22. Do not drown your mind in petty anxieties; if you do, your mind will be dulled, with too little vigour left when the time comes for it to stand up and do its work bravely.

23. Say to yourself that our petty bodies are mortal and frail; pain can reach them from other sources than from wrong or the might of the stronger.

24. Our pleasures themselves become torments: banquets bring indigestion, carousal exhausts us, overindulgence makes us ill.

25. Say: 'I may become poor; I shall then be one among many. I may

be exiled; I shall then regard myself as born in the place I have been sent to.

26. 'They may put me in chains. What then? Am I free from bonds when I do not have chains about me?'

27. To die is to shed those chains, because it is to cease to run the risk of sickness and death.

28. I remember one day you were discussing the well-known saying that many do not suddenly fall on death, but advance towards it by slight degrees, dying a little every day.

29. And this, for many, is true: every day a little of our life is taken from us; even when we are growing, our life is on the wane.

30. We lose our childhood, then our youth. Counting even yesterday, all past time is lost time;

31. The very day which we are now spending is shared between ourselves and death.

32. It is not the last drop that empties the water-clock, but all that which previously has flowed out;

33. Similarly, the final hour when we cease to exist does not of itself bring death; it merely of itself completes the death-process.

34. We reach death at that moment, but we have been a long time on the way. Epicurus upbraids those who desire, as much as those who shrink from, death:

35. 'It is absurd,' he says, 'to run towards death because you are tired of life, when it is your manner of life that has made you run towards death.'

36. And again he says: 'What is so absurd as to seek death, when it is through fear of death that you have robbed your life of peace?'

37. And you may add this: 'People are so thoughtless, nay, so mad, that some, through fear of death, force themselves to die.'

38. Whichever of these ideas you ponder, you will strengthen your mind for the endurance alike of death and of life.

39. And remember: there is an end to nothing; all things are connected in a circle; they flee and they are pursued;

40. Night is close at the heels of day, day at the heels of night; summer ends in autumn, winter rushes after autumn, and winter softens into spring.

41. All nature in this way passes, only to return, what has gone before coming back in different or renewed form,

42. So that what was a human being might in time be in the trees and clouds, for ever different.

Chapter 26: The consolation of the end

1. I was lately telling you that I was within sight of old age. I am now afraid that I have left old age behind.

2. For some other word would now apply to my years, or at any rate to my body; you may rate me in

the class of those who are nearing the end.

3. Nevertheless, I offer thanks to myself, with you as witness; for I feel that age has done no damage to my mind, though I feel its effects on my constitution.

4. Only my vices, and the outward aids to these vices, have reached senility; my mind is strong and rejoices that it has but slight reliance on the body.

5. It has laid aside the greater part of its load. It is alert; it takes issue with me on the subject of old age; it declares that old age is its time of bloom.

6. Let me take it at its word, and let it make the most of the advantages it possesses.

7. My mind bids me do some thinking and consider how much of this peace of mind and moderation of character I owe to wisdom and how much to my time of life;

8. It bids me distinguish carefully what I cannot do and what I do not want to do.

9. For why should one complain or regard it as a disadvantage, if powers which ought to come to an end have failed?

10. 'But,' you say, 'it is the greatest possible disadvantage to be worn out and to die off, or rather, if I may speak literally, to melt away!

11. 'For we are not suddenly smitten and laid low; we are worn away, and every day reduces our powers to a certain extent.'

12. But is there any better end to it all than to glide off to one's proper haven, when nature slips the cable?

13. Not that there is anything painful in a shock and a sudden departure from existence; it is merely because this other way of departure is easy; a gradual withdrawal.

14. I commune thus with myself: 'The showing which we have made up to the present time, in word or deed, counts for nothing.

15. 'All this is but a trifling consideration, and is wrapped in much charlatanism. I shall leave it to others to determine what progress I have made.

16. 'Therefore with no faint heart I am making ready for the day when, putting aside all stage artifice and actor's rouge, I am to pass judgement upon myself,

17. 'Whether I am merely declaiming brave sentiments, or whether I really feel them.

18. 'Put aside the opinion of the world; it is always wavering and always takes both sides.

19. 'Put aside the studies which you have pursued throughout your life; death will deliver the final judgement in your case.

20. 'This is what I mean: your debates and learned talks, your maxims gathered from the teachings of the wise, your cultured conversation,

21. 'All these afford no proof of the real strength of your mind. Even the most timid man can deliver a bold speech.

22. 'What you have done in the past will be manifest only at the time when you draw your last breath.

23. 'I accept the terms; I do not shrink from the decision.' This is what I say to myself, but I would have you think that I have said it to you also.

24. You are younger; but what does that matter? There is no fixed count of our years. You do not know where the end awaits; be ready for it everywhere.

25. It is a wonderful thing to learn thoroughly how to die. You may deem it superfluous to learn a text that can be used only once;

26. But that is just the reason why we ought to think on a thing.

27. When we can never prove whether we really know a thing, we must always be learning it.

28. 'Think on death.' In saying this, we are bidding ourselves to think on freedom.

29. He who has learned to die has unlearned slavery;

30. He is beyond any external power, or, at any rate, he is it. What terrors has any experience of life for him?

31. This is the final consolation: that we will sleep at evening, and be free for ever.

SAGES

Chapter 1

1. The master said: to learn and to practise what is learned time and again is a great pleasure, is it not?
2. To have friends come from afar is happiness, is it not?
3. To be unperturbed when not appreciated by others is noble, is it not?
4. Each day I examine myself on three counts:
5. Whether I am loyal to those on whose behalf I act;
6. Whether I am trustworthy towards my friends;
7. Whether I practise what I teach.
8. In leading a state of a thousand chariots, respect the office and be worthy of trust.
9. Use resources wisely, love the people, do what is timely.
10. At home let the young behave with courtesy; in the world let them behave with brotherly love.
11. Let the young be prudent and trustworthy, loving the people and drawing close to those who are benevolent.
12. Without steadfastness, one cannot command respect, and one's learning will not be sound.
13. If a person advocates loyalty and trustworthiness, he will always have friends who are his equal.

14. How does the master learn? By being gentle, kind, courteous, modest and patient. Such enquiry is different from all others.
15. What is a good person? One who does not seek to be satiated in eating, one who is quick in dealings, prudent in speech, correct in action.
16. The master said: 'Like bone cut, like horn polished, like jade carved, like stone ground.'
17. Does this not tell us that 'poor but happy' is better than 'poor but not servile',
18. And 'rich but benevolent' is better than 'rich but humble'?
19. Do not be concerned about others not appreciating you. Be concerned about not appreciating others.
20. At fifteen, I aspired to learning.
21. At thirty, I established my stand.
22. At forty, I had no illusions.
23. At fifty, I knew my destiny.
24. At sixty, I recognised truth when it came.
25. At seventy, I could follow my heart's wishes without wrongdoing.

Chapter 2

1. Will you know a man? Examine his motives, note his course, take heed whether he is at ease. How can a man hide?

2. Exploring the old and deducing the new makes a teacher.

3. The nobler mind encompasses all and is not partial. The lesser mind is partial and does not encompass all.

4. To learn without thinking is to labour in vain.

5. To think without learning is desolation.

6. When you have erred, be not afraid to correct yourself. Have no associates in study who are not as advanced as yourself.

7. What is knowledge? It is to acknowledge that what is known is known, and that what is not known is not known.

8. What is wealth? Listen carefully and weigh: for the rest, speak prudently.

9. Observe carefully and weigh: for the rest, act prudently.

10. Thus there can be neither accusation nor remorse: that is wealth.

11. Preside with dignity and there is respect, preside with compassion and there is loyalty.

12. Elevate the good and teach the incapable, and there is encouragement.

13. To know what is right and not to do it is to be without courage.

Chapter 3

1. The master said, 'If a person is without benevolence, what use is any outward show to hide the fact?

2. 'In archery, to pierce the target is not the measure, but rather to hit the centre. This has always been the way.

3. 'Those not benevolent cannot long endure adversity. The benevolent are at ease with benevolence. The wise profit from benevolence.

4. 'To hear in the morning that benevolence prevails is to be able to die without regret at night.

5. 'The good set their hearts on benevolence, others set their hearts on possessions.

6. 'The good set their hearts on law, the others set their hearts on privilege.

7. 'The good act before speaking, and afterwards speak according to their actions.

8. 'When we see a man of worth, we should think of equalling him.

9. 'When we see a man of no worth, we should turn inwards and examine ourselves.

10. 'In regard to the aged, give them rest; in regard to friends, give them sincerity; in regard to the young, treat them tenderly.'

11. The master said, 'Admirable indeed is the virtue of a man who has a single bowl of rice, a single gourd of drink, and lives in a mean narrow street, but does not allow his joy to be affected.'

12. The master said, 'With coarse rice to eat, with water to drink, and my bended arm for a pillow, I still have joy in the midst of these things.

13. 'Riches and honours acquired by unrighteousness are to me as a floating cloud.

14. 'Those who know the truth are not equal to those who love it,

15. 'And those who love it are not equal to those who delight in it.

16. 'The man of virtue makes it his first business to overcome difficulty, and makes success a secondary consideration only.

17. 'The wise find pleasure in water, the virtuous find pleasure in hills.

18. 'The wise are active, the virtuous are tranquil. The wise are joyful, the virtuous are long-lived.

19. 'The man of virtue, seeking to be established, seeks to establish others;

20. 'Wishing to be enlarged himself, he seeks to enlarge others.'

21. The master said, 'When I walk along with two others, they may serve me as my teachers.

22. 'I will select their good qualities and follow them, their bad qualities and avoid them.

23. 'Having not and yet affecting to have, empty and yet affecting to be full, straitened and yet affecting to be at ease: it is difficult with such characteristics to have constancy.

24. 'Is virtue a thing remote? I wish to be virtuous, and lo! virtue is at hand.'

25. The master said, 'In letters I am perhaps equal to other men, but the character of the superior man, carrying out in his conduct what he professes, is what I have not yet attained to.'

26. The master said, 'The sage and the man of perfect virtue; how dare I rank myself with them?

27. 'It may simply be said of me, that I strive to become such without satiety, and teach others without weariness.'

28. When a country is well governed, poverty and a mean condition are things to be ashamed of.

29. When a country is ill governed, riches and honour are things to be ashamed of.

30. The commander of the forces of a large state may be carried off, but the will of even a common man cannot be taken from him, if he refuses to let it go.

31. The wise are free from perplexities, the virtuous from anxiety, and the bold from fear.

32. One asked the master about death. The master said, 'While you do not know about life, how can you know about death?'

Chapter 4

1. The master said, 'To govern oneself is the way to the good. Is therefore the way to the good found by a man himself or found by others for him?

2. 'To perfect one's positive qualities without weariness, and to overcome bad qualities, is the way to the good.'

3. Asked about the relationship between good and bad qualities, the master said, 'It is like that between the wind and the grass. The grass must bend, when the wind blows across it.'

4. The master said, 'They think that

distinction consists in being heard throughout the land. But this is not distinction, it is notoriety.

5. 'The person of distinction is solid and straightforward, and loves what is right.

6. 'He examines people's words, and looks at their countenances.'

7. Asked how to exalt virtue, correct evil and do away with delusions, the master said, 'By making your first business to do what is to be done, and treating success as a secondary consideration, that is how to exalt virtue.

8. 'By assailing your own bad qualities and not delaying to do so while you assail the bad qualities of others, that is how to correct evil.'

9. Asked about benevolence, the master said, 'It is to love all humankind.'

10. Asked about knowledge, he said, 'It is to know humankind.'

11. Asked about friendship, he said, 'Faithfully admonish your friend, and skilfully lead him forward.'

12. Asked what his first step would be on taking office, the master said, 'To rectify names.

13. 'If names be not correct, language is not in accordance with the truth of things, and nothing can be done with success.'

14. The master said, 'Do not desire to have things done quickly; do not look at small advantages.

15. 'Seeking to have things done quickly prevents their being done thoroughly.

16. 'Looking at small advantages prevents great affairs from being accomplished.'

Chapter 5

1. The master said, 'The superior man is easy to serve and difficult to please.

2. 'If you try to please him in ways not accordant with right, he will not be pleased.

3. 'In his employment of men he uses them according to their capacity.'

4. The master said, 'The inferior man is difficult to serve, and easy to please.

5. 'If you try to please him in ways not accordant with right, he may be pleased.

6. 'But in his employment of men he wishes them to be equal to everything.

7. 'The firm, the enduring, the simple, the modest: such people are close to virtue.

8. 'Boasting, resentment, covetousness, ignorance: these are the marks of inferiority.'

9. The master said, 'It is hard not to complain when one is poor, but it is easy not to be proud when one is rich.

10. 'Who is the good man? He who, when tempted by gain, thinks of righteousness;

11. 'When faced with danger, summons his courage;

12. 'And who never forgets an old promise, however far back it extends.

13. 'When times are good, it is because people learn with a view to their own improvement.

14. 'When times are bad, it is because people learn to win the approbation of others.'

15. The master said, 'The superior man is modest in his speech, but exceeds in his actions.'

16. The master said, 'The way of the superior man is threefold, but I am not equal to it:

17. 'Virtuous, he is free from anxieties; wise, he is free from perplexities; bold, he is free from fear.'

18. The master said, 'I will not be concerned at people not knowing me; I will be concerned at my own want of ability.'

19. Someone asked the master, 'What do you say of the principle that injury should be recompensed with kindness?'

20. The master replied, 'With what then will you recompense kindness?

21. 'Recompense injury with justice, and kindness with kindness.'

Chapter 6

1. The master was one day playing on a musical drum by a river, when a man carrying a straw basket passed by.

2. The man said, 'His heart is full who so beats the musical drum!'

3. The master said, 'Deep water must be crossed with one's clothes on;

4. 'Shallow water may be crossed with one's clothes held up.

5. 'He who requires more from himself than from others, will keep himself from being an object of resentment.

6. 'When a person is not in the habit of saying, "What do I think of this? What shall I do in this case?" there is indeed little hope for him.

7. 'When a number of people are together for a whole day without their conversation turning to questions about the good, theirs is a hard case.'

8. The master said, 'To do one's best with humility and sincerity: that is what it is to be a superior man.

9. 'The superior man is distressed by his want of ability. He is not distressed by being unknown.

10. 'What the superior man seeks is in himself. What the inferior man seeks is in others.

11. 'The superior man is not a partisan. He seeks to grasp all things with justice.

12. 'The superior man dislikes not having a good reputation after his death.

13. 'The superior man does not value others solely on account of their words,

14. 'Nor does he put aside good words on account of their speaker's reputation, even if it is bad.

15. 'The superior man cannot be known in little matters; he is proved by great things.

16. 'The inferior man cannot be entrusted with great things; his failings will be seen in little matters.'

17. The master said, 'In my dealings with others, whose evil do I blame, whose goodness do I praise, beyond what is just?

18. 'If sometimes I give high praise, there must be grounds for it in my examination of that individual.'

19. The master said, 'False words undo virtue. Want of forbearance in small things undoes great things.

20. 'When the multitude hate a man, it is necessary to examine the case.

21. 'When the multitude love a man, it is necessary to examine the case.

22. 'For the multitude can hate what should be loved, and love what should be hated.'

Chapter 7

1. What is it to have faults? It is to have faults and not to reform them.

2. The master said, 'Rightness is more to man than fire or water.

3. 'I have seen men die from treading on water or fire, but I have never seen a man die from treading the course of rightness.

4. 'There are three friendships which are advantageous. These are friendships with the upright, with the sincere, and with those of much observation.

5. 'There are three friendships which are injurious. These are friendships with those of specious airs, those who are insinuatingly soft, and those with glib tongues.

6. 'There are three kinds of enjoyment which are advantageous. These are discriminating studies, speaking of the goodness of others, and possessing worthy friends.

7. 'There are three kinds of enjoyment which are injurious. These are extravagant pleasures, idleness and sauntering about, and feasting.

8. 'Three errors are committed by those who stand in the presence of a man of virtue and station.

9. 'One is speaking out of turn, this is rashness.

10. 'Another is keeping silent when it is time to speak, this is concealment.

11. 'A third is speaking without looking interlocutors in the eye, this is prevarication.

12. 'There are three things that the superior person guards against.

13. 'In youth, he guards against excess. In the vigour of maturity, he guards against quarrelsomeness. In old age, he guards against covetousness.

14. 'There are three things of which the superior man stands in awe. He stands in awe of the command of reason. He stands in awe of great men. He stands in awe of the wisdom of sages.

15. 'The inferior person stands in awe only of what has power to harm his advantage, whether it is good or bad.

16. 'In youth he indulges in excess, in maturity he is quarrelsome, in old age covetous.

17. 'He speaks out of turn, conceals his meaning, looks no one in the eye.

18. 'He is idle and indulgent, and his poor choice of friends confirms him in the ways of vice and inferiority.'

Chapter 8

1. The master said, 'Most people cannot bear to see the sufferings of others; this is the good in our nature.

2. 'If someone should see a child about to fall into a well, he will feel alarm and distress,

3. 'Not to gain favour with the child's parents, nor to seek the praise of their neighbours,

4. 'Nor from fear of a reputation for being unmoved by such a thing.

5. 'From this we may perceive that commiseration is essential to man, that feelings of shame and dislike are essential to man,

6. 'That feelings of modesty and complaisance are essential to man, and that the feeling of approving and disapproving is essential to man.

7. 'The feeling of commiseration is the principle of benevolence.

8. 'The feeling of shame and dislike is the principle of righteousness.

9. 'The feeling of modesty and complaisance is the principle of propriety.

10. 'The feeling of approving and disapproving is the principle of knowledge.

11. 'Men have these four principles just as they have four limbs.

12. 'When men wilfully do not live according to these principles, they play the thief with themselves; they steal away their own better nature.

13. 'Since all men have these four principles in themselves, let them give full development and completion to them,

14. 'And the result will be like a fire which has begun to burn, or a spring which has begun to flow.

15. 'Let the principles have their complete development, and they will suffice to love and protect all.

16. 'Let them be denied development, and they will not suffice for a man even to honour his parents.'

17. The master said, 'All things are already complete in us. There is no greater delight than to be conscious of sincerity when one examines oneself.

18. 'Let a man not do what his own sense of rightness tells him not to do, and let him not desire what his sense of rightness tells him not to desire: to act thus is all he has to do.

19. 'Benevolence is the natural state of our minds, and rightness is our path.

20. 'How lamentable is it to neglect the path, and not pursue it; to lose this benevolence, and not know how to seek it again!

21. 'When men's dogs or sheep are lost, they know enough to look for them; but if they lose their virtue, they either do not know how to find it again, or do not care.

22. 'The great end of learning is nothing else but to seek to know oneself and to maintain one's understanding of rightness.'

Chapter 9

1. The master said, 'The trees of the mountain were once beautiful.

2. 'But being situated on the borders of a large state, they were hewn down with axes.

3. 'Could they still retain their beauty? And yet, through the powers of life,

4. 'Day and night, and with the nourishing influence of rain and dew,

5. 'Their stumps produced buds and sprouts springing forth.

6. 'But then came cattle and goats, and browsed upon the succulent sprouts, stripping them.

7. 'To these things is owed the bare appearance of the mountain which, when people see it, they think was never finely wooded.

8. 'But is what they see the nature of the mountain?

9. 'And so also of what properly belongs to man: shall it be said that the mind of anyone was originally without the possibility of benevolence and rightness?

10. 'The way in which a man loses his proper goodness is like the way that the trees are felled by axes.

11. 'When its principles are hewn down day after day, can the mind retain its beauty?

12. 'But there is a development of its life day and night,

13. 'And in the calm air of the morning, just between night and day, the mind feels something of those desires and aversions which are proper to humanity;

14. 'But the feeling is not strong, and it is hindered and destroyed by what takes place during the day.

15. 'This destruction taking place again and again, the restorative influence of quiet times is not sufficient to preserve the mind's proper goodness.

16. 'And when this proves insufficient, man's nature ceases to be much different from that of the irrational animals.

17. 'When they see this, people think that the mind never had powers of natural goodness.

18. 'But does this condition represent the feelings proper to humanity?

19. 'If it receive its proper nourishment, there is nothing which will not grow.

20. 'If it lose its proper nourishment, there is nothing which will not decay away.

21. 'So it is with the minds and feelings of people, and their principles of benevolence and rightness.'

Chapter 10

1. The master said, 'In good years the children of the people are mostly good, while in bad years most of them abandon themselves to evil.

2. 'It is not owing to any difference of the powers conferred by nature that they are thus different. The abandonment to evil is owing to circumstances.

3. 'Consider what happens to barley. Let it be sown and covered: if the ground and the time of sowing are the same, it grows rapidly anywhere;

4. 'And when its full time is come, it is found to be ripe.

5. 'If there are inequalities in different fields of barley, they are owing to the difference of the soil,

6. 'To the unequal nourishment of rains and dews, to the different ways in which farmers have gone about their work.

7. 'Thus all things which are the same in kind are like one another.

8. 'Why should we be in doubt with regard to man, as if he were a solitary exception to this rule?

9. 'The sage and we are the same in kind, if we allow the possibility of wisdom to flourish within us.

10. 'If a man made hempen sandals without knowing the size of his customers' feet, yet I know that he will not make them like baskets.

11. 'As the feet of men are more or less the same size, neither like the feet of a mouse nor the feet of an elephant,

12. 'So are the pleasures of their mouths in sweet and salt savours, and of their ears in the harmonies of music;

13. 'So do most people enjoy the mild weather of autumn, and the beauty of the maidens as they bring water from the well.

14. 'What is it that most people approve in the behaviour of their neighbours and friends?

15. 'I say it is the four principles of our nature, and the guidance of rightness.

16. 'The sages knew before I was born what my mind approves, along with the majority of other men, so that we can live in harmony.

17. 'Therefore the principles of our nature and the determinations of righteousness are agreeable to my mind,

18. 'Just as sweet and savoury delicacies are agreeable to my mouth.'

Chapter 11

1. The master said, 'If a man loves others but no affection is shown to him in return, let him turn inwards and examine his own benevolence.

2. 'If he is charged with governing others, and his rule is unsuccessful, let him turn inwards and examine his wisdom.

3. 'If he treats others politely, and they do not return his politeness, let him turn inwards and examine his own feeling of respect.

4. 'When we do not, by what we do, realise what we desire, we must turn inwards, and examine ourselves in every point.'

5. The master was asked, 'All are equally men, but some are great men, and some are little men. How is this?'

6. He replied, 'Those who follow that part of themselves which is great are great men; those who follow that part which is little are little men.'

7. The master was then asked, 'All are equally men, but some follow that part of themselves which is great, and some follow that part which is little. How is this?'

8. The master answered, 'The senses of hearing and seeing do not think, and are obscured by external things.

9. 'When one thing comes into contact with another, as a matter of course one leads the other away.

10. 'To the mind belongs the office of thinking. By thinking, it gets the right view of things; by neglecting to think, it fails to do this.

11. 'These – the senses and the mind – are our best possession. Let a man first stand fast in the supremacy of the nobler part of his constitution,

12. 'And the inferior part will not be able to take it from him. It is simply this which makes the great man.'

Chapter 12

1. The master was asked, 'Since you say the will is chief and the natural passions are subordinate,

2. 'How can we keep the will firm without doing violence to our natural passions?'

3. The master replied, 'When the will alone is active, it moves the passions. When passions alone are active, they move the will.

4. 'Natural passions are great, and exceedingly strong. If nourished by rectitude, they are the helpmates and assistants of rightness and reason.

5. 'Natural passions are directed by the accumulation of right deeds; this is not obtained by accidental acts of rightness.

6. 'There must be a constant practice

of rightness. Yet let us not be like the farmer who grieved that his growing corn was not higher, and therefore tried to pull it longer;

7. 'Returning home he said, "I am tired today. I have been helping the corn to grow long."

8. 'His son ran to look at the field and found the corn broken and withered.

9. 'There are few in the world who do not deal with their passions as if they were assisting the corn to grow long.

10. 'What they do is not only of no benefit to the passions, but injures them.

11. 'Others make the opposite mistake and consider the passions of no benefit, and let them alone; they do not weed their corn.

12. 'We must learn that the passions directed by reason can be part of our better selves, and must be allowed their due, but in proportion to rightness and benevolence.'

Chapter 13

1. The master said, 'What distinguishes the superior man from others is what he preserves in his heart: namely, benevolence and a sense of the right.

2. 'The benevolent man loves others. The man of rightness shows respect to others.

3. 'He who loves others is more often loved by them than he who hates them.

4. 'He who respects others is more often respected in return than is the disrespectful man.

5. 'Consider: here is a man who treats another in a perverse and unreasonable manner.

6. 'The superior man in such a case will say, "I must have been wanting in benevolence; I must have been wanting in propriety: how should this have happened otherwise?"

7. 'He examines himself, and is especially benevolent. He turns to consider himself, and is especially observant of propriety.

8. 'Suppose the perversity and unreasonableness of the other, however, remain the same.

9. 'The superior man will again rebuke himself: "I must have been failing to do my utmost."

10. 'Not often has there been anyone of complete sincerity who failed to move others.

11. 'Not often has there been one who lacked sincerity who was often able to move others.

12. 'The great man is he who does not lose a child's heart, the original good heart with which every man is born.'

13. A disciple said, 'Your principles are lofty and admirable, but learning them may well be likened to climbing on the clouds – something which cannot be achieved.

14. 'Why not adapt your teachings so that those who wish to follow them can consider them attainable, and so daily exert themselves?'

15. The master said, 'A great artificer does not, for the sake of a stupid workman, alter or do away with the marking line.

16. 'A skilled instructor of archery does not, for the sake of an inept archer, change his rule for drawing the bow.

17. 'The superior man draws the bow, but does not discharge the arrow. Such is his standing exactly in the middle of the right path.

18. 'Those who are able to follow him will follow him.'

Chapter 14

1. The master said, 'The superior man gives thoughtful consideration to nine things.

2. 'In regard to the use of his eyes, he wishes to see clearly.

3. 'In regard to the use of his ears, he wishes to hear distinctly.

4. 'In regard to his attitude towards others, he is keen to be benign.

5. 'In regard to his prevailing mood, he wishes it to be calm.

6. 'In regard to his speech, he is keen that it should be sincere.

7. 'In regard to his conduct of business, he is keen that it should be scrupulous.

8. 'In regard to his doubts, he is keen to question others.

9. 'In regard to what angers him, he is careful to consider the difficulties that might flow from expressing anger, and meditates a better course in response.

10. 'In regard to being offered the chance of material gains, he first thinks of honesty.'

11. The master said, 'To contemplate good, and to pursue it as if it could not be reached;

12. 'To contemplate evil, and to shrink from it as one would shrink from putting one's hand in boiling water;

13. 'These I have seen in the best men, and approved.'

14. The master said, 'By nature people are very much alike. By practice, they diverge widely apart.

15. 'Only the wisest of the highest class and the stupidest of the lowest class cannot be changed, or diverted from their path.'

16. The master was asked what constitutes perfect virtue.

17. He said, 'Generosity, sincerity, earnestness and kindness: these together constitute perfect virtue.

18. 'It is said, "If a thing is really hard, it cannot be ground into thinness. If a thing is really white, it will not darken when steeped in dye."'

Chapter 15

1. The master said, 'There are six becloudings. The first is to love benevolence without love of learning: this leads to foolish simplicity.

2. 'The second is to love knowing without love of learning: this leads to thoughtlessness.

3. 'The third is to love sincerity without love of learning: this leads to disregard of consequences.

4. 'The fourth is to love straightfor-wardness without love of learning: this leads to insolence.

5. 'The fifth is to love boldness without love of learning: this leads to quarrelsomeness.

6. 'The sixth is to love firmness without love of learning: this leads to extravagance.'

Chapter 16

1. The master urged his pupils to study poetry. 'For,' he said, 'it stimulates the mind, prompts self-contemplation,

2. 'Encourages sociability, distils the experience of refined minds, and teaches about the world.'

3. He said, 'Not to read poetry is to stand with one's face to the wall.

4. 'He who, from day to day, does not forget what he has yet to learn,

5. 'And from month to month does not forget what he has yet to attain to, may indeed be said to love learning.'

Chapter 17

1. The master said, 'The superior man learns in order to reach the utmost of his principles.

2. 'The officer, having discharged his duties, should apply himself to learning,

3. 'The scholar, having completed his learning, should apply himself to be an officer.

4. 'The faults of the great are like eclipses of the sun and moon.

5. 'All men see them; when they occur, all look up and take note of them.'

6. His pupils said of the master, 'He is like a house with towering walls.

7. 'If one find not the door to enter thereby, the treasures within are hidden from view.

8. 'To be admitted, one must be invited. Once invited, a pupil may contemplate the treasures, and carry away as many as he can hold.'

9. For the master said to them all, 'What is it to study in the house of a master, but to become masters of yourselves,

10. 'And to build a house of your own in which others may come to collect treasures that you have made?

11. 'For the only true master is oneself, and the only true life is the life ruled by your master.

12. 'You are here within the walls of my house, but only as a starting-place for your own task,

13. 'Which is to build your own house for your own life, there to live independently, with honour, justice, strength and wisdom.

14. 'This is the teaching of all sages worthy of the name: that one must only be a pupil in order to cease being a pupil;

15. 'That one must study in order to learn; and that one must learn in order to live.

16. 'For in the brief season of life the first responsibility is to live, and to enrich life in oneself and others,

17. 'So that the final history of things may be a history of good.'

SONGS

1

The moon cannot equal the radiance of
    your face,
Nor the rose your beauty;
My desire's habitation is the curve of
    your eyebrow,
No king has quarters such as that.

What will the sighs of my heart do,
If like breath on a mirror they cloud
    your face?
I fear the narcissus: that your black-
    hearted eyes
Will gaze on no one but yourself,
    unashamed.

Bring me a heavy pitcher of wine;
I cannot speak for those who have not
    crossed this threshold,
Who have not washed their sleeves in
    their heart's blood,
And suffered this transgression of love.

2

Thick grow the green rush leaves,
The dewfall on them turns to frost:
My love is somewhere on this stream –
I went up-river to seek him,
But the way was hard and long.
I went down-river to seek him,
And there in mid-water he was:
Even he!

Close grow the green rush leaves,
Their white dew not yet dry.
My love is at the water's side –
Upstream I sought him,
But the way was long and hard,
Downstream I sought him,
And there on a mid-water ledge
I saw him:
Even he!

3

Hear the deer call,
Nibbling the black southernwood of
    the fields.
A lucky guest has visited me:
Let me play my zither, blow my
    reed-organ,
Take up the basket of gifts and
    offerings.
Here is one who loves me,
And will teach me the way of the land.

Hear the deer call,
Nibbling the white southernwood of
    the fields.
I have a lucky guest, whose name is
    bright:
He is a pattern to the people.
Take up the good wine and the bread:
Let us feast our guest to comfort him,
And gladden his heart with music.

Hear the deer call,
Nibbling the wild garlic of the fields.
I bring good wine and bread
To comfort my guest who brings such
    fortune;
I play my zither, and blow the
    reed-organ,
To delight his heart with music.

4

We plucked the bracken while the
    shoots were soft:
Oh to go back, to go back!
Our hearts are sad, our sad hearts burn:
And no news comes from home.

What splendid thing is that?
It is the flower of the cherry tree:
It is the plume on the chariot of the
    chief,
The war-chariot ready yoked
With its four eager steeds.
We long to go back, to go back,
But the campaign is not over,
And no news comes from home.

We yoke the teams of four,
We ready the ivory bow-ends,
The fish-skin quivers:
The enemy is swift and strong;
How should we dare to tarry?

Long ago, when we started,
The willows spread their shade.
Now as we go on
The snowflakes fly.
Our march is long, we thirst, we
    hunger:
Our hearts are stricken with sorrow:
But no one listens when we cry

'To go back, to go back!
Our hearts burn with sadness.'
And no news comes from home.

5

I wake, and hasten to the window,
Expecting to see the first green buds of
    spring;
But find that the rains of autumn have
    already begun.

When did the years pass,
That I did not notice?
When did spring become autumn,
Whose rain falls at my window,
When I rose with hope to see
The first green buds of spring?

6

A cup of wine, under the flowering
    trees;
I drink alone, for no friend is near.
Raising my cup I beckon the bright
    moon,
For he, with my shadow, will make
    three.
The moon, alas, is no drinker of wine;
Listless, my shadow creeps at my side.
Yet with the moon as friend and the
    shadow as slave
I must make merry before night is
    spent.
Hearing my songs, the moon flickers
    her beams;
In the dance I weave, my shadow
    tangles and breaks.
While we were sober, three shared the
    fun;
Now we are drunk, each goes his own
    way.

May we long share our odd midnight
      feasts,
And meet at last on the cloudy river of
      the sky.

                    7
My friend is lodging high in the Eastern
      Hills,
Loving the beauty of valleys and
      tree-clad slopes.
In summer he lies in the empty woods,
And is still asleep when the sun pours
      warmth on them.
A pine-tree wind dusts his sleeves and
      coat;
A pebbled stream cleans his heart and
      thoughts.
I envy you, who far from strife and talk
Are high-propped on a pillow of blue
      cloud.

Here the fields are chill; the sparse rain
      has stopped;
The colours of nature teem on every
      side.
With leaping fish the blue pond is full;
With singing thrushes the green boughs
      droop.
The flowers of the field have powder on
      their cheeks;
The mountain grasses are bent level at
      the waist.
By the bamboo stream the last frag-
      ments of cloud,
Blown by the wind, scatter slowly away.

                    8
Do not ask me to sing.
That belongs to better times; the lute
And my voice cannot agree,

And neither of them agree
With my untuned fortunes.
Music is the child of mirth, not grief;
This grief's too great for songs and
      smiling eyes.
The raven's harsh call, the wolf's cry,
The midnight screech owl,
Blizzard wind or cracking ice:
That is the only music for this,
Or better: silence;
Not music but silence,
Not the sounding string, but solitude.

                    9
Do you know where the lemon blos-
      soms blow,
Where golden oranges in foliage glow,
Where the breeze falls from an azure
      sky,
And the myrtle and laurel stand high?
Do you know the mansion with the
      white wall,
The blackened chimney and the fire-lit
      hall?
That is the place I would have you
      know,
The place where, with you, I would
      now go.

                    10
At the end of spring
The flower of the pear tree gathers and
      turns to fruit;
The swallows' eggs have hatched.
When the seasons' changes thus
      confront the mind
What comfort is there in philosophy?
It can teach me to watch the days and
      months fly
Without grieving that youth slips away;

If the fleeting world is a dream
What does it matter whether one is
    young or old.
But ever since the day my friend left my
    side
And has lived in exile in a far city,
There is one wish I cannot quite
    abandon:
That from time to time we may meet
    again.

11

In waters still as a burnished mirror's
    face,
In the depths of the river, trout and
    grayling swim.
Idly I come with my bamboo rod
And hang my hook by the stream's
    bank.
A soft breeze blows on my fishing gear,
Gently swaying my three yards of line.
Though my body sits waiting for fish to
    rise,
My heart has wandered to the land of
    nothingness.
Long ago a white-headed man
Also fished at this same river-side;
A hooker of men, not of fish,
When seventy years old he caught a
    king.
But when I cast my hook in the stream
I have no thought of fish or men.
Lacking the skill to capture either prey,
I only bask in the autumn water's light;
When I tire of this, my fishing also
    stops,
And I turn homeward for a cup of
    wine.

12

My house is poor; those that I love have
    left me;
My body is sick; I cannot join the feast.
There is not a single face before my eyes
As I lie alone in my cottage room.
My broken lamp burns with a feeble
    flame;
My tattered curtains are crooked and
    do not meet.
On the doorstep and window sill
I hear the new snow fall.
As I grow older, gradually I sleep less;
I wake at midnight and sit up in bed.
If I had not learned the art of sitting
    and forgetting,
How could I bear this loneliness?
Stiff and stark my body cleaves to earth;
Unimpeded my mind yields to change.
So has it been through the long years,
Through twenty thousand nights!

13

I hug my pillow and do not speak a
    word;
In my empty room no sound stirs.
Who knows that, all day a-bed,
I am not ill, nor even asleep?

Turned to jade are the rosy cheeks
That long ago I had as a boy;
To my sick temples the winter frost
    now clings.
Do not wonder that my body sinks to
    decay;
Though my limbs are old, my heart is
    older yet.

14

Washed by the rain, dust and grime are laid;
Skirting the river, the road's course is flat.
The moon has risen on the last remnants of night;
The travellers' speed profits by the early cold.
In the silence I whisper a song;
Darkness breeds sombre thoughts.
On the lotus-bank hovers a dewy breeze;
Through the rice-furrows trickles a singing stream.
At the noise of our bells a dog stirs from sleep;
At the sight of our torches a roosting bird wakes.
Dawn glimmers through the misty shapes of trees –
For ten miles, till day at last breaks.

15

When the sun rose I was still in bed;
An early oriole sang in the eaves.
I thought of the royal park's trees at dawn,
From which the spring birds greeted the king,
When I served there in his retinue.

Pencil in hand, on duty in the palace office,
At the height of spring, when I paused from work,
Morning and evening, was this the voice I heard?
Now in my exile the oriole sings again
In the dull stillness of this far town:

The bird's note cannot be changed,
All the difference lies in the listener's heart.
If only he could forget that he lives
Exiled at the world's end,
The oriole would sound the same as when
Its song filled the palace garden.

16

I dreamed that I was back in the city,
I saw again the faces of friends.
And in my dream, under an April sky,
They led me by the hand to wander among spring's breezes.
Together we came to the village of tranquillity,
We stopped our horses at the gate of friends;
When they saw us coming, smiles lit their faces.
They pointed at the flowers in the western court,
And opened flasks of wine in the summerhouse.
They said none of us had changed,
They regretted that joy will not stay;
That friends meet only for a while,
Then part again with scarcely time for greeting.
I woke, and stretched out my hands to them:
There was nothing there at all.

17

Here among the river gorges there is no lack of men.
They are people one meets, not people one cares for.
At my front door guests arrive:

They are people one sits with, not
  people one knows.
When I look up through the lattice,
  there are clouds and trees;
When I look down at the desktop, there
  are inkwells and depositions.
I eat, sleep, get up, work, sit in the
  garden to await the breeze;
But everywhere and all day there is an
  emptiness.
Beyond the city walls lives a hermit;
  with him I can be at ease,
For he can drink a flagon of wine, and
  recite
Long-lined poems while the sun sets,
Finding its way down among tangled
  winter branches.

Some afternoon, when the clerks have
  gone home,
At a season when the path by the river
  bank is dry,
I beg you, take up your staff of bamboo
  wood
And find your way to my door where
  the plum trees stand.

18

Heat and cold, dusk and dawn have
  crowded upon one another;
Suddenly it is many years since I arrived
  here.
Through my closed doors I hear
  nothing but the morning and
  evening drum.
From my upper windows I see the ships
  that come and go,
In vain the starlings tempt me with
  their song
To stray beneath the flowering trees;

In vain the green rushes lure me to sit
  by the pond.
There is one thing and one alone I
  never tire of:
Hearing the stream that trickles over
  stones
And splashes its way among rocks
In the shade of the dark wood.

19

The papers that lie on my desk are
  simple and few;
My house by the moat is leisurely and still.
In the autumn rain berries fall from the
  boughs;
At the evening bell the birds return to
  the wood.
A broken sunlight quivers over the
  south porch
Where I lie on my couch in idleness.

20

Men's hearts love gold and silver;
Men's mouths covet wine and flesh.
Not so the old man of the stream;
He drinks from his gourd and asks
  nothing more.
South of the stream he cuts firewood
  and grass,
North of the stream he has four walls
  and a roof.
Yearly he sows an acre of land,
In spring he drives two yellow calves.
In these things he finds repose;
Beyond these he has neither wish nor
  care.
By chance I met him at the water's side;
He took me home and gave me tea.
He asked my rank and pay; doubting
  my tale

He laughed loud and long, saying,
'High officials do not sleep in a barn.'

21

Can the single cup of wine we drank
    this morning
Have made my heart so glad?
This is a joy that comes only from
    within,
Which those who witness will never
    understand.
I have two brothers
And grieved bitterly that both were far
    away;
This spring, back through the high
    gorges of the river
I came to them safely, ten thousand
    leagues.
I am freed at last from the thoughts
    that grieved me,
As though a sword had cut a rope from
    my neck.
Limbs grow light when the heart has
    shed its care;
Suddenly I seem to be flying, for very
    joy,
To the sun-painted clouds and the sky.

22

My friend, drink your cup of wine,
Then set it down and listen to what I
    say.
Do not sigh that your home is far away,
Do not mind that success seems far
    away.
Only hope that as long as life lasts
You and I may never be forced to part.

23

There is silence over the peaks.
In all the treetops there is peace;
Hardly a breath of wind.
The birds are silent and still.
Nothing moves, not a dry leaf
Stirs on the grass,
Not a single soft plume of thistle
Floats.
Only wait: soon
You too will rest.

24

Below the hall, beside the steps,
The pine trees grow in irregular array,
Without order, some tall and some low,
The tallest ten roods tall, the lowest ten
    feet low.
They are like wild things; no one knows
    who planted them.
They touch the walls of my blue-tiled
    house,
Their roots are deep in the terrace of
    white sand.
Every night they are visited by wind
    and moonlight,
Rain or fine they are free from dust.
In the autumn gales they whisper a
    private tune,
In the summer sunlight they yield a
    cool shade.
At the height of spring the fine evening
    rain
Decorates their leaves with hanging
    pearls.
At the year's end, the time of great snow
Burdens their branches with glittering
    jade.
When the people heard I had bought
    this house

They mocked, and called me mad
To move all my family here for the sake
    of a few pines.
And still I hurry to business, my belt
    buckled
And my sandals covered in dust;
And from time to time my heart
    reproves me
That I am not fit to be master of my
    own pine trees,
Who teach their lessons in each season
    of the year.

25

We had ridden long and were still far
    from the inn;
My eyes grew dim, and for some
    moments I dozed.
In my right hand the whip dangled,
In my left hand the reins slackened.
Suddenly I woke and turned to my
    groom,
Who told me that I slept for ten paces.
Body and mind had changed places;
Swift and slow had turned to their
    contraries.
For those few steps as I swayed in the
    saddle
My dream had lasted through aeons of
    time:
True indeed is the saying of the wise,
That a thousand years are but a
    moment of sleep.

26

The sun's early light shines on my
    house-beams,
The first banging of open doors
Echoes like a drumroll in the courtyard.
The dog lies curled on the stone step

Because the ground is still wet with dew.
On my window sill the birds chatter
To announce that the day is fine.
With lingering fumes of last night's
    wine
My head is still heavy;
With new doffing of winter garments
My body feels light and free.

27

I sought the hermit among the moun-
    tain pines
And by the brook that rises there.
I asked a child fishing on its bank;
He said, 'My master has gone to seek
    for herbs,
He is on this mountain, certainly,
But you cannot see him because of the
    clouds.'

28

By woods and water, whose houses are
    these
With high gates and wide-stretching
    meadows?
From their blue gables gilded fishes
    hang,
By their red pillars carved courses run.
Their spring arbours, warm with caged
    mist,
Their autumn yards cold with
    moonlight,
To the stem of the pine tree amber
    beads cling;
The willow oozes ruby-red drops.
Who are the masters of these estates?
They are state officers, counsellors and
    courtiers;
All their lives they have never seen what
    they own,

But know their possessions from a
    bailiff's map only.

29

The western wind has just begun to
    blow,
Yet already the first leaf flies from the
    bough.
On the drying paths I walk in my
    summer shoes,
In the first touch of cold I don my
    quilted coat.
Through shallow ditches the floods seep
    away,
Through sparse osiers a slanting light
    gleams.
In the early dusk, down an alley of
    green moss,
The garden-boy is leading the geese home.

30

I have finished with burdens and ties.
    No changes
Disturb the quiet of my mind, or
    impair my rest.
For ten years now body and mind
Have rested in hermit peace.
And all the more, in these last lingering
    years,
What I shall need is little:
A single rug to keep me warm in
    winter,
One meal to last me through the day.
No matter that my house is small;
One cannot sleep in two rooms at once!
No matter that I have few horses,
One cannot ride in two coaches at
    once!
Few are as fortunate as I am, among the
    peoples of the world;

Even fools are wise in the affairs of
    others;
In their own business even sages err.
To have little and to want no more
Is to be rich, and wise, and free.

31

We are growing old together, you and I,
Let us ask ourselves, what age is like?
The dull eye is closed before night falls,
The idle head is still uncombed at
    noon;
Propped on a staff we sometimes shuffle
From the southern porch to the garden
    gate;
Or sit all day behind closed doors.
One dare not look in the mirror's
    polished face,
One cannot read small-letter books.
Deeper and deeper grows the love of
    old friends,
Fewer and fewer one's dealings with
    young men.
One thing only, the pleasure of idle
    talk,
And summoning of memories,
Remains great as ever, when you and I
    meet.

32

What is the best course for me now,
But to take my belongings to the tavern
And sit there happily with a wine cup.
Let me avoid the company of false
    hearts,
Let me wash my own heart clean
Of all the stains that worldliness
    brings;
Let me have no companions
But a flask of wine and a book.

If I lift my cloak above the world's dust
I shall rise far up, in independence,
Like the crown of the tall cypress.
When I see the cup-bearer's face
And the wine gleaming in the cup
I feel ashamed of the worldly things I
    boasted of.
My slight frame is not able to bear this
    grief,
Now that she is gone: my poor heart
    cannot bear
The burden of her absence.
Think of me as a carouser in the
    wine-house,
Do not trouble my grieving heart,
For if I complain others will seek
    vengeance;
The dust of injury lies on my heart,
Yet I would not sully its bright mirror
Filled with the image of love.

33

Dawn's breeze returns
And with it the lapwing
Returning from the southern desert;
I hear again the dove's song
Singing softly of roses;
The tulip who understands the lily's
    whispers
Has returned
And the friend whom the poet wronged
Has forgiven him and returns too,
Walking to his door with soft returning
    tread.

34

I cannot cease desiring until my desire
    is requited;
Until my mouth has tasted my love's
    red mouth,

Or until from these lips that sought her
    lips
The breath has fled. Others may find an
    equal love;
On her doorstep I have laid myself
    down,
To be covered by dust when life and
    love
Have mingled and together flown.

35

My breath is ready to depart; but the
    grief in my heart,
Beating there without cease, refuses to
    let it go.
For she will not once give, not once,
With her sweet mouth, the peace my
    longing craves;
My breathing is a single long drawn
    sigh,
For the thought of her red mouth burns
    me like fire;
When will that mouth come close and
    whisper
What this longing heart desires to hear?

36

When I am gone open my tomb to see
The smoke that rises from it to wreathe
    about your feet,
For even there my heart will be burning
    for you:
Even from my funeral cloths the smoke
    will rise.
Oh beloved, come to the meadows
    waiting for your feet,
So that the thorns might blossom into
    flowers,
And fruit come to the boughs which
    have known

Perpetual winter only since you went
    away.

37

I search the gardens to find petals
As soft and perfumed as your cheek;
The west wind fans the meadows,
In every garden the poet seeks your
    face,
Asking you to show yourself, to dazzle
    the world
And all who dwell in it
With your loveliness.

Each curl of your luxurious tresses
Is a hook that catches my heart.
My heart is torn into a thousand
    wounds by those barbs,
From each a red drop starts, and earns
    the praise
Of other sad lovers, who understand
The poet's longings and his sighs.

38

Everything around me shines like the
    moon;
Everything is scented with benediction.
How beautiful is life; and how beautiful
    are you,
Young girl, you who are like a thought
    of peace:
Your beauty belongs to all time.
O let us hate only war and destruction.
When we walk by the river at sunset,
When the water ripples and we hear the
    boatman's song
From where the white sails flutter, far off,
We will know that his words are true:
Today by the river as we walk hand in
    hand

There is no suffering,
Today there is only the scented world,
Shining like your beauty, like the
    moon.

39

The words of love we spoke
Have stored themselves in our history
To await in secret another time:
One day they will fall, as seeds, with
    rain to earth,
And grow green all over the world.

40

Another dawn will never come
That finds us waking together.
I know this, and little by little
Give up the love that wants such dawns
    again.
And yet: something within me laughs,
Laughs and shakes it head,
At the thought of ever giving up this
    love
That wants such dawns again.

41

You were the morning, I was a candle in
    the dawn.
I surrendered my heart to your smile on
    awakening.
Such was the pattern of your tresses on
    my breast
That they will make my grave a bed of
    violets.
I opened the doors of my desire to you,
And you crossed the threshold:
I am the slave of what I saw in you,
And though your beauty is displayed to
    everyone,
No one sees your amorous look as I do.

Oh beloved, if like a breeze you pass by
    my tomb
I will rise in that narrow pass and tear
    my shroud,
Summoned by the lightness of your
    footfall.

42

A hot afternoon; I lay drowsing on my
    bed, limbs spread
To catch the breeze of the half-opened
    window.
The light in my room was dim
As twilight in a dark green forest,
Or the glimmer before dawn;
Such light as shy girls like for modesty.
Behold then she came, in a loose slip,
Her hair tumbling down her gleaming
    neck.
I pulled her slip away, not tearing it
    though of gauze,
And she pretended to try keeping it
    about her;
But yielded effortlessly, and stood
    naked,
Naked before my eyes: not a flaw on
    her body.
What shoulders, arms, I saw and
    touched!
What breasts so formed for my caress!
How her belly curved beneath her
    slender waist,
How curved her flanks, her warm
    thighs!
I pressed her naked body against mine,
    and kissed:
Who does not know the rest? Drowsy
    with love we rested:
May many such afternoons be mine!

43

Ring, go to her, encircle her beautiful
    finger;
May she receive you with a glad heart
    and take you
Straightway, where I kissed;
Smoothly fit her finger, lucky ring.
I, envious of my gift, would take its
    place
To encircle her close;
Then when I wished to touch her breasts,
Or reach inside her tunic, I would slip
    from her finger,
However tight and clinging the fit,
And with wonderful art fall into her
    garment's folds.
Again, to close a letter up, she would
    touch me to her moist lips
Before she pressed the wax that seals its
    secret.
She would wear me as she steps into the
    bath,
Though I think her naked limbs would
    rouse my passion.
A vain wish? Away then, little gift:
Show her what loyalty comes with you,
And what desire.

44

Forbear to wonder what the Cantabrian
    or Scythian meditate,
Divided from us by the unsleeping sea;
Leave thought for the necessities of life,
    which needs little.
Youth and beauty are swiftly away,
Old age turns its back on wanton loves.
The same glory does not remain in the
    flower,
Nor does the ruddy moon shine with
    the same face:

Why fatigue yourself with thoughts?
While we can, let us recline under the
    tall pine,
In a shade fragrant with roses,
And wait while the cups of ardent
    Falernian wine
Cool in the passing stream:
And let us call wanton Lyde from her
    house,
To hasten with her ivory lyre, her hair
Tied in a graceful knot
In the manner of the Spartan maids.

45

What slender youth, bathed in
    perfumes,
Embraces you among many a rose, O
    Pyrrha,
In a pleasant arbour?
For whom do you tie up your golden
    hair
In simple elegance?
Alas! how often will he lament your
    faithlessness,
Like a sailor who set out on a sparkling
    sea
Then sees, surprised,
The water roughening and darkened by
    gales!
He who now enjoys you,
Fondly thinking you golden, ever
    lovely,
Is ignorant of the treacherous future
That awaits him at your hands.
O wretched youth, to whom, he untried,
You now appear so dazzling!
As for me, I have hung up the dripping
    garments
In which I nearly drowned while in
    your arms.

46

Tell me, Lydia, why strong Sybaris
Shuns the sun-drenched field of
    exercise,
Why he rides no more among his
    comrades,
Mastering his Gallic stallion with iron
    bit?
Why does he avoid the yellow Tiber's
    foam,
Why does he neglect to oil his limbs
For the wrestling-ground,
Or show his arms bruised with weapon
    practice,
He who once threw the discus, the
    javelin,
Further than all?
Is this the work of love, Lydia,
Or just the work of your charms?

47

It is poetry's will that I celebrate her,
Her bright darting eyes, her breast
    faithful to mutual love;
Who can with grace step into the dance
Or join arms with the virgins of the
    festival?
Would anyone change a single tress of
    her hair
For all the riches of Achaemenes,
Or the wealth of fertile Phrygia?
Especially when she turns her neck to
    meet your burning kisses,
Or with gentle cruelty denies what she
    would
With more delight
Have ravished than the petitioner:
And sometimes eagerly embraces for
    herself?

48

The caged bird owes no allegiance.
Where tonight she lies, no one can give
   us news;
Nor any knows, save the watching moon.

The wall is low around my garden;
The lists in the bailiff's lodge are seldom
   checked.
Were we sometimes unkind?
When the shadows thickened among
   the pines
She crept away, concealed by silence.

The caged bird owes no allegiance,
The wind-tossed flower does not cling
   to the tree.

Where she lies tonight, no one can give
   us news;
Nor any knows, save the watching moon.

49

The mountain path is covered in fallen
   leaves,
So many, so many.
Looking for my lost lover I cannot find
   the path,
Walking the path I am like a boat in
   water,
Leaving no track behind.
Between the branches I see the evening
   sky;
When I gaze into the clouds I see
The smoke of her funeral pyre.
Our former life is now a dream;
The house we left
Has become a home for wildflowers
   and butterflies;
And its walls are covered in ivy.

50

Look to today.
You remember yesterday,
You envision tomorrow,
Today you live.

Live well today,
Yesterday is a good memory,
Tomorrow a good hope.

Neglect today,
Yesterday is remorse,
Tomorrow a trial.

51

Still and clear, the first weeks of May,
When trees are green and bushes soft
   and wet;
When the wind has stolen the shadows
   of new leaves
And birds linger on the last boughs that
   bloom.
Towards evening as the sky grew clearer
   yet
And the south-east was still clothed in
   red,
To the highest terrace we carried our jar
   of wine;
While we waited for the moon, our
   cups moved slow.
Soon, soon her golden shape rose from
   the forest in the east,
Swiftly, as though she had waited for us
   to come.
The beams of her light shone in every
   place,
On towers and halls dancing to and fro.
Till day broke we sat in her clear light
Laughing, singing, yet never growing
   tired.

In the city, where men scramble for
    profit and fame,
How many know such nights as this?

                    52
At my closed door autumn grasses grow.
What could I do to ease a rustic heart?
I planted trees, more than a hundred
    saplings.
When I see their beauty, as they grow
    by the stream-side,
I feel again as though I lived in the hills,
And many a time on public holidays
Round their railing I walk till night
    comes.
Do not say that their roots are still
    weak,
Do not say that their shade is still small;
Already I feel both in garden and house
Day by day a fresher air moves.
But most I love, lying at my window,
To hear in their branches the murmur
    of the breeze.

                    53
Green spring receives the vacant earth;
The white sun shines;
Spring wind provokes each sprout and
    flower
To burst and burgeon anew.
Do not hide in those dark caves where
    winter lurks, my thoughts!
O thoughts come back again! Do not
    stray!
Come back again:
Go not east or west, north or south!

O thoughts go not east,
For eastward a mighty water drowns
    earth's other shore;

Tossed on its waves and heaving with its
    tides
The nameless terrors of the ocean ride,
Clouds gather low, fogs enfold the sea
And gleaming ice drifts past:
O thoughts go not east,
To where dangerous surges
Toss the fragile ships of men and flood
    them over,
Bearing them to the bottom of the
    deep!

O thoughts go not south, where mile
    on mile
The earth is burnt away and poisonous
    serpents
Slither through the flames;
Where on precipitous paths and deep in
    woods
Tigers and leopards prowl, water-
    scorpions wait,
And the king python rears his giant
    head.
O thoughts, go not south,
Where the slow-moving tortoise
    breathes disease
And beasts' eyes glare from the black
    forest shade!

O thoughts go not west,
Where desert wastes of sand stretch
    endlessly;
And barbarians rage, swine-headed,
    hairy-skinned,
With bulging eyes, who in wild laugh-
    ter shake their weapons
And prey on travellers lost in the waste
    of burning dunes.
O thoughts go not west where thirst
    and perils wait!

O thoughts go not north, to the frozen
    peaks
Where trees and grasses dare not grow;
Where a river runs too wide to cross,
    too deep to plumb,
And the sky is white with snow.
Go not north where cold winds cut and
    kill.
O thoughts seek not the north's treach-
    erous icy voids!

O thoughts come back to idleness and
    peace.
In quietude enjoy the meadows of your
    home,
There work your will and follow your
    desires
Till sorrow is forgotten;
Let carefree hours bring you many
    pleasant days
And length of life.
O thoughts come back to joys beyond
    all telling!
Where at harvest-time the corn stacks
    high,
Where pies are cooked of millet and
    bearded maize,
And guests enjoy steaming bowls of soup
And savour the pungency of peppered
    herbs,
To which the artful cook adds slices of
    sweet fowl,
Pigeon and yellow heron and black
    crane.
Come back, O thoughts;
Taste again the feasts of your youth,
    succulent and rich,
With salad of minced radishes in
    brine,
With hot spice of southernwood.

O thoughts come back to taste the
    meats you love!

The four strong liquors are warming at
    the fire
To be smooth on the drinker's throat.
How fragrant rise their fumes, how cool
    their taste!
Unfermented spirit blended with white
    yeast
Distils the essence of cheer and
    forgetfulness.
O thoughts come back and let your
    yearnings cease!
Tunes from small-throated flutes
Gladden the feasters, and old songs are
    sung:
The ballad-singer's voice rises alone, and
    recalls memories.
O thoughts come back to the hollow
    mulberry tree!
There eight and eight the dancers sway,
Weaving their steps to the poet's voice.
Musicians tap their bells and beat their
    chimes
Keeping harp and flute to their
    measure.
Then rival singers compete in melody,
    till not a tune
Is left unsung that human voice could
    sing.
O thoughts come back and listen to
    their song!

Then women enter whose red lips and
    dazzling teeth
Entrance the eye;
Trained in every art they discourse of
    poetry
And strum the lute,

And to their knowledge of history and
    letters
Add soft hands and delicate wrists,
    graceful as the spring.
O thoughts come back and let them
    ease your woe!
Then enter other girls with laughing
    lips
And sidelong glances under moth-eye
    brows;
Whose cheeks are fresh and red;
Girls soft of heart and long of limb,
Whose beauty by intelligence is
    matched.
Rose-glowing cheeks and ears with
    curving rim,
High-arching eyebrows, as with
    compass drawn,
Soft hearts and loving gestures – all are
    there;
Small waists and necks as slender as the
    clasp of brooches.
O thoughts come back to those whose
    tenderness
Drives anger and sadness away!
Last enter those whose every action is
    contrived to please;
Black-painted eyebrows and white-
    powdered cheeks.
They diffuse sweet scents; their long
    sleeves brush
The faces of feasters whom they pass,
They pluck the coats of those who will
    not stay.
O thoughts come back to pleasures of
    the night!

And at the first ray of dawn already is
    hung
The shooting target, where bow in hand

And arrows under arm, archers salute
    each other,
Each willing to yield his rights of
    precedence
Who shall go first;
Here is courtesy, and here leisure;
Here the exercise of skill in the fresh
    morning light.
O thoughts come back to these
    pleasures
And the quiet meadows of home!

A summerhouse with spacious rooms
And a high hall with beams stained red;
A little closet in the southern wing
Reached by a private stair.
And round the house a covered way
    runs
Where horses are trained.
And sometimes riding, sometimes afoot
You shall explore, O thoughts, the park
    in spring;
Your jewelled axles gleaming in the sun
And yoke inlaid with gold;
Or amid orchids and sandalwood trees
You shall stroll through shaded woods.
O thoughts come back and live for
    these delights!
Peacocks shall fill your gardens; you
    shall rear
The roc and phoenix, and red
    jungle-fowl,
Whose cry at dawn assembles river
    storks
To join the play of cranes and ibises;
Where the wild swan all day
Pursues the glint of kingfishers
Flashing amongst the reeds.
O thoughts come back to watch the
    birds in flight!

He who has found such delights
Shall feel his cheeks glow
And the blood dancing through his
    limbs.
Stay with me, O thoughts, and share
The span of days that happiness will
    bring;
See sons and grandsons succeed in their
    crafts, enriched;
O thoughts come back and bring
    prosperity
To house and stock!

The roads that lead abroad teem thick
    as clouds
With travellers going a thousand miles
    away.
Are they wise in council; by their aid
    will rulers relieve
The discontents of humble men
And help the lonely poor?
Will there be deeds to repair
The wrongs endured by every tribe of
    men?
O thoughts come back and leave the
    unjust world,
Come back to where the good are
    praised;
Come back to where the wise are
    sought!
O thoughts, come back, come back! Go
    not
East or south, north or west;
Come back to the quiet meadows of
    home,
To the pavilions of repose where there,
    at last, is rest.

54

That I could shrink the surface of the
    world,
So that suddenly I might find you
    standing at my side!

In old days those who went to fight
Had one year's leave in every three.
But in this war the soldiers never
    return;
They fight on till they die:
That is their discharge.
I thought of you, so unsoldierlike,
Trying to learn to march and drill,
To load a gun, to shoot and kill.
That a young man such as you,
Poet, scholar, lover,
Would ever come home again
Seemed as likely as that the sky should
    fall.

Since I heard the news that you were
    coming back,
Twice I have visited the high hall of
    your home.
I found your brother mending your
    horse's stall;
I found your mother sewing new
    clothes for you.
I am half afraid; perhaps it is not true;
Yet I never weary of watching the road
    for you.
Each day I go to the city gate
With a flask of wine, lest you should
    come thirsty.

Oh that I could shrink the surface of
    the world,
So that suddenly I might find you
    standing at my side!

55

Wake up, cup-bearer, arise! and bring
My thirsty lips the bowl they praise.
I thought love would be easy,
But I have stumbled, and fallen.
I begged the breeze to blow to my face
The fragrance of musk in her hair,
The fragrance that sleeps in the night of
    her hair –
Yet nothing comes but weeping.
Hear the tavern-keeper's counsel: 'With
    red wine
Dye the carpet on which you lie.'
He knows; he knows the way.
Where shall I rest, when all the still
    night long
Beyond the gateway, oh heart of my
    heart,
I hear the bells of lamentation and the
    cry,
'Bind up your burden, and depart!'

The tide runs high, night is clouded
    with fears,
In my ears eddying whirlpools clash
    and roar;
How shall my drowning voice strike
    their ears
Whose lighter vessels have gained the
    shore?
I sought something to be my own; the
    unsparing years
Have brought me only a dishonoured
    name.
What cloak shall cover my misery
When each jesting mouth repeats my
    shame!
Oh hold fast what the wise have said:
'If at last you gain your life's desire,
Cast the world aside, leave it for dead;

There is no ease otherwise for the heart
Than to bind up your burden, and
    depart!'

56

The garden birds sang to the rose
Newly opened in the clear dawn:
'Lower your head! Within this garden
Many as fair as you have bloomed and
    died!'
Laughing she replied,
'That I am born to fade does not grieve
    me.
But you do wrong to vex with bitter
    words
The moment when I am most myself.'

The tavern step shall be your hostelry,
Love's riches come only to those
Who supplicate on its dusty threshold
The ruby-red wine that flows
From life's jewelled goblet; otherwise
A thousand tears will thread your
    eyelashes
For such temerity as denies
That love in the fallen rose's petal lies.

Last night when the garden slept
In the silver arms of the moon,
A breeze stole through its alleys
And lifted the hyacinth's purple head.
'Where is the cup, the mirror of the
    world?
Where is love, like the wakened rose
Blossoming in the garden where its
    kind
Bloomed and died, so many, before?'
The breeze knew not; but sighed, 'Alas!
That happiness should sleep so long.'

Love's secret does not dwell on the lips
    of men;
Its place is secret and unrevealed. O
    friend!
Come where there is idle laughter,
    where wine
Graces the feast: patience and wisdom
    are launched
On a sea of tears, and soon we must
    sleep without end.

57

Light of my eyes and harvest of my
    heart,
Mine at least in changeless memory!
When you found it easy to leave, what
    you left
Was the harder journey for us to take.
Oh you who stand by, help me lift my
    load,
Let pity be the comrade of my road!

If only life could re-enter at the
    deserted door,
And the cold body breathe again and
    burn;
Come! touch my eyes; I am blind to all
But your face; open their gates and let
    me see
By the love we bore each other, and its
    grace,
Once more your face.

58

You ask why I live in the green
    mountain;
I smile but stay silent, for my heart is
    free.
As the leaves of the peach tree float
    downstream

To distant places unknown,
As the hummingbird flashes away to
    the woods,
And smoke curls up to the clouds,
I go likewise, and am found no more:
Neither in the villages of the plain
Nor the habitations of men;
But live high with the winds
Where all five directions are visible at
    once,
Alone, without a care.

59

There are no coins in my pocket, and a
    flagon of wine
Costs as much as an estate to one who
    is poor.
A plate of food costs even more; but
    what does it matter?
I cannot eat, even if I had bowl and
    spoon.
I would cross the river, but ice has
    stopped the ferry;
I would climb the mountain, but the
    pass is blocked with snow;
I would sit by the pond and fish, lazy in
    the afternoon,
But suddenly I dream of flying to the
    sun.
It is hard to journey, hard, for there are
    so many turnings:
Which shall I take?
I will climb on the wind one day and
    ride,
Over the heavy waves, with a cloud for
    a sail,
And cross the deep sea to other lands.

60

In the capital as the year draws to a
    close
A great snowfall cloaks the palace
    courtyard,
And through the blizzard, on their way
    from court,
In fine crimson robes the dukes and
    barons ride.
They can enjoy the snowfall's beauty
    and bracing wind;
To the rich they do not signify hunger
    and cold.
At a grand gate the riders and coaches
    gather,
Candles are lit in the tower and music
    spills out,
Happy guests press knee to knee,
Warmed by wine they open their fur
    coats
To show off silk linings and silver
    buttons.
The host is a high dignitary of the
    Punishments Board,
The guest of honour is the Minister of
    Justice.
It was dusk when the feasting and
    music began,
Now it is past midnight, and the revel
    continues.
What do they care that in the gaol
    tonight
The prisoners are freezing to death?

61

Yesterday the villagers pitched a tent on
    the green,
Brought their hogs and calves to sell;
Their wives laid out cakes and flower
    displays,
And when dusk fell they lit a bonfire
To roast a pig on a spit,
Lifting their beer mugs, talking quietly
    while the spit turned,
Themselves turning over gossip and old
    news.
In the strong firelight they ate when the
    roast was ready,
Faces gleaming,
And in the shadows the fiddler tuned
    his fiddle for the revel to come.

62

This isolated hilltop has been dear to
    me always.
And this hedge also, that draws a line
    under the sky.
Sitting, looking, I wonder idly
What is beyond the horizon: and I
    imagine
Great silences, infinite spaces,
Unearthly stillness. Then for a while I
    am not afraid.
I hear the wind breathing in the trees,
And it is the voice of that distance,
Calling to mind the idea of time
    without time,
The dead ages past and mute,
The unbounded present ever arriving
With tumult and noise. My thoughts
Founder in those immensities;
And it is sweet to sink and drown in
    them.

63

The days of my youth are long over,
Now the days of my prime dwindle in
    their turn.
With what sad regrets I walk again
In this cold deserted place!

In the middle of the garden I stand
   alone,
The moonlight blanching the paths,
The wind cold and damp, leaving
   frosted dews
On the autumn lettuce, tangled and
   gone to seed.
The orchard trees are withered too;
All that is left are chrysanthemums
Newly opened under the wattle fence.
I had brought wine and a cup, and
   meant to drink;
But the sight of these stayed my hand.
I remember how quickly my moods
   could change
From sad to gay when I was young;
If I had wine, no matter what season:
Even before I tasted it my heart grew
   glad.
But now that age approaches, moments
   of gladness
Are harder and harder to get. I fear that
   when I am old
Not even the fiercest liquor will
   comfort me.
Therefore I ask you, chrysanthemums,
   why you bloom so late:
Though I know well that it is not for
   my sake. Yet,
Reminded by you, I will forget age and
   sorrow for this while,
And drink a cup to you.

64

What can this mean? What a strange
   new life!
What could disturb you so? I no longer
   know you,
Heart, now that you are overtaken like
   this,

Old loves, old griefs forgotten, new
   turbulence instead:
Are you caught by the beautiful youth
   whose eyes,
Shining at you, prevent you from
   running away,
Even though you cry out: Let me go!
   Let me go!
It is the thread which cannot be untied
   that leads you back,
Every path leads back, you are held fast:
   what a change!
How old must you grow before this
   kind of enchantment
No longer catches you, but leaves you
   free?

65

Come to the dance with me, fair one,
   come:
The dance crowns the feast day when
   evening falls.
If you are not my love, yet still you can
   be,
And if you will be, come, dance with
   me.
Without you what would a feast day
   be?
If you love me, all life is feasting:
Without you what would a dance be?
Come dance with me;
Let us spin in the dance, let us steal
   dizzied away
To whisper in the evening woods:
Come love, dance with me,
Come crown the feast with dance, and
   love.

66

You see how the high hills stand out
   white with snow,
And the struggling trees can scarcely
   bear the load
Of deep drifts on their branches. The river
Is frozen with sharp ice, even the air
   cracks with cold.
Pile on the logs, build the fire higher,
Bring out the two-handled jug:
Leave everything to its own devices,
The razor-edged wind fighting the
   heaving sea,
The trees shaking and snapping under
   their glittering burden;
Do not ask about tomorrow, but count
   the time as profit,
And give your thoughts to youth's
   enjoyments:
The dances in the square, the laughter
   of a girl
Hiding in a secret corner, which gives
   her away:
And a pledge snatched from her willing
   fingers
Which pretend reluctance, but brush
   your fingers with fire
When they touch.

67

The man caught in the open sea longs
   for calm.
He is filled with fear when a cloud
   obscures the moon,
And the stars' sure gleam is lost to view.
Why ambition, when life is so short?
Why trade peace of mind for these
   ventures,
Our homes for other suns, our rest for
   arduous strife?

Spoiling care climbs the bronze side of
   ships,
It hunts the cavalry, swifter than stags
Or the east wind that hurries the clouds
   before it:
Every hero fell at the throw of its
   quivering lance.
It is like the bolt of lightning that splits
   the oak,
And sets the forests to raging fire in
   summer's drought.
None escapes who leaves his rural home
Where his cattle meditate and his sheep
   quietly graze;
Who keeps warm in winter with a wool
   doublet
Twice dipped in home dye;
Who eats the bread he baked from corn
   he milled,
Scorning the envious crowd.

68

Gold loves to go through gates and
   walls,
It defies armed guards and watchmen,
Money throws down gates, unbolts
   doors,
Brings battlements and fortifications
   crumbling down.
Bribes sink ships, win wars, unseat the
   mighty.
Worry and vexed ambition follow
   money,
Appetite for wealth grows hungrier with
   feeding.

Yet the more one denies oneself, the
   more one gains.
Unencumbered, I seek out the camps of
   those who desire nothing;

A deserter, I hasten away from the side
    of wealthy men,
Whose comparison makes me poor: for
    I am wealthy myself
In the absence of my wants,
Rich in already being satisfied.
I have a stream of clear water, a wood of
    a few acres,
My harvest and milch cows, and my
    bleating sheep;
Each morning I find eggs in the straw.
I expand my revenues by shrinking my
    desires,
And live the emperor of my domain.

69

Let us love that we may live:
Let us judge the old women's gossip
Less worth than a broken jar.
Let the sun rise and set and rise again;
When its brief warmth has left us
We must huddle in the earth
An endless night. So kiss me:
Give me a thousand kisses
Then a hundred kisses
Then a thousand kisses more:
When we have kissed many thousand
    kisses
We will be beyond the jealousy
Of those who do not know
How many kisses we shared.

70

She is here! She stays, she has promised!
Banish discontent; I have won;
She could not resist my entreaties
    longer.
Let joy drive out envy:
She has ceased to travel foreign roads,
She says home is best, exchanging

Wide kingdoms for this narrow bed
    with me.
I did not persuade her with gold or
    Indian pearls,
But with poetry.
Now my feet tread the stars; I walk the
    heavens.
She stays: she, the rare, is mine!

71

I was often hurt by your inconstancy,
Yet I never expected betrayal.
See how mistaken I was! Yet when I ask,
You respond in such slow evasive
    terms.
You raise your brush calmly to your
    tresses,
And idly examine your looks in the
    glass.
You go on decorating your breasts with
    Eastern jewels,
Like a beautiful woman preparing for a
    new lover.
Alas! is this where it ends?
So Calypso felt when the Ithacan
    voyager left,
Weeping long ago to the unfeeling
    waves,
Mourning many months with loosened
    hair,
Blaming the unkind sea that took him
    away:
And even though she would never see
    him again,
Still she grieved, thinking of the
    happiness they shared.
So Dido lamented, at the same waves
    and ocean winds
That irretrievably took the Trojan from
    her,

With tears as salt as the sea, deepening
  its depths.
Yet no such stories make you pity me,
  or stop your lying,
O thoughtless girl! Rivers will return to
  their springs,
The seasons will reverse their course,
  before I cease loving you.
Do not let these eyes seem worthless to
  you now,
That were deliberately blind to your
  perfidies.
You swore by your own that had you
  been false,
They would close for ever when I kissed
  them.
Can you look out at the sunlight, and
  not tremble,
Aware of your falsehoods?
Who has brought this pallor to my
  cheeks,
And the unwilling tears to wet them?
If I bewail what has happened
It is to warn those who would love
How beauty betrays.

72

Daphnis, it chanced, had made his seat
  beneath a whispering ilex,
Where Corydon and Thyrsis drove their
  flocks together,
Thyrsis his sheep, Corydon his goats
  swollen with milk, to the meadows;
Both in the bloom of life, Arcadians
  both.
To this place, while I tended my
  myrtles' new shoots,
My he-goat, the lord of the flock, had
  strayed; and I caught sight of
  Daphnis.

When he saw me he called, 'Quick!
  come here, Meliboeus; your goat
  and kids are safe, and if you can
  idle awhile,
Rest beneath this shade with me.
Your steers will come by themselves
  over the meadows to drink;
Here the stream fringes its green banks
  with waving reeds,
And the old oak swarms with humming
  bees.
Come, and hear Corydon and Thyrsis vie
Who shall sing the sweetest.'
What could I do? My new-weaned
  lambs were safe penned at home;
And the match – Corydon against
  Thyrsis – was a mighty one:
I counted their sport above my work.
So in alternate verses the pair
  competed:
These Corydon, those Thyrsis sang in
  turn.

Corydon:
You mossy springs, and lawns softer
  than sleep,
And the green arbutus that shields you
  with scanty shade,
Ward the noontide heat from my flock.
Now comes the summer's parching,
Now the buds swell on the pliant
  tendril.

Thyrsis:
With me you will find a hearth and
  pitchy brands;
With me a good fire blazing and
  doorposts black with soot.
Here we care as little for the freezing
  blasts of winter

As the wolf for the number of sheep
Or rushing torrents their banks.

Corydon:
Here stand junipers and shaggy chestnuts;
Strewn beneath each tree lies its native
 fruit;
Now all nature smiles; but if fair Alexis
 should quit these hills
The rivers would run dry.

Thyrsis:
The field is parched; the grass is athirst,
 dying in the tainted air;
The vines grudge their shade to the
 hills;
But at the coming of my Phyllis all the
 woodland
Springs to green life,
And rain descends in glad showers.

Corydon:
Dearest is the poplar to the shepherd,
The vine to the reveller,
The myrtle to the lover,
The laurel to the poet.
Phyllis loves hazels, and while Phyllis
 loves them,
Neither myrtle nor the poet's laurel
 shall outdo them.

Thyrsis:
Fairest is the ash in the woodlands, the
 pine in the gardens,
The poplar by rivers, the fir on
 mountaintops;
But if you come often to me, the ash in
 the woodlands
And the pine in the gardens will yield
 to you.

So much I remember:
How Thyrsis strove in vain against
 defeat;
From that day Corydon is our only
 Corydon.

73

He delays: for the third time
The wick of the lamp droops and fades.
Would the flame in my breast sink with
 the lamp,
And not burn so strongly with sleepless
 desire.
Ah how often he promised to come in
 the evening,
But he does not scruple to break my heart
As easily as his vow.

74

Slender Melite, though now not young,
Has not lost the graces of youth.
Still her cheeks are rosy, and her eyes
Have not forgotten their brightness
Or how to charm.
Yet her decades are not few.
Her attractiveness seems to teach us
That time cannot subdue nature.
Alas:
At last that cannot be true.

75

I had lovable Juliana all night with me,
And all night she complained piteously:
From the hour when the evening star
 began to mount,
She blamed it for heralding the
 morrow's dawn.
Nothing is just as we would have it:
The servants of love require endless
 nights.

76

Curious to find out if lovely Ereutho
    was fond of me,
I tested her heart by a subtle falsehood.
I said, 'I am going abroad; but please
    remain, my dearest,
Faithful and ever mindful of my love.'
Whereupon she gave a great cry, and
    leapt up,
And beat her breasts with her hands,
And tore the clusters of her braided
    hair,
Begging me not to go.
Then, as if reluctantly complying, I
    consented.
I am happy in my love:
What I anyway wished to do, I granted
    as a favour.

77

Eluding her mother's apprehensive eyes,
The charming girl gave me a pair of
    apples.
I think she had set fire to those red
    apples
With the torch of love: for I burn:
I burn: I burn:
Yet instead of two breasts
My luckless hands fondle two apples.

78

Melissias denies she is in love,
But her demeanour proclaims
    otherwise.
Unsteady is her step and she takes her
    breath in snatches;
Under her eyes are dark purple hollows.
Oh love! turn your flames on this
    rebellious maid
Till she cries aloud, 'I am afire!'

79

I, a fisherman, having reached trembling
    old age,
Give the sea these gifts of all I have:
My pliant rods, my oar, my rudder and
    keel,
My curved and pointed hooks,
My net weighted with lead,
The floats that mark where the fish run,
These well-woven creels,
This flint to strike fire at evening,
My anchor, stay of my unstable boat,
Now lying in the seaweed:
And myself, whom the waves did not
    once before engulf,
But now may cradle my final sleep.

80

I, a shepherd, in my shaky old age,
Lay aside my heavy crook,
But still have my pipe, and play;
For in my wizened body the voice
    remains.
But let no herdsman tell the wolves
Ravening on the mountain
How feeble I have grown in my old years.

81

Where will you find rest?
I think at the bend in the river
Where an old man wearing a straw hat
    and cape
Sits in his lonely boat and fishes.
It pleases us to see
Green willows, still water,
The sun in the east and the rain in the
    west,
Half bright, half cloudy,
Where the river bends.
That is where you may find rest.

82

The storm has ended. Now the eaves
     drip,
And the cicadas begin once more,
     tentatively,
One here, one there.
We sit in silence in the bower,
Holding hands wet with tears.
We cannot speak, thinking of the
     distance
You must go: a thousand miles,
Never to return.
When lovers endure forced partings
It is like the end of autumn, and deep
     frost.
Where will I wake tomorrow, knowing
That I will not sleep again unless
     drunk?
The morning breeze, the pale and
     empty moon,
Tell us that our love's tender words
Have all been said.

83

Around the red pavilion,
Down the door-posts and the panels,
The dawn light runs like silver rain.
We were glad to meet,
We were sad to part.
The moon is always full when lovers
     part:
We see the sharp black shadow become
     two shadows,
Moving away from each other in the
     night garden.
I have not slept, but waited hoping for
     your return,
Sitting at the door while the night waned
And now the silver rain of dawn light
     shows

The empty garden, the presence of your
     absence.

84

I recall the time of heroes,
When he married his bride
With his fan and crimson scarf,
His gaily knotted cloak fluttering in the
     wind,
His laughter when the speech-makers
     told
How he burned the enemy ships to ash
     on the beach,
And collected the weapons of their dead
     as trophies.
You may laugh too at my obsessions
     and memories,
But I recall the time of heroes,
Before great deeds were buried under a
     mountain of days.

85

The whole world grows darker at the
     end of night.
The line of hills, the hedges and copses,
The rooftops and the wisps of smoke
     from their chimneys,
All grow darker at the end of night.
It is like the departure of youth and
     love:
Away go the shadowy shapes of the
     dead past,
Away the still-sharp memories and
     illusions:
All these things on which our nature
     leaned,
From which our hearts learned to
     learn.
What was bright and insistent and for
     ever

Has become impermanent and dim,
Turning darker at the end of night.

86

How well I remember the first time!
And said, if this is love, how hard it is
    to bear!
How badly it has led and governed me,
To what hard ground and briars, what
    thorns;
How laden with sorrows and sore
    lamentations,
How unresting, sleepless and sad.
Why were these sufferings blended with
    such hope,
Such sweet hope and tender desire?
Behind closed eyes exhausted by
    ever-waking
The bright image of the beloved still
    burns.

87

Beautiful beloved, who inspired
    everything I am,
Say what innocence, what remoteness,
    formed you?
In what cool shade born, by what
    murmurous stream
Raised and taught your arts?
I see the darting hummingbird in the
    garden you kept,
The golden firebird and the silver-
    quilled eagle
Waving in their plumes the light of
    tranquil afternoons
When you rested, your cheek on the
    moss pillow
And your hand on the book of sonnets
    written for you.
No one is like you, or has been;

In no valley where the beekeeper tends
    his hives.
On no plain where the farmer ploughs,
No upland meadow where the shepherd
    pipes,
No orchard or field of vines where the
    husbandman toils,
Has there ever been the like of you.
Beautiful beloved: the tune of the
    willow warbler
Marks your waking from slumber,
And the afternoon sun restrains his
    beams where they kiss your brow.

88

Under the sculptor's hammer
The figure increases as the marble
    decreases.
That is a lesson.
Art arrives when there is nothing left to
    take away:
The artist trembles; in the mass of stone
There is a slender figure seeking escape,
Lost before it was found:
One blow, and it is gone, shattered, like
    a dream
Unremembered.

89

How can the statue last longer than its
    maker?
Hard stone outlasts even hard hearts.
There is a live image in the cold stone,
And the chisel cuts it free and gives it
    life.
Its maker becomes ashes after the years
    have bent him down;
Nature is thus defeated by art, though
    nature struck art
Many sharp and heavy blows.

90

Even time and death cannot threaten
  our work
If we work to defeat death and time.
I have seen this in colours, marble,
  brick.
In ink I have seen it: the defeat of death
  and time.
So long as eyes can see, so do works
  remain.
We are not fools that strive to climb
Above the inevitabilities, to leave our
  mark on them.
If we arrive late at novel and lofty
  attempts,
And can stay only a short time,
Nevertheless we depart, though reluc-
  tant, with satisfaction:
This was the promise if we would try,
That trying is the triumph itself.

91

For a moment a solitary white sail shows
Where the azure gleam of sea touches
  sky.
What did the sailors leave behind in
  their homes
So distant? What do they seek by
  travelling so far?
I feel, for I cannot hear from here,
The creak of masts, and flapping canvas.
I feel, for I cannot touch from here,
Straining ropes and salt-damp railings.
The billows rise and the impatient wind
Hurries the waves before it.
What does the sea desire? Storms:
It does not wish the sun's caress,
But awaits with longing the wild rough
  gale
And the lashing squall.

Where then will be that lone white sail,
Far off where sky meets sea?

92

In the mist the road's stones glimmered,
Then suddenly I stepped from its
  obscurity
Into bright night, with sparkling stars
And a pale northern horizon where the
  sun cannot set.
Above, a grave and wonderful sky,
Beneath, a sleeping earth, bathed
In cool blue light:
This was all I sought, all I needed.
I have no regrets for the past,
I wish only freedom and rest,
I would fall asleep by a tree
For ever, not needing dawn or day:
And with all this, rolling round, would
  be one.

93

The clouds are exiles as I am,
Adrift as I am, wandering at the wind's
  behest
In long strings of vapour,
White or bruised to blue by bellies of
  rain
Waiting to be emptied, with high heads
  or strange shapes
That children make play of: as I am.
In the wastes of the sky where the wind
  crosses
Or blows or pulls, the wandering exiles
  unresisting,
My thoughts float as they do, at the
  command of vagaries.
The clouds have no homeland, only
  banishment:
As I do.

94

Though it is hard to die, it is good to
    die:
I shall ask no one's pity,
And no one will pity me.
I won no glory with my lyre,
Nor added lustre to my family's name;
I am as far from my kin
As on the day I began to live.
All ties are broken, all past regrets
    forgotten.
There is no one to ask forgiveness,
Because there is no forgiveness to give.

95

Here on the steppe is a forgotten grave.
It is not a memorial to anyone now,
Except to an affection that once was,
That lifted and piled stones one on
    another,
Many stones, so that wolves could not
    feed here,
Nor vultures. On the cold steppe there
    is a song
Sung for ever by the wind, neither
    ballad nor lament,
But the steppe song, that sings to those
    who live and die
With its huge horizon before their faces,
And its pure air that carries the wolf's
    howl
Far to the world's edge.
The stones' only visitor now is the
    steppe wind
Singing to them neither ballad nor
    lament.

96

Welcome, solitude: companion of the
    wise and good,
From whose piercing eye fools flee and
    villains hide.
I love to walk with you, and listen to
    your whispered talk,
To your innocence and truth, that
    melts
All but the most obdurate hearts.
You wear a thousand pleasing shapes,
Yours is the balmy breath of evening
When the landscape swims away in
    shadows,
Yours is the secrecy of the hermit's cell
Where is never cause for deceits,
Even of the private self.
Welcome; you are what will greet us all
    at last,
On that conclusive evening we find,
    alone,
The landscapes of our lives dissolve to
    shadow.

97

Dusk descends; all things seem to move
    far off;
Above, the evening star shines out,
A gracious lantern. And then the mist
    rises,
And the trees, the fences,
The remote farmhouse chimney, blur
    and dissolve.
Now in the eastern sky I see the moon,
The gleam and glow of the ochre
    moon,
And out of the evening obscurity come
    the willow branches,
Silver and slim.
Moonlight trembles through the play of
    moving shadows,
And its coolness calms the fretful heart.

98

Night embraces the woods,
From these hills the day has gone down
    to the west.
Flowers sleep and stars reflect their
    peace in the lake.
Leave me here, where the shadows of
    the forest firs cover me;
Let the night breeze breathe around me
    like the breath of dreams,
For here over the dark crest of the hill
    lies sorrow:
Beyond it, the battlefield where long
    ago
They laid the hacked and broken bones
    of men
Who died before they lived, far from
    home.
I shall sit here in the shadows and
    remember them.

99

When evening comes and the world
    grows quiet
And the heart too,
When your hand lies weary on your
    knee
And you can hear the tick of the
    pendulum from the clock on the
    wall
Which has not made itself heard all day,
When dusk lies in the corners and the
    nightjar flies outside;
Then you think of the gleam of the
    setting sun
Looking one last time through the
    window,
The sound of children on their way
    home, laughing,
To their supper and sleep,

You think perhaps the day was glad
    after all,
And tomorrow might be gladder.

100

I would be well content if allowed
The use of past experience,
To use the wisdom gleaned from follies
    past,
Acknowledged now;
To try life again, in hope
Of fewer errors on second proof.
But my heart said: could you, in truth?
Will you pardon time wasted,
Morality violated, talent abused,
Judgement ill-made, mercies not done,
Opportunity lost?
It is an evil incident to man
To leave unexamined the springs of
    useful truth,
And to walk the world with eyes shut,
Mind closed, ears stopped,
Heart gated against the greater good.
And one can walk thus only in the
    trodden way.

101

They sent me a present from Annam:
A red cockatoo,
Coloured like the peach-tree blossom,
Speaking the speech of men.
They had done to it what they always
    do
To the learned and eloquent:
They took a cage with stout bars
And shut it inside.

102

My bed has been put behind the
    unpainted screen.

They have shifted the stove next to the
    blue curtain.
My grandchildren read to me some-
    times from their books:
The servants heat my soup on the
    brazier outside.
With a quick pencil I answer goodwill
    notes from my friends,
I feel in my pocket for coins to pay the
    doctor.
When all these trifling things are done
I lie back on my pillow, and sleep with
    my face to the south.

103

Until forty one is distracted by the five
    lusts;
After seventy one is prey to a hundred
    diseases.
But at fifty and sixty one is free from all
    ills.
Calm and still, the heart enjoys rest.
I have put behind me love and greed,
I have put behind me profit and fame;
I am not yet decrepit or decayed;
Strength of limbs remains to me,
And I can seek the river and walk the
    hills;
My heart still loves hearing the flute
    and strings,
My stomach enjoys the new wine and
    the feast.
Do not complain of three-score:
It is the time we obey ourselves best.

104

Do not braid up your hair.
Let it fly unconfined,
Let its ravisher, the wind,
Wanton with it:

Like a clew of golden thread
Unravelled, let it free.
Do not wind up that light in ribands,
Or over-cloud it, like the night;
But let the sun's colour in it
Shake loose and scatter abroad,
Like day.

105

Into the isolated fields two figures
    passed,
Walking slow, into the frozen wood.
Their lips are tight, their eyes dead,
No one hears what they said.
Into the frozen fields two shadows
    passed,
To remember or deny the forgotten
    past.
Do you recall our ecstasy, they asked;
Why should we recall it, they
    answered;
Does my name beat in your heart
    always, they asked;
Never, they answered; and the taste of
    our kisses, they asked,
Do you taste them still?
No, they answered; all is gone, kisses
    too;
Forgotten, like a broken cup, its
    contents spilled.
So through the barren night they
    wandered,
Through the frozen meadows,
Only darkness hearing their words.

106

Worldly concerns are again drawing
    me.
The world seduces me: my thoughts
Grow narrow and covetous.

Once I used to visit you,
Passing there in the early morning;
Stopped my horse at your gate and
    tapped;
You sent your children to lead me in,
And you ran to the door to greet me,
Gown flapping round your bare
    ankles,
Laughing, cap awry.
And we breakfasted together on the
    swept terrace
With its view to the hills and the
    eastern lodge high up,
Its roof visible above the trees.
We talked all day sometimes,
But never spoke of profit or office.
Since we parted, how long has passed?
The leaves were falling then; now I
    hear
The new cicadas sing. And I
Have been drawn back to worldly
    concerns;
The world seduces me again,
Though we never talked of office and
    profit.

107

How great a thing is a cup of wine!
A single cup makes us tell the story of
    our lives.
By the willows that gaze at themselves
    in the pond
We drank and talked of our schooldays
    together,
Amazed at our folly then, and our
    ignorance:
We were ambitious, and never paused
    to sit quietly,
To look at the moon, to listen to the
    oriole sing,

To appreciate the shapes of oak leaves
    and acorns.
Now I listen to the water falling in the
    stream,
And if I have you and a cup of wine
    with me there
I can tell the story of my life again, and
    listen to yours.

108

Do I love you for the fine soft waves of
    hair
That fall about your neck when you
    undress?
Do I love you for the flowers on your
    cheeks, the rose
And the fragrant blossom there of palest
    red?
Do I love you for your coral lips, and
    the kisses I plant there,
Though those kisses may melt
Mightiest tyrants, and waken death to
    life?
Do I love you for those pearl teeth
That guard the music of your voice,
Or that ivory pillar of your neck, or
    your breasts
Soft and fair with rosy nipples
    crowned?
Do I love you, fairest of all fair?

109

Let there be persuasions to joy, O
    love.
Before the quick eye and darting
    affection grow cold,
Before the graces of manner and face
    change or fall,
Before golden hair grows to snow, or
    fresh beauty fades:

Let there be persuasions to joy.
Before time brings his sickle, or his
    wings,
Let us grasp it, and gather what now is,
And live before winter.

110

Have you grown a stranger to peace?
Are you troubled? Take the flagon and a
    cup;
Leave the turmoil of the town, its dust
    and clamour,
Walk up those paths that wind into the
    woods,
And let the sunlight paint patterns
    through the leaves around you,
The chorus of birds sing to you,
The stream falling among the rocks
    soothe you.
In the brevity of life there is little time
    for these self-estrangements.
Go up to the woods;
You will find yourself waiting there,
Flagon and cup ready, peace seated
    beside you.

111

Every petal that falls reduces spring.
Every leaf that falls hurries the year's
    end towards us.
Having studied the world, I wonder at
    man:
How can he be so deaf to that roar,
That thunder of passing time?

112

The butterflies go deeper and deeper
    among the flowers,
The dragonflies hover between drops of
    water

Flung up in the fountain's spray.
Watching them I see that they are
    unconcerned about what troubles
    us,
Which is that our candle of life flutters
    so weakly in the blast of time.
We have so little chance to know each
    other, beloved,
We should never be apart.

113

When born we weep, while others
    round us smile.
May we live that when we die
We smile, and others round us weep.
Do not deceive, do not offer strangers
    wrong;
Act a brother's part in all;
Then shall you smile on the last day,
To have lived as humanity should:
To be mourned as a servant of the
    good.

114

My fugitive years are hasting away:
Soon I must lie with the turf on my
    breast.
To muse on the perishing pleasures of
    man
I went back to those favourite fields
Where I played in childhood;
To the bank of the river where I sat and
    dreamt;
And found all changed.
The poplars were felled that shaded me
    then;
No more could I hear the rustle of their
    leaves,
Or see their image tremble in the river,
Or sit in their shade to rest;

No more could the blackbird find there
retreat
From which to offer his sweet-flowing
song.
Long since they were turned to smoke,
As the years turn to smoke.
Long since the fugitive years have
hastened them away,
And my years with them.

HISTORIES

Chapter 1

1. These are the records of the historian, offered to preserve remembrance of what mankind has experienced,
2. And to give account of the great war between East and West, on which the hinge of history turned;
3. Of how the West defended its birth from the assault of the East,
4. For the East, in its power and sway, and its indifference to liberty, would by victory have turned the course of the world into different paths.
5. Whereas the free hearts of the fathers of the West, smaller in number, weaker in power,
6. Yet stronger in resolve and greater in genius, kept the infant civilisation free.
7. Experience is our first guide; how much better we fare when we recall examples of our ancestors and their deeds,
8. Not least those that instruct and illuminate our way, placing our steps in the path of understanding;
9. Nor should we forget our beginnings, nor those few to whom we, who are now as multitudinous as stars, owe so much.

Chapter 2

1. When the East was Persia, and had already begun to wax great,
2. And the West was Greece, yet an infant in comparison of numbers and wealth,
3. The relation between them was that of a centre to its margins.
4. For the world was Asia, and the small Greek states from the Aegean islands to Italy's foot were mere villages on its distant shore.
5. The Easterners trace to stories of Troy the reason of their first enmity towards the Greeks;
6. But in truth the seeds of conflict lay in the growth of Eastern power,
7. When Croesus, son of Alyattes, a Lydian by birth, extended his dominion over all the nations west of the River Halys.
8. He was the first of the barbarian kings to have dealings with Greeks, forcing some to become his tributaries, and making allies among others.
9. He conquered the Greeks of Asia and the eastern Mediterranean, the Aeolians, Dorians and Ionians, who up to that time had been free.
10. The first Greek city captured by Croesus was Ephesus; thereafter he

took all the Greek cities of that region,

11. And even planned a fleet to attack the islands, but his advisers stopped him;

12. For the Greeks were masters of the waves, and Croesus would have ventured too far in challenging them there.

13. When Croesus had brought under his dominion all the nations west of the Halys – Lydians, Phrygians, Mysians, Mariandynians,

14. Chalybians, Paphlagonians, Thynian and Bithynian Thracians,

15. Carians, Ionians, Dorians, Aeolians and Pamphylians – and his power was at its height, he was visited by Solon the Athenian.

16. Now Solon was deemed the wisest man in Athens by his fellow citizens, so they had asked him to devise laws for them,

17. To quell arguments and divisions in the city, thus helping its citizens live a peaceful and prosperous life together.

18. Solon agreed, saying, 'I do this on condition that none of my laws shall be changed for ten years, to give them time to take effect.'

19. And when he had done his work he left the city and travelled abroad, so that his fellow-citizens could not plead with him to revoke his laws,

20. But more to see new things and gain new knowledge, for this he loved beyond all else.

Chapter 3

1. After travelling in Egypt and the regions of the near East, Solon went to the court of Croesus in Sardis.

2. He knew that this king was the richest and until then the most fortunate of the world's rulers; and he wished to see him in the high state of his fortune and his empire.

3. Croesus for his part wished to impress so renowned a man as Solon.

4. He lodged him in his palace in opulent rooms, and ordered his servants to show him the immense palace treasuries.

5. When Solon had seen all this, he was given a splendid dinner, seated at the right hand of Croesus;

6. And when the eating was over and fresh wine was poured, the king addressed Solon as follows.

7. 'Solon of Athens,' he said, 'we have heard much of your wisdom and your travels through many lands, seeking knowledge of all things.

8. 'I am curious to ask you: who is happiest of all the people you have encountered in your life?'

9. And Croesus expected to be told that he himself was the happiest because he was the richest and most powerful among kings.

10. But Solon answered with truth rather than flattery, saying, 'The happiest man I have ever encountered is Tellus of Athens.'

11. Astonished and disappointed,

Croesus asked in what way Tellus was happiest.

12. Solon said, 'First, because in his time Athens was flourishing;

13. 'Second, he had sons who were both beautiful and good, and he lived to see each of them have children of their own;

14. 'And third, after a life lived in comfort and uprightness, and in favourable standing among all who knew him,

15. 'He died a courageous and honourable death, fighting alongside his countrymen during the war between Athens and Eleusis.

16. 'He was given a public funeral where he fell, and was paid the highest civic honours.'

17. Thus did Solon admonish Croesus by the example of Tellus.

18. But Croesus privately discounted this story, thinking Tellus no more than a good citizen who, though deserving praise,

19. Could not compare with the glory of a rich and universally admired king.

20. So he asked again, 'Who seems to you happiest after Tellus?'

21. To this Solon replied, 'I would give second place to two men jointly, the brothers Cleobis and Biton.

22. 'They were Argives, modestly well off, but of enormous physical strength, who had both won prizes at the Games for their prowess.

23. 'It once happened that there was an important festival which their mother wished to attend, but the oxen did not return from the fields in time to draw her cart thither;

24. 'So the sons hitched themselves to it, and pulled it from their home to the distant place of festival, bearing their mother along.

25. 'Great crowds saw this feat; the men standing by praised the brothers' athleticism, the women praised their mother for having such dutiful sons;

26. 'And their mother herself applauded them before all the company, and laid claim on their behalf to a monument for their filial affection.'

27. Angrily Croesus said, 'Do you set at nothing all my happiness, that I am to come below private men,

28. 'Even men who have not much beyond mere muscles and the respect for a mother that we expect from everyone?'

29. 'O Croesus,' replied Solon, 'you asked me about the condition of man, and I know that human lives are full of trouble and change.

30. 'A long life witnesses many things that one would rather not witness. A man has not so many as a thousand months to live, no, not so many as nine hundred;

31. 'And each day of those months can bring events unlike any other day, and all manner of accidents.

32. 'I see that you are very rich, and rule many lands and peoples, but what you wish me to answer you I

cannot until I have heard of your death,

33. 'For only then can I judge whether your life was happy.

34. 'For we can call no man happy until he is dead, when the good and bad of his life has been added up and understood.

35. 'Do not call the rich man happy then; call him fortunate; do not call him happy until all things have been reckoned up, and the true balance of his life is weighed.

36. 'For assuredly, the rich man is no nearer happiness than the poor man who has all he needs.

37. 'Indeed the rich man has more worries and responsibilities, and more to lose, than the poor man;

38. 'And therefore more reasons not to sleep well at night. Can we call such a man happy?

39. 'It is necessary for us all to remember the end of life: for it often happens that we have great reason to count ourselves happy,

40. 'Only to have everything dashed from our hands, and a bitter cup placed there instead.

41. 'He who unites all the advantages of having what suffices him, and health, and the affection of those close to him,

42. 'And honourable works, and the enjoyment of these things until the day of his death, is alone a man who can be called happy.

43. 'If you are such as this, I will give you that name. But otherwise, let

us call no man happy until he is dead.'

44. Such was the speech that Solon addressed to Croesus, who thought him an arrant fool because he made no account of present good, but advised men always to wait and mark the end;

45. And therefore Solon departed the court of Croesus without largesse or praise from the king, who saw him leave with much indifference.

Chapter 4

1. At this time Croesus feared the growing power of the Persians under Cyrus,

2. So he resolved to attack first in order to prevent Persia growing yet more powerful, thus threatening his safety.

3. Moreover he had designs on the land of Cappadocia, which he wished to add to his empire;

4. And last but not least, he wished to avenge his brother-in-law Astyages, son of Cyaxerxes and king of the Medes,

5. Who had been defeated by Cyrus the Persian, his Medes taken into the growing Persian empire, and himself made prisoner by Cyrus.

6. Croesus therefore sent to Sparta to form an alliance, and found the Spartans willing, having been recipients of Croesus' friendliness in the past.

7. And with this and other encouragements of a more foolish kind,

Croesus began his preparations for war.

8. Even as he did so he was visited by a Lydian named Sandanis, famed for his wisdom, who came and counselled the king in the following words:

9. 'Oh Croesus, you are about to make war against men who dress in animal skins,

10. 'Who are obliged to eat not what they like but what they can get from the unkind and sterile soil of their country;

11. 'Who do not know wine, but only water; who have neither figs nor any good thing to eat.

12. 'If you conquer them, what good can you get from them, seeing that they have nothing good of their own?

13. 'But if they conquer you instead, consider how much that is precious you will lose;

14. 'For once they get the taste for our pleasant things, they will keep hold of them so tightly that we shall never loosen their grasp again.

15. 'For my part I am thankful that the Persians have never considered invading us here in Lydia, and I fear for the outcome of going to war against such a hardy and increasing people.'

16. Croesus ignored this advice, and led his army to the banks of the River Halys, marking the border with Cappadocia.

17. Here he encountered a difficulty about how to cross, for there were then no bridges, and the stream was too deep to ford.

18. His problem was solved by the philosopher Thales of Miletus, who was with the army.

19. Thales had the engineers dig a second course for the river, thus dividing its stream so that it flowed on either side of the army's encampment, making two streams, each easily fordable.

20. After laying waste to the area of the Syrians beyond the Halys, Croesus was confronted by Cyrus' army in the district of Pteria, and a battle was fought.

21. By the time night fell neither army had gained the upper hand;

22. But as he was the invader and in need of reinforcements, being outnumbered by the Persian forces,

23. Croesus chose to return to Sardis, there to collect his allies with a view to renewing the struggle next spring.

24. On his return to Sardis with these plans in mind, Croesus disbanded his mercenary forces and sent messengers to his allies to summon them for the following spring.

25. He never guessed that Cyrus would not do the same.

26. For Cyrus, knowing that Croesus would stand down his army and devote himself to preparations for the following year,

27. Decided to keep his forces together and to march on Sardis.

He marched with such speed that he was himself the herald of his arrival.

28. Despite his cruel disadvantage, Croesus did not lack courage, nor his Lydians skill in war, for they were famous for fighting with long lances from horseback.

29. Croesus therefore led out the remainder of his army onto the great plain before Sardis, and arrayed his famed cavalry before them.

30. Seeing the cavalry, Cyrus adopted a strategy suggested to him by one Harpagus, a Mede,

31. Which was to take the camels of the baggage train and put riders on them armed as cavalrymen. These led the charge, with the foot behind and the Persian cavalry in the rear.

32. The reason for the strategy was that horses detest camels, and are fearful of the sight and smell of them.

33. By this means Cyrus negated the effect of the Lydian cavalry, otherwise so formidable; for the Lydian horses bolted as the camels came towards them, and Croesus lost his advantage.

34. The courage of the Lydians did not fail them. The cavalrymen leaped from their frightened horses and engaged the Persians on foot.

35. The combat was long and bloody, but eventually went to Cyrus. The Lydians retired behind the walls of Sardis, and the Persians laid siege.

Chapter 5

1. On the fourteenth day of the siege Cyrus proclaimed to his army that he would reward the man who first mounted the walls of Sardis. He then attempted an assault of the walls, but without success.

2. As Cyrus' troops retired, a Mardian called Hyroeades resolved to gain entry to Sardis by a place left unguarded because the steep rock cliff below the walls was thought unassailable.

3. For Hyroeades had seen, earlier in the siege, a Lydian soldier climb down the rock to retrieve a helmet he had dropped, and then back up over the wall; and this gave him his hint.

4. Followed by a large group of Persians, Hyroeades climbed the rock and surmounted the wall, surprising the guard within;

5. And they quickly overcame the latter's resistance, and threw open the gates to the Persian army, which entered and subjected the city to pillage.

6. An unusual event involving the unfortunate Croesus himself occurred during the sack of Sardis.

7. The younger son of Croesus was a deaf mute, and no efforts to cure him had succeeded.

8. As the Persian troops overran the city, Croesus in his grief and despair did nothing to preserve himself, but exposed himself to danger.

9. A Persian soldier, not knowing

that he was the king, ran at him to kill him, and Croesus under the burden of his affliction did nothing to avoid the blow.

10. His mute son, in his agony of fear for his father's life, suddenly burst into speech, crying out, 'Man, do not kill Croesus!' He thereafter retained the power of speech for the rest of his life.

11. Croesus was brought before Cyrus, who made him stand in his fetters, with a group of leading Lydians likewise fettered around him,

12. On a pile of goods that had been looted from the city, purposing to set fire to the pile and so make an end of Croesus and his leading men.

13. Standing there Croesus remembered the words of Solon, 'Call no man happy until he is dead,'

14. And he groaned aloud, and cried out the name of Solon, whose wisdom he at last recognised.

15. Hearing him speak a name, Cyrus asked the interpreters to question Croesus as to his meaning, and who it was he called upon.

16. Croesus answered, 'One I would give much to see converse with every monarch.'

17. Pressed by Cyrus to explain, Croesus told him how Solon had come to see him in all his royal splendour,

18. And had made light of it; and that Solon had been right in what he said, speaking words of wisdom that all should hear.

19. Cyrus, learning from the interpreters what Croesus said, relented, thinking that Croesus too was a man,

20. A fellow-man who had once been as fortunate as himself; and that he himself might one day meet the same fate of being conquered and placed on a pyre to be burned alive.

21. Full of the thought that whatever is human is insecure, Cyrus bade his men quench the blaze that they had started.

22. Alas it seemed that the fire had taken too strong a hold, and the Persians were unable to put it out, so that the fate of Croesus appeared to be sealed.

23. But just then it began to rain; and between the efforts of the Persian soldiers and the rain the fire was extinguished,

24. And Croesus and the distinguished Lydians with him were released, to be made more the guests than the captives of Cyrus.

25. And as they then sat at meat together, Cyrus asked the once-great king Croesus why he had attacked Persia, thus bringing ruin to himself;

26. And Croesus told him that he had been encouraged to it by the Greeks, whom he had consulted on the best way to limit the growing power of Persia.

27. Thus was sown the seed of the first enmity between East and West, between Persia and Greece, which

shaped the course of civilisations to come in after time.

Chapter 6

1. As Cyrus and Croesus sat at meat together this first time, the latter gestured towards his hapless former capital city of Sardis, where the Persian troops were looting and pillaging,

2. And he asked Cyrus, 'Oh king, what are your soldiers doing?'

3. And Cyrus replied, 'They are plundering the riches of your city, of course!'

4. To which Croesus replied, 'Not my city, and not my riches; it is your city and your riches they are plundering.'

5. Struck by this remark, Cyrus told his courtiers to withdraw, and asked Croesus what he thought should be done about the plundering.

6. Croesus said, 'Now that I am your captive and your slave, it behoves me to do what I can to serve you, O king, and show you anything that might be to your advantage.

7. 'Your Persians have proud hearts, but they are a poor people, and much less civilised than those they have just conquered.

8. 'If you let them pillage and take great wealth, I can tell you what to expect at their hands.

9. 'The man who gets the most, expect him to rebel against you sooner rather than later, for he will have acquired a taste for riches and the power they bring.

10. 'If you are wise, you will place your bodyguards as sentinels at each of the city gates, to take the booty from the plunderers as they leave,

11. 'Telling them that the tenth part is owed to the crown for the good of all collectively.

12. 'They will see that this is just and will part with some of their booty willingly, and it will affirm their allegiance to you.'

13. Cyrus was beyond measure pleased with this advice, so excellent did it seem to him. He praised Croesus highly,

14. And gave orders to his bodyguard to do as advised. Turning to Croesus he said, 'O Croesus, I see that you are resolved both in speech and action to show yourself a virtuous prince;

15. 'What can I do to show you my gratitude and friendship towards you?'

16. To which Croesus said, 'Let me send these fetters to the Greeks who advised me to make war on you, to show them what their advice has led to.'

17. To this Cyrus agreed, and Croesus was permitted to send some of his Lydians to Greece with the fetters he had worn on what was to have been his funeral pyre,

18. With the message: that they were the first fruits of their advice.

19. Thus it was that Lydia was brought

under the Persian yoke, and that the Persians became lords of all Asia.

Chapter 7

1. The journey of the Persians to this conquest had been long. Before them it was the Assyrians who held the empire of Upper Asia,

2. And did so for five hundred and twenty years before the Medes set the example of revolt,

3. Shaking off their servitude and becoming a free people. Their example inspired other nations to do the same.

4. Thus the nations of Asia obtained the blessings of self-government, but only at first,

5. For they fell again under the sway of kings, in the following manner:

6. A certain Mede named Deioces, son of Phraortes, a man of great intelligence, conceived the desire of obtaining the sovereign power.

7. He saw that the Medes dwelt in scattered villages without central authority, and in consequence lawlessness prevailed throughout the land.

8. Deioces, already a man of mark in his own village, applied himself with zeal to the cause of justice among his fellows.

9. His fellows observed his integrity and chose him as their judge.

10. Soon the neighbouring villages invited him to be their judge also, for they heard of his uprightness.

11. At last the Medes put their confidence in no one else.

12. After a time, Deioces announced that he was wearied with so many appeals from all the villages of the Medes, and wished to retire from the task.

13. But when he did so, lawlessness again broke out, and the people were more discomforted than before, having grown used to order.

14. Their leading men therefore convened in assembly, and debated among themselves what to do.

15. 'We cannot possibly live in this country if matters continue as now,' they said. 'Let us therefore set a king over us, that the land may be well governed,

16. 'And we ourselves may be able to attend to our own affairs, and not be forced to quit our country because of anarchy.'

17. The assembly agreed; and when they began to discuss whom to appoint, every mouth was filled with the name of Deioces.

18. They built him a palace, appointed a guard to serve him, and obeyed his injunction to quit their villages and gather together to build a great city.

19. Thus arose Ecbatana, whose walls are of great strength, rising in circles one within the other.

20. The innermost walls encircled the treasury and citadel; the outermost had nearly the extent of the walls of Athens in its greatest period.

21. Of the outermost wall the battlements were white, of the next circle of wall they were black, of the next scarlet, of the fourth blue, of the fifth orange; all these colours were of paint.

22. But the battlements of the two innermost walls were respectively coated with silver and gold.

23. Moreover Deioces instituted ceremonial proceedings, of which the key was that his subjects never met him directly, but communicated through messengers only.

24. This he did because he reasoned that his peers, being no less well born and having the same or greater qualities,

25. Might from too much observance of him come to regret electing him king, and be pained at the sight of his lordship over them;

26. Whereas if they did not see him they would come to think of him as quite a different man from themselves, and hold him in awe.

Chapter 8

1. Thus Deioces collected the Medes into a nation, and ruled over them with strict justice.

2. Now these are the tribes of which they consisted: the Busae, the Paretaceni, the Struchates, the Arizanti, the Budii and the Magi.

3. Having reigned fifty-three years, Deioces was succeeded by his son Phraortes.

4. This prince, not satisfied with a dominion which did not extend beyond the single nation of the Medes, began by attacking the Persians;

5. And marching an army into their country, brought them under the Median yoke before any other people.

6. After this success, being now at the head of two nations, both powerful, he proceeded to conquer Asia, overrunning province after province.

7. At last he engaged in war with the Assyrians to whom Nineveh belonged, who were formerly the lords of Asia.

8. At present they stood alone because their allies had deserted to the Medes, yet still their internal condition was as flourishing as ever.

9. On the death of Phraortes his son Cyaxares ascended the throne. He was still more warlike than his ancestors, and first gave organisation to an Asiatic army,

10. Dividing the troops into companies, and forming distinct bodies of spearmen, archers and cavalry, who before his time had been mingled in one mass, and confused together.

11. He it was who fought the Lydians on the occasion when an eclipse of the sun turned day into night, and who brought under his dominion the whole of Asia east of the Halys.

12. This prince, collecting together all the nations which recognised his

sway, marched against Nineveh, resolved to avenge his father.

13. A battle was fought, in which the Assyrians suffered defeat; and Cyaxares had already begun the siege of the place,

14. When a numerous horde of Scythians, under their king Madyes, son of Protohyes, burst into Asia in pursuit of the Cimmerians whom they had driven out of Europe; and entered the Median territory.

15. The Scythians surprised the Medes by taking an indirect route into Media, marching to the north with the Caucasus on their right;

16. And from here they invaded the land of the Medes, and conquered it in a single battle. By this means the Scythians became masters of Asia.

17. After this they marched forward with the design of invading Egypt. But when they reached Palestine, Psammetichus the Egyptian king met them with gifts, and prevailed on them to advance no further.

18. So they returned, for the most part neither pillaging nor doing damage to the lands they passed through, save for some incidents in the city of Ascalon in Syria.

19. The Scythians kept their dominion over Asia for twenty-eight years, during which time their insolence and oppression spread ruin on every side.

20. For besides the regular tribute,

they exacted arbitrary additional imposts from the neighbouring peoples, increasing resentment among them; and they plundered whomever they could.

21. At length Cyaxares and the Medes invited the greater part of the Scythians to a banquet and made them drunk with wine,

22. After which they massacred them, and freed the Medians from their yoke.

23. Thus the Medes regained their empire, and conquered Nineveh, and all Assyria except for Babylon.

Chapter 9

1. Cyaxares reigned over the Medes forty years, and was succeeded by his son Astyages.

2. This king had a daughter, Mandane, whom he married to a Persian of good family and quiet demeanour,

3. Not wishing any Mede to marry his daughter lest such a son-in-law should become ambitious of usurping his throne.

4. All Persians regarded Medes as inferior in rank to themselves, and Cyaxares thought that by marrying Mandane to a Persian he would be safe from the ambition of usurpers.

5. Now this Persian was called Cambyses, and he took Mandane to his home.

6. But Cyaxares was of a suspicious and anxious temper, and he soon began to think that from the

womb of his daughter would flow a line of sons,

7. Who, because of their royal connection, would think that Persians had a right to the throne, and would become dangerous.

8. So he sought to recall Mandane, and when he learned that she was with child he determined to destroy the baby when it was born.

9. He called a loyal and favourite servant named Harpagus to him, and instructed him as follows:

10. 'Harpagus, I beseech you not to neglect the business I am going to charge you with.

11. 'For your king's sake you must take the child born of Mandane my daughter, and carry it to your home, and there slay it and bury it.'

12. Harpagus replied, 'O king, never have I disobliged you in anything, and be sure that in all future time I never will.

13. 'If this is your will, it is for me to serve with diligence.' So he went and fetched the child, which was dressed in the garb of death, and weeping for its hard fate he hastened back to his home.

14. There he found his wife and told her what Astyages had commanded him. And she said, 'Will you do it?'

15. 'No,' replied Harpagus, 'I cannot. First, this child is my own kin. Second, the king is old, and when he dies his daughter Mandane will succeed him;

16. 'And if I slay her child I shall be in fearful danger. But yet, if the child continues to live, I shall be in danger also: from the king.'

17. Said his wife, 'Alas, what is to be done?' And he replied, 'The child must die; but not by my hand or the hand of our kin; it must be killed by someone belonging to Astyages.'

18. So saying he sent a messenger to fetch a certain Mitradates, a herdsman in the employment of Astyages, who tended flocks in the fastness of mountains far from the city;

19. A fit place for the child to be disposed of, being remote and full of wild beasts. These mountains lie north of Ecbatana, towards the Euxine, and are covered in forests.

20. When Mitradates came to Harpagus' house, the latter instructed him, saying, 'The king requires you to take this baby and expose it in the wildest part of the mountains, there to be consumed by the wild beasts.

21. 'If you do not do this the king will subject you to the most painful of deaths.' Mitradates saw the child lying amidst the fearful and weeping inhabitants of Harpagus' house,

22. Swaddled in gold and wrappings of beautiful colours, itself panting and whimpering because untended and unfed.

23. Trembling under this dreadful instruction, Mitradates took the

child and returned to the
mountains,

24. Where his wife, Spaco, one of
the king's female slaves, was just
then daily expecting a child of her
own.

25. Discussing the burden imposed on
them by Harpagus, they became
yet more troubled and afraid on
their own account;

26. And the anxieties made Spaco fall
into labour, and because she was
fearful and wretched, the baby she
delivered was stillborn.

27. 'Wife,' said Mitradates, 'when I
left Harpagus' house with this
child in my arms, a servant
accompanied me for part of the
way, and told me all:

28. 'That this is the offspring of
Mandane, the king's daughter, and
Cambyses the Persian, and the
king wishes it to be killed for fear
that it or its father will usurp his
throne.'

29. So saying he unswaddled the
whimpering baby, which he and
his wife saw was fine and
beautiful;

30. And Spaco burst into tears, and
clasped her husband's knees,
beseeching him on no account to
expose the child to so cruel a
death.

31. 'Take the body of our own child,
stillborn but now, and lay it in the
mountains,' she implored him,
'and let us bring up this child as
our own.

32. 'When we show the remains of our

dead child, it will be thought the
other;

33. 'And so you will not be charged
with disobedience to the will of
the king. Our own child will have
a royal funeral, and this beautiful
baby will live.'

34. So Mitradates and Spaco dressed
the corpse of their own baby in the
gold and royal cloths, and
Mitradates took it to the wildest
places;

35. And after three days he fetched it
again, mauled by the beasts, and
carried it to the city to show
Harpagus.

36. The latter was satisfied, and had
the child buried with royal pomp
at his own bidding.

Chapter 10

1. Now the child brought up as
the herdsman's son they named
Cyrus.

2. He grew strong and noble, and as
early as the age of ten displayed
great command and intelligence.

3. He took charge of his playmates,
who elected him their king,

4. And he ordered them, and
arranged them in troops and led
them into pretend battles.

5. One of his playmates was the son
of a noble Mede of distinction,
and this boy refused to obey
Cyrus' boyish commands,

6. Not only because of his supposed
lowly rank as a herdsman's son,
but because he was a Persian.

7. Angered by the Median youth's

refusal to obey, Cyrus took a whip and chastised him.

8. Outraged, the boy complained to his father, who as a high courtier went to King Astyages to complain.

9. The king wished to please his noble courtier, and summoned the herdsman and his supposed son Cyrus to answer for the latter's behaviour.

10. When they came to the palace Astyages said to Cyrus, 'Have you, the son of so mean a fellow, dared to behave rudely to the son of a noble of my court?'

11. To which Cyrus replied, 'My lord, I only treated him as he deserved.

12. 'I was chosen king in play by the boys of our village, because they thought me the best for it. He himself was one of those who chose me.

13. 'All the others did my bidding; but he refused, and made light of them,

14. 'Until at last he got his due reward. If for this I deserve punishment, here I am ready to submit to it.'

15. While the boy was speaking Astyages was struck with a suspicion who he was.

16. He thought he saw something in the character of his face like his own, and there was a nobleness about the answer he made;

17. Besides which his age seemed to tally with the time when his grandchild was exposed.

18. Astonished at all this, Astyages could not speak for a while. At last, recovering himself with difficulty,

19. And wishing to be quit of the noble Mede who had complained, that he might examine the herdsman alone,

20. He said to the Mede, 'I promise to settle this business that neither you nor your son shall have any cause to complain.'

21. The courtier left the presence chamber, and the king's attendants took Cyrus to an inner room, leaving Astyages and the herdsman alone.

Chapter 11

1. Astyages then enquired about the boy, and Mitradates at first insisted that he and his wife Spaco were the true parents.

2. But when Astyages ordered him to be tortured for the truth, Mitradates broke down in terror and told Astyages everything,

3. Ending with supplications and tears to be forgiven for what he had done.

4. Astyages was very little concerned with the herdsman, but was outraged at the disloyalty of Harpagus, whom he summoned immediately.

5. When Harpagus came the king asked him, 'By what death did you slay the child of my daughter Mandane?'

6. Seeing the herdsman in the

room, Harpagus did not try to dissemble.

7. 'Sir,' he said, 'When you gave the child into my hands I considered with myself how I could carry out your wishes,

8. 'And yet, while guiltless of any unfaithfulness towards you, avoid steeping my hands in blood which was in truth your own.

9. 'And this was how I contrived it. I sent for this herdsman, and gave the child to him, telling him that by the king's orders it was to be put to death.

10. 'And in this I told no lie, for you had so commanded.

11. 'Moreover, when I gave him the child, I enjoined him to lay it somewhere in the wilds of the mountains, until it was dead; and I threatened him with punishment if he failed.

12. 'Afterwards, when he had done according to all that I commanded, and the child had died, I sent some of the most trustworthy of my eunuchs,

13. 'Who viewed the body for me, and then I had the child buried. This, sir, is the simple truth, and this is the death by which the child died.'

14. Thus Harpagus related the whole story in a plain, straightforward way; upon which Astyages, letting no sign escape him of the anger he felt,

15. Began by repeating to him all that he had just heard from the herdsman, and then concluded with saying,

16. 'So the boy is alive, and it is best as it is. For the child's fate was a great sorrow to me, and the reproaches of my daughter went to my heart.

17. 'Truly this has turned out well. Go home then, and send your own son to be with this newcomer who is my grandson,

18. 'And tonight, let us have a banquet at which you will be guest of honour alongside my grandson, to rejoice in these events.'

19. Harpagus, on hearing this, bowed and went home rejoicing to find that his disobedience had turned out so fortunately.

20. The moment he reached home he called for his son, his only child, a youth of thirteen years, and told him to go to the palace, and do whatever Astyages should direct.

21. Then, in the gladness of his heart, he went to his wife and told her what had happened.

22. Astyages, meanwhile, took the son of Harpagus, and slew him, and cut him in pieces, and roasted some portions before the fire, and boiled others;

23. And when all were duly prepared, he kept them ready for use.

24. The hour for the banquet came, and Harpagus appeared, and with him the other guests, and all sat down to the feast.

25. Astyages and the rest of the guests had joints of meat served to them;

but on the table of Harpagus, nothing was placed except the flesh of his own son,

26. All except the hands and feet and head, which were laid by themselves in a covered basket.

27. When Harpagus seemed to have eaten his fill, Astyages called out to him to know how he had enjoyed the repast.

28. On his reply that he had enjoyed it excessively, they whose business it was brought him the basket, and bade him open it, and take out what he pleased.

29. Harpagus accordingly uncovered the basket, and saw within it the remains of his son.

30. The sight, however, did not rob him of his self-possession. Being asked by Astyages if he knew what beast's flesh it was that he had been eating,

31. He answered that he knew very well, and that whatever the king did was agreeable.

32. After this reply, he took with him such morsels of the flesh as were uneaten, and went home, intending to bury them.

33. Such was the manner in which Astyages punished Harpagus.

34. But Harpagus concealed in his heart his own desire for revenge on Astyages; and he waited until the time was ready.

Chapter 12

1. Astyages meanwhile, seeing that his grandson was a fine youth, but not wishing to have a Persian for an heir,

2. Decided to send him to his daughter Mandane and her husband, the real parents, thinking by this means to be rid of responsibility for him.

3. There in Persia Cyrus grew amain, and when Harpagus believed him to be ready, he sent him a letter concealed in the belly of a hare,

4. Telling him to rise against Astyages and take the empire of the Medes for his own.

5. 'Whether Astyages appoint me his general, or some other noble Mede, does not signify;

6. 'For we are all ready to revolt against his tyrannical rule, and see him overthrown,' Harpagus wrote.

7. Cyrus considered with himself how he might best inspire the Persians to revolt against Astyages.

8. The idea he devised was as follows. He took a roll of paper, and called the Persians to an assembly.

9. Flourishing the roll aloft he said, 'King Astyages has appointed me your general.

10. 'I command each of you to go home and fetch your reaping-hook.' He then dismissed the assembly.

11. Now the Persian nation is made up of many tribes. Those Cyrus assembled and persuaded to revolt from the Medes were the principal ones on which all the others are dependent.

12. They are the Pasargadae, the

Maraphians and the Maspians, of whom the Pasargadae are the noblest.

13. The Achaemenidae, from which spring all the Perseid kings, is one of their clans.

14. The rest of the Persian tribes are the Panthialaeans, the Derusiaeans, the Germanians, who are engaged in husbandry;

15. The Daans, the Mardians, the Dropicans and the Sagartians, who are nomads.

16. When, in obedience to the orders they had received, the Persians came with their reaping-hooks,

17. Cyrus led them to a tract of ground, about twenty furlongs each way, covered with thorns, and ordered them to clear it before evening.

18. They accomplished their task; upon which he issued a second order to them, to take a bath the following day, and again come to him.

19. Meanwhile he collected together all his father's flocks, both sheep and goats, and all his oxen,

20. And slaughtered them, and made ready to give a feast to the entire Persian army.

21. Wine, too, and bread of the choicest kinds were prepared for the occasion.

22. When the morrow came, and the Persians appeared, he bade them recline on the grass, and enjoy themselves.

23. After the feast was over, he requested them to tell him 'which they liked best, today's work, or yesterday's?'

24. They answered that 'The contrast was indeed strong: yesterday brought them nothing but what was laborious, today everything that was pleasant.'

25. Cyrus instantly seized on their reply, and explained his purpose in these words:

26. 'Men of Persia, thus do matters stand with you. If you choose to listen to my words, you may enjoy these and ten thousand similar delights,

27. 'And never condescend to any slavish toil; but if you will not listen, prepare yourselves for unnumbered toils as hard as yesterday's.

28. 'Now therefore follow my bidding, and be free. For myself I am ready to undertake your liberation;

29. 'And you, I am sure, are no whit inferior to the Medes in anything, least of all courage.

30. 'Revolt, therefore, from Astyages, without a moment's delay.'

Chapter 13

1. The Persians, who had long been impatient of the Median yoke, now that they had found a leader, were delighted.

2. Meanwhile Astyages, informed of Cyrus' doings, sent a messenger to summon him.

3. Cyrus replied, 'Tell Astyages that I shall appear in his presence sooner than he will like.'

4. Astyages, when he received this message, instantly armed all his subjects,

5. And, as if he had lost his senses, appointed Harpagus as their general, forgetting how greatly he had injured him.

6. So when the two armies met, only a few of the Medes fought; others deserted openly to the Persians; while the greater number counterfeited fear, and fled.

7. Astyages, on learning the shameful flight and dispersion of his army, broke out into threats against Cyrus,

8. And directly armed all the Medes who had remained in the city, both young and old;

9. And leading them against the Persians, fought a battle, in which he was utterly defeated, his army destroyed, and he himself captured.

10. Harpagus then, seeing him a prisoner, came near, and exulted over him with jeers.

11. Among other cutting speeches he made, he alluded to the supper where the flesh of his son was given him to eat,

12. And asked Astyages to answer him now, how he enjoyed being a slave instead of a king?

13. Astyages looked in his face, and asked him in return, why he claimed as his own the achievements of Cyrus?

14. 'Because,' said Harpagus, 'it was my letter which made him revolt, and so I am entitled to the credit of the enterprise.'

15. Then Astyages declared that in that case he was at once the silliest and the most unjust of men:

16. The silliest, if when it was in his power to put the crown on his own head, he had placed it on the head of another;

17. The most unjust, if on account of that supper he had brought slavery on his own people, the Medes.

18. For, supposing that he was obliged to invest another with the kingly power, and not retain it himself, yet justice required that a Mede, rather than a Persian, should receive the dignity.

19. Now, however, the Medes, who had been no parties to the wrong of which he complained, were made slaves instead of lords,

20. And slaves moreover of those who till recently had been their subjects.

21. Thus after a reign of thirty-five years, Astyages lost his crown, and the Medes, in consequence of his cruelty, were brought under the rule of the Persians.

22. The Medes' empire over the parts of Asia beyond the Halys had lasted one hundred and twenty-eight years, except during the time when the Scythians had the dominion.

23. Cyrus kept Astyages at his court during the remainder of his life, without doing him any further

injury, because he was his grandfather.

24. Such were the circumstances of the birth and upbringing of Cyrus, and such were the steps by which he mounted the throne.

25. It was at a later date that he was attacked by Croesus, and over-threw him, as related in an earlier portion of this history.

26. Cyrus' overthrow of Croesus made him master of the whole of Asia.

Chapter 14

1. After the conquest of Lydia by the Persians, the Ionian and Aeolian Greeks sent ambassadors to Cyrus at Sardis, and prayed to become his tributaries as they had been to Croesus.

2. Cyrus listened attentively to their proposals, and answered them by a fable.

3. 'There was a certain piper,' he said, 'who was walking one day by the seaside, when he espied some fish;

4. 'So he began to pipe to them, imagining they would come out to him on the land.

5. 'But when he found that his hope was vain, he took a net, and enclosing a great number of them, drew them ashore.

6. 'The fish then began to leap and dance; but the piper said, "Cease your dancing now, as you did not choose to dance when I piped to you."'

7. Cyrus gave this answer because, when he urged the Ionians and

Aeolians to revolt from Croesus, they refused;

8. But now, when his work was done, they offered allegiance. It was in anger, therefore, that he made this reply.

9. The Ionians, on hearing it, set to work to fortify their towns, and held meetings at the Panionium,

10. Which were attended by all excepting the Milesians, with whom Cyrus had concluded a separate treaty, allowing them the terms they formerly had with Croesus.

11. The other Ionians resolved, with one accord, to send ambassadors to Sparta to beg assistance.

12. Now the Ionian Greeks of Asia, who meet at the Panionium, have built their cities in a region where the air and climate are the most beautiful in the world:

13. For no other region is as pleasant as Ionia, neither above it nor below it, nor east nor west of it.

14. For in other countries either the climate is too cold and damp, or else the heat and drought are sorely oppressive.

15. The Ionians do not all speak the same language, but have four different dialects.

16. Towards the south the main city is Miletus, next to which lie Myus and Priene; all these three are in Caria and have the same dialect.

17. Their cities in Lydia are Ephesus, Colophon, Lebedus, Teos, Clazomenae and Phocaea. The

inhabitants of these towns have a dialect of their own.

18. There are three other Ionian towns, two in the isles, namely, Samos and Chios; and one on the mainland, namely Erythrae.

19. Of these Chios and Erythrae have the same dialect, while Samos has a language of its own.

20. Of the Ionians at this period, the Milesians were in no danger of attack, as Cyrus had received them into alliance.

21. The islanders also had as yet nothing to fear, since Phoenicia was still independent of Persia, and the Persians themselves were not a seafaring people.

22. The Milesians had separated from the common cause solely on account of the extreme weakness of the Ionians:

23. For, feeble as the power of the entire Hellenic race was at that time, of all its tribes the Ionic was by far the feeblest and least esteemed, not possessing a single state of any mark except Athens.

24. The Athenians and most of the other Ionic States went so far in disliking the name 'Ionia' as not to use it.

25. But the twelve cities in Asia always gloried in the name; thus they gave the civic hall which they built for themselves the name of the Panionium.

26. The Ionians founded twelve cities in Asia, and refused to enlarge the number,

27. On account of their having been divided into twelve States when they lived in the Peloponnese before being driven out by the Achaeans.

28. It is incorrect to maintain that these Ionians are more Ionian than the rest, since the truth is that no small portion of them were Abantians from Euboea, who are not even Ionians in name;

29. And, besides, there were mixed up with the emigration of Minyae from Orchomenus, Cadmeians, Dryopians, Phocians from the several cities of Phocis, Molossians, Arcadian Pelasgi, Dorians from Epidaurus, and many other distinct tribes.

30. Even those who came from the Prytaneum of Athens, and reckon themselves the purest Ionians of all, brought no wives with them to the new country,

31. But married Carian girls, whose fathers they had slain. Hence these women made a law, which they bound themselves to observe,

32. And which they handed down to their daughters after them, 'That none should ever sit at table with her husband, or call him by his name';

33. Because the invaders slew their fathers, their husbands and their sons, and then forced them to become their wives. It was at Miletus that these events took place.

34. The kings, too, whom they set

over themselves, were either Lycians, of the blood of Glaucus, son of Hippolochus, or Pylian Caucons of the blood of Codrus, son of Melanthus; or else from both those families.

35. But since these Ionians valued their name more than any of the others did, let them pass for pure-bred Ionians; though truly all are Ionians who have their origin from Athens.

Chapter 15

1. Originally the Aeolians had twelve cities upon the mainland, like the Ionians, but the Ionians deprived them of Smyrna in the following way:

2. Certain men of Colophon had been engaged in a sedition there, and being the weaker party, were driven into banishment.

3. The Smyrnaeans received the fugitives, who, after a time, watching their opportunity, while the inhabitants were celebrating a feast outside the walls, shut the gates, and so captured the town.

4. The Aeolians of the other States came to their aid, and terms were agreed between the parties,

5. The Ionians consenting to give up all the moveables, and the Aeolians making a surrender of the place.

6. The expelled Smyrnaeans were distributed among the other States of the Aeolians, and were everywhere admitted to citizenship.

7. Of the Aeolian islands, Lesbos contains five cities. Arisba, the sixth, was taken by the Methymnaeans, their kinsmen, and the inhabitants reduced to slavery.

8. Tenedos contains one city, and there is another on the Hundred Isles.

9. The Aeolians of Lesbos and Tenedos, like the Ionian islanders, had at this time nothing to fear from Persia.

10. The other Aeolians decided in their common assembly to follow the Ionians, whatever course they should pursue.

11. When the deputies of the Ionians and Aeolians, who had journeyed with all speed to Sparta, reached the city, they chose one of their number, Pythermus, a Phocaean, to be their spokesman.

12. In order to draw together as large an audience as possible, he clothed himself in a purple garment, and so attired stood up to speak.

13. In a long discourse he besought the Spartans to come to the assistance of his countrymen, but they were not to be persuaded, and voted against sending help.

14. The deputies accordingly went their way. But the Lacedaemonians, notwithstanding their refusal,

15. Dispatched a penteconter to the Asiatic coast with certain Spartans on board, for the purpose of observing what Cyrus might do to Ionia.

16. On their arrival these Spartans sent the most distinguished of their number, one Lacrines, to Sardis with a message to warn Cyrus, in the name of the Lacedaemonians, against molesting any city of Greece.

17. On hearing the herald, Cyrus asked some Greeks who were standing by, 'Who are these Lacedaemonians, and how numerous are they, that they dare to send me such a message?'

18. When he had heard their reply, he turned to Lacrines and said, 'I have never yet been afraid of any men, who have a set place in the middle of their city where they come together to cheat and lie.

19. 'If I live, the Spartans shall have troubles enough of their own, without concerning themselves about the Ionians.'

20. Cyrus intended these words as a reproach against all Greeks because of the marketplaces in their cities where they buy and sell,

21. Which was a custom unknown to the Persians, who did not have a single marketplace in their whole country.

22. After this interview Cyrus left Sardis, putting Tabalus, a Persian, in charge of the city, but appointing Pactyas, a native Lydian, to collect the treasure belonging to Croesus and other Lydians.

23. Cyrus himself proceeded towards Ecbatana, taking Croesus with

him, not regarding the Ionians as important enough to be his immediate object.

24. Larger designs were in his mind. He wished to war in person against Babylon, the Bactrians, the Sacae and Egypt; he therefore determined to assign to one of his generals the task of conquering the Ionians.

25. No sooner, however, was Cyrus gone from Sardis than Pactyas induced his Lydian countrymen to rise in revolt against him and his deputy Tabalus.

26. With the vast treasures at his disposal Pactyas went down to the sea, and employed them in hiring mercenary troops,

27. While at the same time he engaged the coastal people to join his army. He then marched on Sardis, where he besieged Tabalus.

28. When Cyrus, on his way to Ecbatana, received this news, he said to Croesus, 'Where will all this end? It seems that Lydians will not cease to trouble both themselves and others.

29. 'It might be best to sell them all for slaves. What I have done is as if I had killed the father but spared the child.

30. 'You, who were more than a father to your people, I have carried off, and to that people I have entrusted their city. Can I be surprised at their rebellion?'

31. Alarmed at the thought that Cyrus would lay Sardis in ruins, Croesus

replied: 'O king, your words are reasonable;

32. 'But do not, I beseech you, give vent to your anger and destroy an ancient city, guiltless alike of the past and the present trouble.

33. 'I caused the one, and in my own person now pay for it. Pactyas has caused the other; let him bear the punishment.

34. 'Grant forgiveness to the Lydians, and to make sure of their never troubling you more, forbid them to keep any weapons of war,

35. 'Command them to wear tunics under their cloaks, and to put buskins on their legs,

36. 'And make them bring up their sons to playing musical instruments and shopkeeping.

37. 'So will you soon see them become women instead of men, and there will be no more fear of their rebelling.'

38. Croesus thought this a better fate for the Lydians than being sold into slavery, and for this reason gave such advice to Cyrus, in a desperate attempt to save his people.

39. The advice pleased Cyrus, who consented. Thereupon he summoned a Mede called Mazares and charged him to issue orders to the Lydians in accordance with Croesus' advice.

40. Further, he commanded him to sell as slaves all who had joined the Lydians in their attack on Sardis,

41. And above all to bring Pactyas

with him alive on his return. Having given these orders Cyrus continued his journey back to Persia.

Chapter 16

1. Pactyas, when news came of the approach of the Persian army, fled in terror to Cyme.

2. The Median general Mazares, who had marched on Sardis with a detachment of the army of Cyrus, finding on his arrival that Pactyas and his troops were gone, immediately entered the town.

3. And first of all he forced the Lydians to obey the orders of his master, and change (as they did from that time) their entire manner of living.

4. Next, he dispatched messengers to Cyme, commanding Pactyas to be handed to him.

5. Although some of the Greeks tried to hide Pactyas, he was at length betrayed to the Persians by the citizens of Chios,

6. Who as their reward were given a tract of land in Mysia opposite Lesbos.

7. Meanwhile Mazares, after he received Pactyas from the Chians, made war on those who had taken part in the attack on Tabalus,

8. And in the first place took Priene and sold the inhabitants into slavery, after which he overran the whole plain of the Maeander and the district of Magnesia,

9. Both of which he gave up for

pillage to the soldiery. He then suddenly sickened and died.

10. Upon his death Harpagus, the Mede who had served and then betrayed king Astyages, and helped place Cyrus on the throne, was sent to the coast to assume the command.

11. He entered Ionia, and took the cities by means of a clever tactic:

12. Forcing the enemy to hide within their defences, he heaped mounds of earth against their walls, and thus captured the towns. Phocaea was the first city he took.

13. Now the Phocaeans were the first Greeks who made long sea voyages, and it was they who made the Greeks acquainted with the Adriatic and with Tyrrhenia, with Iberia, and the city of Tartessus.

14. The vessel they used in their voyages was not the round-built merchant ship, but the long penteconter.

15. On the Phocaeans' arrival at Tartessus, the king there, Arganthonius, took a liking to them. This monarch reigned over the Tartessians for eighty years.

16. He regarded the Phocaeans with so much favour as, at first, to beg them to quit Ionia and settle in whatever part of his country they liked.

17. When he found that he could not prevail upon them to agree to this, and hearing that the Mede was growing great in their neighbourhood,

18. He gave them money to build a wall about their town, and certainly he must have been generous,

19. For the town wall was many furlongs in circuit, built of great blocks of stone skilfully joined.

20. Harpagus, having advanced against the Phocaeans, laid siege to them. Instead of attacking he first offered terms.

21. 'It would content me,' he said, 'if the Phocaeans would agree to throw down one of their battlements, and dedicate one dwelling house to the king.'

22. The Phocaeans, vexed at the thought of becoming slaves, asked a single day to think about the offer, and asked Harpagus during that day to withdraw his forces from the walls.

23. Harpagus replied that he understood well enough what they intended, but nevertheless he granted their request.

24. Accordingly the Persian troops withdrew, and the Phocaeans immediately took the chance to launch their penteconters, and put on board their families and household goods,

25. Leaving only the paintings and works in stone or brass that could not be carried easily; and sailed for Chios. The Persians, on their return, took possession of an empty town.

26. Arrived at Chios, the Phocaeans made offers for the purchase of the

islands called the Oenussae,

27. But the Chians refused, fearing that the Phocaeans would establish a trading centre there, and exclude the Chian merchants from the commerce of those seas.

28. So the Phocaeans, as Arganthonius of Tartessus was now dead, resolved to sail to Cyrnus (Corsica), where, twenty years earlier they had founded a colony called Alalia.

29. Before they set out, however, they sailed once more to Phocaea, and surprising the Persian troops left by Harpagus to garrison the town, killed them all.

30. After this they dropped a heavy mass of iron into the sea, and promised themselves never to return to Phocaea till that mass reappeared on the surface.

31. But as they were preparing to depart for Cyrnus, more than half their number were seized with such sadness and longing to see their city and homes once more, that they decided not to go, and sailed back to Phocaea.

32. The rest of the Phocaeans, who kept their resolve, proceeded without stopping on their voyage,

33. And when they came to Cyrnus they established themselves along with the earlier settlers at Alalia.

34. For five years they annoyed their neighbours by plundering and pillaging on all sides, until the Carthaginians and Tyrrhenians leagued against them, and each sent a fleet of sixty ships to attack them.

35. The Phocaeans manned all their vessels, sixty in number, and met their enemy on the Sardinian Sea.

36. In the battle that followed the Phocaeans were victorious, but their success was an empty victory;

37. They lost forty ships, and the twenty which remained came out of the engagement too damaged for use.

38. The Phocaeans therefore returned to Alalia, and taking their wives and children on board, with such portion of their goods and chattels as the vessels could bear, sailed to Rhegium.

39. The Carthaginians and Tyrrhenians, who had captured many Phocaeans from the crews of the forty vessels that were destroyed, landed their captives on the coast and stoned them all to death.

40. Afterwards the people of Agylla, who had been so horrified by this mass murder, instituted a custom of honouring the dead Phocaeans with magnificent funeral rites, and solemn games both gymnastic and equestrian.

41. Such, then, was the fate that befell the Phocaean prisoners. The other Phocaeans, who had fled to Rhegium, after a while founded the city called Vela, in the district of Oenotria. Thus fared it with the men of the city of Phocaea in Ionia.

Chapter 17

1. They of Teos did and suffered almost the same; for they too, when Harpagus raised his mound against their walls, took ship and sailed to Thrace, and founded there the city of Abdera.

2. The site was one which Timesius of Clazomenae had previously tried to colonise, but without success, for he was expelled by the Thracians.

3. Still the Teians of Abdera regard him to this day as a hero.

4. Of all the Ionians these two states alone, rather than submit to slavery, forsook their fatherland.

5. The others resisted Harpagus no less bravely than those who fled their country, and performed many feats of arms, each fighting in their own defence,

6. But one after another they were defeated; the cities were taken, and the inhabitants submitted, remaining in their respective countries, and obeying the behests of their new lords.

7. Thus was continental Ionia once more reduced to servitude; and when the Ionians of the islands saw their brethren on the mainland subjugated, they also, dreading the like, gave themselves up to Cyrus.

8. It was while the Ionians were in this distress, but still, amid it all, held their meetings, as of old, at the Panionium,

9. That Bias of Priene, who was present at the festival, recommended a project of the highest wisdom, which would, had it been embraced, have enabled the Ionians to become the happiest and most flourishing of the Greeks.

10. He exhorted them 'to join in one body, set sail for Sardinia, and there found a single Pan-Ionic city; so they would escape from slavery and rise to great fortune,

11. 'Being masters of the largest island in the world, exercising dominion even beyond its bounds; whereas if they stayed in Ionia, he saw no prospect of their ever recovering their freedom.'

12. Such was the counsel Bias gave the Ionians in their affliction. Before their misfortunes began, Thales, a man of Miletus, of Phoenician descent, had recommended a different plan.

He counselled them to establish a single seat of government, and nominated Teos as the fittest place for it; 'for that,' he said, 'was the centre of Ionia.'

13. 'Their other cities might still continue to enjoy their own laws, just as if they were independent states.' This also was good advice.

14. The fall of Ionia was the harbinger of Harpagus' conquest of the rest of the independent people in the lower parts of Asia, among them the Carians, the Caunians and the Lycians.

15. Of these nations, the Carians

submitted to Harpagus without performing any brilliant exploits. Nor did the Greeks who dwelt in Caria behave with any greater gallantry.

16. Above Halicarnassus, and further from the coast, were the Pedasians. They alone, of all the dwellers in Caria, resisted Harpagus for a while, and gave him much trouble,

17. Maintaining themselves in a certain mountain called Lida, which they had fortified; but in course of time they also were forced to submit.

18. When Harpagus, after these successes, led his forces into the Xanthian plain, the Lycians of Xanthus went out to fight him:

19. And though but a small band against a numerous host, they engaged in battle, and performed many glorious exploits.

20. Overpowered at last, and forced within their walls, they collected into the citadel their wives and children, all their treasures, and their slaves;

21. And having so done, set fire to the building, and burnt it to the ground with all in it.

22. After this, they bound themselves together by a bond of brotherhood, and sallying forth against the enemy, died sword in hand, not one escaping.

23. Now these were the auguries of the future: that the best of the Greeks would rather die in freedom than live in servitude; and the Persians should have taken warning from this.

Chapter 18

1. While the lower parts of Asia were brought under by Harpagus, Cyrus in person subjected the upper regions, conquering every nation, and not suffering one to escape.

2. When he had brought the rest of the continent under his control, he turned his attention to the Assyrians, and made war on them.

3. Assyria possessed a vast number of great cities, of which the most renowned and strongest at this time was Babylon, which had been made the seat of government after the fall of Nineveh.

4. The city stood on a broad plain, and was an exact square, a hundred and twenty furlongs in length each way, so that the entire circuit was four hundred and eighty furlongs.

5. While such was its size, in magnificence there was no other city that approached it.

6. It was surrounded, in the first place, by a broad and deep moat, full of water,

7. Behind which rose a wall fifty royal cubits in width, and two hundred in height.

8. The wall was built from the spoil of the moat, made directly into bricks in kilns beside the excavation.

9. The cement for the wall was hot bitumen, with a layer of wattled reeds at every thirtieth course of bricks.

10. On the top, along the edges of the wall, they constructed buildings of a single chamber facing one another,

11. Leaving between them room for a four-horse chariot to turn. In the circuit of the wall were a hundred gates, all of brass, with brazen lintels and side-posts.

12. The city was divided into two by the river which runs through the middle: the Euphrates, a broad, deep, swift stream which rises in Armenia, and empties itself into the Erythraean Sea.

13. The city wall was brought down on both sides to the edge of the stream: thence, from the corners of the wall, there was carried along each bank of the river a fence of burnt bricks.

14. The houses were mostly three and four stories high; the streets all ran in straight lines, not only those parallel to the river, but also the cross streets which led down to the waterside.

15. At the river end of these cross streets were low gates in the fence that skirted the stream, which were, like the great gates in the outer wall, of brass, and opened on the water.

16. The outer wall was the main defence of the city. There was, however, a second, inner wall, of

less thickness than the first, but very little inferior to it in strength.

17. The palace of the kings was surrounded by a wall of great strength and size, with gates of solid brass.

18. In the middle of the precinct there was a tower of solid masonry, a furlong in length and breadth, upon which stood a second tower, and on that a third, and so on up to eight.

19. The ascent to the top was on the outside, by a path which winds round all the towers. About halfway up one found seats, so that one could rest on one's way to the summit.

20. Many sovereigns have ruled over Babylon, and lent their aid to the building of its walls and the adornment of its beauties.

21. Among them two were women. Of these, the earlier, called Semiramis, held the throne five generations before the later princess.

22. She raised embankments in the plain near Babylon to control the river, which till then used to overflow and flood the whole country round about.

23. The later of the two queens, whose name was Nitocris, a wiser princess than her predecessor, not only left behind her great works of building which enhanced the city, but also a cunning defence against interference from the Medes.

24. Observing the great power and restless enterprise of the Medes,

who had taken so large a number of cities, and among them Nineveh,

25. And expecting to be attacked in her turn, Nitocris made all possible exertions to increase the defences of her empire.

26. And first, whereas the River Euphrates, which traverses the city, formerly ran with a straight course to Babylon,

27. She, by certain excavations at a distance upstream, rendered it so winding that it comes three times within view of the same village in Assyria called Ardericea;

28. And to this day those who go from the Mediterranean coast to Babylon, having reached the Euphrates to sail down it, touch three times on three different days at this very place.

29. Nitocris also made an embankment along each side of the river, wonderful both for breadth and height,

30. And dug a basin for a lake a great way above Babylon, close alongside the stream, which was sunk everywhere to the point where they came to water,

31. And was of such breadth that the whole circuit measured four hundred and twenty furlongs.

32. When the excavation was finished, Nitocris had stones brought, and bordered the entire margin of the reservoir with them.

33. These two things were done, the river made to wind and the lake excavated, so that the stream might be slacker by reason of the number of curves,

34. And the voyage be rendered circuitous, and that at the end of the voyage it might be necessary to skirt the lake and so make a long round.

35. All these works were on that side of Babylon where the passes lay, and the roads into Media were the straightest,

36. And the aim of the queen in making them was to prevent the Medes from holding intercourse with the Babylonians, and so to keep them ignorant of her affairs.

Chapter 19

1. The expedition of Cyrus was undertaken against the son of this princess, who bore the same name as his father, Labynetus, and was king of the Assyrians.

2. Cyrus introduced the policy whereby the Persian kings, when they go to war, are always supplied with provisions carefully prepared at home, and with cattle of their own.

3. Water too from the River Choaspes, which flows by Susa, is taken with them for their drink, as that is the only water that the kings of Persia taste.

4. Wherever the king travels, he is attended by a number of four-wheeled cars drawn by mules,

5. In which the Choaspes water, ready boiled for use, and stored in

flagons of silver, is moved with him from place to place.

6. Cyrus on his way to Babylon came to the banks of the Gyndes, a stream which, rising in the Matienian mountains, runs through the country of the Dardanians, and empties itself into the River Tigris.

7. The Tigris, after receiving the Gyndes, flows on by the city of Opis, and discharges its waters into the Erythraean Sea.

8. When Cyrus reached the Gyndes, which could only be passed in boats, one of the prized white horses accompanying his march, full of boldness and high mettle, walked into the water, and tried to cross by himself;

9. But the current seized him, swept him along with it, and drowned him in its depths.

10. Cyrus, enraged by this, resolved to break the river's strength so that in future even children should cross it easily without wetting their tunics.

11. Accordingly he delayed his attack on Babylon for a time, and dividing his army into two parts, marked out by ropes one hundred and eighty trenches on each side of the Gyndes, leading off from it in all directions.

12. Setting his army to dig, some on one side of the river, some on the other, he accomplished his intention by the aid of so many hands, but not without thereby losing the whole summer season.

13. Having thus wreaked his vengeance on the Gyndes by dispersing it through three hundred and sixty channels, Cyrus, with the first approach of the ensuing spring, marched forward against Babylon.

14. The Babylonians, camped outside their walls, awaited his coming. A battle was fought at a short distance from the city, in which the Babylonians were defeated, whereupon they withdrew within their defences.

15. Here they shut themselves up, and made light of his siege, having laid in a store of provisions for many years in preparation against this attack;

16. For when they saw Cyrus conquering nation after nation, they were convinced that he would never stop, and that their turn would come.

17. Cyrus was now reduced to great perplexity, as time went on and he made no progress against the place.

18. But then he devised a plan. He placed a portion of his army at the point where the river enters the city, and another where it flows out,

19. With orders to march into the town by the bed of the stream, as soon as the water became shallow enough.

20. He then drew himself off with the unwarlike portion of his host, and made for the place where Nitocris had dug the basin for the river,

where he did exactly what she had done formerly:

21. He turned the Euphrates by a canal into the basin, which was then a marsh; as a result of which the river sank so low that the bed of the stream became fordable.

22. When this happened the Persian warriors who had been left where the river entered the city, finding that the water now reached only about midway up a man's thigh, waded into the town.

23. Had the Babylonians known what Cyrus was about, or had they noticed their danger, they would have destroyed the Persians utterly;

24. For they would have made fast all the street-gates giving onto the river, and mounting on the walls along both sides would have had their enemy trapped.

25. But as it was the Persians took them by surprise and captured the city. Owing to the vast size of the place, the inhabitants of the central parts knew nothing of what had chanced until long after the outer portions of the town were taken,

26. But as they were engaged in a festival, they continued dancing and revelling until far too late.

Chapter 20

1. Such, then, were the circumstances of the first taking of Babylon. With its territory it proved to be the richest and most fruitful of the satrapies of the Persian empire.

2. It alone provided a third of the empire's annual food and supplies, all the rest of Asia together providing two-thirds.

3. When Tritantaechmes, son of Artabazus, held the satrapy of Babylon on behalf of the Persian king, it brought him an artaba of silver every day.

4. He also had, belonging to his own private stud, besides war horses, eight hundred stallions and sixteen thousand mares, twenty to each stallion.

5. Besides which he kept so great a number of Indian hounds, that four large villages of the plain were exempted from all other charges on condition of keeping them in food.

6. Very little rain falls in Assyria, just enough to make the corn sprout, after which the plant is nourished and the ears formed by irrigation from the river.

7. For the river does not, as in Egypt, overflow the corn-lands of its own accord, but is spread over them by hand or the help of engines.

8. The whole of Babylonia is, like Egypt, intersected with canals.

9. The largest of them, which runs towards the winter sun, and is impassable except in boats, is carried from the Euphrates into the Tigris, the river on which the town of Nineveh formerly stood.

10. Of all countries none is so fruitful in grain. It cannot grow the fig, the olive, the vine, or any other

tree of the kind; but in grain it is wonderfully fruitful.

11. The blades of the wheat and barley are often four fingers in breadth. As for millet and sesame, what heights they reach! The fruitfulness of Babylonia must seem incredible to those who have never visited the country.

12. The only oil they use is made from the sesame plant. Palm trees grow in great numbers over the whole of the flat country, and their fruit supplies them with bread, wine and honey.

13. Palms are cultivated like fig trees; for example, Babylonians tie the fruit of the male palms to the branches of the date-bearing palm,

14. To let the gallfly enter the dates and ripen them, and to prevent the fruit from falling off.

15. When Cyrus had conquered the Babylonians, he conceived the desire of bringing the Massagetae under his dominion.

16. Now the Massagetae are said to be a great and warlike nation, dwelling eastward beyond the River Araxes, and opposite the Issedonians. Many regarded them as a Scythian race.

17. The Araxes is said by some to be a greater river than the Ister (Danube). It has forty mouths, all but one of which disappear into marshes. The other mouth flows with a clear course into the Caspian Sea.

18. Now, the sea frequented by the Greeks, the Mediterranean; the sea beyond the Pillars of Hercules, called the Atlantic; and the Erythraean Sea into which the Tigris and Euphrates flow, are all the same sea.

19. But the Caspian is a distinct sea, lying by itself, in length fifteen days' voyage with a rowboat, in breadth, at the broadest part, eight days' voyage.

20. Many and various are the tribes inhabiting its environs, most living on the wild fruits of the forest.

21. In these forests certain trees grow, from whose leaves, pounded and mixed with water, the inhabitants make a dye, with which they paint pictures of animals on their clothes;

22. And the pictures never wash out, but last as though they had been woven into the cloth.

23. On the west the Caspian Sea is bounded by the Caucasus, the most extensive and loftiest of all mountain ranges.

24. To its east is a vast plain, stretching out interminably before the eye, possessed by those Massagetae whom Cyrus now wished to subdue.

Chapter 21

1. At this time the Massagetae were ruled by a queen named Tomyris, who at the death of her husband, the late king, had mounted the throne.

2. To her Cyrus sent ambassadors, with instructions to court her on his part, pretending that he wished to marry her.

3. Tomyris, however, aware that it was her kingdom, and not herself, that he courted, forbade the men to approach.

4. Cyrus, therefore, finding that he did not advance his designs by this deceit, marched towards the River Araxes, openly displaying his hostile intentions.

5. He set to work to construct a bridge, and began building towers on the boats to be used in the passage.

6. While Cyrus was occupied in these labours, Tomyris sent a herald to him, who said, 'King, cease to press this enterprise, for you cannot know if what you are doing will be of advantage to you.

7. 'Be content to rule your own kingdom in peace, and bear to see us reign over the countries that are ours to govern.

8. 'As, however, I know you will not choose to listen to this counsel, since there is nothing you less desire than peace and quietness,

9. 'Come now, if you are so desirous of meeting the Massagetae in arms, leave your useless toil of bridge-making;

10. 'We will retire three days' march from the river bank, and you can come across with your soldiers;

11. 'Or, if you prefer to give us battle on your side of the stream, retire an equal distance and we will come over.'

12. Cyrus, on hearing this, called together the Persian chiefs, asking them to advise what he should do.

13. All the votes were in favour of letting Tomyris cross the stream, and giving battle on Persian ground.

14. But Croesus the Lydian, who was present at the meeting, disagreed with this advice; he therefore rose and said,

15. 'O king! I promised that I would, to the best of my ability, avert impending danger from your house.

16. 'Alas! my own sufferings, by their very bitterness, have taught me to be keen-sighted of dangers.

17. 'My judgement runs counter to that of your other counsellors. If you agree to let the enemy into your country, consider the risk!

18. 'Lose the battle, and with it your whole kingdom is lost. For assuredly, if the Massagetae win they will not return to their homes, but will push forward against the states of your empire.

19. 'Or if you win, why, then you gain far less than if you were across the stream, where you might follow up your victory.

20. 'Rout their army on the other side of the river, and you can push at once into the heart of their country.

21. 'My counsel, therefore, is that we cross the river, push forward as far

as they fall back, then get the better of them by stratagem.

22. 'I am told they are unacquainted with the good things on which the Persians live, and have never tasted the delights of life.

23. 'Let us prepare a feast for them in our camp; let sheep be slaughtered, and wine cups be filled, and let all manner of dishes be prepared: then leaving behind us our worst troops, let us fall back towards the river.

24. 'Unless I much mistake, when they see the good fare set out, they will forget everything else, and feast. Then it will remain for us to do our parts manfully.'

25. Cyrus, preferring the advice Croesus had given, returned answer to Tomyris that she should retire, and he would cross the stream.

26. She did so; and Cyrus, giving Croesus into the care of his son and heir Cambyses, with strict charge to the latter to pay Croesus all respect and treat him well if the expedition failed, crossed the river.

27. After Cyrus had advanced a day's march from the river, he did as Croesus had advised, and, leaving the worthless portion of his army in the camp, drew off with his good troops towards the river.

28. Soon afterwards, a detachment of the Massagetae, one-third of their entire army, led by Spargapises, son of queen Tomyris, fell upon

the troops left behind by Cyrus, and killed them.

29. Then, seeing the banquet prepared, they began to feast. When they had eaten and drunk, and had sunk into sleep, the Persians under Cyrus returned, slaughtered many, and made an even larger number prisoner, Spargapises among them.

30. When Tomyris heard what had happened she sent a herald to Cyrus to say, 'Bloodthirsty Cyrus, do not pride yourself on this poor success:

31. 'It was the grape juice which, when one drinks it, makes one mad, and brings to one's lips such bold words; it was this poison by which you defeated my son, not in fair open fight.

32. 'Now listen to what I advise. Restore my son and leave my land unharmed. Refuse, and I will give you more than your fill of blood.'

33. Cyrus ignored the herald. As for Spargapises, when he became sober, and saw the extent of his calamity, he requested Cyrus to release him from his bonds; then, when his request was granted, and the fetters were removed, he killed himself.

34. Tomyris collected all the forces of her kingdom and gave battle. Of all the combats in which the barbarians have engaged among themselves, this was the fiercest.

35. The Massagetae prevailed; the greater part of the army of the

Persians was destroyed, and Cyrus himself was killed, after reigning twenty-nine years.

36. By order of the queen a search was made among the slain for Cyrus' body, and when it was found she took a skin, and, filling it full of human blood, she dipped the head of Cyrus in the gore, saying,

37. 'I live and have conquered you, and yet I am ruined by you, for you took my son with guile; but thus I make good my threat, and give you your fill of blood.'

Chapter 22

1. On the death of Cyrus, Cambyses his son by Cassandane daughter of Pharnaspes inherited the kingdom, and immediately began a campaign to capture Egypt.

2. Cassandane had died in the lifetime of Cyrus, who had made a great mourning for her at her death, and had commanded all the subjects of his empire to do likewise.

3. Cambyses, regarding the Ionian and Aeolian Greeks as vassals of his father, took them with him in his expedition against Egypt among the other nations under his sway.

4. His war of conquest against Egypt began when Amasis was king of that ancient and wealthy land astride the Nile.

5. But by the time Cambyses arrived with his army in Egypt, Amasis had died at the end of his forty-four-year reign, to be succeeded by his son Psammenitus.

6. At the first battle Cambyses defeated the armies of Psammenitus, whose soldiers fled the battlefield and took refuge behind the walls of Memphis.

7. Cambyses besieged the city for ten days, whereupon it fell; and Psammenitus was taken prisoner and brought to Cambyses' camp.

8. The Persian king resolved to test the fortitude of Psammenitus to see what manner of man he was.

9. He placed him on a seat in the suburb of the vanquished city, his captured nobles with him,

10. And forced him to watch his daughter manhandled along the street, dressed as a slave, and with her the daughters of the Egyptian nobles; and all were subjected to mistreatment.

11. The nobles of Psammenitus wept to see their daughters in this plight, carrying pitchers of water and pushed by soldiers in the dust of the street; but Psammenitus did not weep.

12. Next came Psammenitus' son, and two thousand young men of the same age as he, with ropes around their necks and bridles in their mouths, being driven like beasts to a place of execution outside the city.

13. While the other Egyptians around him wept and tore their clothes at this sight, Psammenitus still did

not weep, but remained silent and still.

14. But then it chanced that an old man who had been a boyhood friend of Psammenitus came into view, hobbling along the ranks of onlookers begging for alms.

15. At this sight the Egyptian king burst into tears, and wept, and called out to the old man by name.

16. Some of the guards watching over Psammenitus went to Cambyses and described what had happened; and Cambyses was astonished, and sent a messenger to Psammenitus,

17. To ask for an explanation of why he had not wept at the disgrace and tribulation of his daughter and son, but had wept so copiously at sight of the old man.

18. To which Psammenitus answered, 'Oh conqueror, my own misfortunes and the loss of my children are too great for tears.

19. 'But the woe of my old friend deserved them. When a man falls into beggary in old age, one may well weep for him.'

20. When Cambyses heard this answer he recognised that it was just, and those who stood about him in his royal tent wept to hear what Psammenitus had said.

21. So he was touched with pity likewise, and sent an order that Psammenitus' son and daughter were to be spared.

22. Alas, it was to late to save Psammenitus' son; he had been the first who was cut to pieces on the execution ground, and lived no more.

23. But Psammenitus was brought to Cambyses' court, and remained there, no longer a prisoner but a guest; for the justice of his pity had earned him a reprieve, and with it the life of his daughter.

24. If this is evidence of humanity in Cambyses, it should be balanced against what he next did,

25. Which was to go from Memphis to Sais, where King Amasis had been buried, and command that his embalmed body be exhumed,

26. For Cambyses held a grudge against Amasis, which was part of his reason for invading Egypt in the first place.

27. When the corpse of Amasis was brought out, Cambyses ordered his attendants to scourge the body,

28. And prick it with goads, and pluck the hair from it, and heap upon it all manner of insults.

29. The body, however, having been embalmed, resisted, and refused to come apart, do what they would to it;

30. So the attendants grew weary of their work; whereupon Cambyses bade them take the corpse and burn it.

31. This was felt by the Egyptians to be a great indignity to their deceased king. It was also among the first marks of madness that was creeping upon Cambyses.

Chapter 23

1. Having designs on the land of the Ethiopians, and wishing to know their strength and dispositions, Cambyses dispatched an embassy there,

2. With gifts for the Ethiopian king comprising a purple robe, a gold chain for the neck, armlets, an alabaster box of myrrh and a cask of palm wine.

3. The Ethiopians are said to be the tallest and handsomest men in the world. In their customs they differ greatly from the rest of mankind, and particularly in the way they choose their kings;

4. For they find out the man who is tallest of all the citizens, and of strength equal to his height, and appoint him to rule over them.

5. The Persian ambassadors, on reaching this people, delivered the gifts to their king, and said,

6. 'Cambyses, king of the Persians, anxious to become your friend, has sent us to bring you these gifts, which are the things he himself most delights in.'

7. To which the Ethiopian, who knew they came as spies, answered, 'The Persian king did not send you with these gifts because he desired my friendship;

8. 'Nor is what you say of yourselves true, for you are here to spy on my kingdom.

9. 'Your king is not a just man, for were he so, he would not covet a land not his own, nor try to bring slavery on a people who never did him wrong.

10. 'Take him this bow, and say, "The Ethiopians thus advise: when the Persians can pull a bow of this strength as easily as an Ethiopian, let him come with an army.

11. '"Until then, let him be thankful that it is not in the heart of the sons of Ethiopia to covet countries which do not belong to them."'

12. So speaking, he unstrung the bow and gave it to the messengers. Then, taking the purple robe, he asked them what it was, and how it had been made.

13. They answered truly, telling him concerning the purple, and the art of the dyer; whereupon he observed that 'the men were deceitful, and their garments also'.

14. Next he took the neck chain and the armlets, and asked about them. So the ambassadors explained their use as ornaments.

15. Then the king laughed, and believing they were fetters, said the Ethiopians had much stronger ones.

16. Thirdly, he inquired about the myrrh, and when they told him how it was made and rubbed upon the limbs, he said the same as he had said about the robe.

17. Last he came to the wine, and having learnt their way of making it, he drank a draught, which greatly delighted him;

18. Whereupon he asked what the Persian king liked to eat, and what

age the longest-lived of the Persians attained.

19. They told him that the king ate bread, and described the nature of wheat; adding that eighty years was the longest term of man's life among the Persians.

20. To this the Ethiopian king remarked that it did not surprise him, if they fed on dirt, that they died so young;

21. Indeed he was sure they never would have lived so long as eighty years, except for the refreshment they got from their wine, which he confessed to be superior to anything that the Ethopians drank.

22. When the spies had seen everything, they returned to Egypt and made report to Cambyses, who was stirred to anger by the words of the Ethiopian king.

23. Immediately he set out on his march against the Ethiopians without making any provision for the sustenance of his army,

24. Or reflecting that he was about to wage war in the uttermost parts of the earth.

25. Like a senseless madman, no sooner did he receive the report of the ambassadors than he began his march,

26. Instructing the Greeks who were with his army to remain where they were, and taking only his land force with him.

27. At Thebes, which he passed on his way, he detached from his main body some fifty thousand men, and sent them against the Ammonians with orders to carry the people into captivity, and burn their civic places.

28. Meanwhile he went on with the rest of his forces against the Ethiopians.

29. Before he had accomplished one-fifth of the distance, all the army's provisions failed; whereupon the men began to eat the sumpter beasts, which were all soon consumed.

30. If, at this time, Cambyses, seeing what was happening, had confessed his mistake, and led his army back, he would have done the wisest thing;

31. But as it was, he took no heed, and continued the march.

32. So long as the earth gave them anything, the soldiers sustained life by eating the grass and herbs;

33. But when they came to the bare sand, some of them committed a horrid deed: by tens they cast lots for a man, who was slain to be the food of the others.

34. When Cambyses heard of this, alarmed at such cannibalism, he gave up his attack on Ethiopia, and retreating by the way he had come, reached Thebes, after he had lost vast numbers of his soldiers.

Chapter 24

1. The men sent to attack the Ammonians started from Thebes, having guides with them,

2. And reached as far as the city Oasis, which is inhabited by Samians, said to be of the tribe Aeschrionia.

3. The place is seven days' journey from Thebes across the desert. Thus far the army is known to have made its way;

4. But thenceforth nothing is known of them, except what the Ammonians report.

5. It is certain they neither reached the territory of Ammonians, nor ever came back to Egypt.

6. The Ammonians say that the Persians set out from Oasis, and had reached about halfway across the desert when, while they were at their midday meal, a strong and deadly wind rose from the south,

7. Bringing with it vast columns of whirling sand, which buried the troops entirely.

8. About the time when Cambyses arrived at Memphis the Egyptians were making festival, arraying themselves in their gayest garments and giving themselves to feasting and jollity:

9. Which, when Cambyses saw, believing that these rejoicings were on account of his failure, he summoned the officers in charge of Memphis, and asked,

10. Why, when he was in Memphis before, the Egyptians had no festival, but waited until now, when he had returned with the loss of so many troops?

11. When the officers answered that this was one of the regular holiday observances of the Egyptians, he would not believe them, and told them that they lied, and condemned them all to death.

12. Then he instructed his troops that any Egyptians found keeping festival were to be put to death. Thus was the feast stopped throughout the land of Egypt.

13. And now Cambyses, who even before had not been quite in his right mind, was forthwith, as the Egyptians say, smitten with madness, and gave himself over to worse crimes.

14. The first of his outrages was the slaying of Smerdis, his brother, whom he had sent back to Persia from Egypt out of envy,

15. Because he drew the bow brought from the Ethiopians by the ambassadors, which none of the other Persians were able to bend.

16. When Smerdis had departed, Cambyses began to fear that he would plot against him, purposing to kill him and rule in his stead.

17. So Cambyses sent his trusted servant Prexaspes into Persia, with instructions to assassinate Smerdis.

18. Prexaspes accordingly went to Susa and slew Smerdis. Some say he killed him as they hunted together, others, that he took him to the Erythraean Sea and there drowned him.

19. This was the first of the outrages that Cambyses committed against his own family. The second was

the slaying of his sister, who had accompanied him to Egypt, and lived with him as his wife.

20. He had made her his wife in the following way. It was not the Persians' custom, before this time, to marry their sisters, but Cambyses fell in love with her,

21. So he called together the royal judges, and put it to them, 'Whether there was any law which permitted a brother to marry his sister?'

22. When Cambyses put his question to the judges, they gave him an answer which was at once true and safe:

23. They did not find any law, they said, allowing a brother to take his sister to wife, but they found a law that the Persian king might do whatever he pleased.

24. And so they neither betrayed the law through fear of Cambyses, nor ruined themselves by maintaining it; but brought a different law to the king's help, which allowed him to have his wish.

25. Cambyses, therefore, married the object of his desire, and soon afterwards took another sister to wife.

26. It was the younger of these who went with him into Egypt, and there suffered death at his hands.

27. Concerning the manner of her death, it is said that Cambyses had put a young dog to fight the cub of a lioness, his wife looking on.

28. Now the dog was getting the worse, when a pup of the same litter broke his chain, and came to his brother's aid; then the two dogs together conquered the lion.

29. This greatly pleased Cambyses, but his sister shed tears. Cambyses asked why she wept,

30. Whereon she told him that seeing the young dog come to his brother's aid made her think of Smerdis, whom there was none to help. For this speech Cambyses put her to death.

Chapter 25

1. Cambyses behaved with madness towards others besides his kindred, including Prexaspes, the man whom he esteemed beyond all the rest of his people,

2. Who carried his messages, and whose son held the office of Cambyses' cupbearer – a matter of no small account among Persians.

3. Cambyses asked him: 'What, Prexaspes, do the Persians say of me?' Prexaspes answered, 'O! sire, they praise you greatly in all things but one: they say you are too much given to wine.'

4. Whereupon Cambyses, full of rage, answered, 'What? they say that I drink too much, and so have gone out of my mind! Then their former speeches about me were untrue.'

5. For once, when the Persians were sitting with him, and Croesus was by, he had asked them what sort of

man they thought him compared to his father Cyrus.

6. They had answered that he surpassed his father, for he was lord of all that his father ever ruled, and further had made himself master of Egypt, and the sea.

7. Then Croesus, who disliked the comparison, said to Cambyses: 'In my judgement, son of Cyrus, you are not equal to your father, for you have not yet left behind you such a son as he had.'

8. Cambyses was delighted when he heard this reply, and praised the judgement of Croesus.

9. Recollecting these answers, Cambyses spoke fiercely to Prexaspes, saying,

10. 'Judge now for yourself, Prexaspes, whether the Persians tell the truth, or whether it is not they who are mad for speaking as they do.

11. 'Look there at your son standing in the vestibule; if I shoot and hit him in the heart, it will be plain the Persians have no grounds for what they say:

12. 'If I miss him, then I allow that the Persians are right, and that I am out of my mind.'

13. So speaking he drew his bow to the full, and struck the boy, who straightway fell down dead.

14. Cambyses ordered the body to be opened, and the wound examined; and when the arrow was found to have entered the heart, the king was overjoyed, and said to the father with a laugh,

15. 'Now you see plainly, Prexaspes,

that it is not I who am mad, but the Persians. I pray you tell me, did you ever see anyone send an arrow with better aim?'

16. Prexaspes, seeing that the king was not in his right mind, and fearing for himself, hid his grief for his son and replied,

17. 'O! my lord, I do not think that anyone in all history could shoot so dexterously.'

18. For this outrage Croesus thought it right to admonish Cambyses, which he did as follows:

19. 'King, do not allow yourself to give way entirely to your youth, and the heat of your temper, but control yourself.

20. 'It is well to look to consequences, and wisdom lies in forethought.

21. 'If you do such things as these, your Persians will eventually rebel against you. It is by your father's wish that I say this; he charged me strictly to give you counsel if it became necessary.'

22. In thus advising Cambyses, Croesus meant nothing but what was friendly. But Cambyses answered him,

23. 'Do you presume to offer me advice? You ruled your own country well when you were a king, and gave sage advice to my father Cyrus at times;

24. 'Yet by misdirection of your own affairs you ruined yourself, and by your own bad counsel, which he followed, you brought ruin upon Cyrus, my father.

25. 'But you will not escape punishment now, for I have long been seeking to find some occasion against you.'

26. As he spoke, Cambyses took up his bow to shoot Croesus; but Croesus ran hastily out, and escaped.

27. So Cambyses ordered his servants to run after him and seize him, and put him to death.

28. The servants, however, who knew their master's humour, thought it best to hide Croesus;

29. So if Cambyses relented, and asked for him, they might bring him out, and get a reward for having saved his life.

30. If, on the other hand, he did not relent, or regret the loss, they might then dispatch him.

31. Not long afterwards, Cambyses did in fact regret the loss of Croesus, and the servants, perceiving it, let him know that he was still alive.

32. 'I am glad,' said he, 'that Croesus lives, but as for you who saved him, you shall not escape my vengeance, but all of you shall be put to death.' And they were killed.

33. Cambyses committed many other such outrages, both upon Persians and upon allies, while he was at Memphis;

34. Among the rest he opened the ancient sepulchres, and examined the bodies that were buried in them, and had no respect for the Egyptians, but mistreated them at will.

35. Thus it appears certain, by many such proofs, that Cambyses was mad; he would not otherwise have set himself to mock the Egyptians' traditions and laws,

36. But would have learned from his successor Darius, who set a good example in this.

37. For Darius, after he had got the kingdom, summoned certain Greeks who were at hand, and asked,

38. 'What he should pay them to eat the bodies of their fathers when they died?' To which they answered, that there was no sum that would tempt them to do such a thing.

39. He then sent for certain Indians, of the race called Callatians,

40. These being men who ate their fathers' corpses to honour them, as they thought, with continued life;

41. And asked them, while the Greeks stood by, 'What he should give them to burn the bodies of their fathers?'

42. The Indians exclaimed aloud, and begged him not to say such a terrible thing.

43. Thus Darius showed the variability of human opinions and traditions, and accepted them, ruling accordingly.

Chapter 26

1. While Cambyses was in Egypt the Greeks were at war with one

another over slights and insults
that different cities felt they had
received from one another.

2. During these troubles some
banished Samians went to Sparta
to seek aid, and were given
audience by the magistrates, before
whom they made a long speech, as
is the way with supplicants.

3. The Spartans answered that by the
end of the speech they had forgotten the first half, and could make
nothing of the second half.

4. Whereupon the Samians begged a
second audience, and at it simply
showed an empty bag, saying, 'The
bag lacks flour.'

5. The Spartans answered that the
Samians did not need to say 'The
bag', but merely, 'lacks flour';
nevertheless they resolved to give
the Samians aid.

6. The Samians were subject to a
concerted attack by their neighbours for wrongs, real and
perceived, done by them in earlier
times.

7. Among these were the
Corinthians, whose grievance
against Samos was that it had
prevented them from taking three
hundred sons of Corcyraean
nobles to be eunuchs as a gift for
an ally.

8. This hard usage of Corcyraean
youths was a punishment imposed
by Periander for the murder of his
son by the Corcyraeans, which
arose as follows.

9. After Periander had put to death

his wife Melissa, it chanced that
on this first affliction a second
followed of a different kind.

10. His wife had borne him two sons,
and one of them had now reached
the age of seventeen, the other
eighteen years, when their
mother's father Procles, tyrant of
Epidaurus, invited them to his
court.

11. They went, and Procles treated
them with much kindness, as was
natural, considering they were his
grandchildren.

12. When time for parting came,
Procles, as he was bidding farewell,
asked, 'Do you know who caused
your mother's death?'

13. The elder son took no account of
this speech, but the younger,
whose name was Lycophron, was
sorely troubled to learn that his
father had killed his mother;

14. So much so, that when he
returned to Corinth he would
neither speak to his father, nor
answer when spoken to. So
Periander at last, growing furious
at such behaviour, banished him
from his house.

15. The younger son gone, he turned
to the elder and asked him what it
was that their grandfather had said
to them.

16. Then the youth related how kind
and friendly Procles had been; but,
not having taken notice of what
Procles said at parting, he did not
mention it.

17. Periander insisted that it was not

possible this should be all; their grandfather must have given them some hint or other; and he went on pressing the youth, till at last he remembered the parting speech and told it.

18. Periander, after he had considered the whole matter, felt unwilling to give way, and sent a messenger to the persons who had opened their houses to his outcast son, and forbade them to harbour him.

19. Then the boy, when he was chased from one friend, sought refuge with another, but was driven from shelter to shelter by the threats of his father,

20. Who menaced all those that took him in, and commanded them to shut their doors against him.

21. Still, as fast as he was forced to leave one house he went to another, and was received by the inmates;

22. For his acquaintance, although in no small alarm at the danger, yet gave him shelter, as he was Periander's son.

23. At last Periander made proclamation that whoever harboured, or even spoke to him, would be fined.

24. On hearing this no one any longer took Lycophron in, or even spoke with him, and he himself did not think it right to do what was forbidden; so he made his lodging in the public porticos.

25. When four days had passed in this way, Periander, seeing how

wretched his son was, that he neither washed nor took any food, felt moved with compassion towards him;

26. And foregoing his anger, he approached him, and said, 'Which is better, my son, to fare as you now do, or to receive my crown and all the good things I possess, on the one condition of submitting yourself to your father?

27. 'See, now, though my own child, and heir to this wealthy Corinth, you have brought yourself to a beggar's life, because you must defy him whom it least behoves you to oppose.

28. 'If there has been a calamity, and you hate me on that account, consider that I feel it too, and am the greater sufferer, because it was by me that the deed was done.

29. 'For yourself, now that you know how much better a thing it is to be envied than pitied, and how dangerous it is to indulge anger against parents, come home with me.'

30. With such words as these did Periander chide his son; but the son made no reply, except to remind his father that he was liable to the fine for speaking to him.

31. Then Periander knew that there was no cure for the youth's disaffection, nor means of overcoming it;

32. So he prepared a ship and sent him away out of his sight to

Corcyra, which island at that time belonged to him.

Chapter 27

1. As for Procles, Periander regarded him as the true author of all his present troubles, and so he went to war with him as soon as his son was gone,

2. And not only made himself master of Epidaurus, but also took Procles himself, and carried him into captivity.

3. As time went by, and Periander grew old, he found himself no longer equal to the management of affairs.

4. Knowing his eldest son to be dull and blockish, he sent to Corcyra and recalled Lycophron to take the kingdom.

5. Lycophron, however, did not even deign to ask the bearer of this message a question.

6. But Periander's heart was set upon the youth, so he sent again to him, this time by his own daughter, the sister of Lycophron, who would, he thought, more than any other person be able to persuade him.

7. When she reached Corcyra, she said to her brother, 'Do you wish the kingdom to pass into strange hands,

8. 'And our father's wealth to be made a prey, rather than yourself return to enjoy it? Come back with me, and cease to punish yourself. It is scant gain, this obstinacy.

9. 'Why seek to cure evil by evil? Mercy, remember, is by many set above justice. Many, also, while pushing their mother's claims, have forfeited their father's fortune.

10. 'Power is a slippery thing; it has many suitors; and he is old and stricken in years. Do not let your own inheritance go to another.'

11. Thus did the sister, who had been tutored by Periander what to say, urge all the arguments most likely to win her brother.

12. But he answered that so long as he knew his father to be still alive, he would never go back to Corinth.

13. When the sister told this to Periander, he sent a message to his son a third time, and said he would himself come to Corcyra, and let his son take his place at Corinth as king.

14. To this Lycophron agreed; and Periander was making ready to travel when the Corcyraeans, being informed of this, and from their hatred of Periander wishing to keep him away, put Lycophron to death.

15. For this reason it was that Periander took vengeance on the Corcyraeans by taking their sons to be eunuchs.

Chapter 28

1. How the Samians angered Periander is as follows. The men who had the Corcyraean youths in

charge touched at Samos on their way to Sardis;

2. Whereupon the Samians, on finding out what was to become of the boys, gave them sanctuary in their city hall,

3. And because the Corinthian sailors were forbidden to enter the Samians' hall to recapture the boys, they tried to starve them into giving themselves up by forbidding anyone to enter the building with food.

4. The Samians therefore invented a festival on the boys' behalf, which they celebrated ever after, as follows:

5. Each evening during the whole time the boys continued there, choirs of youths and virgins danced around the building, carrying in their hands cakes of sesame and honey,

6. In order that the Corcyraean boys might snatch the cakes, and so get enough to live upon.

7. And this went on for so long, that at last the Corinthians gave the boys up, and took their departure, upon which the Samians returned the boys to Corcyra.

8. Thus were the seeds of enmity sown between Corinth and Samos; the two people were thereafter enemies to one another, and the Corinthians bore a grudge for it.

9. Why dwell on the affairs of the Samians? Because three of the greatest works in all Greece were made by them.

10. One is a tunnel under a hill one hundred and fifty fathoms high, carried entirely through the base of the hill, with a mouth at either end.

11. The length of the cutting is seven furlongs, the height and width are each eight feet. Along the whole course there is a second cutting, twenty cubits deep and three feet broad, whereby water is brought into the city, through pipes.

12. The architect of this tunnel was Eupalinus, son of Naustrophus, a Megarian.

13. The second great work is a mole in the sea, which goes all round the harbour, near twenty fathoms deep, and in length above two furlongs.

14. The third is the town hall, the largest of all the halls known to us, whereof Rhoecus, son of Phileus, a Samian, was first architect.

15. Because of these works one likes to dwell on the affairs of Samos; the works of ingenuity and practicality are greater than the works of war, and the expertise of mankind is greater than the example of tyranny.

Chapter 29

1. While Cambyses, son of Cyrus, still lingered in Egypt, two brothers of the Magus tribe revolted against him.

2. One of them, Patizeithes, had been left in Persia by Cambyses as

comptroller of his household; it was he who began the revolt.

3. Aware that Smerdis was dead, and that his death was hidden and known to few Persians, while most believed that he was still alive, Patizeithes laid his plan, and made a bold stroke for the crown.

4. His brother happened greatly to resemble Smerdis, and not only was this brother like Smerdis in appearance, but he was also called Smerdis.

5. Patizeithes, having persuaded his brother to the plan, sat him on the royal throne, and then sent heralds through the land,

6. To Egypt and elsewhere, to make proclamation to the troops that henceforth they were to obey Smerdis the son of Cyrus, and not Cambyses.

7. The heralds made proclamation as they were ordered, and likewise the herald who was sent to Egypt.

8. When the herald reached Ecbatana in Syria, finding Cambyses and his army there, he went straight into the middle of the host, and standing before them made the proclamation which Patizeithes the Magus had commanded.

9. Cambyses no sooner heard him, than believing that what the herald said was true, and imagining that he had been betrayed,

10. He turned his eyes on Prexaspes, and said, 'Is this the way, Prexaspes, that you did my errand?'

11. 'O! my liege,' answered the other, 'there is no truth in the tidings that Smerdis your brother has revolted against you,

12. 'Nor have you to fear any quarrel, great or small, with that man. With my own hands I killed him, and with my own hands I buried him.

13. 'If the dead could leave their graves, expect Astyages the Mede to rise and fight against you; but if the course of nature be the same as always, then no ill can come from this quarter.

14. 'Call that herald, and strictly question him who it was that charged him to bid us obey King Smerdis.'

15. Cambyses approved Prexaspes' words, and the herald was brought before the king.

16. Prexaspes said to him, 'Sirrah, you say that your message is from Smerdis, son of Cyrus. Now answer truly, and you will be allowed to go unharmed.

17. 'Did Smerdis have you in his presence to give you your orders, or did you have them from one of his officers?'

18. The herald answered, 'Truly I have not set eyes on Smerdis son of Cyrus, since the day when King Cambyses led the Persians into Egypt.

19. 'The man who gave me my orders was the Magus that Cambyses left in charge of the household; but he said that Smerdis son of Cyrus sent you the message.'

20. Then Cambyses said to Prexaspes, 'You are free from all blame, Prexaspes, since you did not fail to do what I commanded.

21. 'But tell me, which of the Persians can have taken the name of Smerdis, and revolted against me?'

22. 'I think, my liege,' he answered, 'that I understand the whole business. The men who have risen in revolt are Patizeithes, who was left comptroller of your household, and his brother, named Smerdis.'

23. Cambyses no sooner heard this than, smarting with vexation at his troubles, he sprang hastily onto his horse, meaning to march his army quickly to Susa against the rebels.

24. But as he did so, the button of his sword-sheath fell off, and the bared point pierced his thigh, wounding him sorely.

25. Then Cambyses, feeling that he had got his death-wound, called to his presence all the chief Persians who were with the army, and addressed them as follows:

26. 'Persians, I must tell you now what I have hitherto striven with the greatest care to keep secret.

27. 'I, in my folly, sent Prexaspes to Susa to put my brother to death, because I feared that he would revolt against me, and seize the crown.

28. 'When this great crime was accomplished I lived without fear, never imagining that, after

Smerdis was dead, I need fear revolt from any other.

29. 'But I was mistaken, and slew my brother needlessly, for even so I have lost my crown.

30. 'For it is two of the Magi tribe who have rebelled against me and taken the royal power: Patizeithes, whom I left at Susa to overlook my household, and Smerdis his brother.

31. 'I charge you all, and specially such of you as are Achaemenids, that you do not lamely allow the kingdom to go back to the Medes.

32. 'Recover it one way or another, by force or fraud; by fraud, if it is by fraud that they have seized on it; by force, if force has helped them in their enterprise.

33. 'Do this, and then may your land bring you forth fruit abundantly, and your wives bear children, and your herds increase, and freedom be your portion for ever.'

Chapter 30

1. But the Persians who heard his words put no faith in anything that he said concerning the Magi having the royal power;

2. Instead they believed that he spoke out of hatred towards his brother Smerdis, and had invented the tale of his death to cause the whole Persian race to rise up in arms against him.

3. Thus they were convinced that it was Smerdis the son of Cyrus who

had rebelled and now sat on the throne.

4. For Prexaspes stoutly denied that he had murdered Smerdis, since it was not safe for him to allow that a son of Cyrus had met with death at his hands.

5. Thus Cambyses died, and the Magus now reigned in security, and passed himself off as Smerdis son of Cyrus.

6. And so went by the seven months which were wanting to complete the eighth year of Cambyses.

7. In the eighth month, however, it was discovered who Smerdis the Magian really was, in the following manner.

8. There was a man called Otanes, the son of Pharnaspes, who for rank and wealth was equal to the greatest of the Persians;

9. And he was the first to suspect that the Magus was not Smerdis the son of Cyrus, and to surmise who he really was.

10. He was led to guess the truth by the king never leaving the citadel, and never calling before him any of the Persian noblemen.

11. As soon, therefore, as his suspicions were aroused, he adopted the following measures.

12. One of his daughters, who was called Phaedima, had been married to Cambyses, and was taken to wife, together with the rest of Cambyses' wives, by Smerdis the usurper.

13. Otanes sent her a message, asking her 'Who it was whose bed she shared; was it Smerdis the son of Cyrus, or was it some other man?'

14. Phaedima in reply declared she did not know; Smerdis the son of Cyrus she had never seen, and so she could not tell whose bed she shared.

15. Upon this Otanes sent a second time, and said, 'If you do not know Smerdis son of Cyrus yourself, ask queen Atossa about the man whose bed you share; she cannot fail to know her own brother.'

16. To this the daughter answered, 'I can neither get speech with Atossa, nor with any of the women who lodge in the palace.

17. 'For no sooner did this man obtain the kingdom, than he parted us from one another, and gave us all separate chambers.'

18. This made the matter seem still more plain to Otanes. Nevertheless he sent a third message to his daughter, saying,

19. 'Daughter, you are of noble blood; you will not shrink from the risk which I now ask you to take, even though it could mean your death if discovered.

20. 'When next he passes the night with you, wait till he is fast asleep, then feel his ears. For if you find that he has none, you will know that he is not Smerdis son of Cyrus but Smerdis the Magian.'

21. Now Smerdis the Magian had had his ears cut off in the lifetime of

Cyrus, as a punishment for a crime of no slight heinousness.

22. Otanes' daughter, therefore, when her turn came, and she was taken to the bed of the Magus (in Persia a man's wives sleep with him in their turns), waited till he was sound asleep, and then felt for his ears.

23. She quickly perceived that he had none; and of this, as soon as day dawned, she sent word to her father.

24. Then Otanes went to two of the chief Persians, Aspathines and Gobryas, men it was safe to trust in such a matter, and told them everything.

25. Now they had already themselves suspected how matters stood. When Otanes laid his reasons before them they at once came into his views;

26. And it was agreed that each of the three should take as companion in the work the Persian in whom he placed the greatest confidence.

27. Otanes chose Intaphernes, Gobryas chose Megabyzus, and Aspathines chose Hydarnes. After the number had thus become six, Darius, the son of Hystaspes, arrived at Susa from the province where his father was governor.

28. On his coming it seemed good to the six to take him likewise into their counsels.

29. When they did so Darius said, 'I thought no one but I knew that Smerdis, the son of Cyrus, was not alive, and that Smerdis the Magian ruled over us;

30. 'On this account I hurried back, to raise resistance against the Magian. But as it seems the matter is known to you all, and not to me only, my judgement is that we should act at once, and delay no longer.'

31. Otanes said, 'Son of Hystaspes, you are the child of a brave father, and seem likely to show yourself as gallant as he.

32. 'Beware, however, of rash haste in this matter; we must not hurry, but proceed with caution. We must add to our number before striking a blow.'

33. 'No,' Darius replied; 'if we follow the advice of Otanes we will perish most miserably.

34. 'Someone will betray our plot to the Magians. You ought to have kept the matter to yourselves, and so made the venture;

35. 'But because you have taken others into your secret, including me, we must make the attempt as soon as possible, even today.

36. 'We can easily gain entry to the palace; I can say that I have just arrived and have a message for the king from my father. An untruth must be spoken, where need requires.'

37. Gobryas, agreeing, said, 'Dear friends, when will a fitter occasion offer for us to recover the kingdom, or, if we are not strong enough, at least die in the attempt?

38. 'My vote is that we do as Darius has counselled: march straight to the palace, and immediately set upon the Magian.' So Gobryas spoke, and the rest agreed.

Chapter 31

1. While the seven were thus taking counsel together, it chanced that the Magi had been thinking what they had best do, and had resolved for many reasons to make a friend of Prexaspes.
2. They knew how cruelly he had been outraged by Cambyses, who slew his son with an arrow;
3. They were also aware that it was by his hand that Smerdis the son of Cyrus fell, and that he was the only person privy to that prince's death;
4. And they further found him to be held in the highest esteem by all the Persians.
5. So they summoned him, made him their friend, and bound him by a promise to keep silence about the fraud they were practising, and promised him many gifts of every sort.
6. So Prexaspes agreed, and the Magi, when they found that they had persuaded him so far, went on to another proposal,
7. And said they would assemble the Persians at the foot of the palace wall, and he should mount one of the towers and address them from it, assuring them that Smerdis the son of Cyrus, and none other, ruled the land.

8. Prexaspes said he was ready to do their will; so the Magi assembled the people, and placed Prexaspes on the tower, and told him to make his speech.
9. Prexaspes began by tracing the descent of Cyrus, and all the services that had been rendered by that king to the Persians;
10. And then, in honour of Cyrus' memory, and to the dismay and anger of the Magi, he proceeded to declare the truth,
11. Which he had, he said, until now concealed because it would not have been safe for him to reveal it:
12. So he told how, forced to the deed by Cambyses, he had himself taken the life of Smerdis, son of Cyrus, so that Persia was now ruled by usurping Magi.
13. Last of all, with adjurations to the Persians to recover the kingdom and wreak vengeance on the Magi, he threw himself headlong from the tower into the abyss below.
14. Such was the end of Prexaspes, a man all his life of high repute among the Persians.
15. And now the seven noble Persians, having resolved to attack the usurpers without more delay, set off for the palace, quite unacquainted with what had been done by Prexaspes.
16. The news of his doings reached them on their way, when they had gone about half the distance.
17. Accordingly they turned aside out of the road, and consulted

together. Otanes and his party said they must certainly put off the business, and not make the attack when affairs were in such a ferment.

18. Darius, on the other hand, and his friends, were against any change of plan, and wished to go straight on, and not lose a moment.

19. So they discussed; and quickly the seven became of one accord with Darius, and hastened on towards the palace.

20. At the gate they were received as Darius had foretold. The guards, who had no suspicion that they came for any ill purpose, and held the chief Persians in much reverence, let them pass without difficulty.

21. But when they were in the great court they fell in with certain of the palace eunuchs, who stopped them and asked what they wanted.

22. The seven sought to press on, but the eunuchs would not let them. Then the seven drew their daggers, and stabbing those who tried to withstand them, rushed towards the apartment of the males.

23. Both the Magi brothers were at this time within, discussing the matter of Prexaspes' revelations to the crowd.

24. When they heard the stir among the eunuchs, and their loud cries, they ran out themselves, to see what was happening.

25. Perceiving their danger, they both flew to arms; one had just time to seize his bow, the other got hold of his lance, when straightway the fight began.

26. The one whose weapon was the bow found it of no service at all; the foe was too near, and the combat too close to allow of his using it.

27. But the other made a stout defence with his lance, wounding two of the seven, Aspathines in the leg, and Intaphernes in the eye.

28. This wound did not kill Intaphernes, but it cost him the sight of that eye.

29. The other Magus, when he found his bow of no avail, fled into a chamber which opened out into the apartment of the males, intending to shut the doors.

30. But two of the seven entered the room with him, Darius and Gobryas.

31. Gobryas seized the Magus and grappled with him, while Darius stood over them, not knowing what to do; for it was dark, and he was afraid that if he struck a blow he might kill Gobryas.

32. Then Gobryas, when he perceived that Darius stood doing nothing, asked him why his hand was idle? 'I fear to injure you,' he answered.

33. 'Fear not,' said Gobryas; 'strike, though it be through both.' Darius did as he desired, drove his dagger home, and killed the Magus.

34. Thus were the Magi slain; and the seven, cutting off both the heads, went out of the gates with the

heads in their hands, shouting and
making an uproar.

35. They called out to all the Persians
whom they met, and told them
what had happened, showing them
the heads of the Magi,

36. While at the same time they slew
every Magus who fell in their way.

37. Then the Persians, when they
knew what the seven had done,
and understood the fraud of the
Magi, thought it just to follow the
example set them,

38. And, drawing their daggers, they
killed the Magi wherever they
could find any.

39. Such was their fury that, unless
night had fallen, not a single
Magus would have been left alive.

40. The Persians observe the anniver-
sary of this day with one accord,
and keep it more strictly than any
other in the whole year.

41. It is then that they hold the great
festival, which they call the
Magophonia. No Magus may
show himself abroad during the
whole time that the feast lasts; all
have to remain at home the entire
day.

Chapter 32

1. When the tumult had settled
down the conspirators met
together to consult.

2. Otanes recommended that the
management of public affairs
should be entrusted to the whole
nation.

3. 'To me,' he said, 'it seems

advisable that we should no longer
have a single man to rule over us;
rule by one is neither good nor
pleasant.

4. 'Look at the lengths Cambyses
went in his tyranny. How is it
possible that monarchy should be
a well-adjusted thing, when it
allows a man to do as he likes
without being answerable?

5. 'Such licence is enough to corrupt
the worthiest of men.

6. 'Give a person this power, and
straightway his manifold good
things puff him up with pride,
while envy is so natural to humans
that it cannot but arise in him.

7. 'Pride and envy together include
all wickedness, both of them
leading to deeds of violence.

8. 'It is true that kings, possessing all
that heart can desire, ought to be
void of envy; but the contrary is
seen in their conduct.

9. 'They are jealous of the most
virtuous among their subjects, and
wish their death; while they take
delight in the meanest and basest,
being ever ready to listen to the
tales of slanderers.

10. 'A king, besides, is beyond all
other men inconsistent with
himself. Pay him court in moderation, and he is angry because you
do not show him more respect;

11. 'Show him profound respect, and
he is offended again, because, he
says, you fawn on him.

12. 'But the worst of all is, that he sets
aside the laws of the land, puts

men to death without trial, and subjects women to violence.

13. 'The rule of the many, on the other hand, has, in the first place, the fairest of names, to wit, democracy;

14. 'And further it is free from all the outrages that kings too often commit. In a democracy places are given by lot, the magistrate is answerable for what he does, and measures rest with the commonalty.

15. 'I propose, therefore, that we do away with monarchy, and raise the people to power. For the people are all in all.'

16. Such were the sentiments of Otanes. Megabyzus spoke next, and advised the setting up of an oligarchy:

17. 'In all that Otanes has said to persuade you to put down monarchy,' he observed, 'I fully concur;

18. 'But his recommendation that we should call the people to power seems to me not the best advice.

19. 'For there is nothing so void of understanding, nothing so full of wantonness, as the unwieldy rabble.

20. 'It were folly not to be borne, for men, while seeking to escape the wantonness of a tyrant, to give themselves up to the wantonness of a rude unbridled mob.

21. 'The tyrant, in all his doings, at least knows what he is about, but a mob is altogether devoid of knowledge;

22. 'For how should there be any knowledge in a rabble, untaught, and with no natural sense of what is right and fit?

23. 'It rushes wildly into state affairs with all the fury of a stream swollen in the winter, and confuses everything.

24. 'Let the enemies of Persia be ruled by democracies; but let us choose out from the citizens a certain number of the worthiest, and put the government into their hands.

25. 'For thus both we ourselves shall be among the governors, and power being entrusted to the best men, it is likely that the best counsels will prevail in the state.'

26. After Megabyzus spoke, Darius came forward and said: 'All that Megabyzus said against democracy was well said, I think; but about oligarchy he did not speak advisedly;

27. 'For take these three forms of government – democracy, oligarchy and monarchy – and let them each be at their best, I maintain that monarchy far surpasses the other two.

28. 'What government can possibly be better than that of the very best man in the whole state? The counsels of such a man are like himself, and so he governs the mass of the people to their heart's content;

29. 'While at the same time his measures against evildoers are kept more secret than in other states.

30. 'Whereas in oligarchies, in which men vie with each other in the service of the commonwealth, fierce enmities are apt to arise between man and man, each wishing to be leader, and to carry his own measures;

31. 'Whence violent quarrels come, leading to open strife, often ending in bloodshed. Then monarchy is sure to follow; and this too shows how far that rule surpasses all others.

32. 'Again, in a democracy, it is impossible but that there will be malpractices: which however do not lead to enmities, but to close friendships, which are formed among those engaged in them, who must hold well together to carry out their villainies.

33. 'And so things go on until a man stands forth as champion of the commonalty, and puts down the evildoers.

34. 'Immediately the author of so great a service is admired by all, and from being admired soon comes to be appointed king; so that here too it is plain that monarchy is the best government.

35. 'Lastly, to sum up all in a word, whence, I ask, was it that we got the freedom which we enjoy? Did democracy give it us, or oligarchy, or a monarch?

36. 'As a single man recovered our freedom for us, my argument is that we keep to the rule of one.

37. 'Even apart from this, we ought not to change the laws of our forefathers when they work fairly; for to do so is not well.'

38. Such were the three opinions brought forward at this meeting; the four other Persians voted in favour of the last.

39. Otanes, who wished to give his countrymen a democracy, when he found the decision against him, rose a second time, and said,

40. 'Brother conspirators, it is plain that the king who is to be chosen will be one of ourselves.

41. 'Now, as I have neither a mind to rule nor to be ruled, I shall not enter the lists with you in this matter.

42. 'I withdraw, however, on one condition: none of you shall claim to exercise rule over me or my seed for ever.' The six agreed to these terms, and Otanes withdrew and stood aloof from the contest.

43. And still to this day the family of Otanes continues to be the only free family in Persia;

44. Those who belong to it submit to the rule of the king only so far as they themselves choose; they are bound, however, to observe the laws of the land like the other Persians.

Chapter 33

1. After this the remaining six took counsel together, as to the fairest way of choosing a king:

2. And first, with respect to Otanes, they resolved that it was to be free

to each, whenever he pleased, to enter the palace unannounced, unless the king were in the company of one of his wives;

3. And the king was to be bound to marry into no family excepting those of the conspirators.

4. Concerning the appointment of a king, they resolved the following:

5. They would ride out together next morning into the suburbs of the city, and he whose steed first neighed after the sun was up should have the kingdom.

6. Now Darius had a groom, a sharp-witted knave called Oebares. After the meeting had ended, Darius sent for him, and told him how the king was to be chosen,

7. And said, 'If you have any cleverness, contrive a plan whereby the prize may fall to me.'

8. 'Truly, master,' Oebares answered, 'if it depends on this whether you will be king or no, set your heart at ease, and fear nothing: I have a device which is sure not to fail.'

9. Oebares did as follows: when night came, he took one of the mares, the chief favourite of the horse which Darius rode,

10. And tethering it in the suburb, brought his master's horse to the place;

11. Then, after leading him round and round the mare several times, nearer and nearer at each circuit, he ended by letting them come together.

12. When morning broke, the six

Persians, according to agreement, met together on horseback, and rode out to the suburb.

13. As they went along they neared the spot where the mare was tethered, whereupon the horse of Darius sprang forward and neighed.

14. The five other nobles leaped with one accord from their steeds, and bowed down before him, owning him for their king.

15. Thus was Darius, son of Hystaspes, appointed king; and, except the Arabians, all Asia was subject to him.

16. The Arabians were never subject to the Persians, but had a league of friendship with them from the time when Cambyses invaded Egypt;

17. For had they been unfriendly the Persians could never have made their invasion.

18. And now Darius contracted marriages of the first rank, according to the notions of the Persians:

19. To wit, with two daughters of Cyrus, Atossa and Artystone; of whom Atossa had been twice married before, once to Cambyses, her brother, and once to the Magus, while the other, Artystone, was a virgin.

20. He married also Parmys, daughter of Smerdis, son of Cyrus; and he likewise took to wife the daughter of Otanes, who had made the discovery about the Magus.

21. And now when Darius' power was

established firmly throughout all the kingdoms, the first thing he did was to set up a carving in stone,

22. Which showed a man mounted on a horse, with an inscription in these words following:

23. 'Darius, son of Hystaspes, by aid of his good horse and of his good groom Oebares, got himself the kingdom of the Persians.'

24. Darius arranged his empire into twenty satrapies, reaching from Egypt to Armenia,

25. From the subjected eastern Greeks to India, this last the wealthiest of all the satrapies; and great treasures flowed into his keeping from them.

26. And from the nations that were not in his empire but on its borders he received gifts:

27. From the Ethiopians two choenices of virgin gold, two hundred logs of ebony, five boys and twenty elephant tusks.

28. From the Colchians and their neighbours as far north as the Caucasus he received every five years a hundred boys and a hundred maidens.

29. The Arabs gave him a thousand talents of frankincense every year.

30. All this shows the greatness and wealth of the Persian empire.

Chapter 34

1. And so we come to the period at which Persia's greatness was at its height, having conquered and subjected Asia and Egypt, and spread its dominion across the East;

2. At which time Darius turned his eyes west, towards the happy lands of the Greeks, and proposed to himself to conquer them and all that lay beyond them,

3. And thus to rule all the world according to the Persian way.

4. The immediate prompt for launching this adventure in which the future of the world hung in the balance, was as so often in history, an accident.

5. Leaping to his horse one day, Darius missed his step and fell, injuring his ankle severely, for the bone came out of the socket.

6. The Egyptian doctors about the court attempted to set the injury, but by the violence of their methods made it worse, leaving the king in agony and unable to sleep for five days.

7. Darius asked in his suffering whether there was no one who could help him, whereupon a member of the court said that among those kept prisoner in the palace was a Greek believed to be a notable physician.

8. This was Democedes, who, brought before the king in his rags and fetters, at first tried to deny his skill for fear that if he failed to cure the king he would never again see his beloved Greece.

9. But Darius, suspecting deceit, called for the instruments of

torture to test whether Democedes spoke truly;

10. And at this the Greek confessed that he had some skill, and would try to help Darius.

11. This he successfully did, first by giving the king a concoction that helped him to sleep,

12. And then, in the following weeks, by the gentle Greek arts of manipulating and setting the bones, he soothed the inflamed swelling of the joint and healed its dislocation.

13. Darius had quite lost hope of ever using his foot again, and, being restored, was filled with gratitude.

14. He gave Democedes two sets of golden fetters, which made the Greek ask whether his reward for helping him was to have the sufferings of captivity doubled?

15. Darius was pleased with this speech, and told the eunuchs to take Democedes to see his wives, each of whom plied the Greek with further gifts of gold.

16. Thereafter Democedes dwelt at Susa, dining every day at the king's table, and having everything he wished except the one thing he desired most:

17. Namely, his liberty, so that he could return to his native Greece, which he yearned for.

18. Now one day Atossa, the daughter of Cyrus, once wife to both Cambyses and the usurper Magus, and now wife to Darius, had a boil form on her breast.

19. At first she kept quiet about the sore, but when it burst and spread she sent for Democedes. He said he would make her well if she would grant him whatever he asked,

20. Assuring her that what he asked she would not blush to hear.

21. On these terms he applied his art and soon cured the abcess; and then told Atossa his wish, which was that she should contrive some means for him to return to Greece.

22. She sought to fulfil her promise by addressing Darius as follows, when next she had been summoned to his bed for the night:

23. 'My Lord, it seems strange that with the mighty power that is yours as the foremost ruler of men in the world,

24. 'You sit idle and neither make new conquests nor advance the power of the Persians.

25. 'Surely one so young and rich, with great armies, should undertake some noble achievement to show that Persia is governed by a man.

26. 'Moreover it is good that you should protect your position from enemies within, because idleness in the state breeds revolt.

27. 'Now while you are young you must accomplish some great exploit; for as the body grows in strength the mind too ripens; and as the body ages the mind's powers decay, till at last both body and mind are too dull for anything.'

28. Darius replied, 'Dear lady, you have given voice to the very thoughts in my mind.

29. 'I propose to build a bridge which shall join our continent to the other, Asia to Europe, and carry war into Scythia. Very soon what you suggest I shall do.'

30. But Atossa said, 'Leave Scythia for a while; you might conquer the Scythians any time.

31. 'Take war first into Greece, whose states are famed for their climate and good life.

32. 'I long to be served by some of those Lacedaemonian maids of whom I have heard so much. I want also Argive, and Athenian, and Corinthian women.

33. 'You have here in the court Democedes, who can tell you better than anyone whatever you need to know about Greece, and can serve you as a guide.'

34. 'Since it is your wish that we first try the valour of the Greeks,' said Darius, 'we shall do so.

35. 'I will straight away send some Persians to spy out the land, in company with Democedes;

36. 'And when they have learned all, they can give us a more perfect knowledge of the people and the territories.

37. 'Then I will begin the war.'

Chapter 35

1. Having spoken, Darius wasted no time between words and deed, but when dawn broke he summoned fifteen Persians of note, and told them to take Democedes as their guide and explore the sea coasts of Greece.

2. And he instructed them to bring Democedes back with them, on no account allowing him to escape.

3. Then he called Democedes, and told him what was afoot; and offered him treasures for himself,

4. And a ship full of gold and precious things to take as gifts to his father and brothers in Greece,

5. Both bounties on condition that he would promise to return to Persia when the work of surveying was done.

6. Democedes considered that Darius was trying his loyalty by this offer, and replied that he would leave behind in Susa the treasures offered to himself, to be enjoyed on his return;

7. But that he would accept the gracious gifts for his family.

8. Thereupon Darius sent him and the chosen Persians away to the coast, to Sidon in Phoenicia,

9. Where they fitted out two triremes and a trading vessel loaded with valuable merchandise, and set sail for Greece.

10. The small fleet sailed along the shores of Greece, the crews making careful notes of all they saw, and in this way explored the greater part of the country until at last they reached Tarentum in Italy.

11. There Democedes told his story to

its king, Aristophilides, and what the Persian ships were doing;

12. So the king ordered the rudders to be removed from the Persian ships and arrested their crews as spies, and allowed Democedes to hasten to Crotona, his native city.

13. When Democedes had left, Aristophilides released the Persians and gave them their rudders.

14. Immediately the Persians sailed to Crotona in pursuit of Democedes, and found him in the marketplace, and laid hands on him to drag him to the ships.

15. Some of the Crotoniats, who greatly feared the power of the Persians, were willing to give him up;

16. But others resisted, held Democedes fast, and even struck the Persians with their walking sticks.

17. They, on their part, kept crying out, 'Men of Crotona, beware what you do. It is the king's runaway slave that you are rescuing.

18. 'Do you think Darius will tamely submit to such insults? Do you think that if you carry off the man from us, it will go well with you hereafter?

19. 'Will you not rather be the first persons we will attack? Your city will be the first we burn, and you inhabitants will be led into slavery.'

20. The Crotoniats did not listen to these warnings. Instead they

rescued Democedes and seized the trading ship which the Persians had brought from Phoenicia.

21. Thus robbed, and having lost their guide, the Persians abandoned hope of exploring the rest of Greece, and set sail for Asia.

22. They were delayed by shipwreck on their way, along the coast of Iapygia, but eventually reached Susa and told Darius what had happened.

23. These were the first Persians ever to come to Greece from Asia, sent to spy out the land, and to prepare the way for the invasion of Greece by Persia.

Chapter 36

1. Darius was not slow to respond to the defection of Democedes and the insults of the Crotoniats. First he besieged Samos, and his reason for attacking it first was this.

2. At the time when Cambyses, son of Cyrus, marched against Egypt, vast numbers of Greeks flocked to follow his conquests;

3. Some, as might have been expected, to push their trade; others, to serve in his army; others again, merely to see the land.

4. Among these last was Syloson, son of Aeaces, and brother of Polycrates, at that time an exile from Samos but later its ruler.

5. This Syloson, during his stay in Egypt, met with a singular piece of good fortune.

6. He happened one day to put on a

scarlet cloak, and thus attired went into the marketplace at Memphis,

7. When no less a person than Darius, who was then one of Cambyses' bodyguards, and therefore not at that time a man of great account,

8. Saw him, and taking a strong liking to the cloak, went up and offered to purchase it.

9. Syloson perceived how anxious he was, and by a lucky inspiration answered: 'There is no price at which I would sell my cloak;

10. 'But I will give it to you for nothing, seeing that you like it so much.' Darius thanked him warmly, and accepted the garment.

11. Poor Syloson felt at the time that he had fooled away his cloak in a very simple manner; but afterwards, when Darius became king,

12. Syloson learnt that the person to whom the crown had come was the very man who had coveted his cloak in Egypt, and to whom he had freely given it.

13. So he made his way to Susa, and seating himself at the portal of the royal palace, gave out that he was a benefactor of the king.

14. Then the doorkeeper went and told Darius. Amazed at what he heard, the king said to himself, 'What Greek can have been my benefactor, or to which of them do I owe anything, so lately as I have got the kingdom?

15. 'Scarcely more than one or two have been here since I came to the throne. Nor do I remember that I am in the debt of any Greek.

16. 'However, bring him in, and let me hear what he means by his boast.'

17. So the doorkeeper ushered Syloson into the presence, and the interpreters asked him who he was, and what he had done that he should call himself a benefactor of the king.

18. Then Syloson told the story of the cloak, and said that it was he who had made Darius the present.

19. Hereupon Darius exclaimed, 'O! you most generous of men, are you indeed he who, when I had no power at all, gave me something, albeit little?

20. 'Truly the favour is as great as a very grand present would be nowadays.

21. 'I will therefore give you in return gold and silver without stint, that you may never repent of having rendered a service to Darius, son of Hystaspes.'

22. 'Do not give me silver and gold, O king,' replied Syloson, 'but restore to me Samos, my native land, and let that be your gift to me.

23. 'It belongs now to a slave of my family, who, when Oroetes put my brother Polycrates to death, became its master.

24. 'Give me Samos, I beg; but give it unharmed, with no bloodshed, and no enslavement of its people.'

25. When he heard this, Darius sent off an army under Otanes, one of

the seven, with orders to accomplish all that Syloson had desired. Otanes went down to the coast and made ready to cross over.

26. The government of Samos was at this time held by Maeandrius, son of Maeandrius, whom Polycrates had appointed as his deputy.

27. This person conceived the wish to act like the justest of men, but it was not allowed him to do so. On receiving tidings of the death of Polycrates, he assembled all the citizens, and spoke to them as follows:

28. 'You know that the sceptre of Polycrates, and all his power, has passed into my hands, and if I choose I may rule over you.

29. 'But what I condemn in another I will, if I may, avoid myself. I never approved the ambition of Polycrates to lord it over men as good as himself, nor looked with favour on any of those who have done the like.

30. 'Therefore I lay down my office, and proclaim equal rights.

31. 'All that I claim in return is six talents from the treasury of Polycrates, and a quiet life for myself and my descendants for ever.'

32. One of the leading Samians, by name Telesarchus, rose up and said, 'As if you were fit to rule us, base-born and rascal as you are!

33. 'Think rather of accounting for the monies which you have spent since being given the power.'

34. Maeandrius, therefore, feeling sure that if he laid down the sovereign power someone else would become tyrant in his place, gave up the thought of relinquishing it.

35. Withdrawing to the citadel, he sent for the chief men one by one, under pretence of showing them his accounts, and as fast as they came arrested them and put them in irons.

36. Soon afterwards Maeandrius fell sick: whereupon Lycaretus, one of his brothers, thinking that he was going to die, and wishing to secure the throne for himself more easily, killed all the prisoners. It seemed that the Samians did not choose to be a free people.

37. When the Persians whose business it was to restore Syloson reached Samos, not a man was found to lift up his hand against them.

38. Maeandrius and his partisans expressed themselves willing to quit the island on certain terms, and these terms were agreed by Otanes.

Chapter 37

1. After the treaty was made, the most distinguished of the Persians had their thrones brought, and seated themselves opposite the citadel.

2. Now Maeandrius had a hotheaded brother, Charilaus by name, whom he had emprisoned for some offence:

3. This man heard what was going

on, and peering through his bars, saw the Persians sitting peacefully on their seats,

4. Whereupon he exclaimed aloud, and said he must speak with Maeandrius.

5. When this was reported to him, Maeandrius gave orders that Charilaus should be released from prison and brought to him.

6. No sooner did he arrive than Charilaus began reviling his brother, and strove to persuade him to attack the Persians.

7. 'You mean-minded man,' he said, 'you can keep your brother chained in a dungeon, but when the Persians drive you from power, you look meekly on, though they might so easily be subdued.

8. 'If you, however, are too afraid, lend me your soldiers, and I will make them pay dearly for their coming here. I engage too to send you first safe out of the island.'

9. Maeandrius gave consent, not because he was so foolish as to imagine that his forces could overcome those of the Persians, but because he was jealous of Syloson, and did not wish him to get so quietly an unharmed city.

10. He desired therefore to rouse the anger of the Persians against Samos, so that he might deliver it up to Syloson with its power at the lowest possible ebb;

11. For he knew well that if the Persians met with a disaster they would be furious against the Samians,

12. While he himself felt secure of a retreat at any time that he liked, since he had a secret passage underground leading from the citadel to the sea.

13. Maeandrius accordingly took ship and sailed away from Samos; and Charilaus, having armed all the mercenaries, threw open the gates, and fell upon the Persians.

14. The Persians expected no danger, since they supposed that all was peacefully settled by treaty.

15. At the first onslaught therefore all the Persians of most note, men who were in the habit of using litters, were slain by the mercenaries.

16. The rest of the army quickly came to the rescue, defeated the mercenaries and drove them back into the citadel.

17. Then Otanes, the general, when he saw the calamity which had befallen the Persians, made up his mind to forget Darius' orders,

18. Which had been 'not to kill or enslave a single Samian, but to deliver up the island unharmed to Syloson',

19. And gave the word to his army that they should slay the Samians, both men and boys, wherever they could find them.

20. Upon this some of his troops laid siege to the citadel, while others began the massacre, killing all they

met, some outside, some inside the buildings.

21. So the Persians reduced Samos, and delivered it up to Syloson, emptied of its men.

22. Maeandrius fled from Samos to Lacedaemon, and took there all the riches he had brought away, after which he acted as follows.

23. Having placed upon his board all the gold and silver vessels that he had, and bade his servants to employ themselves in cleaning them,

24. He himself went and entered into conversation with Cleomenes, son of Anaxandridas, king of Sparta, and as they talked, brought him along to his house.

25. There Cleomenes, seeing the plate, was filled with wonder and astonishment;

26. Whereon the other begged that he would carry home with him any of the vessels that he liked.

27. Maeandrius said this two or three times; but Cleomenes here displayed surpassing honesty.

28. He refused the gift, and thinking that if Maeandrius made the same offers to others he would get the aid he sought, the Spartan king went straight to the ephors and told them,

29. 'It would be best for Sparta that the Samian stranger should be sent away from the Peloponnese;

30. 'For otherwise he might persuade himself or some other Spartan to be base.'

31. The ephors took his advice, and let Maeandrius know by a herald that he must leave the city.

Chapter 38

1. Not long after the defeat of the Samian rebellion Otanes decided to repeople the city. He did this as follows.

2. At the time that the army under Otanes sailed for Samos, the Babylonians revolted, having made every preparation for defence.

3. During the time that Smerdis the Magian was king, and while the seven were conspiring, the Babylonians had profited by the troubles,

4. And had made themselves ready for a siege, no one noticing what they were doing.

5. At last when the time came for rebelling openly, they first set apart their mothers, and then each man chose besides out of his whole household one woman, whichever he pleased;

6. These alone were allowed to live, while all the rest were brought to one place and strangled.

7. The women chosen were kept to make bread for the men; while the others were strangled so that they would not consume the stores.

8. When news reached Darius of what had happened, he drew together all his power, and marched straight upon Babylon, laying siege to it.

9. The Babylonians did not care

about his siege, being so well prepared. Mounting upon their battlements they jeered at Darius and his mighty host.

10. One even shouted to them and said, 'Why do you sit there, Persians? Why do you not go home? Till mules foal you will not take our city.'

11. This was by a Babylonian who thought that a mule would never foal.

12. Now when a year and seven months had passed, Darius and his army were quite wearied, unable to find any way to take the city.

13. All stratagems and arts had been used, even the means by which Cyrus conquered the place.

14. At last, in the twentieth month, Zopyrus, son of Megabyzus who was among the seven men that overthrew the Magus,

15. Hit upon a radical and ingenious plan to overthrow Babylon, having reviewed all other ways of capturing the city.

16. His plan was to maim himself and go over to the enemy, pretending to have been savagely punished by Darius for a misdemeanour, and to be rebelling against him therefore.

17. So he cut off his own nose and ears, and then, clipping his hair close and flogging himself with a scourge, he came in this plight before Darius.

18. The king was stirred to wrath at the sight of a man of Zopyrus' lofty rank in such a condition;

19. Leaping down from his throne, he exclaimed aloud, and asked Zopyrus who it was that had disfigured him, and what he had done to be so treated.

20. Zopyrus answered, 'There is not a man in the world but you, O king, that could reduce me to such a plight;

21. 'No stranger's hands have wrought this work on me, but my own only. I maimed myself in order to help us defeat the Assyrians.'

22. Replied Darius, 'Surely you have gone out of your mind! How will your disfigurement induce the enemy to yield one day the sooner?'

23. Zopyrus answered, 'If I had told you what I planned on doing, you would not have allowed me; as it is, I kept my own counsel.

24. 'Now, therefore, we shall take Babylon. I will desert to the enemy as I am, and when I get into their city I will tell them that it is by you I have been thus treated.

25. 'I think they will believe my words, and entrust me with a command of troops.

26. 'You, for your part, must wait till the tenth day after I have entered the town,

27. 'And then place near to the gates of Semiramis a detachment of the army, troops for whose loss you will care little, a thousand men.

28. 'Wait, after that, seven days, and post another detachment, two

thousand strong, at the Nineveh gates;

29. 'Then let twenty days pass, and at the end of that time station near the Chaldaean gates a body of four thousand.

30. 'Let neither these nor the former troops be armed with any weapons but their swords.

31. 'After the twenty days are over, bid the whole army attack the city on every side,

32. 'And put two bodies of Persians, one at the Belian, the other at the Cissian gates;

33. 'For I expect, that, on account of my successes, the Babylonians will entrust everything, even the keys of their gates, to me.

34. 'Then it will be for me and our Persians to do the rest.'

Chapter 39

1. When this plan was agreed Zopyrus fled towards the gates of the town, often looking back, to give himself the air of a deserter.

2. The lookouts on the towers, observing him, hastened down, and setting one of the gates slightly ajar,

3. Questioned him who he was, and on what errand he had come. He replied that he was Zopyrus, and had deserted to them from the Persians.

4. When the doorkeepers heard this they took him at once to the magistrates. Introduced into the

assembly, he began to bewail his misfortunes,

5. Telling them that Darius had maltreated him in the way they could see, only because he had given advice that the siege should be raised, since there seemed no hope of taking the city.

6. 'And now,' he said, 'my coming to you, Babylonians, will prove the greatest gain that you could possibly receive, while to Darius and the Persians it will be the severest loss.

7. 'Truly, he by whom I have been so mutilated shall not escape unpunished. And all the paths of his counsels are known to me.'

8. The Babylonians, seeing a Persian of such exalted rank in so grievous a plight, his nose and ears cut off, his body red with marks of scourging and with blood,

9. Had no suspicion but that he spoke the truth, and was really come to help them. They were ready, therefore, to grant him anything he asked;

10. And on his requesting a command, entrusted to him a body of troops, with whose help he proceeded to do as he had arranged with Darius.

11. On the tenth day after his flight he led out his detachment, and surrounding the thousand men, whom Darius according to agreement had sent, he slew them all.

12. Then the Babylonians, seeing that his deeds were as brave as his

words, were beyond measure pleased, and set no bounds to their trust.

13. He waited, however, and when the next period agreed on had elapsed, again with a band of picked men he went out and defeated the two thousand.

14. After this second exploit, his praise was in all mouths. Once more, however, he waited till the interval appointed had gone by,

15. And then leading the troops to the place where the four thousand were, he put them also to the sword.

16. This last victory gave the finishing stroke to his power; the rejoicing Babylonians committed to him the command of their whole army, and put the keys of their city into his hands.

17. Darius now, still keeping to the plan agreed upon, attacked the walls on every side, whereupon Zopyrus played out the remainder of his stratagem.

18. While the Babylonians, crowding to the walls, did their best to resist the Persian assault, he threw open the Cissian and the Belian gates, and admitted the Persian troops.

19. Such of the Babylonians as witnessed the treachery, took refuge in the citadel; the rest, who did not see it, kept at their posts, till at last they too learnt that they were betrayed.

20. Thus was Babylon taken for the second time. Darius tore down the wall and all the gates; for Cyrus had done neither when he took Babylon.

21. He then chose three thousand of the leading citizens, and caused them to be crucified, while he allowed the remainder still to inhabit the city.

22. Further, wishing to prevent the race of the Babylonians from becoming extinct, he provided wives for them in the room of those whom they had strangled to save their stores.

23. These he levied from the nations bordering Babylonia, who were each required to send a number to Babylon, that in all there were collected no fewer than fifty thousand women.

24. It is from these women that the Babylonians of later times are sprung.

25. As for Zopyrus, he was considered by Darius to have surpassed, in the greatness of his achievements, all other Persians, whether of former or later times,

26. Except only Cyrus, with whom no Persian ever yet dared to compare. Darius, as the story goes, would often say that he had rather Zopyrus were unmaimed, than be master of twenty more Babylons.

27. And he honoured Zopyrus greatly; every year he presented him with all the gifts held in most esteem among Persians;

28. He gave him likewise the

government of Babylon for life, free from tribute, and many other favours.

Chapter 40

1. Now Darius turned his attention to war against the Scythians, which was his first step in carrying his ambition of conquest towards Europe.
2. He dispatched messengers across his empire summoning troops, ships and supplies, and ordering the building of a bridge across the Bosphorus, to connect Asia to Europe.
3. While he was doing so his brother Artabanus came to entreat him not to undertake this expedition, because of the great difficulty of attacking Scythia.
4. But Darius was determined to proceed, and when preparations were complete he marched with his army from Susa.
5. A certain Persian named Oeobazus, the father of three sons, all of whom were to accompany the army,
6. Came and begged the king that he would allow one of his sons to remain with him.
7. Darius answered, as if he regarded him in the light of a friend who had urged a moderate request, that he would allow them all to remain.
8. Oeobazus was overjoyed, expecting that all his children would be excused from service; the king, however, ordered his attendants to take all three sons of Oeobazus and put them to death.
9. Thus they were all left behind, as the king had promised.
10. When Darius reached the territory of Chalcedon on the shores of the Bosphorus, where the bridge had been made, he took ship and sailed to the Cyanean islands.
11. He took his seat on a high point and surveyed the Pontus, which is indeed well worthy of consideration.
12. There is no other sea so wonderful: it extends in length eleven thousand one hundred furlongs, and its breadth, at the widest part, is three thousand three hundred furlongs.
13. The mouth is only four furlongs wide; and this strait, called the Bosphorus, and across which the bridge of Darius had been thrown, is a hundred and twenty furlongs in length, reaching from the Euxine to the Propontis.
14. The Propontis is five hundred furlongs across, and fourteen hundred long. Its waters flow into the Hellespont, the length of which is four hundred furlongs, and the width no more than seven.
15. The Hellespont opens into the wide sea called the Aegean.
16. The way these distances have been measured is the following. In a long day a vessel generally accomplishes about seventy thousand fathoms, in the night sixty thousand.
17. Now from the mouth of the

Pontus to the River Phasis, which is the extreme length of this sea, is a voyage of nine days and eight nights, which makes the distance eleven thousand one hundred furlongs.

18. Again, from Sindica to Themiscyra on the River Thermodon, where the Pontus is wider than at any other place, is a sail of three days and two nights;

19. Which makes three thousand three hundred furlongs. Such is the plan on which thoughtful men have measured the Pontus, the Bosphorus and the Hellespont.

20. After he had finished his survey Darius sailed back to the bridge, which had been constructed for him by Mandrocles, a Samian.

21. He likewise surveyed the Bosphorus, and erected on its shores two pillars of white marble, inscribed with the names of all the nations which formed his army, on one pillar Greek, on the other Assyrian characters.

22. This army was drawn from all the nations under Darius' sway; the whole amount, without counting the naval forces, was seven hundred thousand men, including cavalry. The fleet consisted of six hundred ships.

23. Darius was so pleased with Mandrocles' bridge that he not only gave him all the customary presents, but ten of every kind.

24. Mandrocles, in return, commissioned a picture to be painted showing the whole of the bridge, with King Darius sitting in a seat of honour, and his army crossing over.

25. Darius then passed into Europe, while he ordered the Ionians to enter the Pontus and sail to the mouth of the Ister, in later times called Danube.

26. There he bade them throw a bridge across that stream and to await his coming. The Ionians, Aeolians and Hellespontians were the nations which furnished the chief strength of his navy.

27. So the fleet, threading the Cyanean Isles, proceeded straight to the Ister, and, mounting the river to the point where its channels separate, a distance of two days' voyage from the sea, yoked the neck of the stream.

28. Meantime Darius, who had crossed the Bosphorus by the bridge, marched through Thrace; and happening upon the sources of the River Tearus, pitched his camp and made a stay of three days.

29. This river, famed for its health-giving properties, charmed him so, that he caused a pillar to be erected in this place also, with an inscription saying:

30. 'The fountains of the Tearus afford the best and most beautiful water of all rivers:

31. 'They were visited, on his march into Scythia, by the best and most beautiful of men, Darius, son of

Hystaspes, king of the Persians, and of the whole continent of Asia.'

32. Marching thence, he came to a second river, the Artiscus, which flows through the country of the Odrysians.

33. Here he fixed upon a certain spot, where every one of his soldiers should throw a stone as he passed by.

34. When his orders were obeyed, Darius continued his march, leaving behind him great hills formed by the stones cast by his troops; this was the means to guide their way back.

35. Before arriving at the Ister, the first people he subdued were the Getae.

36. The Thracians of Salmydessus, and those who dwelt above the cities of Apollonia and Mesembria, those called Scyrmiadae and Nipsaeans, gave themselves up to Darius without a struggle;

37. But the Getae obstinately defended themselves, and were forthwith enslaved, notwithstanding that they are the noblest as well as the most just of all the Thracian tribes.

Chapter 41

1. When Darius' land forces reached the Ister and crossed it, he ordered the Ionians to break the bridge, and to follow him with the whole naval force in his land march.

2. They were about to obey his command when the general of the Mytilenaeans, Coes son of Erxander, respectfully addressed him as follows:

3. 'Sire, you are about to attack a country no part of which is cultivated, and in which there is not a single inhabited city.

4. 'Keep this bridge as it is, and leave those who built it to guard it. So if we succeed against the Scythians, we can return by this route;

5. 'But if we fail to find them, our retreat will still be secure.

6. 'For though I have no doubt that we will vanquish the Scythians in battle,

7. 'My dread is that we will be unable to find them, for they will withdraw and hide;

8. 'And then we will suffer much loss while we wander about their territory.'

9. The advice of Coes pleased Darius highly, who replied, 'When I am safe home again in my palace, be sure to come to me, and with good deeds I will recompense you for this good advice.'

10. Having so said, the king took a leather thong, and tying sixty knots in it, called together the Ionian leaders and said,

11. 'My former commands to you concerning the bridge are now withdrawn.

12. 'Look at this thong: from the time that I leave you to march into Scythia, untie one of the knots each day.

13. 'If I do not return before the last

knot is untied, sail home. Meanwhile, understand that you are to guard the bridge with all care.'

Chapter 42

1. The Scythians, apprehending the approach of such a mighty army under the command of the famous Darius, knew they were not strong enough by themselves to fight him.

2. So they sent envoys to the neighbouring nations, and summoned together the kings of the Tauri, the Agathyrsi, the Neuri, the Androphagi, the Melanchaeni, the Geloni, the Budini and the Sauromatae.

3. Each of these tribes had their distinctive customs and histories, of which the most notable are those of the Sauromatae.

4. It is reported that when the Greeks fought with the Amazons in former times, defeating them at the battle of Thermodon,

5. They took all those they had captured and sailed with them, intending to return with them to Greece.

6. But these warrior women, whom the Scythians call 'manslayers', rose up against the crews of the ships and massacred them.

7. But not knowing anything of ships and the sea, of rudders, oars or sails, the Amazons were carried where the wind and waves directed,

8. Beaching at last on the shores of Palus Maeotis, the country of the free Scythians.

9. Here they went ashore, and after finding horses, they mounted them and fell to plundering the Scythian territory.

10. The Scythians could not tell what to make of them; their dress, language, the nation itself were wholly unknown to them;

11. Nor where they had come from. Imagining that they were young men all of the same age, the Scythians went out against them and fought a battle.

12. Some of the bodies of the slain fell into their hands, whereupon they discovered the truth.

13. Accordingly they deliberated, and decided not to kill any more of them, but to send a detachment of their youngest men in about equal numbers to the Amazons,

14. With orders to camp near them, and do as they saw them do; but not to give battle, instead retreating when the Amazons attacked, and following them when they moved off.

15. This they did on account of a strong desire to obtain children from such notable women.

16. The Amazons soon found that the Scythians had not come to do them any harm; and so they on their part ceased to offer them any molestation.

17. And now day after day the camps approached nearer to one another; both parties led the same life,

18. Neither having anything but their arms and horses, so that they were forced to support themselves by hunting.

19. At last an incident brought two of them together; the man easily gained the good graces of the woman,

20. Who bade him by signs (for they did not understand each other's language) to bring a friend the next day to the spot where they had met, promising on her part to bring with her another woman.

21. He did so, and the woman kept her word. When the rest of the youths heard what had taken place, they also sought and gained the favour of the other Amazons.

22. The two camps were then joined in one, the Amazons living with the Scythians as their wives;

23. And the men were unable to learn the tongue of the women, but the women soon caught up the tongue of the men.

24. When they could thus understand one another, the Scythians addressed the Amazons as follows:

25. 'We have parents, and properties; let us give up this mode of life, and return to our nation, and live with them.

26. 'You shall be our wives there no less than here, and we promise you to have no others.'

27. But the Amazons said, 'We could not live with your women; our customs are quite different from theirs.

28. 'To draw the bow, to hurl the javelin, to ride the horse, these are our arts; of womanly employments we know nothing.

29. 'Your women, on the contrary, do none of these things; but stay at home in their waggons, engaged in womanish tasks,

30. 'And never go out to hunt, or to do anything. We should never agree together. But if you truly wish to keep us as your wives, and would conduct yourselves with strict justice towards us,

31. 'Go you home to your parents, bid them give you your inheritance, and then come back to us, and let us and you live together by ourselves.'

32. The youths approved this advice, and followed it. They went and got the portion of goods which fell to them, returned with it, and rejoined their wives,

33. Who then addressed them in these words following: 'We are ashamed, and afraid to live in the country where we now are.

34. 'Not only have we stolen you from your fathers, but we have damaged Scythia by our ravages.

35. 'As you like us for wives, grant the request we make of you. Let us leave this country together, and go and dwell beyond the Tanais.' Again the youths complied.

36. Crossing the Tanais they journeyed eastward a distance of three days' march from that stream, and again northward a distance of

three days' march from the Palus
Maeotis.

37. Here they came to the country
where they now live, and took up
their abode in it.

38. The women of the Sauromatae
have continued from that day to
the present to observe their
ancient customs,

39. Frequently hunting on horseback
with their husbands, sometimes
even unaccompanied; in war
taking the field; and wearing the
same dress as the men.

40. The Sauromatae speak the
language of Scythia, but have
never talked it correctly, because
the Amazons learnt it imperfectly
at the first.

41. Their marriage law lays it down
that no girl shall wed till she has
killed a man in battle.

42. Sometimes it happens that a
woman dies unmarried at an
advanced age, having never been
able in her whole lifetime to fulfil
the condition.

Chapter 43

1. The envoys of the Scythians, in the
assembly of the kings of the
neighbouring nations, told them
that the mighty Persian king,

2. After subduing the whole of the
Asian continent, had built a bridge
over the strait of the Bosphorus,
and crossed into Europe,

3. Where he had reduced the
Thracians, and was now making a

bridge over the Ister, with the aim
of bringing under his sway all the
rest of Europe also.

4. 'Do not stand aloof from the great
struggle now pending,' they said,
'but make common cause with us,
and together let us meet the
enemy.

5. 'If you refuse, we must yield to the
pressure, and either quit our
country or make terms with the
invaders. For what else would be
left for us to do, if we are without
your aid?

6. 'The blow will not light on you
more gently if you do not resist.
The Persian comes against you no
less than against us:

7. 'And will not be content, after we
are conquered, to leave you in
peace. We can bring strong proof
of what we here advance.

8. 'Had the Persian leader indeed
come to avenge the wrongs which
he suffered at our hands when we
enslaved some of his people, and
to war on us only,

9. 'He would have been bound to
march straight upon Scythia,
without molesting any nation by
the way. Then it would have been
plain to all that Scythia alone was
aimed at.

10. 'But what has his conduct been?
From the moment of his entrance
into Europe, he has subjugated
without exception every nation
that lay in his path.

11. 'All the tribes of the Thracians
have been brought under his sway,

and among them even our next neighbours, the Getae.'

12. The assembled princes, after hearing the Scythians, deliberated. At the end opinion was divided: the kings of the Geloni, Budini and Sauromatae were of accord, and pledged assistance to the Scythians;

13. But the Agathyrsian and Neurian princes, together with the sovereigns of the Androphagi, the Melanchaeni and the Tauri, replied as follows:

14. 'If you had not been the first to wrong the Persians, and begin the war, we should have thought the request you make just; we should then have complied with your wishes, and joined our arms with yours.

15. 'Now, however, the case stands thus: you, independently of us, invaded the land of the Persians, and so long as you could, lorded it over them:

16. 'Now that they have power, they are come to do to you the like.

17. 'We, on our part, did no wrong to these men in the former war, and will not be the first to commit wrong now.

18. 'If they invade our land, and begin aggressions upon us, we will not suffer them; but, till we see this come to pass, we will remain at home.

19. 'For we believe that the Persians are not come to attack us, but to punish those who are guilty of first injuring them.'

20. On hearing this reply the Scythians resolved that they would not openly venture any pitched battles with the Persians,

21. But would retire before them, driving off their herds, choking up all the wells and springs as they retreated, and leaving the whole country bare of forage.

22. They divided themselves into three bands, one of which, commanded by Scopasis, was joined by the Sauromatae,

23. And if the Persians advanced in the direction of the Tanais, they planned to retreat along the shores of the Palus Maeotis and make for that river; while if the Persians retired, they should at once pursue and harass them.

24. The two other divisions, the principal one under the command of Idanthyrsus, and the third, of which Taxacis was king, were to unite in one,

25. And joined by the detachments of the Geloni and Budini, were similarly to keep a distance of one day's march from the Persians, falling back as they advanced, and doing the same as the others.

26. And first, they were to take the direction of the nations which had refused to join the alliance, and were to draw the war upon them:

27. So that, if they would not of their own free will engage in the struggle, they would by these means be drawn into it.

28. Afterwards, it was agreed that they

should retire into their own land, and, should it on deliberation appear to them expedient, join battle with the enemy.

29. When these measures had been decided, the Scythians went out to meet the army of Darius, sending out in front the fleetest of their horsemen as scouts.

30. Their waggons with their women and children, and all their cattle, were made to precede them in their retreat, and departed, with orders to keep marching, without change of course, to the north.

Chapter 44

1. The scouts of the Scythians found the Persian host three days' march from the Ister,

2. And immediately took the lead of them at the distance of a day's march, encamping from time to time, and destroying all that grew on the ground.

3. The Persians no sooner caught sight of the Scythian horse than they pursued them, while the enemy retired before them.

4. The pursuit of the Persians was directed towards the single division of the Scythian army, and thus their line of march was eastward towards the Tanais.

5. The Scythians crossed that river and the Persians pursued them. In this way they passed through the country of the Sauromatae, and entered that of the Budini.

6. As long as the march of the Persian army lay through the countries of the Scythians and Sauromatae, there was nothing they could damage, the land being waste and barren;

7. But on entering the territories of the Budini, they came upon a wooden fortress, which was deserted by its inhabitants.

8. The Persians burned it down, then pressed on after the retreating Scythians, till, having traversed the entire country of the Budini, they reached the desert, which extends a distance of seven days' journey above the Budinian territory.

9. When Darius reached the desert he paused, halting his army upon the Oarus. Here he built eight large forts, at an equal distance from one another, sixty furlongs apart.

10. While he was thus occupied, the Scythians he had been following made a circuit by the higher regions, and re-entered Scythia.

11. On their complete disappearance, Darius left his forts half finished, and returned towards the west.

12. He imagined that the Scythians he had seen were the entire nation, and that they had fled in that direction.

13. He now quickened his march, and entering Scythia, fell in with the two combined divisions of the Scythian army, and instantly gave them chase.

14. They kept to their plan of

retreating before him at the distance of a day's march;

15. And they led his hot pursuit of them into the territories of the nations that had refused to become their allies, first into the country of the Melanchaeni.

16. Great disturbance was caused among this people by the invasion first of the Scythians and then of the Persians.

17. So, having harassed them after this sort, the Scythians led the way into the land of the Androphagi, with the same result as before;

18. And thence passed onwards into Neuris, where their coming likewise spread dismay among the inhabitants.

19. Still retreating they approached the Agathyrsi; but this people, which had witnessed the flight and terror of their neighbours, did not wait for the Scythians to invade them,

20. But sent a herald to forbid them to cross their borders, and to forewarn them that, if they made the attempt, it would be resisted by force of arms.

21. The Agathyrsi then proceeded to the frontier, to defend their country against the invaders.

22. As for the other nations, the Melanchaeni, the Androphagi, and the Neuri, instead of defending themselves, when the Scythians and Persians overran their lands, they forgot their threats and fled away in confusion to the deserts lying towards the north.

23. The Scythians, when the Agathyrsi forbade them to enter their country, refrained; and led the Persians back from the Neurian district into their own land.

24. This had gone on so long, and seemed so interminable, that Darius at last sent a horseman to Idanthyrsus, the Scythian king, with the following message:

25. 'You strange man, why do you keep flying before me, when there are two things you might do so easily?

26. 'If you think you can resist my arms, cease your wanderings and come, let us engage in battle.

27. 'Or if you are conscious that my strength is greater than yours, even so you should stop running away;

28. 'You have but to recognise me as lord by bringing me earth and water, and come at once to a conference.'

29. To this message Idanthyrsus, the Scythian king, replied, 'This is my way, Persian. I never fear men or fly from them.

30. 'I have not done so in times past, nor do I now fly from you. There is nothing new or strange in what I do; I only follow my common mode of life in peaceful years.

31. 'Now I will tell you why I do not at once join battle with you. We Scythians have neither towns nor cultivated lands, which might induce us, through fear of their being taken or ravaged, to be in any hurry to fight with you.

32. 'If, however, you must needs come to blows with us speedily, look you now, there are our fathers' tombs; seek them out, and attempt to meddle with them; then you shall see whether or no we will fight with you.

33. 'Till you do this, we shall not join battle, unless it pleases us. As for lords, I acknowledge only myself.

34. 'Earth and water, the tribute you demand, I do not send, but you will soon receive more suitable gifts.

35. 'Last of all, in return for your trying to call yourself my lord, I say to you, "Go weep."'

Chapter 45

1. When the Scythian kings heard the name of slavery they were filled with rage,

2. And dispatched the division under Scopasis to which the Sauromatae were joined,

3. With orders that they should seek a conference with the Ionians, who had been left at the Ister to guard the bridge.

4. Meanwhile the Scythians who remained behind resolved no longer to lead the Persians hither and thither about their country,

5. But to fall upon them whenever they should be at their meals.

6. So they waited till such times, and then did as they had determined.

7. In these combats the Scythian horse always put to flight the horse of the Persians;

8. These last, however, when routed, fell back upon their infantry, who never failed to afford them support;

9. While the Scythians, on their side, as soon as they had driven the horse in, retired again, for fear of the Persian infantry.

10. By night too the Scythians made many similar attacks.

11. A strange thing that greatly advantaged the Persians, and equally disadvantaged the Scythians in their assaults, was the braying of the asses and the appearance of the mules.

12. For the land of the Scythians produced neither ass nor mule, by reason of the cold.

13. So, when the asses brayed, they frightened the Scythian cavalry; and often, in the middle of a charge, the horses would take fright at the noise made by the asses and wheel round, pricking up their ears, and showing astonishment.

14. And thus for a time a stalemate ensued, except that the Persian host suffered attrition, being in a foreign land whose rulers had made waste before them.

15. And little by little the Persians grew worried at their vulnerable position, with dwindling supplies;

16. And they began to take counsel with themselves what they should do.

Chapter 46

1. The Scythians, when they perceived signs that the Persians were becoming alarmed, took steps to induce them not to quit Scythia,

2. In the hope, if they stayed, of inflicting on them the greater injury, when their supplies should altogether fail.

3. To effect this, they would leave some of their cattle exposed with the herdsmen, while they themselves moved away to a distance.

4. The Persians would make a foray, and take the beasts, whereupon they would be highly elated.

5. They did this several times, until at last Darius was at his wits' end;

6. And then the Scythian princes, understanding how matters stood, dispatched a herald to the Persian camp with presents for the king,

7. Which were eight things: a bird, a mouse, a frog and five arrows.

8. The Persians asked the bearer to tell them what these gifts might mean, but he made answer that he had no orders except to deliver them, and return again with all speed.

9. If the Persians were wise, he added, they would find out the meaning for themselves. So when they heard this, they held a council to consider the matter.

10. Darius gave it as his opinion that the Scythians intended a surrender of themselves and their country, both land and water, into his hands.

11. This he conceived to be the meaning of the gifts, because the mouse is an inhabitant of the earth, and eats the same food as man,

12. While the frog passes his life in the water; the bird is as swift and proud as a horse, and the arrows might signify the surrender of all their power.

13. Gobryas, one of the seven conspirators against the Magus, offered a different explanation.

14. 'These tokens say: "Unless, Persians, you can turn into birds and fly into the sky, or become mice and burrow under the ground,

15. "'Or make yourselves frogs, and take refuge in the fens, you will never escape from this land, but die pierced by our arrows."'

16. The single division of the Scythians, which in the early part of the war had been appointed to guard the Palus Maeotis, and had now been sent to parlay with the Ionians stationed at the Ister, addressed them, on reaching the bridge, in these words:

17. 'Men of Ionia, we bring you freedom, if you will only do as we recommend.

18. 'Darius, we understand, enjoined you to keep your guard here at this bridge just sixty days; then, if he did not appear, you were to return home.

19. 'Now, therefore, act so as to be free from blame, alike in his sight, and in ours.

20. 'Tarry here the appointed time, and at the end go your ways.' Having said this, and received a promise from the Ionians to do as they desired, the Scythians hastened back.

21. After sending the tokens to Darius, the Scythian army drew out in battle array against the Persians, and seemed about to come to an engagement.

22. But as they stood in battle array, it chanced that a hare started up between them and the Persians, and set to running;

23. When immediately all the Scythians who saw it rushed off in pursuit, with great confusion and loud cries and shouts.

24. Darius, hearing the noise, enquired the cause of it, and was told that the Scythians were all engaged in hunting a hare.

25. At this he said, 'These men do indeed despise us utterly: and now I see that Gobryas was right about the Scythian gifts.

26. 'As, therefore, his opinion is now mine likewise, it is time we form some wise plan to secure ourselves a safe return home.'

27. 'Sir,' Gobryas rejoined, 'I was sure, before we came here, that this was an impracticable race; since our coming I am yet more convinced of it, especially now that I see them making game of us.

28. 'My advice is, therefore, that, when night falls, we light our fires as we are wont to do at other times,

29. 'And leaving behind us on some pretext that portion of our army which is weak and unequal to hardship, taking care also to leave our asses tethered,

30. 'Let us retreat from Scythia, before our foes march forward to the Ister and destroy the bridge, or the Ionians come to any resolution which may lead to our ruin.'

31. When night came Darius followed Gobryas' counsel, and leaving his sick soldiers, and those whose loss would be of least account, with the asses also tethered about the camp, he marched away.

32. The asses were left that their noise might be heard: the men, really because they were sick and useless,

33. But under the pretence that he was about to fall upon the Scythians with the flower of his troops, and that they meanwhile were to guard his camp for him.

34. Having thus declared his plans to the men he was deserting, and having caused the fires to be lighted, Darius set forth, and marched hastily towards the Ister.

35. The asses, aware of the departure of the host, brayed louder than ever; and the Scythians, hearing the sound, believed that the Persians were still in the same place.

Chapter 47

1. When day dawned, the men who had been left behind, perceiving that they were betrayed by Darius, stretched out their hands towards the Scythians, and spoke as befitted their situation.

2. The Scythians no sooner heard, than they quickly combined their troops in one, and set off in pursuit, straight for the Ister.

3. As, however, the Persian army was chiefly foot, and had no knowledge of the routes, which are not cut out in Scythia;

4. While the Scythians were all horsemen and well acquainted with the shortest way; it so happened that the two armies missed one another,

5. And the Scythians, getting far ahead of their adversaries, came first to the bridge.

6. Finding that the Persians were not yet arrived, they addressed the Ionians, who were aboard their ships, in these words:

7. 'Men of Ionia, the number of your days is out, and you do wrong to remain. Fear doubtless has kept you here until now:

8. 'Now, however, you may safely break the bridge, and hasten back to your homes, rejoicing that you are free.

9. 'Your former lord we undertake so to handle, that he will never again make war on anyone.'

10. The Ionians now held a council. Miltiades the Athenian, who was king of the Chersonesites of the Hellespont, and their commander at the Ister,

11. Recommended the other generals to do as the Scythians wished, and restore freedom to Ionia.

But Histiaeus the Milesian opposed this advice. 'It is through Darius,' he said, 'that we enjoy our thrones in our several states.

12. 'If his power be overturned, I cannot continue lord of Miletus, nor you of your cities. For there is not one of them which will not prefer democracy to kingly rule.'

13. Then the other captains, who, till Histiaeus spoke, were about to vote with Miltiades, changed their minds, and declared in favour of Histiaeus.

14. Having resolved to stay, the Greek leaders further determined to appear to the Scythians to be doing something, when in fact they were doing nothing of consequence.

15. They resolved to break up the Scythian end of the bridge, to the distance of a bowshot from the bank;

16. And to assure the Scythians, while the demolition was proceeding, that there was nothing they would not do to please them.

17. Such were the additions made to the resolution of Histiaeus; who further addressed the Scythians, saying,

18. 'While we demolish the bridge, why do you not go and seek out

Darius, and take your revenge on him?'

19. The Scythians put faith in the promises of the Ionian chiefs, and retraced their steps, hoping to fall in with the Persians.

20. But they missed their enemy's line of march entirely; their own former acts being to blame for it.

21. Had they not ravaged all the pasturages of that region, and filled in the wells, they would have easily found the Persians whenever they chose.

22. But, as it turned out, the measures which seemed to them so wisely planned were exactly what caused their failure.

23. They took a route where water was to be found and fodder could be got for their horses, and on this track sought their adversaries,

24. Expecting that they too would retreat through regions where these things were to be obtained.

25. The Persians, however, kept strictly to the line of their former march, never for a moment departing from it;

26. But even so they only gained the bridge with difficulty.

27. It was night when they arrived, and their terror, when they found the bridge broken up, was great; for they thought the Ionians had deserted them.

28. Now there was in the army of Darius an Egyptian who had a louder voice than any other man in the world.

29. This person was told by Darius to stand at the water's edge, and call Histiaeus the Milesian.

30. Histiaeus, hearing him at the first summons, brought the fleet to make good the bridge once more and convey the army across.

31. By these means the Persians escaped from Scythia, while the Scythians sought for them in vain, again missing their track.

32. And hence the Scythians are accustomed to say of the Ionians, by way of reproach, that, if they be looked upon as freemen,

33. They are the basest and most dastardly of all mankind; but if they be considered as under servitude,

34. They are the most faithful of slaves, and the most fondly attached to their lords.

Chapter 48

1. But this failed venture of Darius into Europe was the cause of reflection among many,

2. Who saw it as a sign that the power of the great king was not unlimited, as all had feared;

3. And it gave rise to ambition and emulation in the hearts of some, while among Persians it made the desire to conquer Europe greater.

4. And now truly the main chapter began in the struggle between Persia and Greece, east and west, and the place it began was Miletus, subject to Darius and ruled by Histiaeus.

5. To him the king granted a favour for his service in Scythia, which was to give him the best architect of the time to come to Miletus and embellish it;

6. But when Darius saw that Histiaeus had begun to build walls round Miletus, he reflected,

7. And decided to summon Histiaeus to be his counsellor at Susa, thus preventing him from growing powerful and insubordinate in his own city.

8. Histiaeus gave the deputy governership of Miletus to his nephew Aristagoras,

9. An ambitious man who sought by several means to increase his own consequence, including a failed expedition against Naxos and the Cyclades, which were not under Persian sway.

10. When the Naxian expedition failed, Aristagoras, fearing the displeasure of Darius, decided to seek Greek help in a rebellion of Miletus against Persian rule.

11. He went first to Sparta and attempted to persuade its king Cleomenes to the venture,

12. Showing him an engraved map of the Persian empire and describing the great riches that the Spartans would acquire if they conquered Darius.

13. And as he spoke he offered Cleomenes more and more money to undertake the venture;

14. But Gorgo, the eight-year-old daughter of Cleomenes, said,

'Father, come away before this man corrupts you and your kingdom.'

15. Then Aristagoras went to Athens, which after Sparta was the most powerful of the Greek states;

16. And there proved that it is easier to persuade a multitude than a single man;

17. For whereas in Sparta he had to deal with Cleomenes, here he had to deal with the Athenian people as a whole: and this proved the simpler task.

18. Accordingly he appeared before them, and, as he had done at Sparta, spoke to them of the good things there were in Asia,

19. And of the Persian mode of fight, how they used neither shield nor spear, and were very easy to conquer.

20. All this he urged, and reminded them also that Miletus was a colony from Athens, and therefore ought to receive their help, since they were so powerful;

21. And in the earnestness of his entreaties he cared little what he promised, till at last he won them over.

22. The Athenians voted that twenty ships should be sent to help Ionia, under the command of Melanthius, a man of mark in every way.

23. These ships were the beginning of mischief both to the Greeks and to the barbarians.

24. When the Athenian fleet joined

Aristagoras at Miletus, he assembled his allies and proceeded to attack Sardis,

25. Not however leading the army himself, but appointing as commanders Hermophantus and his own brother Charopinus. He himself remained in Miletus.

26. The Ionians sailed to Ephesus, and, leaving their ships at Coressus, took guides and went up country with a great host.

27. They marched along the River Cayster, and, crossing over the ridge of Timolus, fell on Sardis and took it, no man opposing them;

28. The whole city fell to them, except the citadel, which Artaphernes defended in person with a large force.

29. But though they took the city, they did not succeed in plundering it; for, as the houses in Sardis were built of reeds,

30. And even the few of brick had reed thatching for their roofs, one of them was no sooner fired by a soldier than the flames ran speedily from house to house.

31. As the fire raged, the Lydians and such Persians as were in the city, enclosed on every side by the flames and finding themselves unable to get out,

32. Came in crowds into the marketplace, and gathered on the banks of the Pactolus.

33. This stream, which comes down from Mount Timolus, and brings

the Sardians a quantity of gold dust, runs directly through the marketplace.

34. So the Lydians and Persians, thus crowded together, were forced to stand on their defence;

35. And the Ionians, when they saw the enemy in part resisting, in part pouring towards them in dense crowds, took fright,

36. And retreating to the ridge called Timolus, went back to their ships when night came.

37. As soon as what had happened was known, all the Persians who were stationed west of the Halys drew together, and brought help to the Lydians.

38. Finding when they arrived that the Ionians had already withdrawn, they pursued them, and caught them at Ephesus.

39. The Ionians turned and fought, but suffered greatly the worse, great numbers of the Greeks being slain by the Persians.

40. The Athenians forsook the Ionians after this, and, though Aristagoras sent ambassadors begging further help, they refused.

41. Still the Ionians continued their efforts to wage war against Darius, which their recent conduct towards him now made unavoidable.

42. Sailing into the Hellespont, they brought Byzantium, and all the other cities in that quarter, under their sway.

43. They went to Caria, and won the

greater part of the Carians to their side; while Caunus, which had formerly refused to join them, after the burning of Sardis came over likewise.

44. Also Cyprus; all the Cyprians, excepting those of Amathus, joined the Ionian cause.

Chapter 49

1. When Darius heard of the burning of Sardis by the Athenians and Ionians,

2. And at the same time learnt that the author of the league was Aristagoras the Milesian, he no sooner understood what had happened,

3. Than, laying aside all thought of the Ionians, who would, he was sure, pay dear for their rebellion, he asked, 'Who are these Athenians?'

4. And, being informed, called for his bow, and placing an arrow on the string, shot upward into the sky, saying, as he let fly the shaft,

5. 'This is my promise: to be revenged on the Athenians!'

6. Thenceforth he ordered one of his servants, when his dinner was spread before him every day, to repeat these words to him three times: 'Master, remember the Athenians.'

7. Then Darius summoned Histiaeus of Miletus, whom he had kept at his court, and said, 'Your lieutenant, to whom you gave Miletus in charge, has raised a rebellion.

8. 'He has brought men from Europe to contend with me, and, prevailing on the Ionians, whose conduct I shall know how to avenge, to join with this force, he has robbed me of Sardis.

9. 'Can this have been done without your knowledge and advice? Beware lest it be found out that you are to blame for this.'

10. Histiaeus answered, 'If my lieutenant has done as you say, be sure he has done it out of his own ambition.

11. 'But I cannot believe that he and the Milesians have done this! Yet if they really have rebelled, see how ill advised it was to remove me from the sea coast.

12. 'The Ionians, it seems, have waited till I was no longer there, and then tried what they long desired to try;

13. 'Whereas, if I had been there, not a single city would have stirred.

14. 'Allow me therefore to go to Ionia, to restore matters to their former footing, and arrest Aristagoras, who has caused all the trouble.

15. 'Having done that, I promise I will not put off the clothes in which I reach Ionia till I have made Sardinia, the biggest island in the world, your tributary.'

16. So Histiaeus spoke, wishing to deceive the king; and Darius, persuaded by his words, let him go.

17. As these events were unfolding, matters were afoot in Cyprus.

18. Artybius, a Persian general,

planned to invade Cyprus with a great army of infantry, while at the same time the Phoenicians were to attack Cyprus with their fleet.

19. Onesilus, chief among the princes of Cyprus, urgently sent heralds to all parts of Ionia asking for help.

20. At the same time the Persians crossed in their ships from Cilicia, and proceeded by land to attack Salamis;

21. While the Phoenicians, with the fleet, sailed round the promontory called 'the Keys of Cyprus'.

22. Onesilus called together the captains of the Ionians who had come to help, and said,

23. 'Men of Ionia, we Cyprians leave it to you to choose whether you will fight with the Persians or with the Phoenicians.

24. 'If you wish to try your strength on land against the Persians, come on shore and ready yourselves for battle; we will take your ships and engage the Phoenicians.

25. 'If, on the other hand, you prefer to encounter the Phoenicians, let that be your task:

26. 'Only be sure, whichever you choose, acquit yourselves so that Ionia and Cyprus may preserve their freedom.'

27. The Ionians answered, 'The commonwealth of Ionia sent us here to guard the sea, not to make over our ships to you.

28. 'We will keep the post assigned to us. For your part, remember what you suffered when you were the slaves of the Medes, and behave like warriors.'

29. The Persians advanced into the plain before Salamis, and the Cyprians ranged themselves in order of battle against them,

30. Placing them so that the choicest troops were set to oppose the Persians, and Onesilus, of his own accord, took post opposite Artybius the general.

31. Now Artybius rode a horse which had been trained to rear up against foot soldiers, attacking with its forelegs and teeth.

32. Onesilus, informed of this, called to him his shield-bearer, who was a Carian, courageous and skilled in war; and asked him what was to be done about Artybius' horse.

33. 'Have no fear of the horse's tricks,' said the Carian. 'This is the last time he will perform them.'

34. The two hosts then joined battle both by sea and by land. The Ionians, who that day fought as they have never done before or since, defeated the Phoenicians.

35. Meanwhile as the two armies engaged in a sharp struggle on land, Artybius charged his horse at Onesilus;

36. The horse reared and kicked, but as he did so the Carian cut at him with a reaping hook, severing the front legs from the body.

37. The horse fell upon the spot, and Onesilus killed Artybius as he fell with him.

38. In the thick of the fight Stesanor,

tyrant of Curium, who commanded a large body of troops, defected to the Persians.

39. At this the Curians also defected; whereupon victory went to the Persians.

40. The Cyprian army was routed, vast numbers were slain, among them Onesilus, and Aristocyprus, king of the Solians, son of Philocyprus whom Solon the Athenian, when he visited Cyprus, praised in his poems beyond all other sovereigns.

41. Thus, after enjoying a short period of freedom, the Cyprians were again enslaved.

42. As for the Ionians who had won the sea fight, when they found that Onesilus had lost they left Cyprus, and sailed home.

43. But Daurises, who was married to one of the daughters of Darius, together with Hymeas, Otanes and other Persian captains, who were likewise married to daughters of the king,

44. Pursued the Ionian fleet, defeated them, and by forcing them to divide their efforts among their various cities, proceeded in succession to take and sack each one of them.

Chapter 50

1. As the cities fell one after another, Aristagoras the Milesian, in truth a man of little courage, began to seek ways to escape.

2. Now convinced that it was vain to fight Darius, he called his

comrades together, and with them made a plan to conquer Thrace and there make a refuge.

3. They set out to do so, but were killed in the attempt. So ended the life of Aristagoras.

4. Meanwhile Histiaeus, tyrant of Miletus, who had been allowed by Darius to leave Susa, arrived at Sardis.

5. The Sardian satrap Artaphernes asked him why Ionia had rebelled; he answered that he did not know,

6. And that it had astonished him greatly, pretending to be unaware of the whole business.

7. Artaphernes, however, who saw that he was dealing dishonestly, and who had in fact full knowledge of the outbreak, said to him,

8. 'Histiaeus: this shoe is of your stitching; Aristagoras has merely been the wearer.'

9. Histiaeus, alarmed at this, fled away to the coast as soon as night fell.

10. Thus he forfeited his word to Darius, and betrayed his deceit.

11. Crossing to Chios, he was there arrested by the inhabitants, who accused him of intending some mischief against them on Darius' behalf.

12. But when the truth was laid before them, and they found that Histiaeus was in reality Darius' foe, they set him free again.

13. But his efforts were to no avail. He was rejected by the people of Miletus, who had tasted their

freedom by the revolt, and did not want a tyrant back again.

14. Histiaeus therefore went to the Hellespont, and began gathering an army and a fleet, principally of men of Lesbos,

15. Together with those he impressed into service who sailed from the Euxine and fell into his hands.

16. But though he captured Chios and made it his headquarters, and even before he met his end in battle with the Persian general Harpagus, his cause was already hopeless,

17. For the Ionians had once again been defeated and enslaved by Persia, after Darius sent a great army and fleet against Miletus.

18. At the battle for Miletus the Ionians assembled a fleet of many ships from their allies, under the command of a Phocaean named Dionysius.

19. He attempted to drill and train the sailors to make them effective for battle, but they complained under the work he imposed,

20. And when the Phoenicians sailed against them in the seas around Miletus, the Samians sailed away rather than fight, and the Lesbians also, and after them the greater part of the Ionians.

21. Of those who stayed to fight the greatest sufferers were the brave Chians, who lost nearly half their hundred ships.

22. When Dionysius saw that all was lost he likewise fled, and became a pirate in Sicily, plundering Carthaginians and Tyrrhenians.

23. When they had defeated the Ionians at sea the Persians besieged Miletus, driving mines under the walls and using every device and stratagem,

24. Until the city fell, six years from the time that the revolt broke out under Aristagoras.

25. All the citizens were enslaved; those whose lives were spared were moved to the city of Ampe at the mouth of the Tigris River,

26. And Miletus was kept by the Persians for themselves, and the hill-country nearby given to the Carians of Pedasus.

27. Those who mourned the downfall of Miletus most were the Athenians, for Miletus had been founded by them in earlier times.

28. They showed their affliction in many ways, and not least by their treatment of the poet Phrynichus,

29. For when his play *The Capture of Miletus* was staged, the whole theatre burst into tears,

30. And the people sentenced him to a fine of a thousand drachmas for reminding them of the misfortunes of their kin.

31. They likewise passed a law that his play should never again be staged.

32. Samos too ceased to be a Greek city, but not because its citizens were removed by the Persians;

33. Instead, the Samians chose to quit their city and start a new life in

Sicily rather than become slaves to Darius.

34. At first they proposed to settle at Kale-Acte; but opportunity offered to capture the beautiful city of Zancle, which they did, and lived there thereafter.

Chapter 51

1. Having recaptured Miletus, the Persians proceeded to attack the islands off the coast, Chios, Lesbos and Tenedos, which were reduced without difficulty.
2. Whenever they became masters of an island, the barbarians, in every single instance, netted the inhabitants.
3. Netting is the practice in which men join hands so as to form a line across from the north coast to the south, and then march through the island hunting out every inhabitant.
4. The Persians also took all the Ionian towns on the mainland.
5. And now the Persian generals made good all the threats with which they had menaced the Ionians before the battle.
6. For no sooner did they get possession of the towns than they picked out the best-favoured boys and made them eunuchs,
7. While the most beautiful girls they tore from their homes and sent as presents to the king, at the same time burning the cities themselves.
8. Thereafter the Persians proceeded to the Hellespont, and took all the

towns which lie on the left shore as one sails into the straits.

9. For the cities on the right bank had already been reduced by the land force of the Persians.
10. The places which border the Hellespont on the European side are the Chersonese, which contains a number of cities,
11. Perinthus, the forts in Thrace, Selybria and Byzantium.
12. The Byzantines at this time, and their opposite neighbours, the Chalcedonians, instead of awaiting the coming of the Phoenicians,
13. Quitted their country, and sailing into the Euxine, took up their abode at the city of Mesembria.
14. The Phoenicians, after burning all the places above mentioned, proceeded to Proconnesus and Artaca, which they likewise burned;
15. This done, they returned to the Chersonese, being minded to reduce those cities which they had not ravaged in their former cruise.
16. They left Cyzicus alone, because its inhabitants had made terms with Oebares son of Megabazus, the satrap of Dascyleium, and had submitted themselves to the king.
17. In the Chersonese the Phoenicians subdued all the cities, excepting Cardia.
18. And now Darius put into execution his plan to capture the cities of Greece, and in particular Athens, the mother of Miletus, about which he had made his

promise by firing an arrow into the sky.

19. He appointed Mardonius son of Gobryas, one of the seven who had freed Persia from the Magus, to lead a great invasion force by land and sea,

20. To cross the Hellespont and proceed against Eretria and Athens. It was however an unlucky expedition.

21. First Mardonius captured Thasos, for the Thasians did not even lift a hand in their defence, and were quickly reduced by the sea force.

22. On land the army added the Macedonians to the slaves of the king. From Thasos the fleet stood across to the mainland, and sailed along the shore to Acanthus, from where an attempt was made to double Mount Athos.

23. But here a violent north wind sprang up, against which nothing could contend, shattering a large number of the ships and driving them aground.

24. Nearly three hundred ships were destroyed, and more than twenty thousand men were lost,

25. Some dashed violently against the rocks, some dying of cold, most drowning.

26. While this happened to the fleet, on land Mardonius and his army were attacked by night in their camp by the Brygi, a tribe of Thracians;

27. And great numbers of Persians were slain, even Mardonius himself receiving a wound.

28. The Brygi, nevertheless, did not succeed in maintaining their freedom, for Mardonius would not leave the country till he had made them subjects of Persia.

29. Still, though he brought them under the yoke, the blow they had given his army, and the destruction of the fleet, forced him to retreat;

30. And so this armament, having failed, returned to Asia. This was the second unsuccessful sortie into Europe by Persia.

Chapter 52

1. After this Darius resolved to make better preparation for conquering the Greeks,

2. And first he investigated which of them were inclined to resist him and which to make their submission.

3. He therefore sent heralds all round Greece, with orders to demand everywhere earth and water as marks of submission.

4. At the same time he sent other heralds to the various coastal towns which paid him tribute, and required them to provide ships of war and horse-transports.

5. These cities accordingly began their preparations. The heralds who had been sent into Greece obtained what the king demanded from a large number of states,

6. And likewise from all the islanders they visited. Among these last were the Eginetans, who, equally with

the rest, consented to give earth and water.

7. When the Athenians heard what the Eginetans had done, believing that it was from enmity to themselves that they had submitted to Darius,

8. And that the Eginetans intended to join Darius in his attack on Athens, they immediately took the matter in hand.

9. In truth it rejoiced them to have such a good pretext; and accordingly they sent embassies to Sparta, making it a charge against the Eginetans that their conduct proved them traitors to Greece.

10. Accordingly Cleomenes, the son of Anaxandridas, who was then one of the two kings of Sparta, went in person to Egina, intending to arrest those whose guilt was the greatest.

11. But a number of the Eginetans resisted; a certain Crius, son of Polycritus, being the foremost. This person told Cleomenes he should not carry off a single Eginetan without it costing him dear; saying,

12. 'The Athenians have bribed Cleomenes to make this attack, for which he has no warrant from his own government, otherwise both the Spartan kings would have come together.'

13. Hereupon Cleomenes, finding that he must quit Egina, asked Crius his name; and when Crius told him he said,

14. 'Get your horns tipped with brass as quickly as possible, O Crius! For you will soon have to face great danger.'

15. Meanwhile in Sparta the other king, Demaratus son of Ariston, was bringing charges against Cleomenes,

16. Moved not so much by love of the Eginetans as by jealousy and hatred of his colleague.

17. Cleomenes therefore was no sooner returned from Egina than he pondered how he might unseat Demaratus.

18. He used an old story that Demaratus was not the true son of his father, and hence not entitled to the Spartan throne;

19. Once persuading the Spartans that this was so, Cleomenes was able to substitute Leotychides for him, and reduce Demaratus to the rank of a magistrate.

20. Then Cleomenes and Leotychides attacked the Eginetans, who quickly surrendered; and the Spartans took the ten wealthiest and noblest men of the city as hostages,

21. And gave them to the Athenians to hold, for the Athenians were the greatest enemies of Egina.

22. Now it was not long after this that Cleomenes went mad and had to be restrained, and while under restraint committed suicide;

23. So then the Eginetans sent ambassadors to Sparta to complain about the hostages kept by Athens,

24. The Lacedaemons assembled a court of justice and gave sentence, saying that Leotychides had grossly affronted the people of Egina,

25. And should be handed to the ambassadors, to be led away in place of the men whom the Athenians held hostage.

26. The ambassadors were about to lead Leotychides away when Theasides the son of Leoprepes, a man greatly esteemed in Sparta, intervened and said:

27. 'What are you minded to do, men of Egina? To lead away the king of the Spartans, whom his countrymen have given into your hands?

28. 'Though now in anger they have passed this sentence, yet the time will come when they will punish you, if you do this, by destroying your country.'

29. On hearing this the Eginetans changed their plan, and, instead of taking Leotychides away captive, agreed with him that he should come with them to Athens, and get back their men.

30. The Athenians refused, and sent Leotychides and the Eginetans away. In revenge the latter captured an Athenian ship and imprisoned the noble youths who were aboard;

31. So the Athenians mustered a fleet and attacked Egina, defeating it in a sea battle.

32. This strife among the Greeks encouraged Darius in his plans.

33. Still every day a servant repeated three times, 'Remember the Athenians',

34. And about his court were a number of Greek exiles, not least among them the Pisistraditae, descendents of that Pisistratus who had once been tyrant of Athens,

35. Who had been driven out, and were always accusing their countrymen.

36. Darius now appointed Datis and Artaphernes to the head of his armed forces, and instructed them to reduce Eretria and Athens, and bring their citizens captive to Susa in chains.

Chapter 53

1. The new commanders took the army to Cilicia to meet the fleet and horse transports. Once embarkation was complete the fleet, consisting of six hundred triremes, sailed for Ionia.

2. Instead of proceeding along the shore to the Hellespont and Thrace, the fleet loosed from Samos and traversed the Icarian Sea through the islands,

3. Mainly because they feared the danger of doubling Mount Athos, where the year before their predecessors had suffered so grievously.

4. But another reason was their earlier failure to take Naxos, which they now planned to capture.

5. The Naxians, seeing their danger, fled into the hills. Some were captured by the Persians and put

to death, and the city itself was looted and burned.

6. This done, the Persians sailed to the other islands. When they approached Delos they found that the citizens had fled as the Naxians had done.

7. Datis sent them a message saying, 'Why have you fled? Why do you judge us so harshly?

8. 'I have enough sense to spare you, even if the king had not already ordered me to do so; come back to your dwellings in safety.'

9. Then he sailed against Eretria, taking with him both Ionians and Aeolians.

10. After he left, the Delians returned home, thinking that the Persians were not so bad after all. Little did they guess the evils about to fall on them.

11. For in the three generations of Darius, Xerxes the son of Darius, and Artaxerxes the son of Xerxes (Xerxes means 'Warrior', and Artaxerxes means 'Great Warrior'), more woes befell Greece than in the twenty generations preceding Darius;

12. Woes caused in part by the Persians, but in part arising from the contentions among the Greeks' own chief men concerning the supreme power.

13. After loosing from Delos the Persians proceeded to touch at other islands, taking troops from each, and carrying off a number of the children as hostages.

14. In this way they came at last to Carystus; but here the Carystians refused to give hostages, and refused to bear arms against their neighbours, meaning Athens and Eretria.

15. So the Persians laid siege to Carystus, and wasted the country round, until at length the inhabitants were forced to submit.

16. Meanwhile the Eretrians, understanding that the Persian forces were coming against them, asked the Athenians for assistance.

17. Athens readily assigned four thousand men, landholders to whom they had allotted the estates of the Chalcidean Hippobatae.

18. At Eretria, however, things were in no healthy state; for though they had aid from Athens, yet they could not agree among themselves how to act.

19. Some wished to leave the city and take refuge in the heights of Euboea; others, hoping for rewards from the Persians, were getting ready to betray their country.

20. When these things came to the ears of Aeschines, the son of Nothon, one of the first men in Eretria,

21. He made known the whole state of affairs to the Athenians who had already arrived, advising them to return home to their own land and not perish with his countrymen.

22. The Athenians listened to his counsel, and, crossing over to Oropus, escaped the danger.

23. The Persian fleet now drew near and anchored on the coast of Eretria.

24. They proceeded to disembark their horses and make ready to attack. But the Eretrians were not minded to offer battle;

25. Their only care, after they had decided not to quit the city, was to defend their walls.

26. And now their fortress was assaulted in good earnest, and for six days great numbers died on both sides.

27. But on the seventh day two of the citizens betrayed the city to the Persians.

28. These no sooner entered than they plundered and burnt everything, and carried away all the inhabitants as slaves.

29. The Persians, having thus subjected Eretria, set sail for Attica, planning to deal with the Athenians as they had dealt with the Eretrians.

30. And, because there was no place in Attica so convenient for their horse as Marathon,

31. And Marathon lay moreover quite close to Eretria, Hippias, son of Pisistratus, took them there.

32. When news of this reached the Athenians, they likewise marched their troops to Marathon, and there stood on the defensive,

33. Having at their head ten generals, of whom one was Miltiades.

Chapter 54

1. Now Miltiades' father, Cimon, son of Stesagoras, had been banished from Athens by the tyrant Pisistratus.

2. During his banishment he had won the four-horse chariot race at Olympia, whereby he gained the very same honour which had before been carried off by his half-brother on his mother's side, also called Miltiades.

3. At the next Olympiad Cimon won the prize again with the same mares; upon which he caused Pisistratus to be proclaimed the winner,

4. Having made an agreement with him that on yielding him this honour he should be allowed to come back to his country.

5. Afterwards, still with the same mares, he won the prize a third time; whereupon he was put to death by the sons of Pisistratus, whose father was no longer living.

6. They set men to lie in wait for Cimon secretly by night, and they murdered him near the government-house.

7. He was buried outside the city, beyond what is called the Valley Road; and right opposite his tomb were buried the mares that had won the three prizes.

8. The same success had likewise been achieved only once before, by the mares of Evagoras the Lacedaemonian.

9. At the time of Cimon's death Stesagoras, the elder of his two sons, was in the Chersonese, where he lived with Miltiades his uncle;

10. The younger, who was called Miltiades after the founder of the Chersonesite colony, was with his father in Athens.

11. It was this Miltiades who now commanded the Athenians, having been elected general by the free choice of the people.

12. Before they left Athens the generals sent a herald to Sparta, one Pheidippides, who was by birth an Athenian, and by profession and practice a trained runner.

13. By sustained fast running he reached Sparta on the very next day after leaving Athens: a famous feat of speed and endurance.

14. On his arrival he went to the rulers and said, 'Men of Lacedaemon, the Athenians ask you to hasten to their aid, and not allow that state, which is the most ancient in all Greece, to be enslaved by the barbarians.

15. 'Eretria is already carried away captive; and Greece is weakened by the loss of no mean city.'

16. The Spartans wished to help the Athenians, but were unable to do so immediately because they were in the midst of an important civic festival which had to be completed, obliging them to wait several days before marching.

17. Even as the Athenians arranged themselves in order of battle they were joined by the Plataeans, who came in full force to their aid.

18. The Plataeans had in former times put themselves under the rule of the Athenians, who had already undertaken many labours on their behalf.

19. The Athenian generals were divided in their opinions: some advised not to risk battle, because they were too few to engage such a host, while others were for fighting at once;

20. And among these last was Miltiades. He therefore, seeing that opinions were divided, and that the less worthy counsel appeared likely to prevail, resolved to go to the Polemarch, and have a conference with him.

21. For the man on whom the lot fell to be Polemarch at Athens was entitled to give his vote with the ten generals. The Polemarch at this juncture was Callimachus of Aphidnae.

22. To him Miltiades went, and said: 'It rests with you, Callimachus, either to bring Athens to slavery,

23. 'Or, by securing her freedom, to leave to all future generations a memory beyond even Harmodius and Aristogeiton.

24. 'For never since the time that the Athenians became a people were they in such great danger as now.

25. 'If they submit to Persia, the woes they will suffer under the revenge of Hippias are already decided;

26. 'If, on the other hand, they fight

and win, Athens may become the first city in Greece.

27. 'Now, we generals are ten in number, and our votes are divided; half of us wish to engage, half to avoid a combat.

28. 'If we do not fight, I look to see a great disturbance at Athens which will shake men's resolution, and then I fear they will choose to surrender.

29. 'But if we fight before such failure of resolve shows itself among our citizens, we can win.

30. 'On you we depend; add your vote to my side and our country will be free, and the first state of Greece.

31. 'If you vote with the others, the reverse will follow.'

32. Miltiades won Callimachus over, and his vote gave the decision for combat.

33. At this the other generals who were in favour of battle gave the full command to Miltiades.

Chapter 55

1. In the Athenian battle array Callimachus the Polemarch led the right wing;

2. After this followed the tribes, according as they were numbered, in an unbroken line; last of all came the Plataeans, forming the left wing.

3. As they marshalled on the field of Marathon, in order that the Athenian front might be of equal length with the Persian,

4. The ranks of the centre were diminished, and it became the weakest part of the line, while the wings were both made strong with a depth of many ranks.

5. When the army was set in array Miltiades gave the order and the Athenians charged the barbarians at a run.

6. Now the distance between the two armies was little short of eight furlongs. The Persians, therefore, when they saw the Greeks coming on at speed, made ready to receive them.

7. But it seemed to them that the Athenians had lost their senses, and were bent on their own destruction;

8. For they saw a mere handful of men running at them unaccompanied by horsemen or archers.

9. Such was the opinion of the barbarians; but the Athenians in close array fell on them, and fought in a manner worthy of being recorded.

10. They were the first of the Greeks who introduced the custom of charging the enemy at a run,

11. And they were likewise the first who dared to face men clad in Persian garb.

12. Until this time the very name of the Persians had been a terror to the Greeks.

13. The two armies fought together on the plain of Marathon for a length of time;

14. And in the mid battle, where the Persians themselves and the Sacae

had their place, the barbarians were victorious,

15. And broke and pursued the Greeks into the inner country; but on the two wings the Athenians and Plataeans defeated the enemy.

16. Having done so, they allowed the routed barbarians to flee at their ease, and joining the two wings in one,

17. Fell upon those who had broken their own centre, and fought and conquered them. These likewise fled,

18. And now the Athenians pursued the runaways and cut them down, chasing them all the way to the shore, where they laid hold of the ships and called for fire.

19. It was in the struggle here that Callimachus the Polemarch died, after greatly distinguishing himself;

20. Stesilaus too, the son of Thrasilaus, one of the generals, was slain;

21. And Cynaegirus, the son of Euphorion, having seized on a vessel of the enemy's by the ornament at the stern, had his hand cut off by the blow of an axe, and so perished;

22. As likewise did many other Athenians of note and name.

23. Nevertheless the Athenians captured seven of the vessels, while in the remainder the barbarians pushed off to sea,

24. And taking aboard their Eretrian prisoners from the island where they had left them, doubled Cape Sunium, hoping to reach Athens before the return of the Athenians.

25. The Alcmaeonidae were accused by their countrymen of suggesting this course to them;

26. They had, it was said, an understanding with the Persians, and made a signal to them, by raising a shield, after they were embarked in their ships.

27. The Persians accordingly sailed round Sunium. But the Athenians with all possible speed marched back to the defence of their city,

28. And succeeded in reaching Athens before the appearance of the barbarians, and encamped at Cynosarges.

29. The barbarian fleet arrived, and anchored off Phalerum, which was at that time the harbour of Athens;

30. But after resting awhile on their oars, seeing that the Athenian army had arrived before them, they departed and sailed away to Asia.

31. There fell in this battle of Marathon, on the side of the Persians, about six thousand four hundred men. The Athenians lost one hundred and ninety-two.

32. Shortly after the departure of the Persians, two thousand Spartans arrived at Athens, having marched as quickly as they could to join the fight.

33. So eager had they been that their march took three days only.

34. Though too late for the battle, they wished to see the Persians,

and so went to the battlefield of
Marathon to look on the slain.

35. After giving the Athenians praise
for their achievement, they
departed again for home.

Chapter 56

1. When news of the defeat at
Marathon reached Darius, his
anger against the Athenians grew
even fiercer, and he became more
eager than ever to conquer Greece.

2. Instantly he sent heralds throughout his empire to raise fresh levies
at an even greater rate than before,
with ships, horses, men and
provisions in yet greater
abundance.

3. For three years all Asia was in
commotion, readying itself for
war; the best and bravest were
enrolled for service, and made
preparations accordingly.

4. In the fourth year of preparations
there was a revolt in Egypt.

5. Enraged, Darius resolved to send
an army against Egypt as well as
Greece, and chose to lead it
himself.

6. Immediately a contention arose
among his sons, because it was the
tradition in Persia that if a king
was about to go to war, he should
appoint an heir.

7. Darius had three sons by his first
wife, a daughter of Gobryas.

8. By Atossa the daughter of Cyrus
he had four sons. Artabazanes was
the eldest of the first brood, and
Xerxes the eldest of the second.

9. Artabazanes claimed the inheritance as eldest of all the sons, while
Xerxes pointed out that he was the
grandson of Cyrus, first liberator
of the Persians and founder of
their royal house.

10. Before Darius had pronounced on
the matter, it happened that the
Spartan Demaratus, the son of
Ariston, who had been deprived of
his crown at Sparta,

11. And had afterwards, of his own
accord, gone into banishment,
came to Susa, and there heard of
the quarrel of the princes.

12. He went to Xerxes and advised
him, in addition to all that he had
urged before, to argue that when
he was born Darius was already
king,

13. But when Artabazanes came into
the world, Darius was a mere
private person.

14. It would therefore be neither right
nor seemly that the crown should
go to anyone but Xerxes.

15. 'For at Sparta,' said Demaratus,
'the law is that if a king has sons
before he comes to the throne, and
another son is born to him
afterwards, the latter child is heir
to his father's kingdom.'

16. Xerxes followed this counsel, and
Darius, persuaded that he had
justice on his side, appointed him
heir.

17. Many say that even without this,
the crown would have gone to
Xerxes; for his mother Atossa was
all-powerful.

18. Having appointed his heir, and made his preparations, Darius was ready to depart in conquest of Greece and the reconquest of Egypt; but death intervened, ending his thirty-six years of reign.

19. Xerxes mounted the throne, and at first was indifferent to the idea of conquering Greece, which seemed unimportant and marginal, whereas the loss of Egypt concerned him far more.

20. But Mardonius, who had great influence with him, persuaded him otherwise, saying,

21. 'Sire, it is not fitting to let the Athenians escape without punishment, after doing Persia such a great injury.

22. 'Subdue Egypt, yes; but then lead the army against Athens. In this way you will prevent future rebellions and insults, by showing that the Persian will never leave either unpunished.'

23. Mardonius also said, 'Europe is a wondrous beautiful region, rich in all kinds of cultivated trees, and the soil excellent: no one, save you, is worthy to be king of such a land.'

24. He said this because he longed for further adventures, and hoped to become satrap of Greece under the king.

25. He was helped by the coincidence that at the same time the kings of Thessaly sent an invitation to Xerxes to enter Greece,

26. Promising him all their assistance in the venture. And further, the Pisistratidae, who had come to Susa, urged the same, and persuaded him even more than the Thessalonians.

Chapter 57

1. When therefore Egypt was subdued, Xerxes undertook to conquer Greece.

2. He called together an assembly of the noblest Persians to hear their opinions, saying,

3. 'I need not remind you of the deeds of Cyrus and Cambyses, and my own father Darius, how many nations they conquered, and added to our dominions.

4. 'You well know what great things they achieved. For myself, I will say that, from the day I mounted the throne,

5. 'I have not ceased to consider by what means I may rival those who have preceded me in this post of honour, and increase the power of Persia as much as any of them.

6. 'I have decided on a way to win glory, and at the same time get possession of a land which is as large and as rich as our own,

7. 'Indeed, which is even more varied in the fruits it bears; while at the same time we obtain satisfaction and revenge.

8. 'My intent is to throw a bridge over the Hellespont and march an army through Europe against Greece,

9. 'That thereby I may obtain

vengeance from the Athenians for the wrongs committed by them against the Persians and my father.

10. 'Your own eyes saw the preparations of Darius against these men; but death came upon him, and foiled his hopes of revenge.

11. 'On his behalf, therefore, and that of all Persians, I undertake the war,

12. 'And pledge myself not to rest till I have burned Athens, which has dared to injure me and my father.

13. 'I see many advantages added to this war. Once we have subdued Athens, and those neighbours of theirs in Sparta,

14. 'We shall extend the Persian territory as far as the sky reaches. The sun will then shine on no land beyond our borders;

15. 'For I will pass through Europe from one end to the other, and with your aid make all the lands it contains into one country.

16. 'For thus there will be no city, no country left in all the world, which will withstand our arms.

17. 'By this course we shall bring all mankind under our rule, alike those who are guilty and those who are innocent of doing us wrong.

18. 'For yourselves, if you wish to please me, do as follows: when I announce the time for the army to meet, hasten to the muster with good will.

19. 'To the man who brings with him the most gallant array I will give the gifts which our people consider most honourable.

20. 'But to show that I am not self-willed in this matter, I lay the business before you, and give you full leave to speak your minds openly.'

21. Then Mardonius spoke. 'You have spoken truly; and best of all is your resolve.

22. 'It were indeed a monstrous thing if, after conquering and enslaving the Sacae, the Indians, the Ethiopians, the Assyrians, the Egyptians and many other mighty nations,

23. 'Not for any wrong that they had done us, but only to increase our empire, we should then allow the Greeks, who have done us such injury, escape our vengeance.

24. 'What is it that we fear in them? Not surely their numbers, not the greatness of their wealth? They have neither!

25. 'We know their way of fighting; we know how weak their power is; already we have subdued their children who dwell in our country, the Ionians, Aeolians and Dorians.

26. 'I myself have had experience of these men when I marched against them by order of your father;

27. 'And though I went as far as Macedonia, and came not far short of reaching Athens itself, yet not a single person ventured to come out against me to battle.

28. 'And yet, I am told, these same

Greeks wage wars against one another in the most foolish way.

29. 'For no sooner is war proclaimed than they search out the smoothest and fairest plain, and there assemble and fight;

30. 'Whence it comes that even the conquerors depart with great loss: I say nothing of the conquered, for they are destroyed altogether.

31. 'Now surely, as they are all of one speech, they ought to interchange heralds, and make up their differences by any means rather than battle;

32. 'Or, at the worst, if they must fight, they ought to post themselves as strongly as possible.

33. 'But, notwithstanding that they are so foolish in warfare, yet these Greeks, when I led my army against them to the very borders of Macedonia, did not so much as think of offering me battle.

34. 'Who then will dare, O king! to meet you in arms, when you come with all Asia's warriors at your back, and all her ships?

35. 'For my part I do not believe the Greek people will be so unwise.

36. 'Grant, however, that I am mistaken, and that they are foolish enough to fight us;

37. 'In that case they will learn that there are no such soldiers in the whole world as we.

38. 'Nevertheless let us spare no pains; for nothing comes without trouble; but all that men acquire is got by taking pains.'

Chapter 58

1. The other Persians were silent; all feared to raise their voice against Xerxes' plan.

2. But Artabanus, the son of Hystaspes and uncle of Xerxes, trusting to his relationship, was bold to speak.

3. 'O king!' he said, 'it is impossible, if no more than one opinion is uttered, to make choice of the best: a man is forced then to follow whatever advice may have been given him;

4. 'But if opposite speeches are delivered, then choice can be exercised.

5. 'I counselled your father, Darius, who was my own brother, not to attack the Scythians, a race of people who had no town in their whole land.

6. 'He thought however to subdue those wandering tribes, and would not listen to me, but marched an army against them, and before he returned home lost many of his bravest warriors.

7. 'You, O king! are about to attack a people far superior to the Scythians, a people distinguished above others both by land and sea. It is fit therefore that I tell you what danger you incur hereby.

8. 'You say you will bridge the Hellespont, and lead your troops through Europe against Greece.

9. 'Now suppose some disaster befall you by land or sea, or by both. It

could happen; for the men are reputed valiant.

10. 'Indeed one may measure their prowess from what they have already done;

11. 'For when Datis and Artaphernes led their huge army against Attica, the Athenians by themselves defeated them.

12. 'But grant they are not successful on both elements. Still, if they man their ships, and, defeating us by sea, sail to the Hellespont, and there destroy our bridge: that, sire, were a fearful hazard.

13. 'I remember how narrowly we escaped disaster once, when your father, after throwing bridges over the Thracian Bosphorus and the Ister,

14. 'Marched against the Scythians, and they tried every means to induce the Ionians, who had charge of the bridge over the Ister, to break the passage.

15. 'On that day, if Histiaeus, king of Miletus, had sided with the other princes, and not set himself to oppose their views, the empire of the Persians would have come to an end.

16. 'Surely it were a dreadful thing even to hear this said, that the king's fortunes depended wholly on one man.

17. 'Think then no more of incurring so great a danger when no need presses, but follow the advice I offer.

18. 'Break up this meeting, and when you have thought the matter over by yourself, and settled what you will do, tell us your decision.

19. 'I know nothing in the world that so profits a man as taking good counsel with himself.

20. 'Moreover, hurry always brings disasters, from which huge sufferings arise;

21. 'But in delay lie many advantages, not always apparent at first sight, but such as in course of time are seen of all. Such is my counsel, O king!

22. 'And you, Mardonius, son of Gobryas, forbear to speak foolishly concerning the Greeks, who are men that ought not to be lightly esteemed by us.

23. 'For by reviling the Greeks, you encourage the king to lead his troops against them; and it seems to me that you want this for your own benefit.

24. 'If, however, it turns out that we must go to war with this people, at least allow the king to abide at home in Persia.

25. 'Then let you and me stake our children on the issue. If things go well for the king, as you say they will, let me and my children be put to death;

26. 'But if they fall out as I predict, let your children suffer, and you too, if you happen to come back alive.

27. 'But if you refuse this wager, and still resolve to march an army against Greece,

28. 'I am certain that some of those you leave behind here will one day

receive the sad tidings that
Mardonius has brought a great
disaster on the Persian people,

29. 'And himself lies a prey to dogs
and birds somewhere in the land
of the Athenians, or else in that of
the Spartans;

30. 'Unless indeed you perish sooner
by the way, experiencing in your
own person the might of those
men on whom you wish to induce
the king to make war.'

31. Angrily Xerxes said, 'Artabanus,
you are my father's brother; that
saves you from punishment for
your stupid words.

32. 'But I will lay one shame on you:
you will not come with me to
conquer the Greeks, but will tarry
here with the women.

33. 'It is henceforth either the Greeks
or the Persians: one must conquer;
there is no middle way.'

34. So he spoke; but in the night he
was troubled by what Artabanus
had said, and changed his mind,
and told the Persians so the next
morning;

35. At which they all rejoiced, and
made grateful obeisances to him.

36. Yet the second night he changed
his mind yet again, and told them
so; and this time, because he had
been discussing long with
Artabanus,

37. And had persuaded his uncle to
support him in his resolve, he was
able to tell the Persians that
Artabanus at last agreed too; and
so the expedition was decided.

Chapter 59

1. Reckoning from the recovery of
Egypt, Xerxes spent four years
collecting his host and making all
ready for the invasion of Greece.

2. So many nations furnished men,
ships and supplies, that no greater
host had ever been assembled for
war, or more careful preparations
made.

3. These included laying up stores at
way stations, building bridges and
digging a great channel across the
isthmus of Athos.

4. Meanwhile the satraps of the
provinces of the empire had vied
with each other in fitting out in
brilliant array the armies they
levied.

5. When these came together, a vast
host, Xerxes led them across the
River Halys, and marched through
Phrygia to the city of Celaenae.

6. Here Xerxes and his army were
magnificently entertained by
Pythius, a citizen so wealthy that
in the time of Darius he had sent
the king a golden plane tree, and
was reputed to be second in wealth
only to Xerxes himself.

7. So pleased was Xerxes by Pythius'
generosity that he promised him
lifelong friendship, and added to
this store of wealth with further
gifts.

8. When the army crossed the
Maeander they passed by the city
of Callatebus, where the men
make honey and harvest wheat
and the fruit of the tamarisk.

9. Xerxes there found a plane tree so beautiful that he presented it with golden ornaments, and put it under the care of one of his favourite guards.

10. When he reached Sardis, the capital of Lydia, Xerxes sent heralds to all Greece demanding gifts of earth and water as tokens of submission, and asking them to prepare feasts to welcome him.

11. To two cities only he did not send these demands: Athens and Sparta.

12. Then Xerxes set forward to Abydos, where the bridge across the Hellespont had just been finished by his engineers.

13. It was a double bridge, one half built by Phoenicians and the other by Egyptians.

14. The former had used cables of white flax, the latter ropes of papyrus. It is seven furlongs from Abydos to the European coast.

15. The bridge was fine to see, and ready for use; but before Xerxes could cross with his host, a violent storm arose, and the bridge was broken to pieces, all the work destroyed and submerged in the raging water.

16. Xerxes was extremely angry at this, and ordered the Hellespont to be given three hundred lashes as punishment, and a pair of fetters thrown into it.

17. It is even said that he ordered his branders to heat their branding irons and brand the Hellespont.

18. It is certain that he commanded those who scourged the waters to utter, as they lashed them, these words:

19. 'You bitter water, your lord punishes you because you have wronged him without cause. King Xerxes will cross you, whether you will or no.

20. 'You deserve this punishment as a treacherous and unsavoury river.'

21. When this absurd task had been completed, other master builders were brought to the Hellespont, and fashioned a new bridge.

22. They joined together triremes and penteconters, three hundred and sixty to support the bridge on the side of the Euxine Sea, and three hundred and fourteen to sustain the other;

23. And these they placed at right angles to the sea, and in the direction of the current of the Hellespont, thus relieving the tension of the shore cables.

24. Having joined the vessels, they moored them with anchors of great size,

25. So that the vessels towards the Euxine could resist the winds which blow from the straits,

26. And those of the more western bridge facing the Aegean might withstand the southerly and south-easterly winds.

27. A gap was left in the penteconters in no fewer than three places, to afford a passage for such light craft as chose to enter or leave the Euxine.

28. When all this was done, they made

the cables taut from the shore by the help of wooden capstans.

29. This time, instead of using the two materials separately, they assigned to each bridge six cables, two of white flax, four of papyrus.

30. Both cables were of the same size and quality; but the flaxen were the heavier, weighing more than a talent the cubit.

31. When the bridge was complete, tree trunks were sawn into planks to match the width of the bridge,

32. And these were fastened side by side on the tightened cables. Brushwood was arranged on the planks, after which earth was heaped on the brushwood, and trodden into a solid mass.

33. Lastly a bulwark was set up on either side of the causeway, high enough to prevent the sumpter beasts and horses from seeing over it and taking fright at the water.

Chapter 60

1. While the host of Xerxes was approaching the bridge at Abydos the sun, shining in a clear sky, was suddenly eclipsed, causing momentary consternation to Xerxes himself and all his men.

2. But the one most unnerved was Pythius, who had royally enter-tained Xerxes on arriving in Lydia;

3. And he asked him if, of the five sons marching with the army, he might be spared just one to stay at home and guard his old age and wealth.

4. Angered, Xerxes said, 'All my kin and people are marching to this war with me, yet you wish to have a son exempted from the duty!

5. 'That son forfeits his life as your punishment for asking!' At this he ordered the youth to be killed and cut in two,

6. One half of the corpse being placed on one side, and the other on the other side of the road along which the army marched towards the Hellespont.

7. On arriving at Abydos, Xerxes had a throne of white marble set on a hill so that he could overlook the Hellespont, the bridge, the great host of his army and his fleet on the waters, all in one sweeping view from this vantage point.

8. He ordered a sailing race among the fleet, which the Phoenicians won; and he was delighted with the sight of such a mighty host and armament.

9. But as he looked at so many ships, and the plains thronging with men as far as the eye could see, he suddenly began to weep.

10. Then Artabanus, his uncle, asked him: 'Why do you weep, who were rejoicing just now at the sight of such a magnificent host bent on securing kingship of the world for you?'

11. And Xerxes said, 'There came on me a sudden pity, when I thought of the brevity of men's lives, and considered that of all this host, so numerous as it is, not one will be alive a hundred years from now.'

12. To which Artabanus replied, 'And yet there are sadder things than that. Short as our time is, there is no man, whether here among this multitude or elsewhere,

13. 'Who is so happy, as not to have felt the wish – I will not say once, but many a time – that he were dead rather than alive.

14. 'Calamities fall upon us; sicknesses vex and harass us, and make life weary even though short.

15. 'So death, through the wretchedness of our life, is a most sweet refuge to our kind.'

16. 'You speak the truth,' said Xerxes, 'and so let us turn our thoughts from it, because the truth is sad.

17. 'And tell me, uncle, whether the sight of this great army and navy here before us pleases you as it does me.'

18. Artabanus replied, 'No one could feel otherwise, if he is on the same side as such a host!

19. 'But I worry about two dangers that are especially difficult to overcome.'

20. 'Can any dangers withstand an army and a navy so great as these?' asked Xerxes, astonished.

21. 'Precisely because they are so great in number and extent, these dangers – one can say: these enemies to you – are the greater,' replied Artabanus.

22. 'They are: the land, and the sea. Nowhere on the margins of the sea is there a harbour big enough for your fleet;

23. 'If a storm arises, there is no way the whole fleet can find protection together.

24. 'And the land: by distance, increasing as you go further from home, and by becoming quickly insufficient to provide food and fodder for such a huge army and its animals, it will contrive to defeat you.'

25. Xerxes said, 'There is good sense in what you say. But do not fear everything alike, or count every risk.

26. 'If we thought only of difficulties we would never venture anything. Far better to have a stout heart, and accept the possibility of evils, than to step timidly and travel nowhere.

27. 'Success for the most part attends those who act boldly, not those who weigh everything.

28. 'You see the height the power of Persia has reached – never would it have grown to this point if they who sat on the throne before me had thought like you, or listened to councillors of such a mind.'

29. And Xerxes sent Artabanus home to Susa, tired of his caution and opposition.

Chapter 61

1. The next day, when the sun rose, Xerxes ordered the first of his host across the bridge.

2. Sumpter beasts, camp followers, and at their head the choice Ten Thousand of the Persian army,

followed by troops of many other nations, crossed over.

3. On the second day the cavalry crossed, and the regiments of spearmen, and Xerxes himself, and the rest of the army.

4. At the same time the fleet sailed to the far shore. As soon as Xerxes had reached the European side, he stood to contemplate his army as they crossed under the lash.

5. And the crossing continued during seven days and seven nights, without rest or pause.

6. It is said that here, after Xerxes had made the passage, a Hellespontian exclaimed,

7. 'Why has the whole race of mankind come to the destruction of Greece? What has Greece done, to deserve such a vengeance?'

8. For Xerxes had brought one million seven hundred thousand men from many nations of Asia, India, Arabia and Africa, each with its own type of weapon and clothing, and its own skills in war.

9. In the fleet were one thousand two hundred triremes, and each ship had a company of soldiers alongside the seamen.

10. There were many men of note and courage in the army and navy, and many noble rulers.

11. And there was one woman, Artemisia, who ruled over the Halicarnassians, the men of Cos, of Nisyrus and of Calydna;

12. She brought five triremes to the Persian fleet and they were, next to the Sidonian, the most famous ships in the fleet.

13. She likewise gave to Xerxes sounder counsel than any of his other allies.

14. So Xerxes began his march into Macedonia. Every city he passed added men to his army, and the coastal towns provided yet further seamen to his fleet.

15. Every city, in response to the demand he had sent by heralds before him, had made food and drink ready for him and his forces.

16. No sooner had the heralds brought their message, than in every city the inhabitants made a division of their stores of corn,

17. And proceeded to grind flour of wheat and of barley for many months together.

18. They purchased the best cattle and fattened them; and fed poultry and waterfowl to be ready for the army;

19. While they likewise prepared gold and silver vases and drinking-cups, and everything else needed for the service of the table.

20. These last preparations were made for the king only, and those who sat with him; for the rest of the army plain food was provided.

21. On the arrival of the Persians, a tent ready pitched for the purpose received Xerxes, who took his rest therein, while the soldiers remained under the open sky.

22. When the dinner hour came, great

was the toil of those who entertained the army;

23. While the guests ate their fill, and
then, after passing the night at the
place, took down the royal tent
next morning, and packing its
contents, carried them all off,
leaving nothing behind.

24. At last Xerxes reached Therma, to
which he had ordered his fleet,

25. And from there he could see the
Thessalian mountains, Olympus
and Ossa, both very high.

26. He took a boat to view the mouth of
the River Peneus, which collects all
the waters of the rivers of Thessaly, a
land ringed by its mountains, and
discharges them into the sea.

Chapter 62

1. When Xerxes returned to Therma
he found waiting for him the
heralds he had sent to the cities of
Greece, demanding earth and
water; and learned which had
complied, and which had refused.

2. Among those who sent earth and
water were the Thessalians,
Dolopians, Enianians,
Perrhaebians,

3. The Locrians, Magnetians,
Malians, Achaeans of Phthiotis,
Thebans, and the Boeotians
generally, except those of Plataea
and Thespiae.

4. In the cities that had refused to
submit there was great alarm and
anxiety, for news of the vast host
of the Persians had reached
everywhere in Greece.

5. In Athens the citizens debated
whether to abandon their city and
fly, or to stay and fight.

6. Among them a citizen of the first
rank, Themistocles, nerved them
by saying, 'We are defended by the
best circuit of wooden walls of any
city;

7. 'I mean our fleet.' He said this
because he had previously given
Athens excellent advice, which was
as follows.

8. The city authorities had accumu-
lated a large sum in the treasury,
and were about to share it among
the citizens, who would have
received ten drachmas apiece,

9. When Themistocles persuaded
them not to distribute the money,
but to use it to build two hundred
ships to help them in their war
against the Eginetans.

10. It was thus the Eginetan war
which proved the saving of Greece;
for thereby was Athens forced to
become a maritime power.

11. Now, with the looming threat of
Xerxes, they resolved to build yet
more ships, and to equip them
well.

12. The Greeks who were loyal to the
Grecian cause assembled in one
place, and there consulted, and
exchanged pledges with each other.

13. They agreed that, before any other
step was taken, the feuds and
enmities between the different
states should first be appeased.

14. There were many such; but one
was of more importance than the

rest, namely, the war then still continuing between the Athenians and Eginetans.

15. When this business was concluded, the Greeks sent spies into Asia to take note of Xerxes' affairs.

16. At the same time they resolved to send ambassadors to the Argives, and conclude a league with them against the Persians;

17. And likewise they dispatched messengers to the people of Corcyra, and to those of Crete, exhorting them to send help to Greece.

18. Their wish was to unite the entire Greek name in one, and so to bring all to join in the same plan of defence, because the approaching dangers threatened all alike.

19. And they sent also to Gelo, the son of Deinomenes, in Sicily.

20. Now the power and wealth of Gelo, as king of Syracuse, was very great, far greater than that of any other single Grecian state.

21. The spies who went to Sardis before Xerxes set forth to the Hellespont were caught while noting the Persian strength,

22. And were just about to be put to death when Xerxes reprieved them, gave them free access to everything in his army,

23. And then sent them home, saying that he would prefer the Greeks to know his great strength than to be ignorant of it.

24. This was like his decision when, at the Hellespont, some Greek ships carrying corn from the Euxine to the Peloponnese were stopped, and the Persians made to capture them.

25. But Xerxes, on hearing what they carried and wither they were bound, said, 'We too are going there; let them carry our corn for us.'

26. And the seamen were able to report on the great armament of the Persians when they reached home, instilling fear.

27. Among those who chose not to aid their fellow-Greeks in opposing Xerxes were the Argives.

28. They had received a message from Xerxes when he first planned his invasion, saying that the Persians regarded themselves as springing from Perseus, founder also of Argos, and that they were therefore kin;

29. And that it was wrong for kin to war on each other, or for the Argives to join the Greeks in opposing Xerxes.

30. Having lately lost many citizens in fighting with Sparta, the Argives were only too happy to find an excuse to stand aside from the war;

31. And used a stratagem to deny the call for aid from their fellow-Greeks. This was to ask for equal generalship of the army, which they knew the Spartans, with their two kings, could not accept.

Chapter 63

1. Of greater moment was the embassy to Gelo, who had made Syracuse great and wealthy.

2. When the Greek envoys reached Syracuse, they said, 'We have been sent to you by the Lacedaemonians and Athenians, with their respective allies, to ask your help against the barbarian.

3. 'Doubtless you have heard of his invasion, bringing out of Asia all the forces of the East, to carry war into Europe, claiming that he only intends to attack Athens, but really bent on subjecting all the Greeks.

4. 'Help us maintain the freedom of Greece; your power is great, and your portion in Greece, as lord of Sicily, is no small one.

5. 'If all Greece join together in one, we will be a mighty host, and we shall be a match for our assailants;

6. 'But if some turn traitors, and others refuse aid, and only a small part of the whole body remains sound, all Greece may perish.

7. 'For do not hope that the Persian, when he has conquered our country, will be content and not advance against you next.

8. 'Take your measures beforehand, and consider that you defend yourself when you aid us.'

9. Gelo replied, 'You have the face to ask this when you refused to aid me against the Carthaginians.

10. 'Now that I am powerful, however, you come to me! But I will not treat you as you treated me.

11. 'I am ready to help, and to furnish as my contribution two hundred triremes, twenty thousand soldiers, two thousand cavalry, and an equal number of archers, slingers and light horsemen,

12. 'Together with corn for the whole Grecian army as long as the war lasts.

13. 'These services, however, I promise on one condition – that you appoint me commander of all the Grecian forces during the war with the barbarian.

14. 'Unless you agree to this, I will neither send aid, nor come myself.'

15. To this neither the Spartans could agree as regards the land forces, nor the Athenians as regards the sea forces.

16. The envoys said, 'We came here in search of an army, not a general! The Spartans are undisputed for their excellence at arms,

17. 'And the Athenians, the most ancient nation in Greece, the only Greeks who have never changed their abode,

18. 'The people who are said by the poet Homer to have sent to Troy the man best able of all the Greeks to array and marshal an army – may be allowed to boast somewhat of themselves.'

19. Gelo replied: 'Strangers, you have, it seems to me, no lack of commanders, but you are likely to lack men to receive their orders.

20. 'As you are resolved to yield nothing and claim everything, you

had best make haste back to Greece, and say that the best hope of succour has been lost to her.'

21. Nevertheless Gelo anxiously kept watch on matters in Greece, to see how affairs stood;

22. And was ready to send earth and water to Xerxes if, as he feared would indeed happen, the Greeks were overcome.

Chapter 64

1. As for the Corcyraeans, whom the envoys visited on their way to Sicily, and gave the same message as to Gelo,

2. They readily promised their help, declaring that the ruin of Greece was a thing which they could not tamely stand by to see;

3. For should she fall, they themselves must submit to slavery the very next day; so they were bound to help to the uttermost of their power.

4. But though they answered so smoothly, when the time came for their aid to be sent, they were of quite a different mind.

5. They manned sixty ships, but it was long before they put to sea with them;

6. And when they had so done, they went no further than the Peloponnese, where they lay to with their fleet off the Lacedaemonian coast, about Pylos and Taenarum;

7. Like Gelo, watching to see what turn the war would take. For they did not believe the Greeks could win, and expected that the Persians would become master of the whole of Greece.

8. They acted as they did in order that they might be able to say to Xerxes: 'O king! though the Greeks sought to obtain our aid in their war with you,

9. 'And though we had a force of no small size, and could have furnished a greater number of ships than any Greek state except Athens,

10. 'Yet we refused, since we would not fight against you, nor do anything to cause you annoyance.'

11. The Corcyraeans hoped that a speech like this would gain them better treatment from the Persians than the rest of the Greeks.

12. At the same time, they had an excuse ready to give their countrymen, which they used when the time came;

13. For when reproached, they replied that they had fitted out a fleet of sixty triremes, but the Etesian winds did not allow them to double Cape Malea,

14. And this hindered them from reaching Salamis – it was not from any bad motive that they missed the sea fight.

15. The Thessalians, however, did not submit to Persia until they were forced to do so; they gave plain proof that they preferred to ally with their fellow-Greeks.

16. No sooner did they hear that

Xerxes was about to invade Europe than they dispatched envoys to meet with all the states inclined to the Grecian cause.

17. These envoys addressed their countrymen as follows: 'Fellow Greeks, it behoves you to guard the pass of Olympus;

18. 'For thus will Thessaly be kept safe, as well as the rest of Greece. We are quite ready to take our share in this work;

19. 'But you must send us a strong force: otherwise we will have to make terms with the Persians.

20. 'We ought not to be left, exposed as we are in front of all the rest of Greece, to die in your defence alone and unassisted.

21. 'If you do not choose to send us aid, you cannot force us to resist the enemy;

22. 'For there is no force so strong as inability. We shall therefore do our best to secure our own safety.'

23. Seeing the force of this argument, the Greeks resolved to send a body of infantry to Thessaly by sea, to defend the pass of Olympus.

24. Accordingly a force was collected, which passed up the Euripus, and disembarked at Alus, on the coast of Achaea.

25. They occupied the defile of Tempe, which leads from Lower Macedonia into Thessaly along the course of the Peneus, having the range of Olympus on the one hand and Ossa on the other.

26. The Greek force amounted to ten thousand heavy-armed men, who were joined by the Thessalian cavalry.

27. The commanders were, for the Lacedaemonians, Evaenetus, the son of Carenus, who had been chosen out of the Polemarchs;

28. And for the Athenians, Themistocles, the son of Neocles.

29. The force did not however maintain its station for more than a few days, because envoys came from Alexander, the son of Amyntas, the Macedonian,

30. And counselled them to leave Tempe, telling them that if they remained in the pass they would be trodden underfoot by the invading army,

31. Whose numbers they recounted, and likewise the multitude of their ships.

32. Also they warned that the Persians might enter by another pass, leading from Upper Macedonia into Thessaly through the territory of the Perrhaebi, and by the town of Gonnus;

33. The pass by which soon afterwards the army of Xerxes indeed made its entrance. The Greeks therefore went back to their ships and sailed away to the Isthmus of Corinth.

Chapter 65

1. On their return to the Isthmus the Greeks considered where they should take their stand.

2. The opinion that prevailed was that they should guard the pass of Thermopylae,

3. For Thermopylae was narrower than the Thessalian defile, and at the same time nearer to them.

4. Of the hidden pathway over the mountain, by which the Greeks who later fell at Thermopylae were intercepted, they had no knowledge,

5. Until, on their arrival there, it was shown to them by the Trachinians.

6. At the same time it was resolved that the fleet should proceed to Artemisium, in the region of Histiaeotis,

7. For, as those places are near to one another, it would be easy for the fleet and army to hold communication.

8. These places seemed to the Greeks fit for their purpose, because in the narrow pass of Thermopylae the barbarians could make no use of their vast numbers, nor of their cavalry.

9. And when news reached them of the Persians being in Pieria, immediately they left the Isthmus,

10. And proceeded, some on foot to Thermopylae, others by sea to Artemisium, making all speed.

11. The fleet of Xerxes now departed from Therma; and ten of the swiftest ships ventured to stretch across directly for Sciathus,

12. At which place there were three Greek ships keeping a lookout, one a ship of Troezen, another of Egina, and the third from Athens.

13. The Greek sailors no sooner saw the barbarians approaching in the distance than they all hurriedly took to sail.

14. The barbarians at once pursued, and the Troezenian ship, which was commanded by Prexinus, fell into their hands.

15. The Eginetan trireme, under its captain Asonides, gave the Persians much trouble,

16. One of the marines, Pythes, the son of Ischenous, distinguishing himself beyond all the others who fought that day.

17. After the ship was taken this man continued to resist, and did not cease fighting till he fell quite covered with wounds.

18. The Persians who served as men-at-arms in the squadron, finding that he was not dead, but still breathed,

19. And being anxious to save his life because he had behaved so valiantly, dressed his wounds with myrrh, and bound them with cotton bandages.

20. Then, when they had returned to their own station, they displayed their prisoner admiringly to the whole host,

21. And behaved towards him with much kindness; but all the rest of the Eginetan ship's crew were treated merely as slaves.

22. The third, a trireme commanded by Phormus of Athens, took to flight and ran aground at the mouth of the River Peneus.

23. The barbarians got possession of the ship but not of the men. For

the Athenians had no sooner run their vessel aground than they leapt out, and made their way through Thessaly back to Athens.

24. When the Greeks stationed at Artemisium learnt what had happened by fire-signals from Sciathus,

25. So terrified were they that, quitting their anchorage-ground at Artemisium, and leaving scouts to watch the foe on the highlands of Euboea,

26. They removed to Chalcis, intending to guard the Euripus.

27. Meantime three of the ten vessels sent by the Persians advanced as far as the sunken rock called 'The Ant' between Sciathus and Magnesia, and there set up a stone pillar brought for that purpose.

28. After this, the course now being clear, the main Persian fleet set sail from Therma, eleven days from the time that the king left it with the army.

29. A day's voyage without a stop brought them to Sepias in Magnesia, and to the strip of coast which lies between the town of Casthanaea and the promontory of Sepias.

Chapter 66

1. As far as this point then, and on land as far as Thermopylae, the armament of Xerxes had been free from mischance;

2. And its numbers were still very great. First there was the original complement of twelve hundred and seven ships which came with the king from Asia,

3. The contingents of the nations severally amounting, if we allow to each ship a crew of two hundred men, to two hundred and forty-one thousand, four hundred.

4. Each of these vessels had on board, besides native soldiers, thirty fighting men, who were either Persians, Medes or Sacans; which gives an addition of thirty-six thousand, two hundred and ten.

5. To these numbers can be added the crews of the penteconters; which may be reckoned, one with another, at eighty men each.

6. There were three thousand such vessels, the men on board accordingly numbering two hundred and forty thousand. This was the sea force brought by the king from Asia; and it amounted in all to five hundred and seventeen thousand, six hundred and ten men.

7. The number of foot soldiers was one million, seven hundred thousand; that of the horsemen eighty thousand;

8. To which must be added the Arabs who rode on camels, and the Libyans who fought in chariots, about twenty thousand.

9. The whole number of the land and sea forces added together amounts to two million, three hundred and seventeen thousand, six hundred and ten men.

10. Such was the force brought from

Asia, without including the camp followers, or taking any account of the provision-ships and their crews.

11. To the amount thus reached we have still to add the forces gathered in Europe.

12. The Greeks dwelling in Thrace and in the islands off its coast gave to Xerxes' fleet one hundred and twenty ships; the crews of which amounted to twenty-four thousand men.

13. Besides these, footmen were provided by the Thracians, the Paeonians, the Eordians, the Bottiaeans, by the Chalcidean tribes,

14. By the Brygians, the Pierians, the Macedonians, the Perrhaebians, the Enianians, the Dolopians, the Magnesians, the Achaeans and by all the dwellers upon the Thracian seaboard;

15. And the forces of these nations amounted to three hundred thousand men. Adding these numbers to the force out of Asia brings the sum of Xerxes' fighting men to two million, six hundred and forty-one thousand, six hundred and ten.

16. Estimating very conservatively the camp attendants and the corn-bark and other freight-ship crews at an equal number, yields a figure of five million, two hundred and eighty-three thousand, two hundred and twenty as the total number of men brought by

Xerxes, the son of Darius, as far as Sepias and Thermopylae.

17. And to this still must be added the vast number of women who followed the camp to grind the corn, and also the many concubines, and the eunuchs;

18. Nor can the baggage horses and other sumpter beasts, nor the Indian hounds which followed the army, be calculated, by reason of their multitude.

19. It is no surprise that the water of the rivers was found too scant for the army in some instances;

20. Rather it is a marvel how the provisions did not fail, when the numbers were so great.

21. For if each man consumed no more than a choenix of corn a day, there must have been used daily by the army one hundred and ten thousand, three hundred and forty medimni,

22. And this without counting what was eaten by the women, the eunuchs, the sumpter beasts and the hounds.

23. Among all this multitude of men there was not one who deserved more than Xerxes himself to wield so vast a power.

Chapter 67

1. When Xerxes' fleet reached the strip of coast between the city of Casthanaea and Cape Sepias, the ships of the first row were moored to the land, while the remainder swung at anchor further off.

2. The beach extended only a little way, so that the majority of ships had to anchor offshore, row upon row, eight deep.

3. In this manner they passed the night. But at dawn calm and stillness gave place to a raging sea,

4. And a violent storm, driven by a strong gale from the east – a wind which the people in those parts call Hellespontias.

5. Those who perceived the wind rising, and were so moored as to allow of it, forestalled the tempest by dragging their ships up the beach, thereby saving themselves and their vessels.

6. But the ships which the storm caught out at sea were driven ashore, some near the place called Ipni, at the foot of Pelion; others on the beach itself;

7. Others again on the rocks about Cape Sepias; while a portion were dashed to pieces near the cities of Meliboea and Casthanaea. There was no resisting the tempest.

8. Those who put the loss of the Persian fleet in this storm at its lowest say that four hundred ships were destroyed, a countless multitude of men died, and a vast treasure was engulfed.

9. Ameinocles, the son of Cretines, a Magnesian, who farmed land near Cape Sepias, found the wreck of these vessels a source of great gain to him;

10. Many gold and silver drinking-cups were cast up long afterwards by the surf, which he gathered;

11. While treasure-boxes too, and golden articles of all kinds and beyond count, came into his possession.

12. Ameinocles grew to be a man of great wealth in this way; but in other respects things did not go over-well with him:

13. He too, like other men, had his own grief – the calamity of losing his offspring.

14. As for the number of the provision craft and other merchant ships which perished, it was beyond count.

15. Such was the loss that the commanders of the sea force, fearing lest in their shattered condition the Thessalians would attack,

16. Raised a high barricade around their station out of the wreck of the vessels cast ashore.

17. The storm lasted three days, and at last ceased on the fourth day.

18. The scouts left by the Greeks about the highlands of Euboea hastened down from their stations on the second day of the storm,

19. And acquainted their countrymen with what had befallen the Persian fleet.

20. These no sooner heard what had happened than they sailed back with all speed to Artemisium, expecting to find very few ships left to oppose them.

21. Meanwhile the Persians, when the wind lulled and the sea grew smooth, drew their ships down to the water, and proceeded to coast along the mainland.
22. Having rounded the extreme point of Magnesia, they sailed straight into the bay that runs up to Pagasae.
23. Fifteen of the Persian ships which had lagged behind the rest, happening to catch sight of the Greek fleet at Artemisium, mistook it for their own,
24. And sailing down into the midst of it, fell into their hands. The commander of this unlucky squadron was Sandoces, the son of Thamasius, governor of Cyme, in Aeolis.
25. This Sandoces was one of the royal judges, and had been crucified by Darius some time before, on the charge of taking a bribe to determine a cause wrongly;
26. But while he yet hung on the cross, Darius remembered that the good deeds of Sandoces towards the king's house were more numerous than his evil deeds;
27. And so, realising that he had acted with more haste than wisdom, he ordered Sandoces to be taken down from the cross and set at large.
28. Thus Sandoces escaped destruction at the hands of Darius, and was alive at this time;
29. But he was not fated to come off so cheaply from his second peril;

for as soon as the Greeks saw the ships making towards them, they guessed their mistake, and putting to sea, took them without difficulty.
30. Aridolis, tyrant of Alabanda in Caria, was on board one of the ships, and was made prisoner;
31. As also was the Paphian general, Penthylus, the son of Domonous, who was on board another.
32. This person had brought with him twelve ships from Paphos, and, after losing eleven in the storm off Sepias, was taken in the remaining one as he sailed towards Artemisium.
33. The Greeks, after questioning their prisoners as much as they wished concerning the forces of Xerxes, sent them away in chains to the Isthmus of Corinth.

Chapter 68

1. Xerxes meanwhile, with the land army, had proceeded through Thessaly and Achaea, and three days earlier had entered the territory of the Malians.
2. In Thessaly he matched his own horses against the Thessalian, which he heard were the best in Greece, but the Greek coursers were left far behind in the race.
3. All the rivers in this region had water enough to supply his army, except only the Onochonus;
4. But in Achaea, the largest of the streams, the Apidanus, barely held out.

5. From hence Xerxes passed into Malis, along the shores of a bay in which there is an ebb and flow of the tide daily.

6. By the side of this bay lies a piece of flat land, in one part broad, but in another very narrow indeed,

7. Around which runs a range of lofty hills, enclosing all Malis within them, and called the Trachinian cliffs after the nearby city of Trachis. Here in the Trachinia Xerxes pitched his camp.

8. On their side the Greeks occupied the narrow pass that they call Thermopylae, meaning 'The Hot Gates';

9. But the natives, and those who dwell in the neighbourhood, merely call them Pylae, that is, 'The Gates'.

10. Here then the two armies took their stand; the one master of all the region lying north of Trachis,

11. The other of the country extending southward of that place to the edge of the continent.

12. The Greeks who at this spot awaited the coming of Xerxes were the following:

13. From Sparta, three hundred men-at-arms; from Arcadia, a thousand Tegeans and Mantineans, five hundred of each people;

14. A hundred and twenty Orchomenians, from the Arcadian Orchomenus; and a thousand from other cities;

15. From Corinth, four hundred men; from Phlius, two hundred; and from Mycenae eighty.

16. Such was the number from the Peloponnese. There were also present, from Boeotia, seven hundred Thespians and four hundred Thebans.

17. Besides these troops, the Locrians of Opus and the Phocians had obeyed the call of their countrymen,

18. And sent the former all the force they had, the latter a thousand men.

19. For envoys had gone from the Greeks at Thermopylae among the Locrians and Phocians, to call on them for assistance, and to say,

20. They were themselves but the vanguard of the host, sent to precede the main body, which might every day be expected to follow them.

21. The sea was in good keeping, watched by the Athenians, the Eginetans, and the rest of the fleet.

22. There was no cause why they should fear; for after all the invader was merely a man;

23. And there never had been, and never would be, a man who was not liable to misfortunes from the very day of his birth,

24. And those misfortunes greater in proportion to his own greatness. The assailant therefore, being only a mortal, must needs fall from his glory.

25. Thus urged, the Locrians and the Phocians had come with their troops to Trachis.

Chapter 69

1. The various states each had captains of their own under whom they served;

2. But the one to whom all especially looked up, and who had the command of the entire force, was the Spartan, Leonidas.

3. Now Leonidas was the son of Anaxandridas, who was the son of Leo, who was the son of Eurycratidas, who was the son of Anaxander, who was the son of Eurycrates, who was the son of Polydorus, who was the son of Alcamenes, who was the son of Telecles, who was the son of Archelaus, who was the son of Agesilaus, who was the son of Doryssus, who was the son of Labotas, who was the son of Echestratus, who was the son of Agis, who was the son of Eurysthenes, who was the son of Aristodemus, who was the son of Aristomachus, who was the son of Cleodaeus, who was the son of Hyllus, who was the son of Hercules.

4. The force with Leonidas was sent forward by the Spartans in advance of the main body, that the sight of them might encourage the allies to fight,

5. And hinder them from going over to the Persians, as it was likely they might have done had they seen that Sparta was backward.

6. They intended presently to leave a garrison in Sparta, and hasten in full force to join the army.

7. The rest of the allies intended to act similarly; for it happened that the Olympic festival fell exactly at this same period.

8. None of them looked to see the contest at Thermopylae decided so speedily;

9. Wherefore they were content to send forward a mere advance guard. Such accordingly were the intentions of the allies.

10. The Greek forces at Thermopylae, when the Persian army drew near to the entrance of the pass, were seized with fear;

11. And a council was held to discuss a retreat. It was the wish of the Peloponnesians generally that the army should fall back to the Peloponnese, and there guard the Isthmus.

12. But Leonidas, who saw with what indignation the Phocians and Locrians heard of this plan, gave his voice for remaining where they were,

13. While they sent envoys to the several cities to ask for help, since they were too few to make a stand against Xerxes' army.

14. While this debate was going on, Xerxes sent a mounted spy to observe the Greeks, and note how many they were, and see what they were doing.

15. He had heard, before he came out of Thessaly, that a few men were assembled at this place, and that at their head were certain Lacedaemonians under Leonidas.

16. The horseman rode up to the camp, and looked about him, but did not see the whole army;

17. For such as were on the further side of the wall, which had been rebuilt and was now carefully guarded, it was not possible for him to behold;

18. But he observed those on the outside, who were encamped in front of the rampart.

19. It chanced that at this time the Spartans held the outer guard, and were seen by the spy,

20. Some of them engaged in gymnastic exercises, others combing their long hair.

21. At this the spy greatly marvelled, but he counted their number, and when he had taken accurate note of everything, he rode back quietly;

22. For no one pursued him, or paid any heed to his visit.

23. On hearing his report Xerxes, who had no means of surmising the truth – namely, that the Spartans were preparing to do or die manfully – thought it laughable that they should be engaged in such employments.

24. He sent for the Spartan Demaratus, and told him what he had heard, and questioned him about it, for he wished to understand the meaning of the Spartans' behaviour.

25. Demaratus said, 'I told you before, O king! about these men, when we had just begun our march upon Greece;

26. 'You only laughed at my words, but I tried to tell you the truth.

27. 'These men have come to dispute the pass with us; and it is for this that they are now making ready.

28. 'It is their custom, when they are about to hazard their lives, to adorn their heads with care.

29. 'Be assured, however, that if you can beat the men who are here and their fellow Lacedaemonians who remain in Sparta,

30. 'There is no other nation in the world that will venture to lift a hand in their defence.

31. 'You have now to deal with the first kingdom and town in Greece, and with the bravest of its men.'

Chapter 70

1. But Xerxes could not believe that so small a force could contend with his multitudes, or would even try to;

2. So he waited four days, expecting the Greeks to run away.

3. When on the fifth he found that they were still there, thinking that their stand was mere impudence and recklessness, he grew angry,

4. And sent against them the Medes and Cissians, with orders to take them alive and bring them into his presence.

5. The Medes rushed forward and charged the Greeks, but fell in vast numbers: others took the places of the slain, and would not be beaten off, though they suffered terrible losses.

6. In this way it became clear to all, and especially to the king, that though he had plenty of combatants, he had very few warriors.

7. The struggle, however, continued during the whole day.

8. The Medes, having met such a rough reception, withdrew from the fight; and their place was taken by the band of Persians under Hydarnes, who were the king's special guard:

9. It was thought they would soon finish the business. But when they joined battle with the Greeks, it was with no better success;

10. Matters went much as before, the two armies fighting in a narrow space,

11. The barbarians using shorter spears than the Greeks, and gaining no advantage from their numbers.

12. The Lacedaemonians fought in a way worthy of note, and showed themselves far more skilful than their adversaries.

13. They often turned their backs, and made as if to run away, at which the barbarians would rush after them with much noise and shouting;

14. Then the Spartans would suddenly wheel and face their pursuers, in this way destroying vast numbers of the enemy.

15. Some Spartans fell in these encounters, but only a few.

16. At last the Persians, finding all their efforts unavailing, withdrew to their quarters.

17. It is said that Xerxes, watching the battle, thrice leaped from the throne on which he sat, in terror for his army.

18. Next day the combat was renewed, but with no better success for the Persians.

19. The Greeks were so few that the barbarians hoped to find them disabled, by reason of their wounds, from offering further resistance; and so they once more attacked.

20. But the Greeks were drawn up in detachments according to their cities, and bore the brunt of the battle in turns,

21. All except the Phocians, who had been stationed on the mountain to guard the pathway.

22. So, when the Persians found no difference between that day and the preceding, they again retired to their quarters.

Chapter 71

1. Now, as Xerxes was in great dilemma, and at a loss how he should deal with the emergency,

2. Ephialtes, the son of Eurydemus, a man of Malis, came to him.

3. Stirred by the hope of receiving a rich reward at the king's hands, he had come to tell him of the pathway which led across the mountain to the rear of Thermopylae;

4. By which disclosure he brought destruction on the band of Greeks who had so far resisted the barbarians.

5. This Ephialtes afterwards, from fear of the Lacedaemonians, fled into Thessaly;

6. And during his exile, in an assembly of the Amphictyons held at Pylae, a price was set on his head by the Pylagorae.

7. When some time had gone by, he returned from exile, and went to Anticyra, where he was slain by Athenades, a native of Trachis.

8. Athenades did not slay him for his treachery, but for another reason:

9. Yet the Lacedaemonians honoured Athenades none the less. Thus did Ephialtes perish a long time afterwards.

10. Xerxes was delighted by Ephialtes' information, and immediately dispatched Hydarnes and the picked Persian guardsmen to follow him over the secret path.

11. They left just as the lamps were being lit in the evening, and went quickly and silently along,

12. Beginning at the Asopus, where that stream flows through the cleft in the hills,

13. Then along the ridge of the mountain which is called, like the pathway over it, Anopaea, and ends at the city of Alpenus,

14. The first Locrian town as one comes from Malis; pasing by the stone called Melampygus and the seats of the Cercopians.

15. Here the path is at its narrowest point.

16. The Persians marched all night, with the mountains of Oeta on their right hand, and on their left those of Trachis. At dawn they found themselves close to the summit.

17. The hill was guarded by a thousand Phocian men-at-arms, who were placed there to defend not just the pathway but also their own country.

18. They had volunteered for this service, and had pledged themselves to Leonidas to maintain the post.

19. Now, during all the time that the Persians were making their way up, the Greeks were unaware of them.

20. But the whole mountain was covered with groves of oak, and it happened that the air was very still, so that the leaves which the Persians stirred as they passed by made a loud rustling.

21. Hearing this the Phocians jumped up and flew to their arms.

22. In a moment the barbarians came in sight, and, perceiving men arming themselves, were greatly amazed;

23. For they had fallen in with an enemy where they expected no opposition.

24. Hydarnes, alarmed at the sight, and fearing lest the Phocians might be Lacedaemonians, inquired of Ephialtes to what nation these troops belonged.

25. Ephialtes told him, whereupon Hydarnes arrayed his Persians for battle.

26. The Phocians, galled by the showers of arrows to which they were exposed, and imagining themselves the special object of the Persian attack,

27. Fled hastily to the crest of the mountain, and there made ready to meet death;

28. But while their mistake continued, the Persians, not thinking it worth their while to delay on account of Phocians, passed on and descended the mountain with all possible speed.

Chapter 72

1. The Greeks at Thermopylae received the first warning of the destruction which dawn was bringing them,

2. From deserters who brought news that the Persians were marching round by the hills: it was still night when these men arrived.

3. Last of all, scouts came running down from the heights, and brought the same account, when the day was just beginning to break.

4. Then the Greeks held a council to consider what they should do. Opinions were divided: some were strong against quitting their post, while others argued the opposite.

5. So when the council had broken up, part of the troops departed and went home to their several states;

6. Part however resolved to remain, and to stand by Leonidas to the last.

7. It is said that Leonidas himself sent away the troops who departed, because he tendered their safety,

8. But thought it unseemly that either he or his Spartans should quit the post they had been especially sent to guard.

9. It is likely that Leonidas gave the order because he perceived the allies to be out of heart and unwilling to encounter the danger to which his own mind was made up.

10. He therefore commanded them to retreat, but said that he himself could not retreat with honour; knowing that, if he stayed, glory awaited him and the Spartans.

11. So the allies, when Leonidas ordered them to retire, obeyed him and departed.

12. Only the Thespians and the Thebans remained; and of these the Thebans were kept back by Leonidas as hostages, very much against their will.

13. The Thespians, on the contrary, stayed willingly, refusing to retreat, and declaring that they would not forsake Leonidas and his followers.

14. So they stayed with the Spartans, and died with them. Their leader was Demophilus, the son of Diadromes.

15. At sunrise Xerxes made his preparations, then waited until the time of morning when it is usual for city forums to fill, before beginning his advance.

16. Ephialtes had advised this because the descent of the mountain is much quicker, and the distance much shorter, than the way round the hills.

17. So the barbarians under Xerxes began to approach; and the Greeks under Leonidas, as they now went out determined to die,

18. Advanced much further than on previous days, until they reached the more open portion of the pass.

19. Hitherto they had held their station within the wall, and from this had sallied out to fight at the point where the pass was narrowest.

20. Now they joined battle beyond the defile, and made great slaughter among the barbarians, who fell in heaps.

21. Behind them the captains of the Persian squadrons, armed with whips, urged their men forward with continual blows.

22. Many were thrust into the sea, and there perished; a still greater number were trampled to death by their own soldiers;

23. No one heeded the dying. For the Greeks, reckless of their own safety and desperate,

24. Since they knew that, as the mountain had been crossed, their destruction was at hand,

25. Exerted themselves with the most furious valour against the barbarians.

26. By this time the spears of most of the Greeks were shivered, so with their swords they cut down the ranks of the Persians;

27. And here, as they strove, Leonidas fell fighting bravely, together with many other famous Spartans, whose names are imperishable on account of their great worthiness, all three hundred of them.

28. There fell too at the same time many famous Persians: among them, two sons of Darius, Abrocomes and Hyperanthes, his children by Phratagune, the daughter of Artanes.

29. And now there arose a fierce struggle between the Persians and the Lacedaemonians over the body of Leonidas, in which the Greeks four times drove back the enemy, and at last by their bravery succeeded in carrying away the body.

30. This combat was scarcely ended when the Persians with Ephialtes approached; and the Greeks, informed that the Persian elite troops were closing in behind them, made a change in the manner of their fighting.

31. Drawing back into the narrowest part of the pass, and retreating even behind the cross wall, they posted themselves on a hillock,

32. Where they stood drawn up together in one close body, except only the Thebans.

33. This hillock is at the entrance of the pass, where the stone lion now stands which was set up in honour of Leonidas.

34. Here the Greeks defended them-selves to the last, such as still had swords using them, and the others resisting with their hands and teeth;
35. Till the barbarians, who in part had pulled down the wall and attacked them in front, in part had gone round, and now encircled them on every side,
36. Overwhelmed the remnant beneath showers of missiles.

Chapter 73
1. Thus nobly did the whole body of Lacedaemonians and Thespians behave;
2. But one man is said to have distinguished himself above the rest, namely, Dieneces the Spartan.
3. A speech he made before the Greeks fought the Persians remains on record.
4. One of the Trachinians told him, such was the number of the barbarians, that when they shot their arrows the sun would be darkened by their multitude.
5. Dieneces, not at all frightened at these words, answered, 'Our Trachinian friend brings us excellent tidings.
6. 'If the barbarians darken the sun, we shall have our fight in the shade.'
7. Next to Dieneces a pair of Spartan brothers are reputed to have made themselves conspicuous: they were Alpheus and Maro, the sons of Orsiphantus.

8. There was also a Thespian who gained greater glory than any of his countrymen: he was Dithyrambus, the son of Harmatidas.
9. The slain were buried where they fell, and in their honour, nor less in honour of those who died before Leonidas sent the allies away, an inscription was set up, which said:
10. 'Here did four thousand men from Pelops' land/against three hundred thousand bravely stand.' This was in honour of all.
11. Another was for the Spartans alone: 'Go, stranger, and to Lacedaemon tell/that here, obey-ing her orders, we fell.'
12. These inscriptions, and the pillars likewise, were all set up by the Amphictyons.
13. The Thebans under the command of Leontiades remained with the Greeks, and fought against the barbarians only so long as neces-sity compelled them.
14. No sooner did they see victory inclining to the Persians, and the Greeks under Leonidas hurrying with all speed towards the hillock,
15. Than they moved away from their companions, and with hands upraised advanced towards the barbarians,
16. Exclaiming, as was indeed true, that they for their part wished well to the Persians, and had been among the first to give earth and water to the king;

17. Force alone had brought them to Thermopylae; and so they must not be blamed for the slaughter which had befallen the king's army.

18. These words, the truth of which was attested by the Thessalians, sufficed to obtain the Thebans the grant of their lives.

19. However, their good fortune was not without some drawback; for several of them were slain by the barbarians on their first approach;

20. And the rest, who were the greater number, had the royal mark branded upon their bodies by the command of Xerxes; Leontiades, their captain, being the first to suffer.

21. Thus fought the Greeks at Thermopylae. And Xerxes, after the fight was over, called for Demaratus to question him; and began as follows:

22. 'Demaratus, you are a worthy man; your truth-speaking proves it. All has happened as you warned. Now then, tell me,

23. 'How many Lacedaemonians are there left, and of those left how many are such brave warriors as these? Or are they all alike?'

24. 'King!' replied the other, 'the whole number of the Lacedaemonians is very great; and many are the cities which they inhabit.

25. 'But what you really need to know is that there is a city of Lacedaemon called Sparta, which contains within it about eight thousand full-grown men.

26. 'They are, one and all, equal to those who have fought here. The other Lacedaemonians are brave men, but not such warriors as these.'

27. 'Tell me now, Demaratus,' said Xerxes, 'how we can subdue these Spartans with least loss to ourselves.

28. 'You must know all the paths of their counsels, since you were once their king.' Demaratus answered, 'I advise this: send three hundred vessels from your fleet to attack the shores of Laconia.

29. 'There is an island called Cythera in those parts, not far from the coast, concerning which Chilon, one of our wisest men, remarked,

30. 'That Sparta would be better off if that island sank to the bottom of the sea, so constantly did he expect that it would give occasion to a project such as I now recommend.

31. 'Send your ships to that island, and the Spartans will keep their troops at home, fearing an attack on their very gates.

32. 'They will not then give any help to the rest of the Greeks. In this way all Greece can be subdued; and then Sparta, left to herself, will be powerless.

33. 'But if you will not take this advice, I will tell you what will happen. When you reach the Peloponnese, you will find the Isthmus of Corinth, a narrow neck

of land, where all the Peloponnesians will be gathered together;

34. 'And there you will have to fight bloodier battles than any you have yet witnessed. If you follow my plan, the Isthmus and the cities of the Peloponnese will yield to you without a battle.'

Chapter 74

1. Achaeamenes, brother of Xerxes, and commander of the fleet, immediately spoke, fearing that Xerxes would do as Demaratus advised.

2. 'Demaratus is wrong, and speaks from resentment of your success. We have lost four hundred vessels by shipwreck;

3. 'If three hundred more are sent away, our enemies will become a match for us.

4. 'Let us keep our whole fleet in one body, and it will be dangerous for them to venture an attack, as they will certainly be no match for us.

5. 'Besides, while our sea and land forces together advance, the fleet and army can each help the other; but if they are parted, no aid will come from one to the other.

6. 'Keep all together; if the Lacedaemonians come out against the Persians to battle, they will not be able to repair the disaster which has befallen them here.'

7. Xerxes replied, 'Achaeamenes, I agree with you. But Demaratus advised what he thought best; it is

just that his judgement is not so good as yours.

8. 'Never will I believe that he does not wish my cause well; for that is disproved both by his former counsels, and also by the circumstances of the case.

9. 'A citizen does indeed envy any fellow-citizen who is luckier than himself, and often hates him secretly;

10. 'If such a man be called on for counsel, he will not give his best thoughts, unless indeed he is a man of exalted virtue, and such are rarely found.

11. 'But a friend of another country delights in the good fortune of his foreign bond-friend, and will give him, when asked, the best advice in his power.

12. 'Therefore I warn all men not to speak ill of Demaratus, who is my bond-friend.'

13. Then Xerxes proceeded to pass among the slain, looking for the body of Leonidas, whom he knew to have been the Lacedaemonian leader.

14. On finding it he ordered that the head should be cut off, and the torso and limbs crucified upon a cross.

15. This proves most clearly that King Xerxes had more hatred for Leonidas, while he was still in life, than for any other man.

16. He would not otherwise have used his body so shamefully. For the Persians, more than any other

nation, usually pay high honours to those who are valiant in battle.

Chapter 75

1. Meanwhile the Greek fleet lay at Artemisium, two hundred and seventy ships not counting the penteconters, under the command of the Spartan Eurybiades, son of Eurycleides.
2. A Spartan had been appointed admiral because the allies recognised that if a Lacedaemonian did not take the command, they would break up the fleet, for never would they serve under the Athenians.
3. From the outset, even before the embassy went to Sicily to solicit alliance, there had been a talk of entrusting the Athenians with the command at sea;
4. But the allies were averse to the plan, so the Athenians did not press it, for there was nothing they had so much at heart as the salvation of Greece,
5. And they knew that, if they quarrelled among themselves about the command, Greece would be defeated.
6. In this they were right, for internal strife is a thing as much worse than war carried on by a united people, as war itself is worse than peace.
7. When the Greek fleet arrived at Artemisium, and saw the number of Persian ships at anchor near Aphetae,

8. And the abundance of Xerxes' troops everywhere, they were full of alarm at what they saw,
9. And began to speak of drawing back from Artemisium towards the inner parts of their country.
10. When the Euboeans heard this, they went to Eurybiades, and begged him to wait while they removed their families to safety.
11. But he refused, so they went to Themistocles, the Athenian commander, to whom they gave a bribe of thirty talents, on his promise that the fleet would remain and risk a battle in defence of Euboea.
12. Themistocles succeeded in keeping the fleet by giving Eurybiades five talents out of the thirty, which he gave as if they came from himself;
13. And having in this way persuaded the admiral, he approached Adeimantus, the son of Ocytus, the Corinthian leader,
14. Who was the only remonstrant now, and who still threatened to sail away from Artemisium and not wait for the other captains.
15. Themistocles said to him, 'Would you forsake us? By no means! I will pay you better for remaining than the Persian would for leaving your friends,'
16. And immediately sent on board Adeimantus' ship a present of three talents of silver.
17. So these two captains were won by gifts, and came over to the views

of Themistocles, who was thereby able to gratify the Euboeans.

18. He made his own gain on the occasion; for he kept the rest of the money, and no one knew of it. The commanders who took the gifts thought that the sums were furnished by Athens.

19. So it came to pass that the Greeks stayed at Euboea and there gave battle to the enemy. Now the battle took place as follows.

20. The barbarians reached Aphetae early in the afternoon, and then saw, as they had previously heard reported, that a fleet of Greek ships, few in number, lay at Artemisium.

21. At once they were eager to engage, fearing that the Greeks would flee, and hoping to capture them before they could escape.

22. They did not think it wise to make straight for the Greek station, in case the enemy saw them approaching, and thus escaped;

23. In which case night might fall before they overtook the fugitives; for the Persians were resolved not to let a single person slip through their hands.

24. They therefore contrived a plan to send two hundred ships around Euboea by Caphareus and Geraestus, so reaching the Euripus without being seen because they sailed outside the island of Sciathos.

25. This was to enclose the Greeks on every side; the ships detached would block the Greeks' line of retreat, while the rest of the Persian fleet would attack from the front.

26. Now the Persians had with them a man named Scyllias, a native of Scione, who was the most expert diver of his day.

27. At the time of the shipwreck off Mount Pelion he had recovered for the Persians much of what they lost, at the same time taking care to obtain a good share of the treasure for himself.

28. He had been wishing to go over to the Greeks for some time, but no good opportunity had offered itself till now.

29. So he slipped away, and no sooner reached Artemisium than he gave the Greek captains a full account of the damage done by the storm,

30. And likewise told them of the ships sent to make the circuit of Euboea.

31. On hearing this the Greeks held a council, at which they resolved on a plan: to remain at their moorings until midnight, then put out to sea, and attack the ships which were on their way round the island.

32. Later in the day, when they found that no one meddled with them, they formed a new plan, which was to wait till near evening,

33. And then sail out against the main body of the barbarians, for the purpose of testing the Persian mode of fighting and skill in manoeuvring.

34. When the Persians saw the Greeks boldly sailing towards them with their few ships, they thought them mad, and went out to meet them,

35. Expecting, as indeed seemed likely enough, that they would capture all their vessels with the greatest ease.

36. Such of the Ionians as wished well to the Grecian cause but served unwillingly in the Persian fleet, seeing their countrymen surrounded, were sorely distressed; for they felt sure that not one of them would escape.

37. On the other hand, such as saw with pleasure the attack on Greece, now vied eagerly with each other who should be the first to make prize of an Athenian ship, and thereby secure himself a rich reward from the king.

38. For through both the fleets none were so much admired as the Athenians.

39. The Greeks, at a signal, brought the sterns of their ships together into a small compass, and turned their prows on every side towards the barbarians;

40. After which, at a second signal, although enclosed within a narrow space, and closely pressed upon by the foe, yet they fell bravely to work,

41. And captured thirty ships of the barbarians, at the same time taking prisoner Philaon, the son of Chersis, and brother of Gorgus king of Salamis, a man of much repute in the Persian fleet.

42. The first to capture a Persian ship was Lycomedes the son of Aeschreas, an Athenian, who was afterwards given the prize for valour.

43. Victory was still doubtful when night came, and put a stop to the combat. The Greeks sailed back to Artemisium,

44. And the barbarians returned to Aphetae, much surprised at the result, which was far different from what they expected.

45. In this battle only one of the Greeks who fought on the side of Xerxes deserted and joined his countrymen.

46. This was Antidorus of Lemnos, whom the Athenians rewarded for his desertion by a present of land in Salamis.

Chapter 76

1. Evening had barely arrived when heavy rain – it was about midsummer – began to fall, which continued the whole night, with terrible thundering and lightning from Mount Pelion.

2. The bodies of the slain and the broken pieces of damaged ships drifted in the direction of Aphetae, and floated about the prows of the Persian vessels there, disturbing the action of the oars.

3. The barbarians were greatly dismayed by the storm, expecting certainly to perish, as they had fallen into such a multitude of misfortunes.

4. For before they recovered from the tempest and the wreck of their vessels off Mount Pelion, they had been surprised by a sea fight which had taxed all their strength,

5. And now the sea fight was scarcely over when they were exposed to floods of rain, and the rush of swollen streams into the sea, and violent thundering.

6. If those who lay at Aphetae passed a comfortless night, far worse were the sufferings of those who had been sent to make the circuit of Euboea;

7. The storm fell on them out at sea, and the result was calamitous. They were sailing near the Hollows of Euboea, when the wind began to rise and the rain to pour:

8. Overpowered by the force of the gale, they were driven onto rocks, and were entirely lost.

9. In the days following, the Persians and Greeks fought each other repeatedly off Artemisium, the latter making greater slaughter among the former than the other way round.

10. But then news reached the Greek fleet of the defeat at Thermopylae, and after its captains discussed what to do, it was decided to retreat further down the coast of Greece.

11. As the fleet made its escape by night from the anchorage at Artemisium, Themistocles sent some of his swifter boats to watering places along the coast,

12. With instructions to the sailors to cut messages in the rocks to the Ionians who were with the Persian fleet, saying,

13. 'Men of Ionia, you do wrong to fight against your own fathers, and to give your help to enslave Greece.

14. 'Come over, if possible, to our side: if you cannot, then stand aloof from the contest, and persuade the Carians to do likewise.

15. 'If neither of these things be possible, and you are hindered, by a force too strong to resist, from venturing upon desertion,

16. 'At least when we come to blows fight backwardly, remembering that you are sprung from us,

17. 'And that it was through you we first provoked the hatred of the barbarian.'

18. Themistocles had a twofold plan in this: he considered that either the Ionians would by moved by his words, or Xerxes would begin to suspect their loyalty, and keep them from sea battles.

19. When the Persians saw that the Greeks had gone, they advanced to Artemisium, and then along the coast to Histiaea, which they easily captured.

20. There they heard of the victory at Thermopylae, and Xerxes invited as many as wished to see the battlefield to visit it.

21. Huge numbers hastened to see it, and there saw the four thousand

dead Greeks, and a mere one thousand dead Persians,

22. For Xerxes had ordered that a trench be dug and the great mass of his slaughtered troops be buried in it.

23. No one was fooled by this; but there was rejoicing at the victory nevertheless.

24. At this time there came a few deserters from Arcadia to join the Persians, poor men who had nothing to live on, and needed employment.

25. The Persians brought them to the king, who asked what the Greeks were doing? The Arcadians answered,

26. 'They are holding the Olympic Games, seeing the athletic sports and the chariot races.'

27. 'And what,' said the king, 'is the prize for which they contend?' 'An olive wreath,' returned the others.

28. On hearing this, Tritantaechmes, the son of Artabanus, said, 'What! What manner of men are these against whom we have come to fight?

29. 'Men who contend with one another, not for money, but for honour!'

Chapter 77

1. The army of Xerxes now advanced into the land of the Phocians, and wasted it with fire and sword,

2. Plundering and then burning the cities of Drymus, Charadra, Erochus, Tethronium, Amphicaea, Neon, Pedieis, Triteis, Elateia, Hyampolis and Parapotamii.

3. Their citizens had fled into the mountains, and therefore escaped the fate of their homes;

4. But at Abae the Persians captured a number of them, and killed some of their women by repeatedly raping them, before stripping the city of its goods and setting it alight.

5. Now Xerxes set himself to march towards Athens, entering Boeotia by the country of the Orchomenians.

6. The Boeotians had one and all embraced the cause of the Persians, and their towns were in the possession of Macedonian garrisons,

7. Whom Alexander had sent there, to make it manifest to Xerxes that the Boeotians were on his side.

8. Meanwhile, the Greek fleet, which had left Artemisium, proceeded to Salamis at the request of the Athenians, and there cast anchor.

9. The Athenians had requested them to take up this position, in order that they might carry their women and children out of Attica, and plan what course to follow thereafter.

10. They had hoped to see the Peloponnesians drawn up in full force to resist the enemy in Boeotia, but that did not happen;

11. On the contrary, they learnt that the Greeks of those parts, only concerning themselves about their

own safety, were building a wall across the Isthmus,

12. And intended to guard the Peloponnese, and let the rest of Greece take its chance.

13. It was this news that made Athens request that the combined fleet should anchor at Salamis.

14. So while the rest of the fleet lay off this island, the Athenians cast anchor along their own coast.

15. Immediately on their arrival a proclamation was issued that every Athenian should save his family and household as he best could;

16. Whereupon some sent their families to Egina, some to Salamis, but the greater number to Troezen. This removal was made with all possible haste.

17. And now the remainder of the Grecian sea force, hearing that the fleet which had been at Artemisium was come to Salamis,

18. Joined it at that island from Troezen, orders having been issued previously that the ships should muster at Pogon, the port of the Troezenians.

19. The vessels collected were many more in number than those which had fought at Artemisium, and were supplied by more cities.

20. The admiral was the same who had commanded before, namely Eurybiades the Spartan.

21. The city which sent by far the greatest number of ships, and the best sailors, was Athens. There were three hundred and seventy

eight ships in all, most of them triremes.

Chapter 78

1. As the captains of the fleet were discussing their strategy, some advising that they should withdraw to the Isthmus so that, if they were defeated, they could return to their homes,

2. Word came that the Persians had entered Attica, and were ravaging and burning everything.

3. For the army under Xerxes had just arrived at Athens from its march through Boeotia, where it had burnt Thespiae and Plataea,

4. Both of which cities were forsaken by their inhabitants, who had fled to the Peloponnese;

5. And now it was laying waste all the possessions of the Athenians.

6. Thespiae and Plataea had been burnt by the Persians, because they knew from the Thebans that neither of those cities had espoused their side.

7. Since the Persians had crossed the Hellespont and begun their march on Greece, four months had gone by;

8. One, while the army made the crossing and delayed about the region of the Hellespont; and three while they proceeded from there to Attica, which they entered in the archonship of Calliades.

9. They found Athens empty; a few people only remained in the citadel, either keepers of the

treasures, or men of the poorer sort.

10. These persons having fortified the citadel with planks and boards, held out against the enemy.

11. The Persians camped on the hill opposite the citadel, which is called Mars' Hill by the Athenians, and began the siege of the place,

12. Attacking the Greeks with arrows to which rags of flaming tow were attached.

13. Those within the citadel found themselves in a woeful case, for their wooden rampart betrayed them, catching fire; but still they resisted.

14. It was in vain that the Pisistratidae came and offered terms of surrender – the defenders stoutly refused all parley,

15. And among their other modes of defence, rolled down masses of stone on the barbarians as they were climbing up to the gates:

16. So that Xerxes was for a long time perplexed, and could not contrive any way to take them.

17. At last some Persians found a secret way up a steep part of the precipice behind the citadel, and forced an entry.

18. They opened the gates to the main force, which rushed in and killed all those who did not throw themselves to their deaths from the walls.

19. Then they pillaged the citadel and set it alight. Xerxes, thus completely master of Athens,

dispatched a horseman to Susa, with a message to Artabanus, informing him of his success.

20. Meanwhile, at Salamis, the Greeks no sooner heard what had befallen the Athenian citadel,

21. Than they fell into such alarm that some of the captains did not wait for the council to come to a vote,

22. But hastily boarded their vessels, and set sail as though they would take to flight immediately.

Chapter 79

1. The rest, who stayed at the council board, voted that the fleet should sail from Salamis and give battle at the Isthmus.

2. Night now drew on; and the captains, dispersing from the meeting, proceeded on board their respective ships.

3. Themistocles, as he entered his own vessel, was met by Mnesiphilus, an Athenian, who asked him what the council had decided to do.

4. On learning that the idea was to sail to the Isthmus, and there give battle on behalf of the Peloponnese, Mnesiphilus exclaimed:

5. 'If these men sail away from Salamis, you will have no fight at all for our one fatherland;

6. 'They will all scatter to their own homes, and neither Eurybiades nor anyone else will be able to stop them. Greece will be brought to ruin by this bad counsel.

7. 'Make haste, and see if there is any possible way to persuade Eurybiades to change his mind, and stay here.'

8. Themistocles managed to persuade Eurybiades to reconvene the council of captains,

9. And when they had gathered, he quickly and eagerly began to speak, as men tend to do when they are anxious.

10. The Corinthian captain, Adeimantus son of Ocytus, said, 'Themistocles, at the Games they who start too soon are scourged.'

11. 'True,' Themistocles replied, 'but they who wait too late are not crowned.'

12. Then instead of using the arguments he had beforehand given to Eurybiades about the risk of the allies all going their separate ways, since this might offend those present,

13. He used a different argument. 'Eurybiades,' he said, 'it rests with you to save Greece if you will listen to my advice.

14. 'If we withdraw to the Isthmus we will be at a disadvantage, having to fight in the open sea against the greater numbers of the enemy.

15. 'Moreover we will thereby already have lost Salamis, Megara and Egina. The land and sea force of the Persians will advance together,

16. 'And our retreat will only draw them towards the Peloponnese, and so bring all Greece into peril.

17. 'If we stay here we will fight in a

narrow sea with few ships against many, and that will give us a great victory;

18. 'A narrow sea is favourable to us, a wide sea favourable to them. Salamis will be preserved, where we have placed our wives and children.

19. 'And indeed, the very point on which we set most store, namely defending the Peloponnese, is secured as much by this course as by the other;

20. 'For whether we fight here or at the Isthmus, we achieve the same end.'

21. When Themistocles had spoken, Adeimantus the Corinthian again attacked him, and told him to be silent, since he was a man without a city or a country,

22. Because Athens had been taken, and was in the hands of the barbarians; and he urged that Themistocles should show of what state he was envoy, before he gave his voice with the rest.

23. Themistocles bitterly reproached Adeimantus, and reminded the captains that with two hundred ships at his command, all fully manned for battle,

24. He had both city and territory as good as theirs; since there was no Grecian state which could resist his men at sea.

25. Then he turned to Eurybiades, and addressing him with still greater warmth and earnestness, said,

26. 'If you stay here, and behave like a

brave man, all will be well; if not, Greece will fall to ruin. For the whole fortune of the war depends on our ships.

27. 'But if you are not persuaded by my words, we Athenians will take our families on board, and go, just as we are, to Siris, in Italy, which is ours from of old.

28. 'You then, when you have lost allies like us, will hereafter call to mind what I have now said.'

29. At these words, Eurybiades changed his mind, because he feared that if he withdrew the fleet to the Isthmus the Athenians would sail away,

30. And he knew that without the Athenians the rest of their ships would be no match for the enemy fleet.

31. He therefore decided to remain, and give battle at Salamis.

Chapter 80

1. The men belonging to Xerxes' fleet, after they had seen the Spartan dead at Thermopylae,

2. And crossed the channel from Trachis to Histiaea, waited there for three days,

3. And then sailed down through the Euripus, in three more days reaching Phalerum.

4. The Persian forces both by land and sea when they invaded Attica were not less numerous than they had been on their arrival at Sepias and Thermopylae,

5. Despite their losses in the storm

and at Thermopylae, and again in the sea fights off Artemisium.

6. For various nations had since joined the king: the Malians, the Dorians, the Locrians and the Boeotians,

7. Each serving in full force in his army except the last, who did not number in their ranks either the Thespians or the Plataeans;

8. And together with these, the Carystians, the Andrians, the Tenians and the other people of the islands, who all fought on this side except the five states already mentioned.

9. For as the Persians penetrated further into Greece, they were joined continually by fresh nations.

10. Reinforced by the contingents of all these various states, the barbarians reached Athens.

11. The rest of the sea forces came safe to Phalerum, where they were visited by Xerxes, who had conceived a desire to go aboard and learn the wishes of the fleet.

12. So he came and sat in a seat of honour, and the sovereigns of the nations and the captains of the ships were sent to appear before him,

13. And as they arrived took their seats according to the rank assigned them by the king.

14. In the first seat sat the king of Sidon; after him, the king of Tyre; then the rest in their order.

15. When the whole company had taken their places, one after

another, and were set down in orderly array, Xerxes, to try them, sent Mardonius and questioned each, whether a sea fight should be risked or not.

16. All said that the Greeks should be given battle at sea, all except Artemisia, who said, 'Spare the ships, and do not risk a sea battle;

17. 'These people are far superior to yours in seamanship. Anyway what need is there to risk it? You are master of Athens, which is the purpose of your invasion;

18. 'And the whole of Greece lies subject at your feet. If you keep the fleet close and march on the Peloponnese, you will easily accomplish all your aims.

19. 'But if you fight at sea and lose, I tremble to think of the danger to your land army.'

20. The friends of Artemisia were anxious for her, in case her words offended the king,

21. And her enemies rejoiced, that having been in such favour with Xerxes she might now even forfeit her life.

22. But he was pleased beyond all others with the reply of Artemisia; and whereas, even before this, he had always esteemed her, he now praised her more than ever.

23. Nevertheless, he gave orders that the advice of the majority should be followed; for he thought that at Euboea the fleet had not done its best, because he himself was not there to see its work;

24. Whereas this time he resolved that he would be an eyewitness of the combat.

25. Orders were now given to the Persian fleet to stand out to sea; and the ships proceeded towards Salamis, and took up the stations to which they were directed, without hindrance from the Greeks.

26. The day, however, was too far spent for them to begin the battle, so they prepared to engage on the morrow.

27. The Greeks, meanwhile, were in great distress and alarm, more especially those of the Peloponnese, who were troubled that they had been kept at Salamis to fight on behalf of the Athenian territory,

28. And feared that, if they should suffer defeat, they would be besieged in an island, while their own country was left unprotected.

29. The same night the land army of the barbarians began its march towards the Peloponnese, where, however, all that was possible had been done to prevent the enemy from forcing an entrance by land.

30. As soon as news reached the Peloponnese of the death of Leonidas and his companions at Thermopylae, the inhabitants flocked together from the various cities,

31. And encamped at the Isthmus, under the command of Cleombrotus, son of

Anaxandridas, and brother of Leonidas.

32. Here their first care was to block up the Scironian Way; after which it was decided to build a wall across the Isthmus.

33. The number assembled amounted to many tens of thousands, and there was not one who did not give himself eagerly to the work, bringing stones, bricks, timber and baskets filled with sand.

34. Not a moment was lost therefore, and the work was soon finished.

Chapter 81

1. The Greeks at Salamis, on the other hand, when they heard that Xerxes was marching towards the Isthmus, were greatly alarmed for the Peloponnese.

2. At first they murmured together in low voices, each with his fellow, secretly, and marvelled at the folly shown by Eurybiades;

3. But presently the smothered feeling broke out, and another assembly was held, at which the former debate was resumed,

4. One side maintaining that it was best to sail to the Peloponnese and risk battle there, instead of abiding at Salamis and fighting for a land already taken by the enemy;

5. While the other, which consisted of the Athenians, Eginetans, and Megarians, was urgent to remain and have the battle fought where they were.

6. Themistocles, when he saw that the Peloponnesians would carry the vote against him,

7. Went out secretly from the council, and, instructing a certain man in what to say, sent him on board a merchant ship to the Persian fleet.

8. This man was Sicinnus, one of Themistocles' household slaves, who had served as tutor to his sons;

9. In after times, when the Thespians were admitting persons to citizenship, Themistocles made him a Thespian, and rich.

10. When Sicinnus reached the Persian fleet he delivered his message to the leaders in these words:

11. 'The Athenian commander has sent me to you privily, without the knowledge of the other Greeks.

12. 'He is a well-wisher to the king's cause, and would rather success should attend on you than on his countrymen;

13. 'So he bids me tell you that fear has seized the Greeks and they are meditating a hasty flight.

14. 'Therefore it is open to you to beat them in battle if you will hinder their escaping.

15. 'They no longer agree among themselves, so they will make little resistance – indeed, it is likely you may see a fight already begun between such as favour and such as oppose your cause.'

16. The messenger, when he had thus expressed himself, departed and was seen no more.

17. Then the Persian captains, believing what the messenger had said, proceeded to land a large body of troops on the islet of Psyttaleia, which lies between Salamis and the mainland;

18. After which, about midnight, they advanced their western wing towards Salamis, so as to enclose the Greek fleet.

19. At the same time the forces stationed near Ceos and Cynosura moved forward, and filled the whole strait as far as Munychia with their ships.

20. This advance was made to prevent the Greeks from escaping, and to keep them in Salamis, to take vengeance on them for the battles fought near Artemisium.

21. The Persian troops were landed on the islet of Psyttaleia, because, as soon as the battle began, the men and wrecks were likely to drift in that direction, as the isle lay in the very path of the coming fight;

22. And they would thus be able to save their own men and destroy those of the enemy.

23. All these movements were made in silence, so that the Greeks would be unaware of them; and they occupied the whole night, so that the men had no time to get their sleep.

24. Meanwhile, among the Greek captains at Salamis, the strife of words was growing fierce.

25. As yet they did not know that they were surrounded, but imagined that the barbarians remained in the same places as the day before.

26. In the midst of their arguing, Aristides, the son of Lysimachus, who had crossed from Egina, arrived in Salamis.

27. He was an Athenian, and had been ostracised by the community, even though there was not a man so worthy and just in all Athens as he.

28. He arrived at the council, and, standing outside, called for Themistocles.

29. Now Themistocles was not his friend, but his most determined enemy. However, under the pressure of the great dangers impending, Aristides forgot their feud,

30. And called Themistocles out of the council, since he wished to confer with him, because he had heard before his arrival of the impatience of the Peloponnesians to withdraw the fleet to the Isthmus.

31. As soon as Themistocles came out, therefore, Aristides addressed him in these words.

32. 'Our rivalry at all times, and especially at the present season, ought to be a struggle, which of us shall most advantage our country.

33. 'I have seen with my own eyes what I now report: that, however much the Corinthians or Eurybiades himself may wish it, they cannot now retreat;

34. 'For we are enclosed on every side by the enemy.

35. 'Go in to them, and make this known.' 'This is good news,' said Themistocles; 'and know that what the Persians have done was at my instance;

36. 'It was necessary, as our men would not fight here of their own free will, to make them fight whether they would or not.

37. 'But come, as you have brought the news, go in and tell it. If I speak to them, they will not believe me.'

38. So Aristides entered the assembly, and spoke to the captains: he had come, he told them, from Egina, and had but barely escaped the blockading vessels;

39. The Greek fleet was entirely enclosed by the ships of Xerxes, and he advised them to get ready to fight. Having said so much, he withdrew.

40. And now another contest arose; for the greater part of the captains would not believe the news.

41. But while they still doubted, a Tenian trireme, commanded by Panaetius, the son of Sosimenes, deserted from the Persians and joined the Greeks, bringing full intelligence.

42. For this reason the Tenians were inscribed upon the memorials as among those who overthrew the barbarians.

43. With this ship, which deserted to their side at Salamis, and the Lemnian vessel which came over before at Artemisium, the Greek fleet was brought to the full number of three hundred and eighty ships.

Chapter 82

1. The Greeks now, no longer in doubt, made ready for the coming fight.

2. At dawn all the men-at-arms were assembled, and speeches were made to them, of which the best was by Themistocles;

3. Who throughout contrasted what was noble with what was base, and bade them, in all that came within the range of man's nature and constitution, always to make choice of the nobler part.

4. Then he told them to go at once on board their ships, which they accordingly did; and the Greeks now put to sea with all their fleet.

5. The fleet had scarcely sailed when it was attacked by the Persians.

6. At once most of the Greeks began to back water, and were about to reach shore, when Ameinias of Palline, one of the Athenian captains, darted out in front of the line at an enemy ship.

7. The two vessels became entangled, and could not separate, whereupon the rest of the fleet came up to help Ameinias, and engaged with the Persians.

8. Against the Athenians, who held the western extremity of the line towards Eleusis, were placed the Phoenicians;

9. Against the Lacedaemonians,

whose station was eastward towards the Piraeus, were placed the Ionians.

10. Of these last a few only followed the advice of Themistocles, to fight backwardly; the greater number did far otherwise.

11. The names of trierarchs who captured vessels from the Greeks include Theomestor, the son of Androdamas, and Phylacus, the son of Histiaeus, both Samians.

12. For this service Theomestor was made tyrant of Samos by the Persians, while Phylacus was enrolled among the king's benefactors, and presented with a large estate in land.

13. By far the greater number of the Persian ships engaged in this battle were disabled, either by the Athenians or by the Eginetans.

14. For as the Greeks fought in order and kept their line, while the barbarians were in confusion and had no plan in anything they did, the issue of the battle could not be other than it was.

15. Yet the Persians fought far more bravely here than at Euboea, and indeed surpassed themselves; each did his utmost through fear of Xerxes, for each thought that the king's eye was upon himself.

16. Artemisia distinguished herself more than any other Persian leader, and in such a way as raised her even higher than before in Xerxes' esteem.

17. For after confusion had spread through the king's fleet, and her ship was closely pursued by an Athenian trireme,

18. She, having no way to fly, since in front of her were a number of friendly vessels, and she was nearest of all the Persians to the enemy, resolved on a measure which in fact proved her safety.

19. Pressed by the Athenian pursuer, she bore straight against one of the ships of her own party, a Calyndian, which had Damasithymus, the Calyndian king, himself on board, and sank it.

20. The commander of the Athenian trireme, when he saw her bear down on one of the enemy's fleet, thought immediately that her vessel was Greek,

21. Or else had deserted from the Persians, and was now fighting on the Greek side; he therefore gave up the chase, and turned away to attack others.

22. Thus she saved her life, and Xerxes observed, 'My men have behaved like women, my women like men!'

23. There fell in the battle Ariabignes, one of the chief commanders of the Persian fleet, who was son of Darius and brother of Xerxes;

24. And with him perished a vast number of men of high repute, Persians, Medes and allies.

25. Among the Greeks only a few died; for, as they were able to swim, all those that were not slain by the enemy escaped from the

sinking vessels and swam to
Salamis.

26. On the barbarian side more
perished by drowning than in any
other way, because they did not
know how to swim.

27. The greatest destruction took place
when the ships which had been
first engaged began to retreat;

28. For those stationed in the rear,
anxious to display their valour
before the eyes of the king, made
every effort to force their way to
the front, and so became entangled with their own retreating
forces.

29. In this confusion certain
Phoenicians, belonging to ships
which had been sunk,

30. Came before the king and laid the
blame of their defeat on the
Ionians, saying that they were
traitors, and had wilfully destroyed
the vessels.

31. But the consequence of their
complaint was that Xerxes
condemned them instead of the
Ionians.

32. For exactly as they spoke, a
Samothracian vessel bore down on
an Athenian and sank it, but was
attacked and crippled immediately
by one of the Eginetan squadron.

33. Now the Samothracians were
expert with the javelin, and aimed
their weapons so well,

34. That they cleared the deck of the
vessel that had disabled their own,
after which they sprang on board,
and took it.

35. Xerxes, when he saw the exploit,
turned fiercely on the Phoenicians
– ready, in his extreme vexation, to
find fault with anyone – and
ordered their heads to be cut off,

36. To prevent them, he said, from
casting the blame of their own
misconduct upon braver men.

Chapter 83

1. During the whole battle Xerxes sat
at the base of the hill called
Aegaleos, near Salamis;

2. And whenever he saw any of his
own captains perform a worthy
exploit he enquired about him,
and the man's name was taken
down by his scribes, together with
the names of his father and his
city.

3. The Greeks who gained the
greatest glory in the battle of
Salamis were the Eginetans, and
after them the Athenians.

4. The individuals of most distinction were Polycritus the Eginetan,
and two Athenians, Eumenes of
Anagyrus and Ameinias of Palline;
the latter of whom had pressed
Artemisia so hard.

5. If he had known that the vessel
carried Artemisia, he would never
have given up the chase until he
had either taken her, or else been
taken himself.

6. For a reward of ten thousand
drachmas had been offered to
anyone who should make her
prisoner.

7. The Athenians say that

Adeimantus, the Corinthian commander, at the moment when the two fleets joined battle, was seized with fear,

8. And spread his sails, and hastened to escape; on which the other Corinthians, seeing their leader's ship in flight, followed it.

9. They had not gone far when a bark drew near to their ships and its occupants called out, saying,

10. 'Adeimantus, while you play a traitor's part, by withdrawing all these ships, and flying away from the fight,

11. 'The Greeks you have deserted are defeating their foes as completely as they ever wished.'

12. Adeimantus would not believe what the men said; whereupon they told him he might take them with him as hostages, and put them to death if he did not find the Greeks winning.

13. Then Adeimantus put about, both he and those who were with him; and they rejoined the fleet when the victory was already gained.

14. Such is the tale that the Athenians tell concerning Corinthians; these latter however do not allow its truth.

15. On the contrary, they declare that they were among those who distinguished themselves most in the fighting. And the rest of Greece bears witness in their favour.

16. But these disputes in after-time arose because Salamis was a

famous victory, which saved Greece, and thereby Europe and the future of its civilisation.

Chapter 84

1. Xerxes, when he saw the extent of his defeat, began to be afraid lest the Greeks might sail straight to the Hellespont,

2. And break down the bridges there, in which case he would be trapped in Europe, at great risk of perishing.

3. He therefore decided to fly; but, as he wished to hide his purpose alike from the Greeks and his own people,

4. He set to work to carry a mound across the channel to Salamis, and at the same time began fastening a number of Phoenician merchant ships together, to serve as both a bridge and a wall.

5. He made many other warlike preparations, as if he were about to engage the Greeks again at sea.

6. Now, when these things were seen, all grew fully persuaded that the king was bent on remaining, and intended to push the war in good earnest.

7. Mardonius, however, was not deceived; for long acquaintance enabled him to read all the king's thoughts.

8. Meanwhile, Xerxes, though engaged in this way, sent off a messenger to carry intelligence of his misfortune to Persia.

9. Persian messengers travelled very fast.

The entire plan is a Persian invention;
and this is the method of it:

10. Along the whole line of road there
are men stationed with horses,
equal in number to the number of
days that the journey takes,
allowing one man and horse to
each day.

11. These men will not be hindered
from accomplishing at their best
speed the distance they have to go,
either by snow, rain or heat, or by
the darkness of night.

12. The first rider delivers his dispatch
to the second and the second to
the third;

13. And so it is borne from hand to
hand along the whole line, like the
light in the torch-race. The
Persians give this riding the name
of 'Angarum'.

14. At Susa, on the arrival of the first
message, which said that Xerxes
was master of Athens, such was the
delight of the Persians who had
remained behind,

15. That they strewed the streets with
myrtle boughs, and burnt incense,
and fell to feasting and merriment.

16. When the second message reached
them concerning Salamis, so great
was their dismay that they all rent
their garments, and cried aloud,
and wept without stint.

17. They laid the blame of the disaster
on Mardonius; and their grief on
the occasion was less on account of
the damage done to their ships,
than anxiety about the king's safety.

18. Their fears did not cease until

Xerxes himself, by his arrival, put
an end to them.

19. Now Mardonius saw that as he
had been the one to urge Xerxes to
conquer Greece, he would be
blamed for the failure of the
expedition.

20. So he said to Xerxes, 'Master, our
fate does not hang on a few planks
lost at sea, but on our great army
of infantry and cavalry.

21. 'The Greeks will never prevail
against them. Let us attack the
Peloponnese; or if you are resolved
to return to Persia,

22. 'Let me have 300,000 of the better
troops, and I will subdue the
Peloponnese in your name,

23. 'And bring you the heads of the
Spartan chiefs and the chiefs of the
other nations there, putting them
all beneath your sway.'

24. Xerxes was delighted by these
words, and called the other chief
Persians to consult about
Mardonius' proposal.

25. The person he especially asked was
Artemisia, who had proved herself
a wise counsellor and knew what it
was best to do.

26. Artemisia said, 'As your affairs now
stand, it seems to me you would
do better to return home.

27. 'As for Mardonius, if he prefers to
remain, and undertakes to do as he
has said, give him the troops he
desires.

28. 'If he succeeds, yours is the
conquest; for your slaves will have
accomplished it.

29. 'If, on the other hand, he fails, we suffer no great loss, so long as you are safe, and your house in no danger.

30. 'The Greeks, while you live and your house flourishes, must be prepared to fight many battles for their freedom;

31. 'Whereas if Mardonius falls, it matters nothing; the Greeks will have gained a poor triumph: merely a victory over one of your slaves!

32. 'Remember also, you go home having gained the purpose of your expedition; for you have burnt Athens!'

33. This advice of Artemisia pleased Xerxes well; for she had exactly uttered his own thoughts.

Chapter 85

1. As a mark of distinction Xerxes entrusted to Artemisia the conveyance of his natural sons to Ephesus.

2. He sent with them one of his chief eunuchs, a man named Hermotimus, a Pedasian, whose responsibility it was to tutor these sons.

3. This Hermotimus took a cruel vengeance on one who had done him an injury.

4. As a youth he had been made a prisoner of war, and when his captors sold him, he was bought by a certain Panionius, a native of Chios, who made his living by a very nefarious traffic.

5. Whenever he could get any boys of unusual beauty, Panionius made them eunuchs, and taking them to Sardis or Ephesus sold them for high prices.

6. For the barbarians value eunuchs more than others, since they regard them as more trustworthy.

7. Many were the slaves that Panionius, who made his living by this practice, had thus created; and among them was Hermotimus.

8. However, Hermotimus was not without luck, for after a while he was sent from Sardis, together with other gifts, as a present to the king.

9. Nor was it long before he came to be esteemed by Xerxes more highly than all his other eunuchs.

10. Now, when the king was on his way to Athens with the Persian army, and paused for a time at Sardis, Hermotimus made a journey on business into Mysia;

11. And there, in a district which is called Atarneus but belongs to Chios, he happened to fall in with Panionius.

12. Recognising him at once, he entered into friendly talk with him, describing the numerous blessings he had enjoyed because Panionius had made him a eunuch,

13. And promised him all manner of favours in return, if he would bring his household to Sardis and live there.

14. Panionius was overjoyed, and,

accepting the offer, came and brought his wife and children with him.

15. Then Hermotimus, when he had got Panionius and all his family into his power, addressed him as follows:

16. 'You, who get a living by viler deeds than anyone else in the world, what wrong did I or any of mine do to you or yours, that you made me the nothing I now am?

17. 'Ah! surely you thought you would never be punished for your crimes.

18. 'But justice has delivered you into my hands; and you cannot complain of the vengeance which I am resolved to take on you.'

19. So saying, Hermotimus commanded the four sons of Panionius to be brought, and forced the father to make them eunuchs with his own hand.

20. Unable to resist, he did as Hermotimus required; and then his sons were made to treat him in the same way.

21. Thus did Hermotimus exact requital from Panionius.

Chapter 86

1. Xerxes sent for Mardonius, and told him to choose from all his army such men as he wished, and see that he made his achievements equal his promises.

2. When night fell he ordered the captains of what remained of his fleet to sail for the Hellespont as fast as possible, to guard the bridges for the king's return.

3. On their way, as they sailed by Zoster, where certain narrow points of land project into the sea,

4. They mistook the cliffs for vessels, and fled far away in alarm.

5. Discovering their mistake, however, after a time, they joined company once more, and proceeded on their voyage.

6. Next day the Greeks, seeing the land force of the barbarians encamped in the same place,

7. Thought that their ships must still be lying nearby, and began to prepare for another attack.

8. Soon however news came that the Persian fleet had gone; whereupon it was instantly resolved to pursue.

9. The Greeks sailed as far as Andros; but, seeing nothing of the Persians, stopped there, and held a council.

10. Themistocles advised that the Greeks should press the pursuit, and make all haste to the Hellespont, in order to break down the bridges.

11. Eurybiades, however, delivered a contrary opinion. 'If,' he said, 'we break down the bridges, it would be the worst thing that could possibly happen for Greece.

12. 'The Persian, supposing himself compelled to remain in Europe, would be sure never to give us peace.

13. 'He could not afford inaction, which would ruin all his affairs,

and leave him no chance of ever getting back to Asia;

14. 'Indeed, it would even cause his army to perish by famine: whereas, if he stirred himself, and acted vigorously,

15. 'It was likely that the whole of Europe would eventually become subject to him;

16. 'Since, by degrees, the various towns and tribes would either fall before his arms, or agree to submit;

17. 'And in this way, his troops would find food sufficient, since each year the Greek harvest would be theirs.

18. 'As it was, the Persian, because he had lost the sea fight, intended evidently to remain no longer in Europe.

19. 'The Greeks ought to let him go; and when he was gone from among them, and had returned into his own country,

20. 'There would be time for them to contend with him for the possession of that.'

21. The other captains of the Peloponnesians agreed with this.

22. Finding the majority against him, Themistocles changed round, and addressing himself to the Athenians,

23. Who of all the allies were most nettled at the enemy's escape, and who eagerly desired, if the other Greeks would not stir, to sail on by themselves to the Hellespont and break the bridges, said:

24. 'I have often myself witnessed, and I have heard the same from others, that men who have been conquered, and driven quite to desperation, have renewed the fight, and retrieved their former disasters.

25. 'We have now had the great good luck to save both ourselves and all Greece by the repulse of this vast cloud of men;

26. 'Let us be content and not press them too hard, now that they have begun to retreat.

27. 'At present all is well with us – let us abide in Greece, and look to ourselves and our families.

28. 'The barbarian is gone – we have driven him off – let each go home, and sow his land diligently.

29. 'In the spring we will take ship and sail to the Hellespont and to Ionia!'

30. All this Themistocles said, dissembling, in the hope of establishing a claim upon Xerxes;

31. For he wanted to have a safe retreat in case any mischance should befall him at Athens – which indeed came to pass afterwards.

32. But at this time his fellow Athenians were ready to do whatever he advised, since they had always esteemed him a wise man, and he had lately proved himself truly well-judging.

Chapter 87

1. Privately now Themistocles lost no time in sending messengers in a light bark to Xerxes,

2. Choosing for this purpose men he could trust even if they should be put to torture.

3. Among them was the house-slave Sicinnus, the same whom he had made use of previously.

4. When the men reached Attica, all the others stayed in the boat, but Sicinnus went up to the king, and said,

5. 'I am sent by Themistocles, son of Neocles, leader of the Athenians, and the wisest and bravest man of the allies.

6. 'He says to you: "Themistocles the Athenian, anxious to render you a service, has restrained the Greeks,

7. '"Who were impatient to pursue your ships, and to break up the bridges at the Hellespont. Now, therefore, return home at your leisure."'

8. Now the Greeks, having resolved that they would neither pursue the barbarians, nor sail for the Hellespont to destroy the bridge,

9. Laid siege to Andros, intending to take the town by storm. Themistocles had required the Andrians to pay a sum of money;

10. And they had refused, being the first of all the islanders to do so.

11. To his declaration, that the money must needs be paid, as the Athenians had brought with them two mighty warriors, Persuasion and Necessity,

12. They replied that Athens might well be a great and glorious city,

since she was blest with such excellent fortune;

13. But they were wretchedly poor, stinted for land, and cursed with two weak governors, who always dwelt with them and would never quit their island; to wit, Poverty and Helplessness.

14. Accordingly the Andrians would not pay. For the power of Athens could not possibly be stronger than their inability.

15. This reply, coupled with the refusal to pay the sum required, caused their city to be besieged by the Greeks.

16. Meanwhile Themistocles, who never ceased his pursuit of gain, sent threatening messages to the other islanders with demands for different sums,

17. Employing the same messengers and the same words as he had used towards the Andrians.

18. If, he said, they did not send him the amount required, he would bring the fleet on them, and besiege them till he took their cities.

19. By these means he collected large sums from the Carystians and the Parians, who, when they heard that Andros was already besieged,

20. And that Themistocles was the best esteemed of all the captains, sent the money through fear.

21. In this way Themistocles, during his stay at Andros, obtained money from the islanders, unbeknown to the other captains.

Chapter 88

1. Xerxes and his army waited only a few days after the sea fight, and then withdrew into Boeotia by the road they had followed on their advance.
2. It was the wish of Mardonius to escort the king a part of the way; and as the time of year was no longer suitable for war,
3. He thought it best to winter in Thessaly, and wait for the spring before he attacked the Peloponnese.
4. After the army arrived in Thessaly, Mardonius made choice of the troops that were to stay with him;
5. And, first of all, he took the whole body called the 'Paragons', except only their leader, Hydarnes, who refused to leave the king.
6. Next, he chose the Persians who wore breastplates, and the thousand picked horse;
7. Likewise the Medes, the Sacans, the Bactrians and the Indians, foot and horse equally.
8. These nations he took entire: from the rest of the allies he culled a few men,
9. Taking either such as were remarkable for their appearance, or else such as had performed, to his knowledge, some valiant deed.
10. The Persians furnished him with the greatest number of troops, men who were adorned with chains and armlets.
11. Next to them were the Medes, who in number equalled the Persians, but in valour fell short of them.
12. The whole army, reckoning the horsemen with the rest, amounted to 300,000 men.
13. At the time when Mardonius was making choice of his troops, and Xerxes still continued in Thessaly,
14. The Lacedaemonians decided to seek satisfaction at the hands of Xerxes for the death of Leonidas, and take whatever he chose to give them.
15. So the Spartans sent a herald with all speed into Thessaly, who arrived while the entire Persian army was still there.
16. He said, 'King of the Persians, the Lacedaemonians and the Heracleids of Sparta require satisfaction due for bloodshed, because you slew their king, who fell fighting for Greece.'
17. Xerxes laughed, and for a long time said nothing. At last, however, he pointed to Mardonius, who was standing by him, and said,
18. 'Mardonius here shall give Sparta the satisfaction they deserve.' And the herald accepted the answer, and went his way.
19. After this Xerxes left Mardonius in Thessaly, and marched away himself, at his best speed, towards the Hellespont.
20. In forty-five days he reached the place of passage, with scarcely a fraction of his former vast army left.

21. All along their line of march, in every country where they chanced to be, his soldiers seized and devoured whatever corn they could find belonging to the inhabitants;

22. While, if no corn was to be found, they gathered the grass that grew in the fields, and stripped the trees, whether cultivated or wild, alike of their bark and their leaves, and so fed themselves.

23. They left nothing anywhere, so hard were they pressed by hunger. Plague and dysentery attacked the troops while still on their march, and greatly thinned their ranks.

24. Many died; others fell sick and were left behind in the different cities that lay along the route, the inhabitants being strictly charged by Xerxes to tend and feed them.

25. Of these some remained in Thessaly, others in Siris of Paeonia, others again in Macedonia.

Chapter 89

1. The Persians, having journeyed through Thrace and reached the passage, found that the bridges had been broken and dispersed by storms.

2. They therefore entered the ships of the fleet that awaited them, and crossed the Hellespont to Abydos.

3. At Abydos the troops halted, and, obtaining more abundant provision than they had on their march, fed without stint;

4. From which cause, added to the change in their water, great numbers of those who had hitherto escaped perished.

5. The remainder, together with Xerxes himself, came safe to Sardis.

6. Another story is told of the return of the king. It is said that when Xerxes on his way from Athens arrived at Eion on the Strymon, he gave up travelling by land,

7. And, entrusting Hydarnes with the conduct of his forces to the Hellespont, embarked himself on board a Phoenician ship, and so crossed into Asia.

8. On his voyage the ship was assailed by a strong wind blowing from the mouth of the Strymon, which caused the sea to run high.

9. As the storm increased, and the ship laboured heavily, because of the number of the Persians who had come in the king's train, and now crowded the deck,

10. Xerxes was seized with fear, and called out to the helmsman in a loud voice, asking him if there were any means whereby they might escape the danger.

11. 'No means, master,' the helmsman answered, 'unless we could be quit of these too numerous passengers.'

12. Xerxes, they say, on hearing this, addressed the Persians as follows: 'Men of Persia,' he said, 'now is the time for you to show what love you bear your king.

13. 'My safety, as it seems, depends wholly on you.' So spoke the king;

and the Persians instantly made obeisance, and then leapt into the sea.

14. Thus was the ship lightened, and Xerxes got safely to Asia.

15. As soon as he reached the shore he sent for the helmsman, and gave him a golden crown because he had preserved the life of the king;

16. But because he had caused the death of a number of Persians, he ordered his head to be struck from his shoulders.

17. Such is the other account given of the return of Xerxes; but it seems unworthy of belief, alike in other respects, and in what relates to the Persians.

18. For had the helmsman made any such speech to Xerxes, there is not one man in ten thousand who will doubt that this is what the king would have done:

19. He would have made the men on the ship's deck, who were not only Persians, but Persians of the highest rank, quit their place and go down below to take the oars,

20. Casting into the sea an equal number of the rowers, who were Phoenicians.

21. But the truth is, that the king returned into Asia by land, on the same road as the rest of the army.

22. There is another strong proof of this. It is certain that Xerxes passed through Abdera on his way back from Greece, where he made a contract of friendship with the inhabitants,

23. And presented them with a golden scymitar, and a tiara broidered with gold.

24. The Abderites declare, though somewhat improbably, that from the time of the king's leaving Athens he never once loosed his girdle till he came to their city, since it was not till then that he felt himself in safety.

25. Now Abdera is nearer to the Hellespont than Eion and the Strymon, where Xerxes, according to the other tale, took ship.

Chapter 90

1. When the spoils of war had been divided among them and monuments made to their victory from the chiefest spoils,

2. The Greeks sailed to the Isthmus, where a prize of valour was to be awarded to the man who, among them all, had shown the most merit during the war.

3. When the chiefs were all come, they took the ballots to give their votes for the first and for the second in merit.

4. Then each man gave himself the first vote, since each considered that he himself was the worthiest;

5. But most of the second votes were given to Themistocles.

6. In this way, while the others received but one vote apiece, Themistocles had for the second prize a large majority of the suffrages.

7. Envy, however, hindered the chiefs

from coming to a decision, and they all sailed away to their homes without making any award.

8. Nevertheless Themistocles was regarded everywhere as by far the wisest man of all the Greeks; and the whole country rang with his fame.

9. As the chiefs who fought at Salamis, notwithstanding that he was entitled to the prize, had withheld the honour from him,

10. Themistocles went without delay to Lacedaemon, in the hope that he would be honoured there.

11. And the Lacedaemonians received him handsomely, and paid him great respect.

12. The prize of valour, which was a crown of olive, they gave to Eurybiades;

13. But Themistocles was given a crown of olive too, as the prize of wisdom and dexterity.

14. He was likewise presented with the most beautiful chariot that could be found in Sparta;

15. And after receiving abundant praises, he was, upon his departure, escorted as far as the borders of Tegea by the three hundred picked Spartans who are called the Knights.

16. Never was it known, either before or since, that the Spartans escorted a man out of their city.

Chapter 91

1. Meanwhile hostilities were still taking place in the north.

2. Artabazus, the son of Pharnaces, a man always held in high esteem by the Persians, but who, after the affair of Plataea, rose still higher in their opinion,

3. Escorted King Xerxes as far as the Hellespont, with sixty thousand of the chosen troops of Mardonius.

4. When the king was safe in Asia, Artabazus set out upon his return;

5. And on arriving near Palline, and finding that Mardonius had gone into winter quarters in Thessaly, and was in no hurry for him to rejoin the camp,

6. He thought it his bounden duty, as the Potidaeans had just revolted, to occupy himself in reducing them to slavery.

7. For as soon as the king had passed their territory, and the Persian fleet had retreated from Salamis, the Potidaeans revolted from the barbarians openly;

8. As likewise did all the other inhabitants of that peninsula.

9. Artabazus therefore laid siege to Potidaea; and having a suspicion that the Olynthians were likely to revolt shortly, he besieged their city also.

10. Now Olynthus was at that time held by the Bottiaeans, who had been driven from the parts about the Thermaic Gulf by the Macedonians.

11. Artabazus captured the city and led out all the inhabitants to a marsh in the neighbourhood, and there killed them.

12. After this he delivered the place into the hands of the people called Chalcideans, having first appointed Critobulus of Torone to be governor.

13. Such was the way in which the Chalcideans got Olynthus.

14. When Olynthus had fallen, Artabazus pressed the siege of Potidaea even more vigorously; and was aided by one Timoxenus, captain of the Scionaeans, who entered into a plot to betray the town to him.

15. Whenever Timoxenus wished to send a letter to Artabazus, or Artabazus to send one to Timoxenus, the letter was written on a strip of paper,

16. And rolled round the notched end of an arrow-shaft; the feathers were then put on over the paper, and the arrow shot to some agreed place.

17. But after a while the plot was discovered, in this way: Artabazus shot an arrow, intending to send it to the accustomed place, but, missing his mark, hit one of the Potidaeans in the shoulder.

18. A crowd gathered about the wounded man, as commonly happens in war; and when the arrow was pulled out, they noticed the paper,

19. And straightway carried it to the captains who were present from the various cities of the peninsula.

20. The captains read the letter, and, finding who the traitor was,

nevertheless resolved, out of regard for the city of Scione, that as they did not wish the Scionaeans to be thenceforth branded with the name of traitors, they would not bring any charge of treachery against him.

21. After Artabazus had continued the siege for three months, it happened that there was an unusual ebb of the tide, which lasted a long time.

22. When the barbarians saw that what had been sea was now no more than a swamp, they determined to push across it into Palline.

23. When the troops had already made two-fifths of their passage, and three-fifths still remained before they could reach Palline, the tide came in with a very high flood.

24. All who were not able to swim perished immediately; the rest were slain by the Potidaeans, who bore down on them in their ships.

Chapter 92

1. As for that part of the Persian fleet which had survived Salamis and reached the coast of Asia,

2. After it had taken the king and his army across the Hellespont to Abydos, it passed the winter at Cyme.

3. On the first approach of spring, there was an early muster of the ships at Samos, where some of them had remained throughout the winter.

4. Most of the men-at-arms who served on board were Persians or Medes,

5. And the command of the fleet had been taken by Mardontes, son of Bagaeus, and Artayntes son of Artachaeus;

6. While there was likewise a third commander, Ithamitres, the nephew of Artayntes, whom his uncle had appointed to the post.

7. They did not dare to venture further west than Samos, however, remembering what a defeat they had suffered,

8. And there was no one to compel them to approach any nearer to Greece.

9. They therefore remained at Samos, and kept watch over Ionia, to hinder it from breaking into revolt.

10. The whole number of their ships, including those furnished by the Ionians, was three hundred.

11. It did not enter into their thoughts that the Greeks would attack Ionia;

12. On the contrary, they supposed that Salamis would content the Greeks, more especially as they had not pursued the Persian fleet when it fled that battle.

13. The Persian sailors despaired, however, of gaining any success by sea themselves, though by land they thought that Mardonius was sure of victory.

14. So they remained at Samos, and discussed how they might harass the enemy, at the same time as they eagerly waited to hear how Mardonius fared.

15. As for the Greeks, the approach of spring, and the knowledge that Mardonius was in Thessaly, roused them.

16. Their land force was not yet come together, but their fleet, consisting of one hundred and ten ships, proceeded to Egina, under the command of Leotychides.

17. This Leotychides, who was both general and admiral, was the son of Menares, the son of Agesilaus, the son of Hippocratides, the son of Leotychides, the son of Anaxilaus, the son of Archidamus, the son of Anaxandrides, the son of Theopompus, the son of Nicander, the son of Charillus, the son of Eunomus, the son of Polydectes, the son of Prytanis, the son of Euryphon, the son of Procles, the son of Aristodemus, the son of Aristomachus, the son of Cleodaeus, the son of Hyllus, the son of Hercules.

18. He belonged to the younger branch of the royal house. All his ancestors, except the two next in the above list to himself, had been kings of Sparta.

19. The Athenian vessels were commanded by Xanthippus, the son of Ariphron.

20. When the whole fleet was gathered at Egina, ambassadors from Ionia arrived at the Greek station;

21. They had just come from visiting

Sparta, where they had been entreating the Lacedaemonians to liberate their native land.

22. One of these ambassadors was Herodotus, the son of Basileides. Originally they were seven in number; and the whole seven had conspired to slay Strattis, the tyrant of Chios;

23. One, however, of those engaged in the plot betrayed the enterprise; and the conspiracy being in this way discovered, Herodotus and the remaining five left Chios,

24. And went straight to Sparta, whence they had now proceeded to Egina, their object being to beseech the Greeks to liberate Ionia.

25. It was not, however, without difficulty that they were induced to advance even so far as Delos.

26. All beyond that region seemed to the Greeks full of danger; the places were quite unknown to them, and to their fancy swarmed with Persian troops;

27. As for Samos, it appeared to them as far off as the Pillars of Hercules. So it came to pass that at the very same time that the barbarians were hindered by their fears from venturing any further west than Samos,

28. The urgings of the Chians failed to induce the Greeks to advance any further east than Delos. Terror guarded the mid region.

Chapter 93

1. Mardonius now sent an envoy to Athens, to propose peace to them, and a league with them against the Peloponnese.

2. Hearing this, the Spartans lost no time in sending envoys to Athens also; and it so happened that these envoys were given their audience at the same time as Mardonius' envoy:

3. For the Athenians had waited and made delays, because they felt sure that the Lacedaemonians would hear that an ambassador had arrived from the Persians.

4. They contrived this on purpose, so that the Lacedaemonians might hear them deliver their sentiments to the Persians.

5. The Spartan ambassadors said, 'We are sent here by all Lacedaemonia to entreat that you will not do a new thing in Greece, nor agree to the terms which are offered you by the barbarian.

6. 'Such conduct on the part of any of the Greeks would be alike unjust and dishonourable; but in you it would be worse than in others.

7. 'For it would surely be an intolerable thing that the Athenians, who have always hitherto been known as a nation to which many men owed their freedom,

8. 'Should ever become the means of bringing all other Greeks into slavery.

9. 'We feel, however, for the heavy

calamities which press on you – the loss of your harvest these last two years, and the ruin in which your homes have lain for so long a time.

10. 'We offer you, therefore, on the part of the Lacedaemonians and the allies, sustenance for your women and for the unwarlike portion of your households, so long as the war endures.

11. 'Do not be seduced by Mardonius. He does as is natural for him to do; a tyrant himself, he helps forward a tyrant's cause.

12. 'You Athenians should know that with barbarians there is neither trustworthiness nor truth.'

13. At this the Athenians turned to the ambassadors of Mardonius and said, 'We know, as well as you do, that the power of the Persian is many times greater than our own:

14. 'Nevertheless we so firmly cling to freedom that we shall always offer what resistance we may to tyranny, and would rather die than be slaves.

15. 'Do not seek to persuade us into making terms with Xerxes or his servant Mardonius – say what you will, you will never gain our assent.

16. 'Return at once, and tell Mardonius that our answer to him is this: "So long as the sun keeps his present course, we will never join alliance with Xerxes.

17. '"Nay, we shall oppose him unceasingly, and never yield."'

18. To the Spartan ambassadors the Athenians said, 'It was natural no doubt that the Lacedaemonians should be afraid we might make terms with the barbarian;

19. 'But nevertheless it was a base fear in men who knew so well of what temper and heart we are.

20. 'Not all the gold that the whole earth contains – not the fairest and most fertile of all lands – would bribe us to side with the Persians and help them enslave our countrymen.

21. 'Even if we could have brought ourselves to such a thing, there are many powerful motives which would now make it impossible.

22. 'The chief of these is the burning and destruction of our city, which forces us to make no terms with its destroyer,

23. 'But rather to pursue him with our resentment to the uttermost.

24. 'Again, there is our common brotherhood with the Greeks: our common language, the shared history, the common character which we bear;

25. 'If the Athenians betray these, it would not be well. Know then now, if you did not know it before, that while one Athenian remains alive, we will never join alliance with Xerxes.

26. 'We thank you, however, for your forethought on our behalf, and for your wish to give our families sustenance, now that ruin has fallen on us; the kindness is complete on your part;

27. 'But for ourselves, we will endure as we may, and not be a burden to you. Such is our resolve.

28. 'Be it your care now to lead out your troops with all speed; for if we guess rightly, the barbarian will not wait long before he invades our territory again, but will set out so soon as he hears our answer.

29. 'Now then is the time for us, before he enters Attica, to go forward ourselves into Boeotia, and give him battle.'

30. When the Athenians had thus spoken, the ambassadors from Sparta returned in good heart to their own country.

Chapter 94

1. When Mardonius heard the Athenians' answer he immediately broke camp and led his army with all speed from Thessaly towards Athens,

2. Forcing the several nations through whose land he passed to furnish him with additional troops.

3. The chief men of Thessaly, far from repenting of the part they had taken in the war hitherto, urged on the Persians more earnestly than ever.

4. Thorax of Larissa in particular, who had helped to escort Xerxes on his flight to Asia, now openly encouraged Mardonius in his march towards Attica.

5. When the army reached Boeotia the Thebans advised Mardonius to stop,

6. And by sending gifts to various of the great men of Greece, to sow division among them, making it easier to conquer them.

7. But Mardonius had too strong a desire to take Athens a second time,

8. Not least so that by fire-signals along the islands he could tell Xerxes in Sardis that he was once again master of that city, ten months after it had first fallen to the Persians.

9. So he pressed forward; and the Athenians, as before withdrawing all their families and goods to Salamis, left a deserted and still ruined city to him.

10. On reaching the city Mardonius again sent a message offering the Athenians terms, hoping that now that they saw all Attica under Persian sway, their stubbornness would yield.

11. When Mardonius' message was delivered to the Athenians at Salamis, one of their councillors, Lycidas, gave it as his opinion that the proposal ought to be put before the assembly of the people.

12. When they heard this the other councillors and the body of Athenians waiting outside were exceedingly angry, and immediately surrounded Lycidas, and stoned him to death.

13. When the Athenian women heard of what he said, they hastened to the house of his wife and children, and stoned them to death too.

14. Meanwhile the Athenians had sent messengers to Sparta,

15. To reproach the Lacedaemonians for being too slow to send troops to oppose the Persian advance, so that the Athenians had had to abandon their city a second time.

16. Now, the Lacedaemonians had been celebrating a festival, and placing battlements on the wall across the Isthmus, which is why they had not yet mustered to aid Athens.

17. The messengers said, 'Xerxes again offers to give us our country back, and to conclude an alliance with us on fair and equal terms, and to bestow on us any other land we like.

18. 'But although we are fully aware that it is far more to our advantage to make peace with the Persian than to continue fighting him, we shall not, of our own free will, consent to any terms of peace.

19. 'Thus do we, in all our dealings with the Greeks, avoid what is base and counterfeit:

20. 'But you, who were so lately full of fear lest we made terms with the Persian, having learnt of what temper we are, and assured yourselves that we would not prove traitors,

21. 'And moreover having brought your wall across the Isthmus to an advanced state, cease altogether to care about us.

22. 'You agreed with us to go out and meet the Persian in Boeotia; but when the time came, you were false to your word, and looked on while the barbarian host advanced into Attica.

23. 'We Athenians are angered with you therefore; and justly, for you have not done what is right.

24. 'But we urge you to make haste to send your army, that we may even yet meet Mardonius in Attica.

25. 'Now that Boeotia is lost to us, the best place for the fight within our country will be the plain of Thria.'

26. Although the ephors delayed for ten days to give an answer to the Athenian ambassadors,

27. Either out of shame or because the wall across the Isthmus was not yet quite finished, they at length sent the army.

28. This was after Chileus the Tegean urged them that if the Athenians were conquered by the Persians, no wall would save the Peloponnese, because the way would be open all round its coasts for an invasion.

29. So a body of five thousand Spartans, each accompanied by seven helots, was dispatched under the command of Pausanias, the son of Cleombrotus.

30. The chief power belonged of right at this time to Pleistarchus, the son of Leonidas; but as he was still a child, Pausanias, his cousin, was regent in his place.

Chapter 95

1. When Mardonius learnt that the Spartans were on their march, he

no longer cared to remain in Attica.

2. Hitherto he had kept quiet, wishing to see what the Athenians would do, and had neither ravaged their territory, nor done it any harm;

3. For he continued to hope that the Athenians would come to terms.

4. As, however, he found that his persuasions were of no avail, he determined to withdraw from Attica before Pausanias reached the Isthmus.

5. First, however, he burned Athens, and cast down level with the ground whatever remained standing of the walls and other buildings.

6. His reason for retreating was that Attica is not a country where horse can act with advantage;

7. And further, that if he suffered defeat in a battle, no escape was open to him, except through defiles in the hills, where a handful of troops might stop all his army.

8. So he determined to withdraw to Thebes, and give the Greeks battle in the neighbourhood of a friendly city, and on ground well suited for cavalry.

9. After he had quitted Attica and was already on his march, Mardonius heard that a body of a thousand Lacedaemonians, distinct from the army of Pausanias, and sent on in advance, had arrived in the Megarid.

10. When he heard it, wishing, if possible, to destroy this detachment first, Mardonius considered with himself how he might do so.

11. With a sudden change of march he made for Megara, while his cavalry, pushing on in advance, entered and ravaged the Megarid.

12. This was the westernmost point in Europe to which this Persian army ever penetrated.

13. Then Mardonius received another message, by which he learnt that the forces of the Greeks were collected together at the Isthmus;

14. Which news caused him to draw back, and leave Attica for the territory of the Thebans.

15. And now, although the Thebans had espoused the cause of Persia, yet Mardonius cut down all the trees in these parts;

16. Not from any enmity towards the Thebans, but on account of his own urgent need,

17. For he required a rampart to protect his army, and a refuge in case the battle should go against him.

18. His army at this time lay on the Asopus, and stretched from Erythrae, along by Hysiae, to the territory of the Plataeans.

19. The rampart, however, was not made to extend so far, but formed a square of about ten furlongs each way.

20. While the barbarians were employed in this work, a certain citizen of Thebes, Attaginus, the son of Phrynon, gave a banquet,

and invited Mardonius, together with fifty of the noblest Persians.

21. Fifty noble Thebans also were asked; and the two nations were not arranged separately, but a Persian and a Theban were set side by side upon each couch.

22. After the feast was ended, and the drinking had begun, the Persian who shared Thersander's couch addressed him in the Greek tongue,

23. And enquired of him from what city he came.

24. He answered, that he was of Orchomenus; whereupon the other said,

25. 'Since we have eaten at one table, and drunk from one cup, I will tell you what I think, and perhaps this will be a useful warning for you:

26. 'Of these Persians you see here feasting, and the army in the camp nearby, in a little while, hardly any of these men will still be alive.'

27. As he spoke, the Persian wept; at which the Theban said, 'Surely you should tell your fear of this to Mardonius, and the Persians who are next him in honour?'

28. But the other replied, 'Dear friend, no one believes warnings, however true.

29. 'Many of us Persians know our danger, but we are constrained by necessity to do as our leader bids us.

30. 'In truth it is the worst of human ills, to abound in knowledge and yet have no power over action.'

Chapter 96

1. When Mardonius had held his camp in Boeotia during the first invasion of Greece a year beforehand,

2. All the Greeks of those parts who were friendly to the Persians sent troops to join his army, and these troops accompanied him in his attack upon Athens.

3. The Phocians alone abstained, and took no part in the invasion;

4. For, though they had espoused the Persian cause, it was much against their will, and only because they were compelled to do so.

5. However, a few days after the arrival of the Persian army at Thebes on this second occasion,

6. A thousand of their heavy-armed soldiers came up, under the command of Harmocydes, one of their most distinguished citizens.

7. No sooner had these troops reached Thebes, than some horsemen came to them from Mardonius, with orders that they should take up a position upon the plain, away from the rest of the army.

8. The Phocians did so, and forthwith the entire Persian cavalry drew near them: whereupon there went a rumour through the Greek force encamped with the Persian that Mardonius was about to destroy the Phocians.

9. The same conviction ran through the Phocian troops themselves; and Harmocydes, their leader,

addressed them with words of encouragement:

10. 'Phocians,' said he, 'it is plain that the Persians have resolved to take our lives,

11. 'Perhaps because of the accusations of the Thessalians, or for some other treachery.

12. 'Now, then, is the time for you to show yourselves brave men. It is better to die fighting and defending ourselves, than tamely to allow them to slay us in this shameful fashion.

13. 'Let them learn that they are barbarians, and that the men whose death they have plotted are Greeks!'

14. So spoke Harmocydes; and the Persian horse, having encircled the Phocians, charged them, as if about to deal out death, with bows bent, and arrows ready to fly;

15. Here and there some did indeed discharge their weapons.

16. But the Phocians stood firm, keeping close to one another, and serrying their ranks as much as possible:

17. Whereupon the horse suddenly wheeled round and rode off. It is not known with certainty whether the Persians came, at the behest of the Thessalians, to destroy the Phocians,

18. But seeing them prepared to stand on their defence, and fearing to suffer damage at their hands, they retreated, having orders from Mardonius to do so.

19. Perhaps Mardonius' intent was to try the temper of the Phocians and see whether they had courage.

20. Whatever the reason, when the horsemen retired Mardonius sent a herald to the Phocians, saying,

21. 'Fear not, Phocians; you have shown yourselves valiant men, much unlike the report I had heard of you.

22. 'Now therefore be forward in the coming battle. You will not readily outdo either the king or myself in services.' Thus ended the affair of the Phocians.

Chapter 97

1. The Lacedaemonians, when they reached the Isthmus, pitched their camp there;

2. And the other Peloponnesians, hearing or seeing that they were on the march, joined them.

3. All went out in one body from the Isthmus and marched as far as Eleusis.

4. There they were joined by the Athenians, who had come across from Salamis.

5. On reaching Erythrae in Boeotia they learned that the barbarians were encamped on the Asopus;

6. Wherefore they themselves, after considering how they should act, disposed their forces opposite the enemy on the slopes of Mount Cithaeron.

7. When Mardonius saw that the Greeks would not come down into the plain, he sent his cavalry under Masistius to attack them.

8. Now Masistius was a man of much repute among the Persians, and rode a Nisaean charger magnificently caparisoned, complete with a golden bit.

9. So the cavalry advanced against the Greeks, and made attacks on them in divisions, doing them great damage at each charge, and shouting insults at them.

10. It happened that the Megarians occupied the position most open to attack, where the ground offered the best approach to the cavalry.

11. Finding themselves hard pressed, they sent a herald to the Greek leaders, saying,

12. 'We cannot, brothers-in-arms, continue to resist the Persian horse in the post we have occupied from the first, if we are left without help.

13. 'So far, although hard pressed, we have held out against them.

14. 'Now, however, unless you send others to take our place, we shall have to quit our post.'

15. Pausanias, when he received this message, enquired among his troops if there were any who would volunteer to relieve the Megarians.

16. None were willing to go, so the Athenians offered themselves;

17. And a body of picked men, three hundred in number, commanded by Olympiodorus, the son of Lampo, undertook the service.

18. Selecting the whole body of

archers to accompany them, these men relieved the Megarians.

19. After the struggle had continued for a while, it ended in the following way.

20. As the barbarians continued charging in divisions, the horse of Masistius, which was in front of the others, received an arrow in his flank, the pain of which caused him to rear and throw his rider.

21. Immediately the Athenians rushed upon Masistius as he lay, caught his horse, and when he himself resisted, slew him.

22. At first, however, they were not able to kill him, for his armour hindered them. He had on a breastplate formed of golden scales, with a scarlet tunic covering it.

23. Thus the blows, all falling upon his breastplate, took no effect, till one of the soldiers, perceiving the reason, drove his weapon into his eye and so slew him.

24. All this took place without any of the other horsemen seeing it: they had neither observed their leader fall from his horse, nor beheld him slain;

25. For he fell as they wheeled round and prepared for another charge, so that they were quite ignorant of what had happened.

26. However when they halted, and found that there was no one to marshal their line, Masistius was missed;

27. And instantly his soldiers,

understanding what must have befallen him, with loud yells charged the Athenians in one mass, hoping to recover the body.

28. When the Athenians saw that, instead of coming up in squadrons, the whole body of horse was charging them at once, they called out to the other troops to hasten to their aid.

29. As the infantry was moving to their assistance, the fighting raged fiercely around the corpse of Masistius.

30. The three hundred, so long as they fought by themselves, had greatly the worse of the encounter, and were forced to retire and yield the corpse to the enemy;

31. But when the reinforcements arrived, the Persian horse could no longer hold their ground and fled without carrying off the corpse, having incurred in the attempt further losses.

32. They retired about two furlongs, and discussed what was best to do. Being without a leader, it seemed to them fittest to return to Mardonius.

33. There Mardonius and all the Persian army made great lamentation for Masistius.

34. They shaved the hair from their heads, and cut the manes from their warhorses and their sumpter beasts,

35. While they vented their grief in such loud cries that all Boeotia resounded with the clamour,

36. Because they had lost the man who, next to Mardonius, was held in the greatest esteem, both by the king and by the Persians generally.

37. So the barbarians, after their own fashion, paid honours to the dead Masistius.

Chapter 98

1. The Greeks, on the other hand, were greatly emboldened by what had happened,

2. Seeing that they had not only stood their ground against the attacks of the cavalry, but had compelled them to retreat.

3. They placed the corpse of Masistius on a cart, and paraded it along the ranks of the army.

4. Now the body was a sight which well deserved to be gazed upon, being remarkable both for stature and for beauty;

5. And it was to stop the soldiers from leaving their ranks to look at it, that they resolved to carry it round.

6. After this the Greeks determined to quit the high ground and go nearer Plataea,

7. As the land there seemed far more suitable for an encampment than the country about Erythrae, being better supplied with water.

8. At this place, and more especially to a spring-head called Gargaphia, they encamped once more in their order.

9. Here, in the marshalling of the nations, a fierce argument arose

between the Athenians and the Tegeans, both of whom claimed to have one of the wings assigned to them.

10. On each side were brought forward the deeds which they had done, whether in earlier or in later times;

11. But at length the deeds of the Athenians at Marathon and Salamis carried the argument in their favour, over the ancient claims of the Tegeans from long-ago wars.

12. When the disposition of the army had been settled, it was drawn up in the following order:

13. Ten thousand Lacedaemonian troops held the right wing, five thousand of whom were Spartans;

14. And these five thousand were attended by a body of thirty-five thousand Helots, who were only lightly armed; seven Helots to each Spartan.

15. The place next to themselves the Spartans gave to the Tegeans, on account of their courage and of the esteem in which they held them.

16. They were all fully armed, and numbered fifteen hundred men.

17. Next came the Corinthians, five thousand strong; and with them Pausanias had placed, at their request, the band of three hundred who had come from Potidaea in Palline.

18. Six hundred Arcadians of Orchomenus came next; then the Sicyonians, three thousand; then the Epidaurians, eight hundred;

19. Then the Troezenians, one thousand; then the Lepreats, two hundred; the Mycenaeans and Tirynthians, four hundred;

20. The Phliasians, one thousand; the Hermionians, three hundred; the Eretrians and Styreans, six hundred; the Chalcideans, four hundred; and the Ambraciots, five hundred.

21. After these came the Leucadians and Anactorians, who numbered eight hundred; the Paleans of Cephallenia, two hundred;

22. The Eginetans, five hundred; the Megarians, three thousand; and the Plataeans, six hundred.

23. Last of all, but first at their extremity of the line, were the Athenians, who, to the number of eight thousand, occupied the left wing, under the command of Aristides, son of Lysimachus.

24. All these, except the Helots, were heavy-armed troops, or Hoplites; and they amounted to thirty-eight thousand seven hundred men.

25. The light-armed troops consisted of the thirty-five thousand Helots, who were all well equipped for war;

26. And of thirty-four thousand five hundred other slaves belonging to the Lacedaemonians and the rest of the Greeks, nearly at the rate of one light to one heavy armed.

27. Thus the entire number of the light-armed was sixty-nine thousand five hundred.

28. The Greek army, therefore, which mustered at Plataea, was only eighteen hundred men short of one hundred and ten thousand;

29. And this amount was exactly made up by the Thespians who were present in the camp;

30. For eighteen hundred Thespians, being the whole number left, were likewise with the army; but these men were without arms.

31. Such was the array of the Greek troops when they took post on the Asopus.

Chapter 99

1. The barbarians under Mardonius, when the mourning for Masistius was at an end, and they had learnt that the Greeks were in Plataea, moved likewise towards the River Asopus.

2. On their arrival Mardonius marshalled them against the Greeks in the following order.

3. Against the Lacedaemonians he posted his Persians; and as the Persians were far more numerous he drew them up with their ranks deeper than common,

4. And extended their front so that part faced the Tegeans; and here he took care to choose out the best troops to face the Spartans,

5. While against the Tegeans he arrayed those on whom he could not so much depend.

6. This was done on the advice of the Thebans. Next to the Persians he placed the Medes, facing the Corinthians, Potidaeans, Orchomenians and Sicyonians;

7. Then the Bactrians, facing the Epidaurians, Troezenians, Lepreats, Tirynthians, Mycenaeans and Phliasians;

8. After them the Indians, facing the Hermionians, Eretrians, Styreans and Chalcidians; then the Sacans, facing the Ambraciots, Anactorians, Leucadians, Paleans and Eginetans;

9. And last of all, facing the Athenians, the Plataeans and the Megarians, he placed the troops of the Boeotians, Locrians, Malians and Thessalians, and also the thousand Phocians.

10. The whole nation of the Phocians had not joined the Medes;

11. On the contrary, there were some who had gathered themselves into bands about Parnassus, and made expeditions from thence,

12. Whereby they distressed Mardonius and the Greeks who sided with him, and so did good service to the Grecian cause.

13. Besides those mentioned above, Mardonius likewise arrayed against the Athenians the Macedonians and the tribes dwelling about Thessaly.

14. Here have been named the greatest of the nations marshalled by Mardonius on this occasion, all those of most renown.

15. Mixed with these were men of divers other peoples, as Phrygians,

Thracians, Mysians, Paeonians and the like;

16. Ethiopians again, and Egyptians, both of the Hermotybian and Calascirian races, whose weapon is the sword, and who are the only fighting men in that country.

17. The number of the barbarians was three hundred thousand; that of the Greeks who had made alliance with Mardonius is not known, but guessed to be near fifty thousand strong.

18. The troops thus marshalled were all foot soldiers. As for the horse, it was drawn up by itself.

Chapter 100

1. Each side now waited for what it thought would be its best opportunity to begin the battle.

2. Since neither side felt quite ready, the two armies remained in camp opposite each other for ten days;

3. But the Persian horse harassed the Greeks, and captured some of their supply trains as they approached from the direction of the Peloponnese.

4. At last Mardonius, fearing to run out of supplies, and urged by some of his advisers that more men were joining the Greek army each day, resolved to give battle.

5. In the night before the eleventh day Alexander of Macedon, whose troops were in the Persian's host,

6. Secretly rode to the Greek lines and sent a message to the generals,

telling them that the attack was imminent.

7. When they heard this, the generals conferred; and Pausanias said to the Athenians,

8. 'You have fought the Persians at Marathon, and know their style of fighting; I suggest you take the right wing opposite them,

9. 'And we Spartans will exchange to your current place on the left wing, for we have fought the Boeotians and Thessalians before, and know how they fight.'

10. To this the Athenians readily agreed, having themselves thought that this would be a good idea.

11. But when Mardonius saw the changeover occurring, he likewise exchanged his wings; and when the Greeks changed back, he followed suit.

12. And then he sent a mocking message to the Spartans, saying, 'Lacedaemonians, men say that you are the bravest of mankind,

13. 'And admire you because you never turn your backs in flight nor quit your ranks, but always stand firm, and either die at your posts or else destroy your adversaries.

14. 'But in all this which they say concerning you there is not one word of truth; for now have we seen you, before battle was joined or our two hosts had come to blows, flying and leaving your posts,

15. 'Wishing the Athenians to make the first trial of our arms, and

taking your own station against our slaves.'

16. Then Mardonius offered a fight in equal between the pick of the Persian guards and the Spartans; but receiving no reply to his challenge, ordered the cavalry to attack.

17. Now the Persian cavalry fired arrows from horseback as they attacked, and sorely distressed the Greek troops, who could not bring them to close combat.

18. Moreover the Persians at this time choked up and spoiled the fountain of Gargaphia, from which the whole Greek army drew its water.

19. Accordingly the Greek generals met together and laid a new plan.

20. If the Persians did not attack in full force that day, they resolved to move the army to a new position at a place called 'The Island',

21. Formed by the divided arms of the River Oeroe on a tract of land before Plataea, about ten furlongs from the River Asopus and the fountain of Gargaphia.

22. In this place they would have abundant water and would be less vulnerable to the Persian cavalry, which could not so easily harass them there.

23. Having resolved to move their ground during the second watch of night so as to be less visible, the Greeks continued to suffer through the rest of the day from the attrition of the Persian cavalry.

24. When night fell and the attacks ceased, the army began to get ready for its move.

25. But the greater number of the men were not minded to take the new ground, but wanted to flee into the city of Plataea and hide behind its walls.

Chapter 101

1. Meanwhile one of the generals who had not been at the meeting earlier, Amompharetus, now refused to retreat;

2. And while the Spartan leaders Pausanias and Euryanax were arguing with him, the Athenians, who had kept their station, sent a horseman to find out what was happening,

3. For they distrusted the Lacedaemonians, who often said one thing and did another.

4. Just at the moment when the Athenian herald arrived, Amompharetus, still disputing, took up a vast rock with both hands, and placed it at the feet of Pausanias, saying,

5. 'With this pebble I give my vote not to run away from the barbarians.'

6. Pausanias, in reply, called him a fool and a madman, and, turning to the Athenian herald, instructed him to tell his countrymen how he was occupied,

7. And ask them to approach nearer, and retreat or not according to the movements of the Spartans.

8. The herald returned to the

Athenians; and the Spartans continued to dispute till morning began to dawn.

9. Then Pausanias, who as yet had not moved, gave the signal for retreat, expecting that Amompharetus, when he saw the rest of the Lacedaemonians in motion, would be unwilling to be left.

10. No sooner was the signal given, than all the army except the Pitanates began their march, and retreated along the line of the hills, the Tegeans accompanying them.

11. The Athenians likewise set off in good order, but proceeded by a different way from the Lacedaemonians.

12. For while the latter clung to the hilly ground and the skirts of Mount Cithaeron, on account of their fear of the enemy Persian cavalry, the former took themselves to the low country and marched through the plain.

13. As for Amompharetus, at first he did not believe that Pausanias would really dare to leave him behind; he therefore kept his men at their post;

14. When, however, he saw Pausanias and his troops were now some way off, Amompharetus, thinking himself forsaken in good earnest, ordered his band to take their arms, and led them towards the main army.

15. Now the army was waiting for them at a distance of about ten furlongs, having halted on the bank of the River Moloeis at a place called Argiopius.

16. They had stopped there so that, in case Amompharetus and his band should really not quit the spot where they were drawn up, they might have it in their power to move back and lend them assistance.

17. Amompharetus, however, and his companions rejoined the main body; and at the same time the whole mass of the barbarian cavalry arrived and began to harass them.

18. The Persian cavalry had followed their usual practice and ridden up to the Greek camp, when they discovered that it was deserted.

19. So they pushed forward without stopping, and, as soon as they overtook the Greeks, pressed them heavily.

Chapter 102

1. When Mardonius heard that the Greeks had quit their place he summoned Thorax of Larissa, and his brothers Eurypylus and Thrasideius, and said,

2. 'O sons of Aleuas! what do you say now, when you see the Greek camp empty?

3. 'Why, you told me the Lacedaemonians never fled from battle, but were brave beyond the rest of mankind.

4. 'Yet you saw them change their place in the line; and now, as all

may see, they have run away during the night.

5. 'In truth they have shown plainly that they are men of no worth, and if they have distinguished themselves among Greeks then Greeks in general are even of less worth.

6. 'I can readily excuse you, who, knowing nothing of Persians, praised these men from your acquaintance with certain exploits of theirs;

7. 'But I marvel at Artabazus, that he should have been afraid of the Lacedaemonians, and have therefore given us such poor counsel,

8. 'Bidding us to remove to Thebes, and allow ourselves to be besieged there by the Greeks.

9. 'But now we must not allow them to escape us, but must pursue them till we overtake them.'

10. When he had so spoken, he immediately crossed the Asopus, and led the Persians forward at a run directly on the track of the Greeks, whom he believed to be in actual flight.

11. He could not see the Athenians; for, as they had taken the way of the plain, they were hidden from his sight by the hills;

12. He therefore led his troops against the Lacedaemonians and the Tegeans only.

13. When the commanders of the other divisions of the barbarians saw the Persians pursuing the Greeks so hastily, they all seized

their standards and hurried after, in great disorder and disarray.

14. On they went with loud shouts and in a wild rout, thinking to swallow up the runaways.

15. Pausanias sent a horseman to the Athenians with a message saying,

16. 'Men of Athens! now that the great struggle has come, which is to decide the freedom or the slavery of Greece,

17. 'We two people, Lacedaemonians and Athenians, are deserted by all the other allies, who have fled away during the night.

18. 'Nevertheless, we are resolved what to do; we must endeavour, as best we may, to defend ourselves and to succour one another.

19. 'Come to our aid, sore pressed as we are by the enemy. Should you yourselves be so straitened that you cannot come, at least send us your archers, and be sure you will earn our gratitude.

20. 'We acknowledge that throughout this whole war there has been no zeal to be compared to yours; we therefore do not doubt that you will do us this service.'

21. The Athenians, as soon as they received this message, were anxious to go to the Spartans' aid;

22. But as they marched they were attacked by the Greeks who had sided with Xerxes, whose place in the line had been opposite theirs.

23. Accordingly the Lacedaemonians, and the Tegeans, whom nothing

could induce to quit their side,
were left to resist the Persians.

24. Many fell on the Spartan side, and
a still greater number were
wounded, for the Persians had
made a rampart of their wicker
shields, and shot such clouds of
arrows from behind them, that the
Spartans were sorely distressed.

25. Goaded by the hail of arrows, the
Tegeans rushed forward against
the enemy, and the
Lacedaemonians followed their
attack; while the Persians, on their
side, left shooting their bows, and
prepared to meet them.

26. And first the combat was at the
wicker shields. When these were
swept down a fierce contest
followed, which lasted long, and
ended in a hand-to-hand struggle.

27. The barbarians many times seized
the Greek spears and broke them,
for in boldness and warlike heart
they were not inferior to the
Greeks;

28. But they were without bucklers,
untrained, and far below the
enemy in skill at arms.

29. Sometimes singly, sometimes in
bodies of ten, now fewer and now
more in number, they dashed
upon the Spartan ranks, and
perished.

30. Wherever Mardonius fought in
person, mounted on a white horse
and surrounded by the elite of the
Persians, the fight went most
against the Greeks.

31. So long as Mardonius was alive,

this body resisted all attacks, and,
while they defended their own
lives, struck down many Spartans.

32. But after Mardonius fell, and the
troops with him, which were the
main strength of the Persian army,
the remainder yielded to the
Lacedaemonians, and ran hastily
away, without preserving any
order,

33. And took refuge in their own
camp, within the wooden defence
which they had raised in the
Theban territory.

34. Their light clothing, and want of
bucklers, were their downfall: for
they had to contend against men
heavily armed, while they themselves were without such defence.

35. Mardonius was slain by
Aeimnestus, a man famous in
Sparta; his killing of Mardonius
was the vengeance owed to the
Spartans for the death of Leonidas.

36. And thus did Pausanias, son of
Cleombrotus, grandson of
Anaxandridas, and of the same
ancestry as Leonidas,

37. Win a victory exceeding in glory
all those to which knowledge of
earlier times extends.

Chapter 103

1. Artabazus, the son of Pharnaces,
who had disapproved from the
first of Xerxes' leaving Mardonius
behind,

2. And then had made great endeavours to dissuade Mardonius from
risking a battle, when he found

that the latter was bent on acting otherwise, did as follows.

3. He had a force under his command amounting to nearly forty thousand men. Knowing how the battle was likely to go,

4. As soon as the two armies began to fight he led his soldiers forward in an orderly array, bidding them to follow him at the same pace as himself.

5. He then pretended to lead them to the battle. But when, advancing before his army, he saw that the Persians were already in flight, instead of keeping the same order he wheeled his troops round and retreated;

6. Nor did he seek shelter behind the walls of Thebes, but hurried on into Phocis, resolved to make his way to the Hellespont with all speed.

7. As for the Greeks with Mardonius' forces, while most of them played the coward on purpose, the Boeotians, on the contrary, had a long struggle with the Athenians.

8. Those of the Thebans who were attached to the Persians especially displayed great zeal;

9. Far from retreating, they fought with such fury that three hundred of the best and bravest among them were slain by the Athenians.

10. But at last they too were routed, and fled away; not, however, in the same direction as the Persians and the crowd of allies,

11. Who, having taken no part in the battle, ran off without striking a blow, but to their own city of Thebes.

12. This clearly shows how completely the rest of the barbarians were dependent on the Persian troops,

13. That they all fled at once, without ever coming to blows with the enemy, merely because they saw the Persians running away.

Chapter 104

1. And so it came to pass that the whole army of Mardonius took to flight, except only the Persian and Boeotian cavalry.

2. These did good service to the fleeing infantry, by advancing close to the enemy, and protecting the fugitives from the Greeks.

3. The victors however pressed on, pursuing and slaying the remnant of the Persian army.

4. Meantime, while the Persian flight continued, news reached the Greeks who were drawn up round the Heraeum, and so were absent from the battle, that Pausanias was gaining the victory.

5. Hearing this, they rushed forward without any order, the Corinthians taking the upper road across the skirts of Cithaeron and the hills,

6. While the Megarians and Phliasians followed the level route through the plain.

7. These last had almost reached the enemy when the Theban cavalry saw them,

8. And, observing their disarray,

dispatched against them the squadron led by Asopodorus, the son of Timander.

9. He charged them with such effect that he left six hundred of their number dead on the plain,

10. And, pursuing the rest, compelled them to seek shelter in Cithaeron. So these men perished without honour.

11. The Persians, and the multitude with them, who fled to the wooden fortress, were able to ascend into the towers before the Lacedaemonians came up.

12. Thus placed, they strengthened the defences as well as they could;

13. And when the Lacedaemonians arrived, a sharp fight took place at the rampart.

14. So long as the Athenians were away, the barbarians kept off their assailants, and had much the best of the combat, because the Lacedaemonians were unskilled in the attack of walled places:

15. But on the arrival of the Athenians, a more concerted assault was made.

16. In the end the valour of the Athenians prevailed; they gained the top of the wall, and, breaking a breach through it, enabled the Greeks to pour in.

17. The first to enter were the Tegeans, and they it was who plundered the tent of Mardonius;

18. Where, among other booty, they found the manger from which his horses ate, made of solid brass.

19. As soon as the wall was broken the barbarians no longer kept together in any array,

20. Nor was there one among them who thought of making further resistance;

21. In truth, they were all half dead with fright, huddled as so many thousands were into such a confined space.

22. With such tameness did they submit to be slaughtered by the Greeks, that of the three hundred thousand men who composed the army,

23. Omitting the forty thousand by whom Artabazus was accompanied in his flight, no more than three thousand survived the battle.

24. Yet of the Lacedaemonians from Sparta, only ninety-one died in this battle; of the Tegeans, sixteen; of the Athenians, fifty-two.

25. On the side of the barbarians, the greatest courage was manifested, among the foot soldiers, by the Persians;

26. Among the horse, by the Sacae; while Mardonius himself, as a man, bore off the palm from the rest.

27. Among the Greeks, the Athenians and the Tegeans fought well; but the prowess shown by the Lacedaemonians was beyond either.

28. The bravest man by far on that day was Aristodemus, the same who alone escaped from the slaughter of the three hundred at

Thermopylae, and who on that account had endured disgrace and reproach:

29. Next to him were Posidonius, Philocyon, and Amompharetus the Spartan.
30. The Spartans, however, who took part in the fight, when the question of who had distinguished himself most came to be talked over,
31. Decided that Aristodemus, who, on account of the blame which attached to him, had manifestly courted death,
32. And had therefore left his place in the line and behaved like a madman, had done very notable deeds;
33. But that Posidonius, who, with no such desire to lose his life, had quitted himself no less gallantly, was by so much a braver man than he.
34. Perhaps, however, it was envy that made them speak in this way.

Chapter 105

1. These then were the most distinguished of those who fought at Plataea.
2. As for Callicrates, the most beautiful man, not among the Spartans only, but in the whole Greek camp;
3. He was not killed in the battle, but by an arrow fired by the harassing Persian cavalry beforehand.
4. While his comrades advanced to

the fight, he was carried out of the ranks, very unwilling to die, as he showed by the words he addressed to Arimnestus, one of the Plataeans:

5. 'I grieve,' said he, 'not because I have to die for my country, but because I have not lifted my arm against the enemy,
6. 'Nor done any deed worthy of me, much as I have desired to achieve something.'
7. The Athenian who is said to have distinguished himself most was Sophanes, son of Eutychides, of the Deceleian canton.
8. Two stories are told about him: according to one, he wore an iron anchor, fastened by a bronze chain to the belt which secured his breastplate;
9. And this, when he came near the enemy, he stuck in the ground so that, when they made their charge,
10. It would be impossible for him to be driven from his post; but as soon as the enemy fled, he would pluck up his anchor and pursue them.
11. The other story is contradictory to the first, relating that Sophanes, instead of having an anchor fastened to his breastplate,
12. Bore the device of an anchor upon his shield, which he never allowed to rest, but made to run round continually.
13. Another glorious deed was likewise performed by this same Sophanes:
14. At the time when the Athenians

were laying siege to Egina, he took up the challenge of Eurybates the Argive, a winner of the Pentathlum, and slew him.

Chapter 106

1. Pausanias made a proclamation that no one should take booty, instead ordering the Helots to collect it and bring it all to one place.

2. So the Helots went through the Persian camp, where they found many tents richly adorned with furniture of gold and silver,

3. Couches covered with plates of the same, and golden bowls, goblets and other drinking-vessels.

4. On the carriages were bags containing silver and golden kettles;

5. And on the bodies of the slain were bracelets and chains, and scymitars with golden ornaments;

6. Not to mention embroidered apparel, of which no one made any account.

7. The Helots at this time stole many things of much value, which they sold in after times to the Eginetans;

8. However, they brought in no small quantity, chiefly things they could not hide.

9. And this was the beginning of the great wealth of the Eginetans, who bought the gold of the Helots as if it had been mere brass.

10. When all the booty had been brought together it was divided among the soldiers, each of whom received less or more according to his deserts;

11. And in this way a distribution was made of the Persian concubines, gold, silver, beasts of burden, and all the other valuables.

12. As for Pausanias, the portion which was set apart for him consisted of ten specimens of each kind of thing: women, horses, talents, camels and whatever else there was in the spoil.

13. It is said that the following circumstance happened at this time.

14. Xerxes, when he fled from Greece, left his war tent with Mardonius. When Pausanias saw the tent with its adornments of gold and silver, and its hangings of divers colours,

15. He commanded the Persian bakers and cooks to make a banquet of the kind they had made for Mardonius.

16. Then Pausanius, beholding the couches of gold and silver daintily decked out with their rich covertures,

17. And the tables of gold and silver laid, and the feast itself prepared with all magnificence, was astonished at the good things which were set before him.

18. Then he commanded his own followers to make ready a Spartan supper.

19. When the suppers were both served, and it was apparent how vast a difference lay between the two, Pausanias laughed,

20. And sent his servants to call the Greek generals. On their coming, he pointed to the two boards, and said:

21. 'I sent for you, O Greeks, to show you the folly of this Persian captain, who, when he enjoyed such fare as this, must needs come here to rob us of our penury.'

22. Such, it is said, were the words of Pausanias to the Grecian generals.

23. During many years afterwards, the Plataeans used often to find on the field of battle concealed treasures of gold, and silver, and other valuables.

24. More recently they discovered the following: the flesh having fallen away from the bodies of the dead, and their bones having been gathered together into one place,

25. The Plataeans were able to see a skull without any seam, made entirely of a single bone;

26. Likewise a jaw, both the upper bone and the under, wherein all the teeth, front and back, were joined together and made of one bone;

27. Also, the skeleton of a man not less than five cubits in height.

28. The Greeks, after sharing the booty on the field of Plataea, proceeded to bury their own dead, each nation apart from the rest.

29. The Lacedaemonians made three graves; in one they buried their youths, among whom were Posidonius, Amompharetus, Philocyon and Callicrates;

30. In another, the rest of the Spartans; and in the third, the Helots. Such was their mode of burial.

31. The Tegeans buried all their dead in a single grave; as likewise did the Athenians theirs, and the Megarians and Phliasians those who were slain by the Persian cavalry.

Chapter 107

1. After the Greeks had buried their dead at Plataea they held a council, at which it was resolved to attack Thebes, and to require that those who had joined the Persians should be delivered into their hands.

2. Two Thebans who had been chief in making alliance with Persia were especially named, Timagenidas and Attaginus.

3. If the Thebans should refuse to give these men up, it was determined to besiege the city, and never cease till it should surrender.

4. After this resolve, the army marched on Thebes; and having demanded the men, and been refused, began the siege,

5. Laying waste the country all around, and making assaults upon the wall in divers places.

6. When twenty days were gone by, and the violence of the Greeks did not slacken, Timagenidas said to his countrymen,

7. 'Men of Thebes, since the Greeks have stated that they will never

desist till either they take Thebes or we are delivered to them, we do not wish the land of Boeotia to suffer any longer on our behalf.

8. 'If it be money that they desire, and their demand of us be no more than a pretext,

9. 'Let money from the treasury of the state be given them; for the state, and not we alone, embraced the cause of Xerxes.

10. 'If, however, they really want our persons, we are ready to be delivered to them and to stand trial.'

11. The Thebans thought this offer very right and reasonable; so they dispatched a herald to Pausanias, and told him they were willing to deliver up the men.

12. As soon as an agreement had been concluded upon, Attaginus made his escape from the city; his sons, however, were surrendered in his place;

13. But Pausanias refused to hold them guilty, since children, he said, could have had no part in such an offence.

14. The rest of those whom the Thebans gave up had expected to obtain a trial, and in that case their trust was to escape by means of bribery;

15. But Pausanias, afraid of this, dismissed at once the whole army of allies, and took the men with him to Corinth, where he killed them all.

16. Such were the events which happened at Plataea and at Thebes.

Chapter 108

1. The Persian general Artabazus son of Pharnaces, who had fled from Plataea with his forty thousand troops, soon reached Thessaly.

2. The inhabitants received him hospitably, and enquired about the rest of the army, since they were still ignorant of what had taken place at Plataea.

3. Knowing that if he told the truth, he would risk perishing with his whole army,

4. For if the facts were once known, all who learnt them would be sure to attack him,

5. Artabazus kept everything secret, and said, 'I am hastening into Thrace, as I am sent with this force on special business from the main army.

6. 'Mardonius and his host are close behind me, and may be looked for shortly. When he comes, receive him as you have received me;

7. 'Show him every kindness. Be sure you will never hereafter regret it, if you so do.'

8. Then he took his departure, and marched his troops at their best speed through Thessaly and Macedon to Thrace, following the inland route, which was the shortest.

9. He himself succeeded in reaching Byzantium; but a great part of his army perished on the road,

10. Many being cut to pieces by the Thracians, and others dying from hunger and excess of toil.

11. From Byzantium Artabazus set sail, and crossed the strait to Asia.

12. On the same day that the blow was struck at Plataea, another defeat befell the Persians at Mycale in Ionia.

13. While the Greek fleet under Leotychides was still lying inactive at Delos, there arrived an embassy from Samos,

14. Consisting of three men, Lampon, son of Thrasycles, Athenagoras, son of Archestratidas, and Hegesistratus, son of Aristagoras.

15. The Samians had sent them secretly, concealing their departure both from the Persians and from their own tyrant, Theomestor, son of Androdamas, whom the Persians had made ruler of Samos.

16. When the ambassadors came before the Greek captains, Hegesistratus spoke to them,

17. Saying that the Ionians only needed to see them arrive in order to revolt from the Persians, and that the Persians would not stay to fight;

18. 'Or if they did, it would be to offer them the finest booty that they could anywhere expect to gain';

19. And at the same time he urged them to deliver from bondage a Grecian race, and to drive back the barbarians.

20. 'This,' he said, 'might very easily be done, for the Persian ships are poor craft, no match for yours';

21. Adding, moreover, that 'if there was any suspicion that the Samians intended treachery, we are ourselves ready to be hostages, and to return on board the ships of the Greeks to Asia.'

22. Leotychides accepted, the Samians pledged their faith, and a treaty of alliance was made.

23. This done, two of the ambassadors immediately sailed away, Hegesistratus remaining with Leotychides and the fleet.

24. The Greeks put to sea and sailed across from Delos to Samos. Arriving off Calami on the Samian coast, they dropped anchor and prepared for battle.

25. The Persians, however, no sooner heard of the Greeks' arrival than they sailed away to the mainland after dismissing the Phoenician ships.

26. For it had been resolved in council not to risk a battle, since the Persian fleet was no match for the Greeks.

27. They fled to the mainland to be under the protection of their land army, which now lay at Mycale, and consisted of the troops left behind by Xerxes to keep guard over Ionia.

28. This was an army of sixty thousand men, under the command of Tigranes, a Persian of more than common beauty and stature.

29. The Persian captains sailed for Gaeson and Scolopoeis, which are in the territory of Mycale.

30. Here they drew the ships up on

the beach, and surrounded them with a rampart of stones and tree trunks,

31. Cutting down for this purpose all the fruit trees which grew near, to the chagrin of the local people,

32. And defending the barrier by means of stakes firmly planted in the ground.

33. They were prepared either to fight a battle, or undergo a siege.

Chapter 109

1. The Greeks, when they understood that the barbarians had fled to the mainland, were annoyed at their escape:

2. Nor could they decide at first what to do, whether to return home or proceed to the Hellespont.

3. In the end they decided to do neither, but to make sail for the continent.

4. So they prepared for a sea fight, with boarding-bridges and everything else necessary, and sailed to Mycale.

5. Now when they came to the Persian camp they found no one to come out to meet them, but observed the ships dragged ashore within the barrier,

6. And a strong land-force drawn up in battle array on the beach.

7. Leotychides therefore sailed along the shore, keeping as close to land as possible, and by the voice of a herald addressed the Ionians:

8. 'Men of Ionia: the Persians will not understand me, because they do not speak our tongue, but you listen to me.

9. 'When we join battle with them, before everything else remember Freedom; and next, remember our watchword.'

10. In saying this Leotychides was using the same ploy as Themistocles had used at Artemisium:

11. Either the barbarians would not know what he said, and the Ionians would be persuaded to revolt from them;

12. Or if his words were reported to the former, they would mistrust their Greek soldiers. The trick worked, as subsequent events showed.

13. The Greeks then brought their ships to land, disembarked, and arrayed themselves for battle.

14. When the Persians saw them marshalling, their first act was to disarm the Samians, whom they now suspected of complicity with their enemies.

15. For it had happened lately that a number of the Athenians who had been made prisoners by the troops of Xerxes were brought to Asia on board the barbarian fleet;

16. And these men had all been ransomed by the Samians, who sent them back to Athens, well provided for the journey.

17. On this account, as much as on Leotychides' ruse, the Samians were suspected.

18. After disarming them, the Persians next dispatched the Milesians to

watch the paths leading to the heights of Mycale,

19. Because (so they said) the Milesians were well acquainted with that region: their true object, however, was to remove them to a distance from the camp.

20. In this way the Persians sought to secure themselves against such of the Ionians as they thought likely to rebel.

21. They then joined shield to shield, and made themselves a breastwork against the enemy.

Chapter 110

1. The Greeks now, having finished their preparations, advanced towards them.

2. As they did so news flew through the Persian host that the Greeks had fought and conquered the army of Mardonius in Boeotia.

3. Before the rumour reached them, the Greeks were full of trepidation, not so much on their own account, as for their countrymen, and for Greece herself.

4. But when they heard the news, their fear vanished and they charged at their enemies vigorously.

5. The Hellespont and the Islands formed the prize for which they were about to fight.

6. The Athenians, and the force drawn up with them, who formed one half of the army, marched along the shore, where the country was low and level;

7. But the way for the Lacedaemonians, and the troops with them, lay across hills and a torrent-course.

8. Hence, while the Lacedaemonians were making their way round, the Athenians on the other wing had already closed with the enemy.

9. So long as the wicker bucklers of the Persians lasted, they made a stout defence, and had not even the worst of the battle;

10. But when the Athenians and their allies, wishing to make the victory their own and not to share it with the Lacedaemonians,

11. Cheered each other on with shouts, and attacked them with the utmost ferocity, at last the face of things changed.

12. For, bursting through the line of shields and rushing forwards in a body, the Greeks fell upon the Persians;

13. Who, though they bore the charge and for a long time held their ground, yet at length tried to take refuge in their fortifications.

14. Here the Athenians themselves, together with those who followed them in the line of battle, the Corinthians, Sicyonians and Troezenians,

15. Pressed so closely on the heels of their foes, that they entered along with them into the fortress.

16. And now that their fortress was taken, the barbarians no longer offered resistance, but fled hastily away, all except the Persians.

17. They still continued to fight in knots of a few men against the Greeks, who kept pouring into the intrenchment.
18. And here, while two of the Persian commanders fled, two died: Artayntes and Ithamitres, who were leaders of the fleet, escaped,
19. While Mardontes, and the commander of the land force, Tigranes, died fighting.
20. The Persians were still holding out when the Lacedaemonians and their section of the army arrived, and joined in the remainder of the battle.
21. The number of Greeks who fell in the struggle here was not inconsiderable; the Sicyonians especially lost many, including Perilaus, their general.
22. The Samians who served with the Medes, and who, although disarmed, still remained in the camp,
23. Seeing from the very beginning of the fight that the victory was doubtful, did all that lay in their power to help the Greeks.
24. And the other Ionians likewise, beholding their example, revolted and attacked the Persians.
25. As for the Milesians, who had been ordered to watch the mountain paths,
26. Guided the flying Persians by wrong roads, which brought them into the presence of the enemy;
27. And at last they set upon them with their own hands, and showed themselves the hottest of their adversaries.
28. Ionia, therefore, on this day revolted a second time from Persia.
29. In this battle the Greeks who behaved with the greatest bravery were the Athenians;
30. And among them the palm was borne off by Hermolycus, son of Euthynus, a man accomplished in the Pancratium.
31. After the Athenians, the most distinguished on the Greek side were the Corinthians, Troezenians and Sicyonians.
32. The Greeks, when they had killed most of the barbarians, either in the battle or in the rout,
33. Set fire to the Persian ships and the rampart round them, first removing all the booty and carrying it down to the beach.
34. Besides other plunder they found many caskets of money.

Chapter III

1. The Greeks then sailed to Samos, and there discussed what to do about the Ionians.
2. Ionia they proposed to abandon to the barbarians; and the question was, in what part of their own possessions in Greece they should settle the Ionian people.
3. For it seemed to them impossible that they should be ever on the watch to protect Ionia; but otherwise there could be no hope that the Ionians would escape the vengeance of the Persians.

4. The Peloponnesian leaders proposed that the seaport towns of those Greeks who had sided with Xerxes should be taken from them, and given to the Ionians.

5. The Athenians, on the other hand, were unwilling that any removal should take place, and disliked the Peloponnesians holding councils concerning their colonists.

6. So, as they set themselves against the change, the Peloponnesians yielded with a good will.

7. At this the Samians, Chians, Lesbians, and other islanders who had helped the Greeks at this time,

8. Were received into the league of the allies; and promised to be faithful and not desert the common cause.

9. After this the Greeks sailed to the Hellespont, where they meant to destroy the bridges, which they supposed still stood across the strait.

10. The barbarians who escaped from the battle – a scanty remnant – took refuge in the heights of Mycale, whence they made good their retreat to Sardis.

11. During the march to Sardis, Masistes, son of Darius and brother of Xerxes, who had been present at the disaster, had words with Artayntes, the general,

12. On whom he showered reproaches, and said there was no punishment he did not deserve to suffer for bringing such grievous hurt on the king's house.

13. Artayntes bore the reproaches for a while, but at last he fell into a rage, and drew his scymitar to kill Masistes.

14. A certain Halicarnassian called Xenagoras, son of Praxilaus, who stood behind Artayntes at the time, seeing him do this,

15. Seized him and threw him to the ground; which gave time for Masistes' guards to come to his aid.

16. By this conduct Xenagoras gained the favour not of Masistes only, but of Xerxes himself,

17. For he had saved the king's brother from death; and he was rewarded by being appointed governor of Cilicia.

18. Except this, nothing happened on the road, and the remnant of the army safely reached Sardis.

19. At Sardis they found Xerxes, who had been there ever since he had fled to Asia after this defeat at Salamis.

Chapter 112

1. During the time that Xerxes abode at Sardis, he fell in love with the wife of his brother Masistes.

2. He sent her messages, but failed to win her consent; and he did not dare to use violence, out of regard to Masistes.

3. This the woman knew well enough, which is why she had the boldness to resist him.

4. So Xerxes, finding no other way, devised a marriage between his

own son Darius and a daughter of this woman, thinking that he might better obtain his ends thereby.

5. Accordingly he betrothed the two, and after the usual ceremonies were completed, went to his capital city of Susa.

6. When he received his new daughter-in-law, whose name was Artaynta, into his palace, a change came over him;

7. Losing all love for the wife of Masistes, he conceived a passion for Artaynta, who very soon returned his love.

8. After a while the affair was discovered by Xerxes' wife Amestris.

9. She had woven a long robe of many colours, very curiously made, as a gift for her husband.

10. Xerxes, who was greatly pleased with it, immediately put it on; and went in it to visit Artaynta.

11. She happened on this day to please him greatly in their pleasures in bed, so he bade her ask him for whatever she liked,

12. And promised that, whatever it was, he would grant it. She then boldly asked for the robe.

13. Hereupon Xerxes tried all possible means to avoid the gift; not that he grudged to give it, but because he dreaded Amestris,

14. Who already suspected, and would now, he feared, detect his love.

15. So he offered Artaynta cities instead, and heaps of gold, and an army which should obey no other leader. (The last of these is a thoroughly Persian gift.)

16. But, as nothing could make her change her mind, at last he gave her the robe.

17. Artaynta greatly rejoiced, and often wore the garment and was proud of it.

18. But it quickly came to the ears of Amestris that the robe had been given to Artaynta.

19. She felt no anger against Artaynta; but, looking upon Artaynta's mother, the wife of Masistes, as the cause of the mischief, she determined to kill her.

20. She waited until her husband gave the great royal banquet in celebration of his birthday, the feast called 'Tykta'.

21. This is the only day in the year on which the king soaps his head, and distributes gifts to the Persians.

22. Amestris waited for this day, and then asked Xerxes to please give her, as her present, the wife of Masistes.

23. He refused; for it seemed to him monstrous to give into the power of another a woman who was not only his brother's wife,

24. But was also wholly guiltless of what had happened – the more especially as he knew what Amestris intended.

25. At length, however, wearied by her importunity,

26. And constrained by the law of the feast, which required that no

request made at the king's board should be denied,

27. He yielded, but with a very ill will, and gave the woman into her power.

28. Having so done, the king called his brother and said,

29. 'Masistes, you are my brother, and a good man. I ask you, live no longer with the wife you now have.

30. 'I will give you instead my own daughter in marriage.'

31. Masistes, greatly astonished, answered, 'My lord, how strange of you to ask this!

32. 'You tell me put away my wife, who has borne me three good sons, and daughters besides,

33. 'One of which you have taken to be your son's wife – you ask me to put away this wife, who pleases me greatly, and marry a daughter of yours!

34. 'In truth, O king! to be accounted worthy to wed your daughter is a great honour;

35. 'Yet I am wholly unwilling to part with my wife. Do not force me to this.'

36. Xerxes angrily replied, 'I will tell you what you have gained by these words.

37. 'I will not give you my daughter; nor will you live any longer with your own wife. So you will learn, in time to come, to take what is offered.'

38. Masistes, when he heard this, withdrew, only saying, 'Master, you have not yet taken my life.'

39. While these words were passing between Xerxes and his brother, Amestris sent for the spearmen of the royal bodyguard,

40. And caused the wife of Masistes to be mutilated in a horrible fashion.

41. Her two breasts, her nose, ears and lips were cut off and thrown to the dogs; her tongue was torn out by the roots, and thus disfigured, she was sent back to her home.

42. Masistes, who knew nothing of what had happened, but was fearful that some calamity impended, ran hastily to his house.

43. There, finding his wife so savagely used, he took counsel with his sons, and, accompanied by them and certain others, set out to Bactria,

44. Intending to stir up revolt in that province, and hoping to do great hurt to Xerxes:

45. Which he would have accomplished, if he had reached the Bactrian and Sacan people, for he was loved by them both,

46. And was moreover satrap of Bactria. But Xerxes, hearing of his designs, sent an armed force on his track,

47. Which killed him on the road, with his sons and followers.

Chapter 113

1. Meanwhile the Greeks, who had left Mycale and sailed for the Hellespont,

2. Were forced by contrary winds to

anchor near Lectum, from where they afterwards sailed to Abydos.

3. On arriving they discovered that the Hellespont bridges, which they had thought were still standing, were destroyed.

4. Leotychides and the Peloponnesians under him were keen to return home; but the Athenians under their captain Xanthippus wished to remain to make an attempt on the Chersonese.

5. So, while the Peloponnesians sailed home, the Athenians crossed from Abydos to the Chersonese, and laid siege to Sestos.

6. Now, as Sestos was the strongest fortress in that region, the news had no sooner gone abroad that the Greeks were at the Hellespont,

7. Than great numbers of people flocked in panic to Sestos from the neighbouring towns.

8. Among them came a certain Oeobazus, a Persian from the city of Cardia,

9. Where he had kept the shore cables which had been used in the construction of the bridges.

10. Sestos was guarded by its own Aeolian inhabitants, but contained also some Persians and a great multitude of their allies.

11. The whole district was ruled by the satrap Artayctes, a Persian, but a cruel and wicked man.

12. When Xerxes was marching against Athens, Artayctes had craftily possessed himself of the treasures belonging to Protesilaus, the son of Iphiclus, which were at Elaesus in the Chersonese.

13. For at this place is the tomb of Protesilaus, with a great store of wealth, vases of gold and silver, works in brass, garments and other treasures,

14. All which Artayctes made his prey, having got the king's consent by saying to him,

15. 'Master, in this region there is the house of a Greek, who, when he attacked your territory, was killed.

16. 'Give me his house, so that hereafter men will fear to carry arms against you.'

17. He easily persuaded Xerxes to agree, for there was no suspicion in the king's mind.

18. And Artayctes could say in a certain sense that Protesilaus had borne arms against the land of the king,

19. Because the Persians considered all Asia to belong to them, and to their king for the time being.

20. So when Xerxes allowed his request, Artayctes brought all the treasures from Elaesus to Sestos, and made the forfeit land into cornfields and pasture.

21. It was this Artayctes who was now besieged by the Athenians.

22. He was ill prepared for defence, because had he not in the least expected the Greeks' coming.

23. When it was now late in the autumn, and the siege continued, the Athenians began to murmur

that they were kept abroad too long;

24. And, seeing that they were not able to take the place, urged Xanthippus to lead them back to their own country.

25. But he refused to move until either the city fell or the Athenian people ordered them home. So the soldiers patiently endured.

26. Meanwhile those within the walls were reduced to the last straits, forced to boil the very thongs of their beds for food.

27. At last, when these too were finished, Artayctes and Oeobazus, with the native Persians, fled away from the place by night,

28. Having let themselves down from the wall at the back of the town, where the blockading force was scantiest.

29. As soon as day dawned, the Chersonese signalled the Greeks from the walls, and let them know what had happened, at the same time opening the city gates.

30. Some of the Greeks entered the town, while a more numerous body of them set out in pursuit of the enemy.

31. Oeobazus fled into Thrace; but there the Apsinthian Thracians seized and killed him.

32. As for Artayctes and the troops with him, who had been the last to leave the town, they were over-taken by the Greeks not far from Aegospotami,

33. And defended themselves stoutly for a time, but were at last either killed or taken prisoner.

34. The prisoners were bound with chains and brought back to Sestos, Artayctes and his son among them.

35. Artayctes offered the Greeks wealth if they would release him and his son, but he failed to persuade Xanthippus,

36. And in any case the men of Elaeus wished to avenge Protesilaus, entreating Xanthippus that Artayctes might be put to death;

37. And Xanthippus himself was of the same mind. So they took Artayctes to the tongue of land where the bridges of Xerxes had been fixed, and there crucified him.

38. As for Artayctes' son, they stoned him to death before his father's eyes as he hung nailed to the cross.

39. This done, the Athenians sailed back to Greece, carrying with them, besides other treasures and mementoes, the shore cables from the bridges of Xerxes.

Chapter 114

1. So Greece expelled the Persians; so the cradle of the West repelled the East, then more powerful and more ambitious;

2. And which, if it had prevailed, would have commenced a far different history for the world.

3. Therefore do the Greeks of that time merit gratitude, for they saved the brightest hopes of the

human race, which then stood in jeopardy of dying in their infancy.

4. In the former days of Cyrus an ancestor of Artayctes, one Artembares, had urged the king to conquer the greener and more fertile lands of Europe, saying,

5. 'When shall we have a fairer opportunity to do this, now that we are lords of so many nations, and rule all Asia?'

6. But Cyrus had disdainfully replied, 'You can do so if you like, but do not expect to remain rulers if you do, and prepare to be ruled by others;

7. 'For soft countries give rise to soft men; no country produces delight-ful fruits, and at the same time warlike men.'

8. Now the Persians of that day thought Cyrus wise, and they chose to stay in their harsh and churlish land and exercise lord-ship, rather than to cultivate plains and be the slaves of others.

9. But in the days of Xerxes it was proved that there were men who did not choose to be slaves of others, yet at the same time cultivated their olives and vines,

10. And speculated on all things under the sun: on the origin and nature of the universe, on the right and the good, and on the mind of man.

11. These were the fathers of the civilisation that sprang from them, which, though the East never ceased to try conquering them either in body or mind or both,

12. And sometimes succeeded for long periods, yet the ideal survived, and through the centuries found continual rebirth,

13. So that as one travels towards the setting sun one finds successors to Athens, none of them perfect, as Athens was never perfect,

14. Yet inspired in the hearts of their better citizens by the hope of becoming more so.

15. For they remember what the inheritors of those who defeated Xerxes' host heard, which were such words as these:

16. 'Let us take pride in what we are and what we might become, if we value our freedom and the good opinion of those who will come after us.

17. 'We are free people, or capable of being so, in mind no less than in our institutions.

18. 'This freedom was hard won, and might easily be lost; but not if we are vigilant.

19. 'And for the sake of that vigilance, let us remind ourselves what we are.

20. 'Our affairs are in the hands of the many, not the few.

21. 'There exists equal justice to all in their private disputes, but the claim of excellence is also recognised;

22. 'And when a citizen is in any way distinguished, he is appointed to the public service not as a matter of privilege, but as the reward of merit.

23. 'Neither is poverty an obstacle, but a man may benefit his country whatever the obscurity of his condition.

24. 'There is no exclusiveness in our public life, and in our private business we are not suspicious of one another, nor angry with our neighbour if he does what he likes;

25. 'We do not turn sour looks on him, which, though harmless, are not pleasant; for we value tolerance and fairness in all things.

26. 'While we are thus unconstrained in our private business, let there also be a noble attitude in our public acts,

27. 'Where we are prevented from doing wrong by respect for the laws, having a particular regard to those which are ordained for the protection of the weak and injured,

28. 'As well as those unwritten laws which bring upon a transgressor the reprobation of the general sentiment.

29. 'Nor have we forgotten to provide ourselves many kinds of relaxations from toil; we have our recreations throughout the year;

30. 'Our homes are comfortable and secure; and the delight we daily feel in all these things brings us cheer.

31. 'Because of the greatness of our civilisation the fruits of the whole earth flow in upon us; so that we enjoy the goods of other climes as freely as our own.

32. 'Let us be lovers of the beautiful and the good, and let us recall that our strength lies not only in our powers of deliberation,

33. 'But in the knowledge which is gained by deliberation preparatory to action.

34. 'For we have a peculiar power of thinking before we act, and of acting, too,

35. 'Whereas other men are courageous from ignorance, but hesitate upon reflection.

36. 'And they are surely to be esteemed the bravest hearts who, having the clearest sense of both the pains and pleasures of life, do not on that account shrink from challenges.

37. 'In doing good, again, we are unlike others; we make our friends by conferring, not by receiving favours.

38. 'Now he who confers a favour is the firmer friend, because he would rather by kindness keep alive the memory of an obligation;

39. 'But the recipient is colder in his feelings, because he knows that in requiting another's generosity he will not be winning gratitude, but only paying a debt.

40. 'We alone do good to our neighbours not upon a calculation of interest, but in the confidence of freedom and with a frank and fearless heart.

41. 'Let the individual in his own person have the power of adapting himself to the most varied forms

of action with the utmost versatility and grace.

42. 'This is no passing and idle word,
but a counsel of wisdom; and it is
supported by the position to
which these qualities have raised
the state of mankind.

43. 'For in the hour of trial the best
are always superior to the report of
them.

44. 'And the endeavours of the best
shall assuredly not be without
witnesses; there are mighty
monuments of their achievements
which make them the wonder of
all ages.

45. 'Of how few can it be said that
their deeds, when weighed in the
balance, have been found equal to
their fame!

46. 'For even those who come short in
other ways may justly plead the
efforts they have made for the

good; they have blotted out their
failures with their successes thereby.

47. 'Such was the way of all who
strove to make, promote or defend
something worthwhile, of whatever kind;

48. 'They merited the name of human
being, and of friend. The value of
such is not to be expressed in
words.

49. 'Anyone can discourse for ever
about the advantages of courage
and determination,

50. 'But instead of listening to
discourses only, let us day by day
fix our eyes on the good, until we
become filled with the love of it.

51. 'And then we will have helped
fulfil the promise that lay in the
victory of the Greeks over the
Persians:

52. 'To be free in honour, and wise in
freedom.'

PROVERBS

Chapter 1: Action

1. Action is the proper fruit of knowledge.
2. Great actions speak great minds.
3. Actions need no trumpet.
4. For the sake of one good act, a hundred ill acts might be forgiven.

Chapter 2: Adversity

1. Adversity is the first path to truth.
2. There is no education like adversity.
3. Though it makes no one rich, it makes many wise.
4. It has few friends, but proves those it has.
5. Adversity flatters no one, it tries virtue and tests courage.
6. Gold is tested by fire, brave men by adversity.

Chapter 3: Advice

1. Advice is what the wise do not need and fools do not take.
2. Who will not be advised cannot be helped.
3. Advice most needed is least heeded.
4. If the advice be good, it matters not who gave it.
5. None can act upon advice but those who need it.
6. Advice after mischief is like medicine after death.
7. Be adviser to all, security for none.
8. Less advice, more hands.
9. In advising a friend, seek to help, not please.
10. It is bad advice that cannot be altered.
11. When well, we easily advise the sick.
12. The advice of fools is worth nothing.
13. Do not hazard your wealth on a pauper's advice.
14. Whispered advice is not worth a pea.

Chapter 4: Affliction

1. Affliction is like the blacksmith's hammer; it shapes as it smites.
2. Everyone has enough courage to bear others' afflictions.

Chapter 5: Age

1. A head that is white is no maid's delight.
2. Age, like love, cannot be hid.
3. Age will not be defied.
4. Age should think, youth should do.
5. All would live long, but none would be old.
6. Old age makes us wiser and more foolish.
7. The autumn of the beautiful is beautiful.
8. We do not count our years until we have nothing left to count.

9. Age makes many white but not better.

10. Few know how to be old well.

11. Age plants more wrinkles in the mind than the face.

12. Old is as one's heart.

13. Age comes uncalled.

14. Old people see best in the distance.

15. Old age and the wear of time teach many things.

16. The old age of an eagle is better than the youth of a sparrow.

17. What else are the elderly but voice and shadow?

18. Old age is more to be feared than death.

Chapter 6: Ambition

1. Ambition is the growth of every clime.

2. Ambition obeys no law but its own.

3. Ambition spends unwisely what avarice collected.

4. They shoot higher who aim at the sun than those who aim at a tree.

5. Low ambition and thirst of praise: marks of the worthless.

6. One does not heed the rungs of the ladder by which one climbs.

7. There is nothing humbler than ambition when it first starts to climb.

8. There is no eel so small but it hopes to become a whale.

Chapter 7: Anger

1. Anger rides a mad horse.

2. Anger sharpens valour.

3. Anger is a bad counsellor.

4. Anger is never without a reason, but seldom has a good one.

5. Anger makes dull people witty but keeps them poor.

6. Anger punishes itself.

7. Those who are angry seldom want woe.

8. Beware the fury of a patient man.

9. The dog bites the stone, not the thrower.

10. Anger blinds the eye to truth.

11. However weak the hand, anger gives it strength.

12. Hidden wrath causes harm.

13. The remedy for anger is delay.

14. Anger is a fool.

Chapter 8: Appetite

1. One always has a good appetite at another's feast.

2. The full stomach turns even from the honey of Hybla.

3. Seek appetite by toil.

4. A stomach seldom empty despises common food.

5. Where reason rules, appetite obeys.

6. The poor lack meat for their stomach, the rich lack stomach for their meat.

Chapter 9: Argument

1. A contentious person never lacks words.

2. A noisy arguer is always right.

3. It were endless to dispute everything disputable.

4. People may be convinced, but never pleased, against their will.

5. To treat your adversary with respect

is to give him an advantage he is not entitled to.

6. A quarrel is fought with noise or fists, an argument with logic.

Chapter 10: Art

1. Art has an enemy called ignorance.
2. Art is not a thing, but a way.
3. Art may err, but nature never.
4. Art is its own expression.
5. Art strives for form, and hopes for beauty, or truth; or both.
6. Great art is eternity arrested for an instant.
7. All the arts are brothers.
8. Each art is a light to the others.
9. The perfection of art is to conceal art.
10. What takes effect by chance is not art.

Chapter 11: Artists

1. A great artist can paint a great picture on a small canvas.
2. An artist is a dreamer who dreams reality.
3. Every artist was first an amateur.
4. The art of every artist is his autobiography.
5. Nothing can come from the artist that is not in the human being.
6. Scratch an artist and you surprise a child.
7. Great artists are simplifiers.

Chapter 12: Aspiration

1. Who stays in the valley shall never surmount the hill.
2. What defines you is not what you do, but what you would do.

3. One is complete only if one desires to be more.

Chapter 13: Avarice

1. The covetous do nothing well until they die.
2. Avarice and happiness do not share a home.
3. Avarice is a spur to industry.
4. It is not lack but abundance that breeds avarice.
5. They who covet are always poor.
6. Poverty lacks much, avarice lacks everything.
7. Misers fear to use their gains.
8. The miser is as bereft of what he has as of what he lacks.

Chapter 14: Beauty

1. Everything has its beauty but not everyone sees it.
2. All heiresses are beautiful.
3. Beauty and folly are old companions.
4. Beauty and honesty seldom agree.
5. Beauty carries its dower in its face.
6. Beauty is its own excuse.
7. Beauty is a natural superiority.
8. Beauty provokes thieves sooner than gold.
9. Where beauty is, there will be love.
10. Beauty is as good as ready money.
11. Beauty opens locked doors.
12. Most women would rather be beautiful than good.
13. Beauty is the purgation of superfluities.
14. There is beauty enough where there is goodness enough.

15. Rare is the union of beauty and modesty.
16. Beauty is a short-lived reign.
17. Beauty is a fading flower.
18. When the candles are out all women are fair, with money in hand all men are handsome.

Chapter 15: Beginnnings

1. At first everything is difficult.
2. All glory comes from daring to begin.
3. Better never begin than never end.
4. Who begins many things ends few.
5. The first step is as good as half over.
6. What begins with tow will not end as silk.
7. Things are always at their best at the beginning.
8. All beginnings are small.

Chapter 16: Belief

1. Believe not all you see or half you hear.
1. He does not believe who does not live accordingly.
2. Each person's own belief is true.
3. Who believes everything, misses; who believes nothing, misses.
4. People believe what they wish were true.
5. Quick believers need broad shoulders.
6. A belief is not true because it is useful.
7. Who quick believes late repents.
8. Who knows much believes less.

Chapter 17: Benefit

1. Benefits, like flowers, please when fresh.
2. Benefits turn to poison in bad minds.
3. The last benefit is the most remembered.
4. When benefited, remember it; when benefiting, forget it.
5. Write injuries in dust, benefits in marble.
6. Who confers a benefit loves more than the one benefited.
7. Benefits are acceptable only if they can be repaid.
8. Benefits are traced on sand, injuries on brass.
9. To accept a benefit is to sell one's freedom.
10. To benefit the worthy is to benefit all.

Chapter 18: Birth

1. No one can help being born.
2. We are not completely born until we are dead.
3. I wept when I was born, and every day shows why.
4. No one is born with an axe in hand.
5. No one is born a partisan of this or that cause; all such are made.

Chapter 19: Blindness

1. The sky is not less blue because the blind cannot see it.
2. A pebble and a diamond are alike to the blind.
3. Better be blind than see ill.
4. Better half blind than both eyes out.

5. People are most blind in their own cause.
6. The blind eat many a fly.
7. Blind men should judge no colours.
8. The eyes are blind when the mind is elsewhere.
9. Among the blind close your eyes.

Chapter 20: Blushing

1. Whoever blushes is not quite a brute.
2. People blush less for their crimes than their weaknesses.
3. Rather see a young man blush than turn pale.
4. When the guilty blush it is a sign of mending.
5. Rather bring blood to the cheek than let it out of the body.

Chapter 21: Boldness

1. The bold never lack a weapon.
2. Bold knaves thrive without a grain of sense, while the good starve for want of impudence.
3. Boldness is an ill keeper of promises.
4. Great boldness is seldom without some absurdity.
5. It is a bold mouse that breeds in the cat's ear.
6. Boldness is a bulwark.
7. Boldness leads to the highest or the lowest.

Chapter 22: Books

1. Something is learned every time a book is opened.
2. A book may be as great a thing as a battle.
3. Books are ships that traverse the seas of time.
4. Books cannot always please, however good; minds are not always craving for food.
5. Books give no wisdom where there was not wisdom before.
6. Rather a study full of books than a purse full of money.
7. There is nothing so old as a new book.
8. The best companions are good books.
9. The books that help most are those that prompt most thought.
10. The virtue of books is to be readable.
11. There is no frigate like a book to take us to lands far away.
12. Wear the old coat and buy the new book.
13. The world may know me by my book, and my book by me.
14. Word by word the great books are written.
15. The reader's fancy makes the fate of books.

Chapter 23: Borrowing

1. A borrowed cloak does not keep one warm.
2. Borrowed clothes never fit well.
3. Better buy than borrow.
4. Creditors have better memories than debtors.
5. With a horse of your own you can borrow another.
6. Who borrows must pay again with shame or loss.
7. They that borrow, sorrow.

8. If you would know the value of money, try borrowing some.
9. Borrowing is the mother of trouble.
10. Borrowing thrives but once.

Chapter 24: Bread

1. Acorns were good till bread was found.
2. Bread and cheese are shields against death.
3. Eaten bread is forgotten.
4. Whose bread I break, his song I sing.
5. Others' bread has seven crusts.
6. Another's bread costs dear.
7. I know what I say when I ask for bread.
8. A knife is soon found for bread.

Chapter 25: Breeding

1. Better unborn than unbred.
2. Birth is much, breeding is more.
3. They are not well bred that cannot abide ill breeding in others.
4. Vipers breed vipers.
5. What is born of a cat will catch mice.

Chapter 26: Bribes

1. A bribe will enter without knocking.
2. All have their price.
3. Bribery and theft are first cousins.
4. Few people have virtue to withstand the highest bidder.
5. Honesty stands at the gate, bribery enters in.
6. A greased mouth cannot say no.

Chapter 27: Burdens

1. Every ass thinks his own load heaviest.
2. Let every pedlar carry his own pack.
3. Light burdens are heavy when borne far.
4. None knows the weight of another's burden.
5. The back is shaped to the burden.
6. It is base to flinch under a burden.
7. The burden grows light when well borne.
8. Place the burden on the slow donkey.
9. The burden is light on another's shoulder.

Chapter 28: Business

1. Whoever does not smile should not open a shop.
2. Fuel is not sold in the forest, nor fish by a lake.
3. Drive your business or it will drive you.
4. Everyone lives by selling something.
5. Ill ware is never cheap.
6. Keep your shop and it will keep you.
7. Good merchandise finds a ready buyer.
8. Do not buy everything that is cheap.
9. Buy at a fair, sell at home.
10. There are more foolish buyers than foolish sellers.
11. The buyer needs a hundred eyes, the seller needs not one.

Chapter 29: Chance

1. Chance may win what mischance lost.
2. He who leaves nothing to chance will do little ill, but will do little anyway.
3. Something must be left to chance.
4. Too late to grieve when the chance is past.
5. He that waits on chance is never sure of his dinner.
6. Chance is always on the side of the prudent.
7. Chance and valour are blended in one.
8. Chance is another master.
9. Chance and justice are unequally matched.
10. Probabilities direct the conduct of the wise.
11. What chance made yours is not really yours.
12. Whom chance passes by, it finds them at last.

Chapter 30: Character

1. Character is easier kept than recovered.
2. Character is what you are in the dark.
3. No one climbs beyond the limits of character.
4. There is much unmapped territory within us.
5. People show their character by what they laugh at.
6. Character is nurtured amidst the tempests of the world.
7. Character is destiny.
8. Character is habit long continued.
9. Character is the result of conduct.
10. Trust more in character than promises.
11. To the bad character good doctrine avails nothing.
12. One's character is the arbiter of one's fortune.

Chapter 31: Charity

1. Who gives to be seen will not help in the dark.
2. Better feed ten drones than let one bee starve.
3. Better to give one than promise two.
4. Rather not live than to live by alms.
5. They give twice who give quickly.
6. Do good, and ask not for whom.

Chapter 32: Cheapness

1. Cheap things are not good, good things are not cheap.
2. Cheap bargains are dear.
3. The cheap buyer takes bad meat.
4. To buy cheap, buy of a needy fool.

Chapter 33: Children

1. A pet child has many names.
2. Children and drunkards speak truth.
3. A spoiled child never loves its mother.
4. Better a little chiding than a great heartbreak.
5. Children and fools have merry lives.
6. Children and fools must avoid edged tools.
7. Children are certain cares but uncertain comforts.

8. Children are poor men's riches.

9. Children have wide ears and long tongues.

10. Children pick up words as pigeons pick peas.

11. Children suck the mother when young, and the father when old.

12. Children when young make parents fools; when older, make them mad.

13. For a little child a great mourning.

14. Give the child his will and he will turn out ill.

15. Happy are those who are happy in their children.

16. Those without children do not know love.

17. Better to have one plough going than two cradles.

18. As the twig is bent, the tree inclines.

19. Late children, early orphans.

20. The child says nothing but what is heard by the fire.

21. The sports of children satisfy the child.

22. Unruly children make their sire stoop.

23. When children stand still, they have done some ill.

24. Children have more need of example than criticism.

25. Better the child should cry than the parent.

26. The neighbour's children are always the worst.

27. What the parents spin the children must reel.

28. You can do anything with children if only you will play with them.

29. Children are deceived with candies and men with promises.

30. Better bind children with respect than fear.

Chapter 34: Company

1. A crowd is not company.

2. Company in misery makes it light.

3. Company keeps your mind from coarsening.

4. Ill company is like a dog, which dirties most those it most loves.

5. The company makes the feast.

6. If you live with the lame you learn to limp.

7. Jackdaw to jackdaw.

8. Who lies down with dogs will rise with fleas.

9. No road is long in good company.

10. The smaller the company, the better the feast.

Chapter 35: Conceit

1. Conceit is the comfort of little men.

2. To be full of oneself is to be empty.

3. Those who are in love with themselves will have no rivals.

4. He thinks his farthing good silver.

Chapter 36: Confidence

1. Confidence is a plant of slow growth.

2. No one can be forced into trust.

3. Skill and confidence make an unconquerable army.

4. Confidence arises from caution.

Chapter 37: Conscience

1. An evil deed has a witness in the bosom.

2. A burdened conscience needs no hangman.
3. A clear conscience bears any trouble.
4. A good conscience is a soft pillow.
5. A guilty conscience never feels safe.
6. Conscience tells us what is honour.
7. A quiet conscience sleeps through thunder.
8. Who has no conscience has nothing.
9. The worm of conscience consorts with the owl.
10. A clear conscience is a wall of brass.
11. A bad conscience is a snake in one's breast.

Chapter 38: Contentment

1. Those who are content can never be ruined.
2. A contented mind is a kingdom.
3. Better a little with content than much with contention.
4. Contentment lodges oftener in cottages than castles.
5. Contentment surpasses wealth.

Chapter 39: Courage

1. If you do not enter the tiger's den, you cannot get his cubs.
2. Courage is never out of fashion.
3. Courage scorns the death it cannot shun.
4. Courage should have eyes as well as arms.
5. It is easier to use a weapon than to show courage.
6. The test of courage is bearing defeat without losing heart.
7. Where the brave man is, is the thickest of the battle.
8. Courage does more than rage can.
9. You cannot know your courage until you have tasted danger.
10. All are brave when the enemy flies.
11. They need heels who have no heart.
12. Courage in danger is half the battle.
13. Courage champions right.
14. True courage grapples misfortune.
15. It is the courage, not the weapon, that wins.
16. There is always safety in valour.

Chapter 40: Courtesy

1. All doors open to courtesy.
2. Courtesy costs nothing.
3. Courtesy unanswered does not last long.
4. Do not limp before the lame.
5. The courteous learn their courtesy from the discourteous.

Chapter 41: Cowardice

1. To see what is right and not do it, is cowardice.
2. A coward's fear can make a coward valiant.
3. Cowards are cruel.
4. Cowards die many deaths.
5. Cowards in scarlet pass for men of war.
6. Cowards show no mercy.
7. Many would be cowards if they had courage enough.
8. There grows no herb to heal a coward's heart.
9. Better be a coward than a fool.
10. One coward makes ten.

11. The coward makes threats only when he is safe.
12. Strength is no use to the coward.
13. Who cannot strike the ass may strike the saddle.
14. Cowards call themselves cautious, misers call themselves thrifty.

Chapter 42: Credit

1. Better take eight than sell for ten on credit.
2. They who have lost their credit are dead to the world.
3. They pay severely who require credit.
4. No man ever lost credit but he who had none to begin with.
5. The poor have no credit.
6. Who loses credit has nothing else to lose.

Chapter 43: Crime

1. Crimes may be secret, but are never secure.
2. They act the third crime who defend the first.
3. They who do what they should not, will feel what they would not.
4. The contagion of crime is like the plague.
5. We easily forget crimes known only to ourselves.
6. One may thrive on crime, but not for long.
7. Crime needs crime to conceal it.
8. To share your friend's crime is to make it your own.
9. No crime is founded on reason.
10. Criminals are punished to amend others.

11. No one lives who is without a crime.
12. Successful crime is called virtue.
13. Who is content with one crime only?
14. Who profits from a crime commits the crime.

Chapter 44: Custom

1. Custom is the plague of the wise and the idol of fools.
2. Custom meets us at the cradle and leaves us only at the grave.
3. Custom reconciles us to everything.
4. Tyrant custom makes a slave of reason.
5. A cake and a bad custom ought to be broken.
6. Custom is a deceiving schoolteacher.
7. So many countries, so many customs.
8. A good custom is surer than law.
9. Choose the best; custom will make it easy.
10. We care more about what is done against custom than against nature.

Chapter 45: Danger

1. Who loves danger will perish by it.
2. As soon as there is life there is danger.
3. Danger and delight grow on one stalk.
4. Danger is next neighbour to security.
5. Danger is the best remedy for danger.
6. Danger is the spur of great minds.
7. Danger will wink at opportunity.

8. Dangers bring fears, fears bring more dangers.
9. Dangers foreseen are soonest prevented.
10. Who fears danger in time seldom feels it.
11. They that would sail without danger will never go to sea.
12. If the danger seems slight, time to beware.
13. There is no one who is not dangerous to someone.
14. No danger, no glory.
15. Danger comes the sooner when despised.
16. They are happy whom others' perils make wary.
17. Who dares dangers overcomes them before incurring them.
18. The danger that is nearest we least dread.
19. Without danger the game is cold.
20. Fear the goat from the front, the horse from behind, and human beings all round.
21. One who would scratch a bear must have iron nails.

Chapter 46: Death
1. Few have luck, all have death.
2. The dead feel no cold.
3. The deathbed reveals the heart.
4. The dying can do nothing easy.
5. A good death honours a whole life.
6. Gentle death is the ebb of care.
7. Death has many doors to let out life.
8. Death is only an incident in life.
9. Death makes high and low equal.
10. Death is the period of all pain.
11. Death opens the gate of fame and shuts the gate of envy.
12. Death takes no bribes.
13. Death will seize the doctor too.
14. Happy are they who die before they call for death.
15. Who fears death lives not.
16. They that once are born, once must die.
17. How sweet is death to those who weep.
18. It is as natural to die as to be born.
19. It is not death but dying which is terrible.
20. Peace, rest and sleep are all we know of death.
21. The dead are soon forgotten.
22. The dead have few friends.
23. The doors of death are always open.
24. To be content with death is better than to desire it.
25. To live in the hearts we leave behind is not to die.
26. We weep when we are born, not when we die.
27. Death pays all debts.
28. It is only the dead who do not return.
29. There is no dying by proxy.
30. To die quickly is a privilege.
31. All men are born richer than they die.
32. It is not death but a shameful death that is dreadful.
33. The whole earth is a sepulchre for the famous.
34. To die well is a chief part of virtue.
35. It takes four of the living to carry one dead from the house.

36. Death is rest from labour and misery.
37. Death is sometimes a gift.
38. Death overtakes all who flee.
39. They have gone to the majority.
40. It is uncertain where death awaits you, so expect it everywhere.
41. The fear of death is worse than death.
42. The life of the dead is in the memory of the living.
43. The earth rests lightly on those on whom life lay heavily.
44. There is a remedy for everything but death.
45. A good death is better than a bad life.
46. Death reveals truth.
47. The young might, the old must.

Chapter 47: Debt

1. Whoever is in debt lives in a net.
2. A pound of care pays not a penny of debt.
3. Better to bed supperless than to rise indebted.
4. Debt is the mother of folly and crime.
5. Who gets out of debt gets rich.
6. Industry pays debts, despair increases them.
7. Loans and debts make worries and frets.
8. Never spend money before you have it.
9. Out of debt, out of danger.
10. Speak not of my debts unless you mean to pay them.
11. It is an empty purse which is full of other people's money.
12. Debt is the worst kind of poverty.
13. They are rich enough who owe nothing.
14. Debts turn the free into slaves.
15. A light debt makes a debtor, a heavy debt makes an enemy.
16. Debt and gratitude are different things.
17. Debt is grievous to an honourable person.
18. The sick sleep, but debtors lie awake.
19. You cannot pay debts with tears.

Chapter 48: Deceit

1. Deceit invites deceit.
2. They cry wine and sell vinegar.
3. If the world will be gulled, must it be gulled?
4. One dupe is as impossible as one twin.
5. The easiest person to deceive is oneself.
6. There is a twofold pleasure in deceiving the deceiving.
7. Distrust justifies deceit.
8. One might outwit another, but not all the others.
9. The surest way to invite deceit is to think oneself cleverer.
10. We are often deceived by what we love.
11. Who would not be deceived must have as many eyes as hairs on his head.

Chapter 49: Deeds

1. A deed well done pleases the heart.
2. Better not the deed than to weep it done.

3. Our deeds shape us as much as we them.
4. Our deeds are sometimes better than our thoughts.
5. The reward for a good deed is the deed itself.
6. The shortest answer is doing.
7. We know better than we do.
8. We live in deeds, not years.
9. Living requires less life than doing.
10. A good person is silent about a good deed.
11. All are the children of their works.

Chapter 50: Delay

1. Delay is better than disaster.
2. Delay in revenge gives a heavier blow.
3. Delay is preferable to error.
4. Desire is nourished by delay.
5. We hate delay, yet it makes us wise.
6. We may delay, but time will not.
7. Every delay that postpones pleasure is long.
8. Who delays, gathers.

Chapter 51: Desire

1. Desire has no rest.
2. First deserve, then desire.
3. They begin to die who cease to desire.
4. Desire often outlives performance.
5. The fewer desires, the more peace.
6. We live in our desires, not in our achievements.
7. People are led by their desires like a horse in halter.
8. There is no desire for what is unknown.

9. We most desire what we ought not to have.

Chapter 52: Despair.

1. Despair is an evil counsellor.
2. Despair and boldness both banish fear.
3. Despair ruins some, presumption ruins many.
4. To despair of winning is to assure defeat.
5. Despair doubles strength.
6. Despair often wins battles.

Chapter 53: Difficulty

1. Who accounts all things easy will have many difficulties.
2. Everything is difficult before it is easy.
3. Difficulty is the daughter of idleness.
4. A difficulty is a light; an impossibility is the sun.
5. Many things difficult to design are easy in performance.
6. Nothing is too difficult to a willing mind.
7. It is difficulties that show what men are.
8. Even easy things become difficult when done reluctantly.
9. The greater the difficulty, the greater the glory.

Chapter 54: Disease

1. Diseases are the tax on ill pleasures.
2. A disease will have its course.
3. Each season has its own disease.
4. Who was never ill dies the first fit.
5. Sickness comes on horseback, but goes away on foot.

6. Sickness is felt, health not at all.
7. There is no curing the sick who believe themselves well.
8. No one is ever untouched by disease and sorrow.
9. Meet the disease on its way.
10. To hide disease is fatal.
11. The beginning of health is to know the disease.

Chapter 55: Doubt

1. An honest person can never surrender an honest doubt.
2. Who doubts nothing knows nothing.
3. The wise are prone to doubt.

Chapter 56: Dreams

1. All men of action are dreamers.
2. Foolish people have foolish dreams.
3. Love's dreams seldom come true.
4. None thrive for long on the happiest dreams.
5. The more people dream, the less they believe.

Chapter 57: Drunkenness

1. Liquor talks loud when it escapes the jug.
2. The best cure for drunkenness is to see a drunk.
3. A drunkard can soon be made to dance.
4. Let drunkards alone and they will fall by themselves.
5. What is in the sober person's heart is on the drunkard's tongue.
6. Drunkenness is voluntary madness.

Chapter 58: Eating

1. One must eat though every tree were a gallows.
2. Better bide the cook than the doctor.
3. More have been killed by suppers than cured by doctors.
4. Eat, and welcome; fast, and heartily welcome.
5. Eat enough, and it will make you wise.
6. Who feasts every day never makes a good meal.
7. The laziest are never lazy at board.
8. It is good to be merry at meat.
9. The sincerest love is the love of food.
10. To lengthen life, lessen meals.
11. Stop short of your appetite.
12. Unquiet meals make unquiet digestions.
13. We never repent at eating too little.
14. Who would eat the kernel must break the shell.
15. Who eats too much does not know how to eat.
16. The rich eat when they will, the poor when they can.

Chapter 59: Education

1. People may be educated beyond their intelligence.
2. Better build schoolrooms for the child than prisons for the adult.
3. Genius without education is like silver in the moon.
4. There is nothing so worthwhile as an instructed mind.
5. The secret of education lies in respecting the pupil.

6. What sculpture is to marble,
   education is to the mind.
7. Nature is stronger than education.
8. Too much education can hinder as
   greatly as too little.
9. Education is an ornament in
   prosperity and a refuge in adversity.
10. The foundation of society is the
    education of youth.
11. Only the educated are free.
12. Education leads to treasure.
13. Only the ignorant despise
    education.

Chapter 60: Enemies

1. No one is without enemies.
2. An enemy's mouth seldom speaks
   well.
3. Even from a foe one may learn
   wisdom.
4. The wise dread their enemies.
5. One enemy can do more hurt than
   ten friends can do good.
6. There is no little enemy.
7. Though your enemy be a mouse,
   watch him like a lion.
8. Your enemies make you wise.
9. Enmity is anger waiting for
   revenge.
10. No tears are shed when an enemy
    dies.
11. Better a good enemy than a bad
    friend.

Chapter 61: Envy

1. Envy and wrath shorten life.
2. Envy does not enter an empty
   house.
3. No one is made richer by envy.
4. Bad eyes never see good.

5. People have most what they envy
   most.
6. Nothing sharpens sight like envy.
7. The envious shall never lack woes.
8. It is better to be envied than pitied.
9. Envy takes no holidays.
10. I would rather my enemies envy me
    than I them.
11. The envious grow thin at others'
    prosperity.

Chapter 62: Error

1. The errors of the learned are
   learned errors.
2. Error can be sincerely enough
   believed to count as truth.
3. Error can only be defended by
   error.
4. Error is a hardy plant that flourishes in any soil.
5. Error, like straws, floats on the
   surface; the pearls lie deep below.
6. Honest error is to be pitied, not
   ridiculed.
7. No one prospers so suddenly as by
   other people's errors.
8. One error breeds twenty more.
9. Love truth, but pardon error.
10. The wisest may err.

Chapter 63: Evil

1. Bad people leave their mark
   wherever they go.
2. Putrid flesh is all of a flavour.
3. A bad tree does not yield good
   apples.
4. A bad reaper never has a good
   sickle.
5. Bad is the wool that cannot be
   dyed.

6. Evil conduct is the root of misery.
7. Better good afar than evil at hand.
8. Evil is quickly learned.
9. Evil is wrought by want of thought as well as want of heart.
10. Evil deserves the evil it gets.
11. Humanity creates the evil it endures.
12. None but the base delight in baseness.
13. Of one ill come many.
14. Evil often triumphs but never conquers.
15. Doing evil to avoid evil is still evil.
16. The worse the evil, the calmer we face it.
17. No time is too brief for the wicked to work evil in.
18. The authors of great evils know best how to remove them.
19. An evil life is a kind of death.

Chapter 64: Experience

1. They know the water best who have waded through it.
2. An ounce of wit bought is better than a pound of wit taught.
3. Experience is good if not bought too dear.
4. Experience is the mother of knowledge, the father of wisdom.
5. Experience keeps an expensive school, but fools will learn in no other.
6. They are wrong to blame the sea who have twice survived shipwreck.
7. They are wise who learn from others' woes.
8. They come home wisest who come home whipped by their own follies.

9. Put an old cat to an old rat.
10. Sad experience leaves no room for doubt.
11. The wise learn from others' harm, the fool from his own.
12. I know by my own pot how others boil.
13. One bitten by a serpent is afraid of ropes.
14. A frog in a well knows nothing of the sea.
15. Who suffers, remembers.

Chapter 65: Failure

1. Failure teaches success.
2. Have the heart to fight and lose.
3. Failure is not in the lexicon of youth.
4. To fail in an immense ambition is to know the fiercest despair.
5. They who do not fly high will fall less far.
6. Not every fall is a failure.
7. Hasty climbers have sudden falls.
8. They fail badly who cannot rise again.
9. It is easier to fail than to succeed; easiest not to try at all.
10. When a tree is falling, all cry 'Down with it!'
11. To dare is to brave the thought of failure.
12. Not everything that shakes falls.

Chapter 66: Fame

1. All fame is dangerous; good brings envy, bad brings shame.
2. Fame is a magnifying glass.
3. Fame is but the breath of the people.

4. Fame is proof that people are gullible.
5. Fondness of fame is avarice of air.
6. Fame is fickle and partial.
7. Fames comes unlooked for, if it comes at all.
8. Fame is as ephemeral as the famous.

Chapter 67: Fathers

1. It is not a father's anger but his silence that a son dreads.
2. The father, in praising the son, praises himself.
3. He that loves the tree loves the branch.
4. No man is responsible for his father.
5. One father might support ten children, but ten children rarely support one father.
6. One father is more than a hundred schoolmasters.
7. A father loves his children in hating their faults.
8. He that has his father for judge goes safely to trial.

Chapter 68: Fault

1. A fault denied is twice committed.
2. Everyone blames their faults on the times.
3. He is faultless to a fault.
4. Faults are thick where love is thin.
5. Faults done by night blush by day.
6. They are lifeless who are faultless.
7. In every fault there is folly.
8. People hate faults they do not themselves commit.
9. The greatest fault is to be conscious of none.

10. Those who seek only faults, find nothing else.
11. The hunchback sees only his neighbour's hump.
12. We never confess our faults except through vanity.
13. The fault of another is a good teacher to an apt pupil.
14. Who desires a faultless mule must walk.
15. Let a fault be concealed by its nearness to a virtue.

Chapter 69: Fear

1. Fear is the mother of safety and the father of courage.
2. They who fear you present, will hate you absent.
3. Fear is the parent of cruelty.
4. Fear is stronger than love.
5. Fear springs from ignorance.
6. Fear kills more than disease.
7. Foolish fear doubles danger.
8. Share your courage, keep your fear to yourself.
9. Nothing is as rash as fear.
10. Nothing is terrible except fear itself.
11. The fearless man is his own salvation.
12. To fear the worst can cure the worse.
13. Fear tames lions.
14. If many fear you, fear the many.
15. Fear does not guard duty.
16. Fear makes people believe the worst.
17. Fear, not mercy, restrains the wicked.
18. Fear feels no pity when extreme danger threatens.

19. It is torment to fear what cannot be overcome.
20. Terror closes the ears and eyes.

Chapter 70: Flattery

1. A flatterer is one who either despises you or wishes to cheat you.
2. Flattery corrupts both the giver and the receiver.
3. Flatterers look as much like friends as wolves look like dogs.
4. Flattery is perfume, to be smelt not swallowed.
5. Flattery sits in the parlour while plain speech is kicked out of doors.
6. They put honey in their mouths who have none in their pot.
7. Who loves to be flattered is worthy of the flatterer.
8. Friend and flatterer do not meet in the same person.
9. More flies are caught with a drop of honey than a lake of vinegar.
10. It is easier to flatter than praise.
11. A flatterer is a secret enemy.
12. Who paints me before, blackens me behind.
13. Who delight in being flattered, later pay by regret.
14. Flattery is so much bird lime.
15. Let anyone daub you with honey and you will never lack flies.
16. Better flatter fools than fight them.

Chapter 71: Folly

1. Folly has the wings of an eagle and the eyes of an owl.
2. Folly grows without watering.
3. Folly makes itself sick.
4. Happy those who learn from their youthful follies.
5. If folly were grief, every house would weep.
6. If others had not been foolish, we would be.
7. It is folly to drown on dry land.
8. It is folly to try to buy reputation.
9. It is folly to sing twice to the deaf.
10. One person's folly is another's fortune.
11. Who live without folly are not as wise as they think.
12. Folly is self-inflicted misfortune.
13. It is better to advise folly than punish it.
14. Wealth excuses folly.
15. The shame lies not in one's folly, but in not learning from it.

Chapter 72: Fools

1. The fool's mind dances on the tip of his tongue.
2. Fools are like other people as long as they are silent.
3. A fool may ask more questions in an hour than the wise can answer in seven years.
4. Fools are sometimes right.
5. A fool does not see the same tree as the wise.
6. A fool's tongue is long enough to cut his own throat.
7. A rich fool is a wise person's treasurer.
8. Everyone is a fool sometimes, and none is a fool always.
9. Everyone has a fool in his sleeve.
10. A fool is one who deals with fools.

11. Fools bite each other, where the wise agree.
12. Fools cut their fingers, the wise their tongues.
13. Fools set stools for the wise to stumble over.
14. Fools tie knots, and the wise untie them.
15. They are not wise who cannot sometimes play the fool.
16. Most fools think they are only ignorant.
17. One fool praises another.
18. The fool wanders, the wise travel.
19. The wise draw more advantage from their enemies than fools from their friends.
20. Every fool has a bigger fool to praise him.
21. Hairdressers learn their trade on fools' heads.
22. If fools ate no bread, wheat would be cheap.
23. With fools it is always holiday.
24. Do not speak of stones to fools lest they throw them at your head.
25. Fools say what they know, the wise know what they say.
26. Better a slap from a wise person than a kiss from a fool.
27. Better to lose with the wise than win with a fool.

Chapter 73: Forgiveness
1. Good to forgive, best to forget.
2. Forgive others sooner than yourself.
3. The offender never pardons.
4. Who forgives readily only invites offence.
5. One pardons in the degree that one loves.
6. To understand is to forgive.
7. Forgiveness is better than revenge.

Chapter 74: Freedom
1. Better be a free bird than a captive king.
2. Restraint from ill is freedom to the wise.
3. To have the blessings of freedom requires the pains of getting and keeping it.
4. You are free at the moment you wish to be free.
5. The free never grow old.
6. They who have lost their freedom have nothing else to lose.
7. No bad person is free.
8. None are free who lack self-mastery.

Chapter 75: Friends
1. The road is never long to a friend's house.
2. A judicious friend is better than a zealous friend.
3. They are not all friends who speak us fair.
4. Be slow to choose friends, slower in changing them.
5. Better be a nettle to your friend than his echo.
6. They are friends who give help rather than pity.
7. The best mirror is an old friend.
8. I will be your friend, but not your vices' friend.
9. A false friend, like a shadow, attends only in sunlight.

10. Promises get friends, performances keep them.
11. The only way to have a friend is to be one.
12. The vanquished have no friends.
13. Be a friend to yourself, and others will befriend you.
14. Relatives are given, friends chosen.
15. A friend to all is a friend to none.
16. Prosperity makes friends and adversity tries them.
17. Where there are friends there is wealth.
18. They who have a thousand friends have not one to spare.
19. A friend can be treated without ceremony, but not without civility.
20. Friendship is a commerce between equals.
21. Friendship is not to be valued by material advantages.

Chapter 76: Genius

1. Genius can only breathe in the air of liberty.
2. Genius is of no country.
3. Genius is mainly energy.
4. Genius is a compound of labour and diligence.
5. Genius is patience.
6. Genius is the capacity for hard work.
7. Genius is the capacity for avoiding hard work.
8. Genius must be born and can never be taught.
9. Genius rusts for want of use.
10. Hunger is the handmaid of genius.
11. Rules and models destroy genius.
12. Genius is able to do what talent cannot.

13. Adversity reveals genius, prosperity hides it.

Chapter 77: Gluttony

1. A full belly is the mother of evil.
2. A full belly makes a dull brain.
3. A full stomach neither fights well nor flees well.
4. An empty stomach hears nobody.
5. They who do not mind their bellies will mind little else.
6. The belly hates a long lecture.
7. The belly robs the back.
8. The stomach thinks that the throat has been cut.
9. When the belly is full, the bones are at rest.
10. When the belly is full, the mind is with the maids.
11. No clock is more regular than the stomach.
12. The belly is a bad adviser.
13. A gross belly does not make a refined mind.
14. It is hard to argue with the stomach, for it has no ears.
15. Empty stomach, no sleep.

Chapter 78: Goodness

1. Good people are a public good.
2. Take good will for part payment.
3. Not to serve the good is to serve the bad.
4. They can never be good who are not obstinate.
5. Good that comes too late is no good.
6. Few things are good for nothing at all.
7. Good and evil can be close neighbours.

8. Do not say that none are good.
9. Be called good rather than fortunate.
10. The good make others good.
11. What is good is never plentiful.
12. If you put good in, you can take good out.

Chapter 79: Gratitude

1. Do not cut down the tree that gives you shade.
2. Praise the bridge that carried you over.
3. Mere words are empty thanks.
4. Most people's gratitude is but the hope of receiving more.
5. Gratitude soon grows old and dies.

Chapter 80: Grief

1. Grief makes one hour ten.
2. Grief told brings a little peace.
3. Grief instructs the wise.
4. New grief awakens the old.
5. The cure for grief is action.
6. Little griefs make us tender, great griefs make us hard.
7. Of all ills common to humankind, grief is greatest.
8. They who conceal grief find no remedy for it.
9. Light griefs can speak; great griefs are dumb.
10. There is no grief that time does not lessen.
11. The crown of sorrows is remembrance of happier times.
12. When sorrow sleeps, do not wake it.
13. The longest sorrow at last finds relief.

14. Nothing comes too soon but grief.

Chapter 81: Habit

1. People's natures are alike, it is their habits that divide them.
2. Habits are first cobwebs, then cables.
3. Habit is ten times nature.
4. It is hard to break a bad custom.
5. It is easier to prevent bad habits than reform them.
6. Man is an animal of habit.
7. Unresisted habits become necessities.
8. Much injustice is caused by habit.

Chapter 82: Haste

1. Fools haste to no speed.
2. A hasty person never lacks trouble.
3. Haste trips on its own heels.
4. They hasten well who have patience.
5. The hasty fish lives in an empty pond.
6. They tire quickly who hasten too much.
7. Be patient, to finish more quickly.
8. The hasty arrive as late as the slow.
9. Great haste makes error.
10. Haste is the parent of failure.
11. Haste and prudence never meet.
12. Who pours in haste spills most to waste.

Chapter 83: Hate

1. People never understand those they hate.
2. Hate never ages.
3. Hate and mistrust are born of blindness.
4. Hatred is self-punishment.
5. Hatred has the sharpest eyes.

6. A true man hates no one.
7. Hatred sinks us below those we hate.
8. Hatred renewed is fiercer than first hatred.
9. Hatred proclaimed loses its chance of revenge.
10. We hate those we have injured.
11. Whom people fear they hate, whom they hate they wish dead.

Chapter 84: Health

1. A cool head and warm feet live long.
2. Whoever is healthy is young.
3. Who lives by medicine lives miserably.
4. Better to lose health like a spendthrift than waste it like a miser.
5. They destroy their health who labour to protect it.
6. Better lack a supper than have a hundred doctors.
7. Health comes when the feet do more than the mouth.

Chapter 85: Honesty

1. Honest people do not make themselves dogs for the sake of a bone.
2. An honest person is a citizen of the world.
3. Honest people fear neither light nor dark.
4. Clean hands are better than full ones.
5. It is never too late to be honest.
6. Honesty is rarely the way to wealth.

Chapter 86: Hope

1. Hope is the pauper's income.
2. Hope is a good breakfast but a poor supper.
3. Who lives by hope must die of hunger.
4. Hope is a bad guide, but good company on the way.
5. Without hope the heart must break.
6. Never quit certainty for hope.
7. None so well but hopes to be better.
8. If hope breaks, patience must hold.
9. Hope makes the fool rich.
10. To cease to hope is to cease to fear.
11. Great hopes make great men.

Chapter 87: Idleness

1. All things are easy to industry, difficult to sloth.
2. An idle head is a box for the wind.
3. An idle youth, a needy age.
4. Poison comes from standing water.
5. Idle dogs worry sheep.
6. Idle people have least leisure.
7. Idle people have most labour.
8. Idleness is the mother of poverty and the nurse of vice.
9. Idleness destroys.
10. Idleness travels so slowly that poverty soon overtakes him.
11. To do nothing is in everyone's power.
12. To do nothing is to be nothing.
13. Indolence is the sleep of the mind.
14. The idle breathe but do not live.

Chapter 88: Ignorance
1. An ignorant person is one who walks by night.
2. A person without knowledge is like one who is dead.
3. Our lives are shortened more by lack of knowledge than by lack of years.
4. The tragedy of ignorance is complacency.
5. There is no slavery but ignorance.
6. To be ignorant of one's ignorance is the malady of ignorance.
7. Better unborn than untaught.

Chapter 89: Justice
1. Delay of justice is injustice.
2. Justice is impossible without wisdom.
3. The extremity of justice is unjust.
4. Where there is justice, it is freedom to obey.
5. Any time is the proper time for justice.

Chapter 90: Kindness
1. Kindness is more binding than a loan.
2. A kind heart loses nothing.
3. The nearer the kindred, the less the kindness.

Chapter 91: Knowledge
1. To know one's ignorance is the best part of knowledge.
2. A man is what he knows.
3. Investment in knowledge pays the best interest.
4. Who knows little often repeats it.
5. Knowledge comes, wisdom lingers.
6. Knowledge is a treasure-house, practice is the key to it.
7. Knowledge is the only elegance.
8. The desire for knowledge increases with its acquisition.
9. They know enough who know how to learn.
10. Those who thirst for knowledge, get it.
11. Better to know something about everything than everything about one thing.
12. There is only one good: knowledge. There is only one evil: ignorance.
13. Who knows nothing never doubts.
14. Who knows most believes least.
15. Who knows most forgives most.
16. A learned man has always riches in himself.
17. All wish to know, but none wish to pay the fee.

Chapter 92: Laughter
1. A maid that laughs is half taken.
2. A fool laughs because others laugh.
3. Laughter is sunshine in a house.
4. All things are cause either for laughing or weeping.
5. People show their characters in what they laugh at.
6. No one is sadder than one who laughs too much.
7. Ill-timed laughter is dangerous.
8. What is worse than to be laughed at?

Chapter 93: Law
1. Agree, for the law is costly.
2. Who goes to law holds a wolf by the ears.

3. A rich knave is a libel on the law.

4. Bad laws are the worst tyranny.

5. The best way to be rid of bad laws is to apply them rigorously.

6. Law cannot persuade where it cannot punish.

7. Let law govern man if reason governs the law.

8. Law is a bottomless pit.

9. Law is a pickpocket.

10. Laws should be servants, not masters.

11. Laws are like cobwebs, that catch small flies but let foxes break through.

12. Much law, little justice.

13. Petty laws breed great crimes.

14. Law manufactures a crime, then punishes it.

15. Unnecessary laws are bad laws.

16. Laws are useless when people are pure, broken when people are impure.

17. Where law ends, tyranny begins.

18. The noise of weapons drowns the voice of law.

19. Arms and laws do not dwell together.

20. A lean compromise is better than a fat lawsuit.

21. The more laws, the more offenders.

22. The prince is not above the laws.

23. Fear not the law, but the judge.

Chapter 94: Leisure

1. A life of laziness and a life of leisure are not the same thing.

2. To have leisure requires good use of time; the idle have least leisure, the self-disciplined most.

3. Those who use time well are least at leisure when at leisure; for they use leisure to improve their mind's estate, and to nourish friendship.

4. Leisure is the reward of labour, the mother of philosophy, a bringer of gifts.

5. Leisure is the repair of life, knitting up the ends frayed by labour and striving.

6. Leisure is the womb of innovations, the brother of art, the companion of love.

7. Leisure is the stream that replenishes the reservoir, with waters clean and cool.

Chapter 95: Lending

1. Will you make an enemy? Let him borrow from you.

2. It is better to give a dollar than lend a cent.

3. Lend to a foe and make a friend; lend to a friend and make a foe.

4. What we spent we have; what we gave came back doubled; what we lent we lost.

5. Loans do not come laughing home, but stay abroad as enemies.

6. If you would lend, lend only what you can lose.

7. If you have enough to lend, you have enough to give; and gain more by it.

Chapter 96: Liars

1. Liars begin by deceiving others, and end by deceiving themselves.

2. Old folk and great travellers lie by licence; lawyers lie for pay.

3. Why say 'Show me a liar and I'll show you a thief'? Because liars steal trust.
4. When the liar speaks true, is he believed? Does the liar believe even the honest man?
5. The liar more readily takes an oath.
6. The liar is sooner caught than one who cannot run.
7. The liar is less happy than the sufferer for truth.
8. The liar has no real friend.
9. Liars have least respect for other people.
10. Liars have least respect from other people.

Chapter 97: Liberty

1. Lean liberty is better than fat slavery.
2. Liberty is not licence.
3. The price of liberty is unsleeping vigilance.
4. Better a crust in liberty than sweetmeats in prison.
5. Liberty is the breath of progress.
6. Liberty is the free man's country.

Chapter 98: Lies

1. Half the truth is often a great lie.
2. Who hears much, hears many lies.
3. The cruellest lies are often told in silence.
4. Lies grow with repetition.
5. There is no lie so reckless as lacks some proof.
6. You can travel far with a lie, but you cannot come back.

Chapter 99: Life

1. Life is short and full of blisters.
2. A long life might not be good enough, but a good life is long enough.
3. To live well is to live long.
4. Life is all in this present hour.
5. Life is short and time is swift.
6. They do not live more who live longer.
7. Life is a school of probability.
8. Life is a lesson in humility.
9. Life is a loom, weaving illusions.
10. Life is a winter's day and a winter's way.
11. The secret of life is not to do what you like, but to like what you do.
12. Many do not live, but linger.
13. Do not look for a golden life in an iron age.
14. While I live, let it not be in vain.
15. Not life itself, but living ill, is evil.
16. They live badly who are always about to begin living.
17. We live not as we wish but as we can.
18. As long as one lives, one must continue learning how to live.

Chapter 100: Love

1. Love makes any place agreeable.
2. We have a choice to begin love, but not to end it.
3. Love knows no laws or conditions.
4. Dry bread is better with love than a fat capon with fear.
5. They who have love in their hearts have spurs in their sides.
6. Hope is a lover's staff.
7. The lover is no judge of beauty.

8. In love there is no lack.
9. Labour is light where love pays.
10. Love and ambition do not keep fellowship.
11. Love and pride are both roads to lunacy.
12. Love and sorrow were born twins.
13. Love built on beauty fades as soon as it ages.
14. Hasty love is soon hot and soon cold.
15. Love is more than great riches.
16. Love is master where he will.
17. Love is the noblest frailty of the mind.
18. Calf love, half love; old love, cold love.
19. Love is the salt of life.
20. Love is too young to know what conscience is.
21. Love has neither reason nor law.
22. Love keeps out the cold better than a cloak.
23. Love knows no measure.
24. There is beggary in the love that can be counted.
25. Love laughs at locksmiths.
26. The lover is a monarch.
27. Love needs no instruction.
28. Pity is one remove from love.
29. She loves enough who does not hate.
30. Come blows, love goes.
31. Love is a hearth for forbidden fires.
32. Love is a talkative passion.
33. Love is an egoism of two.
34. Love is stronger than death.
35. Love makes time pass; time makes love pass.
36. Love never dies of starvation, but often of indigestion.
37. The beloved is always right.
38. Love lessens women's delicacy, and increases men's.
39. Love's anger is fuel to love.
40. Lovers take pleasure from their misfortunes.
41. Love excuses its own faults.
42. Love is blind, but sees far.
43. Love abounds in honey and poison.
44. Love is the same in everyone.
45. Love is credulous.
46. What love commands, it is not safe to despise.
47. The lover loves much who weeps.
48. Love is the child of illusion, and the parent of disillusion.
49. Affection bends the judgement to her ply.
50. When affection speaks, truth is not always by.

Chapter 101: Mankind

1. Good people and bad people are both less so than they seem.
2. Humans are animals that make bargains.
3. Man is a gaming animal.
4. Man is a substance clad in shadows.
5. People are beasts when shame deserts them.
6. Man is to man the surest ill.
7. Human beings are mankind's greatest enemy.
8. Customs vary, but human nature is always the same.
9. Nature revolves, but humanity advances.
10. No one is born learned and wise.

11. A human being is a mere reed, but a thinking reed.
12. For mankind, nothing is certain but death.
13. Nothing is more glorious or more wretched than humanity.
14. People too often talk wisely but live foolishly.

Chapter 102: Manners

1. Good breeding is the fruit of good sense.
2. As in the hall, so on the hill.
3. The sum of good manners is, 'After you.'
4. Good manners consist in small sacrifices.
5. Manners make the man.
6. Manners are morals.
7. As the times, so the manners.
8. Evil communications corrupt good manners.
9. Office corrupts manners.

Chapter 103: Mind

1. A vacant mind is open to all suggestions, as a mountain cave to echoes.
2. Fat bodies, lean minds.
3. If the brain sows no corn, it grows thistles.
4. Whatever afflicts people, their minds are free.
5. In the end, mind vanquishes sword.
6. It is good to polish the mind against other minds.
7. It is the mind that ennobles, not the blood.
8. A noble mind is free to all.
9. Light minds love trifles.

10. The wise master their minds, fools are mastered by them.
11. Pain of mind is worse than pain of body.
12. The mind alone cannot suffer exile.
13. The mind is the man.
14. To relax the mind is to lose it.
15. The mind rules, the body serves.

Chapter 104: Misers

1. A miser's money takes the place of wisdom.
2. Misers put their backs and bellies into their pockets.
3. The miser gives straw to his dog and bones to his ass.
4. A miser spoils the coat by scanting the cloth.
5. Niggard father, spendthrift son.
6. The miser is always poor.
7. What misers have is of as much use to them as what they have not.

Chapter 105: Moderation

1. Measure is medicine.
2. The best things carried to excess are wrong.
3. In everything there is a measure.
4. Enough is enough for the wise.

Chapter 106: Money

1. One handful of money is stronger than two handfuls of truth.
2. A person without money is a bow without an arrow.
3. Help me to money and I will help myself to friends.
4. Everyone bastes the fat hog while the lean one burns.
5. For lack of money one cannot speed.

6. If money goes before, all ways lie open.
7. Money begets money.
8. Money is ace of trumps.
9. Money is often lost for want of money.
10. When fishing for man, money is the best bait.
11. Money is welcome though it come in dirty clothes.
12. Money makes us laugh.
13. Money makes mastery.
14. Money makes the pot boil.
15. Money makes, and money mars.
16. Ready money is a ready remedy.
17. The love of money and the love of learning seldom meet.
18. Liberty is the price paid for money.
19. Money is perfumed, wherever found.
20. There is no companion like money.
21. To have money is a fear, to lack it is a grief.
22. They need honey on their tongues who have no money in their purses.
23. Money has wings.
24. Money is never out of season.
25. Mention money, and the world is silent.
26. The person with both mind and money employs the latter well.
27. Money is the sinew of affairs.
28. The love of money grows with the amount of money.
29. You must spend money if you wish to make it.
30. When money speaks, truth is silent.

Chapter 107: Mothers

1. Better the child cry than the mother sigh.
2. A child may have too much of a mother's blessing.
3. Light-heeled mothers make leaden-heeled daughters.
4. Men are what their mothers make them.
5. Mothers' darlings make milksop heroes.
6. The kick of the dam does not hurt the colt.
7. Mother love is always in its spring.
8. Who takes the child by the hand takes the mother by the heart.
9. Children are the anchors that hold their mothers to life.
10. A bustling mother makes a slothful child.
11. The mother's breath is always sweet.
12. No mother has a homely child.
13. A mother's wrath does not survive the night.
14. A mother will understand what her dumb child says.
15. When the child falls the mother weeps; when the mother falls the child laughs.
16. More than one mother can make a tasty soup.
17. Judge someone not by the words of his mother but by the comments of his neighbours.

Chapter 108: Nature

1. To know nature, consult nature.
2. It cannot be nature, if it is not sense.
3. Nature is the true law.

4. Nature obeys necessity.

5. Nature pardons no mistakes.

6. To command nature one must obey it.

7. The volume of nature is the book of knowledge.

8. Wisdom and nature never say different things.

9. Nature always returns.

10. Nature does nothing in vain.

Chapter 109: Necessity

1. Necessity breaks iron.

2. Necessity is the argument of tyrants and the creed of slaves.

3. Necessity makes an honest man a knave.

4. Necessity never makes a good bargain.

5. We do what we must, and call it by good names.

6. Necessity is a strict teacher.

7. Every act of necessity is disagreeable.

8. The wise never oppose necessity.

9. Necessity knows no shame.

Chapter 110: Opinion

1. Only little minds are alienated by differences of opinion.

2. Erroneous opinions can be tolerated where reason is free to combat them.

3. Opinion in good people is knowledge in the making.

4. So many heads, so many opinions.

5. A man who never alters his opinion is like standing water, which breeds reptiles.

6. Opinion is the queen of the world.

7. Those who never retract an opinion love themselves more than truth.

Chapter 111: Opportunity

1. Every opportunity grasped is two new opportunities made.

2. Hoist sail in a fair wind.

3. Opportunity seldom comes labelled.

4. Who seizes the right moment is the right person for the moment.

5. Know your opportunity.

Chapter 112: Pain

1. Where we feel pain we lay a hand.

2. An hour of pain is as long as a day of pleasure.

3. Great pain for little gain makes a man weary.

4. If pains be a pleasure, profit will follow.

5. Pain is forgotten when gain comes.

6. Those who do not feel pain seldom think others feel it.

7. There is a pleasure akin to pain.

8. No matter which finger you bite, it will hurt.

9. Nothing comes without pains except dirt and long nails.

Chapter 113: Patience

1. Grain by grain the hen fills her belly.

2. They who can have patience can have what they will.

3. How poor are those without patience.

4. Patience achieves more than force.

5. Patience is a plaster for all sores.

6. Patience opens every door.

7. Every misfortune is subdued by patience.
8. Patience provoked often turns to fury.
9. Be patient, and shuffle the cards.
10. With patience and time the mulberry becomes a silk gown.

Chapter 114: Peace

1. Peace breeds, strife consumes.
2. Better a lean peace than a fat victory.
3. By wisdom peace, by wisdom plenty.
4. Peace begins where ambition ends.
5. Peace has greater victories than war.
6. When people find no peace within, they will find it nowhere else.

Chapter 115: People

1. The mob has many heads but no brains.
2. The people pay with ingratitude.
3. The tyranny of a multitude is a multiplied tyranny.
4. To worship the people is to be worshipped.
5. Trust not the many-minded populace.
6. Nothing is so uncertain as the judgements of the mob.
7. It is easy to side with the crowd.

Chapter 116: Philanthropy

1. Mankind will not be reasoned out of the feeling of humanity.
2. We praise those who love their fellow human beings.
3. What good thing you do, do not defer it.
4. What is done for another is done for oneself.
5. Only those live who do good.

Chapter 117: Philosophy

1. Philosophy is the sweet milk of adversity.
2. Clarity is the sincerity of philosophers.
3. Philosophy is doubt.
4. Let philosophers be wise for themselves.
5. Philosophy does the going, and wisdom is the goal.
6. Philosophy is the mother of the arts.
7. The true medicine of the mind is philosophy.
8. To enjoy freedom, be the slave of philosophy.

Chapter 118: Pleasure

1. If you long for pleasure you must labour to get it.
2. After pleasant scratching comes painful smarting.
3. Fly the pleasure that bites tomorrow.
4. Follow pleasure and it will flee, flee pleasure and it will follow.
5. For one pleasure a thousand griefs are proved.
6. Pleasure makes hours short.
7. Pleasure is the greatest incentive to vice.
8. Rarity gives zest to pleasure.
9. There is no pleasure unalloyed.

Chapter 119: Politics

1. All politicians die by swallowing their own lies.
2. The honest politician is the one who, when bought, stays bought.
3. Few politicians die, and none resign.
4. Politicians neither love nor hate.
5. Old politicians chew on past wisdom.
6. Party is the madness of the many for the gain of the few.
7. There is no gambling like politics.
8. Vain hope, to make people happy by politics.
9. When great questions end, little parties begin.
10. Office shows the person.

Chapter 120: Poverty

1. Those guilty of poverty easily suspect themselves.
2. Who licks his knife has little for others.
3. Who has a low door must stoop.
4. It is easier to praise poverty than to bear it.
5. Poverty, not will, consents.
6. Poverty is not a vice but an inconvenience.
7. Poverty is the mother of health.
8. Poverty is the worst guard of chastity.
9. There is no virtue that poverty cannot destroy.
10. Poverty is the mother of crime.
11. Riches follow poverty better than poverty follows riches.
12. Light purse, heavy heart.
13. Poverty is a kind of leprosy.
14. The poor are never free.
15. Poverty is never believed, though speaking truth.
16. Contented poverty is an honourable estate.
17. Little goods, little cares.
18. It is natural for the poor to count their sheep.
19. Money moves slowly towards poverty.
20. There are many things the ragged dare not say.
21. To have nothing is not poverty.
22. Poverty is a shirt of fire.

Chapter 121: Power

1. If you would have power, pretend to have power.
2. Increase of power leads to increase of wealth.
3. Power weakens the wicked.
4. The greater the power, the more dangerous its abuse.
5. Power corrupts.
6. Partnership with power is never safe.
7. Power acquired by guilt is never used for good.

Chapter 122: Praise

1. A man's praise stinks in his own mouth.
2. All praise their own wares.
3. Faint praise is abuse.
4. Who loves praise loves temptation.
5. Let all praise the bridge they go over.
6. Praises are wages.
7. Praise makes good men better and bad men worse.

8. Undeserved praise is satire.
9. In doing what we ought we deserve no praise.
10. Unless new praise arises, the old is lost.
11. One has only to die to be praised.
12. The refusal of praise is the desire to be twice praised.

Chapter 123: Prosperity

1. Prosperity reveals vice, adversity virtue.
2. Prosperity is a great teacher, adversity a greater.
3. Prosperity lets go the bridle.
4. Prosperity makes friends, adversity tries them.
5. The rich are never sure that they are loved for themselves.

Chapter 124: Proverbs

1. Proverbs are the daughters of experience.
2. A proverb is a short sentence formed of long experience.
3. There is no proverb which is untrue.
4. A short saying often contains much wisdom.
5. A proverb is the wit of one and the wisdom of many.
6. Patch grief with proverbs.
7. Proverbs lie on the lips of fools.
8. The wise make proverbs and fools repeat them.

Chapter 125: Prudence

1. The prudent seldom err.
2. Commend the sea, but keep ashore.
3. Who walks barefoot must not plant thorns.

4. Always have two irons in the fire.
5. Precaution is better than cure.
6. Prudence is always in season.
7. Chance fights on the side of the prudent.
8. Prudence keeps life safe, but does not always make it happy.

Chapter 126: Reason

1. Listen to reason, or it will make itself felt.
2. Reason rules the wise and cudgels the fool.
3. What reason weaves, passion undoes.
4. Few have strength enough to follow reason all the way.
5. Reason does not come before years.
6. Nothing is lasting when reason does not rule.
7. Reason is the lamp of life.
8. Reason panders to will.

Chapter 127: Reputation

1. A good name keeps its lustre in the dark.
2. A good reputation is a fair estate.
3. A wounded reputation is seldom cured.
4. Better not named than ill spoken of.

Chapter 128: Resolution

1. Be resolved and the thing is done.
2. Never tell your resolution beforehand.
3. Set a stout heart to a steep hill.

Chapter 129: Revenge

1. Revenge never comes too late.
2. Those who meditate revenge keep their own wounds green.
3. They meditate revenge who least complain.
4. It costs more to revenge injuries than to bear them.
5. Living well is the best revenge.
6. The noblest vengeance is to forgive.
7. Revenge may have leaden feet, but strikes with iron hands.
8. Revenge is a fruit best left to ripen.
9. Revenge is a confession of pain.

Chapter 130: Riches

1. People are rich in proportion to the number of things they do not need.
2. They are not fit for riches who are afraid to use them.
3. Where wealth accumulates, people decay.
4. Better to live rich than die rich.
5. The rich have no faults.
6. Riches are got with pain, kept with care, and lost with grief.
7. Superfluous wealth can only buy superfluities.
8. The pride of the rich makes the labours of the poor.
9. The rich person's wealth is the greatest enemy of his health.
10. Wealth is a good servant and a bad master.
11. Without a rich heart, wealth is an ugly beggar.
12. Rich people are at home everywhere.
13. A golden bit does not make a better horse.
14. They most enjoy riches who least need them.
15. The foolish sayings of the rich pass for wisdom.

Chapter 131: Right

1. Right wrongs no one.
2. The greatest right is the right to be wrong.
3. We are not satisfied to be right unless we prove others to be wrong.
4. Better do right without thanks than wrong without punishment.

Chapter 132: Self-control

1. They are strong who conquer others, they are mighty who conquer themselves.
2. Few are fit to be entrusted to themselves.

Chapter 133: Shame

1. Shame lasts longer than poverty.
2. Where there is shame, in time there may be grace.
3. Who is lost to shame is lost.
4. Who has no shame owns the world.
5. In the land of the naked, clothes make shame.

Chapter 134: Silence

1. Speech is often repented, silence rarely.
2. Even silence may be eloquent.
3. He is not a fool who knows how to keep silent.
4. Silence catches a mouse.
5. The wise say nothing in dangerous times.
6. The silence of the people is a warning to the king.

7. Beware a silent dog and still water.
8. Silence is strength.
9. Silent people are dangerous.

Chapter 135: Success

1. Life begins only in success.
2. Nothing is so impudent as success.
3. Success alters manners.
4. Success is never blamed.
5. Success is the child of audacity.
6. Success makes a fool seem wise.
7. Many fail where one succeeds.
8. Success has many friends.

Chapter 136: Teaching

1. Better untaught than ill taught.
2. They teach ill who teach all.
3. Let them love the doctrine for the teacher's sake.
4. To teach is to learn.

Chapter 137: Temptation

1. An open box tempts an honest person.
2. A bad padlock invites a picklock.
3. I was taken by a morsel, says the fish.
4. It is easy to keep a castle that was never assaulted.
5. Do not tempt a desperate person.
6. The less the temptation, the greater the crime.
7. Who is worse, tempter or tempted?

Chapter 138: Thieves

1. A thief thinks everyone steals.
2. A thief knows a thief as a wolf knows a wolf.
3. The thief is a gentleman when stealing has made him rich.
4. Call someone a thief and he will steal.
5. They that will steal an egg will steal an ox.
6. Little thieves are hanged, but great ones escape.
7. To make thieves honest, trust them.

Chapter 139: Thought

1. A moment's thinking is an hour in words.
2. A thought can take you prisoner.
3. If people thought more they would act less.
4. Think today, speak tomorrow.
5. There is no harvest of thought without a seed-time of character.
6. Our thoughts are often worse than we are.
7. A human is merely a reed, the weakest in nature; but a thinking reed.

Chapter 140: Time

1. Time subdues all things.
2. An inch of time cannot be bought by an inch of gold.
3. There is a time to fish, and a time to dry nets.
4. A little time is enough to hatch a great mischief.
5. As well have no time as make no good use of it.
6. Present time lost is all time lost.
7. Lost time is never found.
8. Nothing treads so silently as the foot of time.
9. In time the savage bull bears the yoke.
10. Time flies but leaves its shadow.

11. Time has a taming hand.
12. Time heals sorrow.
13. Time is the rider that breaks youth.
14. Time wasted is existence, time used is life.
15. To choose time is to save time.
16. Those who use time worst most complain of its brevity.
17. Time is the wisest of all counsellors.
18. There is no appeal from time past.

Chapter 141: Truth

1. Truth is often paradoxical.
2. Better suffer for truth than prosper by falsehood.
3. To withhold truth is to bury gold.
4. All great truths begin as blasphemies.
5. A truth-teller finds all doors closed.
6. A lie travels round the world while truth is still tying its shoes.
7. Not all truths should be told.
8. Craft needs clothes, but truth loves to go naked.
9. Face to face the truth comes out.
10. Half the truth is often a great lie.
11. He who finds a truth lights a torch.
12. Truth gives wings to strength.
13. The truth explains everything.
14. In too much disputing the truth is lost.
15. To fool the world, tell the truth.
16. Truth is heavy; few can bear it.
17. Truth may languish but can never perish.

Chapter 142: Virtue

1. Where there is no virtue there is no liberty.
2. Virtue is not hereditary.
3. Virtue never grows old.
4. Virtue and sense are one.
5. In justifying itself virtue debases itself.
6. Virtue is sufficient for happiness.
7. Conquer by virtue.
8. Virtue is praised, and starves.
9. Virtue overcomes envy.
10. Poverty does not destroy virtue, nor does prosperity bestow it.

Chapter 143: War

1. War can only breed war.
2. The first blow is as much as two.
3. Few die well who die in battle.
4. There was never a good war or a bad peace.
5. War is death's feast.
6. To die or conquer are the terms of war.
7. War devours the brave and spares the coward.
8. War seeks its victims among the young.
9. There is little reason in arms.
10. War is sweet to those who have not experienced it.
11. When war rages, the laws are dumb.
12. After a war many heroes present themselves.

Chapter 144: Wisdom

1. A flow of words is no proof of wisdom.
2. The doors of wisdom are never shut.
3. It is sometimes wisdom to seem a fool.
4. Wisdom asks fruit, folly asks flowers.

5. Wisdom does not always go by years.
6. The wise seek wisdom, the fool has found it.
7. The wise hide their wisdom, the fool displays his folly.
8. One's chief wisdom consists in knowing one's weakness.
9. In youth and beauty wisdom is rare.
10. The wise are beyond harm.
11. All countries are home to the wise.
12. They are wise enough who have enough wit for their own affairs.
13. They seem wise who thrive.
14. We are wiser than we know.
15. No one is wise all the time.
16. It is easier to be wise for others than for oneself.
17. The wise are strong.
18. The wise learn many things from their foes.
19. No one is wise enough alone.
20. No one is the only wise one.

Chapter 145: Youth

1. Green wood makes a hot fire.
2. Youth is the fever of reason.
3. Youth is drunkenness without wine.
4. Reckless youth makes rueful age.
5. If youth knew; if age could.

THE LAWGIVER

Chapter 1

1. If one listens to the wisdom of those who sat in the councils of kings, and witnessed the government in many lands;

2. One learns that whereas it is possible to rule lives and bodies, it is not so easy to try ruling minds – but nor is it right,

3. For the human mind is a kingdom in itself, and wise rulers know where the borders of their own kingdoms lie.

4. If people's minds were as easily controlled as their tongues, every king would sit safely on his throne, and government by compulsion would cease;

5. For all subjects would shape their lives according to the intentions of their rulers,

6. And would count a thing true or false, good or evil, just or unjust, in obedience to their dictates.

7. But no one's mind can lie wholly at the command of another,

8. For no one can willingly give away the natural right of free reason and judgement, even if compelled to do so.

9. For this reason government which attempts to control minds is accounted tyrannical,

10. An abuse of sovereignty and a usurpation of the rights of subjects; To seek to prescribe what must be accepted as true, or rejected as false, or what opinions should actuate men, is wrong.

11. All these questions fall within a person's natural right, which he cannot abdicate even with consent,

12. Even under the lash of tyranny over body and life.

13. Judgement can be biased in many ways, sometimes to a great degree,

14. So that while exempt from direct external control, it may be so dependent on another person's words, that it can be said to be ruled by him;

15. That is the way of proselytisers, demagogues and teachers of the young and credulous,

16. Who use their authority to fill others with beliefs and ideas of their own choosing;

17. But although this influence carries far, it has never gone so far as to invalidate this truth:

18. That every person's understanding is his or her own, and that minds are as diverse as palates.

19. Demagogues have gained at times such a hold over popular

judgement that they were accounted superhuman,

20. And believed to speak and act with special authority;

21. Nevertheless even the most famous of them could not escape murmurs and evil interpretations.

22. How much less then can other monarchs avoid them!

23. Yet such unlimited power, if it exists at all, must belong to a monarch,

24. And least of all to a democracy where the whole or a great part of the people wield authority collectively.

25. However unlimited, therefore, the power of a sovereign may be, it can never prevent people from forming judgements according to their own intellects, or being influenced by their emotions.

26. Since, therefore, no one can abdicate the freedom of judgement and feeling; since all are by in-defeasible natural right the owner of their own thoughts,

27. It follows that people thinking in diverse and contradictory fashions, cannot, without disastrous results, be compelled to speak only accord-ing to the dictates of the supreme power.

28. Not even the most experienced, to say nothing of the multitude, know how to keep silence.

29. The ultimate aim of government is not to rule, or restrain, by fear, nor to exact obedience,

30. But rather to free all the people

from fear, that they may live in security;

31. Which is to strengthen their natural right to exist and work without injury to themselves or others.

32. So the object of government is not to change people from rational beings into beasts or puppets,

33. But to enable them to develop themselves in security, and to employ their reason unshackled;

34. Neither showing hatred, anger or deceit, nor watched with the eyes of jealousy and injustice.

35. In short, the true aim of govern-ment is liberty.

Chapter 2

1. Because it is impossible to preserve peace unless individuals compro-mise their right of acting entirely on their own judgement,

2. They justly cede the right of free action in appropriate and necessary cases, though not the right of free reason and judgement;

3. For people cannot act against the authorities without danger to the state, though their feelings and judgement may be at variance therewith;

4. They may even speak against them, provided that they do so from rational conviction,

5. Not from fraud, anger or hatred, and provided that they do not attempt to introduce any change on their private authority.

6. For instance, supposing a person

shows that a law is repugnant to reason, and should be repealed;

7. If he submits his opinion to the judgement of those who, alone, have the right of making and repealing laws,

8. And meanwhile acts in nowise contrary to that law, he has deserved well of the state, and has behaved as a good citizen should;

9. But if he accuses the authorities of injustice, and stirs up the people against them,

10. Or seditiously strives to abrogate the law without their consent, he is merely an agitator and rebel.

11. Thus we see how people may declare and teach what they believe, without injury to the authority of their rulers, or to the public peace;

12. Namely, by leaving in their hands the power of legislation as it affects action,

13. And by doing nothing against their laws, though they be compelled often to act in contradiction to what they believe, and openly feel, to be best.

14. Such a course can be taken without detriment to justice and dutiful-ness, nay, it is the one which a just and dutiful person would adopt.

15. Hence, so long as people act in obedience to the laws of the rulers, they in nowise contravene their reason,

16. For in obedience to reason they transferred the right of controlling some of their actions to the rulers.

17. From freedom of thought and expression inconveniences may sometimes arise,

18. But what question was ever settled so wisely that no abuses could possibly spring therefrom?

19. Whoever seeks to regulate every-thing by law is more likely to arouse vices than to reform them.

20. It is best to grant what cannot be abolished, even though it be in itself harmful.

21. How many evils spring from luxury, envy, avarice, drunkenness and the like,

22. Yet these are tolerated – vices as they are – because they cannot be prevented by legal enactments.

23. How much more then should free thought be granted, seeing that it is in itself a virtue and that it cannot be crushed!

Chapter 3

1. Besides, the evil results can easily be checked, not to mention that such freedom is necessary for progress in science and the liberal arts:

2. For people do not follow such pursuits to advantage unless their judgement be entirely free and unhampered.

3. But let it be granted that freedom may be crushed, and people be so bound down, that they do not dare to utter a whisper, save at the bidding of their rulers;

4. Nevertheless this can never be carried to the pitch of making them think according to authority,

5. So that the necessary consequences

would be that people would daily be thinking one thing and saying another,

6. To the corruption of mutual trust, that mainstay of government, and to the fostering of flattery and perfidy,

7. Whence spring stratagems, and the corruption of every good art.

Chapter 4

1. It is possible by violence and its threat to impose uniformity of speech, but not where freedom otherwise lives;

2. For there the more that rulers strive to curtail freedom of speech, the more obstinately are they resisted;

3. Not indeed by the avaricious, the flatterers, and those who think that goodness consists in filling their stomachs and purses,

4. But by those whom good education, sound morality and virtue have rendered more free.

5. People resent the branding as criminal of opinions they believe to be true,

6. And the proscription as wicked of that which inspires them to morality;

7. Hence they are ready to forswear the laws and conspire against the authorities,

8. Thinking it not shameful but honourable to stir up seditions and perpetuate any crime with this end in view.

9. Such being the constitution of human nature, we see that laws

directed against opinions affect the generous-minded rather than the wicked,

10. And are adapted less for coercing criminals than for offending the upright;

11. So that they cannot be maintained without great peril to the state.

12. Moreover, such laws are almost always useless, for those who hold that the opinions proscribed are sound, cannot possibly obey the law;

13. Whereas those who already reject them as false, accept the law as a kind of privilege,

14. And make such boast of it that authority is powerless to repeal it, even if such a course be subsequently desired.

15. And, lastly, how many divisions have arisen from the attempt of authorities to decide by law the intricacies of opinion!

16. If people were not allured by the hope of getting the law and the authorities on their side,

17. Of triumphing over their adversaries in the sight of an applauding multitude,

18. And of acquiring honourable distinctions, they would not strive so maliciously, nor would such fury sway their minds.

19. This is taught not only by reason but by daily examples,

20. For laws of this kind prescribing what all the people shall think and forbidding anyone to speak or write to the contrary, have often been passed,

21. As concessions to the anger of those who cannot tolerate people of enlightenment and freedom,

22. And who, by such harsh and crooked enactments, can easily turn the loyalty of the masses into fury and direct it against whom they will.

23. How much better would it be to restrain popular anger, instead of passing inutile laws which can only be broken by those who love virtue and the liberal arts,

24. Thus paring down the state till it is too small to harbour people of talent.

25. What greater misfortune for a state than that honourable people should be sent into exile like criminals because they hold diverse opinions which they cannot disguise?

26. What can be more hurtful than that people who have committed no crime or wickedness should, because they are enlightened, be treated as enemies and put to death,

27. And that the scaffold, the terror of evildoers, should become the arena where the highest examples of tolerance and virtue are displayed to the people with all the marks of ignominy that authority can devise?

28. He that knows himself to be upright does not fear the death of a criminal, and shrinks from no punishment;

29. His mind is not wrung with remorse for any disgraceful deed:

30. He holds that death in a good cause is no punishment, but an honour, and that death for freedom is glory.

31. What purpose then is served by the death of such people, what example is proclaimed?

32. The cause for which they die is unknown to the idle and the foolish, hateful to the turbulent, loved by the upright.

33. The only lesson we can draw from such scenes is to flatter the persecutor, or else to imitate the victim.

Chapter 5

1. If formal assent is not to be esteemed above conviction, and if governments are to retain authority and not be compelled to yield to agitators,

2. It is imperative that freedom of judgement should be granted, so that people may live together in harmony,

3. However diverse, or even openly contradictory their opinions may be.

4. We cannot doubt that such is the best system of government and open to the fewest objections,

5. Since it is the one most in harmony with human nature.

6. In a democracy everyone submits to the control of authority over his actions, but not over his judgement and reason;

7. That is, seeing that all cannot think alike, the voice of the majority has the force of law, subject to repeal if circumstances bring about a change of opinion.

8. In proportion as the power of free judgement is withheld we depart from the natural condition of humanity, and the government becomes more tyrannical.

9. Laws seeking to settle controversies of opinion and outlook are more likely to irritate than to reform, and thus can give rise to extreme licence.

10. Further, it was seen that divisions do not originate in a love of truth, which is a source of courtesy and gentleness,

11. But rather in an inordinate desire for supremacy.

12. From all these considerations it is clearer than the sun at noonday,

13. That controversialists are those who condemn other men's writings, and seditiously stir up the quarrelsome masses against their authors, rather than those authors themselves,

14. Who generally write only for the learned, and appeal solely to reason.

15. Thus the real disturbers of the peace are those who, in a free state, seek to curtail the liberty of thought and expression,

16. Which they are unable to tyrannise over as they can with people's actions.

Chapter 6

1. Among those who have studied the ways of government and rulers, there is much practical wisdom,

2. Which applies as much to the rule of what is less than a state than to states themselves.

3. Nothing makes leaders more esteemed than undertaking great enterprises and setting a fine example,

4. Or anyway an unusual example, gaining for themselves the reputation of being remarkable individuals.

5. A leader is also respected when he is either a true friend or a severe enemy,

6. When, without any reservation, he declares himself in favour of one party against the other;

7. Which course will always be more advantageous than standing neutral,

8. Because if others come into conflict, and are of such a character that one has either to fear the winner or not,

9. It will always be more advantageous to declare oneself and contend strenuously;

10. For those who win do not want doubtful friends, and those who lose will not befriend one who stood by as they endeavoured.

11. It will always happen that those who are not one's friend will demand one's neutrality,

12. While those who are one's friend will entreat one to side with them.

13. And irresolute leaders, to avoid present difficulties, generally follow a neutral path,

14. And are generally therefore ruined. But when a leader declares himself gallantly in favour of one side, if

the party with whom he allies himself conquers,

15. Although the victor may be powerful and may have him at his mercy, yet he is indebted to him, and there is established a bond of amity;

16. And people are rarely so shameless as to become a monument of ingratitude later.

17. Victories after all are never so complete that the victor must not show some regard, especially to justice.

18. But if he with whom one allies oneself loses, one may be sheltered by him, and while he is able he may aid one, and become a companion to a fortune that may rise again.

19. In the second case, when those who fight are of such a character that one has no anxiety as to who may win, so much the more is it greater prudence to be allied.

20. But let it be noted that a leader ought to take care never to make an alliance with one more powerful than himself for the purposes of contending with others, unless necessity compels him;

21. Because if the more powerful leader wins, one is at his discretion,

22. And leaders ought to avoid as much as possible being at the discretion of anyone.

23. Never let any government imagine that it can choose perfectly safe courses.

24. Rather let it expect to have to take very doubtful courses, because it is found in ordinary affairs that one never seeks to avoid one trouble without running into another;

25. But prudence consists in knowing how to distinguish the character of troubles, and for choice to take the lesser evil.

Chapter 7

1. A leader ought to show himself a patron of ability, and to honour the proficient in every art.

2. At the same time he should encourage his followers to practise their callings peaceably,

3. And make them know that there is no risk that the reward of their efforts will be denied them or taken from them,

4. But they will receive reward and the enjoyment from it freely.

5. Further, he ought to fete his followers at convenient times, and show himself an example of courtesy and liberality;

6. Nevertheless, always maintaining the right relationship of his position,

7. For too great familiarity loosens the bonds between leader and led, and in the end undoes both.

Chapter 8

1. The leader must consider how to avoid what will make him disliked or contemptible, so that he need fear no reproach.

2. It makes him most disliked to be selfish, and to ignore the feelings and wishes of those he leads.

3. When neither the position nor the pride of followers is impugned, the majority of them are content,

4. And the leader has only to contend with the ambition of a few, to whom he can respond with ease in many ways.

5. It makes him contemptible to be considered fickle, frivolous, mean-hearted, irresolute, from all of which a leader should guard himself as from a rock;

6. And he should endeavour to show in his actions courage, fortitude and magnanimity;

7. And in his private dealings with his subjects let him show that his judgements are firm,

8. And maintain himself in such reputation that no one can hope either to deceive him or to persuade him against doing what is right.

9. That leader is esteemed who conveys this impression of himself, and he who is esteemed is not easily conspired against;

10. For, provided it is well known that he is an excellent man and revered by his people, he can only be attacked with difficulty.

11. For this reason a leader ought to have two fears, one from within, on account of his followers, the other from without, on account of external circumstances.

12. From the latter he is defended by being well prepared and having good allies.

13. If he is well prepared he will have good friends, and affairs will always remain quiet within when they are quiet without.

14. And even should affairs outside be disturbed, if he has carried out his preparations and has conducted himself honourably,

15. As long as he does not despair, he will resist every difficulty that his own powers and resource can overcome.

16. But concerning his followers, when affairs outside are disturbed he has only to fear that they will turn against him secretly,

17. From which a leader can easily secure himself by keeping the fidelity of his followers, which is in turn secured by keeping them properly satisfied with him.

18. For this reason a leader ought to reckon disaffections of little account when his followers hold him in esteem;

19. But when they are hostile to him, and bear hatred towards him, he ought to fear everything and everybody.

20. And well-ordered states and wise leaders have taken every care not to drive the other senior people to opposition, and to keep the people satisfied and contented,

21. For this is one of the most important objects a leader can have.

22. Neither could there be a better or a more prudent arrangement, or a greater source of security for a leader,

23. Than that he ought to leave affairs of reproach to be managed by

others, while keeping those of grace
in his own hands.

24. Let others make recriminations,
give unwelcome orders, make
dismissal or demotion;

25. The leader should be the one to
reward and praise.

Chapter 9

1. The choice of assistants is of the
greatest importance to a leader, and
their worth is according to his
powers of discrimination.

2. Here is his primary skill, in
appointing good assistants to
manage his affairs.

3. For the first opinion one forms of a
leader, and of his understanding, is
by observing those he has around
him;

4. When they are capable and faithful
he may always be considered wise,
because he has known how to
recognise the capable and to keep
them faithful;

5. But when they are otherwise one
cannot form a good opinion of
him, for the prime error he made
was in choosing them.

6. But to enable a leader to form an
opinion of his assistant there is one
test that never fails;

7. When he sees the assistant thinking
more of his own interests than of
his leader's,

8. And seeking inwardly his own
profit in everything, such a one will
never make a good assistant, nor
will he ever be trustworthy;

9. For he who has the state of another

in his hands ought never to think of
himself, but always of his principal,

10. And never pay any attention to
matters in which the leader is not
concerned.

11. But to keep his assistant faithful the
leader ought to study him, honouring him, advancing him,

12. Doing him kindnesses, rewarding
him well and sharing his plans and
cares.

13. At the same time let him see that
the assistant cannot stand alone,

14. So that rewards and praises may
not make him desire more than
both, and that cares may not make
him timid.

15. When, therefore, leaders and their
assistants are thus disposed, they
can trust each other,

16. But when it is otherwise, the
outcome will always be unsatisfac-
tory for one or the other.

Chapter 10

1. In order to know how wrong is
sometimes done by those who lead,

2. Hear what is said by advisers who
teach leaders that they must
sometimes do wrong in order to
lead.

3. They say: 'Everyone admits how
praiseworthy it is in a leader to
keep faith, and to live with integrity and not with craft.

4. 'Yet history shows that those leaders
who have done great things have
held good faith of little account,
and in the end have overcome any
who relied on their word.

5. 'There are two ways of resolving disputes, the one by agreement, the other by contest; the first method is proper to mankind, the second to beasts.

6. 'But because the first has frequently proved insufficient, men have often taken recourse to the second.

7. 'Therefore it is necessary to understand how leaders are apt to conduct themselves in both ways as appropriate.

8. 'A wise leader cannot, nor ought he to, keep faith when such observance may be turned against him, and when the reasons that caused him to pledge it exist no longer.

9. 'If men were entirely good this precept would not hold, but because they are often bad, and will not keep faith with each other, no one is bound to keep faith when it is injurious to himself.

10. 'Nor will there ever be wanting to a leader legitimate reasons to excuse this.

11. 'But this means that it is necessary to know how to disguise this characteristic, and to dissemble when required.

12. 'Men are so simple, and so subject to present necessities, that he who seeks to deceive will always find someone who will allow himself to be deceived.

13. 'Accordingly it is unnecessary for a leader to have all the good qualities that men admire, but it is very necessary to appear to have them.

14. 'To have such qualities and always to exercise them is injurious, but to appear to have them is useful;

15. 'To appear merciful, faithful, humane, upright, and to be so, but with a mind so framed that should you require not to be so, you may be able to change to the opposite.

16. 'A leader cannot observe all those things for which men are esteemed,

17. 'Being often forced, in order to maintain his situation, to act contrary to fidelity, friendship and humanity.

18. 'Therefore it is necessary for him to be ready to adapt as the winds and variations of fortune force it;

19. 'Not to diverge from the good if he can avoid doing so, but, if compelled, then to know how to set about it.

20. 'For this reason, a leader ought to take care that he never lets anything slip from his lips that is not replete with the above-named qualities,

21. 'That he may appear to those who see and hear him altogether merciful, faithful, humane and upright.

22. 'There is nothing more necessary to appear to have than this last quality, inasmuch as men judge generally more by the eye than by the hand,

23. 'Because it belongs to everybody to see us, to few to come in touch with us directly.

24. 'Everyone sees what a man appears to be, few really know what he is, and those few dare not oppose

themselves to the opinion of the many.

25. 'History teaches that when a leader has the credit of gaining and holding his success, the means will always be considered honest, and he will be praised by everybody;

26. 'Because ordinary folk are always taken by what a thing seems to be and by what comes of it;

27. 'And in the world there are only such, for the few find a place there only when the many have no ground to rest on.'

28. Are such advisers right, who teach dissembling in pursuit of success, and the appearance of virtue when virtue itself cannot triumph, but with its opposite in its place?

29. It can be said that they have history on their side, but not philosophy.

Chapter 11

1. Every state is a community of some kind, and every community is established with a view to some good;

2. For people always act in order to obtain that which they think good.

3. But, if all communities aim at some good, the state or political community,

4. Which is the highest of all, and which embraces all the rest,

5. Aims at good in a greater degree than any other, and at the highest good.

6. Some people think that the qualifications of a statesman, king, householder and master are the same,

7. And that they differ, not in kind, but only in the number of their subjects.

8. For example, the ruler over a few is called a master; over more, the manager of a household;

9. Over a still larger number, a statesman or king, as if there were no difference between a great household and a small state.

10. The distinction which is made between the king and the statesman is that when the government is personal, the ruler is a king;

11. When, according to the rules of political science, the citizens rule and are ruled in turn, then he is called a statesman.

12. But it is not true that governments differ only in degree; they differ in kind, as will be evident to anyone who considers the matter.

13. As in other departments of science, so in politics, the compound should always be resolved into the simple elements or least parts of the whole.

14. We must therefore look at the elements of which the state is composed,

15. In order that we may see how the different kinds of rule differ from one another, and whether we can understand each one clearly.

16. For it is obvious that government too is the subject of a single science, which has to consider what government is best and of what sort it must be,

17. To be most in accordance with our

aspirations, if there were no external impediment,

18. And also what kind of government is adapted to particular states. For the best is often unattainable,

19. And therefore the true legislator and statesman ought to be acquainted, not only with that which is best in the abstract,

20. But also with that which is best relative to circumstances.

Chapter 12

1. We should be able further to say how a state may be constituted under any given conditions;

2. Both how it is originally formed and, when formed, how it may be longest preserved.

3. We ought, moreover, to know the form of government which is best suited to states in general;

4. And we should consider, not only what form of government is best, but also what is possible and what is easily attainable by all.

5. There are some who would have none but the most perfect; for this, many natural advantages are required.

6. Others, again, speak of a more attainable form, and, although they reject the constitution under which they are living, they extol some one in particular.

7. Any change of government which has to be introduced should be one which men, starting from their existing constitutions, will be both willing and able to adopt,

8. Since there is quite as much trouble in the reformation of an old constitution as in the establishment of a new one, just as to unlearn is as hard as to learn.

9. The same political insight will enable a man to know which laws are best, and which are suited to different constitutions;

10. For the laws are, and ought to be, relative to the constitution, and not the constitution to the laws.

11. A constitution is the organisation of offices in a state, and determines what is to be the governing body, and what is the end of each community.

12. But laws are not to be confounded with the principles of the constitution;

13. They are the rules according to which the magistrates should administer the state, and proceed against offenders.

14. Therefore we must know the varieties, and the number of varieties, of each form of government, if only with a view to making laws.

15. For the same laws cannot be equally suited to all oligarchies or to all democracies,

16. Since there is certainly more than one form both of democracy and of oligarchy.

Chapter 13

1. We may classify governments into three forms: monarchy, aristocracy and constitutional government,

2. And recognise three corresponding forms to which each tends: tyranny, oligarchy and democracy.

3. It is obvious which of the three is worst. If monarchy is not a mere name, it must exist by virtue of some great personal superiority in the king;

4. So tyranny, as the opposite of such virtue, is the worst of governments, and is thus necessarily the farthest removed from a well-constituted form.

5. Oligarchy is little better, for it is a long way from aristocracy, supposed to mean 'rule by the best'. It simply means rule by a clique, who alone are free.

6. And therefore democracy, with all its imperfections, is the most tolerable of the three.

7. What is the best constitution for most states, and the best life for most men,

8. Neither assuming a standard of virtue which is above the ordinary, nor ideals which are an aspiration only?

9. We must answer having regard to the life which the majority are able to share, and to the form of government which states can realistically attain;

10. For the end of community is the happiness of the members, and that happiness must be attainable.

11. The happy life is the life according to virtue lived without impediment, and that virtue is a mean, or middle path.

12. Then the life which is lived along a mean attainable by everyone, must be the best.

13. And the same principles of virtue and vice are characteristic of cities and of constitutions;

14. For the constitution is, so to speak, the life of the city.

15. Those constituting the mean of a society are those neither too rich nor too poor to be interested in the benefit of all,

16. But who wish the whole to be in harmony with itself. This is the middle section of society.

17. The legislator should always include the middle class in his government:

18. If he makes his laws oligarchical, to the middle class let him look; if he makes them democratical, he should equally by his laws try to attach this class to the state.

19. There only can the government ever be stable where the middle class exceeds one or both of the others,

20. And in that case there will be no fear that the rich will unite with the poor against the government.

21. For neither of them will ever be willing to serve the other,

22. And if they look for some form of government more suitable to both, they will find none better than this,

23. For the rich and the poor will never consent to rule in turn, because they mistrust one another.

24. The arbiter is always the one trusted, and he who is in the middle is an arbiter.

25. The more perfect the admixture of

the political elements, the more stable and lasting will the constitution be.

26. Many even of those who desire to form aristocratical governments make a mistake,

27. Not only in giving too much power to the rich, but in attempting to overreach the people.

28. There comes a time when out of a false good there arises a true evil,

29. Since the encroachments of the rich are more destructive to the constitution than those of the people.

Chapter 14

1. Those who would duly enquire about the best form of a state ought first to determine which is the best kind of life for people;

2. While this remains uncertain the best form of the state must also be uncertain,

3. For, in the natural order of things, those may be expected to lead the best life who are governed in the best manner that their circumstances admit.

4. We ought therefore to ascertain which is generally the best kind of life,

5. And whether the same life is or is not best for the state and for individuals alike.

6. What is the best life? No one will dispute the propriety of that partition of goods which separates them into three classes,

7. Namely, external goods, goods of the body and goods of the mind; or

deny that the happy man must have all three.

8. For no one would maintain that he is happy who has little courage or temperance or justice or prudence,

9. Who is afraid of every insect which flutters past, who will commit any crime, however great, to gratify his appetites,

10. Who will sacrifice his dearest friend for the sake of a farthing, and is as feeble and false in mind as a child or a madman.

11. These propositions are universally acknowledged as soon as they are uttered, but men differ about the degree or relative superiority of this or that good.

12. Some think that a moderate amount of virtue is enough, and they set no limit to their desires of wealth, property, power and reputation.

13. To whom we reply by an appeal to facts, which easily prove that people do not acquire or preserve virtue by the help of external goods, but external goods by the help of virtue;

14. And that happiness, whether consisting in pleasure or virtue, or both,

15. Is more often found with those who are most highly cultivated in their mind and in their character, and have only a moderate share of external goods,

16. Than among those who possess external goods to a useless extent, yet are deficient in higher qualities.

17. This is not only a matter of experience, but, if reflected upon, will easily appear to be in accordance with reason.
18. For, whereas external goods have a limit, like any other instrument,
19. And all things useful are of such a nature that where there is too much of them they must either do harm, or be of little use, to their possessors,
20. Yet every good of the mind, the greater it is, is also of greater use.
21. It is for the sake of the mind that goods external and goods of the body are eligible at all,
22. And all wise men ought to choose them for the sake of the mind, and not the mind for the sake of them.
23. Let us acknowledge then that each one has just so much happiness as he has virtue and wisdom, and acts virtuously and wisely.
24. Herein lies the difference between good fortune and happiness;
25. For external goods come of themselves, and chance is the author of them,
26. But no one is just or temperate by or through chance.
27. In like manner, the happy state may be shown to be that which is best and which acts rightly;
28. And it cannot act rightly without doing right actions, and neither individual nor state can do right actions without virtue and wisdom.
29. Thus the courage, justice and wisdom of a state have the same

form and nature as these qualities in an individual.
30. Let this then be the lawgiver's first aim: to require of the state that it should be worthy of its best citizens,
31. And of its citizens that they should be just, wise and temperate.

Chapter 15

1. Philosophers who urge people to take lessons from them, but give no real instruction or advice, are like those who trim the lamps, but fail to pour in oil.
2. An understanding of life dedicated to affairs of state, of its practice and not merely its theory, requires a grasp of the precepts of statecraft.
3. At the basis of political activity there must be a strong foundation of judgement and reason,
4. So that choice of policy arises not from mere impulse due to empty opinion or contentiousness.
5. Some engage in public affairs but then weary of them or become disgusted by them,
6. But are not able to retire from them without difficulty;
7. They are in the same predicament as persons who have gone aboard a vessel to be rocked by the waves,
8. And then have been driven out into the open sea; they turn their gaze outside, seasick and much disturbed, but obliged to stay where they are and endure their plight.
9. Such people cast the greatest

discredit upon public life by regretting their course and being unhappy.

10. Some, after hoping for glory, fall into disgrace or, after expecting to be feared by others on account of their power,

11. Are drawn into affairs which involve dangers and popular disorders.

12. But the person who has entered upon public life from conviction and reasoning, as the activity most befitting him and most honourable,

13. Is not frightened by any of these things, nor is his conviction changed.

14. Neither is it right to enter upon public life as a gainful trade, as did those who used to invite each other to 'come to the golden harvest' as they called the orators' platform.

15. Those who make themselves up for political competition or the race for glory, as actors do for the stage,

16. Must necessarily regret their action, since they must either serve those whom they think they should rule, or offend those whom they wish to please.

17. Those who, like men who fall into a well, stumble into public life for the wrong reasons, must inevitably regret their course,

18. Whereas those who enter into it quietly, as the result of preparation and reflection,

19. Will be moderate in their conduct of affairs and will not be discomposed by anything,

20. Inasmuch as they have honour itself and nothing else as the purpose of their actions.

21. So, after thus determining their choice in their own minds, statesmen must apply themselves to the understanding of the character of the citizens,

22. Which shows itself as in the highest degree a compound of all their individual characters and is powerful.

23. For any attempt on the part of the statesman to produce by himself a change of character and nature in the people will not easily succeed,

24. Nor is it safe, but it is a matter that requires a long space of time and great power.

25. But just as wine is at first controlled by the character of the drinker, but gradually, as it warms and mingles with him, itself forms the drinker's character and changes him,

26. Just so the statesman, until by reputation and public confidence he has established his leadership, must accommodate himself to the people's character as he finds it,

27. And make that the object of his efforts, knowing by what things the people are naturally pleased and led.

28. Ignorance of their characters leads to mistakes and failures;

29. The statesman who has attained power and won the people's confidence can then try to train the character of the citizens,

30. Leading them gently towards that

which is better and treating them with mildness;

31. For it is a difficult task to change the multitude.

Chapter 16

1. But he who would be a statesman, since he is to live as on an open stage,

2. Must educate his character and put it in order; and because it is not easy to banish evil from one's character wholly,

3. He must at least remove and repress those faults which are most flourishing and conspicuous.

4. For example, Themistocles, when he was thinking of entering public life,

5. Withdrew from drinking parties and carousals; he was wakeful at night, was sober and deeply thoughtful,

6. Explaining to his friends that the examples of great men would not let him sleep.

7. And Pericles also changed his personal habits of life, so that he spoke carefully and with forethought,

8. Always showed a composed countenance, and trod only one path – that which led to the assembly and the senate.

9. For a populace is not a simple and easy thing for any chance person to subject to that control which is salutary;

10. But one must be satisfied if the multitude accepts authority

without shying, like a suspicious and capricious beast, at face or voice.

11. Since, then, the statesman must not treat even these matters carelessly, he ought not to neglect the things which affect his life and character,

12. To keep them clear of blame and ill report of every kind.

13. For not only are statesmen held responsible for their public words and actions,

14. But people are curious and pry into all their concerns,

15. Wishing to know about their dinners, love affairs, marriages, amusements and every serious interest.

16. What need is there, for instance, to speak of Alcibiades, who,

17. Though he was most active of all the citizens in public affairs and was undefeated as a general,

18. Was ruined by his audacious and dissolute habits in private life,

19. And, because of his extravagance and lack of restraint, deprived the state of the benefit of his other good qualities?

20. Why, the Athenians blamed Cimon for wine-drinking,

21. And the Romans, having nothing else to say, blamed Scipio for sleeping;

22. And the enemies of Pompey the Great, observing that he scratched his head with one finger, reviled him for it!

23. For, just as a mole or a wart on the face is more unpleasant than

brand-marks, mutilations, or scars on other parts of the body,

24. So small faults appear great when observed in the lives of leaders and statesmen on account of the opinion which the majority has of governing and public office,

25. Regarding it as a great thing which ought to be clean of all eccentricities and errors.

26. With good reason, therefore, did Livius Drusus the tribune gain in reputation because,

27. When many parts of his house were exposed to the view of his neighbours and an artisan promised to conceal them for only five coins,

28. Drusus replied, 'Take ten coins and make the whole house open to view, that all the citizens may see how I live.'

29. For he was a man of temperate and well-ordered life.

30. And perhaps he had no need of that exposure to the public view;

31. For the people see through the characters, counsels, acts and lives of public men, even those that seem to be very thickly cloaked;

32. They love and admire one man and dislike and despise another quite as much for his private as for his public practices.

33. 'But,' you say, 'do not states put in office men who live licentiously and wantonly?'

34. They do, but it is just like pregnant women who long for sweetmeats,

35. And seasick persons for salt pickles

and the like, which then a little later they vomit up and detest.

36. So the people, because of the luxury of their own lives or through sheer perversity,

37. Or for lack of better leaders, make use of those who happen to turn up, though they dislike or even despise them,

38. Then take pleasure in hearing defamatory and critical things said about them.

39. And remember how the Roman people, when Carbo promised something, unanimously voted that they did not trust him.

40. And at Lacedaemon, when a dissolute man named Demosthenes made a desirable motion, the people rejected it,

41. But the ephors chose by lot one of the elders and told him to make that same motion, in order that it might be made acceptable to the people,

42. Thus pouring, as it were, from a dirty vessel into a clean one.

Chapter 17

1. The foregoing shows how great is the importance, in a free state, of confidence or lack of confidence in a statesman's character.

2. However, we should not on this account neglect the charm and power of eloquence and ascribe everything to virtue,

3. But, considering oratory to be, not the creator of persuasion but certainly its co-worker, we should

qualify Menander's view that 'The speaker's nature, not his speech, persuades',

4. For both his nature and his speech do so; unless, indeed, one is to affirm that just as the helmsman, not the tiller, steers the ship,

5. And the rider, not the rein, turns the horse, so political virtue, employing not speech but the speaker's character as tiller or rein, sways a state,

6. Laying hold of it and directing it, as it were, from the stern, which is the easiest way of turning an animal about.

7. Great kings and emperors of the past dressed themselves in purple robes, carried sceptres, and surrounded themselves with guards and much ceremony,

8. Yet although they enslaved multitudes by this show, as if they were superior beings,

9. They still desired to be orators, and did not neglect the charm of speech,

10. Trying to soften by persuasion and overcoming by charms the fierce hearts of the people,

11. Whenever it was not politic or possible to do it by threat or force.

12. How, then, is it possible that a private person of ordinary costume and mien, who wishes to lead a state,

13. May gain power and rule the multitude, unless he possesses persuasion and attractive speech?

14. Now the pilots of ships employ others to give orders to the rowers,

15. But the statesman needs to have in himself the mind that steers and also in himself the speech that gives orders,

16. That he may not require some other man's voice and be obliged to say,

17. As Iphicrates did when defeated through the eloquence of Aristophon's orators,

18. 'My opponents' actor is better, but my play is superior.'

19. The spokesman who employs speech as his only instrument, moulding and adapting some things,

20. And softening and smoothing off those which are hindrances to his work,

21. Such as would be knots in wood or flaws in iron, is an ornament to the state.

22. For this reason the government of Pericles, though in name a democracy, was in fact the rule of the foremost man because of his power of oratory.

23. For Cimon also was a good man, as were Ephialtes and Thucydides,

24. But when the last named was asked by Archidamus, king of the Spartans, whether he or Pericles was the better wrestler, he replied,

25. 'Nobody can tell; for whenever I throw him in wrestling, he says he was not thrown and wins by persuading the onlookers.'

26. And this brought not only reputation to Pericles but safety to the state;

27. For while it was swayed by him it preserved its existing prosperity and refrained from foreign entanglements.
28. But Nicias, whose policy was the same, but who lacked powers of persuasion, could not restrain or master the people,
29. But against his will went off to Sicily at the prompting of their intemperance, and together with them suffered disaster.

Chapter 18

1. The wolf, they say, cannot be held by the ears; but one must lead a people or a state chiefly by the ears,
2. Not, as some who have no practice in speaking, and seek uncultured and inartistic holds upon the people, by pulling them by the belly,
3. With banquets or gifts of money or arranging ballet dances or gladiatorial shows, by which they curry favour with the people.
4. For leadership of a people is leadership of those who are persuaded by speech;
5. But enticing the mob by such means is exactly like catching and herding irrational beasts.
6. The speech of the statesman, however, must not be theatrical,
7. As if he were making a speech for show and weaving a garland of words for their own sake and not for the sake of serious matter;
8. On the other hand it must not, as Pytheas said of the speech of

Demosthenes, smell of the lamp and elaborate literary labour,
9. With sharp arguments and with periods precisely measured by rule and compass.
10. No, just as musicians demand that the touch upon the strings exhibit feeling, not mere technique,
11. So the speech of the statesman, counsellor and ruler must not exhibit shrewdness or subtlety,
12. And it must not be to his credit to speak fluently or artistically or distributively;
13. But his speech must be full of unaffected character, true high-mindedness, a father's frankness, foresight, and thoughtful concern for others.
14. His speech must also have, in a good cause, a charm that pleases and a winning persuasiveness;
15. In addition to nobility of purpose it must possess grace arising from appropriate and persuasive thoughts.
16. And political oratory, much more than that used in a court of law, admits maxims, historical examples and metaphors,
17. By means of which those who employ them sparingly and at the proper moment move their audiences exceedingly;
18. As did Phocion when he said, with reference to the victory of Leosthenes,
19. That the furlong race of the war was good, but he was fearful about the long-distance race.

20. And in general, sobriety and clarity of style are most fitting for political speech;
21. Rhetorical efforts and grand periods are especially inappropriate in times of danger or war,
22. For as has been said, 'None should talk foolishly when near the steel.'
23. However, derision and ridicule are sometimes proper parts of the statesman's speech if employed, not as insults or buffoonery, but for needful reproof and disparagement.
24. That sort of thing is most laudable in rejoinders and replies; but when employed of set purpose and without provocation, it carries a suspicion of malice.
25. But for one who employs wit in self-defence the occasion makes it pardonable and at the same time pleasing,
26. As when Demosthenes, in reply to a man who was suspected of being a thief and who mocked him for writing at night, said,
27. 'I am aware that I offend you by keeping a light burning.'
28. Witty too was Xenaenetus' rejoinder to the citizens who reviled him for running away when he was general:
29. 'Yes,' he said, 'it was to keep you company, my dears.'
30. But in jesting one must guard against going too far, perhaps offending by jesting at the wrong moment or humiliating the speaker.
31. Polyeuctus said that Demosthenes was the greatest orator, but that Phocion was the cleverest in speaking, because his speech contained the most meaning in the fewest words.
32. And Demosthenes, though he affected to despise other orators, used to say when Phocion rose to speak, 'The cleaver of my speeches is getting up.'
33. In sum then, the aspiring statesman must, in addressing the people, seek to employ well-considered, not empty, speech,
34. And to use precaution, knowing that even the great Pericles used to prepare carefully before making a public speech,
35. So that no single utterance foreign to the matter in hand might occur to him.
36. Yet also the orator must always keep his speech nimble and in good practice for making apt rejoinders;
37. For occasions arise quickly and often bring with them in public affairs sudden developments.
38. That is why Demosthenes was inferior to many, as they say, because he drew back and hesitated when the occasion called for the opposite course.
39. And Theophrastus tells us that Alcibiades, because he planned not only to say the right thing, but to say it in the right way,
40. Often while actually speaking would search for words and arrange them into sentences, thereby causing hesitation and stumbling.

41. But the man who is so moved by events and the opportunities they offer that he springs to his feet is the one who most thrills the crowd and carries it with him.

42. And the statesman must bring to the struggle of statecraft, a struggle which is important, and calls for all one's fighting power,

43. Not just education and fore-thought, but good health and stamina, that he may not be frequently so weary that he is defeated by mere hecklers.

44. Cato, when he had no hope of winning his cause by persuasion because the senate was gained over beforehand by favours and interests,

45. Used to get up and speak the whole day, thus destroying his opponents' opportunity, and showing the worth of stamina.

Chapter 19

1. There are two entrances to public life and two paths leading to it:

2. One the quick and brilliant road to reputation, by no means without risk; the other more prosaic and slower, but safer.

3. For some men launch out at once into political life with some conspicuous great or daring action,

4. Like men who launch a vessel from a promontory that juts out into the sea;

5. They think Pindar is right in saying 'To a work's beginning we must set a front that shines afar.'

6. People are more ready to accept a beginner because they are surfeited with those they are accustomed to,

7. Just as spectators at a show are glad to see a new performer; and authority and power that has a brilliant and rapid growth takes envy's breath away.

8. For, as Ariston says, fire does not cause smoke, nor does reputation cause envy, if it blazes up quickly at the start;

9. But those who grow great gradu-ally and slowly are attacked one from one side, another from another;

10. Hence many men wither away before coming to full bloom as statesmen.

11. Remember Pompey, who demanded a Triumph although he had not yet been admitted to the senate;

12. When Sulla voted against it, Pompey said to him, 'More welcome the rising than the setting sun';

13. And Sulla, when he heard this, withdrew his opposition.

14. Nowadays, when the affairs of states less often involve leadership in wars, the overthrowing of tyrannies, acts of alliances,

15. What opening for a conspicuous and brilliant public career could a young man find?

16. There remain the public lawsuits, and embassies abroad,

17. Which demand a man of ardent temperament and one who

possesses both courage and intellect.

18. But there are many excellent lines of endeavour that are neglected in our cities which a man may take up,

19. And also many practices resulting from evil custom, that have insinuated themselves to the shame or injury of the state,

20. Which a man may remove, and thus turn them to account for himself.

21. Indeed in past times a just verdict gained in a great suit,

22. Or good faith in acting as advocate for a weak client against a powerful opponent,

23. Or boldness of speech on behalf of the right against a wicked ruler,

24. Has opened to some men a glorious entrance into public life.

25. And not a few also have grown great through the enemies they have made by attacking men whose position made them enviable or caused them to be feared;

26. For when such a man is overthrown his power passes at once, and with better reputation, to the man who overcame him.

27. For attacking, through motives of envy, a good man who, on account of his virtue, is leader of the state,

28. As Pericles was attacked by Simmias, Themistocles by Alcmeon, Pompey by Clodius, and Epameinondas by Menecleides the orator,

29. Is neither conducive to a good reputation nor advantageous in any other way;

30. For when the people have committed a wrong against a good man and then repent of their anger,

31. They think the easiest way to excuse themselves for this offence is the most just, namely,

32. To destroy the man who was the author of it and persuaded them to commit it.

33. On the other hand, to revolt against a bad man who by shameless audacity and cunning has made affairs subject to himself,

34. Such as Cleon and Cleophon were at Athens, and to pull him down and humble him,

35. Provides a glorious entrance upon the stage of public life.

36. And I am not ignorant of the fact that some men by curtailing the power of an oppressive and oligarchical senate,

37. As Ephialtes did at Athens and Phormio at Elis,

38. Have gained at the same time both power and glory;

39. But to one who is just entering upon public life there is a great risk in this.

40. Therefore Solon made a better beginning, when Athens was divided into three factions called the Diacrians ('hill-folk'), the Pedieans ('plains-folk'), and the Paralians ('coast-folk');

41. For he entangled himself with none of them, but acted for all in common and said and did

everything to bring about concord among them,

42. So that he was chosen lawgiver to reconcile their differences and in this way established his rule.

Chapter 20

1. So many, then, and of such kinds are the more conspicuous ways of entering upon a public career.

2. But the safe and leisurely way has been chosen by many famous men – Aristeides, Phocion, Pammenes the Theban, Lucullus at Rome, Cato, the Lacedaemonian Agesilaus.

3. For just as ivy rises by twining itself about a strong tree, so each of these men, by attaching himself while still young to an older man,

4. And while still obscure to a man of reputation, being gradually raised up under the shelter of his power and growing great with him,

5. Fixed himself firmly and rooted himself in the affairs of state.

6. For Aristeides was made great by Cleisthenes, Phocion by Chabrias, Lucullus by Sulla,

7. Cato by Maximus, Epameinondas aided Pammenes and Lysander Agesilaus.

8. But Agesilaus, through untimely ambition and jealousy of Lysander's reputation, insulted and quickly cast aside the guide of his actions;

9. But the others in noble and statesmanlike fashion cherished their teachers until the end and joined in honouring them,

10. Enhancing in turn with their own radiance, and illuminating, like the heavenly bodies that face the sun, that which caused themselves to shine.

11. Certainly Scipio's detractors said that he was the actor, but his friend Laelius the real author of his deeds;

12. Laelius, however, was not puffed up by any of those sayings, but continued always eagerly to exalt Scipio's virtue and renown.

13. And Pompey's friend Afranius, even though he was of humble station,

14. Nevertheless expected to be elected consul, but when Pompey favoured other candidates, he relinquished his ambition,

15. Saying that gaining the consulship would be to him not so much glorious as painful and trouble-some, if it were against Pompey's will and without his co-operation;

16. And so after waiting only one year he both gained the office and retained the friendship.

17. Those who are thus led to renown by the hand of others gain favour with many,

18. And at the same time, if anything unpleasant happens, are less disliked;

19. And that is why Philip advised Alexander to gain friends as long as he could while another man was king,

20. By having pleasant relations with others and maintaining friendly ties with them.

21. But anyone who is entering upon a

public career should choose as his leader a man who is not merely of established reputation and powerful,

22. But one who is all this on account of real worth. For just as not every tree will accept and support the vine which entwines about it, but some trees stifle and ruin its growth,

23. So in states, the men who are not lovers of what is noble, but merely lovers of honours and of office,

24. Do not give young men opportunities for public activities,

25. But through envy repress them and, to speak figuratively, wither them up by depriving them of glory, their natural nourishment.

26. So Marius, after having achieved many successes in Libya and Gaul with the help of Sulla, ceased to employ him and cast him off, being angered by his growth in power.

27. Sulla, however, exalted Pompey from the time of his youth, rising up and uncovering his head when he came near;

28. And also by giving the other young men opportunities for leadership,

29. And by urging some on even against their will, he filled his armies with ambition and eagerness;

30. And he gained power over them all by wishing to be, not the only great man, but first and greatest among many great men.

31. Such, then, are the men to whom young statesmen should attach themselves and cling closely,

32. Not snatching glory away from them, like Aesop's wren who was carried up on the eagle's shoulders, then suddenly flew out and got ahead of him,

33. But receiving it from them in goodwill and friendship, knowing that no one can ever command well who has not first learned rightly to obey, as Plato says.

Chapter 21

1. Next comes the decision to be made concerning friends, and here we approve neither the idea of Cleon nor of Themistocles.

2. For Cleon, when he first decided to take up political life, brought his friends together and renounced his friendship with them,

3. As something which often weakens and perverts the right and just choice of policy in political life.

4. But he would have done better if he had cast out of his character avarice and love of strife, and cleansed himself of envy and malice;

5. For the state needs, not men who have no friends or comrades, but good and self-controlled men.

6. As it was, he drove away his friends, but a hundred cursed flatterers circled and fawned around him instead,

7. And he subjected himself to the masses to win their favour, making the basest and most unsound

element of the people his associates against the best.

8. But Themistocles on the other hand, when someone said that he would govern well if he showed himself equally impartial to all, replied,

9. 'May I never take my seat on such a throne that my friends shall not have more from me than those who are not my friends!'

10. He also was wrong; for he subordinated the government to his friendship, putting the affairs of the community and the public below private favours and interests.

11. And yet when Simonides asked for something that was not just, he said to him:

12. 'He is not a good poet who sings contrary to metre, nor is he an equitable ruler who grants favours contrary to law.'

13. For the architect chooses subordinates and handicraftsmen who will not spoil his work but will co-operate to perfect it.

14. The statesman who is, as Pindar says, the best of craftsmen and the maker of lawfulness and justice, should choose friends whose convictions are like his own,

15. Who will aid him and share his enthusiasm for what is noble;

16. And must avoid those who are always wrongfully and by violent means trying to divert him to various other uses.

17. A politician of the latter sort will be found to be no better than a builder or a carpenter who through ignorance and error makes use of such squares and rulers and levels as are sure to make his work crooked.

18. For friends are the living and thinking tools of the statesman, and he ought not to slip with them when they go wrong,

19. But he must be on the watch that they do not err even through ignorance.

20. It was this that disgraced Solon and brought him into disrepute among the citizens;

21. For when he made up his mind to lighten debts and to introduce the cancellation of debts, he told his friends about it, and they did a very wrong thing;

22. They secretly borrowed large sums of money before the law was published,

23. And later, after its publication, they were found to have bought splendid houses and much land with the loans they no longer needed to repay.

24. Solon, who was wronged by them, was nevertheless accused of sharing in their wrongdoing.

25. For the principles that govern a statesman's conduct do not force him to act with severity against the moderate errors of his friends;

26. On the contrary, they make it possible for him, after he has once made the chief public interests safe,

27. Out of his abundant resources to assist his friends, take his stand beside them, and help them out of their troubles.

28. And there are also favours which arouse no ill-will, such as aiding a friend to gain an office,

29. Putting into his hands some honourable administrative function or some friendly foreign mission,

30. For example one which includes honours to a ruler or negotiations with a state concerning friendship and concord;

31. And if some public activity be laborious, but conspicuous and important,

32. The statesman can first appoint himself to the post and then choose his friend as assistant,

33. For such concession to one's friends adorns those who give praise no less than those who receive it.

34. Then, besides, a man ought to ascribe to his friends a share in his own good and kindly acts of favour;

35. He should tell those who have been benefited to praise and show them affection as the originators and advisers of the favours.

36. But base and absurd requests he should reject, not harshly but gently,

37. Informing the askers by way of consolation that the requests are not in accord with their own excellence and reputation.

38. Epameinondas exemplifies this most admirably: after refusing to let the pedlar out of prison at Pelopidas' request,

39. And then letting him out a little later when his mistress asked it, he said, 'Favours of that sort, Pelopidas, are fit for courtesans to receive, but not for generals.'

40. But Cato acted harshly and arbitrarily when he was quaestor, and Catulus the censor, one of his most intimate friends, asked for the acquittal of a man who was being tried,

41. By saying: 'It is a disgrace that you, whose duty it is to train us young men to honourable conduct, have to be thrown out by our servants.'

42. For he might, while refusing the favour in fact, have avoided harshness of speech,

43. By producing the impression that the offensive quality of his action was not due to his own will, but was forced upon him by law and justice.

Chapter 22

1. The administration of affairs frequently gives the man in public life this sort of chance to help his friends.

2. Hand over to one friend a case at law which will bring in a good fee as advocate in a just cause,

3. To another introduce a rich man who needs legal oversight and protection, and help another to get some profitable contract or lease.

4. Epameinondas even told a friend to go to a certain rich man and ask for a talent, saying that it was he who bade him give it;

5. And when the man who had been

asked for it came and asked him the reason, he replied:

6. 'Because this man is a good man and poor, but you are rich since you have appropriated much of the state's wealth.'

7. And Xenophon says that Agesilaus delighted in enriching his friends, he being himself above money.

8. But since, to quote Simonides, 'all larks must grow a crest', and every public career bears its crop of enmities and disagreements, the public man must take care over these matters.

9. So most people commend Themistocles and Aristeides who, whenever they went on an embassy or in command of an army,

10. Laid down their private enmity at the frontier, then took it up again later.

11. And some people are also immensely pleased by the conduct of Cretinas of Magnesia.

12. He was a political opponent of Hermeias, a man who was not powerful, but was ambitious, with a brilliant mind,

13. And when the Mithridatic war broke out, seeing that the state was in danger,

14. He told Hermeias to take over the command and manage affairs, while he himself withdrew;

15. Or, if Hermeias wished him to be general, then Hermeias should remove himself,

16. That they might not by ambitious strife with one another destroy the state.

17. The challenge pleased Hermeias, and saying that Cretinas was more versed in war than himself, he went away with his wife and children.

18. And as he was departing Cretinas escorted him, first giving him out of his own means such things as were more useful to exiles than to people besieged in a city,

19. After which by his excellent military leadership he saved the state when it was on the brink of destruction.

20. For if it is a noble thing and the mark of an exalted individual to be willing to make peace with a personal enemy for the sake of those things for which we ought even to give up a friend,

21. Certainly Phocion and Cato and their like acted much better,

22. For they would allow no personal enmity to have any bearing whatsoever upon political differences,

23. But were stern and inexorable only in public contests against sacrificing what was for the common good;

24. Yet in private matters they treated kindly and without anger their political opponents.

25. For the statesman should not regard any fellow-citizen as an enemy,

26. Unless some man, such as Aristion, Nabis or Catiline, should appear who is a running sore to the state.

27. Those who are in other ways out of harmony he should, like a skilful musician, bring into unison by

gently tightening or relaxing the strings of his control,

28. Not attacking angrily and insultingly those who err, but making an appeal designed rather to make a moral impression.

29. If his opponents say or do anything good, the statesman should not be vexed by their honours,

30. Nor should he be sparing of complimentary words for their good actions;

31. For if we act in this way our blame, where it is needed, will be thought justified,

32. And we shall make them dislike evil by exalting virtue and showing through comparison that good actions are more worthy and fitting than the other kind.

Chapter 23

1. And I think also that the statesman should give testimony in just causes even for his opponents,

2. Should aid them in court against malicious prosecutors,

3. And should discredit calumnies about them if such accusations are alien to the principles he knows that they profess;

4. Just as the infamous Nero, a little before he put Thrasea to death, whom he hated and feared intensely,

5. Nevertheless when someone accused him of a bad and unjust decision in court, said: 'I wish Thrasea were as good a friend to me as he is a most excellent judge.'

6. And it is not a bad method for confounding persons of a different kind,

7. Men who are naturally vicious and prone to evil conduct, to mention to them some enemy of theirs who is of finer character,

8. And to say: 'He would not have said that or done that.'

9. Cato, although he had opposed Pompey in the violent measures which he and Caesar applied to the state,

10. When war broke out between them advised handing over the leadership to Pompey, saying:

11. 'The men who can bring about great evils can also end them.'

12. For blame which is mingled with praise and contains nothing insulting, but merely frankness of speech,

13. And arouses not anger, but a pricking of the conscience and repentance,

14. Appears both kindly and healing; but abusive speech is not at all fitting for statesmen.

15. Jeering and scurrility bring disgrace upon the speakers of them rather than upon those spoken of,

16. And moreover they bring confusion into the conduct of affairs and they disturb councils and assemblies.

17. Therefore Phocion did well when he stopped speaking and yielded the floor to a man who was reviling him,

18. And then, when the fellow had at last become silent, came forward again saying:

19. 'Well, then, about the cavalry and the heavy infantry you have heard already;

20. 'It remains for me to discuss the light infantry and the targeteers.'

21. But since many men find it hard to endure that sort of thing quietly, and abusive speakers are often, and not without general benefit, made to shut their mouths by the retorts they evoke,

22. Let the reply be brief in wording, showing no temper and no extreme rancour,

23. But urbanity mingled with playfulness and grace which somehow or other has a sting in it.

24. There are men who enter upon every kind of public service, as Cato did, claiming that the good citizen ought, so far as in him lies, to omit no trouble or diligence;

25. And they commend Epameinondas because, when through envy and as an insult he had been appointed telmarch by the Thebans, he did not neglect his duties,

26. But saying that not only does the office distinguish the man, but also the man the office,

27. He advanced the telmarchy to a position of great consideration and dignity,

28. Though previously it had been nothing but a sort of supervision of the alleys for the removal of dung and the draining of water in the streets.

29. All such are helped by the remark of Antisthenes which has been handed down to memory;

30. For when someone expressed surprise that he himself carried a dried fish through the marketplace, he said, 'Yes, but it is for myself';

31. But I, on the other hand, say to those who criticise me for standing and watching tiles being measured or concrete or stones being delivered,

32. That I attend to these things, not for myself, but for my native town.

33. For there are many other things in regard to which a man would be petty who attended to them himself for his own sake,

34. But if he does it for the public and for the state's sake, he is not ignoble;

35. On the contrary his attention to duty and his zeal are all the greater when applied to little things.

Chapter 24

1. But there are others who think the conduct of Pericles was more dignified and splendid, one of whom is Critolaus the Peripatetic,

2. Who claims that just as the Salaminia and the Paralus, ships at Athens, were not sent out to sea for every service, but only for necessary and important missions,

3. So the statesman should reserve himself for the most momentous and important matters.

4. The statesman ought to find the people fond of him when he comes

to them and to leave a longing for him when he is not there;

5. Which Scipio Africanus accomplished by spending much of his time in the country,

6. Thereby at one and the same time removing the weight of envy and giving a breathing space to those who thought they were oppressed by his glory.

7. Timesias of Clazomenae was in other respects a good man in his service to the state, but by doing everything himself he had aroused rancour;

8. But of this he was unaware until the following incident took place:

9. Some boys were playing a game of knocking a knucklebone out of a hole when he was passing by;

10. And the boy who had struck at it said: 'I'd like to knock the brains out of Timesias as truly as this has been knocked out of the hole.'

11. Timesias, hearing this and understanding that dislike of him had permeated all the people,

12. Returned home and told his wife what had happened; and directing her to pack up and follow him, he went immediately away from his house and out from the city.

13. And it appears that Themistocles, when he met with the same treatment from the Athenians, said,

14. 'Why, my dear people, are you tired of receiving repeated benefits?'

15. Now of such sayings some are well said, others are not.

16. For so far as goodwill and solicitude for the common weal are concerned, a statesman should not hold aloof from any part of public affairs, but should pay attention to them all and inform himself about all details;

17. Nor should he hold himself aloof, waiting for the extreme necessities and fortunes of the state;

18. But perform other duties by means of different instruments operated by different agents,

19. Thus giving a turn or a twist to the instruments while they sit apart, as a ship's captain makes use of sailors, lookout men and boatswains,

20. Some of whom they often call to the stern and entrust with the tiller,

21. Just so it is fitting that the statesman should yield office to others and should invite them to the orators' platform in a gracious and kindly manner,

22. And he should not try to administer all the affairs of the state by his own speeches, decrees and actions,

23. But should have good, trustworthy men and employ each of them for each particular service according to his fitness.

24. So Pericles made use of Menippus for the position of general,

25. Humbled the Council of the Areopagus by means of Ephialtes,

26. Passed the decree against the Megarians by means of Charinus,

27. And sent Lampon out as founder of Thurii.

28. For, when power seems to be distributed among many, not only

does the weight of hatreds and
enmities become less troublesome,

29. But there is also greater efficiency
in the conduct of affairs.

30. For just as the division of the hand
into fingers does not make it weak,
but renders it a more skilful
instrument for use,

31. So the statesman who gives to
others a share in the government
makes action more effective by
co-operation.

32. But he who through insatiable
greed of fame or power puts the
whole burden of the state upon
himself,

33. And sets himself even to tasks for
which he is not fitted by nature or
by training,

34. As Cleon set himself to leading
armies, Philopoemen to commanding ships and Hannibal to
haranguing the people – such a
man has no excuse when he makes
mistakes.

35. So, being no persuasive speaker,
you went on an embassy,

36. Or being easy-going, you undertook administration,

37. Being ignorant of accounting, you
were treasurer,

38. Or when old and feeble, you took
command of an army.

39. But Pericles divided the power with
Cimon so that he should himself be
ruler in the city and Cimon should
man the ships and wage war against
the barbarians;

40. For one of them was more gifted for
civic government, the other for war.

41. And Eubulus the Anaphlystian also
is commended because, although
few men enjoyed so much confidence and power as he,

42. Yet he administered none of the
Hellenic affairs and did not take
the post of general,

43. But applied himself to the finances,
increased the revenues, and did the
state much good thereby.

Chapter 25

1. Since there is in every democracy
an inclination to malice and
fault-finding directed against men
in public life,

2. And they suspect that many
desirable measures, if there is no
party opposition and no expression of dissent, are done by
conspiracy,

3. And this subjects a man's associations and friends to calumny,

4. Statesmen ought not to let any real
enmity or disagreement against
themselves subsist.

5. When the populace are suspicious
about some important and salutary
measure,

6. The statesmen when they come to
the assembly ought not all to
express the same opinion, as if by
previous agreement,

7. But two or three of the friends
should dissent and quietly speak on
the other side, then change in their
position as if they had been
convinced;

8. For in this way they draw the
people along with them, since they

appear to be influenced only by the public advantage.

9. In small matters, however, which do not amount to much, it is not a bad thing to let one's friends really disagree,

10. Each following his own reasoning that in matters of the highest importance their agreement upon the best policy may not seem to be prearranged.

11. Now the statesman is always by nature ruler of the state, like the queen bee in the hive,

12. And bearing this in mind he ought to keep public matters in his own hands;

13. But offices which are called 'authoritative' and are elective he ought not to seek too eagerly or often, for love of office is neither dignified nor popular;

14. Nor should he refuse them, if the people offer them and call him to them in accordance with the law,

15. But even if they be too small for a man of his reputation, he should accept them and exercise them with zeal.

16. For it is right that men who are adorned with the highest offices should in turn adorn the lesser,

17. And that statesmen should show moderation, giving up and yielding some part of the weightier offices, and adding dignity and grandeur to the minor offices,

18. That we may not be despised in connection with the latter, nor envied on account of the former.

19. And when entering upon any office whatsoever, one must not only call to mind those considerations of which Pericles reminded himself when he assumed the cloak of a general:

20. 'Take care, Pericles; you are ruling free men, you are ruling Greeks, Athenian citizens,'

21. But one must also say to oneself: 'You who rule are a subject, ruling a state controlled by proconsuls, the agents of peace;

22. 'These are not the spearmen of the plain, nor is this ancient Sardis, nor the famed Lydian power.'

23. One should imitate the actors, who, while putting into the performance their own passion, character and reputation,

24. Yet listen to the prompter and do not go beyond the degree of liberty in rhythms and metres permitted by those in authority over them.

25. For to fail in one's part in public life brings not mere hissing or catcalls or stamping of feet.

26. Furthermore when we see little children trying playfully to bind their fathers' shoes on their feet or fit their crowns upon their heads, we only laugh,

27. But the officials in the cities, when they foolishly urge the people to imitate the deeds, ideals and actions of their ancestors, however unsuitable they may be to the present times and conditions, stir up the common folk,

28. And though what they do is

laughable, what is done to them is no laughing matter, unless they are merely treated with utter contempt.

Chapter 26

1. The statesman, while making his native state readily obedient to its laws, must not further humble it;
2. Nor, when the leg has been fettered, go on and subject the neck to the yoke,
3. As some do who, by referring everything, great or small, to the sovereign power,
4. Bring the reproach of slavery upon their country, or rather wholly destroy its constitutional government, making it timid and powerless in everything.
5. For just as those who have become accustomed neither to dine nor to bathe except by the physician's orders do not even enjoy that degree of health which nature grants them,
6. So those who invite the government's decision on every decree, meeting of a council, granting of a privilege or administrative measure,
7. Force their government to be their master more than it desires.
8. And the cause of this is chiefly the greed and contentiousness of the foremost citizens;
9. For either, in cases in which they are injuring their inferiors, they force them into exile from the state,
10. Or, in matters concerning which they differ among themselves, since they are unwilling to occupy an inferior position among their fellow-citizens, they call in those who are mightier;
11. And as a result senate, popular assembly, courts and the entire local government lose their authority.
12. But the statesman should soothe the ordinary citizens by granting them equality, and the powerful by concessions in return,
13. Thus keeping them within the bounds of the local government and solving their difficulties as if they were diseases, making for them, as it were, a sort of political medicine;
14. He will prefer to be himself defeated among his fellow-citizens rather than to be successful by outraging and destroying the principles of justice in his own city,
15. And he will beg everyone else to do likewise, and will teach them how great an evil is contentiousness.
16. But as it is, not only do they not make honourable and gracious compromises with their fellow-citizens and tribesmen at home and with their neighbours and colleagues in office,
17. But they carry their dissensions outside and put them in the hands of lawyers, to their own great injury and disgrace.
18. For when physicians cannot entirely eradicate diseases, they turn them outwards to the surface of the body;
19. But the statesman, if he cannot keep the state entirely free from

troubles, will at any rate try to cure and control whatever disturbs it,

20. Keeping it meanwhile within the state, so that it may have as little need as possible of physicians and medicine drawn from outside.

21. For the policy of the statesman should be that which holds fast to security and avoids the tumultuous and mad impulse of empty opinion.

22. For he must not create storms himself, and yet he must not desert the state when storms fall upon it;

23. He must not stir up the state and make it reel perilously, but when it is reeling and in danger, he must come to its assistance and employ his frankness of speech as an anchor.

24. You would not see the man who is really a statesman cowering in fear,

25. Nor would you see him throwing blame upon others and putting himself out of danger,

26. But you will see him serving on embassies, sailing the seas,

27. And even though he had no part in the wrongdoing of the people, taking dangers upon himself on their behalf.

28. For this is noble; and besides being noble, one man's excellence and wisdom, by earning admiration,

29. Has often mitigated anger which has been aroused against the whole people and has dissipated the threatened terror and bitterness.

30. Something of that sort seems to have happened in the case of Pompey regarding Sthenno,

31. When, as he was going to punish the Mamertines for revolting, Sthenno told him that he would be doing wrong if he should destroy many innocent men for the fault of one man;

32. For, he said, it was he himself who had caused the city to revolt by persuading his friends and compelling his enemies.

33. This so affected Pompey that he let the city go unpunished and also treated Sthenno kindly.

34. But Sulla's guest-friend, practising virtue of the same sort but not having to do with the same sort of man, met with a noble end.

35. For when Sulla, after the capture of Praeneste, was going to slaughter all the rest of the citizens but was letting that one man go on account of his guest-friendship,

36. The latter declared that he would not be indebted for his life to the slayer of his fatherland,

37. And then mingled with his fellow-citizens and was cut down with them.

Chapter 27

1. Deeming every public office to be something great and important, we should respect one who holds an office, and understand the difficulty of its performance;

2. But the honour of an office resides in honesty and diligence, and in concord with colleagues, much more than in titles and uniforms or a purple-bordered robe.

3. But those who consider that serving together in a campaign or in school is the beginning of friendship,

4. But regard joint service in the generalship or other office as the cause of enmity, have failed to avoid one of the three evils;

5. For either they regard their colleagues as their equals and are themselves factious, or they envy them as their superiors, or despise them as their inferiors.

6. But a man ought to conciliate his superior, add prestige to his inferior, honour his equal,

7. And be affable and friendly to all, considering that they have been made all alike by vote of the people,

8. And that they bear goodwill towards one another as a heritage, from their country.

9. Scipio was criticised in Rome because, when he entertained his friends on a feast day, he did not include his colleague Mummius;

10. For even if in general the two men did not consider themselves friends,

11. On such occasions they usually thought it proper to show honour and friendliness to each other on account of their office.

12. Inasmuch, therefore, as the omission of so slight an act of courtesy brought a reputation for haughtiness to Scipio, a man in other respects admirable,

13. How can anyone be considered honourable and fair-minded who detracts from the dignity of a colleague in office,

14. Or maliciously flouts him by actions which reveal ambitious rivalry,

15. Or is so self-willed that he arrogates and annexes to himself everything, in short, at the expense of his colleague?

16. I recollect that when I was still a young man I was sent with another as envoy to the proconsul;

17. The other man was somehow left behind. I alone met the proconsul and accomplished the business.

18. Now when I came back and was to make the report of our mission, my father left his seat and told me in private not to say 'I went', but 'we went',

19. Not 'I said', but 'we said', and in all other ways to associate my colleague in a joint report.

20. For that sort of thing is not only honourable and kind, but it also takes the sting out of any envy of our reputation.

21. Most people say and believe that it is the business of political teaching to cause men to be good subjects;

22. For, they say, the subject class is in every state larger than the ruling class;

23. And each official rules but a short time, whereas he is ruled all the time, if he is a citizen of a democracy;

24. So that it is a most excellent and useful thing to learn to obey those in authority, even if they happen to

be deficient in power and reputation.

25. For it is absurd that in a tragedy the chief actor often makes his entrance after a hireling who takes third-class parts,

26. And addresses him in humble fashion just because the latter wears the diadem and sceptre,

27. But that in real affairs and in government the rich and famous man belittles and despises the official who is plebeian and poor,

28. Thereby using his own high standing to insult and destroy that of the state, instead of enhancing it rather and adding to the office the esteem and power derived from himself.

29. So at Sparta the kings gave precedence to the ephors,

30. And if any other Spartans were summoned, they did not walk slowly in obeying the summons,

31. But by running eagerly at full speed through the marketplace they exhibited to their fellow-citizens their rejoicing in paying honour to the state.

32. They did not behave like some uncultured and unmannerly persons who, as if swaggering in the excess of their own power,

33. Abuse the umpires at the games, revile the chorus at festivals and jeer at generals and gymnasiarchs,

34. Not knowing and not understanding that it is often more glorious to pay honour than to receive it.

35. For to a man who has great power

in the state greater distinction accrues through serving in the bodyguard and the escort of an official than through being so served and escorted by him,

36. Or rather the latter brings him dislike and envy, but the former brings true reputation, that which comes from goodwill;

37. And by being seen sometimes at the official's door, by greeting him first, and by putting him in the best place in walking alongside him,

38. A man adds lustre to the state without taking anything from himself.

39. It is also a service to the people sometimes to endure the evil speech and anger of a man in office,

40. Putting off requital to the right time; for then either we shall respond to him after his term of office is ended,

41. Or in the delay our gain will be the cessation of anger.

Chapter 28

1. One should, however, deal always and with every official in zeal, forethought for the common good, and wisdom;

2. If they are worthy men, voluntarily suggesting and pointing out to them things to be done, and allowing them to make use of well-considered ideas so that they will be held in high esteem as benefactors of the community.

3. But if there is in them any

reluctance, delay or ill-will in putting such suggestions into effect,

4. Then one ought to come forward oneself and address the people,

5. And not neglecting or slighting the public interests on the ground that because someone else is in office it is not proper for him to meddle in the administration of affairs.

6. For the law always gives the first rank in the government to him who does what is right and recognises what is advantageous.

7. For example: there was in the army a man named Xenophon, neither a general nor a captain,

8. But perceiving what was needed and daring to do it, he put himself in command and saved the Greeks.

9. Certainly it is good to make innovations, not for the sake of small or casual matters, but in cases of necessity, or for glorious causes,

10. As Epameinondas did when contrary to the law he added four months to his tenure of office, in which time he invaded Laconia and carried out his measures at Messene;

11. So that if any accusation or blame be brought against us on this account we may have necessity as our defence,

12. Or the greatness and glory of the action as compensation for the risk.

13. A saying is recorded of Jason, monarch of Thessaly, which he always repeated when taking punitive measures against individuals:

14. 'It is inevitable that those should act unjustly in small matters who wish to act justly in great matters.'

15. This is recognisable at once as the saying of a despot; a far more statesmanlike precept is this:

16. 'Win the favour of the people by giving way in small things in order that in greater matters you may oppose them stubbornly and thus prevent them from committing errors.'

17. For a statesman who is always very exact and strenuous about everything,

18. Never yielding at all, but always inexorable,

19. Gets the people into the habit of opposing him and being out of temper with him.

20. It is better that he sometimes joins them graciously, as at public games and spectacles in the theatre, and sometimes pretends not to see or hear their errors,

21. Just as we treat the errors of the young people in a family, in order that the force of rebukes – like that of a medicine – may not become exhausted or stale, but may in matters of greater importance retain its full strength and credit.

22. He thereby takes a stronger hold upon the people and persuades them into compliance.

23. But to the people the statesman will, so far as is possible, permit no outrageous conduct towards the citizens,

24. No confiscation of others' property,

nor distribution of public funds, but by persuasion, arguments and law he will oppose desires of that sort.

25. For by nourishing and increasing such destructive desires Cleon and his partisans produced in the state, as Plato says, 'a swarm of drones with stings'.

Chapter 29

1. When something important and useful but requiring much conflict and serious effort is to be accomplished,

2. Try to select from among your friends those who are most powerful, or from among the most powerful those who are easiest to get along with;

3. For they are least likely to act against you and most likely to work with you, if they possess wisdom without contentiousness.

4. And, moreover, you should know your own nature, so that for any purpose for which you are naturally less fitted than others, choose as colleagues men who are more able than yourself,

5. As Diomedes, about to go on a scouting expedition, chose as companions men of prudence and passed over the men of courage.

6. For actions are thus more equally balanced, and contention does not arise among men whose ambitions proceed from different virtues and abilities.

7. So, if you are not a good speaker, take an orator as your assistant in a lawsuit or your colleague in an embassy;

8. If you are too lofty of speech and not persuasive in addressing the masses, choose a man who is winning and conciliatory in his oratory;

9. And if you are physically weak and incapable of hard work, choose a strong man who is fond of labour, as Nicias chose Lamachus.

10. So statesmen, by uniting for one purpose not only men's persons and funds,

11. But also their abilities and virtues, if they are in agreement, can gain greater reputation in connection with the same action than by other means.

12. Ambition, although it is a more pretentious word than 'covetousness', is no less pernicious in the state;

13. For there is more daring in it; one does not find it in slothful and abject people, but in the most vigorous and impetuous,

14. And the surge which comes from the masses, raising ambition on the crest of the wave and sweeping it along by shouts of praise, often makes it unrestrained and unmanageable.

15. Therefore, just as Plato said that young people should be told from childhood that it is not proper to ornament their bodies,

16. Because within they possess virtue, a far more precious thing,

17. So let us moderate ambition, saying
that we have in ourselves honour,
an ornament uncorrupted, undefiled and unpolluted by envy and
fault-finding,

18. Which increases along with
reasoning and forethought
concerning our acts and public
measures.

19. Therefore we have no need of
honours painted, modelled or cast
in bronze, in which even that
which is admired is really the work
of another;

20. For the person who has a public
statue raised to him is not the main
object of admiration, but instead it
is the sculptor who is praised.

21. When Rome was beginning to be
full of portrait statues, Cato refused
to let one be made of himself,
saying,

22. 'I prefer to have people ask why
there is not a statue of me rather
than why there is one.'

23. Such honours arouse envy, and the
people think that they are themselves under obligations to men
who have not received honours,

24. But that those who have received
them are oppressors of the people,
being in effect men who demand
payment for their services.

25. But if it is not easy to reject some
mark offered by the kindly sentiment of the people, when it is so
inclined, then one may accept a
dignified reward;

26. A mere inscription suffices, a tablet,
a decree or a green branch such as

27. Epimenides received from the
Acropolis after saving the city.

27. Anaxagoras, giving up the honours
which had been granted him,
requested that on the day of his
death the children be allowed a day
off school.

28. And to the seven Persians who
killed the usurping Magi, the
privilege was granted that they and
their descendants should wear their
headdress tilted forward over the
forehead; for this was their secret
sign when they undertook their act.

29. And there is something that
indicates public-mindedness, too,
about the honour received by
Pittacus;

30. For, when he was told to take as
much as he wished of the land
which he had gained for the
citizens,

31. He took only as much as he could
throw a javelin over.

32. And the Roman Cocles received as
much as he – and he was lame
– could plough around in one day.

33. For the honour should not be
payment for the action, but a
symbol, that it may last for a long
time, as those just mentioned have
lasted.

34. But of all the three hundred statues
of Demetrius of Phalerum, not one
lasted; they were all destroyed while
he was still living; and those of
Demades were melted down into
chamber pots.

35. Things like that have happened to
many honours, they having become

offensive, not only because the recipient was worthless, but also because the gift bestowed was too great.

36. And therefore the best and surest way to ensure the duration of honours is to reduce their cost;

37. Those that are great and top-heavy are, like ill-proportioned statues, quickly overturned.

38. The statesman will not despise the true honour and favour founded upon the goodwill of those who remember his actions,

39. Nor will he disdain reputation and avoid 'pleasing his neighbours', as Democritus demanded.

40. For not even the greeting of dogs nor the affection of horses is to be spurned by huntsmen and horse-trainers,

41. But it is both advantageous and pleasant to instil into animals which live with us such a disposition towards us as is welcome.

42. We lead unruly horses and runaway dogs by force of bits and dog-collars;

43. But nothing makes a man willingly tractable and gentle to another man except trust in his goodwill and belief in his nobility and justice.

44. And therefore Demosthenes is right in declaring that the greatest safeguard states possess against tyrants is distrust;

45. For that part of the mind with which we trust is most easily taken captive.

Chapter 30

1. The first and most important advantage to the reputation of statesmen is the trust which gave them an entrance into public affairs;

2. And the second is the goodwill of the multitude, which is a weapon of defence for the good against the slanderous and wicked, keeping off envy.

3. In the matter of power, make the low-born equal to the nobles, the poor to the rich, and the private citizen to the office-holders.

4. When truth and virtue are added to this, the goodwill that results will be a steady fair wind behind one's endeavours.

5. Of all kinds of love, that which is engendered in states and peoples for an individual because of his virtue is at once the strongest and best;

6. But those falsely named and falsely granted honours derived from giving theatrical performances, making distributions of money or offering gladiatorial shows, are like harlots' flatteries,

7. Since the masses always smile upon him who gives to them and does them favours, granting him an ephemeral and uncertain reputation.

8. And so he who first said that the people were ruined by the first man who bought his favour was well aware that the multitude loses its strength when it succumbs to bribe-taking;

9. But those also who give such bribes should bear in mind that they are destroying themselves when they purchase reputation by great expenditures,

10. Thus making the multitude strong and bold in the thought that they have power to give and take away something important.

11. We ought not, however, on this account to be niggardly about the customary public contributions, if we are in prosperous circumstances;

12. Since the masses are more hostile to a rich man who does not give them a share of his private possessions than to a poor man who steals from the public funds,

13. For they think the former's conduct is due to arrogance and contempt of them, but the latter's to necessity.

14. First, then, let the gifts be made without bargaining for anything; for so they gladden the recipients more completely;

15. And secondly they should be given for a worthwhile reason connected with the public good, for example, education;

16. For at the same time there springs up in the minds of the masses a strong disposition to associate the benefaction with real benefit.

17. Just as Plato wished to withhold the Lydian and the Ionian musical modes from the education of the young,

18. Because the first arouses a sense of mourning and grief, and the second arouses feelings of pleasure and lasciviousness,

19. So you must, if possible, remove from the state all those free exhibitions which excite and nourish the murderous and brutal or the scurrilous and greedy appetites,

20. Or if you cannot do that, avoid them and oppose the multitude when they demand them.

21. But always make the objects of your expenditures useful and moderate, having as their purpose either what is good or what is necessary,

22. Or at any rate what is pleasant and agreeable without anything harmful or outrageous in it.

23. But if your property is moderate and in relation to your needs strictly circumscribed,

24. It is neither ignoble nor humiliating at all to confess your poverty and to withdraw from among those who have the means for public expenditures,

25. Instead of borrowing money and making yourself at once a pitiful and a ridiculous object in the matter of your public contributions;

26. For men are plainly seen to lack resources when they keep annoying their friends or truckling to money-lenders;

27. So that it is not reputation or power, but rather shame and contempt, which they acquire by such expenditures.

28. And therefore it is always desirable

in connection with such things to remember Lamachus and Phocion;

29. For the latter, when the Athenians called upon him to contribute and repeatedly raised a clamour, said,

30. 'I should be ashamed if I gave you a contribution and did not pay Callicles here what I owe him,'

31. Pointing to his money-lender. And Lamachus always, when he was general, entered in his accounts money for shoes and a cloak for himself.

32. It is not ignoble to confess poverty, and poor men, if by reason of their virtue they enjoy freedom of speech and public confidence,

33. Have no less influence in their cities than those who give public entertainments and exhibitions.

34. The statesman must, then, do his best to control himself in such matters and not go down into the plain on foot to fight with cavalry;

35. If he is poor, he must not produce foot-races, theatrical shows and banquets in competition with the rich for reputation and power,

36. But he should vie with those who try always to lead the state on the strength of virtue and wisdom, combined with reason,

37. For in such are found not only nobility and dignity, but also the power to win and attract the people, a thing 'more desirable than gold coins of Croesus'.

Chapter 31

1. For the good man is neither presumptuous nor offensive, and the prudent man is not over-blunt in his speech,

2. But in the first place he is affable and generally accessible and approachable for all,

3. Keeping his house always unlocked as a harbour of refuge for those in need, and showing his solicitude and friendliness,

4. Not only by acts of service, but also by sharing the griefs of those who fail and the joys of those who succeed;

5. And he is in no way disagreeable or offensive by reason of the number of servants who attend him at the bath or by appropriating seats at the theatre,

6. Nor is he conspicuous for invidious exhibitions of luxury and extravagance;

7. But he is on an equal level with others in his clothing and daily life,

8. In the bringing up of his children and as regards the servants who wait upon his wife,

9. As one who wishes to live like the masses and be friendly with them.

10. And, moreover, he shows himself a kindly counsellor, an advocate who accepts no fee, and a kind-hearted conciliator when husbands are at variance with their wives or friends with one another.

11. He spends no small part of the day engaged in the public business on the orators' platform of the senate or the assembly,

12. And thenceforth all the rest of his life he draws services and commissions from every quarter.

13. But since he is always devoting his thoughts to the public weal and regards public office as his life and his work, not, like most people, as an interruption to leisure and a compulsory expense,

14. By all these and similar qualities he turns and attracts the people towards himself,

15. For they see that the flatteries and enticements of others are spurious and counterfeit when compared with his care and forethought.

16. The multitude, even if at first they reject a good and wise man,

17. Afterwards, when they have become acquainted with his truthfulness and his character, consider him alone a statesmanlike, public-minded man and a ruler,

18. Whereas they consider and call the others, one a provider of choruses, one a giver of banquets, and one a director of athletics.

19. Then, just as at banquets, though Callias or Alcibiades pay the bill, it is Socrates to whom they listen, and Socrates on whom all eyes are turned,

20. So in states in which the conditions are sound Ismenias makes contributions, Lichas gives dinners and Niceratus provides choruses,

21. But it is Epameinondas, Aristeides and Lysander who are the rulers, public men and generals.

22. So, observing these things, we must not be humiliated or overwhelmed by the reputation with the masses gained from theatres, kitchens and assembly halls,

23. Remembering that it lasts but a short time and ends the minute the gladiatorial and dramatic shows are over, since there is nothing honourable or dignified in it.

Chapter 32

1. Those who are skilled in keeping bees think that the hive which hums loudest is thriving and in good condition;

2. But he who has the care of the rational and political swarm will judge its happiness chiefly by their quietness and tranquillity.

3. He will accept and imitate to the best of his ability the other precepts of Solon,

4. But will wonder in great perplexity why that great man prescribed that in case of factional disorder whoever joined neither faction should be deprived of civic rights.

5. For in a body afflicted with disease, the beginning of a change to health does not come from the diseased parts,

6. But it comes when the condition in the healthy parts gains strength and drives out that which is contradictory to nature;

7. And in a people afflicted with faction, if it is not dangerous and destructive but is destined to cease sometime, there must be a strong

and permanent admixture of sanity and soundness;

8. For to this element there flows from the men of understanding what is akin to it, and then it permeates the part which is diseased;

9. But states which have fallen into disorder are ruined unless they meet with some external necessity and chastisement,

10. And are thus forcibly compelled by their misfortunes to be reasonable.

11. Yet certainly it is not fitting in time of disorder to sit without feeling or grief,

12. Singing the praises of your own impassiveness and of the inactive and blessed life, and rejoicing in the follies of others;

13. On the contrary, at such times you should by all means put on the buskin of Theramenes, conversing with both parties and joining neither;

14. For you will appear to be, not an outsider by not joining in wrongdoing,

15. But a common partisan of all by coming to their aid;

16. And your not sharing in their misfortunes will not arouse envy, if it is plain that you sympathise with all alike.

17. But the best thing is to see to it in advance that factional discord shall never arise, and to regard this as the noblest function of what may be called the art of statesmanship.

18. For observe that the greatest blessings which states can enjoy – peace, liberty, plenty and concord – are not the easiest to achieve for long periods; and yet they are the most desirable and productive.

19. At such times the arts flourish, the young are educated, trade increases and with it prosperity for all,

20. The health of the people and the land increases, and the wise statesman who maintains equilibrium within the state and among its neighbours is praised by all, so long as the people count their blessings;

21. For the long continuance of such times makes the people grow lazy, restless, self-indulgent and ungrateful.

22. There remains, then, for the statesman, of those activities which fall within his province, only this – and it is the equal of any of the other good things:

23. Always to instil concord among those who dwell with him, and to remove strifes, discords and all enmity.

24. He will talk, as in the case of quarrels among friends, first with the persons who think they are the more aggrieved,

25. And will appear to share their feeling of wrong and anger;

26. Then he will try in this way to mollify them and teach them that those who let wrongs go unheeded are superior to those who are quarrelsome and try to compel and overcome others,

27. Not only in reasonableness and character, but also in wisdom and greatness of heart,

28. And that by yielding in a small thing they gain their point in the best and most important matters.

29. Then he will instruct his people both individually and collectively and will call attention to the weak condition of affairs,

30. In which it is best for wise men to accept one advantage. For what dominion, what glory is there for those who are victorious?

31. What sort of power is it which a small edict of a proconsul may annul or transfer to another man and which, even if it last, has nothing in it seriously worthwhile?

Chapter 33

1. For just as a conflagration does not often begin in public spaces, but some lamp left neglected in a house or some burnt rubbish in a back yard causes a great flame and works public destruction,

2. So disorder in a state is not always kindled by contentions about public matters,

3. But frequently differences arising from private affairs and offences pass thence into public life and throw the whole state into confusion.

4. Therefore it behoves the statesman above all things to remedy or prevent these,

5. That some of them may not arise at all and some may be quickly ended,

and others may not grow great and extend to public interests,

6. But may remain merely among the persons who are at odds with one another.

7. He should do this by noticing himself and pointing out to others that private troubles become the causes of public ones and small troubles of great ones,

8. If they are overlooked and do not in the beginning receive treatment or soothing counsel.

9. For example, at Syracuse there were two young men, intimate friends,

10. One of whom, being entrusted with his friend's beloved for safe keeping, seduced him while the other was away;

11. Then the latter, as if to repay outrage with outrage, committed adultery with the offender's wife.

12. Thereupon one of the elder men came forward in the senate and moved that both be banished before the state reap the result and be infected with enmity through them.

13. His motion, however, was not carried, and from this beginning disorder arose which caused great distress and overthrew the most excellent government.

14. Therefore the statesman should not despise such offences as may, like diseases in a person, spread quickly,

15. But he should take hold of them, suppress them and cure them.

16. For by attention, as Cato says, the great is made small and the small is reduced to nothing.

17. And for this there is no more persuasive device than for the statesman to show himself in his private differences mild and conciliatory,

18. Persisting without anger in his original reasons for disagreement, and treating no one with contentiousness, anger or any other passion which injects bitterness into disputes.

19. For we put soft gloves on the hands of those who compete in the boxing-school, that the contest may not have a fatal result, its blows being soft and not painful;

20. And in law suits against one's fellow-citizens it is better to treat the causes of disagreement pure and simple in one's pleading,

21. And not, by sharpening and poisoning matters with bad words, malice and threats, to make them incurable, great and of public importance.

22. For a man who acts with gentleness and care towards those with whom he has difficulties will find that others also yield to him;

23. And rivalries affecting public interests, if private enmities are done away with, become of slight importance and do no serious or incurable harm.

ACTS

Chapter 1

1. It has been well said that we should contemplate what the great did in the past, not just out of curiosity but to educate ourselves for the present.

2. Nobility and moral beauty have an active attraction, and invite all who live in later times to nobility again;

3. Not by imitation alone, but by stimulating thought about how to live, out of the bare contemplation of how some of the great once lived.

4. It is said, and rightly: to know what was done is to know better what to do now.

5. Nothing is more fitted to interest reflective minds than accounts of the variety of circumstance in human affairs,

6. Which, whether prompting admiration for achievement or lamentation for what was suffered, always offers instruction:

7. The untroubled recollection of past endeavours has a charm of its own to those who shared them,

8. While to those who did not share them, but who look upon them with interest and sympathy, there is much to be gained.

9. And yet those of great name are never faultless. Fame either heightens or hides flaws, so that memorials of them distort them into paragons or pariahs.

10. But why can there not be a juster appreciation of the alloy that is man, despite which some rise into the permanent annals of history,

11. Leaving their best achievements as examples to posterity, while we admit the base metal there inmixed?

12. The virtues of the great serve us as a looking glass, in which we may see how to adjust and adorn our own lives,

13. Their faults and frailties admonishing by example likewise, and the whole made of both serving as a manual of humanity.

14. Contemplating lives can be compared to associating with those we thus contemplate;

15. We receive and entertain in our inquiry each successive guest, view their qualities and select from their actions all that is noblest to know.

16. By the study of history and the familiarity acquired in writing, we habituate our memories to receive and retain images of the best and worthiest.

17. We are thus enabled to raise

thought above what is base to better examples of our forerunners famous for their success,

18. Who leave no doubt whether they owe their achievements to luck, or their own character and conduct.

19. Of the many portraits one might paint to this end, only a few are necessary,

20. For from the few one can discern the many.

Chapter 2: Lycurgus of Sparta

1. Lycurgus, the lawgiver of Sparta, was the second son of that city's king and younger brother of Polydectes, who became king after their father's death.

2. Their father was killed in a riot, for Sparta was then troubled with faction, the people unruly and undisciplined;

3. And the father of Lycurgus and Polydectes was stabbed by one of his subjects while trying to bring order.

4. Soon afterwards Polydectes died also, leaving the right of succession to Lycurgus; and reign he did, until it was discovered that Polydectes' widow was pregnant;

5. Upon which Lycurgus immediately declared that the kingdom belonged to her issue, if it were male, and that he himself exercised authority only as the child's guardian.

6. A secret overture was made to him by the queen, that she would destroy the infant, on condition that he would marry her when he came to the crown.

7. Abhorring the woman's wickedness, Lycurgus pretended not to reject her proposal,

8. But, making show of agreeing, dispatched a messenger with thanks,

9. And to dissuade her from aborting herself, which would impair her health, if not endanger her life, he himself, he said, would ensure that the child should be killed as soon as born.

10. By such artifices having drawn on the woman to her time of birth, when he heard that she was in labour, he sent persons to observe all that passed,

11. With orders that if it were a girl they should give it to the women, but if a boy, they should bring it to him wherever he was, and whatever doing.

12. He was at supper with the principal magistrates when the queen produced a boy, who was immediately brought to him at the table;

13. He, taking him into his arms, announced: 'Men of Sparta, here is our king';

14. And laid the child in the king's place, and named him Charilaus, that is, joy of the people;

15. Because all were transported with joy at Lycurgus' noble heart. His reign had lasted only eight months, but he was honoured by the citizens,

16. Who obeyed him because of his

virtues more than because he was regent.

17. Some, however, envied and opposed his growing influence; chiefly the kindred of the queen mother, who pretended to have been treated injuriously.

18. Her brother Leonidas, in a heated debate with Lycurgus, said he was certain they would soon see the latter king,

19. Thus suggesting suspicions and preparing the way for an accusation of him.

20. Similar hints were spread about by the queen mother and her adherents.

21. Troubled by this, and suspecting the outcome, Lycurgus thought it wisest to avoid their envy by a voluntary exile,

22. And to travel abroad until his nephew reached marriageable age, and, by having a son, secured the succession.

23. Setting sail, therefore, he first went to Crete, where, having considered the different city governments there,

24. And having made acquaintance with their principal men, he resolved to make use in Sparta of those of their laws he admired, though much he rejected as useless.

25. Among the persons there renowned for learning and wisdom in state matters was one Thales,

26. Who though by outward

profession a poet, was one of the ablest lawgivers in the world.

27. Lycurgus persuaded Thales to go to Sparta, where the songs he composed, which were exhortations to discipline and concord,

28. And the measure and cadence of the verse conveying order and tranquillity,

29. Had so great an influence on the listeners, that they were insensibly softened and civilised,

30. Insomuch that they renounced their private feuds and animosities, and were reunited in common virtue.

31. So that it may truly be said that Thales prepared the way for Lycurgus' later reforms.

32. From Crete Lycurgus sailed to Asia, with design, as is said, to examine the difference between the societies of the Cretans, which were sober and temperate, and those of the Ionians, a people of luxurious habits.

33. Here he first read Homer's works, in the library of the family of Creophylus;

34. And having observed that they contained serious lessons of state and morality, set himself eagerly to transcribe and order them, thinking they would be of good use in his own country.

35. They had, indeed, already obtained some slight repute among the Greeks, and scattered portions, as chance conveyed them, were in the hands of individuals;

36. But Lycurgus first made Homer's works really known.
37. The Egyptians say that he visited them, and some Greek writers also record this.
38. But as for his voyages into Spain, Africa and the Indies, and his conferences there with the Gymnosophists, there is slender evidence only.
39. Lycurgus was much missed at Sparta, and often sent for, 'for we have kings', they said, 'with the name of royalty, but as for the qualities of their minds, they are no different from their subjects';
40. Adding, that in him alone was the true foundation of sovereignty: a nature made to rule, and a genius to gain obedience.
41. The kings too wished him home, for they looked on his presence as a bulwark against the people.

Chapter 3

1. So Lycurgus returned, and finding matters in bad posture, applied himself to a thorough reformation,
2. Resolving to change the whole face of the commonwealth; for what could a few new laws only, and a partial alteration, avail?
3. He resolved to act as physicians do in the case of a patient suffering a complication of diseases:
4. By force of medicine reducing and exhausting him, to change his whole temperament, and put him on a totally new regimen.
5. Having resolved that his laws should be the best, and the resulting commonwealth the most famous in the world,
6. He set himself to make allies of the leading Spartans, exhorting their help in his great undertaking.
7. He described the plan first to his particular friends, and then, by degrees, gained others, and animated them all to his designs.
8. When all was ripe for action, he gave orders to thirty of his principal allies to be ready armed at the marketplace at dawn, in order to quell the opposite party.
9. Things growing to a tumult, King Charilaus, thinking this a conspiracy against his person, took sanctuary;
10. But, being soon after undeceived, and having the promise of their loyalty, quitted his refuge and joined them.
11. Among the many changes Lycurgus now made, the first and greatest in importance was the establishment of a senate,
12. Which having a power equal to the king's, and, as Plato expresses it, allaying and qualifying the fiery strength of the royal office, gave steadiness and safety to the commonwealth.
13. For the state, which before had no firm basis, but leaned sometimes towards absolute monarchy and sometimes towards mob rule, found in the senate a central weight, like ballast in a ship;
14. The twenty-eight senators

supporting the kings against the people, but supporting the people against royal absolutism.

15. The senate had no building to meet in. Lycurgus thought that ornament was not a help but a hindrance in their counsels,

16. By diverting their attention from the business before them to statues and pictures,

17. And to roofs curiously fretted, the usual embellishments of such places among the other Greeks.

18. The people assembled in the open air, and heard the kings and senators.

19. It was not allowed to any of their order to give advice, but only either to ratify or reject what was proposed to them by the king or senate.

20. But because it happened afterwards that the people, by adding or omitting words, perverted the sense of propositions,

21. The kings inserted into the Rhetra, or grand covenant, a clause saying that if the people did this it would be lawful for the leaders to refuse ratification.

22. Although Lycurgus had used all the qualifications possible in the constitution of his commonwealth,

23. Yet those who succeeded him found the oligarchical element still too dominant,

24. And to check its high temper, established the office of ephor, a hundred and thirty years after Lycurgus' death.

25. Elatus and his colleagues were the first who had this dignity conferred upon them in the reign of King Theopompus,

26. Who, when his queen criticised him one day that he would leave the regal power less than he had received it from his ancestors, said in answer, 'No, it will be greater; for it will last longer.'

27. For, indeed, the kings' prerogative being thus reduced within reasonable bounds, they were at once freed from jealousies and consequent danger,

28. And never experienced the calamities of their neighbours at Messene and Argos,

29. Who, by maintaining the royal prerogative too strictly for want of yielding a little to the populace, lost all.

30. Indeed, whoever will examine the sedition and misgovernment in the bordering nations to whom Sparta was near related in blood and situation, will find in them the best reason to admire the wisdom of Lycurgus.

31. For these three states, in their first rise, were equal, or, if there were any odds, they lay on the side of the Messenians and Argives,

32. Who, in the first allotment, were thought to have been luckier than the Spartans; yet their happiness did not endure,

33. Partly the tyrannical temper of their kings and partly the ungovernableness of the people quickly

bringing upon them such disorders,

34. As clearly to show how truly great a blessing the Spartans had had in Lycurgus.

35. After the creation of the senators, Lycurgus' next task, and indeed the most hazardous, was a new division of lands.

36. For there was an extreme inequality among the people;

37. Their state was overloaded with indigent and necessitous persons, while its whole wealth had centred upon very few.

38. To expel from the state arrogance and envy, luxury and crime,

39. And those yet more inveterate diseases of want and superfluity,

40. Lycurgus therefore persuaded rich and poor alike to renounce their properties,

41. And to accept a new division of the land, so that all should live together on an equal footing;

42. Merit to be their only road to eminence, and the disgrace of evil, and credit of worthy acts, the one measure of difference between man and man.

43. Upon their consent, he divided the country into thirty thousand equal shares, and the area around the city of Sparta into nine thousand; these he redistributed.

44. A share was enough to yield seventy bushels of grain annually for a man, and twelve for his wife, with a suitable proportion of oil and wine.

45. This he thought sufficient to keep their bodies in health and strength; superfluities they were better without.

46. It is reported, that, as he returned from a journey shortly after the land redistribution, the ground being newly reaped, seeing the stacks all standing equal and alike, he smiled, and said,

47. 'Laconia looks like one family estate divided among a band of brothers.'

Chapter 4

1. Not contented with this, he resolved to make a division of movables too, that there might be no odious distinction or inequality left amongst them;

2. But finding that it would be dangerous to do it openly, he defeated their avarice by the following stratagem:

3. He commanded that all gold and silver coin should be called in, and that only money made of iron should be current, a great weight and quantity of which was worth little;

4. So that to lay up twenty or thirty pounds required a large closet, and to move it nothing less than a yoke of oxen.

5. With the diffusion of this money, a number of vices were at once banished;

6. For who would steal, or accept as a bribe, a thing which it was not easy to hide, nor a credit to have?

7. In the next place, Lycurgus outlawed all superfluous arts; but here he might have spared his pains, for they would have gone of themselves after the gold and silver, the money which remained being not so proper payment for curious work;

8. For, being of iron, it was scarcely portable, neither could they use it to buy from other Greeks, who ridiculed it.

9. So there was now no way of purchasing foreign goods and small wares;

10. Merchants sent no shiploads into Laconian ports; no rhetoric master, no itinerant medicine man, no harlot monger, silver-smith, engraver or jeweller, set foot in a country which had no money;

11. So that luxury, deprived little by little of that which fed and fomented it, died away of itself.

12. For the rich had no advantage here over the poor, as their expensive possessions were shut up at home doing nothing.

13. In this way the Spartans became excellent artists in ordinary and necessary things:

14. Beds, chairs and tables, and such staple utensils in a family, were admirably well made there;

15. Their cup, particularly, was much in demand, and eagerly bought up by soldiers, as Critias reports;

16. For its colour was such as to prevent water, drunk upon necessity and disagreeable to look at, from being noticed;

17. And its shape was such that the mud stuck to the sides, so that only the cleaner part came to the drinker's mouth.

18. For this also, they had to thank their lawgiver, who, by relieving the artisans of the trouble of making useless things,

19. Set them to show their skill in giving beauty to things of daily use.

Chapter 5

1. The third and most masterly stroke of this great lawgiver, by which he delivered a yet more effective blow against luxury and the desire of riches,

2. Was the ordinance he made that they should all eat in common, of the same bread and meat,

3. And should not spend their lives at home, lying on costly couches at splendid tables,

4. Delivering themselves into the hands of their tradesmen and cooks, to fatten like greedy brutes,

5. And to ruin not only their minds but their bodies which, enfeebled by indulgence, would stand in need of long sleep, warm bathing, freedom from work,

6. And, in a word, as much care and attendance as if they were continu-ally sick.

7. It was certainly an extraordinary thing to have brought about such a result,

8. But a greater yet to have taken

away from wealth, as Theophrastus observes, not merely the property of being coveted, but its very nature of being wealth.

9. For the rich, being obliged to go to the same table as the poor, could not make use of their abundance, nor so much as please their vanity by looking at or displaying it.

10. The common table ordinance in particular exasperated the wealthier men.

11. They collected in a body against Lycurgus, and from ill words came to throwing stones,

12. So that at length he was forced to run out of the marketplace, and seek sanctuary to save his life.

13. He managed to outrun all except one Alcander, a young man otherwise not ill accomplished, but hasty and violent, who came up so close to him,

14. That when Lycurgus turned to see who was near, Alcander struck his face with a stick, and put out one of his eyes.

15. Lycurgus, so far from being daunted by this accident, stopped short and showed his disfigured face and eye to his countrymen;

16. They, ashamed at the sight, escorted him safely home, and delivered Alcander into his hands to be punished.

17. Lycurgus, having thanked them, dismissed them all, except Alcander;

18. And, taking him with him into his house, neither did nor said anything severely to him, but bade Alcander to wait on him at table.

19. The young man, who was of an ingenuous temper, without murmuring did as he was commanded;

20. And being thus admitted to live with Lycurgus, he had an opportunity to observe in him, besides his gentleness and calmness, an extraordinary sobriety and an indefatigable industry,

21. And so, from an enemy, became one of his most zealous admirers.

Chapter 6

1. The public repast of Sparta had several names in Greek; the Cretans called them 'andria', because the men only came to them.

2. The Lacedaemonians called them 'phiditia', that is, by changing l into d, the same as 'philitia', love feasts, because by eating and drinking together they had opportunity of making friends.

3. Or perhaps from 'phido', parsimony, because they were so many schools of sobriety.

4. Or perhaps the first letter is an addition, and the word at first was 'editia', from 'edode', eating.

5. They met by companies of about fifteen, and each of them stood bound to bring in monthly a bushel of meal, eight gallons of wine, five pounds of cheese, two pounds and a half of figs and a

small sum of money for meat or fish.

6. Besides this, when any of them had been hunting, he donated a part of the venison he had killed;

7. For such occasions were the only excuses allowed for supping at home.

8. The custom of eating together was observed strictly for a great while afterwards;

9. Insomuch that King Agis himself, after having vanquished the Athenians, sending for his commons at home, because he desired to eat privately with his queen, was refused by the polemarchs; when he complained they made him pay a fine.

10. The Spartans sent their children to these tables as to schools of temperance;

11. Here they were instructed in state affairs by listening to experienced statesmen;

12. Here they learned to converse with pleasantry, to make jests without scurrility, and to take teasing without ill humour.

13. In this point of good breeding the Lacedaemonians excelled particularly, but if any man were uneasy under it, upon the least hint given, no more was said to him.

14. It was customary also for the eldest in the company to say to each of them, as they came in, 'Through this' (pointing to the door) 'no words go out.'

15. When anyone desired to be admitted into any of these little societies, he was to go through the following probation:

16. Each man in the company took a little ball of soft bread, which they were to throw into a basin carried by a waiter on his head.

17. Those favouring the candidate dropped their ball into the basin without altering its figure;

18. Those who disliked him flattened it between their fingers, and this signified a negative vote.

19. If there were just one of these flattened pieces in the basin, the suitor was rejected, so desirous were they that all the members of the company should be agreeable to each other.

20. The basin was called 'caddichus', and the rejected candidate had a name thence derived.

21. The most famous dish of the common table was black broth, which was so much valued that the older men fed only upon that, leaving the meat to the younger men.

22. After drinking moderately, every man went home without lights,

23. For the use of them was forbidden, so that they might accustom themselves to march boldly in the dark.

Chapter 7

1. Lycurgus would never put his laws into writing; there is a Rhetra expressly forbidding it.

2. For he thought that the most

material points, being imprinted on the hearts of the youth by a good discipline, would be sure to remain, and would find a stronger security there.

3. It was his design that education should effect every end and object of the law.

4. And as for things of lesser importance, as pecuniary contracts and such like, the forms of which have to be changed as occasion requires,

5. He thought it best to prescribe no positive rules, willing that they should be alterable according to circumstances, as determined by men of sound judgement.

6. One of the Rhetras was, that their laws should not be written;

7. Another was particularly levelled against luxury, for by it was ordained that the ceilings of the houses should only be wrought by the axe, and their gates and doors smoothed only by the saw.

8. Epameinondas' famous dictum about his own table, that 'Treason and a plain dinner like this do not keep company together,' may be said to have been anticipated by Lycurgus, for luxury and a plain house could not well be companions.

9. He would lack sense who would furnish simple rooms with silver-footed couches, purple coverlets and gold plate.

10. Doubtless Lycurgus had good reason to think that they would proportion their beds to their houses, and their coverlets to their beds, and the rest of their goods and furniture to these.

11. It is reported that King Leotychides, the first of that name, was so little used to the sight of any kind of decorated work,

12. That, being entertained at Corinth in a stately room, he was much surprised to see the timber and ceiling so finely carved, and asked his host whether the trees grew so in his country.

13. A third ordinance of Rhetra was, that they should not make war often, or long, with the same enemy,

14. Lest they should train and instruct them in war, by habituating them to defend themselves.

15. And this is what Agesilaus was blamed for, a long time after; it being thought that, by his continual incursions into Boeotia, he made the Thebans a match for the Spartans;

16. And therefore Antalcidas, seeing him wounded one day, said that he was well paid for making the Thebans good soldiers despite themselves.

17. For the good education of the youth, which Lycurgus thought the most important and noblest work of a lawgiver,

18. He went so far back as to take into consideration their very conception and birth, by regulating marriages.

19. Aristotle is wrong in saying that,

after Lycurgus had tried all ways to reduce the women to more modesty and sobriety, he was at last forced to leave them as they were,

20. Because in the absence of their husbands, who spent the best part of their lives away at war, their wives, whom they had to leave absolute mistresses at home,

21. Took great liberties and assumed the superiority; and were treated with overmuch respect and called by the title of lady or queen.

22. The truth is, Lycurgus took in their case, also, all the care that was possible;

23. He ordered the maidens to exercise themselves with wrestling, running, throwing the discus and casting the dart,

24. To the end that the fruit they conceived might, in strong and healthy bodies, take firmer root and find better growth,

25. And that with this greater vigour, might better undergo the pains of childbearing.

26. And to take away their excessive tenderness and all acquired womanishness, he ordered that the girls should go naked in the processions, as well as the young men,

27. And dance, too, in that condition, at feasts, singing certain songs, while the young men stood around, seeing and hearing them.

28. On these occasions the maidens now and then made, by jests, a

reflection on those youths who had misbehaved themselves in the wars;

29. And again sang encomiums upon those who had acted gallantly, and by these means inspired the younger men with an emulation of their glory.

30. Those that were thus commended went away proud, elated and gratified with their honour among the maidens;

31. And those who were rallied were as sensibly touched as if they had been formally reprimanded;

32. So much the more, because the kings and the elders, as well as the rest of the city, saw and heard all that passed.

33. Nor was there anything shameful in this nakedness of the girls; modesty attended them, and all wantonness was excluded.

34. It taught them simplicity and a care for good health, and gave them some taste of higher feelings, admitted as they thus were to the field of noble action and glory.

35. Hence it was natural for them to think and speak as Gorgo, for example, the wife of Leonidas, is said to have done,

36. When some foreign lady told her that the women of Lacedaemon were the only women in the world who could rule men;

37. 'With good reason,' Gorgo replied, 'for we are the only women who bring forth men.'

38. These public processions of the

maidens, and their appearing naked in their exercises and dancings, were incitements to marriage,

39. Operating upon the young with the rigour and certainty, as Plato says, of love, if not of mathematics.

40. But besides all this, to promote it yet more effectually, those who continued bachelors were partly disfranchised by law;

41. For they were excluded from the public processions in which the young men and maidens danced naked,

42. And, in wintertime, the officers compelled them to march naked themselves round the marketplace,

43. Singing a song to their own disgrace, that they justly suffered this punishment for disobeying the law to marry and have children.

44. Moreover, they were denied the respect paid by younger men to their elders;

45. No man, for example, found fault with what was said to Dercyllidas, though so eminent a commander;

46. Upon whose approach one day a young man, instead of rising, retained his seat, remarking, 'No child of yours will make room for me.'

Chapter 8

1. In their marriages, the brides were never of tender years, but in their full bloom and ripeness.

2. After being carried off by her man, the bride had her hair clipped close, dressed in man's clothes, and lay on a mattress in the dark;

3. Afterwards came the bridegroom, in his everyday clothes, sober and composed, as having supped at the common table,

4. And, entering privately into the room where the bride lies, untied her virgin girdle, and took her to himself;

5. And, after staying some time together, he returned composedly to his own apartment, to sleep as usual with the other young men.

6. And so he continued to do, spending his days and nights with the young men, visiting his bride in secret, and with circumspection;

7. She, for her part, using her wit to find favourable opportunities for their meeting, when company was out of the way.

8. In this manner they lived a long time, insomuch that they sometimes had children by their wives before ever they saw their faces by daylight.

9. Their interviews, being thus difficult and rare, served not only for continual exercise of self-control,

10. But brought them together with their bodies healthy and vigorous, and their affections unsated and undulled by easy access and long continuance with each other;

11. While their partings were always early enough to leave unextinguished in each of them some remaining fire of longing and mutual delight.
12. After guarding marriage with this modesty and reserve, Lycurgus was equally careful to banish jealousy.
13. For this object, excluding all licentious disorders, he made it honourable for men to agree to their wives consorting with those they thought fit, that so they might have children by them;
14. Ridiculing those in whose opinion such favours are so wrong as to shed blood and go to war about it.
15. Lycurgus allowed a man who was advanced in years and had a young wife to recommend some virtuous and approved young man,
16. That she might have a child by him, who might inherit the good qualities of the father, and be a son to himself.
17. On the other side, an honest man who had love for a married woman upon account of her modesty and the well-favouredness of her children,
18. Might, without formality, beg her company of her husband, that he might raise, as it were, from this plot of good ground, worthy and well-allied children for himself.
19. And indeed, Lycurgus was of the view that children were not so much the property of their parents as of the whole commonwealth,
20. And therefore would not have his

citizens begot by the first-comers, but by the best men that could be found;
21. The laws of other nations seemed to him absurd and inconsistent, where people would be so solicitous for their dogs and horses as to exert interest and pay money to procure fine breeding,
22. And yet kept their wives shut up, to be made mothers only by themselves, who might be foolish, infirm or diseased;
23. As if it were not apparent that children of a bad breed would prove their bad qualities first upon those who were rearing them,
24. And well-born children, in like manner, their good qualities.
25. These regulations, founded on natural and social grounds, were certainly so far from that scandalous liberty which was afterwards charged upon Spartan women,
26. That they knew not what was meant by the word adultery.

Chapter 9

1. Nor was it in the power of the father to dispose of a newborn if he thought it unfit;
2. He had to carry it before assessors, whose business it was carefully to examine the infant;
3. If they found it healthy and vigorous, they gave order for its rearing, and allotted to it one of the nine thousand shares of land for its maintenance,
4. But, if they found it misbegotten,

they ordered it to be taken to the chasm called Apothetae,

5. Thinking it neither for the good of the child itself, nor in the public interest, that it should be brought up.

6. The women did not bathe the newborn children in water, as in other countries, but in wine, to prove the temper of their bodies,

7. From a notion that weakly children faint away upon their being thus bathed, while those who are strong acquire firmness by it.

8. Much care and art was used by the nurses; they had no swaddling bands;

9. The children grew up free and unconstrained in limb, not dainty about their food,

10. Not afraid in the dark, or of being left alone, and without peevishness or crying.

11. On this account Spartan nurses were valued in other countries.

12. Lycurgus would not have teachers bought out of the slave market, nor those who charged fees;

13. Nor could fathers themselves educate their children after their own fancy;

14. But when seven years old they were enrolled in companies where they lived under the same order and discipline, doing their exercises and playing together.

15. Of these, the one who made the best showing was made captain; they kept their eyes upon him,

16. So that their whole education was one continued exercise of ready and perfect obedience.

17. The older men were spectators of their performances, and often stirred disputes among them,

18. To find out their different characters, and see which would be valiant, which a coward, in real conflicts.

19. They taught them just enough reading and writing to serve;

20. The chief care was to make them good subjects and soldiers, and to teach them to endure pain and conquer in battle.

21. As they grew older their discipline was proportionately increased; their heads were close-clipped, they went barefoot and played naked.

22. After they were twelve years old, they were forbidden to wear undergarments, and made one coat last a year.

23. Their bodies were hard and dry, with little acquaintance of baths and unguents; these indulgences were allowed only on particular days in the year.

24. They lodged together in little bands upon beds made of the rushes from the River Eurotas.

25. If it were winter, they mingled some thistledown with the rushes for warmth.

26. By the time they reached this age none of the more hopeful boys

obeyed him and patiently accepted his discipline,

lacked a lover to bear him company.

27. The old men, too, had an eye upon them, coming often to the grounds to observe them contend in wit and strength,

28. And this with as much interest as if they were their fathers, tutors or magistrates;

29. So they were never without someone present to remind them of their duty, and punish neglect of it.

30. One of the best men in the city was appointed to take charge of them;

31. He arranged them into their bands, and chose their captains from among the most temperate and boldest of the Irens,

32. Who were usually twenty years old, two years out of the boys' group.

Chapter 10

1. A young man chosen as Iren was the boys' captain when they fought and their master at home,

2. Using them for the offices of his house; sending the eldest of them to fetch wood, and the less able to gather salads;

3. And these they must either go without or steal; which they did by getting cunningly into gardens or the eating-houses.

4. If they were caught they were whipped, not for stealing but for being found out.

5. They stole all the other food they could, watching all opportunities when people were asleep or careless.

6. If they were caught, they were punished not only by whipping but by hunger also,

7. Being reduced to their ordinary allowance, which was very slender,

8. This to induce them to help themselves and exercise their energy and cunning.

9. This hard and spare fare, and the work of getting it, had another purpose:

10. It conduced to beauty of shape; for a dry and lean habit is a better subject for nature's configuration, which the gross and overfed are too heavy to submit to properly.

11. Just as we find that women who take physic whilst they are with child bear leaner and smaller but better-shaped and prettier children.

12. So seriously did the Spartan children go about their stealing,

13. That it is reputed that a youth, having stolen a young fox and hid it under his coat,

14. Suffered it to tear out his very bowels with its teeth and claws, and died rather than let it be discovered.

15. The Iren used to stay with the boys after supper, and bade one of them to sing; to another he put a question requiring a thoughtful answer,

16. For example, who was the best

man in the city? What he thought of such an action of such a man?

17. Thus the boys were taught early to pass careful judgement on persons and things, and to keep themselves informed.

18. If they had not an answer ready they were looked upon as dull and careless, with little sense of honour;

19. Besides this, they were to give a good reason for what they said, and in as few and comprehensive words as possible.

20. He that failed of this, or answered not to the purpose, had his thumb bitten by the master.

21. Sometimes the Iren did this in the presence of the older men and magistrates, that they might see whether he punished them justly and proportionately,

22. And when he did amiss, they would not reprove him before the boys, but afterwards called him to account and corrected him.

Chapter 11

1. The boys' lovers and favourers, too, had a share in their honour or disgrace;

2. There goes a story that one of them was fined by the magistrates, because the lad he loved cried out effeminately when fighting.

3. And though this sort of love was approved among them, yet rivalry did not exist,

4. And if several men's fancies met in one person, it was rather the beginning of an intimate friendship,

5. In which they all jointly conspired to render the object of their affection as accomplished as possible.

6. They taught them, also, to speak with a natural and graceful raillery, and to comprehend much matter of thought in few words.

7. For Lycurgus disapproved of discourse which did not contain its matter in few words.

8. Children in Sparta, by habits of silence, came to give brief, just and sententious answers.

9. King Agis, when an Athenian laughed at the Spartans' short swords, and said that the jugglers on the stage swallowed them with ease, answered,

10. 'We find them long enough to reach our enemies.' As their swords were short and sharp, so were their sayings;

11. They reach the point and arrest the attention of hearers better than any.

12. Lycurgus spoke thus, as appears by his answer to one who would set up a democracy in Lacedaemon;

13. 'Begin, friend,' said he, 'and set it up in your family.'

14. When a man named Hecataeus was criticised for speaking not one word all suppertime, Archidamidas answered in his vindication,

15. 'He who knows how to speak, knows also when.'

Chapter 12

1. When they were at war the Spartans' exercises were generally more moderate, their fare not so hard, nor the rule of their officers so strict,

2. So that they were the only people in the world to whom war gave repose.

3. When their army was drawn up for battle, and the enemy near, the soldiers set their garlands on their heads, the pipers began to play and the king began the paean of advance.

4. It was both a magnificent and a terrible sight to see them march to their flutes, without any disorder in their ranks,

5. Without any discomposure in their minds, or change in their countenances; but calmly moving with the music towards the deadly fight.

6. Men, in this temper, were not likely to be afraid or furious, but deliberate in valour and assurance.

7. After they had routed an enemy, they pursued till they were assured of victory,

8. And then sounded a retreat, thinking it unworthy of Grecians to kill men who had yielded.

9. This manner of dealing with enemies not only showed magnanimity, but policy;

10. For, knowing that they killed only those who resisted, and gave quarter to the rest,

11. Opponents generally thought their best safety was surrender.

Chapter 13

1. The discipline of the Spartans continued after they were full-grown men.

2. No one was allowed to live after his own fancy; the city was a camp, in which every man had his share of provisions and business,

3. And looked upon himself as born to serve not himself but his country.

4. Therefore if they had no other duties, they went to see the boys exercising, to teach them something useful or to learn it better themselves.

5. Indeed, one of the highest blessings Lycurgus procured his people was the abundance of leisure which proceeded from his forbidding them to follow any mean or mechanical trade.

6. Of the money-making that depends on troublesome going about and doing business, they had no need in a state where wealth had no honour.

7. The Helots tilled their ground for them, and paid them yearly the appointed quantity, without any trouble of theirs.

8. Upon the prohibition of gold and silver, all lawsuits immediately ceased,

9. For there was now neither avarice nor poverty among them, but equality, where everyone's wants were supplied,

10. And independence, because those wants were so small.

11. All their time, except when at war, was taken up by the choral dances and festivals,

12. In hunting, and in attendance on the exercise-grounds and places of public conversation.

13. Those who were under thirty years were not allowed in the marketplace,

14. But had the necessaries of their family supplied by their relations and lovers;

15. Nor was it to the credit of older men to be seen too often in the marketplace;

16. It was esteemed more suitable for them to frequent the exercise-grounds and places of conversation, not money-making and watching market prices.

17. Thus Lycurgus bred up his citizens in such a way that they neither would nor could live by themselves;

18. They were to make themselves one with the public good.

19. To inure the young to the sight of death, Lycurgus allowed the citizens to bury their dead within the city,

20. So that their youth might be accustomed to such spectacles, and not be afraid to see a dead body,

21. Or fear to touch a corpse or to tread on a grave. The time appointed for mourning was eleven days and no more.

22. Thus Lycurgus cut off all superfluity, so in things necessary there was nothing so trivial which did

not express a homage to virtue or scorn of vice.

23. He filled Lacedaemon with examples of good conduct; with the constant sight of which, from their youth upwards, the people could hardly fail to be formed and advanced in virtue.

24. And this was the reason why he forbade them to travel abroad and go about acquainting themselves with foreign rules of morality, the habits of ill-educated people and different views of government.

25. And he banished from Lacedaemon all strangers who would not give good reason for coming there;

26. Not because he was afraid that they should learn anything to their good, but rather lest they should introduce something bad in example or teaching.

27. With strange people, strange words must be admitted; these novelties produce novelties in thought;

28. And on these follow views and feelings whose discordant character destroys the harmony of the state.

29. Lycurgus was as careful to save his city from the infection of foreign bad habits, as men usually are to prevent the introduction of the plague.

Chapter 14

1. I see no sign of unfairness in the laws of Lycurgus, though some

who grant that they make good soldiers, criticise them as lacking in justice.

2. Both Aristotle and Plato had this opinion alike of the lawgiver and his government,

3. And especially the ordinance by which the magistrates secretly dispatched some of the ablest young men into the countryside,

4. Carrying only daggers and some provisions, to hide in the daytime but to come out at night and kill all the Helots they could find;

5. And even sometimes murdering them by daylight, as they worked in the fields.

6. Aristotle, in particular, adds that the ephors, so soon as their office was created, used to declare war against the Helots,

7. That they might be massacred without a breach of law. It is confessed on all hands that the Spartans treated the Helots very badly;

8. For apart from the murders and cruelty committed upon them as just described,

9. It was common to force them to drink to excess, then lead them into their public halls, that the children might see what a sight a drunken man is;

10. They made them perform low dances and sing ridiculous songs, forbidding them expressly to meddle with any of a better kind.

11. And accordingly, when the Thebans invaded Laconia, and captured many Helots, they could by no means persuade them to sing the verses of Terpander, Alcman or Spendon,

12. 'For,' said the Helots, 'the masters do not like it.' As someone truly observed, in Sparta he who was free was most so, and he that was a slave there, was the greatest slave in the world.

13. I think these outrages on the Helots began at a later time, after the great earthquake, when the Helots made a general insurrection,

14. And, joining with the Messenians, laid the country waste. For I cannot persuade myself that Lycurgus was so barbarous,

15. Judging from his disposition to justice and gentleness in other ways.

16. And yet, is this frightful cruelty to slaves all the criticism that can be offered?

17. Much more criticism might be made: that no one belonged to himself, but to the state only, without personal freedom;

18. That Sparta was preserved in its institutions and manners by a strict limitation of knowledge and an impoverished austerity;

19. That to make a whole society an army is as much as to make it a tribe of ants merely;

20. That the arts of civilisation and philosophy were excluded for what elsewhere they were valued,

21. Namely, their promise of

innovation and the expansion both of knowledge and the human character.

22. In short, that though Sparta had the camaraderie and discipline of the military camp, it had little else.

23. And such might even be said in balance with the well-ordering of the state, the health of its citizens,

24. The sensible liberality of its morals and its safety from conquest and enslavement by foreigners.

25. How might a state combine these benefits without the imitations and severity that made Sparta a place, in effect, of self-imposed siege?

26. For who now can imagine being a Spartan?

Chapter 15

1. When Lycurgus saw that his institutions had taken root in the minds of his countrymen, that custom had rendered them familiar, and that his commonwealth was now able to go alone,

2. He planned to make it enduring, and, as far as human forecast could reach, to deliver it unchangeable to posterity.

3. He called an assembly of the people, and told them that as he thought everything was now well established,

4. He desired that they would observe the laws without the least alteration until he returned from a journey he now proposed.

5. They consented readily, and bade

him hasten back; and promised to maintain the established polity until he did so.

6. Having taken leave of his friends and family, and to ensure that the Spartans should never be released from the promise they had made, he resolved, of his own act, now to end his life.

7. He was then at an age when life is still tolerable, yet might be quitted without regret.

8. This latter he did by fasting, thinking it a statesman's duty to make his very death, if possible, an act of service to the state, and even at the end of life to give some example of virtue.

9. He was not deceived in his expectation that he would secure to his countrymen the advantages he had spent his life obtaining for them,

10. For Sparta continued the chief city of Greece for five hundred years, in strict observance of his laws, during the reign of fourteen kings down to the time of Agis son of Archidamus.

11. And even then, the creation of ephors made in Agis' day was so far from diminishing, that it much heightened the balanced character of the government,

12. So that it continued Lycurgus' monument afterwards, until the Pyrrhic victory of its defeat of Athens in that war which Thucydides later recorded.

Chapter 16: Solon of Athens

1. Solon the lawgiver and teacher of Athens was the son of Execestides, a man of moderate wealth and influence in the city, but of noble stock; his mother was cousin to the mother of Pisistratus.

2. He and this latter were at first great friends, partly because they were kin, and partly because of Pisistratus' noble qualities and beauty.

3. They say Solon loved him; which is the reason that when afterwards they differed about the government,

4. Their enmity never produced any violent passion, for they remembered their old kindnesses, and retained, though in its embers, the once strong fire of their love.

5. As this shows, Solon was not proof against beauty, nor did he lack courage to stand up to passion and meet it.

6. Solon's father ruined the family estate by his benefits and kindnesses to others,

7. So Solon applied himself to trade, though he had friends enough willing to help him;

8. But as one descended from a family who were accustomed to do kindnesses rather than receive them, he preferred independence.

9. Some say that he travelled to get learning and experience rather than money.

10. But in his time, as Hesiod says, work was shameful to none, nor was trade disrespected, but was a desirable calling,

11. For it brought home the good things that barbarous nations enjoyed, was the occasion of friendship with their kings, and a great source of experience.

12. Some add that Thales the philosopher and Hippocrates the mathematician traded; and that Plato defrayed the expense of his travels by selling oil in Egypt.

13. Solon's softness and profuseness, his popular rather than philosophical tone about pleasure in his poems, have been ascribed to his trading life;

14. For, having suffered a thousand dangers, it was natural they should be recompensed with enjoyments;

15. But that he accounted himself poor rather than rich is evident from his lines,

16. 'Some wicked men are rich, some good are poor, We will not change our virtue for their store; Virtue's a thing that none can take away, But money changes owners every day.'

17. At first Solon used his poetry not for any serious purpose, but to amuse his idle hours;

18. Afterwards he introduced moral and political thoughts, which he did, not to record them as an historian,

19. But to justify his actions, and to correct, chastise, and prompt the Athenians to noble performances.

20. Some say that he intended to put his laws into heroic verse.

21. In philosophy, as most of the wise men then, he chiefly esteemed the political part of morals; in physics, he was empirical and plain.

22. It is probable that at that time Thales alone had raised philosophy above mere practice into speculation;

23. And the rest of the wise men were so called from prudence in political concerns.

24. Solon was acquainted with both Thales and Anacharsis.

25. It is reported that the latter, visiting Athens, knocked at Solon's door, and told him that he, being a stranger, wished to be his guest, and to begin a friendship with him.

26. When Solon said, 'It is better to make friends at home,' Anacharsis replied, 'Well, you are at home; therefore make friends with me.'

27. Solon, pleased by this repartee, received him kindly, and kept him there some time.

28. He told Anacharsis about his compilation of laws; which when Anacharsis heard about them, he laughed at Solon for imagining that the dishonesty and covetousness of his countrymen could be restrained by written laws,

29. Which, he said, were like spiders' webs, and would catch the weak and poor, yet be easily broken by the mighty and rich.

30. To this Solon rejoined that men keep their promises when neither side can get anything by breaking them;

31. And he would so fit his laws to the citizens, that all should understand it was more eligible to be just than to break them.

32. But Anacharsis proved the more right in the long run.

33. Anacharsis, being once at the assembly, expressed his wonder at the fact that in Greece wise men spoke and fools decided.

Chapter 17

1. Solon went, they say, to Thales at Miletus, and wondered that Thales had no wife and children.

2. To this, Thales made no answer for the present; but, a few days after, procured a stranger to pretend that he had just come from Athens;

3. And Solon enquiring what news there, the man, according to his instructions, replied, 'None but a young man's funeral, which the whole city attended;

4. 'For he was the son of an honourable man, the most virtuous of the citizens, who was not then at home, but had been travelling a long time.'

5. Solon replied, 'What an unfortunate man to have lost a son! What was his name?'

6. 'I have forgotten it,' said the man, 'only there was great talk of his wisdom and his justice.'

7. Thus Solon was drawn on by every answer, and his fears heightened, till at last, being extremely concerned,

8. He mentioned his own name, and

asked the stranger if that young man was called Solon's son;

9. And the stranger assenting, Solon began to beat his head, and to do and say all that is usual with men in transports of grief.

10. But Thales took his hand, and, with a smile, said, 'These things, Solon, keep me from marriage and rearing children, which are too great for even your constancy to support;

11. 'However, be not concerned at the report, for it is a fiction.'

12. This was an unkind manner of teaching. Moreover, it is irrational and poor-hearted not to seek good things for fear of losing them,

13. For upon the same account we should not allow ourselves to seek wealth, glory or wisdom, since we may fear to be deprived of all these;

14. Nay, even virtue itself, than which there is no richer possession.

15. Now Thales, though unmarried, could not be free from concern, unless he likewise felt no care for his friends, his kinsmen or his country;

16. Yet we are told he adopted his sister's son. For the mind of man, having a principle of kindness in itself,

17. And being born to love, as well as perceive, think and remember, must feel a connection with someone or something, even a dog or horse.

18. We must not guard against the loss of wealth by being poor, or the loss of friends by refusing to have friends, or the loss of children by having none;

19. Instead, it is by morality and reason that we must guard against the affliction that the loss of such things brings.

Chapter 18

1. Now, when the Athenians were tired with a tedious and difficult war that they conducted against the Megarians for the island of Salamis,

2. And made a law that it should be death for any man, by writing or speaking, to assert that the city ought to recover it,

3. Solon, vexed at the disgrace, and perceiving that thousands of the youth wished for somebody to oppose that decision, devised a stratagem;

4. He counterfeited madness, then secretly composed some elegiac verses, and getting them by heart, that they might seem extempore,

5. Ran into the agora with a cap upon his head, and, the people gathering about him, sang that elegy which begins:

6. 'I am a herald come from Salamis the fair, My news from thence my verses shall declare.'

7. The poem contains one hundred verses, very elegantly written. When it had been sung, his friends commended it,

8. And especially Pisistratus exhorted the citizens to obey its call;

9. Insomuch that they revoked the law, and renewed the war under Solon's conduct.

10. With Pisistratus he sailed to Colias, and, finding the women celebrating a festival according to the custom of the country,

11. He sent a trusty friend to Salamis, who should pretend himself a renegade, to advise them that if they desired to seize the chief Athenian women, to come at once to Colias.

12. The Megarians immediately sent their men with him; and Solon, seeing them sail from the island,

13. Commanded some beardless youths, dressed in the women's clothing and secretly armed with daggers, to dance and play near the shore till the enemies had landed.

14. The Megarians were allured with the appearance, and coming to shore, jumped out, eager who should first seize a prize.

15. Not one of them escaped; and the Athenians set sail for Salamis and captured it.

16. Others give a different account of the island's capture.

17. They say that Solon, sailing by night with five hundred Athenian volunteers in several fisher-boats and one thirty-oared ship,

18. Anchored in a bay of Salamis that looks towards Nisaea;

19. And the Megarians who were then on the island, hearing only an uncertain report, hurried to their arms, and sent a ship to reconnoitre.

20. This ship Solon took, and manned it with Athenians, and gave them orders to sail round the island as secretly as possible;

21. Meanwhile he and the other soldiers marched against the Megarians by land, and while they were fighting, those from the ship took the city.

22. For these exploits, Solon grew famous and powerful.

Chapter 19

1. Soon afterwards the Athenians again fell into their old quarrels about the government,

2. There being as many different parties as there were diversities in the country.

3. The Hill quarter favoured democracy, the Plain, oligarchy, and those that lived by the Seaside stood for a mixed government,

4. And so each hindered either of the other parties from prevailing.

5. The disparity of fortune between the rich and the poor, at that time, was at a height;

6. So the city seemed in a truly dangerous condition, with despotic power seeming to be the only means possible for freeing it from disturbances.

7. All the people were in debt to the rich; and either they tilled their

land for their creditors, paying them a sixth part of the increase,

8. Or else they mortgaged their own bodies for the debt, and might be seized, and either sent into slavery at home, or sold to strangers.

9. Some, for no law forbade it, were forced to sell their children, or fly their country to avoid the cruelty of their creditors.

10. But the bravest of them began to combine together and encourage one another to stand firm and choose a leader,

11. To liberate the condemned debtors, redistribute the land and change the government.

12. Then the wisest of the Athenians, perceiving that Solon was the only one not implicated in the troubles,

13. For he had not joined in the exactions of the rich, and was not involved in the necessities of the poor,

14. Pressed him to succour the commonwealth and resolve the differences.

15. Solon himself says that he engaged in state affairs reluctantly at first, being afraid of the pride of one party and the greediness of the other;

16. But he accepted the office of archon and was empowered as arbitrator and lawgiver,

17. The rich consenting because he was wealthy, the poor because he was honest.

18. There was a saying of his current before his appointment,

19. That when things are even there never can be war, and this pleased both parties,

20. The one taking him to mean, when all have their fair proportion; the others, when all are absolutely equal.

21. So the chief men pressed Solon to take the government into his own hands, and, when he was once settled, to manage it freely and according to his determination.

22. The common people, thinking it would be difficult to change matters by law and reason, were willing to have one wise and just man set over the affairs as king.

23. But Solon did not choose to be made king. His familiar friends chided him for opposing monarchy, as if the virtue of the ruler could not make it a lawful form;

24. Solon replied to his friends, that it was true a tyranny was a very fair spot, but there was no way down from it.

25. Yet, though he refused the kingship, he was not too mild in the affair;

26. He did not show himself mean and submissive to the powerful, or make his laws to please those that chose him.

27. For where the laws were already good, he altered nothing,

28. For fear lest, changing everything and disordering the state, it would be difficult to recompose it to a tolerable condition;

29. But what he thought he could

effect by persuasion upon the pliable, and by force upon the stubborn, this he did.

30. And, therefore, when he was afterwards asked if he had left the Athenians the best laws that could be given, he replied, 'The best they could receive.'

Chapter 20

1. The way that the Athenians have of softening the badness of a thing, by ingeniously giving it some pretty and innocent name,

2. For example: calling harlots, mistresses; tributes, customs; a garrison, a guard; and the jail, the chamber,

3. Seems originally to have been Solon's idea, who called cancelling debts 'relief'.

4. For the first thing he settled was that all existing debts should be forgiven,

5. And no man, for the future, should mortgage his own body as security.

6. Some say the debts were not cancelled, but the interest only lessened, which sufficiently pleased the people,

7. Together with raising the value of their money; for he made a pound, which before equalled seventy-three drachmas, now worth a hundred;

8. So that, though the number of pieces in the payment was equal, the value was less;

9. Which proved a considerable

benefit to those that had great debts, and no loss to the creditors.

10. While he was planning the debt relief arrangements, a most vexatious thing happened;

11. For when he had resolved to take off the debts, and was considering the proper way of doing it, he told some of his friends, Conon, Clinias and Hipponicus,

12. In whom he had a great deal of confidence, that he would not meddle with the lands, but only free the people from their debts;

13. Upon which, using the advantage of this knowledge, they quickly borrowed considerable sums of money, and purchased several large farms;

14. And when the law was enacted, they kept the possessions, and would not return the money;

15. Which brought Solon into suspicion and dislike, as if he himself had been concerned in the trick.

16. But he presently stopped this suspicion, by releasing his debtors of five talents (for he had lent so much), according to the law;

17. Others say fifteen talents. His unfaithful friends, however, were ever afterward called Chreocopidae, repudiators.

18. His debt relief scheme pleased neither party, for the rich were angry for their money, and the poor were angry that the land was not divided equally.

19. That was what Lycurgus had done, but Solon did not have the same

power to effect such a thing, being only a citizen of the middle class;

20. Yet he acted to the height of his power, having nothing but the goodwill of his citizens to rely on;

21. And that he offended the majority, who looked for another result, is the mark that he had been fair.

Chapter 21

1. Solon repealed all of Draco's laws, except those concerning homicide, because they were far too severe, and the punishments too great;

2. For in the Draconian law death was the penalty for almost all offences,

3. So that those convicted of idleness, or for stealing a cabbage or an apple, had to suffer the same as murderers.

4. As was well said, Draco's laws were written not with ink, but with blood;

5. When asked why he made death the punishment of most offences, Draco replied, 'Small ones deserve it, and I have no higher for the greater ones.'

6. Next, Solon, being willing to keep the magistracies in the hands of the rich, and yet to receive the people into the other part of the government,

7. Took an account of the citizens' estates, and arranged the orders according to their wealth;

8. But though those who had less than a certain income were not admitted to any office of state,

they could come to the assembly, and act as jurors;

9. Which at first seemed nothing, but afterwards was found an enormous privilege, as almost every matter of dispute came before them to decide.

10. Even in the cases which he assigned to the archons' cognisance, he allowed an appeal to the courts.

11. Besides, it is said that he was obscure and ambiguous in the wording of his laws, on purpose to increase the honour of the courts;

12. For since differences could not be adjusted by the letter, citizens would have to bring their causes to the judges, who were thus made masters of the laws.

13. He mentions this equalisation in one of his poems: 'Such power I gave the people as might do,

14. 'Abridged not what they had, and gave them new. Those that were great in wealth and high in place, My counsel likewise kept from all disgrace.

15. 'Before them both I held my shield of might, And let not either touch the other's right.'

16. When he had constituted the Areopagus of those who had been yearly archons,

17. Of which he himself was a member, observing that the people, now free from debt, were unsettled and imperious,

18. He formed another council of four

hundred, a hundred out of each of the four tribes,

19. Which was to inspect all matters before they were propounded to the people,

20. And to take care that nothing but what had been first examined should be brought before the general assembly.

21. The upper council, or Areopagus, he made inspectors and keepers of the laws,

22. Conceiving that the commonwealth, held by these two councils, like anchors, would be less liable to tumults, and the people more at quiet.

23. Amongst his other laws, one is very surprising, which disfranchises all who stand neuter in political controversy;

24. For he would not have anyone remain insensible of the public good,

25. But everyone must at once join with the good party and those that have the right upon their side,

26. To assist and venture with them, rather than keep out of harm's way and watch who would get the better.

Chapter 22

1. Regarding marriage, Solon made a law that the bride and bridegroom shall be shut in a chamber to eat a quince together;

2. And that the husband of an heiress shall consort with her thrice a month;

3. For though there be no children, yet it is an honour which a husband ought to pay to a virtuous wife;

4. For it takes off all petty differences, and will not permit their little quarrels to proceed to a rupture.

5. In all other marriages he forbade dowries to be given;

6. The wife was to have three suits of clothes, a little household stuff, and that was all;

7. For he would not have marriages contracted for gain or an estate, but only for love, kind affection, and birth of children.

Chapter 23

1. Another commendable law of Solon's is that which forbids men to speak evil of the dead,

2. For it is unfair to asperse those that are gone, and politic to prevent perpetuations of discord.

3. He likewise forbade speaking evil of the living in the courts of justice, the public offices, or at the games.

4. Doing so incurred a fine of three drachmas to the person, and two to the public.

5. For never to be able to control passion shows a weak nature and ill-breeding;

6. Even though always to moderate it is very hard, and to some impossible.

7. He is likewise much commended for his law concerning wills; for

before him none could be made, but all the wealth and estate of the deceased belonged to his family.

8. But by introducing wills, he allowed people without children to bestow their estate on whom they pleased,

9. Showed that he esteemed friendship a stronger tie than kindred,

10. And affection a stronger tie than necessity; and made every man's estate truly his own.

11. Yet Solon allowed only legacies not extorted by the frenzy of a disease, imprisonment, force, or the persuasions of a wife;

12. With good reason thinking that being seduced into wrong was as bad as being forced,

13. And that between deceit and necessity, flattery and compulsion, there was little difference, since both can suspend the exercise of reason.

14. Observing Athens to be filled with persons that flocked from all parts into Attica for security of living,

15. And that most of the country was barren and unfruitful,

16. And that traders at sea import nothing to those that could give them nothing in exchange,

17. He turned his citizens to trade, and made a law that no son should be obliged to support an ageing father who had not bred him up to a calling.

18. It is true that Lycurgus, having a city free from all strangers, and land large enough for twice the population,

19. And above all, an abundance of slaves about Sparta, did well to relieve his citizens from laborious and mechanical occupations, and keep them only to the art of war.

20. But Solon, fitting his laws to the state of things, and not making things to suit his laws,

21. And finding the ground scarce rich enough to maintain the husbandmen, and altogether incapable of feeding an unoccupied and leisurely multitude,

22. Brought trades into credit, and ordered the Areopagites to examine how every man got his living, and to chastise the idle.

23. Solon's laws in general about women are his strangest; for he permitted anyone to kill an adulterer that found him in the act;

24. But if anyone forced a free woman, a hundred drachmas was the fine; if he enticed her, twenty;

25. Except those that sell themselves freely, that is, harlots, who go openly to those that hire them.

26. He made it unlawful to sell a daughter or a sister, unless, being yet unmarried, she was found wanton.

27. Since Attica has few rivers, lakes or large springs, and many relied on wells they had dug,

28. There was a law made, that, where there was a public well within four furlongs, all should draw at that;

29. But, when it was farther off, they should try to make a well of their own;

30. And, if they had dug ten fathoms deep and could find no water, they had liberty to fetch a pitcherful of four gallons and a half a day from their neighbours' well;

31. For he thought it prudent to make provision against want, but not to supply laziness.

32. He permitted only oil to be exported, and those that exported any other fruit, the archon was solemnly to fine a hundred drachmas.

33. He made a law concerning hurts and injuries from beasts,

34. In which he commanded the master of any dog that bit a man to deliver him up with a log about his neck, four and a half feet long; a happy device for men's security.

35. He permitted only those foreigners to be made free of Athens who were in perpetual exile from their own country, or came with their whole family to trade.

36. He did this not to discourage strangers, but to invite them to a permanent participation in the privileges of the government;

37. And, besides, he thought those would prove the more faithful citizens who had been forced from their own country, or voluntarily forsook it.

38. All his laws he established for a hundred years, and wrote them on wooden tables; and the council and people made solemn promises to abide by them.

Chapter 24

1. Now when these laws were enacted, and some came to Solon every day, to commend or dispraise them,

2. And to advise, if possible, to leave out, or put in something,

3. And many criticised, and desired him to explain, and tell the meaning of such and such a passage,

4. He, knowing that to do it was useless, and not to do it would get him ill-will,

5. And desirous to bring himself out of all straits, and to escape all displeasure and exceptions,

6. It being a hard thing, as he himself says, 'In great affairs to satisfy all sides',

7. Decided to travel, and as an excuse bought a trading vessel, and, having obtained leave for ten years' absence,

8. Departed, hoping that by that time his laws would have become familiar.

9. His first voyage was to Egypt, and he lived, as he himself says, 'Near Nilus' mouth, by fair Canopus' shore',

10. And spent some time in study with Psenophis of Heliopolis, and Sonchis, the most learned of all Egyptians;

11. From whom he learned the story of Atlantis. Solon proposed putting this into a poem, and bringing it to the knowledge of the Greeks.

12. From thence he sailed to Cyprus, where he was feted by Philocyprus, one of the kings there,

13. Whose city lay in a strong but incommodious hilly situation.

14. Solon persuaded him, since there lay a fair plain below, to remove, and build there a pleasanter and more spacious city.

15. And he assisted in gathering inhabitants, and in fitting it both for defence and for convenience of living;

16. Insomuch that many flocked to Philocyprus, and the other kings imitated the design; and, therefore, to honour Solon, he called the city Soli.

17. Solon himself, in his Elegies, addressing Philocyprus, mentions this foundation in these words:

18. 'Long may you live, and fill the Solian throne, Succeeded still by children of your own;

19. 'And from your happy island while I sail, Let Cyprus send me a favouring gale.'

Chapter 25

1. That Solon should discourse with Croesus on these travels, some think is not agreeable with chronology;

2. But I cannot reject so famous and well-attested a narrative, and, what is more, so worthy of Solon's wisdom and greatness of mind.

3. They say, therefore, that Solon, visiting Croesus at his request, was in the same condition as an inland man when first he goes to see the sea;

4. For as he fancies every river he meets with to be the ocean, so Solon, as he passed through the court,

5. And saw a great many nobles richly dressed, and proudly attended with a multitude of guards and footboys, thought each one was the king,

6. Till he was brought to Croesus himself, who was decked with every possible rarity and curiosity,

7. In ornaments of jewels, purple and gold, that could make a grand and gorgeous spectacle of him.

8. Now when Solon came before him, and seemed not at all surprised, nor gave Croesus those compliments the king expected,

9. But showed himself to be a man that despised the gaudiness and petty ostentation of it,

10. Croesus commanded his servants to open his treasure houses, and take Solon to see his sumptuous furniture and luxuries, though he did not wish it;

11. For Solon could judge of him well enough by the first sight of him. When he returned from viewing all, Croesus asked him if he had ever known a happier man than he.

12. And when Solon answered that he had known one Tellus, a fellow-citizen of his own,

13. And told him that this Tellus had been an honest man, had had good children, a competent estate,

and died bravely in battle for his country,

14. Croesus took him for an ill-bred fellow and a fool, for not measuring happiness by the abundance of gold and silver,

15. And preferring the life of a private man before so much power and empire.

16. He asked him, however, again, if, besides Tellus, he knew any other man more happy.

17. And Solon replying said, 'Yes, Cleobis and Biton, who were loving brothers, and extremely dutiful to their mother,

18. 'For when the oxen delayed her, they harnessed themselves to the wagon, and drew her to the festival,

19. 'Her neighbours all calling her happy, and she herself rejoiced; then, after feasting, the brothers went to rest,

20. 'And never rose again, but died in the midst of their honour a painless and tranquil death.'

21. 'What,' said Croesus, angrily, 'and do you not reckon me amongst the happy men at all?'

22. Solon, unwilling either to flatter or exasperate him more, replied,

23. 'The Greeks, O king, have all the gifts of nature in moderate degree; and so our wisdom, too, is a homely thing;

24. 'And this, observing the numerous misfortunes that attend all conditions, forbids us to grow insolent upon our present enjoyments,

25. 'Or to admire any man's happiness that may yet, in course of time, suffer change.

26. 'For the uncertain future has yet to come, with every possible variety of fortune;

27. 'And he only who lives virtuously and harmoniously until his end, we call happy;

28. 'To salute as happy one that is still in the midst of life and hazard, we think as little safe and conclusive as to crown and proclaim as victorious the wrestler that is still in the ring.'

29. After this, he was dismissed, having given Croesus some pain, but no instruction.

30. Aesop, who wrote the fables, being then at Sardis at Croesus' invitation, and very much esteemed,

31. Was concerned that Solon was so ill received, and gave him this advice:

32. 'Solon, let your converse with kings be either short or seasonable.'

33. 'Nay, rather,' replied Solon, 'either short or reasonable.'

34. So at this time Croesus despised Solon; but when he was overthrown by Cyrus,

35. Had lost his city, was taken alive, condemned to be burnt, and laid bound on the pyre before all the Persians and Cyrus himself,

36. He cried out as loud as possibly he could three times, 'O Solon!'

37. And Cyrus, being surprised, and asking who or what this Solon

was, whom alone he invoked in this extremity,

38. Croesus told him the whole story, saying, 'He was one of the wise men of Greece, whom I sent for,

39. 'Not to be instructed, or to learn anything that I wanted, but that he should see and be a witness of my happiness;

40. 'The loss of which was, it seems, to be a greater evil than the enjoyment was a good;

41. 'For when I had them they were goods only in opinion, but now the loss of them has brought upon me intolerable and real evils.

42. 'And he, conjecturing from what then was, this that now is, bade me look to the end of my life, and not rely and grow proud upon uncertainties.'

43. When this was told, Cyrus, who was a wiser man than Croesus, and saw in the present example Solon's maxim confirmed,

44. Not only freed Croesus from punishment, but honoured him as long as he lived;

45. And Solon had the glory, by the same saying, to save one king and instruct another.

Chapter 26

1. While Solon was gone the citizens of Athens began to quarrel among themselves again.

2. One named Lycurgus led the Plain; Megacles, the son of Alcmaeon, led the Seaside;

3. And Pisistratus led the Hill, the area of the poorest people, and greatest enemies to the rich;

4. So though the city still used Solon's new laws, yet all desired a change of government,

5. Hoping that a change would be better for them, and put them above the other factions.

6. Affairs standing thus, Solon returned, and was reverenced by all, and honoured;

7. But his old age would not permit him to be as active as formerly;

8. Yet, by privately conferring with the heads of the factions, he endeavoured to compose the differences, Pisistratus appearing the most tractable;

9. For he was extremely smooth and engaging in his language, a great friend to the poor, and moderate in his resentments;

10. And what nature had not given him, he had the skill to imitate; so that he was trusted more than the others,

11. Being accounted a prudent and orderly man, one that loved equality, and would be an enemy to any that moved against the present settlement.

12. Thus Pisistratus deceived the majority of people; but Solon knew his character, and understood his intentions, better than anyone else;

13. Yet did not hate him for this, but endeavoured to tame his ambition, and often told him and others,

14. That if anyone could cure him of

his desire of absolute power, none would make a more virtuous man or excellent citizen.

15. Thespis was at this time beginning to act tragedies, and because this was a new thing it much captivated the multitude.

16. Solon, being by nature fond of hearing and learning something new,

17. And now, in his old age, living idly and enjoying himself with music and wine, went to see Thespis act;

18. And after the play was done, addressed him, and asked him if he was not ashamed to tell so many lies before such a number of people;

19. And Thespis replying that it was no harm to say or do so in play, Solon vehemently struck his staff against the ground and said:

20. 'If we honour and commend such play as this, we shall soon find it in our business.' And soon enough it was, as a trick played by Pisistratus showed.

21. For Pisistratus wounded himself, and was brought into the marketplace in a chariot pretending to suffer,

22. On purpose to stir up the people, as if he had been thus treated by his political opponents. A great many were enraged, but Solon, going up to him, said,

23. 'This is a bad copy of Homer's Odysseus; you do, to trick your countrymen, what he did to deceive his enemies.'

24. After this the people were eager to protect Pisistratus, and met in assembly, where a motion was put that Pisistratus should be allowed fifty clubmen to guard his person.

25. Solon, knowing that Pisistratus did this to have a private army with which to capture the government, opposed the motion,

26. But observing that the poor were tumultuously bent on gratifying Pisistratus, and the rich were fearful and wished to keep out of harm's way,

27. He departed, saying he was wiser than some and stouter than others;

28. Wiser than those who did not understand Pisistratus' plan,

29. Stouter than those who, though they understood it, were afraid to oppose it.

Chapter 27

1. Now, the people, having passed the law granting Pisistratus a bodyguard, did not watch how many he gathered around him; until he seized the Acropolis.

2. When that was done, and the city was in an uproar, Megacles, with all his family, at once fled;

3. But Solon, though he was now very old, and had none to back him, nevertheless came into the marketplace and made a speech to the citizens,

4. Partly blaming their inadvertency and timidity, and in part urging and exhorting them not to lose their liberty so tamely;

5. And likewise then spoke that memorable saying, that, before, it was an easier task to stop the rising tyranny,

6. But now the greater and more glorious action was to destroy it, when it was begun already, and had gathered strength.

7. But all being afraid to side with him, he returned home, and, taking his sword and shield, he brought them out and laid them in the porch before his door, with these words:

8. 'I have done my part to maintain my country and my laws,' and then he busied himself no more.

9. His friends advising him to flee, he refused; but wrote poems reproaching the Athenians for putting tyrannical power into one man's hands.

10. Many warned him that the tyrant would take his life for this, and asking what he trusted to, that he ventured to speak so boldly, he replied, 'To my old age.'

11. But Pisistratus so extremely courted Solon, so honoured him, obliged him, and sent to see him, that Solon gave him his advice, and approved many of his actions;

12. For the tyrant retained most of Solon's laws, observed them himself, and compelled his friends to obey.

13. And Pisistratus himself, though already absolute ruler, being accused before the Areopagus of murder, came quietly to clear

himself; but his accuser did not appear.

14. And he added other laws, one of which is that the maimed in the wars should be maintained at the public charge;

15. In this Pisistratus followed Solon's example, who had decreed it in the case of a soldier named Thersippus;

16. And Theophrastus asserts that it was Pisistratus, not Solon, that made that law against laziness, which was the reason that the country became more productive, and the city more tranquil.

17. Thus Solon survived after Pisistratus seized the government; Heraclides Ponticus says that Solon lived many years after Pisistratus began his tyranny,

18. Whereas Phanias the Eresian says he lived less than two years after it began.

19. The story that his ashes were scattered about the island Salamis is too strange to be easily believed,

20. Yet it is told, amongst other good authors, by Aristotle the philosopher.

Chapter 28: Pericles of Athens

1. The greatest ruler of Athens in its greatest age was Pericles.

2. He was the leading citizen of that city for fifty-five years, and in that time he brought it to pre-eminence both in the Greece of its day, and in the history of the world.

3. In the Athens of Pericles flourished

the philosophy and poetry that makes it the capital of the civilisation it founded,

4. And along with them the very fabric of buildings that to this day are emulated in every notable city of the world,

5. Thereby expressing admiration for the Greek genius over which he presided.

6. Pericles was of the noblest birth both on his father's and on his mother's side.

7. His father Xanthippus defeated the King of Persia's generals at the battle of Mycale.

8. His mother Agariste was the granddaughter of Clisthenes, the man who drove out the tyrannical sons of the despot Pisistratus, and nobly put an end to their usurpation;

9. And moreover made a body of laws, settling a model of government admirably suited for the harmony and safety of the Athenian people.

10. When Pericles was born he was perfectly formed, except that his head was somewhat long and out of proportion.

11. Consequently most images and statues of him show him wearing a helmet. The poets of Athens called him 'Schinocephalos', or squill-head, from 'schinos', a squill or sea-onion.

12. One of the comic poets, Teleclides, describes him when contending with political difficulties as 'fainting underneath the load of his own head:

13. 'And abroad from his huge gallery of a pate sending forth trouble to the state'.

14. And another comic writer, Eupolis, in the play called *The Demi*, has Pericles appear at the end of a line of demagogues to the words,

15. 'And here by way of summary, now we've done, behold, in brief, the heads of all in one.'

16. The master who taught him music was Damon, who, being a sophist, sheltered himself under the profession of music teacher to conceal from people his skill in politics and oratory, and under this pretence taught Pericles.

17. Damon's lyre, however, did not prove altogether successful as a disguise; he was banished from the country by ostracism for ten years, as a dangerous intermeddler and a favourer of arbitrary power,

18. And by this means gave the comedians occasion to satirise him. As, for instance, one comic poet introduces a character who questions him: 'Tell me, if you please, since you're the man who taught Pericles.'

19. Pericles, also, was a student of Zeno, the Eleatic, who treated of natural philosophy in the same manner as Parmenides,

20. But had also perfected himself in an art of his own for refuting and silencing opponents in argument;

21. As Timon of Phlius describes it:
'Also the two-edged tongue of
mighty Zeno, who, say what one
would, could argue it untrue.'

Chapter 29

1. But Pericles' main teacher in his
youth, the man who furnished
him most especially with a weight
and grandeur of sense, superior to
all arts of popularity,

2. And in general gave him his
elevation and sublimity of purpose
and of character, was Anaxagoras
of Clazomenae.

3. This philosopher was called by the
men of those times 'Nous', that is,
mind, or intelligence,

4. In admiration of the great and
extraordinary gift he had displayed
for the science of nature.

5. Pericles entertained a great esteem
for Anaxagoras, and filling himself
with his lofty thought,

6. Derived from it not merely
elevation of purpose and dignity of
language, raised far above the base
and dishonest buffooneries of mob
eloquence,

7. But a composure of countenance,
and a serenity and calmness in all
his movements, which no occur-
rence while he was speaking could
disturb;

8. With a sustained and even tone of
voice, and various other advantages of a similar kind, which
produced a profound effect on his
hearers.

9. Once, after being abused all day
long by some vile and abandoned
fellow in the marketplace,

10. While he was engaged in the
dispatch of some urgent affair, he
continued his business in perfect
silence,

11. And in the evening returned home
composedly, the man still dogging
him at the heels, and showering
him all the way with abuse and
foul language;

12. And when Pericles stepped into his
house, it being by this time dark,
he ordered one of his servants to
take a light, and to go along with
the man and see him safe home.

13. A contrary account of his character is given by Ion, the dramatic
poet, who said that Pericles'
manner in company was somewhat pompous;

14. And that into his high-bearing
there entered a good deal of
disdain and scorn of others.

15. Ion reserved his commendation
for Cimon's ease and natural grace
in society, as an admirer of that
leader, so we cannot altogether rely
on his opinion.

16. Zeno used to tell those who
thought that Pericles' gravity was
an affectation, to go and affect the
like themselves,

17. On the grounds that counterfeit-
ing it might in time make them
acquire a real love and knowledge
of noble qualities.

18. Nor were these the only advantages that Pericles derived from
Anaxagoras' acquaintance;

19. He seems also to have become, by his instructions, superior to the folly that possesses the minds of people unacquainted with science,

20. Eager for silly explanations, and excitable through ignorance of nature.

21. Pericles, while still a young man, stood in considerable apprehension of the people,

22. Because he was thought to look very like the tyrant Pisistratus,

23. And those of great age remarked upon the sweetness of his voice, and his eloquence and rapidity in speaking,

24. And were struck with amazement at the resemblance to Pisistratus in this too.

25. Reflecting also that he was rich, and from a noble family with influential friends,

26. He thought all this might cause him to be banished as a dangerous person to the tranquillity of the state,

27. And therefore he avoided state affairs, but devoted himself intrepidly to military service.

28. But when Aristides died, and Themistocles had been driven out, and Cimon was for the most part kept abroad by military expeditions outside Greece,

29. Pericles, seeing things in this posture, stepped forward into public life, not on the side of the rich and few,

30. But with the many and poor,

contrary to his natural bent, which was far from democratical.

31. Fearing that he might be suspected of aiming at arbitrary power, and seeing Cimon on the side of the aristocracy,

32. And much beloved by the better and more distinguished people, he joined the party of the people, with a view at once both to secure himself and to oppose Cimon.

Chapter 30

1. Pericles immediately entered, also, on quite a new course of life and management of his time.

2. For he was never seen to walk in any street but that which led to the marketplace and council hall,

3. And he avoided invitations from friends to go to supper with them, and ceased all friendly visiting and intercourse whatever;

4. In all the time he had to do with the public, which was not a little, he was never known to go to any of his friends for supper, except once when his near kinsman Euryptolemus married;

5. And then he remained only until drinks were served, when he immediately rose from table and went home.

6. For these friendly meetings are quick to undo any assumed superiority, and a grave exterior is hard to maintain in intimate familiarity.

7. Real excellence, indeed, is most

recognised when most openly looked into;

8. And in really good men, nothing which meets the eyes of external observers so truly deserves their admiration,

9. As their daily common life does that of their nearer friends.

10. Pericles, however, to avoid any feeling of commonness, or any satiety on the part of the people,

11. Presented himself at intervals only, not speaking on every business, nor at all times coming into the assembly,

12. But, as Critolaus says, reserving himself, like the Salaminian galley, for great occasions,

13. While matters of lesser importance were dispatched by friends or other speakers under his direction.

14. Among his lieutenants was Ephialtes, who broke the power of the council of Areopagus,

15. Giving the people, according to Plato's expression, so copious and so strong a draught of liberty, that they grew wild and unruly as an unmanageable horse.

16. The style of speaking that best suited Pericles' manner of life and the dignity of his views took its lead from what Anaxagoras had taught him.

17. Pericles continually deepened the colours of rhetoric with the dye of natural science.

18. For having added to his natural genius a great height of knowledge by the study of philosophy, he

showed himself far superior to all others.

19. Upon which account, they say, Pericles had his nickname of 'Olympian' given him;

20. Though some are of the opinion he was named this from the public buildings with which he adorned the city;

21. And others again, from his great power in public affairs, whether of war or peace.

22. However, the comedies staged at the time, which, both in good earnest and in merriment, let fly many hard words at him,

23. Plainly show that he got that appellation especially from his speaking;

24. They speak of his 'thundering and lightning' when he harangued the people,

25. And of his wielding a dreadful thunderbolt in his tongue.

Chapter 31

1. A saying also of Thucydides, son of Melesias, is on record, spoken by him by way of pleasantry upon Pericles' dexterity.

2. Thucydides was one of the noble and distinguished citizens, and had been his greatest opponent;

3. And when Archidamus, the king of the Lacedaemonians, asked him whether he or Pericles was the better wrestler, he answered:

4. 'When I have thrown him and given him a fair fall, he gets the better of me by insisting that he

had no fall, and makes the bystanders, in spite of their own eyes, believe him.'

5. The truth is, however, that Pericles was so careful about what he said and how he spoke, that whenever he went up to the hustings,

6. He took time to prepare beforehand so that no word might slip from him unawares that was unsuitable to the matter or occasion.

7. Pericles has left nothing in writing behind him, except some decrees; and very few of his sayings are recorded.

8. One is, that when his fellow-general Sophocles, going with him on board ship, praised the beauty of a youth they met on the way,

9. Perciles said, 'Sophocles, a general ought not only to have clean hands but also clean eyes.'

10. And Stesimbrotus tells us that, in his encomium on those who fell in battle at Samos, he said they would always be remembered,

11. 'Because we do not see them themselves, but only by the honours we pay them, and by the benefits they do us;

12. 'Such attributes belong to those who die in the service of their country.'

13. Since Thucydides describes the rule of Pericles as an aristocratical government that went by the name of democracy, but was, indeed, the supremacy of a single great man,

14. While many others say, on the contrary, that by him the common people were first encouraged and led on to such evils as appropriations of subject territory, allowances for attending theatres, payments for performing public duties,

15. And by these bad habits were, under the influence of his public measures, changed from a sober, thrifty people, that maintained themselves by their own labours,

16. To lovers of expense, intemperance and licence, let us examine the cause of this change by looking at the facts.

17. At the first, as has been said, when Pericles opposed Cimon's great authority, he indeed courted the people.

18. Finding himself come short of Cimon in wealth, by which the latter was enabled to caress the poor,

19. Inviting every day some needy citizens to supper, giving clothes to aged people, and pulling down the hedges round his property so that anyone could freely gather what fruit they pleased,

20. Pericles, thus outdone in popular arts, took the advice of one Damonides of Oea and made a distribution of the public moneys;

21. And in a short time having bought the people over, what with moneys allowed for shows and for service on juries, and what with other forms of pay and largesse,

22. He made use of them against the

council of Areopagus of which he himself was not a member, as having never been chosen archon, lawgiver, king or captain.

23. For from ancient times these offices were conferred on persons by lot, and those who had acquitted themselves in the discharge of them were promoted to the court of Areopagus.

Chapter 32

1. And so Pericles, having secured his power with the populace, directed the exertions of his party against this council with such success,

2. That most of the causes and matters which used to be tried there were, by the agency of Ephialtes, removed from its authority.

3. Cimon, also, was banished by ostracism as a favourer of the Lacedaemonians and a hater of the people,

4. Though in wealth and noble birth he was among the first of Athenians, and had won several glorious victories over the barbarians, filling the city with money and spoils of war; as is recorded in the history of his life.

5. But his banishment proves the great influence that Pericles obtained among the people.

6. The ostracism was limited by law to ten years; but the Lacedaemonians, in the meantime, entering with a great army into the territory of Tanagra, and the

Athenians going out to fight against them,

7. Cimon, coming from his banishment before his time was out, put himself in arms and array with those of his fellow-citizens that were of his own tribe,

8. And desired by his deeds to wipe off the suspicion of his favouring the Lacedaemonians, by venturing his own person along with his countrymen.

9. But Pericles' friends, gathering in a body, forced him to retire as a banished man.

10. For which cause also Pericles seems to have exerted himself more in that than in any other battle, and to have been conspicuous for his exposure of himself to danger.

11. All Cimon's friends, also, to a man, fell together side by side, whom Pericles had accused with him of taking part with the Lacedaemonians.

12. Defeated in this battle on their own frontiers, and expecting a new and perilous attack with the return of spring,

13. The Athenians now felt regret and sorrow for the loss of Cimon, and repentance for their expulsion of him.

14. Pericles, being sensible of their feelings, did not hesitate or delay to gratify it, and himself made the motion for recalling him home.

15. He, upon his return, concluded a peace betwixt the two cities;

16. For the Lacedaemonians entertained as kindly feelings towards
him as they did the reverse
towards Pericles and the other
popular leaders.

17. Yet some say that Pericles did not
propose the order for Cimon's
return till some private articles of
agreement had been made between
them, and this by means of
Elpinice, Cimon's sister:

18. That Cimon should go out to sea
with a fleet of two hundred ships,
and be commander-in-chief abroad,

19. With a design to reduce the King
of Persia's territories, and that
Pericles should have the power at
home.

20. This Elpinice, it was thought, had
before this time procured some
favour for her brother Cimon at
Pericles' hands,

21. And induced him to be more
remiss and gentle in urging the
charge when Cimon was tried for
his life;

22. For Pericles was one of the
committee appointed by the
commons to plead against him.

23. And when Elpinice came and
spoke with him on her brother's
behalf, he answered, with a smile,

24. 'O Elpinice, you are too old a
woman to undertake such business
as this.'

25. But, when he appeared to impeach
him, he stood up only once to
speak, merely to acquit himself of
his commission, and went out of
court,

26. Having done Cimon the least
prejudice of any of his accusers.

27. How, then, can one believe
Idomeneus, who charges Pericles
as if he had by treachery procured
the murder of Ephialtes, the
popular statesman,

28. One who was his friend, and of his
own party in all his political
course, out of jealousy, and envy
of his great reputation?

29. This historian, having raked up
these stories, I know not where,
has libelled with them a man who,
although not altogether free from
fault or blame,

30. Yet had a noble heart, and a mind
bent on honour; and where such
qualities are, there can be no cruel
and brutal passions.

31. The truth of what happened to
Ephialtes, as Aristotle has told us,
is this:

32. That having made himself formidable to the oligarchical party by
being an uncompromising asserter
of the people's rights in calling to
account and prosecuting those
who in any way wronged them,

33. He was assassinated by Aristodicus
the Tanagraean on behalf of his
enemies.

Chapter 33

1. Cimon, while he was admiral, died
in Cyprus. And the aristocratical
party, seeing that Pericles was
already the greatest and foremost
man in the city,

2. But nevertheless wishing to set

somebody up against him to blunt the edge of his power to prevent it turning into a monarchy,

3. Put forward Thucydides of Alopece, a discreet person and a near kinsman of Cimon's, to conduct the opposition against him;

4. Who, indeed, though less skilled in warlike affairs than Cimon,

5. Was better versed in speaking and political business, and keeping close guard in the city.

6. By engaging with Pericles on the hustings, in a short time he brought the government to an equality of parties.

7. For he would not allow those who were called the 'honest and good' (that is, persons of worth and distinction) to be scattered among the populace,

8. As formerly, diminishing and obscuring their superiority amongst the masses;

9. But taking them apart by themselves and uniting them in one body, by their combined weight he was able to make a counterpoise to the other party.

10. For, indeed, there was from the beginning a concealed split between the different popular and aristocratical tendencies;

11. But the open rivalry and contention of these two opponents made the gash deep,

12. And severed the city into the two parties of 'the people' and 'the few'.

13. And so Pericles, at that time, more than at any other, gave the reins to the people, and made his policy serve their interest,

14. Contriving continually to have some great public show or solemnity, some banquet, or some procession or other in the town to please them,

15. Coaxing his countrymen like children with such delights and pleasures as were not, however, unedifying.

16. Besides that, every year he sent out sixty galleys, on board which there were numbers of citizens, who were paid for eight months to learn and practise the art of seamanship.

17. He sent a thousand citizens into the Chersonese as planters, to share the land among them by lot,

18. And five hundred more into the isle of Naxos, and half that number to Andros,

19. A thousand into Thrace to dwell among the Bisaltae, and others into Italy, when the city Sybaris, which now was called Thurii, was to be repeopled.

20. And this he did to ease and discharge the city of an idle, and, by reason of their idleness, a meddling crowd of people;

21. And at the same time to meet the necessities and restore the fortunes of the poor townsmen,

22. And to intimidate, also, and check their allies from attempting any change, by posting such garrisons, as it were, in the midst of them.

Chapter 34

1. What gave most pleasure and ornament to Athens, and the greatest admiration and even astonishment to all strangers,

2. And that which now is Greece's only evidence that the power she boasts of and her ancient wealth are no romance or idle story,

3. Was Pericles' construction of the great public buildings.

4. Yet these were the actions in government that his enemies most looked askance at, and cavilled at in the popular assemblies,

5. Crying out that the commonwealth of Athens had lost its reputation and was denigrated abroad for removing the common treasure of the Greeks from the isle of Delos into their own custody;

6. And though their excuse for doing so was to protect it from capture by the barbarians, Pericles had now spent it;

7. And they complained that 'Greece cannot but resent it as an insufferable affront, and consider herself to be tyrannised over openly,

8. 'When she sees the treasure, which was contributed by her upon a necessity for the war, wantonly lavished out by us upon our city,

9. 'To gild her all over, and to adorn and set her forth, as it were some vain woman, hung round with precious stones and statues, which cost a world of money.'

10. But Pericles informed the people that they were in no way obliged to give any account of those moneys to their allies,

11. So long as they maintained their defence, and kept off the barbarians from attacking them;

12. While in the meantime they did not so much as supply one horse or man or ship, but only found money for the service;

13. 'Which money,' he said, 'is not theirs that gave it, but theirs that received it,

14. 'So long as they perform the conditions on which they received it.'

15. And that it was good reason, that, now the city was sufficiently provided and stored with all things necessary for the war,

16. They should convert the overplus of its wealth to such undertakings as would hereafter, when completed, give them eternal honour,

17. And, for the present, while in process, freely supply all the inhabitants with plenty.

18. With their variety of workmanship and of occasions for service, which summon all arts and trades and require all hands to be employed about them,

19. They put the whole city, in a manner, into state-pay; while at the same time she is both beautiful and maintained by herself.

20. For as those who are of age and strength for war are provided for and maintained in the armaments

abroad by their pay out of the
public stock,

21. So, it being Pericles' desire and
design that the undisciplined
multitude that stayed at home
should not go without their share
of public salaries, and yet should
not have them for sitting still and
doing nothing,

22. To that end he thought fit to
bring in among them, with the
approbation of the people, these
projects of buildings and designs
of work,

23. That would be of some continuance before they were finished,
and would give employment to
numerous arts,

24. So that the part of the people that
stayed at home might, no less than
those that were at sea or in garrisons or on expeditions,

25. Have a fair and just occasion of
receiving the benefit and having
their share of the public moneys.

26. The materials were stone, brass,
ivory, gold, ebony and
cypresswood;

27. And the arts or trades that
wrought and fashioned them were
smiths and carpenters, moulders,

28. Founders and braziers, stone-
cutters, dyers, goldsmiths,
ivory-workers, painters, embroi-
derers and turners;

29. And those who conveyed them to
the town for use included
merchants, mariners and ship-
masters by sea,

30. And by land,

cartwrights, cattle-breeders,
wagoners, rope-makers, flax-work-
ers, shoemakers, leather-dressers,
road-makers, miners.

31. And every trade in the same
nature, as a captain in an army has
his particular company of soldiers
under him, had its own hired
company of journeymen and
labourers belonging to it banded
together as in array, to be the
instrument and body for the
performance of the service.

32. Thus, to say all in a word, the
occasions and services of these
public works distributed plenty
through every age and condition.

Chapter 35

1. As the public works rose up, no
less stately in size than exquisite in
form,

2. The workmen striving to outvie
the material and the design with
the beauty of their workmanship,

3. Yet the most wonderful thing of all
was the rapidity of their execution.

4. Undertakings, any one of which
singly might have required, they
thought, several successions and
ages of men for their completion,

5. Were every one of them accomplished in the height and prime of
one man's political service.

6. Although they say, too, that Zeuxis
once, having heard Agatharchus
the painter boast of dispatching
his work with speed and ease,
replied, 'I take a long time.'

7. For ease and speed in doing a

thing do not give the work lasting solidity or exactness of beauty;

8. The expenditure of time allowed to a man's pains beforehand for the production of a thing is repaid by the preservation when once completed.

9. For which reason Pericles' works are especially admired, as having been made quickly, yet having lasted so long.

10. For every piece of his work was immediately antique, even at that time, for its beauty and elegance;

11. And yet in its vigour and freshness looks to this day as if it were just executed.

12. There is a sort of bloom of newness upon those works of his, preserving them from the touch of time,

13. As if they had some perennial essence and undying vitality mingled in the composition of them.

14. Phidias was in charge of all the works as surveyor-general, though upon the various parts other great masters and workmen were employed.

15. Callicrates and Ictinus built the Parthenon;

16. The hall at Eleusis, where the festivals were celebrated, was begun by Coroebus, who erected the pillars that stand upon the floor or pavement, and joined them to the architraves;

17. And after his death Metagenes of Xypete added the frieze and the upper line of columns;

18. Xenocles of Cholargus roofed or arched the lantern on top of the monument to Castor and Pollux;

19. And the long wall, which Socrates says he himself heard Pericles propose to the people, was undertaken by Callicrates.

20. The Odeum, or music room, which in its interior was full of seats and ranges of pillars,

21. And outside had its roof made to slope and descend from one single point at the top,

22. Was constructed in imitation of the King of Persia's Pavilion; this likewise by Pericles' order;

23. Which Cratinus in his comedy called *The Thracian Women* made an occasion of raillery:

24. 'So, we see here, long-pate Pericles appear, since ostracism time, he's laid aside his head, and wears the new Odeum in its stead.'

25. Pericles, also eager for distinction, then first obtained the decree for a contest in musical skill to be held yearly at the Panathenaea,

26. And he himself, being chosen judge, arranged the order and method in which the competitors should sing and play on the flute and on the harp.

27. And both at that time, and at other times also, they sat in this music room to see and hear all such trials of skill.

28. The propylaea, or entrances to the Acropolis, were finished in five

years, Mnesicles being the principal architect.

29. Phidias had the whole work under
his charge, along with the oversight over all the artists and
workmen, through Pericles'
friendship for him;

30. And this, indeed, made him much
envied, and his patron shamefully
slandered with stories,

31. As if Phidias were in the habit of
receiving, for Pericles' use, free-
born women that came to see the
works.

32. The comic writers of the town,
when they got hold of this story,
made much of it, and bespattered
him with all the ribaldry they
could invent,

33. Charging him falsely with the wife
of Menippus, one who was his
friend and served as lieutenant
under him in the wars;

34. And with the birds kept by
Pyrilampes, an acquaintance of
Pericles, who, they pretended,
used to give presents of peacocks
to Pericles' female friends.

35. And how can one wonder at any
number of strange assertions from
men whose whole lives were
devoted to mockery,

36. And who were ready at any time
to sacrifice the reputation of their
superiors to vulgar envy and spite,

37. When even Stesimbrotus the
Thracian has dared to lay to the
charge of Pericles a monstrous and
fabulous piece of criminality with
his son's wife?

38. So very difficult a matter is it to
trace and find out the truth of
anything by history,

39. When, on the one hand, those
who afterwards write it find long
periods of time intercepting their
view,

40. And, on the other hand, the
contemporary records of any
actions and lives,

41. Partly through envy and ill-will,
partly through favour and flattery,
pervert and distort truth.

Chapter 36

1. When the orators who sided with
Thucydides and his party were
crying out against Pericles,

2. As one who squandered away the
public money, and made havoc of
the state revenues,

3. He rose in the open assembly and
put the question to the people,
whether they thought he had laid
out much;

4. And they saying, 'Too much, a
great deal,' 'Then,' said he, 'since it
is so, let the cost not go to your
account,

5. 'But to mine; and let the inscription upon the buildings stand in
my name.'

6. When they heard him say this,
whether it were out of a surprise to
see the greatness of his heart or out
of emulation of the glory of the
works,

7. They cried aloud, bidding him to
spend on, and lay out what he
thought fit from the public purse,

and to spare no cost, until everything was finished.

8. At length, coming to a final
contest with Thucydides which of
the two should banish the other
out of the country,

9. And having gone through this
peril, Pericles threw his antagonist
out, and broke up the confederacy
that had been organised against
him.

10. So that now all schism and
division being at an end, and the
city brought to evenness and unity,

11. He got all Athens and all its affairs
into his own hands, the tributes,
armies, fleets, islands, sea, and
their wide-extended power,

12. Partly over other Greeks and partly
over barbarians;

13. And all that empire which they
possessed, founded and fortified
upon subject nations and royal
friendships and alliances.

14. After this Pericles was no longer
the same man he had been before,

15. Nor as tame and gentle and
familiar as formerly with the
populace,

16. So as readily to yield to their
pleasures and to comply with the
desires of the multitude, as a
steersman shifts with the winds.

17. Quitting that loose, remiss and, in
some cases, licentious court of the
popular will,

18. He turned those soft and flowery
modulations to the austerity of
aristocratical and regal rule;

19. And employing this uprightly and

undeviatingly for the country's
best interests,

20. He was able generally to lead the
people along, with their own wills
and consents, by persuading and
showing them what was to be
done;

21. And sometimes, too, urging and
pressing them forward extremely
against their will,

22. He made them, whether they
would or no, yield submission to
what was for their advantage.

23. In which, to say the truth, he
behaved like a skilful physician,
who, in a complicated and chronic
disease, as he sees occasion,

24. At one time allows his patient the
moderate use of such things as
please him,

25. At another gives him keen pains
and bitter drugs to work the cure.

26. For there arising and growing up,
as was natural, all manner of
distempered feelings among a
people which had so vast a
command and dominion,

27. He alone, as a great master,
knowing how to handle and deal
fitly with each one of them,

28. And, in an especial manner,
making use of hopes and fears as
his two chief rudders,

29. With the one to check the career
of their confidence at any time,

30. With the other to raise them up
and cheer them when under any
discouragement,

31. Plainly showed by this, that
rhetoric, the art of speaking, is as

Plato says the government of the minds of men,

32. And its chief business is to address the affections and passions, which are the strings and keys to the mind, and require a skilful touch to be played on rightly.

Chapter 37

1. The source of Pericles' predominance was not only his power of language, but, as Thucydides assures us, the reputation of his life, and the confidence felt in his character;

2. His manifest freedom from every kind of corruption, and superiority to all considerations of money.

3. Notwithstanding he had made the city of Athens, which was great of itself, as great and rich as can be imagined,

4. And though he was himself as powerful and influential as many kings and absolute rulers,

5. He did not make the personal patrimony left to him by his father greater than it was by a single penny.

6. Thucydides, indeed, gives a plain statement of the greatness of his power;

7. And the comic poets, in their spiteful manner, more than hint at it, styling his companions and friends the new Pisistratidae,

8. And calling on him to abjure any intention of usurpation,

9. As one whose eminence was too great to be any longer proportionable to and compatible with a democracy or popular government.

10. And Teleclides says the Athenians had surrendered up to him 'the tribute of the cities, and with them, the cities too, to do with them as he pleases, and undo;

11. 'To build up, if he likes, stone walls around a town; and again, if so he likes, to pull them down;

12. 'Their treaties and alliances, power, empire, peace and war, their wealth and their success for ever more.'

Chapter 38

1. Nor was all this the luck of some happy occasion; nor was it the mere bloom and grace of a policy that flourished for a season;

2. But having for forty years maintained the first place among statesmen such as Ephialtes and Leocrates and Myronides and Cimon and Tolmides and Thucydides;

3. And then after the defeat and banishment of Thucydides, for no less than fifteen years more,

4. In the exercise of one continuous unintermitted command in the office, to which he was annually re-elected, of General, he preserved his integrity unspotted;

5. Though otherwise he was not altogether idle or careless in looking after his pecuniary advantage;

6. His paternal estate, which of right

belonged to him, he so ordered that it might neither through negligence be wasted or lessened,

7. Nor yet, being so full of business as he was, cost him any great trouble or time with taking care of it;

8. And put it into such a way of management as he thought to be the most easy for himself, and the most exact.

9. All his yearly products and profits he sold together in a lump, and supplied his household needs afterwards by buying everything that he or his family wanted out of the market.

10. Upon which account, his children, when they grew to age, were not well pleased with his management,

11. And the women that lived with him were treated with little cost, and complained of his way of housekeeping,

12. Where everything was ordered and set down from day to day, and reduced to the greatest exactness;

13. Since there was not there, as is usual in a great family and a plentiful estate, anything to spare;

14. But all that went out or came in, all disbursements and all receipts, proceeded as it were by number and measure.

15. His manager in all this was a single servant, Evangelus by name,

16. A man either naturally gifted or instructed by Pericles so as to excel everyone in this art of domestic economy.

17. All this, in truth, was very little in harmony with Anaxagoras' wisdom;

18. If, indeed, it be true that he, by a generous impulse and greatness of heart,

19. Voluntarily quitted his house, and left his land to lie fallow and to be grazed by sheep like a common.

20. But the life of a contemplative philosopher and that of an active statesman are not the same thing;

21. For the one merely employs, upon great and good objects of thought, an intelligence that requires no aid of instruments nor supply of any external materials;

22. Whereas the other, who tempers and applies his virtue to human uses, may have occasion for affluence,

23. Not as a matter of necessity, but as a noble thing; which was Pericles' case, who relieved numerous poor citizens.

24. However, there is a story that Anaxagoras himself, while Pericles was taken up with public affairs,

25. Lay neglected, and that now being grown old, he wrapped himself up with a resolution to die by starving himself.

26. When Pericles heard this he was horror-struck, and instantly ran to Anaxagoras,

27. And used all the arguments and entreaties he could to him, lamenting not so much Anaxagoras' condition as his own,

28. Should he lose such a counsellor as he had found him to be;

29. And that, upon this, Anaxagoras unfolded his robe, and showing his underfed ribs, made answer:

30. 'Pericles,' said he, 'even those who have occasion for a lamp supply it with oil.'

Chapter 39

1. The Lacedaemonians beginning to show themselves troubled at the growth of the Athenian power,

2. Pericles, on the other hand, to elevate the people's sentiments further, and to raise them to the thought of great actions,

3. Proposed a decree, to summon all the Greeks, whether of Europe or Asia, every city, little as well as great,

4. To send their deputies to Athens to a general assembly, or convention,

5. There to consult and advise concerning repairs to the cities which the barbarians had burnt down,

6. And also concerning the navigation of the sea, that they might henceforward pass to and fro and trade securely and be at peace among themselves.

7. Upon this errand there were twenty men above fifty years of age, sent by commission;

8. Five to summon the Ionians and Dorians in Asia, and the islanders as far as Lesbos and Rhodes;

9. Five to visit all the places in the Hellespont and Thrace, up to Byzantium; and five more to go to

Boeotia and Phocis and Peloponnesus,

10. And from thence to pass through the Locrians over to the neighbouring continent as far as Acarnania and Ambracia;

11. And the rest to take their course through Euboea to the Oetaeans and the Malian Gulf,

12. And to the Achaeans of Phthiotis and the Thessalians;

13. All of them to treat with the people as they passed,

14. And persuade them to come and take their part in the debates for settling the peace and jointly regulating the affairs of Greece.

15. Nothing came of this, nor did the cities send deputies, as was desired;

16. Because the Lacedaemonians, suspecting Pericles' intentions, subverted the plan underhandedly.

17. But the plan shows the calibre of Pericles and the greatness of his thoughts.

18. In his military conduct, he gained a great reputation for wariness:

19. He would not by his goodwill engage in any fight which had too much risk;

20. He did not envy the glory of generals whose rash adventures were luckily favoured with brilliant success, however they were admired by others;

21. Nor did he think them worthy of his imitation, but always used to say to his citizens that, so far as lay in his power, they should never die.

22. When Pericles saw Tolmides son of

Tolmaeus, made confident by his former successes and flushed with the honour his military actions had procured him,

23. Making preparations to attack the Boeotians in their own country when there was no likely opportunity,

24. And seeing also that Tolmides had prevailed with the bravest and most enterprising of the youth to enlist themselves as volunteers in the service,

25. He endeavoured to withhold him and to advise him from it in the public assembly,

26. Telling him in a memorable saying of his, which still goes about, that,

27. If he would not take Pericles' advice, yet he would not do amiss to wait and be ruled by time, the wisest counsellor of all.

28. This saying, at that time, was but slightly commended;

29. But within a few days after, when news was brought that Tolmides had been defeated and slain in battle near Coronea,

30. And that many brave citizens had fallen with him, it gained Pericles great repute as well as goodwill among the people,

31. For wisdom and for love of his countrymen.

Chapter 40

1. But of all his expeditions, that to the Chersonese gave most satisfaction and pleasure,

2. Having proved the safety of the Greeks who inhabited there. For he took with him a thousand fresh citizens of Athens to give new strength and vigour to the cities,

3. And by fortifying the neck of land which joins the peninsula to the continent with bulwarks and forts from sea to sea,

4. He put a stop to the inroads of the Thracians, who lay all about the Chersonese,

5. And closed the door against a continual and grievous war, with which that country had been long harassed,

6. Lying exposed to the encroachments of barbarous neighbours.

7. Nor was Pericles less admired and talked of abroad for his sailing around the Peloponnesus,

8. Having set out from Pegae, or The Fountains, the port of Megara, with a hundred galleys.

9. For he not only laid waste the sea-coast, as Tolmides had done before, but also, advancing far up into the mainland with the soldiers he had on board,

10. By the terror of his appearance drove many within their walls;

11. And at Nemea, with main force, routed and raised a trophy over the Sicyonians, who stood their ground and joined battle with him.

12. And having taken on board a supply of soldiers into the galleys out of Achaia, then in league with Athens, he crossed with the fleet to the opposite continent,

13. And, sailing along by the mouth of the River Achelous, overran Acarnania and shut up the Oeniadae within their city walls,

14. And having ravaged and wasted their country, weighed anchor for home with the double advantage of having shown himself formidable to his enemies,

15. And at the same time safe and energetic to his fellow citizens;

16. For there was not so much as any chance miscarriage that happened, the whole voyage through, to those who were under his charge.

17. Entering also the Euxine Sea with a large and finely equipped fleet, he obtained for the Greek cities any new arrangements they wanted, and entered into friendly relations with them;

18. And to the barbarous nations, and kings and chiefs round about them, displayed the greatness of the power of the Athenians,

19. Their perfect ability and confidence to sail wherever they had a mind, and to bring the whole sea under their control.

20. He left the Sinopians thirteen ships of war, with soldiers under the command of Lamachus, to assist them against Timesileus the tyrant;

21. And when this tyrant and his accomplices had been thrown out,

22. Obtained a decree that six hundred of the Athenians that were willing should sail to Sinope and plant themselves there with the Sinopians,

23. Sharing among them the houses and land which the tyrant and his party had previously held.

24. But in other things he did not comply with the giddy impulses of the citizens, nor quit his own resolutions to follow their fancies,

25. When, carried away with the thought of their strength and great success, they were eager to interfere again in Egypt,

26. And to disturb the King of Persia's maritime dominions.

27. Indeed, there were a good many who were, even then, possessed with that profoundly unwise passion for Sicily,

28. Which afterward the orators of Alcibiades' party blew up into a flame.

29. There were some also who dreamt of conquering Tuscany and Carthage,

30. And not without plausible reason in their present large dominion and prosperous course of their affairs.

31. But Pericles curbed this passion for foreign conquest, and unsparingly pruned and cut down their ever busy fancies for a multitude of undertakings;

32. And directed their power for the most part to securing and consolidating what they had already got,

33. Supposing it would be quite enough for them to do, if they could keep the Lacedaemonians in check;

34. To whom he entertained all along a sense of opposition; which, as upon many other occasions,

35. He particularly showed by what he did in the time of the Delphic war.

Chapter 41

1. The Lacedaemonians, having gone with an army to Delphi to recapture it from the Phocians who had taken it from the Delphians;

2. Immediately after their departure, Pericles, with another army, came and restored the Phocians.

3. That he did well and wisely in thus restraining the exertions of the Athenians within the compass of Greece,

4. The events themselves that happened afterward bore sufficient witness.

5. For, in the first place, the Euboeans revolted, against whom he passed over with forces;

6. And then, immediately after, news came that the Megarians were turned their enemies,

7. And a hostile army was on the borders of Attica, under the conduct of Plistoanax, king of the Lacedaemonians.

8. So Pericles hastened back with his army from Euboea, to meet the invasion which threatened at home;

9. And did not venture to engage a numerous and brave army eager for battle; but perceiving that Plistoanax was a very young man,

10. And governed mostly by the counsel and advice of Cleandrides, whom the ephors had sent with him to be a guardian and assistant,

11. He secretly tested this youth's integrity, and, in a short time, having corrupted him with money, persuaded him to withdraw the Peloponnesians from Attica.

12. When the army had retired and dispersed into their several states, the Lacedaemonians in anger fined their king so large a sum of money, that, unable to pay it, he quitted Lacedaemon;

13. While Cleandrides fled, and had sentence of death passed upon him in his absence.

14. This was the father of Gylippus, who later overpowered the Athenians in Sicily.

15. And it seems that this covetousness was an hereditary disease transmitted from father to son;

16. For Gylippus also afterwards was caught in foul practices, and expelled from Sparta for it.

17. When Pericles, in giving up his accounts of this expedition, stated a disbursement of ten talents, as laid out upon fit occasion,

18. The people, without any question, nor troubling themselves to investigate the mystery, freely allowed of it.

19. And some historians, in which number is Theophrastus the philosopher,

20. Have given it as a truth that Pericles every year used to send

privately the sum of ten talents to Sparta,

21. With which he complimented those in office, to keep off the war;

22. Not to purchase peace, but time, that he might prepare at leisure, and be the better able to carry on war hereafter.

Chapter 42

1. Immediately after this, turning his forces against the Euboean rebels with fifty ships and five thousand men,

2. Pericles reduced their cities, and drove out the citizens of the Chalcidians, called Hippobotae, horse-feeders, the chief persons for wealth and reputation among them;

3. And removing all the Histiaeans out of the country, brought in a plantation of Athenians in their place,

4. Making them his one example of severity, because they had captured an Attic ship and killed all on board.

5. After this, having made a truce between the Athens and Sparta for thirty years,

6. He ordered, by public decree, the expedition against the isle of Samos,

7. On the ground that, when they were told to cease their war with the Milesians, they had not complied.

8. And as these measures against the Samians are thought to have been taken to please his mistress Aspasia,

9. This may be a fit point for enquiry about that woman, what art or charming faculty she had that enabled her to captivate, as she did, the greatest statesmen,

10. And to give the philosophers occasion to speak so much about her, and that, too, not to her disparagement.

11. That she was a Milesian by birth, the daughter of Axiochus, is acknowledged.

12. And they say it was in emulation of Thargelia, a courtesan of the old Ionian times, that she made her addresses to men of great power.

13. Thargelia was a great beauty, extremely charming, and at the same time sagacious;

14. She had numerous suitors among the Greeks, and brought all who had to do with her over to the Persian interest,

15. And by their means, being men of the greatest power and station, sowed the seeds of the Median faction up and down in several cities.

16. Aspasia, some say, was courted and caressed by Pericles upon account of her knowledge and skill in politics.

17. Socrates himself would sometimes go to visit her, and some of his acquaintance with him;

18. And those who frequented her company would carry their wives with them to listen to her.

19. Her house was a home for young courtesans. Aeschines tells us that Lysicles, a sheep-dealer, a man of low birth and character,

20. By keeping Aspasia company after Pericles' death, came to be a chief man in Athens.

21. And in Plato's *Menexenus*, though we do not take the introduction as quite serious, still thus much seems to be historical,

22. That she had the repute of being resorted to by many of the Athenians for instruction in the art of speaking.

23. Pericles' inclination for her seems, however, to have proceeded from the passion of love.

24. He had a wife that was near kin to him, who had been married first to Hipponicus, by whom she had Callias, surnamed the Rich;

25. And also she brought Pericles, while she lived with him, two sons, Xanthippus and Paralus.

26. Afterwards, when they did not well agree, nor like to live together, he parted with her, with her own consent, to another man,

27. And himself took Aspasia, and loved her with wonderful affection;

28. Every day, both as he went out and as he came in from the market-place, he saluted and kissed her.

29. In the comedies she goes by the nicknames of 'the new Omphale' and 'Deianira'.

30. Cratinus, in downright terms, calls her a harlot: 'To find him an embodiment of lust bore that harlot past shame, Aspasia by name.'

31. It seems also that he had a son by her.

32. Aspasia, they say, became so celebrated and renowned that Cyrus, who also made war against Artaxerxes for the Persian monarchy,

33. Gave the concubine he loved most the name of Aspasia, who before that was called Milto, a Phocaean by birth.

Chapter 43

1. Pericles, however, was particularly charged with having proposed to the assembly the war against the Samians, from favour to the Milesians, upon the entreaty of Aspasia.

2. For the two states were at war for the possession of Priene; and the Samians, getting the better,

3. Refused to lay down their arms and to have the controversy betwixt them decided by arbitration by the Athenians.

4. Pericles, therefore, fitting out a fleet, went and broke up the oligarchical government at Samos,

5. And taking fifty of the principal men of the town as hostages, and as many of their children, sent them to the isle of Lemnos,

6. There to be kept, though he had offers, as some relate, of a talent apiece for himself from each one of the hostages,

7. And of many other presents from those who were anxious not to have a democracy.

8. Moreover, Pisuthnes the Persian, one of the king's lieutenants, bearing some goodwill to the Samians,

9. Sent him ten thousand pieces of gold to excuse the city. Pericles, however, would have none of this;

10. But after he had dealt with the Samians as he saw fit, and set up a democracy among them, sailed back to Athens.

11. But they immediately revolted, Pisuthnes having privily got away their hostages for them,

12. And provided them with means for the war. Whereupon Pericles came out with a fleet a second time against them, and found them not idle nor slinking away,

13. But manfully resolved to contest the dominion of the sea.

14. The issue was, that after a sharp sea fight around the island of Tragia, Pericles obtained a decisive victory,

15. Having with forty-four ships routed seventy of the enemy's, twenty of which were carrying soldiers.

16. Together with his victory and pursuit, having made himself master of the port, he laid siege to the Samians,

17. And blocked them up, who yet, one way or another, still ventured to make sallies, and fight under the city walls.

18. But after another greater fleet from Athens arrived, and the Samians were now shut up with a close leaguer on every side,

19. Pericles, taking with him sixty galleys, sailed out into the main sea, intending to meet a squadron of Phoenician ships coming for the Samians' relief,

20. And to fight them at as great distance as could be from the island;

21. But this proved a miscalculation. For on his departure, Melissus, the son of Ithagenes, a philosopher,

22. Being at that time the general in Samos, despising either the small number of the ships that were left or the inexperience of the commanders,

23. Prevailed with the citizens to attack the Athenians. And the Samians having won the battle,

24. And taken several of the men prisoners, and disabled several of the ships, were masters of the sea,

25. And brought into port all necessaries they wanted for the war, which they had not before.

26. Aristotle says, too, that Pericles had been once before this worsted by this Melissus in a sea fight.

27. The Samians, that they might requite the affront which had been put on them, branded the Athenian prisoners on their foreheads with the figure of an owl.

28. For so the Athenians had marked Samians before with a Samaena,

which is a sort of ship, low and flat in the prow, so as to look snub-nosed,

29. But wide and large and well-spread in the hold, by which it both carries a large cargo and sails well.

30. And it was so called, because the first of that kind was seen at Samos, having been built by order of Polycrates the tyrant.

31. These brands upon the Samians' foreheads, they say, are the allusion in the passage of Aristophanes, where he says, 'For, oh, the Samians are a lettered people.'

32. Pericles, as soon as news was brought him of the disaster that had befallen his army, made all the haste he could to come in to their relief,

33. And having defeated Melissus, he immediately proceeded to hem them in with a wall, resolving to master them and take the town,

34. Rather with some cost and time than with the wounds and hazards of his citizens.

35. But as it was a hard matter to keep back the Athenians, who were vexed at the delay,

36. And were eagerly bent to fight, he divided the whole multitude into eight parts, and arranged by lot that that part which had the white bean should have leave to feast and take their ease while the other seven were fighting.

37. And this is the reason, they say, that people, when at any time they have been merry and enjoyed

themselves, called it white day, in allusion to this white bean.

38. In the ninth month the Samians surrendered. Pericles pulled down their walls and seized their shipping,

39. And set a fine of a large sum of money upon them, part of which they paid down at once,

40. And they agreed to bring in the rest by a certain time, and gave hostages for security.

41. Duris the Samian makes a tragical drama out of these events, charging the Athenians and Pericles with a great deal of cruelty,

42. Probably with little regard to truth; for no other historians report such a thing.

43. Duris is likely to have exaggerated the calamities which befell his country, to create odium against the Athenians.

44. On his return to Athens Pericles took care that those who died in the war should be honourably buried,

45. And made a funeral harangue, as the custom is, in their commendation at their graves, for which he gained great admiration.

46. As he came down from the stage on which he spoke, the rest of the women came and complimented him, taking him by the hand, and crowning him with garlands and ribbons, like a victorious athlete in the games;

47. But Elpinice, coming near to him, said, 'These are brave deeds,

Pericles, that you have done, and such as deserve our chaplets;

48. 'Who have lost us many a worthy citizen, not in a war with Phoenicians or Medes, like my brother Cimon, but for the overthrow of an allied and kindred city.'

49. As Elpinice spoke these words, Pericles, smiling quietly, replied with this verse: 'Old women should not seek to be perfumed.'

50. Ion says that Pericles indulged very high and proud thoughts of himself for conquering the Samians,

51. Whereas Agamemnon was ten years taking a barbarous city, he had in nine months vanquished and taken the greatest and most powerful of the Ionians.

52. And indeed it was not without reason that he assumed this glory to himself, for, in real truth, there was much uncertainty and great hazard in this great war,

53. If so be, as Thucydides tells us, the Samian state was within a very little of wresting the whole power and dominion of the sea out of the Athenians' hands.

Chapter 44

1. After this, the Peloponnesian war beginning to break out in full tide, Pericles advised the people to help the Corcyraeans, who were being attacked by the Corinthians,

2. And thereby to secure to themselves an island possessed of great naval resources, since the Peloponnesians were already all but in actual hostilities against Athens.

3. The people readily consented to this, so Pericles dispatched Lacedaemonius, Cimon's son, with ten ships, as if out of a design to affront him;

4. For there was a great kindness and friendship betwixt Cimon's family and the Lacedaemonians;

5. So, in order that Lacedaemonius might lie the more open to a charge, or suspicion at least, of favouring the Lacedaemonians and playing false,

6. If he performed no considerable exploit in this service, he allowed him a small number of ships, and sent him out against his will;

7. And indeed he made it somewhat his business to hinder Cimon's sons from rising in the state,

8. Professing that by their very names they were not to be looked upon as native and true Athenians,

9. But foreigners and strangers, one being called Lacedaemonius, another Thessalus and the third Eleus,

10. And they were all three of them, it was thought, born of an Arcadian woman.

11. Being, however, ill spoken of on account of these ten galleys, as having afforded but a small supply to the people that were in need,

12. And yet given a great advantage to those who might complain of the act of intervention,

13. Pericles sent out a larger force afterwards to Corcyra, which arrived after the fight was over.

14. And now the Corinthians, angry and indignant with the Athenians, accused them publicly at Lacedaemon,

15. And the Megarians joined with them, complaining that they were, contrary to common right and the articles of peace sworn among the Greeks,

16. Kept out and driven away from every market and from all ports under the control of the Athenians.

17. The Aeginetans, also, professing to be ill-used, made supplications in private to the Lacedaemonians for redress,

18. Though not daring openly to call the Athenians in question. In the meantime, also, Potidaea, under the dominion of the Athenians, but a colony formerly of the Corinthians,

19. Had revolted, and was beset with a formal siege, and was a further occasion of precipitating the war.

20. Despite all this, there being embassies sent to Athens, and Archidamus, the king of the Spartans,

21. Trying to bring most of the disputes to a fair resolution and to pacify the hearts of the allies,

22. It is likely that war would not have fallen upon the Athenians, if they could have been persuaded to repeal the ordinance against the Megarians.

23. Upon which account, since Pericles was the main opponent of repeal,

24. And stirred the Athenians' passions to persist in their dispute with the Megarians, he was regarded as the sole cause of the war.

25. They say, moreover, that ambassadors went from Sparta to Athens on this very business,

26. And that when Pericles was urging a certain law which made it illegal to take down or withdraw the tablet of the decree, one of the ambassadors, Polyalces by name, said,

27. 'Well, do not take it down then, but turn it; there is no law, I suppose, which forbids that.'

28. Which, though prettily said, did not change Pericles' mind, for he bore much animosity towards the Megarians.

29. Even so, he proposed a decree that a herald should be sent to them, and the same also to the Lacedaemonians, with the accusation against the Megarians;

30. An order which certainly shows equitable and friendly proceeding enough.

31. The herald who was sent, by name Anthemocritus, died on the journey back, and it was believed that the Megarians had killed him.

32. Then Charinus proposed a decree against them, that there should be an irreconcilable and implacable enmity thenceforward between the two commonwealths;

33. And that if any one of the
    Megarians should set foot in
    Attica, he should die;

34. And that the commanders, when
    they take the usual oath, should,
    over and above that,

35. Swear that they will twice every
    year make an inroad into the
    Megarian country;

36. And that Anthemocritus should be
    buried near the Thracian Gates,
    which are now called the Dipylon,
    or Double Gate.

Chapter 45

1. On the other hand, the Megarians,
   utterly denying the murder of
   Anthemocritus,

2. Threw the whole matter upon
   Aspasia and Pericles, availing
   themselves of the famous verses in
   the Acharnians:

3. 'To Megara some of our madcaps
   ran, And stole Simaetha thence,
   their courtesan.

4. 'Which exploit the Megarians to
   outdo, Came to Aspasia's house,
   and took off two.'

5. The true occasion of the quarrel is
   not easy to fathom. But all alike
   charge Pericles with the refusal to
   annul the decree.

6. Some say he met the request with
   a positive refusal, out of a sense of
   pride and a view of the state's best
   interests,

7. Believing that the demand made
   by the embassies was a test of
   Athens' will, and that a concession
   would be taken for weakness;

8. While others say that it was
   out of arrogance and contentiousness, to show his own strength,
   that he slighted the
   Lacedaemonians.

9. The worst motive of all, which is
   confirmed by most witnesses, is
   this: Phidias the sculptor had
   undertaken to make a statue.

10. Now he, being a great friend of
    Pericles, had many enemies
    because of this, who envied and
    maligned him;

11. Who brought an accusation
    against him of stealing gold that
    was to be used in making the
    statue.

12. Though the gold was weighed
    every day and none was found
    missing, still Phidias was commit-
    ted to prison, and there died,

13. Some say, of poison, administered
    by Pericles' enemies, to raise a
    slander, or a suspicion at least, as
    though he had procured it.

14. About the same time, Aspasia was
    charged that she received into her
    house freeborn women for the use
    of Pericles.

15. And Diopithes proposed a decree,
    that public accusations should be
    laid against persons who neglected
    every view of the world but that of
    science,

16. Directing suspicion, by means of
    Anaxagoras, against Pericles
    himself.

17. The people receiving and admit-
    ting these accusations and
    complaints, at length came to

enact a decree, at the motion of Dracontides,

18. That Pericles should bring in the accounts of the moneys he had expended, and lodge them with the Prytanes;

19. And that the judges, carrying their suffrage from the Acropolis, should examine and determine the business in the city.

20. This last clause Hagnon took out of the decree, and moved that the causes should be tried before fifteen hundred jurors,

21. Whether they should be styled prosecutions for robbery, or bribery, or any kind of malversation.

22. Pericles pleaded for the release of Aspasia, shedding, as Aeschines says, many tears at the trial, and personally entreating the jurors.

23. But fearing for Anaxagoras, he sent him out of the city. And finding that in Phidias' case he had lost the confidence of the people,

24. And wishing to avoid impeachment, he kindled the war against Sparta, which hitherto had smouldered quietly, and now blew it up into a flame;

25. Hoping, by that means, to disperse and scatter these complaints and charges;

26. For the city usually threw herself upon him alone, trusting to his sole conduct, when emergencies and great affairs and public dangers arose, by reason of his authority and the sway he bore.

27. These are variously alleged as the reasons which induced Pericles not to allow the people of Athens to yield to the proposals of the Lacedaemonians; but their truth is uncertain.

Chapter 46

1. The Lacedaemonians, for their part, feeling sure that if they could once remove Pericles, they might impose what terms they pleased on the Athenians,

2. Sent them word that they should expel the 'pollution' with which Pericles on the mother's side was tainted, as Thucydides tells us, for her ancestors' part in expelling the sons of Pisistratus;

3. But the issue proved quite contrary to what they expected; instead of bringing Pericles under suspicion,

4. They raised him into yet greater credit and esteem with the citizens, as a man whom their enemies most hated and feared.

5. In the same way, also, before Archidamus, who was at the head of the Peloponnesians, made his invasion into Attica,

6. Pericles told the Athenians beforehand, that if Archidamus, while he laid waste the rest of the country, should spare his estate, either on the ground of friendship or right of hospitality that was betwixt them,

7. Or on purpose to give his enemies an occasion of traducing him; then

he would freely bestow upon the state all his land and the buildings on it for the public use.

8. The Lacedaemonians, therefore, and their allies, with a great army, invaded the Athenian territories under the conduct of King Archidamus, and laying waste the country, marched as far as Acharnae,

9. And there pitched their camp, presuming that the Athenians would never endure that,

10. But would come out and fight them for their country's and their honour's sake.

11. But Pericles looked upon it as dangerous to engage in battle, to the risk of the city itself, against sixty thousand Peloponnesians and Boeotians; for that is how many had invaded;

12. And he endeavoured to appease those who were eager to fight, saying that 'trees, when they are lopped and cut, grow up again in a short time, but men, being once lost, cannot easily be recovered'.

13. He did not convene the people into an assembly, for fear lest they should force him to act against his judgement;

14. But, like a skilful steersman, who, when a sudden squall comes on at sea, makes all his arrangements, sees that all is tight and fast,

15. And then follows the dictates of his skill, taking no notice of the tears and entreaties of the seasick and fearful passengers,

16. So he, having shut the city gates and posted guards, followed his own judgement,

17. Little regarding those who cried out against him; although many of his friends urged him, and many of his enemies threatened and accused him,

18. And many made songs and lampoons upon him, which were sung about the town to his disgrace,

19. Reproaching him with the cowardly exercise of his office of general, and the tame abandonment of everything to the enemy's hands.

20. Cleon was already among his assailants, making use of the feeling against him as a step to the leadership of the people, as appears in the verses of Hermippus:

21. 'Satyr-king, instead of swords, Will you always handle words? Very brave indeed we find them, But a Teles lurks behind them.

22. 'Yet to gnash your teeth you're seen, When the little dagger keen, Whetted every day anew, Of sharp Cleon touches you.'

23. Pericles, however, was unmoved by these attacks, but took all patiently, and submitted in silence to the disgrace they threw upon him and the ill-will they bore him;

24. And sending out a fleet of a hundred galleys to Peloponnesus, he did not go along with it in person,

25. But stayed behind, that he might watch at home and keep the city under his own control, till the Peloponnesians broke up their camp and were gone.

26. Yet to soothe the common people, jaded and distressed with the war, he relieved them with distributions of public moneys,

27. And ordained new divisions of subject land. For having turned out all the people of Aegina, he parted the island among the Athenians according to lot.

28. Some comfort also, and ease in their miseries, they might receive from what their enemies endured.

29. For the fleet, sailing round the Peloponnese, ravaged a great deal of the country, and pillaged and plundered the towns and smaller cities;

30. And by land he himself entered with an army the Megarian country, and made havoc of it all.

Chapter 47

1. Whence it is clear that the Peloponnesians, though they did the Athenians much mischief by land,

2. Yet suffering as much themselves from them by sea, would not have protracted the war to such a length,

3. But would quickly have given it over, as Pericles at first foretold they would, had not accident entered the picture.

4. In the first place, plague seized upon the city, and ate up all the flower and prime of their youth and strength.

5. The people, afflicted in their minds as well as bodies, were enraged like madmen against Pericles,

6. And, like patients grown delirious, sought to lay violent hands on their physician, or, as it were, their father.

7. They had been persuaded by Pericles' enemies that the reason for the plague was the crowding of the country people into the town,

8. Forcing everyone, in the heat of summer, to huddle together in small tenements and stifling hovels,

9. And to follow a lazy course of life within doors, whereas before they lived in the open air.

10. The author of all this, they said, is he who on account of the war has poured a multitude of people in upon us within the walls,

11. And uses all these men that he has here upon no employ or service, but keeps them pent up like cattle,

12. To be overrun with infection from one another, affording them neither shift of quarters nor any refreshment.

13. With the design to remedy these evils, and do the enemy some inconvenience, Pericles got a hundred and fifty galleys ready,

14. And having embarked many tried soldiers, both foot and horse,

15. Was about to sail out, giving great

hope to his citizens, and no less alarm to his enemies, upon the sight of so great a force.

16. When the vessels had their complement of men, and Pericles had gone aboard his own galley,

17. It happened that the sun was eclipsed, and it suddenly grew dark, to the affright of all, for the ignorant did not understand the cause.

18. Pericles, therefore, seeing his steersman seized with fear, took his cloak and held it before the man's face, screening him so that he could not see,

19. And asked him whether he imagined there was any great hurt in this. The steersman answering No,

20. 'Why,' said Pericles, 'and what does that differ from this, only that what has caused that darkness there, is something bigger than a cloak?'

21. This is a story philosophers tell their students. Pericles, however, after putting out to sea, seems not to have done any other exploit befitting such preparations,

22. And when he had laid siege to Epidaurus, which gave him some hope of surrender, miscarried in his design by reason of the plague.

23. For it not only seized upon the Athenians, but upon all others, too, that held any sort of communication with the army.

24. Finding the Athenians ill affected towards him after this, he tried

what he could to re-encourage them.

25. But he could not allay their anger, nor persuade them, till they freely passed their votes on him, and resumed their power,

26. Taking away his command and fining him in a sum of money;

27. Which by their account that say least, was fifteen talents, while they who reckon most, name fifty.

28. The name prefixed to the accusation was Cleon, as Idomeneus tells us; Simmias, according to Theophrastus; and Heraclides Ponticus gives it as Lacratidas.

29. After this, public troubles were soon to leave him unmolested; the people discharged their anger against him in this stroke, and lost their stings in the wound.

30. But his domestic concerns were in an unhappy condition, many of his friends and acquaintances having died in the plague time,

31. And those of his family having long since been in disorder and in a kind of mutiny against him.

32. For the eldest of his lawful sons, Xanthippus by name, being naturally prodigal, and marrying a young and expensive wife,

33. Was highly offended at his father's economy in giving him only a scanty allowance, a little at a time.

34. He therefore borrowed some money in his father's name, pretending it was by his order.

35. The lender coming afterwards to demand the debt, Pericles was so

far from yielding to pay it, that he entered an action against his son.

36. Upon which the young man, Xanthippus, thought himself so ill used and disobliged that he openly reviled his father;

37. Telling first, by way of ridicule, stories about his conversations at home, and the discourses he had with the sophists and scholars that came to his house.

38. As, for instance, how one who was a practiser of the five games of skill,

39. Having with a dart or javelin unawares against his will struck and killed Epitimus the Pharsalian,

40. His father spent a whole day with Protagoras in a serious dispute, whether the javelin, or the man that threw it,

41. Or the masters of the games who appointed these sports, were, according to the strictest and best reason, to be accounted the cause of this mischance.

42. Besides this, Stesimbrotus tells us that it was Xanthippus who spread abroad the infamous story concerning his own wife, Pericles' daughter-in-law,

43. That Pericles had fallen in love with her; and in general that this difference of the young man's with his father,

44. And the breach betwixt them, continued never to be healed or made up till his death; for Xanthippus died in the plague.

Chapter 48

1. In the plague Pericles also lost his sister, and the greatest part of his relations and friends,

2. And those who had been most useful and serviceable to him in managing the affairs of state.

3. However, he did not shrink or give in upon these occasions, nor betray or lower his character and the greatness of his mind under all these misfortunes;

4. He was not seen to weep or mourn, or even attend the burial of any of his friends or relations, till at last he lost his only remaining legitimate son.

5. Subdued by this blow, and yet striving still, as far as he could, to maintain the greatness of his mind,

6. When he came to perform the ceremony of putting a garland of flowers on the head of the corpse, he was vanquished by his passion at the sight,

7. So that he burst into exclamations, and shed copious tears, having never done any such thing in his life before.

8. The city having tried other generals for the conduct of war, and politicians for business of state,

9. When they found there was no one who was of weight enough to be trusted with so great a command,

10. Regretted the loss of him, and invited him again to advise them,

and to reassume the office of general.

11. He was lying at home in dejection and mourning; but was persuaded by Alcibiades and others of his friends to come abroad and show himself to the people;

12. Who on his appearance made their acknowledgements, and apologised for their treatment of him.

13. So he undertook the public affairs once more; and, being chosen general,

14. Requested that the statute concerning base-born children, which he himself had formerly caused to be made, might be suspended;

15. So that the name and race of his family might not, for want of a lawful heir to succeed, be lost and extinguished.

16. The case of the statute was this: Pericles, when long ago at the height of his power in the state,

17. Having then had lawfully begotten children, proposed a law that those only should be reputed true citizens of Athens who were born of parents who were both Athenians.

18. Sometime later the king of Egypt sent a present of forty thousand bushels of wheat to be shared among the citizens.

19. There followed a great many actions and suits about legitimacy by virtue of that edict; cases which, till that time, had never occurred;

20. And several persons suffered by false accusations.

21. There were little less than five thousand who were convicted and sold for slaves as non-citizens;

22. Those who, passing the test, proved to be true Athenians were found on census to be fourteen thousand and forty persons in number.

23. It looked strange that a law which had been carried so far against so many people should be cancelled again by the same man that made it;

24. Yet the present distress which Pericles laboured under in his family broke through all objections,

25. And prevailed with the Athenians to pity him, as one whose misfortunes had sufficiently punished his former arrogance.

26. His sufferings deserved, they thought, their pity, and even indignation,

27. And his request was such as became a man to ask and men to grant; so they gave him permission to enrol his son in the register of his tribe, giving him his own name.

28. This son afterwards, after having defeated the Peloponnesians at Arginusae, was, with his fellow-generals, put to death by the people.

29. About the time when his son was enrolled, it should seem the plague seized Pericles, not with sharp and

violent fits, as it did others that had it, but with a dull and lingering distemper,

30. Attended with various changes and alterations, little by little wasting the strength of his body and undermining the noble faculties of his mind.

31. So that Theophrastus, in his *Morals*, when discussing whether men's characters change with their circumstances,

32. And their moral habits, disturbed by the ailings of their bodies, start aside from the rules of virtue, has left it upon record that Pericles, when he was sick,

33. Showed one of his friends that came to visit him an amulet that the women had hung about his neck;

34. As much as to say, that he was very sick indeed when he would admit of such foolery as that was.

Chapter 49

1. When he was now near his end, the best of the citizens and those of his friends who were left alive, sitting about him,

2. Were speaking of the greatness of his merit, and reckoning up his famous actions and victories;

3. For there were no less than nine trophies, which, as their commander and conqueror of their enemies, he had set up for the honour of the city.

4. They talked thus among themselves, as though he were unable to understand or mind what they said.

5. He listened, however, all the while, and then spoke up, saying that he wondered they should commend things which were as much owed to luck as anything else,

6. And had happened to many other commanders, and, at the same time, should not mention that which was the most excellent and greatest thing of all.

7. 'For,' said he, 'no Athenian, through my means, ever wore mourning.'

8. He was indeed a character deserving our highest admiration not only for his equitable and mild temper, which all along in the many affairs of his life,

9. And the great animosities which he incurred, he constantly maintained;

10. But also for the high feeling which made him regard it the noblest of his honours,

11. That in the exercise of such immense power, he never gratified his envy or his passion.

12. And to me it appears that this one thing gives that otherwise childish and arrogant title of 'Olympian' a fitting and becoming significance;

13. So dispassionate a temper, so unblemished a life in the height of power and place, might well be called Olympian.

14. Not as the poets represent, confounding us with their

ignorant fancies; but in meaning of the metaphor as a truly great man.

15. The course of public affairs after Pericles' death produced a speedy sense of his loss to Athens.

16. Those who had resented him because he eclipsed themselves, after making trial of other leaders,

17. Readily acknowledged that there had never been such a disposition as his, more moderate and reasonable in the height of the power he held,

18. Or more grave and impressive in the mildness with which he used it.

Chapter 50: Cato the Censor

1. Cato was known as the Censor because of the unbending strictness and severity of his moral rule when he held the office of Censor at Rome.

2. He is therefore an example either to be admired or shunned: let his life story suggest which.

3. He was also known as Cato the Younger, for he had a great-grandfather, remembered as Cato the Elder, who did Rome notable military service.

4. This elder Cato had often obtained military prizes, and having lost five horses under him in battle, received, for his valour, the worth of them out of the public exchequer.

5. The family was not however patrician, and the younger Cato

himself was happier working on his farm than speaking in the forum at Rome.

6. He was born at Tusculum, though until he turned to civil and military affairs he lived in the country of the Sabines, where he had inherited a modest estate from his father.

7. He gained early in life a good habit of body by farming, austere living and military service, and seemed to have equal proportions of health and strength.

8. From an early age he practised his eloquence through all the villages of his neighbourhood,

9. Thinking eloquence necessary to anyone intending more than a humble and inactive life.

10. He would never refuse to serve as counsel for those who needed him, and was early reckoned a good lawyer and a capable orator.

11. Not only did he refuse fees for his legal work, but he did not put great value on the honour proceeding from winning court cases,

12. Being much more desirous to distinguish himself in military efforts.

13. While still a youth his breast received scars in combat, being only seventeen years old when he made his first campaign.

14. That was in the time when Hannibal, at the height of his success, was burning and pillaging all Italy.

15. In battle Cato would strike hard, without flinching, stand his ground firmly, present a bold countenance to his enemies, and shout at them with a harsh threatening voice,

16. Justly telling others that such rugged behaviour sometimes terrifies an enemy more than the sword itself.

17. When marching he carried his own weapons, followed by only one servant to carry the provisions.

18. He is said never to have been angry or hasty with servants, but would, when free from his duties, help them in theirs.

19. When he was with the army he used to drink only water, unless, when extremely thirsty, he might mingle it with a little vinegar; or if he found his strength fail him, a little wine.

20. The small country house of Manius Curius, who had been awarded three Triumphs by Rome, happened to be near his farm;

21. So that often visiting there, and contemplating the small compass and plainness of the place,

22. He formed an idea of the mind of the person, who, being one of the greatest of the Romans, and having subdued the most warlike nations,

23. Was contented to dig in so small a piece of ground, and live in such a cottage.

24. Here it was that the ambassadors

of the Samnites, finding Manius boiling turnips in the chimney corner, offered him a present of gold;

25. But he sent them away, saying that he, who was content with such a supper, had no need of gold;

26. And that he thought it more honourable to conquer those who possessed gold, than to possess the gold itself.

27. Cato, after reflecting on these things, used to return home,

28. And reviewing his own farm, his servants and housekeeping, increase his labour, and further retrench his expenses.

29. When Fabius Maximus took Tarentum, Cato, being then just a youth, was a soldier under him;

30. And lodging with one Nearchus, a Pythagorean, desired to understand some of his doctrine.

31. Hearing from him about Plato's doctrines – that pleasure is evil's chief bait and the body the principal calamity of the mind,

32. And that those thoughts which most separate and take the mind from the appetites of the body, most enfranchise and purify it,

33. He fell in love all the more with frugality and temperance.

34. With this exception, he is said not to have studied Greek until when he was quite old;

35. And in rhetoric then to have profited a little by Thucydides, and more by Demosthenes.

36. His writings, however, are

considerably embellished with Greek sayings and stories;

37. Many of these, translated word for word, figure among his own apothegm.

Chapter 51

1. There was a man of the highest rank, and very influential among the Romans, called Valerius Flaccus,

2. Who was singularly skilful in discerning excellence in the young, and disposed to nourish and advance it.

3. He had lands bordering Cato's; nor could he but admire him, when he understood from Cato's servants their master's manner of living,

4. And how he laboured with his own hands; went on foot betimes in the morning to the courts to assist those who wanted his counsel;

5. How, returning home again, when it was winter, he would throw a loose cloak over his shoulders,

6. And in the summer time would work among his domestics, sit with them, eat of the same bread and drink of the same wine.

7. When they spoke of his fair dealing and moderation and his wise sayings, Valerius arranged that he should be invited to supper;

8. And thus becoming personally assured of Cato's superior character,

9. Which, like a plant, seemed only to require culture and a better situation,

10. He persuaded him to apply himself to state affairs at Rome.

11. To Rome, therefore, Cato went, and by his work in the courts soon gained many friends and admirers;

12. But, Valerius chiefly assisting his promotion, he first of all got appointed tribune in the army, and afterwards was made its treasurer.

13. And now becoming eminent and noted, he passed, with Valerius himself, through the greatest commands, being first his colleague as consul, and then censor.

14. But among all the ancient senators, he most attached himself to Fabius Maximus;

15. Not so much for the honour of his person, and greatness of his power, as that he might have before him Fabius' habit and manner of life, as the best examples to follow:

16. And so he did not hesitate to oppose Scipio the Great, who, being then but a young man,

17. Had set himself against the power of Fabius, and to be envied by him.

18. For being sent as treasurer to the army in Sicily where Scipio was commander,

19. When Cato saw him, according to his usual custom, make great expenses, and distribute largesse among the soldiers without sparing,

20. He freely told him that the expense in itself was not the greatest thing to be considered,

21. But that he was corrupting the ancient frugality of the soldiers, by giving them means to abandon themselves to unnecessary pleasures and luxuries.

22. Scipio answered that he had no need for so accurate a treasurer,

23. And that he owed the people an account of his actions, not of the money he spent.

24. Hereupon Cato returned from Sicily, and, together with Fabius,

25. Complained in the senate about Scipio's extravagance, and of his loitering away his time in wrestling matches and comedies,

26. As if he were there not for war, but for holiday; and thus succeeded in getting tribunes sent to recall Scipio to answer the accusations.

27. But Scipio convinced the tribunes, by showing them his preparations for a coming victory,

28. And, being found merely to be living pleasantly with his friends when there was nothing else to do, without neglecting anything of consequence,

29. He was allowed without impediment to set sail towards the war.

Chapter 52

1. Cato grew more and more powerful by his eloquence, so that he was commonly called the Roman Demosthenes;

2. But his manner of life was yet more famous and talked of. For oratorical skill was, as an accomplishment, commonly studied and sought after by all young men;

3. But it was a rare person who would cultivate the habits of bodily labour, or prefer a light supper,

4. And a breakfast which never saw the fire; or be in love with poor clothes and a homely lodging;

5. Or could set his ambition rather on doing without luxuries than on possessing them.

6. For now the state, unable to keep its purity because it had grown so great and populous,

7. And having so many affairs, and people from all parts of the world under its government,

8. Was open to many mixed customs and new examples of living.

9. With reason, therefore, everybody admired Cato, when they saw others sink under labours and grow effeminate by pleasures,

10. And yet saw him unconquered by either;

11. And this not only when he was young and desirous of honour,

12. But also when old and greyheaded, after a Consulship and a Triumph;

13. Like some famous victor in the games persevering in his exercise and maintaining his character to the last.

14. He himself says, that he never wore a suit of clothes which cost more than a hundred drachmas;

15. And that, when he was general and

consul, he drank the same wine as his workmen;

16. And that the meat or fish which was bought in the market for his dinner, did not cost above thirty asses.

17. All which was for the sake of the commonwealth, that so his body might be the hardier for the war.

18. Having a piece of embroidered Babylonian tapestry left him, he sold it,

19. Because none of his farmhouses were so much as plastered.

20. Nor did he ever buy a slave for above fifteen hundred drachmas,

21. As he did not seek for effeminate and handsome ones, but able, sturdy workmen, horse-keepers and cowherds:

22. And these he thought ought to be sold again, when they grew old, and no useless servants fed in his house.

23. In short, he reckoned nothing a good bargain, which was superfluous;

24. But he thought anything unnecessary too expensive, even at half a farthing.

25. He was for the purchase of lands for sowing and feeding, not for gardens.

26. Some imputed these things to petty avarice, but others approved of him,

27. As if he had only the more strictly denied himself to set an example to others.

Chapter 53

1. Should Cato be applauded for this austerity and economy in all things?

2. Certainly it marks an over-rigid temper, for a man to take the work out of his servants as out of brute beasts,

3. Then turn them off and sell them in their old age, thinking there ought to be no further commerce between man and man, than what has some profit by it.

4. We see that kindness or humanity has a larger field than bare justice to exercise itself in;

5. Law and justice we cannot, in the nature of things, employ on others than men;

6. But we may extend our goodness and charity even to irrational creatures;

7. And such acts flow from a gentle nature, as water from an abundant spring.

8. It is doubtless the part of a kind-natured man to keep even worn-out horses and dogs,

9. And not only take care of them when they are young, but also when they are old.

10. The Athenians turned their mules loose to feed freely, when they had done the hardest labour.

11. The graves of Cimon's horses, which thrice won the Olympian races, are yet to be seen close by his own monument.

12. Old Xanthippus, too, entombed his dog, which swam after his galley to Salamis.

13. We are not to use living creatures like old shoes or dishes, and throw them away when they are worn out;

14. But if it were for nothing else, but by way of study and practice in humanity, a man ought always to habituate himself in these things to be kind.

15. As to myself, I would not so much as sell my draught ox on the account of his age,

16. Much less for a small piece of money sell a poor old man, and so chase him from where he has lived a long while,

17. And the manner of living he has been accustomed to; and that more especially when he would be as useless to the buyer as to the seller.

18. Yet Cato, for all this, boasted that he left that very horse in Spain, which he used in the wars when he was consul,

19. Only because he would not put the public to the expense of transporting it home.

20. Whether these acts are to be ascribed to the greatness or pettiness of his mind, let everyone argue as they please.

Chapter 54

1. Despite this, for his general temperance and self-control Cato surely deserves the highest admiration.

2. For when he commanded the army, he never took for himself, and those that belonged to him,

above three bushels of wheat for a month,

3. And somewhat less than a bushel and a half a day of barley for his baggage-cattle.

4. And when he became governor of Sardinia, where his predecessors had been used to require tents, bedding and clothes at the public expense,

5. And to charge the state heavily with the cost of provisions and entertainments for a great train of servants and friends,

6. The difference he showed in his economy was extraordinary.

7. There was hardly anything he would charge to the public purse.

8. He would walk without a carriage to visit the cities, accompanied only by a common town officer.

9. Yet, though he was easy and sparing to all who were under his authority,

10. He showed most inflexible strictness in what related to public justice, and was rigorous and precise in what concerned the laws;

11. So that the Roman government never seemed more terrible, nor yet more mild, than under his administration.

12. His very manner of speaking seemed to have such a kind of idea with it; for it was courteous, and yet forcible;

13. Pleasant, yet overwhelming; facetious, yet austere; sententious, yet vehement:

14. Like Socrates, in the description of Plato, who seemed to those about him to be a simple, blunt fellow,

15. While in fact he was full of such gravity and matter as would even move tears, and touch the very hearts of his auditors.

16. Being once desirous to dissuade the common people of Rome from their unseasonable and impetuous clamour for largesses and distributions of corn, Cato said:

17. 'It is a difficult task, O citizens, to make speeches to the belly, which has no ears.'

18. Reproving, also, their sumptuous habits, he said it was hard to preserve a city where a fish sold for more than an ox.

19. He had a saying, also, that the Roman people were like sheep; for they, when single, do not obey, but when all together in a flock, they follow their leaders:

20. 'So you,' said he, 'when you have got together in a body, let yourselves be guided by those whom singly you would never think of being advised by.'

21. Discoursing of the power of women, he echoed a saying of Themistocles,

22. Who, when his son was making many demands of him by means of the mother, said,

23. 'O woman, the Athenians govern the Greeks; I govern the Athenians, but you govern me, and your son governs you; so let him use his power sparingly, since,

24. simple as he is, he can do more than all the Greeks together.'

24. Another saying of Cato's was that the Roman people did not only fix the value of such and such purple dyes, but also of such and such habits of life:

25. 'For,' he said, 'as dyers most of all dye such colours as they see to be most agreeable, so the young men zealously affect what is most popular with you.'

26. He would say of men who continually desired to be in office that apparently they did not know their way around Rome,

27. Since they could not do without beadles to lead them along its streets.

28. He also reproved the citizens for always choosing the same men as their magistrates:

29. 'For you will seem,' he said, 'either not to esteem government worth much, or to think few worthy to hold it.'

30. Pointing at one who had sold an inherited estate which lay near the sea, he pretended to express his wonder at this man's being stronger than the sea itself;

31. For what it washed away with much effort, he drank away with great ease.

32. When the senate with a great deal of splendour received King Eumenes on his visit to Rome,

33. And the chief citizens strove who should sit nearest the king, Cato regarded him with dislike;

34. And when someone said to him that Eumenes was a good prince, and a friend to Rome:

35. 'It may be so,' said Cato, 'but by nature this same animal of a king is a kind of man-eater';

36. And added that there were never kings who compared with Epameinondas, Pericles, Themistocles, Manius Curius or Hamilcar Barca.

Chapter 55

1. Cato used to say that his enemies envied him because he got up every day before light, and neglected his own business to serve that of the public.

2. He would also say that he had rather be deprived of the reward for doing well, than not to suffer punishment for doing ill;

3. And that he could pardon all offenders but himself.

4. The Romans having sent three ambassadors to Bithynia, of whom one was gouty, another had his skull trepanned and the third seemed little better than a fool;

5. Cato, laughing, said that the Romans had sent an embassy which had neither feet, head nor heart.

6. He used to assert that wise men profited more by fools, than fools by wise men;

7. For that wise men avoided the faults of fools, fools would not imitate the example of wise men.

8. He would profess, too, that he was more taken with young men that blushed, than with those who looked pale;

9. And that he never desired to have a soldier that moved his hands too much in marching, and his feet too much in fighting; or snored louder than he shouted.

10. Ridiculing a fat overgrown man: 'What use,' said he, 'can the state turn a man's body to, when all between the throat and groin is taken up by belly?'

11. A man who was much given to pleasures desired his acquaintance, whereupon Cato begged his pardon, saying he could not be friends with a man whose palate was of a quicker sense than his heart.

12. He would likewise say that the heart of a lover lived in the body of another;

13. And he said that in his whole life he most repented of three things:

14. One was that he had trusted a secret to a woman;

15. Another, that he went by water when he might have gone by land;

16. The third, that he had remained one whole day without doing any business of moment.

17. Addressing an old man who was committing some vice, he said:

18. 'Friend, old age has of itself blemishes enough; do not add to them the deformity of vice.'

19. Speaking to a tribune who was reputed a poisoner, and was very keen to bring in a certain law:

20. 'Young man,' cried he, 'I know not which would be better, to drink what you mix, or confirm what you would put up for a law.'

21. Being reviled by a fellow who lived a profligate and wicked life:

22. 'A contest,' replied he, 'is unequal between you and me; for you can hear ill words easily, and can as easily give them;

23. 'But it is unpleasant to me to give such, and unusual to hear them.'

24. Such was the way Cato expressed himself, in sayings that are memorable.

Chapter 56

1. Being chosen consul with his friend Valerius Flaccus, Cato was given the government of that part of Spain which the Romans call Hither Spain.

2. As he was engaged in pacifying some of the tribes by force, and negotiating with others, a large army of barbarians attacked him,

3. So that there was danger of being disastrously driven from those territories.

4. He therefore called upon his neighbours, the Celtiberians, for help.

5. They demanded two hundred talents, and everybody thought it intolerable that Romans should pay barbarians for aid;

6. But Cato said there was no discredit in it; for if they won, the barbarians would be paid out of the enemy's purse;

7. But if they lost, there would be nobody left either to demand or to pay the reward.

8. However, he won a convincing victory, and all his subsequent affairs went well.

9. By his command the walls of all towns east of the River Baetis were demolished in a single day;

10. There were a great many of them, full of brave and warlike men.

11. Cato himself says that he took more cities – four hundred of them – than he stayed days in Spain.

12. And though the soldiers had gathered much booty in the fights, yet he distributed a pound of silver to each of them,

13. Saying it was better that many Romans should return home with silver, than a few with gold.

14. For himself he says he took nothing beyond what he ate and drank.

15. 'I do not fault those who seek booty,' he said, 'but I had rather compete in valour with the best than in wealth with the richest, or with the most covetous in love of money.'

16. He kept not only himself but his servants from taking booty.

17. One of them, called Paccus, bought three boys from among the captives.

18. When Paccus learned that Cato had heard this, he hanged himself rather than face Cato's wrath.

19. Cato sold the boys, and gave the price to the public exchequer.

Chapter 57

1. Scipio the Great was Cato's enemy, and wishing to limit his achievements and take Spanish affairs into his own hands,

2. He arranged to be appointed his successor there; and, making all haste, put an end to Cato's authority.

3. But Cato, taking with him a convoy of five cohorts of foot, and five hundred horse to attend him home,

4. On the way overthrew the Lacetanians, and finding six hundred Roman deserters hiding among them, had all the deserters beheaded;

5. Scipio pretended indignation at this, but Cato, in mock disparagement of himself, said,

6. 'Rome would become great indeed, if men of higher birth never allowed men of lower birth [meaning himself] to advance the honour of the city.'

7. The senate voted to change nothing established by Cato in Spain,

8. So the Spanish government passed under Scipio to little purpose and in idleness, diminishing Scipio's credit rather than Cato's.

9. Nor did Cato, who received a Triumph from the senate, slacken the reins of virtue, as many do,

10. Who strive more for vainglory than honour, so that having attained the highest honours they pass the rest of their life in idleness, quitting public affairs.

11. But he, as if entering public life for the first time and thirsting after achievements,

12. Exerted himself; and would give up neither his civil nor his military service.

13. He assisted Tiberius Sempronius, as his lieutenant, when the latter went to Thrace and the Danube;

14. And, in the role of tribune, went with Manius Acilius into Greece against Antiochus the Great,

15. Who, after Hannibal, more than anyone struck terror into the Romans.

16. For having reduced once more under a single command almost the whole of Asia,

17. And having subdued many warlike barbarian nations, Antiochus longed to conquer Rome,

18. As if it alone was the only thing worth having as an enemy to fight against him.

19. So he came into Greece pretending that it was to free it from Rome.

20. Manius sent ambassadors to the different Greek cities,

21. And Titus Flamininus quieted most of the troublemakers in them who supported Antiochus, without much difficulty.

22. Cato likewise brought over Corinth, Patrae and Aegium, and spent much time at Athens.

23. It is reputed that he made an oration in Greek, expressing his admiration of the ancient Athenians,

24. And signifying that he came with

pleasure to see the beauty and greatness of their city.

25. But this is a fiction, for he spoke to the Athenians through an interpreter, though he was able to speak Greek;

26. But he wished to observe the usage of his own country, and laughed at those who admired nothing but what was Greek.

27. He professed to believe that the words of the Greeks came only from their lips, while those of the Romans came from their hearts.

Chapter 58

1. Antiochus occupied the narrow passages about Thermopylae, added palisades and walls to the natural fortifications of the place,

2. And camped there, thinking he had done enough to divert the war;

3. And the Romans, indeed, seemed wholly to despair of forcing the passage.

4. But Cato, calling to mind the circuit which the Persians made to attack that place, went out at night, taking part of the army.

5. While they were climbing, the guide missed the way, and wandering along impracticable and precipitous paths, the soldiers were filled with anxiety.

6. Cato, perceiving the danger, commanded the rest to halt, and taking with him one Lucius Manlius, an expert mountaineer,

7. Advanced with much labour and danger, in darkness without moonlight, among wild olive trees and steep crags,

8. There being nothing but precipices and darkness before their eyes, till they found a little pass which they thought led to the enemy camp.

9. They marked some rocks and returned to fetch the army.

10. The way still proved difficult, but at dawn they at last saw the enemy trenches at the foot of the rock.

11. Here Cato halted his forces, and commanded the most reliable troops, the Firmans, to stay by him, saying,

12. 'I desire to take one of the enemy alive, to find out the number, discipline, order and preparation of the enemy;

13. 'But this feat must be an act of great quickness and boldness, such as that of lions, when they dart upon a timorous animal.'

14. The Firmans darted down the mountain and dispersed the enemy guards, capturing one.

15. From him Cato quickly learned that the rest of the forces lay in the narrow passage around the king,

16. And that those who kept the tops of the rocks were six hundred choice Aetolians.

17. Heartened by the smallness of the enemy's number and their carelessness, Cato drew his sword and fell upon them with a great noise of trumpets and shouting.

18. The enemy, perceiving them thus tumbling upon them from the

precipices, flew to the main body, disordering everything there.

19. As Manius was forcing the defences below, pouring his forces into the narrow passages,

20. Antiochus was hit in the mouth by a stone which knocked his teeth out, making him feel such excessive pain that he turned away with his horse;

21. Nor did any part of his army withstand the shock of the Romans.

22. But there seemed no reasonable hope of flight where all paths were so difficult, winding among deep marshes and steep rocks.

23. The fugitives crowded and pressed together in the narrow ways,

24. Destroying one another in their terror of the Roman swords.

25. Cato was never sparing of his own praises, and seldom shunned boasting of his exploits;

26. Which quality he seems to have thought the natural accompaniment of great actions.

27. With these particular exploits against Antiochus he was highly pleased.

28. He wrote that those who saw him that day, pursuing and slaying the enemies,

29. Were ready to assert that Cato owed not so much to the public, as the public to Cato;

30. He adds that Manius the consul, coming hot from the fight, embraced him for a great while, when both were all in a sweat,

31. And cried out with joy that neither he himself, nor all the Romans together, could make him a sufficient recompense.

32. After the fight Cato was sent to Rome, to be the messenger of it;

33. And his news of the victory filled the whole city with joy and celebrations,

34. And the people with the belief that they were invincible on every sea and land.

Chapter 59

1. Such are all the eminent actions of Cato in military affairs. In civil affairs his chief interest was law and order.

2. He prosecuted many, and he would assist in other prosecutions, and even tried to prosecute Scipio;

3. But unsuccessfully, by reason of the nobleness of Scipio's family and the real greatness of Scipio's mind, which enabled him to resist all calumnies.

4. But joining with the accusers against Scipio's brother Lucius, he succeeded in obtaining a sentence against him,

5. Which condemned him to the payment of a large fine; though Lucius was saved by the interposition of the tribunes of the people.

6. Cato himself did not escape with impunity, for if he gave his enemies the least chance he was often in danger of being prosecuted himself.

7. He is reported to have escaped at

least fifty indictments; one when he was eighty-six years old drew from him the saying that it was hard for him,

8. Who had served one generation of men, to plead before another.

9. Neither did he make this the last of his lawsuits;

10. For, four years after, when he was ninety, he accused Servilius Galba:

11. So that his life and actions extended, we may say, as Nestor's did, over three ordinary ages of man.

12. For, having had many contests about affairs of state with Scipio the Great,

13. He continued them down even to Scipio the Younger, who was the adopted grandson of the former.

Chapter 60

1. Ten years after his consulship Cato stood for the office of Censor, which was the summit of all honour, and the highest step in civil affairs;

2. For besides all other power, it had also that of an inquisition into everyone's life and manners.

3. For the Romans thought that no marriage or rearing of children, no feast or drinking bout, ought to be permitted according to individual fancy,

4. Without being examined into; their view was that a man's character is much sooner revealed by such things than by what he does publicly.

5. They therefore chose two persons, one from the patricians, the other from the commons, who were to watch, correct and punish,

6. If anyone too far transgressed the morals or mores of the country; and these they called Censors.

7. The Censors had power to distrain goods, or expel from the senate anyone who lived intemperately.

8. It was also their business to take an estimate of what everyone was worth,

9. And to put down in registers everybody's birth and quality, besides many other prerogatives.

10. The chief nobility opposed Cato's ambition for the office.

11. Jealousy prompted them, who thought that it would be a stain to everybody's nobility,

12. If a man of common birth should rise to the highest office;

13. While others, conscious of their questionable practices and violations of Rome's laws and customs,

14. Were afraid of Cato's austerity, which, in an office of such great power, was likely to prove uncompromising and severe.

15. And so they brought forward seven candidates in opposition to him,

16. Who sedulously set themselves to court the people's favour by fair promises,

17. As though what they wished was indulgent and easy government.

18. Cato, on the contrary, promised no such mildness, but plainly threatening evil livers,

19. Openly declared himself on the hustings, arguing that the city needed a thorough purgation.

20. He called upon the people, if they were wise, not to choose the gentlest, but the roughest of physicians;

21. Such a one, he said, he was, and Valerius Flaccus, one of the patricians, another;

22. Together with him, he had no doubt they would achieve something worthwhile.

23. He added that his opponents sought the office with ill intent,

24. Because they were rightly afraid of those who would exercise it justly.

25. It would seem that the Roman people did not fear Cato's grim countenance,

26. But rejecting those smooth promisers who were ready to do anything to ingratiate themselves, they voted for him,

27. Together with Flaccus, obeying his recommendations as if he had had the actual power of censorship already.

28. Cato named his colleague Flaccus as chief of the senate, and expelled, among many others, Lucius Quintius, for the following reason.

29. It seems Lucius was accompanied in all his commands by a youth whom he had long kept as his lover,

30. And to whom he gave as much power and respect as to the chiefest of his friends and relations.

31. Now it happened that while Lucius was consular governor of a province, the youth said to him in his cups,

32. That he loved him so dearly that 'though there was a gladiator show at Rome, and I have never seen one; and though I long to see a man killed; yet I made all haste to come to you here instead.'

33. Returning his fondness, Lucius replied, 'I can remedy that.'

34. Ordering a condemned prisoner to be brought to him, together with the headsman and axe, Lucius commanded his head to be cut off.

35. Cato asserted that Lucius himself played the part of executioner with his own hand.

36. Afterwards, when there was some show at the theatre, Lucius passed by the seats where former consuls sat,

37. And taking his seat a great way off, excited the compassion of the commoners,

38. Who presently with a great noise made him go forward, and as much as they could, tried to salve over what had happened.

39. Manilius, also, who according to the public expectation would have been next consul, Cato threw out of the senate,

40. Because, in the presence of his daughter, and in open day, he had kissed his wife.

41. Cato said that, as for himself, his wife never came into his arms except when there was great

thunder, for which reason he liked storms.

42. His treatment of Lucius, the brother of Scipio, who had been honoured with a Triumph, occasioned some odium against Cato;

43. For he took his horse from him, and was thought to do it with a design of putting an affront on Scipio Africanus, now dead.

Chapter 61

1. But he gave most general annoyance by retrenching people's luxury, because most of the youth had already been corrupted thereby.

2. Because it seemed impossible to take it away directly, Cato went about it about it obliquely.

3. He caused all dress, carriages, women's ornaments and household furniture whose price exceeded fifteen hundred drachmas,

4. To be rated at ten times the worth; thus making their tax assessments greater.

5. He also ordered that for every thousand asses of property of this kind,

6. Three thousand asses should be paid, so that people, burdened with these extra charges, were persuaded out of their prodigality,

7. Seeing others paying less into the public exchequer who had equally good estates but were more frugal.

8. And thus, on the one side, not only were those disgusted at Cato

who bore the taxes for the sake of their luxury,

9. But those, too, who on the other side laid by their luxury for fear of the taxes.

10. For people in general reckon that an order not to display their riches is equivalent to taking away their riches;

11. Because riches are for display, seen much more in superfluous than in necessary things.

12. This was what amazed Ariston the philosopher: that we account those who possess superfluous things more happy than those who abound in what is necessary and useful.

13. But when Scopas, the rich Thessalian, was asked by one of his friends to give him something of no great utility,

14. Scopas replied, 'In truth it is just these useless and unnecessary things that make my wealth and happiness.'

15. Thus the desire of riches does not proceed from a natural passion within us, but arises rather from vulgar opinion of others.

16. Cato, caring nothing for those who exclaimed against him, increased his austerity.

17. He cut the pipes through which some persons brought the public water into their own houses,

18. And demolished all buildings that jutted into the common streets.

19. He forced down the price of contracts for public works, and

raised it in contracts for farming the taxes to the highest sum;

20. By which proceedings he drew a great deal of hatred on himself.

Chapter 62

1. Yet however much the patricians complained, the commoners liked his censorship very well;

2. They set up a statue to him in the public gardens, and put an inscription on it,

3. Not for his war record, but saying that this was Cato the Censor, who, by good discipline and wise ordinances,

4. Reclaimed the Roman commonwealth when it was declining into vice.

5. Before this honour was done to him he used to laugh at those who loved statues and honours,

6. Saying that they did not see that they were taking pride in the workmanship of brass-founders and painters;

7. Whereas the citizens carried Cato's own best likeness in their breasts.

8. And when any seemed to wonder that he should have never a statue, he said,

9. 'I would much rather be asked, why I have not one, than why I have one.'

10. In short, he would not have any honest citizen endure to be praised, except it might prove advantageous to the commonwealth.

11. Yet still he passed the highest commendation on himself;

12. For he tells us that those who were criticised for doing something wrong used to say, it was not worthwhile to blame them, for they were not Catos.

13. He also adds that they who awkwardly mimicked some of his actions were called left-handed Catos;

14. And that the senate in perilous times would call to him, as to a pilot in a ship,

15. And that often when he was not present in the senate they put off affairs of greatest consequence until he was present.

16. Much of this is true, for Cato had a great authority in the city, alike for his life, his eloquence and his age.

17. He was also a good father, an excellent husband to his wife and an extraordinary economist.

18. And as he did not manage his affairs of this kind carelessly or as things of little moment, I ought to record a little further what was commendable in him in these points.

19. He married a wife more noble than rich; being of opinion that both the rich and the high-born are haughty and proud,

20. But those of noble blood would be more ashamed of base things.

21. A man who beat his wife or child, laid violent hands, he said, on what was most precious;

22. And a good husband he reckoned worthy of more praise than a great senator.

23. He admired the ancient Socrates for nothing so much as having lived a contented life with a wife who was a scold and children who were half-witted.

24. As soon as he had a son born, only public affairs would keep him from his wife's side as she washed and dressed the infant.

25. She herself suckled it, and often gave her breast to her servants' children to produce a kind of natural love between them and her son.

26. When the boy came to years of discretion, Cato himself taught him to read,

27. Although he had as servant a very good grammarian called Chilo, who taught many others;

28. But Cato thought not fit, as he himself said, to have his son reprimanded by a slave,

29. Nor would he have him owe to a servant the obligation of so great a thing as his learning.

30. He himself, therefore, taught him his grammar, his law and his gymnastic exercises.

31. Nor did he only show him how to throw a dart, to fight in armour and to ride,

32. But to box and to endure heat and cold, and to swim over the most rapid and rough rivers.

33. He says, likewise, that he wrote histories, in large characters, with his own hand,

34. So that his son might learn to know about his countrymen and forefathers.

35. Thus, Cato formed and fashioned his son to virtue; nor had he any occasion to find fault with his readiness and docility;

36. But as the boy proved to be of too weak a constitution for hardships, he did not insist on requiring of him an austere way of living.

37. However, though delicate in health, Cato's son proved a stout man in battle, and behaved himself valiantly when Paulus Aemilius fought against Perseus;

38. For when his sword was struck from him by a blow, he so keenly resented losing it,

39. That he turned to some of his friends about him, and taking them along with him again, fell upon the enemy;

40. And having by a hard fight cleared the place, at length found his sword among great heaps of arms,

41. And the dead bodies of friends as well as enemies piled one upon another.

42. Upon which Paulus, his general, much commended the youth; and there is a letter of Cato's to his son, which highly praises his honourable eagerness for the recovery of his sword.

43. Afterwards Cato's son married Tertia, Aemilius Paulus' daughter and sister to Scipio;

44. Nor was he admitted into this

family less for his own worth than for his father's.

45. So Cato's care in his son's education came to a very fitting result.

Chapter 63

1. Cato purchased many slaves out of the captives taken in war, but chiefly bought up the young ones, who were capable of being trained up like whelps and colts.

2. None of these ever entered another man's house, except sent either by Cato himself or his wife.

3. If any one of them were asked what Cato did they were instructed to answer that they did not know.

4. When a servant was at home, he was obliged either to work or sleep,

5. For Cato most preferred those who often slept, accounting them more docile than those who were wakeful, and more alert when refreshed with slumber.

6. Being also of opinion that the great cause of misbehaviour among slaves was their running after pleasures,

7. He fixed a certain price for them to pay for permission amongst themselves, but would suffer no connections out of the house.

8. At first, when he was only a poor soldier, he would not mind what he ate, but looked upon it as pitiful to quarrel with a servant for the belly's sake.

9. But afterwards, when he grew richer and made feasts for friends, as soon as supper was over he used to go with a leather thong and scourge those who had served or cooked carelessly.

10. He always contrived that his servants should be at odds among themselves, being suspicious of any understanding between them.

11. Those who had committed anything worthy of death, he punished if they were found guilty by their fellow-servants.

12. Being very desirous of gain, he took care to invest his money safely;

13. He purchased ponds, hot baths, grounds full of fuller's earth, remunerative lands, pastures and woods,

14. From all of which he drew large returns.

15. He was also given to the form of usury which is considered most odious in traffic by sea, as follows:

16. He desired that those he invested in, should have many partners;

17. And when the number of them and their ships came to fifty, he took one share through Quintio his freedman, who therefore was to sail with the adventurers,

18. And take a part in all their proceedings; so that there was no danger of losing his whole stock, but only a little part, and that with a prospect of great profit.

19. He likewise lent money to those of his slaves who wished to borrow, with which they bought other young ones,

20. Whom, when they had taught and bred them up at his charge, they would sell again at the year's end;

21. But some of them Cato would keep for himself, giving just as much for them as another had offered.

22. But the strongest indication of Cato's avaricious humour was when he took the boldness to affirm that he was a most wonderful man, who left more behind him than he had received.

Chapter 64

1. He had grown old when two famous philosophers, Carneades the Academic and Diogenes the Stoic, came as deputies from Athens to Rome,

2. To seek release from a penalty of five hundred talents laid on the Athenians,

3. In a suit to which they did not appear, in which the Oropians were plaintiffs and Sicyonians judges.

4. All the most studious youth immediately waited on these philosophers, and frequently, with admiration, heard them speak.

5. But the gracefulness of Carneades' oratory, whose ability was really great,

6. And his reputation equal to it, gathered large and favourable audiences.

7. So that it soon began to be told that a Greek, famous even to admiration, winning and carrying all before him,

8. Had impressed so strange a love upon the young men,

9. That quitting all their pleasures and pastimes, they ran mad after philosophy;

10. Which indeed much pleased the Romans in general;

11. They beheld with much pleasure the youth so welcome Greek literature, and frequent the company of learned men.

12. But Cato, seeing this passion for words flowing into the city,

13. Was ill disposed towards it, fearing that the youth should be diverted that way,

14. And come to prefer philosophy instead of arms and military prowess.

15. And when the fame of the philosophers increased in the city,

16. And Caius Acilius, a person of distinction, at his own request, became their interpreter to the senate at their first audience,

17. Cato resolved, under some specious presence, to have all philosophers cleared out of the city;

18. And, coming into the senate, blamed the magistrates for letting these deputies stay so long a time without being dispatched,

19. Though they were persons that could easily persuade the people to what they pleased;

20. That therefore in all haste something should be determined about their petition,

21. So that they could go home again,

and leave the Roman youth to be obedient, as hitherto, to their own laws and governors.

22. He did this not out of any hostility, as some think, to Carneades;

23. But because he wholly despised philosophy, and out of a kind of pride scoffed at the Greek studies and literature;

24. As, for example, he would say that Socrates was a prating seditious fellow, who did his best to tyrannise over his country,

25. To undermine the ancient customs, and to entice and withdraw the citizens to opinions contrary to the laws.

26. Ridiculing the school of Isocrates, he would add that his scholars grew old men before they had done learning with him.

27. And to frighten his son from anything that was Greek, in a more vehement tone than became one of his age,

28. He stated that the Romans would certainly be destroyed when they once began to be infected with Greek literature;

29. Though time indeed has shown the vanity of his prophecy;

30. For the city of Rome rose to its highest fortune while entertaining Grecian learning.

Chapter 65

1. Nor had he an aversion only against Greek philosophers, but against the physicians also;

2. For having, it seems, heard how

Hippocrates, when the king of Persia sent for him with offers of an immense fee,

3. Said that he would never assist enemies of the Greeks;

4. He affirmed that this was a common oath taken by all Greek physicians, and enjoined his son to avoid them.

5. He had himself written a little book of prescriptions for curing the sick in his own family:

6. He never enjoined fasting, but ordered them either vegetables, or the meat of a duck, pigeon or leveret;

7. Such kind of diet being of light digestion, and fit for sick folks, only it made those who ate it dream too much.

8. However, despite priding himself on understanding medicine, he lost both his wife and his son;

9. Though he himself, being of a strong, robust constitution, lived long and healthily,

10. And would often, even in his old age, go to bed with women.

11. When he was past a lover's age he married a young woman, upon the following pretence:

12. Having lost his own wife, he had a young courtesan come privately to visit him;

13. But the house being small, and a daughter-in-law also in it, this practice was quickly discovered;

14. For the young woman seeming once to pass through it a little too boldly,

15. The youth, his son, though he said nothing, seemed to look somewhat indignantly upon her.

16. The old man perceiving and understanding that what he did was disliked,

17. Went away as his custom was, with his usual companions to the market;

18. And among the rest, he called aloud to one Salonius, who had been a clerk under him,

19. And asked him whether he had married off his daughter?

20. Salonius answered, no, nor would he, till he had consulted him.

21. Said Cato, 'Then I have found out a fit son-in-law for you, if he should not displease by reason of his age';

22. Upon this Cato, without any more ado, told him, he desired to have the damsel himself.

23. These words, as may well be imagined, at first astonished the man,

24. Conceiving that Cato was as far off from marrying, as he from a likelihood of being allied to the family of one who had been consul, and had a Triumph;

25. But perceiving him in earnest, he consented willingly.

26. When Cato's son died he bore the loss like a philosopher, and was nothing the more remiss in attending to affairs of state;

27. So that he did not grow languid in his old age, as though public business were a duty once to be discharged, and then quitted;

28. Nor did he, like Scipio Africanus, because envy had struck at his glory, turn from the public,

29. And change and pass away the rest of his life without doing anything;

30. For Cato thought old age was most honourable if it was busied in public affairs;

31. Though he would, now and then, when he had leisure, recreate himself with gardening and writing.

32. He composed various books and histories; and in his youth, he addicted himself to agriculture for profit's sake;

33. For he used to say, he had but two ways of getting money, namely agriculture and parsimony;

34. And now, in his old age, the first of these gave him both occupation and a subject of study.

35. He wrote one book on country matters, in which he treated even of making cakes and preserving fruit,

36. It being his ambition to be curious and singular in all things.

Chapter 66

1. Some say the overthrow of Carthage was Cato's last act of state,

2. For though indeed it was Scipio the younger who gave it the last blow, the war was undertaken chiefly by the counsel and advice of Cato.

3. He had been sent to the

Carthaginians and Masinissa, king of Numidia,

4. Who were at war with one another, to know the cause of their difference.

5. Finding Carthage, not (as the Romans thought) low and in an ill condition,

6. But well manned, full of riches and all sorts of arms and ammunition, and perceiving the Carthaginians in high fettle,

7. He conceived that it was not a time for the Romans to adjust affairs between them and Masinissa,

8. But rather that Rome itself would fall into danger, unless it found means to check this rapid new growth of Rome's ancient irreconcilable enemy.

9. Therefore, returning quickly to Rome, he acquainted the senate,

10. That the former defeats of the Carthaginians had not so much diminished their strength, as it had advanced their ambition;

11. That they were not become weaker, but more experienced in war,

12. And only skirmished with the Numidians to exercise themselves the better to cope with the Romans;

13. And that their treaty with Rome was merely a suspension of war, which awaited a fairer opportunity to break out again.

14. He then shook his gown to let drop some African figs before the senate.

15. As the senators admired their size and beauty, he added that the place that bore them was only three days' sailing from Rome.

16. He never after this gave his opinion, but at the end he would be sure to say, 'Also, Carthage ought utterly to be destroyed.'

17. But Publius Scipio Nasica would always declare his opinion to the contrary, in these words, 'It seems requisite to me that Carthage should still stand.'

18. For seeing his countrymen wanton and insolent, and the people made obstinate and disobedient to the senate by their prosperity,

19. He wished to keep the fear of Carthage alive as a rein on the contumacy of the multitude;

20. For he regarded the Carthaginians as too weak to overcome the Romans, and too great to be despised by them.

21. On the other side, it seemed perilous to Cato that a city which had been always great,

22. And was now grown sober and wise by reason of its former calamities,

23. Should still be lying in wait until the follies and excesses of the Romans made it vulnerable.

24. So that he thought it the wisest course to have all outward dangers removed, when Rome had so many inward ones to contend with.

25. Thus Cato, they say, stirred up the third and last war against the

Carthaginians; but no sooner was the war begun, than he died.

26. He had lived to a great age, over ninety; and left a reputation which invites a mixed approbation: severe, upright, rigorous, of stern principle,

27. But mean and avaricious, in some ways cold and harsh,

28. Opposed to most of the graces of civilisation, and yet a lover of his country and tireless in its service.

29. There were men of great probity in the republican days of Rome's early glory,

30. But few as uncompromising and severe as he.

Chapter 67: Cicero

1. Cicero was a lawyer, orator, philosopher, judge, statesman, defender of the Roman Republic,

2. And what is not less than any of these, he was a master of an exquisite Latin prose style that made him a model for writers many centuries after his own lifetime.

3. He lived at the time when the Roman Republic collapsed and became a monarchy,

4. To his great regret and despite his best efforts. He was a flawed man, but a great Roman.

5. When he was young Cicero was eager for every kind of learning,

6. And so distinguished for his talents that the fathers of other boys would often visit his school to witness the quickness in

learning for which he was renowned.

7. After school Cicero studied with Philo the Academic, whose eloquence the Romans admired above all the other scholars of Clitomachus; and they loved him too for his character.

8. Cicero also sought the company of the Mucii, who were eminent statesmen and leaders in the senate, and acquired from them a knowledge of the laws.

9. For some short time he served in the army under Sylla, in the Marsian war.

10. But seeing Rome beset by factions, and knowing that the tendency of faction is to produce absolute monarchy,

11. He chose a retired life, conversing with learned Greeks and devoting himself to study;

12. Until Sylla took power in Rome, and by his dictatorship quelled the troubled city for a period.

13. At this time one Chrysogonus, who was Sylla's emancipated slave, made a fraudulent purchase of an estate for a mere two thousand drachmas.

14. This estate had belonged to a man put to death by proscription, and Chrysogonus had laid an information about it.

15. When Roscius, the heir of the executed man, complained that the estate was worth greatly more than had been paid,

16. Sylla started a prosecution to

silence him, Chrysogonus himself managing the evidence.

17. None of the advocates, fearing Sylla, dared to assist Roscius.

18. The young man turned to Cicero for help. Cicero's friends encouraged him, saying he was never likely to have a more honourable introduction to public life.

19. So he undertook the defence, won, and thus made his first step to fame.

20. But fearing Sylla, he travelled to Greece, saying it was for his health.

21. And indeed he was lean and meagre, with such a weak stomach that he could take only a spare diet, eating once a day after sunset.

22. In Athens he attended lectures by Antiochus of Ascalon, whose fluency and elegance impressed him, although he did not agree with his doctrines.

23. For Antiochus inclined to the Stoics, while Cicero adhered to the New Academy.

24. He planned to pass his life quietly in the study of philosophy if he did not succeed in public life.

25. On receiving news of Sylla's death, together with letters from his friends at Rome earnestly soliciting him to return to public affairs,

26. Cicero set himself to practise rhetoric, diligently attending the most celebrated rhetoricians of the time, to prepare himself for returning to Rome.

27. He sailed from Athens for Asia and Rhodes. Amongst the Asian masters he conversed with Xenocles of Adramyttium, Dionysius of Magnesia and Menippus of Caria;

28. At Rhodes, he studied oratory with Apollonius, son of Molon, and philosophy with Posidonius.

29. Apollonius, we are told, not understanding Latin, requested Cicero to declaim in Greek.

30. He complied willingly, thinking that his faults would thus be better corrected.

31. After he finished, all his other hearers were astonished, and contended who should praise him most, but Apollonius sat musing in silence for a long time.

32. And when Cicero was discomposed at this, Apollonius said,

33. 'You have my praise and admiration, Cicero, and Greece has my pity and commiseration,

34. 'Because those arts and that eloquence which are the only glories that remain to her, will now be transferred by you to Rome.'

Chapter 68

1. Cicero was cautious when he first returned to Rome, with the result that for a while he was held in little esteem, and was called by the derogatory names of 'Greek' and 'Scholar'.

2. But once he began in earnest in the law courts he far surpassed all other advocates of the bar.

3. He was eloquent, persuasive and witty, and prone to sarcasm, which offended some,

4. So that among his enemies he gained a reputation for ill-nature.

5. He was appointed quaestor during a corn shortage and had Sicily for his province,

6. Where at first he displeased many of the residents by compelling them to send their provisions to Rome.

7. But when they perceived his care, justice and clemency, they honoured him more than any of their previous governors.

8. Some young Romans of noble family, charged with misconduct in military service, were brought before the praetor in Sicily.

9. Cicero undertook their defence, which he conducted admirably, and achieved their acquittal.

10. He returned to Rome with a great opinion of himself for these things.

11. Meeting a friend, he asked what the Romans thought of him, as if the whole city had been filled with admiration for his quaestorship in Sicily.

12. His friend responded, 'Where is it you have been, Cicero?'

13. He was utterly mortified to think that reports of his work had sunk into the city of Rome as into the ocean, without any visible result in reputation.

14. He became less ambitious as a result, though to the last he was passionately fond of praise and esteem, which often interfered with the prosecution of his wisest resolutions.

15. When he began to apply himself with vigour to public business he resolved to do as workmen did, who know the name and use of all their tools;

16. For the politician, men are the tools; and so he set himself to study those he had to deal with:

17. Their names, estates, friends and character. Travelling anywhere in Italy, he could discourse of all the estates he passed, and their owners.

18. Having only a small estate himself, though it was sufficient for his expenses, it was wondered at that he took neither fees nor gifts from his clients,

19. And more especially that he did not do so when he undertook the prosecution of one Verres,

20. Who stood charged by the Sicilians of many evil practices during his praetorship there.

21. Cicero succeeded in getting Verres condemned, not by speaking, but as it were by holding his tongue.

22. For when the trial came on, the Roman praetors, favouring Verres, deferred proceedings by several adjournments to the last day,

23. When there was insufficient time for the advocates to be heard and the cause decided.

24. Cicero, therefore, came forward, and said there was no need of speeches;

25. And after producing and examining witnesses, he required the judges to proceed to sentence. Verres was thus convicted.

26. The Sicilians, in testimony of their gratitude, brought him presents, when he was aedile;

27. Of which he made no private profit himself, but used their generosity to reduce the public price of provisions.

28. Cicero had a pleasant house at Arpi, and farms near Naples and Pompeii, neither of any great value.

29. He lived in a liberal but temperate style with the learned Greeks and Romans that were his familiar friends.

30. He was careful of his health, having a dietary regime, and daily walks and rubbings.

31. By this means he eventually brought himself to better health, capable of supporting many great fatigues and trials.

32. He gave his father's town house to his brother Quintus, and himself lived near the Palatine Hill, to be easily available for consultation.

33. And indeed, no fewer appeared daily at his door than went to Crassus for his riches,

34. Or Pompey for his influence in military appointments, these then being the two most powerful men in Rome.

35. Even Pompey himself used to pay court to Cicero,

36. And Cicero's public actions did much to establish Pompey's authority and reputation in the state.

Chapter 69

1. Numerous distinguished competitors contested Cicero for the praetor's office,

2. But he was chosen before them all, and managed the courts with justice and integrity;

3. And especially won the admiration of the common people for his fair and honest dealing.

4. Yet when Cicero was appointed to the consulship it was with no less applause from the nobles than from the common people,

5. Who all agreed it was for the good of the city; and both parties jointly assisted his promotion.

6. This was because the changes to government made by the dictator Sylla had at first seemed arbitrary,

7. But by time and usage they had come to be generally accepted; yet there were some who wished to subvert his arrangements,

8. Not from good motives but for private gain; and because Pompey was away at the wars in Pontus and Armenia, there was insufficient force at Rome to suppress a revolution.

9. These people had at their head a bold, daring and restless man, Lucius Catiline, a man of noble birth and eminent endowments, but of a vicious and depraved disposition.

10. His delight, from his youth, had been in civil commotions, bloodshed, robbery and sedition; and in such scenes he had spent his early years.

11. Catiline could endure hunger, want of sleep and cold, to an amazing degree.

12. His mind was daring, subtle and versatile, capable of pretending or dissembling whatever he wished.

13. He was covetous of other men's property, and prodigal of his own. He had abundance of eloquence, but little wisdom.

14. His ambition was always pursuing objects extravagant, romantic and unattainable.

15. And since the time of Sylla's dictatorship, he had had a strong desire to seize the government;

16. Nor did he care, provided that he secured power, by what means he did it.

17. His violent temper was daily hurried further into crime by increasing debts, and by his consciousness of guilt.

18. The corrupt morals of the state, too, which extravagance and selfishness, pernicious and contending vices, rendered thoroughly depraved, furnished him with additional incentives to action.

19. This man was chosen by the more unruly citizens as their leader, and a great part of the young men of the city were corrupted by him,

20. He providing everyone with drink and women, and profusely supplying the expense of their debauches.

21. In so populous and corrupt a city it was easy for Catiline to keep about him, like a bodyguard, crowds of these unprincipled and desperate people.

22. For all those profligate characters, who had dissipated their patrimonies by gaming, luxury and sensuality;

23. All who had contracted heavy debts to purchase immunity for their crimes or offences;

24. All assassins or riotous persons from every quarter, convicted or dreading conviction for their evil deeds;

25. All, besides, whom their tongue or their hand maintained by perjury or civil bloodshed;

26. All, in fine, whom wickedness, poverty or a guilty conscience disquieted,

27. Were the associates and intimate friends of Catiline; and with these he planned revolution.

Chapter 70

1. In addition to Rome itself being in an unsettled and dangerous state, there was trouble beyond the city,

2. For at that time the region of Etruria had been encouraged to revolt, as well as a large part of Cisalpine Gaul.

3. Wishing for a platform to carry out his designs, Catiline stood for the consulship, and had great hopes of success,

4. Thinking that his fellow-consul would be Caius Antonius, a man fit to lead neither in a good nor a bad cause, but who might be a useful deputy.

5. To prevent Catiline, the honest portion of the citizenry persuaded Cicero to stand in the election; and Cicero won, alongside Caius Antonius;

6. And Cicero was the only one of the candidates descended from the equestrian rather than the senatorial order.

7. Though Catiline's designs were not yet publicly known, Cicero's consulship faced many difficulties from the start, chief among them the following.

8. Those disqualified by Sylla's laws from holding office were considerable both in power and number, and they came forward to oppose the laws.

9. They had right on their side, but were acting at an inopportune time because the state was in turmoil.

10. The tribunes of the people were also pressing for change.

11. They wished to institute a commission of ten persons with wide powers, including the right to sell public lands in Italy, Syria and Pompey's new conquests;

12. To judge and banish whomever they pleased; to found colonies; to use public money; and to levy soldiers.

13. Several of the nobility favoured this law also, among them Cicero's consular colleague Caius Antonius, who hoped to be one of the Ten.

14. But what worried most nobles was that Antonius was thought to be in league with Catiline,

15. Whose plans he supported because they would free him from his great debts.

16. But Cicero ensured Antonius' support by assigning to him the province of Macedonia, he himself declining that of Gaul.

17. Antonius was thereafter ready to support whatever Cicero did.

18. Now Cicero could attack the conspirators with greater courage.

19. In the senate he argued against the proposed commission of ten, and the senate voted against it.

20. And when the commission's proponents tried again by summoning the consuls before the people's assembly, Cicero not only secured its rejection there too,

21. But so overpowered the tribunes by his oratory, that they abandoned all thought of their other projects.

22. For Cicero was the one man above all others whose eloquence made Romans feel the invincibility of justice,

23. And by the power of his advocacy he freed the right and useful from everything that could cause offence.

24. An incident occurred in the theatre during Cicero's consulship

which showed what his oratory could achieve.

25. Whereas formerly the knights of Rome mingled in the theatre with commoners, the praetor Marcus Otho appointed them their own section in the theatre.

26. The commoners took this as an insult, so when Otho appeared in the theatre they hissed him; the knights, on the contrary, applauded him.

27. The people increased their hissing, the knights their clapping; then the two sections turned on one another, hurling insults, and reduced the theatre to uproar.

28. Cicero was called, and so effectually chided everyone for their behaviour that the crowd now applauded Otho,

29. The people contending with the knights who should give him the greatest demonstrations of honour and respect.

Chapter 71

1. Catiline and his co-conspirators, at first disheartened, soon took courage again.

2. In secret meetings they exhorted one another to capture the government before Pompey's army returned from the eastern wars.

3. The veterans of Sylla's army were Catiline's chief stimulus to action.

4. They had been disbanded and dispersed around Italy,

5. But the greatest number and the fiercest of them lived in the cities of Etruria, where they were dissatisfied and restless.

6. These, under the leadership of one Manlius, who had served with distinction in the wars under Sylla, joined themselves to Catiline,

7. And they came to Rome to assist him with their votes at the consular election, he having resolved to stand again for that office,

8. While also having resolved to assassinate Cicero in the tumult of the hustings.

9. Cicero, suspecting these plans, deferred the day of election and summoned Catiline to the senate, there questioning him about the charges made against him.

10. Catiline believed that there were many in the senate with views similar to his own,

11. And in order to get their support by showing them his mettle, he gave an audacious answer:

12. 'What harm,' said he, 'when I see two bodies, the one lean and consumptive with a head,

13. 'The other great and strong without one, if I put a head to the body that lacks one?'

14. This representation of the senate and the people excited yet greater apprehensions in Cicero.

15. He put on armour, and was attended from his house by many citizens, bent on protecting him.

16. Letting his tunic slip partly from his shoulders,

17. He showed his armour

underneath, thus showing his danger to the spectators;

18. Who, being much moved by it, gathered round to defend him; and Catiline again lost the vote for the consulship.

19. After this Catiline's soldiers in Etruria began to form themselves into companies, the day appointed for the revolution being near.

20. Late one night Cicero was woken by a group of the principal citizens of Rome,

21. Among them Marcus Crassus, Marcus Marcellus and Scipio Metellus.

22. Crassus had that night been secretly brought a bundle of letters by an unknown person. They were directed to various senators,

23. And one of them was for Crassus himself. It did not have a sender's name.

24. He read it, and found that it advised him to leave the city because a great slaughter was intended by Catiline.

25. He did not open the other letters, but took them immediately to Cicero,

26. Being apprehensive of the danger, and to free himself of any suspicion of leaguing with Catiline.

27. Cicero summoned the senate to meet at dawn. He brought the letters with him, and delivered them to their addressees,

28. To be read out loud; they all alike contained an account of the conspiracy.

29. And when Quintus Arrius, a man of praetorian dignity, reported how soldiers were collecting in companies in Etruria,

30. And that Manlius was in motion with a large force near those cities,

31. Waiting for orders from Rome, the senate made a decree granting exceptional powers to the consuls, to do their best to save the state.

32. After Cicero had received this power, he committed all affairs outside Rome to Quintus Metellus, but kept the management of the city in his own hands.

33. Such a large number of people guarded him every day that the marketplace was filled with his followers when he entered it.

Chapter 72

1. Catiline, impatient of further delay, resolved to leave Rome and go to Manlius,

2. But he commanded Marcius and Cethegus to take their swords,

3. And go early in the morning to Cicero's gates, as if to greet him, but there to slay him.

4. Cicero was however warned of this plan. Cethegus and Marcius came at dawn,

5. But being denied entrance they made an outcry at the gates, which excited yet more suspicion.

6. Cicero summoned the senate, and when Catiline arrived with his followers, intending to make his defence,

7. None of the senators would sit

near him, but all of them left the bench where he placed himself;

8. And when Catiline began to speak, they heckled him.

9. Then Cicero stood up and commanded him to leave the city,

10. On the grounds that since he wished to govern the commonwealth with words and the other with arms,

11. It was necessary there should be a wall between them.

Chapter 73

1. Catiline immediately left Rome with three hundred armed men;

2. And assuming, as if he were a magistrate, the rods, axes and military ensigns, he went to Manlius,

3. And having collected a body of twenty thousand men, he marched to various cities, trying to raise revolt.

4. Now that it had come to open civil war, Antonius was sent with troops to fight him.

5. The remainder of Catiline's conspirators still in Rome were kept together and encouraged by Cornelius Lentulus.

6. Though of noble family, Lentulus was a dissolute person, who for his debauchery had been turned out of the senate,

7. And was now holding the office of praetor for the second time,

8. As the custom is with those seeking to regain the dignity of senator.

9. This man, bad in his own nature and now inflamed by Catiline,

10. Resolved to murder all the senators, and as many other citizens as he could,

11. And to set the city on fire, sparing nobody except Pompey's children,

12. Intending to keep them as pledges so that he could reconcile with Pompey, who was still at the eastern wars.

13. The night appointed for this design fell during a festival.

14. Swords, flax and sulphur were hidden in the house of Cethegus;

15. A hundred men were detailed to start fires in different quarters of the city at the same moment, so that everything would be in flames together.

16. Others were appointed to block the aqueducts, and to kill those who tried to carry water to the fires.

17. While these plans were in preparation, it happened that there were two ambassadors from the Allobroges staying in Rome;

18. A nation at that time in a distressed condition, and uneasy under the Roman government.

19. Lentulus and his party judged these men useful instruments to move Gaul to revolt,

20. So they admitted them to the conspiracy and gave them letters to their own leaders, and letters to Catiline.

21. In the former they promised liberty, in the latter they exhorted

Catiline to set all slaves free, and bring them to Rome.

22. They sent a man called Titus, a native of Croton, to accompany the ambassadors and carry the letters to Catiline.

23. Cicero followed the plotting of the conspirators closely, having spies in place to observe all that was done and said,

24. And keeping a secret correspondence with many who pretended to join the conspiracy, including these ambassadors of the Allobroges.

25. He thus knew all the discourse which passed between them and the strangers;

26. And, lying in wait for them by night, he arrested Titus the Crotonian with his letters.

27. The next morning he summoned the senate, where he read the letters aloud and examined the informers.

28. Junius Silanus witnessed that Cethegus said that three consuls and four praetors were to be slain. Piso testified other matters of the like nature;

29. Caius Sulpicius, one of the praetors, was sent to Cethegus' house and found a cache of darts and of armour,

30. And a still greater number of swords and daggers, all newly sharpened.

31. The senate decreed indemnity to Titus the Crotonian in return for his confession.

32. Lentulus was convicted, abjured his praetorial office and put off his senatorial robe edged with purple.

33. He and the other conspirators were then committed to the custody of the praetors.

Chapter 74

1. After giving details of the conspiracy and arrests to the crowds waiting outside,

2. Cicero withdrew to consider what punishment the conspirators should suffer.

3. He was reluctant to inflict the death penalty, partly from clemency,

4. But also in case he should be thought too strict in executing men of the noblest birth and most powerful friendships in the city;

5. And yet, if he treated them mildly, there could only be further danger from them.

6. For there was no likelihood, if they escaped death, that they would be reconciled,

7. But rather, adding new rage to their former wickedness, they would rush into every kind of audacity.

8. Cicero was also worried that as he had a reputation among the people for mildness,

9. They might easily think him timid and unmanly if he did not rigorously apply the law.

10. The next day in the senate Silanus argued that the conspirators should suffer the utmost penalty.

11. Everyone agreed one after another until it came to Julius Caesar's turn.

12. He was then only a young man, at the outset of his career,

13. But he had already set himself on the course which led to Rome becoming a monarchy.

14. No one else foresaw this except Cicero, who had some inkling of Caesar's ambitions and capacities.

15. But quite a few suspected that Caesar was sympathetic to Catiline's views,

16. And some of them believed that Cicero voluntarily overlooked the evidence against him for fear of his friends and power;

17. For it was evident to everybody that if Caesar was accused with the conspirators,

18. They were more likely to be saved with him than he to be punished with them.

19. So when it was Caesar's turn to speak, he opposed execution,

20. Suggesting instead that the conspirators' estates be confiscated,

21. And their persons confined in such cities in Italy as Cicero should approve.

22. To this sentence, as it was moderate, and delivered by a powerful speaker,

23. Cicero himself gave due weight when he stood up to speak.

24. He said that both proposals had merit, and left the matter so in the balance,

25. That Silanus now changed his mind and withdrew his motion for the death sentence.

26. The first man to reject Caesar's motion was Catulus Lutatius.

27. Cato followed, and so vehemently urged in his speech the strong suspicion against Caesar himself of involvement with Catiline,

28. And so filled the senate with anger and resolution,

29. That a decree was passed for the immediate execution of the conspirators.

30. But Caesar opposed the confiscation of their goods,

31. Not thinking it fair that those who rejected the mildest part of his sentence should avail themselves of the severest.

32. And when many insisted upon it, he appealed to the tribunes, but they would do nothing;

33. Till Cicero himself yielded, and remitted that part of the sentence.

Chapter 75

1. Cicero then went to where the conspirators were being kept by the praetors,

2. And took them one by one to the prison, where they were each strangled in turn.

3. As he escorted them through the forum he was surrounded by large, anxious crowds,

4. Who silently and fearfully watched the proceedings.

5. But that evening, when he

returned from the forum to his own house,

6. The citizens received him as he passed with acclamations and applause,

7. Saluting him as the saviour and founder of his country.

8. A bright light shone through the streets from the lamps and torches set up at the doors,

9. And the women showed lights from the tops of houses to honour Cicero,

10. And to see him returning home with a splendid train of the leading citizens;

11. Amongst whom were many who had conducted great wars, celebrated Triumphs,

12. And added to the possessions of the Roman empire, both by sea and land.

13. These, as they passed along with him, acknowledged to one another,

14. That though the Roman people were indebted to several officers and commanders of that age for riches, spoils and power,

15. To Cicero alone they owed the safety and security of all these, for delivering them from such a great and imminent danger.

16. For though it might seem no wonderful thing to prevent a conspiracy and punish the conspirators,

17. Yet to defeat the greatest of all conspiracies with so little disturbance and commotion was very extraordinary.

18. For the greater part of those who had flocked to Catiline, as soon as they heard the fate of his fellow conspirators, abandoned him,

19. And he himself, with his remaining forces, was killed in battle with the army led by Antonius.

Chapter 76

1. And yet there were still some who were ready to speak ill of Cicero, and to seek revenge for his actions;

2. And they had for their leaders some of the magistrates of the following year,

3. Including Julius Caesar, who was one of the praetors, and Metellus and Bestia, the tribunes.

4. These men, beginning their period of office some days before Cicero's consulate expired, would not permit him to make a speech to the people.

5. But it was an advantage for Cicero that Cato was at that time one of the tribunes.

6. For he, being equal in power to the rest and of greater reputation, could oppose their designs.

7. In an oration to the people Cato so highly extolled Cicero's consulate that the greatest honours were decreed him,

8. And Cicero was publicly declared the Father of his Country, the first man to have this title bestowed on him.

9. At this time, therefore, Cicero's authority was very great in the city.

10. But he offended many and invited envy, not by any evil action, but because he was always praising himself.

11. He would talk endlessly of his triumph over Catiline and Lentulus,

12. And he filled his writings with his exalted part in their downfall, to such excess as to render his writings irksome,

13. Though as prose they were exceptionally beautiful.

14. He was also much given to sharp raillery against opponents and mocking them,

15. Which in judicial pleading might be allowable as rhetoric;

16. But he excited much ill-feeling by his readiness to attack anyone for the sake of a jest.

17. This manner, and his proneness to self-praise, clung to him like a disease.

18. But though he was intemperately fond of his own glory, he was free from envying others;

19. On the contrary, he was liberally profuse in praising both the ancients and his contemporaries.

20. And many such sayings of his are also remembered; as that he called Aristotle a river of flowing gold,

21. And said of Plato's *Dialogues* that their language was transcendent.

22. He used to call Theophrastus his special luxury.

23. And being asked which of Demosthenes' orations he liked best, he answered, the longest.

24. And as for the eminent men of his own time, either in eloquence or philosophy,

25. There was not one of them whom he did not, by writing or speaking favourably of him, render more illustrious.

26. He obtained of Caesar, when in power, Roman citizenship for Cratippus the Peripatetic,

27. And got the court of Areopagus, by public decree, to request his stay at Athens,

28. For the instruction of their youth and the honour of their city.

Chapter 77

1. The beginning of Cicero's downfall was owed to one Clodius, who during the Catiline conspiracy had been one of Cicero's staunchest allies.

2. Clodius was a bold youth of noble family, who fell in love with Pompeia, Caesar's wife.

3. He was still beardless, and therefore thought he could get privately into her house dressed as a music-girl.

4. But coming into the large house by night, he lost his way in the passages,

5. And a servant belonging to Caesar's mother, seeing him wandering about, enquired his name.

6. Being obliged to speak, he told her he was looking for one of Pompeia's maids;

7. And she, perceiving that he was not a woman, shrieked out,

8. And called the other servants, who shut the gates, and searched everywhere until they found Clodius hidden in a chamber.

9. As a result Caesar divorced Pompeia, and Clodius was prosecuted.

10. Though Cicero and Clodius had been allied, in the trial Cicero refused to tell untruths about Clodius' whereabouts on the night of the trespass, as Clodius wished of him.

11. Many other citizens also gave evidence against him, for perjuries, disorders, bribing the people and debauching women.

12. Notwithstanding all the evidence against Clodius' character, the judges were frightened by the outcry among the common people,

13. Who united against the accusers and witnesses in the case, so that a guard had to be placed about the judges for their defence;

14. And most of them wrote their sentences on the tablets in such a way that they could not well be read.

15. It was decided, however, that there was a majority for his acquittal, and it was reported that bribery had been involved;

16. In reference to which Catulus remarked, when he next met the judges,

17. 'You were very right to ask for a guard, to prevent your money being taken from you.'

18. And when Clodius upbraided Cicero that the judges had not believed his testimony,

19. 'Yes,' said he, 'twenty-five of them trusted me and condemned you,

20. 'And the other thirty did not trust you, for they did not acquit you till they got your money.'

21. Caesar, though cited, did not give his testimony against Clodius, and declared himself not convinced of his wife's adultery,

22. But said he had put her away because it was fit that Caesar's house should be free not only of the evil fact, but even of the mere rumour of it.

Chapter 78

1. Clodius, having escaped this danger, and been chosen one of the tribunes, immediately attacked Cicero, inciting people against him.

2. The common people he gained over with popular laws;

3. To each of the consuls he decreed large provinces: to Piso, Macedonia, and to Gabinius, Syria;

4. He made a strong party among the poor citizens to support him in his proceedings, and had always a body of armed slaves about him.

5. Of the three men then in greatest power, Crassus was Cicero's open enemy, Pompey indifferently made advances to both, and Caesar was going with an army into Gaul.

6. To Caesar, though not his friend

because what had occurred in the
time of the conspiracy had created
suspicions between them,

7. Cicero applied, requesting an
appointment as one of his lieutenants in the province.

8. Caesar accepted him, and Clodius,
perceiving that Cicero would thus
escape his tribunician authority,
professed to be inclined to a
reconciliation.

9. By this artifice he so freed Cicero
of his fears that the latter resigned
his appointment to Caesar, and
resumed involvement in politics.

10. At which Caesar, being exasperated, joined the party of Clodius
against Cicero,

11. And wholly alienated Pompey
from him; he also declared, in a
public assembly of the people,

12. That he did not think Lentulus
and Cethegus were fairly put to
death without being brought to
trial.

13. And this, indeed, was the crime
charged upon Cicero, and this
impeachment he was summoned
to answer.

14. And so, as an accused man, and in
danger for the result, he changed
his dress,

15. And went round with his hair
untrimmed, in the attire of a
suppliant, to seek the people's
support.

16. But Clodius met him at every
corner, having a band of abusive
and daring fellows about him,

17. Who derided Cicero for his

change of dress and his
humiliation,

18. And often, by throwing dirt and
stones at him, interrupted his
addresses to the people.

19. But almost the whole equestrian
order changed their dress with
him,

20. And no less than twenty thousand
young gentlemen followed him
with their hair untrimmed,
supplicating with him to the
people.

21. And then the senate met, to pass a
decree that all the people should
change their dress as in time of
public sorrow.

22. But the consuls opposing it, and
Clodius with armed men besetting
the senate house,

23. Many of the senators ran out,
crying out and tearing their
clothes.

24. But this sight moved neither
shame nor pity; Cicero must either
fly or determine matters by the
sword with Clodius.

25. He entreated Pompey to aid him,
who had on purpose left the city,
and was staying at his country
house in the Alban Hills;

26. And first Cicero sent his son-in-
law Piso to intercede with him,
and afterwards set out himself.

27. But when Pompey was informed
that Cicero was coming, he would
not stay to see him,

28. Being ashamed at the remembrance of the many times Cicero
had acted on his behalf,

29. And how much of his policy Cicero had directed for his advantage.

30. Now Pompey set aside all former kindness, and, slipping out at another door, avoided the interview.

31. Thus being forsaken by Pompey, and left alone to himself, Cicero turned to the consuls.

32. Gabinius was rough with him, as usual, but Piso spoke more courteously, desiring him to yield and give place for a while to the fury of Clodius,

33. And to await a change of times, and eventually to be, as once before, his country's saviour from the perils that Clodius was causing.

Chapter 79

1. Cicero, receiving this answer, consulted with his friends. Lucullus advised him to stay in Rome, as being sure to prevail at last;

2. Others advised him to fly, because the people would soon desire him again, when they should have enough of the rage and madness of Clodius.

3. This last Cicero approved. Receiving an escort from his friends, in the middle of the night he left the city and went by land through Lucania, intending to reach Sicily.

4. But as soon as it was publicly known that he had left Rome,

Clodius proposed to the people a decree of exile,

5. And by his own order interdicted him fire and water, prohibiting any within five hundred miles in Italy from receiving him into their houses.

6. Most people, out of respect for Cicero, paid no regard to this edict, offering him every attention, and escorting him on his way.

7. But at Hipponium, a city of Lucania, a Sicilian whom Cicero, when consul, had appointed head of the state engineers, and shown many other instances of friendship,

8. Would not receive him into his house, sending him word that he would appoint a place in the country for his reception.

9. Caius Vergilius, the praetor of Sicily, who had been on the most intimate terms with Cicero, wrote to him to forbear coming into Sicily.

10. At these things Cicero, being disheartened, went to Brundusium,

11. And sailed to Dyrrachium, reaching it just as an earthquake and a convulsion in the sea happened at the same time.

12. Although many visited him there with respect, and the cities of Greece contended which should honour him most,

13. He yet continued disheartened and disconsolate, like an unfortunate lover, often casting his looks back upon Italy;

14. And, indeed, he became so dejected by his misfortunes, as none could have expected in a man who had devoted so much of his life to study and learning;

15. And yet he often desired his friends not to call him orator, but philosopher,

16. Because he had made philosophy his business, and had only used rhetoric as an instrument in public life.

17. But the desire of glory has great power in washing the tinctures of philosophy out of the minds of men,

18. And in imprinting instead the passions of the common people, by custom and conversation, in the minds of those that take a part in governing them;

19. Unless the politician be very careful to interest himself only in public affairs themselves, and not in the passions that surround them.

Chapter 80

1. Clodius, having thus driven Cicero away, burned his farms and villas, and afterwards his city house, and built on its site a monument to Liberty.

2. The rest of his property he offered for sale, but nobody came to buy.

3. By these courses he became formidable to the noble citizens, and being followed by the commonalty,

4. Whom he had filled with insolence and licentiousness, he began at last to try his strength against Pompey,

5. Criticising him for the dispositions he left in the countries he had conquered.

6. The disgrace of this made Pompey reproach himself for his cowardice in deserting Cicero.

7. Now changing his mind, he set himself with his friends to contrive Cicero's return.

8. And when Clodius opposed this, the senate made a vote that no public measure should be ratified or passed by them till Cicero was recalled.

9. But when Lentulus was consul, the commotions grew so great because of this,

10. That the tribunes were injured in riots in the forum, and Quintus, Cicero's brother, was left for dead among the slain.

11. The people began to change in their feelings, and Annius Milo, one of their tribunes, was the first who dared summon Clodius to trial for acts of violence.

12. Many of the commoners of the neighbouring cities formed a party with Pompey,

13. Who with their help drove Clodius out of the forum, and summoned the people to vote for Cicero's return.

14. And, it is said, the people never passed any suffrage more unanimously than this.

15. The senate, striving to outdo the

people, sent letters of thanks to those cities which had received Cicero in his exile,

16. And decreed that his house and estates, which Clodius had destroyed, should be rebuilt at the public charge.

17. Thus Cicero returned sixteen months after his exile,

18. And the cities were so glad, and people so zealous to meet him,

19. That what he boasted of afterwards, that Italy had brought him on her shoulders home to Rome, was no exaggeration.

20. And Crassus himself, who had been his enemy before his exile, went out voluntarily to meet him,

21. And was reconciled, to please his son Publius, as he said, who was Cicero's affectionate admirer.

22. Cicero had not been long at Rome when, taking the opportunity of Clodius' absence, he went with a great company to the capitol,

23. And there tore down the tribunician tables, which recorded the acts passed in the time of Clodius.

24. And when Clodius called him in question for this, he answered that he, being of the patrician order,

25. Had obtained the office of tribune against law, and therefore nothing done by him was valid.

26. Cato was displeased at this, and opposed Cicero, not that he commended Clodius,

27. Yet he argued that it was irregular for the senate to vote the illegality of so many decrees,

28. Including those of Cato's own government in Cyprus and Byzantium.

29. This occasioned a breach between Cato and Cicero, which, though it did not come to open enmity, yet made a more reserved friendship between them.

30. After this, Milo killed Clodius, and, being arraigned for the murder, he asked Cicero to be his advocate.

31. The senate, fearing lest the questioning of so eminent a citizen as Milo might disturb the peace of the city, committed the superintendence of the trial to Pompey,

32. For him to maintain the security alike of the city and of the courts of justice.

33. Pompey, therefore, went in the night, and occupying the high grounds about it, surrounded the forum with soldiers.

34. Milo, fearing lest Cicero, being disturbed by such an unusual sight, should conduct his cause the less successfully,

35. Persuaded him to come to the forum in a litter, and there wait till the judges were set and the court filled.

36. On this occasion he did not perform well. Quitting his litter, he saw Pompey posted with his troops above, and seeing weapons shining round the forum,

37. He was so confounded that he could hardly begin his speech for trembling;

38. Whereas Milo was intrepid, disdaining either to let his hair grow or to put on mourning.
39. And this, indeed, seems to have been one principal cause of his condemnation, for the trial was lost.

Chapter 81

1. Shortly afterwards Cicero was appointed by lot to the province of Cilicia,
2. And set sail thither with twelve thousand foot and two thousand six hundred horse.
3. He had orders to bring back Cappadocia to its allegiance to Ariobarzanes, its king; which he effected very completely without recourse to arms.
4. And perceiving that the Cilicians were disposed to revolt, as a result of the great loss the Romans suffered in Parthia and the turbulences in Syria,
5. Cicero soothed them back into fidelity by a gentle course of government.
6. He would accept none of the presents that were offered him by the kings;
7. He remitted the charge of public entertainments, but daily at his own house received the cultured persons of the province, not sumptuously, but liberally.
8. His house had no porter, and from early in the morning he stood or walked before his door, to receive those who came to offer salutations.
9. He is said never once to have ordered any of those under his command to be beaten with rods, or to have their garments rent.
10. He never used contumelious language in his anger, nor inflicted punishment with reproach.
11. He detected an embezzlement, to a large amount, in the public money,
12. And thus relieved the cities from their burdens, at the same time allowing those who made restitution to retain their rights as citizens without further punishment.
13. He engaged too, in war, so far as to defeat the banditti who infested Mount Amanus, for which the army under his command saluted him as imperator.
14. To Caecilius, the orator, who asked him to send some panthers from Cilicia to be exhibited at the theatre in Rome,
15. He wrote, in commendation of his own actions, that there were no panthers in Cilicia,
16. For they were all fled to Caria, in anger that in so general a peace they had become the sole objects of attack.
17. On leaving his province he touched at Rhodes, and tarried for some time at Athens, longing to renew his old studies.
18. There he visited the eminent scholars, and saw his former friends and companions;
19. And after receiving the honours

that were due to him, returned to Rome,

20. Where everything was now just breaking out into a civil war because of the quarrel between Pompey and Caesar.

21. When the senate offered to decree Cicero a Triumph, he told them he had rather, if the then quarrels could be settled, follow the triumphal chariot of Caesar.

22. In private he gave advice to both men, writing many letters to Caesar and personally entreating Pompey, doing his best to soothe and bring to reason both of them.

23. But when matters became incurable, and Caesar was approaching Rome, and Pompey dared not stay, but, with many honest citizens, left the city,

24. Cicero still did not join in the flight, and was reputed to adhere to Caesar.

25. And it is very evident that he was much divided in his thoughts and wavered painfully between both, for he writes in his epistles,

26. 'To which side should I turn? Pompey has the fair and honourable plea for war;

27. 'And Caesar, on the other hand, has managed his affairs better, and is more able to secure himself and his friends,

28. 'So that I know whom I should fly from, not whom I should fly to.'

29. But when Trebatius, one of Caesar's friends, signified to him

by letter that Caesar wished him to join his party,

30. But adding that if he felt too old for the conflict, he should retire to Greece, and stay quietly out of the way of either party,

31. Cicero, wondering that Caesar had not written himself, gave an angry reply, that he should not do anything unbecoming his past life.

32. But as soon as Caesar had marched into Spain, Cicero immediately travelled to join Pompey.

33. And he was welcomed by all but Cato; who, taking him aside privately, chid him for coming to Pompey.

34. As for himself, Cato said, it would have been indecent to forsake that part in the commonwealth which he had chosen from the beginning;

35. But Cicero might have been more useful to his country if he had remained neutral, and used his influence to moderate the result,

36. Instead of coming hither to make himself, without reason or necessity, an enemy to Caesar, and a partner in such great dangers.

37. By this language, partly, Cicero's feelings were altered, and partly, also, because Pompey made no great use of him.

38. Although, indeed, he was himself the cause of this, by his not denying that he was sorry he had come,

39. By his depreciating Pompey's resources, finding fault underhand with his counsels,

40. And continually indulging in jests and sarcastic remarks on his fellow-soldiers.

Chapter 82

1. After Pompey's defeat at the battle of Pharsalia, at which he was not present for health reasons,
2. Cicero was asked by Cato, who had considerable forces and a great fleet at Dyrrachium,
3. To be commander-in-chief, according to law and the precedence of his consular dignity.
4. Cicero declined, and wished no further part in plans for continuing the war.
5. He was consequently in great danger of being killed, for young Pompey and his friends called him traitor, and drew their swords upon him;
6. But Cato interposed, and rescued him from the camp.
7. Afterwards Cicero waited at Brundusium for Caesar, who was delayed by his affairs in Asia and Egypt.
8. When it was reported that Caesar had arrived at Tarentum, and was marching by land to Brundusium,
9. He set off to meet him, in some trepidation about what reception to expect.
10. But there was no necessity for him either to speak or do anything unworthy of himself;
11. For Caesar, as soon as he saw him coming a good way before the rest of the company,
12. Came down to meet him, saluted him, and, leading the way, conversed with him alone for some furlongs.
13. And from that time forward Caesar continued to treat him with honour and respect, so that, when Cicero wrote an oration in praise of Cato,
14. Caesar, in writing an answer to it, took occasion to commend Cicero's own life and eloquence,
15. Comparing him to Pericles and Theramenes. Cicero's oration was called Cato; Caesar's, anti-Cato.
16. And it is also related that when Quintus Ligarius was prosecuted for having been in arms against Caesar,
17. And Cicero had undertaken his defence, Caesar said to his friends,
18. 'Ligarius, there is no question, is a wicked man and an enemy; but why might we not have once more the pleasure of a speech from Cicero?'
19. But when Cicero began to speak, he wonderfully moved Caesar,
20. And proceeded in his speech with such varied pathos, and such a charm of language, that the colour of Caesar's countenance often changed,
21. And it was evident that all the passions of his heart were in commotion.
22. At length, Cicero touching upon the Pharsalian battle, Caesar was so affected that his body trembled,
23. And some of the papers he held dropped from his hands. And thus

he was overpowered, and acquitted Ligarius.

Chapter 83

1. Henceforth, the commonwealth being changed into a monarchy, Cicero withdrew himself from public affairs,

2. And employed his leisure in instructing young men in philosophy;

3. And by the near intercourse he thus had with some of the noblest and highest in rank, he again began to possess great influence in the city.

4. The work he set himself was to compose and translate philosophical dialogues,

5. And to render Greek philosophical terms into Latin, rendering them intelligible and expressible to the Romans.

6. He spent the greatest part of his time at his country house near Tusculum, rarely going to the city, unless to visit Caesar.

7. He was commonly the first amongst those who voted Caesar honours, and sought out new terms of praise for his actions.

8. As, for example, when he said of the statues of Pompey, which had been thrown down and were afterwards set up again by Caesar's orders,

9. That Caesar, by this act of humanity, had not only set up Pompey's statues, but he had fixed and established his own.

10. He wished to write a history of his country, combining with it that of Greece,

11. And incorporating in it all the accounts of the past that he had collected.

12. But his purposes were interfered with by various public and various private misfortunes; for most of which he was himself at fault.

13. For first of all, he put away his wife Terentia, by whom he had been neglected in the time of the war, and sent away destitute of necessaries for his journey;

14. Neither did he find her kind when he returned to Italy, for she did not join him at Brundusium, where he stayed a long time,

15. Nor would allow her young daughter proper servants or the requisite expenses when she undertook a long journey to join him.

16. Also she left him a naked and empty house, and yet had involved him in many large debts.

17. These were alleged as the fairest reasons for the divorce.

18. But Terentia, who denied them all, had the most unmistakable defence furnished her by her husband himself,

19. Who not long after married a young maiden for her beauty and for her riches, to discharge his debts.

20. For the young woman was very rich, and Cicero had the custody of her estate, being left guardian in trust;

21. And being much in debt, was persuaded by friends to marry her, notwithstanding the disparity of age.

22. Mark Antony, who mentions this marriage in his answer to Cicero's Philippics, which are his speeches against Antony,

23. Reproaches him for putting away a wife with whom he had lived many years, adding strokes of sarcasm at Cicero's scholarly habits.

24. Not long after his marriage, Cicero's daughter Tullia died in childbed at Lentulus' house,

25. To whom she had been married after the death of Piso, her former husband.

26. The philosophers from all parts came to comfort Cicero,

27. For his grief was so excessive that he put away his new-married wife, because she seemed to be pleased at the death of Tullia.

Chapter 84

1. Cicero had no concern in the design that was now forming against Caesar,

2. Although, in general, he was Brutus' principal confidant, and one who was as aggrieved at the present, and as desirous for the former state of public affairs, as any other.

3. When Brutus and Cassius assassinated Caesar, and the friends of Caesar had gathered together, there was fear that the city would again descend into civil war.

4. Mark Antony, being consul, convened the senate, and made a short address recommending concord.

5. And Cicero followed him, trying to persuade the senate to imitate the Athenians,

6. And decree an amnesty for what had been done, and to bestow provinces on Brutus and Cassius.

7. But neither of these pleas were effective. For as soon as the common people saw Caesar's body carried through the marketplace,

8. With Antony displaying Caesar's bloodied clothes pierced through in every part with daggers, they were enraged to a frenzy,

9. And went in search of the murderers, taking firebrands to burn their houses.

10. The assassins, however, being forewarned, avoided this danger, and left the city.

11. Antony was delighted by this, and everyone was alarmed at the prospect that he would make himself sole ruler, Cicero more than anyone.

12. For Antony, seeing Cicero's influence reviving in the commonwealth and knowing how closely he was connected with Brutus, was ill-pleased to have him there.

13. Cicero, fearing Antony's intentions, was inclined to go as lieutenant with Dolabella into Syria.

14. But Hirtius and Pansa,

consuls-elect as successors of
Antony, good men and lovers of
Cicero,

15. Entreated him not to leave,
undertaking to put Antony down
if Cicero would stay in Rome.

16. And he, still doubting what to do,
let Dolabella go without him,

17. Promising Hirtius that he would
spend his summer at Athens, and
return when the new consular
terms began.

18. So Cicero set out on his journey;
but on the way news came from
Rome that Antony had made an
astonishing change, and was
managing public affairs at the will
of the senate,

19. And that there was nothing
lacking but Cicero's presence to
bring things to a happy
settlement.

20. And therefore, chastising himself
for his cowardice, Cicero returned
to Rome, and at first all seemed
promising.

21. For such multitudes flocked out to
meet him that the compliments
and civilities which were paid him
at the gates, and at his entrance
into the city, took up almost a
whole day.

Chapter 85

1. The next day Antony convened the
senate, and summoned Cicero
thither.

2. Cicero did not attend, pretending
to be ill with his journey;

3. But the true reason was suspicion

of some design by Antony against
him.

4. Antony was greatly offended, and
sent soldiers, commanding them
to bring Cicero or burn his house;

5. But because many interceded on
Cicero's behalf, he was content to
accept their assurances.

6. Ever after, when the two men met,
they passed one another with
silence, and continued on their
guard,

7. Till Octavius Caesar, afterwards
Augustus, coming from Apollonia,
entered on the first Caesar's
inheritance as his adopted son,

8. And was engaged in a dispute with
Antony about two thousand five
hundred myriads of money, which
Antony detained from Caesar's
estate.

9. Upon this, Philippus, who had
married the mother, and
Marcellus, who had married the
sister of Octavius Caesar,

10. Came with the young man to
Cicero, to ask for the aid of
Cicero's eloquence and political
influence with the senate and
people; and Cicero agreed.

11. He did so partly from his opposition to Antony, but more because
he saw that he could influence
public policy through the young
Octavius Caesar, who went so far
as to call him Father.

12. Though Brutus greatly disliked
this courtship of Cicero by
Octavian, he gave Cicero's son,
then studying philosophy at

Athens, a command in his army, and employed him in various ways, with a good result.

13. Cicero's own power at this time was at the greatest height in the city, and he did whatever he pleased;

14. He drove out Antony, and sent the two consuls, Hirtius and Pansa, with an army to reduce him;

15. And, on the other hand, he persuaded the senate to give Octavius Caesar the lictors and ensigns of a praetor, as though he were his country's defender.

16. After Antony was defeated in battle, and the consuls slain, the armies united, and ranged themselves with Octavius Caesar.

17. And the senate, in awe of the young man, tried by honours to reduce the army's loyalty to him, and to lessen his power;

18. Professing there was no further need of arms now Antony was put to flight.

19. This gave Octavius Caesar such concern that he privately sent friends to persuade Cicero to procure the consular dignity for them both together;

20. Saying Cicero should manage affairs as he pleased with full power, for the young Octavius was only desirous of the name and glory of consul.

21. Moreover Octavius Caesar himself confessed that, fearing ruin and in danger of being deserted, he had made use of Cicero's ambition.

22. And now, more than at any other time, Cicero let himself be deceived, though an old man, by the persuasion of a boy.

23. He joined Octavius Caesar in soliciting votes, and procured the goodwill of the senate,

24. Not without blame at the time on the part of his friends, who guessed what was coming;

25. And he, too, soon enough, saw that he had ruined himself, and betrayed the liberty of his country.

26. For Octavius Caesar, once established as consul, bade Cicero farewell;

27. And reconciling himself to Antony and Lepidus, joined his power with theirs, and divided the government, like a piece of property, with them.

28. Thus united, they made a list of more than two hundred people who were to be put to death.

29. But the greatest contention in their debates was centred upon Cicero.

30. Antony would accept no conditions, unless Cicero was the first to be killed.

31. Lepidus agreed with Antony, and Octavius Caesar opposed them both.

32. They met secretly for three days near the town of Bononia. The place was not far from the army camp, with a river surrounding it.

33. Octavius Caesar, it is said, earnestly defended Cicero for two

days; but on the third day gave
him up.

34. The terms of their mutual concessions were these: that Caesar
should desert Cicero; Lepidus, his
brother Paulus; and Antony,
Lucius Caesar, his uncle by his
mother's side.

35. Thus they let their anger take away
their sense of humanity, and
demonstrated that no beast is
more savage than man when
possessed with power equal to his
rage.

36. While these things were happening, Cicero was with his brother at
his house near Tusculum.

37. Hearing of the proscriptions, they
decided to go to Astura, a villa of
Cicero's near the sea, and to take
ship from there to Macedonia,
where Brutus had his strength.

38. They travelled together in
separate litters, overwhelmed
with sorrow;

39. And often stopping on the way till
their litters came together,
condoled with one another.

40. But Quintus was the more
disheartened because he had no
money for the journey, having
brought nothing with him from
home, and Cicero himself had
only a slender provision.

41. They therefore decided that Cicero
should continue to escape, while
Quintus returned home to provide
necessaries;

42. So they mutually embraced, and
parted with many tears.

43. Quintus, a few days after, was
betrayed by his servants, and was
slain, together with his young son.

Chapter 86

1. Cicero reached Astura, where he
found a vessel and sailed as far as
Circaeum with a prosperous
wind;

2. But when the pilots resolved to sail
on immediately, Cicero went
ashore, either fearing the sea, or
hoping that Octavius Caesar
might still save him;

3. And travelled a hundred furlongs
by land, as if going back to Rome.

4. But again changing his mind, he
returned to the sea, and there
spent the night in fearful and
perplexed thoughts.

5. At last he decided to go by sea to
Capitie, where he had a house, an
agreeable place to retire to in the
heat of summer, when the Etesian
winds are so pleasant.

6. He again went ashore, and on
entering his house, lay down to
rest. His servants, anxious for his
safety, and guessing that assassins
were in search of him,

7. Partly by entreaty and partly by
force took him up, and carried
him in his litter towards the
seaside.

8. But in the meantime, accompanied by a band of soldiers, the
assassins were closing in;

9. They were Herennius, a centurion,
and Popillius, a tribune, whom
Cicero had formerly defended

when prosecuted for the murder of his father.

10. Finding the doors shut, they broke them open. Those within said they did not know where Cicero was,

11. But a youth called Philologus, who had been educated by Cicero in the liberal arts and sciences,

12. And who was an emancipated slave of his brother Quintus, betrayed Cicero,

13. Informing the tribune that the litter was on its way to the sea through the close and shady walks.

14. The tribune, taking a few with him, ran out in pursuit. And Cicero, perceiving Herennius approaching, commanded his servants to set down the litter;

15. And stroking his chin, as he used to do, with his left hand, his person covered with dust, his beard and hair untrimmed,

16. And his face worn with his troubles, he looked steadfastly upon his murderers.

17. Such was the pity of the sight that the greatest part of those that stood by covered their faces while Herennius slew him.

18. And thus he was murdered, stretching forth his neck out of the litter to receive the blow. He was in his sixty-fourth year.

19. Herennius cut off his head, and, by Mark Antony's command, cut off his hands also, by which his Philippics were written;

20. For so Cicero styled those orations

he wrote against Antony, and so they are called to this day.

21. When Cicero's head and hands were brought to Rome,

22. Antony was holding an assembly for the choice of public officers;

23. And when he heard it, and saw them, he cried out, 'Now let there be an end of our proscriptions.'

24. He commanded the head and hands to be fastened up over the rostra, where the orators spoke;

25. A sight which the Roman people shuddered to behold, and they believed they saw there, not the face of Cicero, but the image of Antony's own mind.

26. A long time afterwards Octavius Caesar, visiting one of his daughter's sons, found him with a book of Cicero's in his hand.

27. The boy for fear endeavoured to hide it under his gown; which Octavius Caesar perceiving, he took it from him,

28. And turning over a great part of the book, gave it back, saying, 'My child, this was a learned man, and a lover of his country.'

29. And immediately after he had vanquished Mark Antony, being then consul, he made Cicero's son his colleague in the office;

30. And under that consulship the senate took down all the statues of Antony, and abolished all the other honours that had been given him,

31. And decreed that none of that family should thereafter bear the name of Marcus;

32. And thus the final acts of the punishment of Antony were carried out by the family of Cicero.

EPISTLES

Epistle 1

1. My dear son: you must begin by having a true estimate of our human species,

2. Before you can begin to formulate how you will advance yourself to being one of the better specimens of it.

3. That will be the purpose of these letters to you, as you take your journey among people and places,

4. So that you can combine your experience of them with the experience I offer you.

5. There are those who exalt the human species to the skies, and represent man as a paragon;

6. And there are those who insist on the worst of human nature, and can discover nothing except vanity and folly in man, making him no better than other animals.

7. A delicate sense of morals is apt to give one a disgust of the world, and to make one consider the common course of human affairs with indignation and dislike.

8. For my part I think that those who view mankind favourably and sympathetically do more to promote virtue than those who have a mean opinion of human nature.

9. When a man has a high notion of his moral status, he will naturally endeavour to live up to it, and will scorn to do a base or vicious thing, which might sink him below the figure he makes in his own imagination.

10. Accordingly we find that all the best moralists concentrate on the idea that vice is unworthy of us, as well as being odious in itself.

11. In disputes concerning the dignity or meanness of human nature it is right to begin by accepting that there is a natural difference between merit and demerit, virtue and vice, wisdom and folly.

12. Yet it is evident that in assigning approbation or blame, we are commonly more influenced by comparison than by any fixed standard in the nature of things.

13. When we call an animal big or small, we always do so on the basis of comparing that animal and others of the same species;

14. And it is that comparison which regulates our judgement concerning its size.

15. Suppose this dog and that horse are the same size; we will wonder at the dog for being large, the horse for being small.

16. When I hear any dispute I always

ask myself whether it is a question of comparison that is at issue;

17. And if it is, whether the disputants compare the same objects together, or talk of things that are widely different.

18. In forming our notions of human nature we are apt to compare men and animals, the only creatures endowed with thought that fall under our senses.

19. Certainly this comparison is favourable to mankind. In man we see a creature whose thoughts are not limited by narrow bounds of place or time;

20. Who carries his inquiries into the most distant regions of this globe, and beyond this globe, to the stars;

21. Who looks backward to consider the history of the human race;

22. Who casts his eye forward to see the influence of his actions on posterity,

23. And the judgement that will be made of his character a hundred or a thousand years hence;

24. We see a creature who traces causes and effects to a great length and intricacy,

25. Extracts general principles from particular appearances,

26. Improves his discoveries, corrects his mistakes and makes his errors profitable.

27. On the other side we see an animal – a being the very reverse of this, limited in its observations and reasonings to a few objects which surround it;

28. Without curiosity, without foresight; blindly conducted by instinct, and attaining, in a short time, its utmost perfection, beyond which it is unable to advance a single step.

29. Thus we see what a wide difference there is between humans and the other animals!

30. And how exalted a notion must we entertain of the former, in comparison to the latter therefore!

31. Yet there are two means commonly employed to destroy this conclusion:

32. First, by making an unfair representation of the case, and insisting only on the weaknesses of human nature,

33. And second, by forming a comparison between man and imagined beings of the most perfect wisdom.

34. Among the other excellencies of man, one is that he can form an idea of perfections much beyond what he has experience of in himself;

35. And therefore he is not limited in his conception of wisdom and virtue, but can imagine both in the greatest degree.

36. He can easily exalt his notions and conceive an extent of knowledge, which, when compared to his own, will make his own appear very contemptible,

37. And will cause the difference between human sagacity and that of animals almost to disappear.

38. Given that all the world agree that

human understanding falls infinitely short of perfect wisdom,

39. It is proper we should know when this comparison takes place, that we may not dispute where there is no real difference in our sentiments.

40. Man falls much more short of perfect wisdom, and even of his own ideas of perfect wisdom, than animals do of man;

41. Yet the latter difference is so considerable that nothing but a comparison with the former can make it appear of little moment.

42. It is also usual to compare one person with another; and finding very few we can call wise or virtuous, we are apt to entertain a contemptuous notion of people in general.

43. To see the fallacy of this way of reasoning, we may observe that the honourable appellations of wise and virtuous are not annexed to any particular degree of those qualities of wisdom and virtue;

44. But arise only from the comparison we make between one person and another. When we find a man who attains an uncommon pitch of wisdom, we pronounce him wise:

45. So to say that there are few wise people in the world, is really to say nothing; since it is only by their scarcity that they merit that appellation.

46. Were the lowest of our kind as wise as the greatest that history contains, we should still have reason to say that there are few wise people.

47. For in that case we should exalt our notions of wisdom still higher,

48. And should not pay a singular honour to anyone who was not singularly distinguished by his talents.

Epistle 2

1. As it is usual to compare man with the other species above or below him, or to compare the individuals of the species among themselves;

2. So we often compare together the different motives of human nature, in order to regulate our judgement concerning it.

3. And indeed this is the only kind of comparison which is worth our attention, or decides anything in the present question.

4. If our selfish and vicious principles were much more dominant than our social and virtuous principles, we ought undoubtedly to entertain a contemptuous notion of human nature.

5. But there is much that is mere dispute about words in this controversy. When a man denies the sincerity of public spirit or affection to a country and community, I am at a loss what to think of him.

6. Perhaps he never felt this emotion in so clear and distinct a manner as to remove all his doubts about its reality.

7. But when he proceeds afterwards to reject all private friendship, if no interest or self-love intermix itself, I am then confident that he abuses terms, and misunderstands the ideas they denote;

8. For it is impossible for anyone to be so selfish or stupid as to make no difference between one man and another, and to give no preference to qualities which invite his approbation and esteem.

9. Is he also as insensible to anger as he pretends to be to friendship? And does injury and wrong no more affect him than kindness or benefits?

10. Impossible: he does not know himself: he has forgotten the movements of his heart;

11. Or rather, he makes use of a different language from the rest of his countrymen, and does not call things by their proper names.

12. What does he say of natural affection? Is that also a species of self-love?

13. 'Yes,' he says: 'all is self-love. My children are loved only because they are mine:

14. 'My friend for a like reason: and my country engages me only so far as it has a connection with myself.'

15. So if the idea of self were removed, nothing would affect him! He would be altogether inactive and insensible:

16. Or, if he ever gave himself any movement, it would only be from vanity, and a desire of fame and reputation to his own self.

17. I reply that I am willing to accept his interpretation of human actions, provided he admit the facts:

18. That self-love which manifests itself in kindness to others has a great influence over human actions,

19. And even greater, on many occasions, than that which remains in its original shape and form.

20. For how few are there, who, having a family, children and relations, do not spend more on the maintenance and education of these than on their own pleasures?

21. This, indeed, he justly observes, may proceed from their self-love, since the prosperity of their family and friends is one of their pleasures, as well as their chief honour.

22. But if he is one such of these selfish men, still he will have everyone's good opinion and goodwill, because he cares for his family in this way;

23. Or not to shock his ears with these expressions, the self-love of everyone, and mine among the rest, will then incline us to serve him, and speak well of him.

24. In my opinion, there are two things which have led astray those who have insisted so much on the selfishness of man.

25. In the first place, they found that every act of virtue or friendship was attended with a secret

pleasure; from which they concluded that friendship and virtue could not be disinterested.

26. But the fallacy of this is obvious. The virtuous sentiment produces the pleasure, and does not arise from it.

27. I feel a pleasure in doing good to my friend, because I love him; but do not love him for the sake of that pleasure.

28. In the second place, it has always been found that the virtuous are far from being indifferent to praise;

29. And therefore they have been represented as a set of vainglorious people, who had nothing in view but the applause of others.

30. But this also is a fallacy. It is very unjust to find a tincture of vanity in a laudable action and to depreciate it on that account, or ascribe it entirely to that motive.

31. The case is not the same with vanity as with other passions.

32. Where avarice or revenge enters into any seemingly virtuous action, it is difficult for us to determine how far it enters, and it is natural to suppose it the sole actuating principle.

33. But vanity is so closely allied to virtue, and to love the fame of laudable actions is so close to loving laudable actions for their own sake,

34. That these passions are more capable of mixture than any other kinds of affection;

35. And it is almost impossible to have the latter without some degree of the former.

36. Thus in general, to love the glory of virtuous deeds is a sure proof of the love of virtue itself.

Epistle 3

1. And now, my dear son, to your own progress in the love of virtue!

2. I shall neither deny nor grudge you any money that may be necessary for either your improvement or your pleasures:

3. I mean the pleasures of a rational being. Under the head of improvement, I mean good books, education and lodging;

4. By rational pleasures I mean charities, presents, entertainments and other incidental calls of good company.

5. The only two articles I will never pay for are low riot, and the idle lavishness of negligence and laziness.

6. A fool squanders away, without credit or advantage to himself, more than a man of sense spends in getting both.

7. The latter employs his money as he does his time, and never spends anything of the one, nor a minute of the other, except in something that is either useful or rationally pleasing to himself or others.

8. But the fool buys whatever he does not want, and does not pay for what he does want.

9. He cannot withstand the charms

of fripperies and low pleasures; others conspire with his own self-indulgence to cheat him;

10. In a very little time he is astonished, in the midst of ridiculous superfluities, to find himself lacking the real comforts and necessaries of life.

11. Without care and method, the largest fortune will not, and with them, almost the smallest will, supply all necessary expenses.

12. As far as you can possibly, pay ready money for everything and avoid credit.

13. Pay that money yourself, and not through the hands of others, who always require their portion.

14. Where you must use credit, pay it regularly every month, and with your own hand.

15. Never, from a mistaken economy, buy a thing you do not want, because it is cheap; or from pride, because it is dear.

16. Keep an account in a book of what you receive, and what you pay;

17. For no man who knows what he receives and pays ever runs out.

18. In economy, as well as in the rest of life, have the proper attention to proper objects, and the proper contempt for little ones.

19. A strong mind sees things in their true proportions; a weak one views them through a magnifying medium,

20. Which, like the microscope, makes an elephant of a flea: magnifies all little objects, but blinds one to great ones.

21. The sure characteristic of a sound and strong mind is to find in everything the proper boundaries of things.

22. In manners, this line is good breeding; beyond it, is troublesome ceremony; short of it, is unbecoming negligence and inattention.

23. In morals, it divides puritanism from vice: and, in short, every virtue from its kindred vice or weakness.

Epistle 4

1. Many young people are so light, so dissipated and so incurious, that they can hardly be said to see what they see, or hear what they hear.

2. That is, they hear in so superficial and inattentive a manner that they might as well not see nor hear at all.

3. For instance, if they see a public building, as a college, a hospital, an arsenal, they content themselves with the first glance,

4. And take neither the time nor the trouble of informing themselves of the material parts of them;

5. Which are the constitution, the rules, and the order and economy in the inside.

6. You will, I hope, go deeper, and make your way into the substance of things.

7. You are now come to an age capable of reflection, and I hope

you will do what few people at your age do: exert it for your own sake in the search of truth and sound knowledge.

8. I will confess, for I am not unwilling to discover my secrets to you, that it is not many years since I have presumed to reflect for myself.

9. Till sixteen or seventeen I had no reflection; and for many years after that, I made no use of what I had.

10. I adopted the notions of the books I read, or the company I kept, without examining whether they were just or not;

11. And I rather chose to run the risk of easy error, than to take the time and trouble of investigating truth.

12. Thus, partly from laziness, partly from dissipation, and partly from thinking I was rejecting fashionable notions,

13. I was hurried away by prejudices, instead of being guided by reason; and quietly cherished error, instead of seeking for truth.

14. But since I have taken the trouble of reasoning for myself, you cannot imagine how much my notions of things are altered, and in how different a light I now see them.

15. Yet no doubt I still retain many errors, which, from long habit, have grown into real opinions; alas.

16. Without any extraordinary effort of genius, I have discovered that nature was the same three thousand years ago as it is at present;

17. That men were but men then as well as now; that modes and customs vary often, but that human nature is always the same.

18. And I can no more suppose that men were better, braver or wiser, fifteen hundred or three thousand years ago,

19. Than I can suppose that the animals or vegetables were better then than they are now.

20. Use and assert your own reason; reflect, examine and analyse everything, in order to form a sound and mature judgement;

21. Let no authority impose upon your understanding, mislead your actions or dictate your conversation.

22. Be early what, if you are not, you will when too late wish you had been.

23. Consult your reason betimes: I do not say that it will always prove an unerring guide; for human reason is not infallible; but it will prove the least erring guide that you can follow.

24. Books and conversation may assist it; but adopt neither blindly and implicitly; try both by that best guide, reason.

25. Of all the troubles, do not avoid, as many people do, the trouble of thinking: it is the best and most useful trouble in the world.

26. The herd of mankind can hardly be said to think; their notions are

almost all adoptive; and, in general, I believe it is better that it should be so,

27. As such common prejudices contribute more to order and quiet than their own separate reasonings would do, uncultivated and unimproved as they are.

Epistle 5

1. The day, if well employed, is long enough for everything.
2. One half of it, bestowed upon your studies and your exercises, will finish your mind and your body;
3. The remaining part of it, spent in good company, will form your manners and complete your character.
4. What would I not give to have you read Demosthenes critically in the morning, and understand him better than anybody;
5. At noon, behave yourself better than any person at court;
6. And in the evening, trifle more agreeably than anybody in mixed companies?
7. All this you may do if you please; you have the means, you have the opportunities.
8. Employ them while you may, and make yourself that all-accomplished man that I wish to have you.

Epistle 6

1. In order to judge of the inside of others, study your own; for men in general are very much alike;
2. And though one has one prevailing passion, and another has another, yet their operations are much the same;
3. And whatever engages or disgusts, pleases or offends you, in others will engage, disgust, please or offend others, in you.
4. Observe with the utmost attention all the operations of your own mind, the nature of your passions, and the various motives that determine your will;
5. And you may, in a great degree, know all mankind.
6. For instance, do you find yourself hurt and mortified when another makes you feel his superiority, and your own inferiority, in knowledge, parts, rank or fortune?
7. You will certainly take great care not to make a person whose goodwill, good word, interest, esteem or friendship you would gain, feel that superiority in you, if you have it.
8. If disagreeable insinuations, sneers or repeated contradictions tease and irritate you, would you use them where you wish to engage and please?
9. Surely not, and I hope you wish to engage and please, almost universally.
10. The temptation of saying a smart and witty thing, and the malicious applause with which it is commonly received, has made

more enemies for people who can say them,

11. And, still oftener, people who think they can, but cannot, and yet try;

12. Not only does this make enemies, but it makes implacable ones, and is the surest way to enmity than anything else I know of.

13. If such things shall happen to be said at your expense, reflect seriously upon the sentiments of anger and resentment which they excite in you;

14. And consider whether it can be prudent, by the same means, to excite the same sentiments in others against you.

15. It is a decided folly to lose a friend for a jest; but, in my mind, it is not much less folly to make an enemy of an indifferent and neutral person for the sake of a facetious remark.

16. When things of this kind are said of you, the most prudent way is to seem not to suppose that they are meant of you,

17. But to dissemble and conceal whatever degree of anger you may feel inwardly;

18. But, should they be so plain that you cannot be supposed ignorant of their meaning,

19. Join in the laugh of the company against yourself; acknowledge the hit to be a fair one, and the jest good, and play it off in seeming good humour;

20. But by no means reply in the same way; which only shows that you are hurt, and publishes the victory which you might have concealed.

21. Should the thing said indeed injure your honour or moral character, there is but one proper reply, which I hope you never will have occasion to make.

Epistle 7

1. Consider, therefore, how precious every moment of time is to you now.

2. The more you apply to your business, the more you will taste your pleasures.

3. The exercise of the mind in the morning whets the appetite for the pleasures of the evening,

4. As much as the exercise of the body whets the appetite for dinner.

5. Business and pleasure, rightly understood, mutually assist each other, instead of being enemies, as silly or dull people often think them.

6. No man tastes pleasures truly, who does not earn them by previous business,

7. And few people do business well, who do nothing else.

8. Thus work and pleasure are friends and helpers to each other, and relieve and sweeten each other.

9. Remember that when I speak of pleasures, I always mean the pleasures of a rational being, and not the brutal ones of a swine.

10. I mean good food, not gluttony;

good wine, far short of drunkenness;

11. Pleasant play, without the least gaming; and gallantry, without debauchery.

12. There is a line in all these things which men of sense, for greater security, take care to keep a good deal on the right side of;

13. For sickness, pain, contempt and infamy lie immediately on the other side of that line.

14. Men of sense and merit, in all other respects, may have had some of these failings;

15. But those few examples, instead of inviting us to imitation, should only put us the more upon our guard against weaknesses.

Epistle 8

1. To reflect upon people, their nature, their characters, their manners, will help you to form yourself, as well to know others.

2. It seems as if it were nobody's business to communicate such knowledge to the young.

3. Their masters teach them the languages or the sciences, but are generally incapable of teaching them the world:

4. Their parents likewise seem incapable, or at least neglect doing it,

5. Either from indifference, or from being too busy, or from an opinion that merely throwing them into the world is the best way of teaching it to them.

6. This last notion is in a great degree true; that is, the world can doubtless never be well known by theory: practice is absolutely necessary;

7. But surely it is of great use to the young, before they set out for that country full of mazes, windings and turnings,

8. To have at least a general map of it, made by some experienced traveller.

Epistle 9

1. A certain dignity of manners is absolutely necessary, to make even the most valuable character either respected or respectable.

2. Horse-play, romping, frequent and loud fits of laughter, jokes, waggery and indiscriminate familiarity will sink both merit and knowledge into a degree of contempt.

3. They compose at most a merry fellow; and a merry fellow was never yet a respectable man.

4. Indiscriminate familiarity either offends your superiors, or else makes you their dependant and follower.

5. It gives your inferiors just, but troublesome and improper, claims of equality.

6. A joker is near akin to a buffoon; and neither of them is the least related to wit.

7. Whoever is admitted or sought for in company upon any other account than that of merit and manners, is never respected there,

8. But only made use of: 'We will have such a one,' people say, 'for he sings prettily; we will invite such a one to a ball, for he dances well;

9. 'We will have such a one at supper, for he is always joking and laughing; we will ask another, because he drinks a great deal.'

10. These are all vilifying distinctions, mortifying preferences, and exclude all ideas of esteem and regard.

11. Whoever is invited into company for the sake of any one thing singly, is singly that thing and will never be considered in any other light;

12. Consequently he is never respected for himself, let his merits be what they will.

13. This dignity of manners, which I recommend so strongly to you, is not pride: far from it.

14. It is not only as different from pride as true courage is from blustering,

15. Or true wit from joking; but is absolutely inconsistent with it; for nothing vilifies and degrades more than pride.

16. The pretensions of the proud man are more often met with contempt than with indignation;

17. As we offer ridiculously too little to a tradesman who asks ridiculously too much for his goods;

18. But we do not haggle with one who only asks a just and reasonable price.

19. Abject flattery and indiscriminate agreement degrade as much as indiscriminate contradiction and contrariness disgust.

20. But a modest assertion of one's own opinion, and a complaisant acquiescence to other people's, preserve dignity.

21. Vulgar expressions and awkward movements attract dislike, as they imply a low turn of mind, a low education and low company.

22. Frivolous curiosity about trifles, and a laborious attention to little objects which neither require nor deserve a moment's thought, lower a man; who from thence is thought incapable of greater matters.

23. One man very sagaciously marked out another for a little mind, from the moment that the latter told him he had used the same pen three years, and that it was still good.

Epistle 10

1. My son, a certain degree of exterior seriousness in looks and motions gives dignity,

2. Without excluding wit and decent cheerfulness, which are always serious themselves.

3. A constant smirk upon the face, and restlessness of the body, are strong indications of futility.

4. Whoever is in a hurry, shows that the thing he is about is too big for him. Haste and hurry are very different things.

5. I have only mentioned some of those things which may, and do, in the opinion of the world, lower and sink characters, in other respects valuable enough;

6. But I have taken no notice of those that affect and sink the moral characters. These latter are sufficiently obvious.

7. A man who has patiently been kicked may as well pretend to courage, as a man blasted by vices and crimes may pretend to dignity of any kind.

8. But an exterior decency and dignity of manners will keep even such a man longer from sinking, than otherwise he would be.

9. Pray read frequently, and with the utmost attention, even learn by heart, that incomparable chapter in Cicero's *Offices*, upon decorum. It contains whatever is necessary for the dignity of manners.

10. A vulgar, ordinary way of thinking, acting or speaking implies a low education, and a habit of low company.

11. Young people contract it at school, or on the street, if they are too often used to converse there;

12. But if they are to frequent good company, they need attention and observation very much, if they are to lay bad habits aside;

13. And, indeed, if they do not, good company will be very apt to lay them aside.

14. The various kinds of vulgarisms are infinite; some samples may help one guess at the rest.

15. A vulgar man is captious and jealous, eager and impetuous about trifles.

16. He suspects himself to be slighted, thinks everything that is said is meant at him:

17. If the company happens to laugh, he is persuaded they laugh at him;

18. He grows angry and testy, says something very impertinent, and draws himself into a scrape,

19. By showing what he likes to call a strong character, and asserting himself.

20. A sensible man, by contrast, does not suppose himself to be either the sole or principal object of the thoughts, looks or words of the company;

21. And never suspects that he is either slighted or laughed at, unless he is conscious that he deserves it.

22. And if, which very seldom happens, the company is absurd or ill-bred enough to do either, he does not care,

23. Unless the insult be so gross and plain as to require satisfaction of another kind.

24. As he is above trifles, he is never vehement and eager about them; and, wherever they are concerned, rather acquiesces than wrangles.

25. A vulgar man's conversation always savours strongly of the lowness of his education and company.

26. It turns chiefly upon his domestic

affairs, daily work, the excellent order he keeps in his own family and the little anecdotes of the neighbourhood;

27. All which he relates with emphasis, as interesting matters. He is a man of gossip.

28. Vulgarism in language is the next and distinguishing characteristic of bad company and a bad education.

29. A reflective man avoids nothing with more care than platitude.

30. Proverbial expressions and trite sayings are the rhetorical flowers of the vulgar man.

31. Would he say that men differ in their tastes, he both supports and adorns that opinion by a good old saying, as he respectfully calls it, that 'one man's meat is another man's poison'.

32. If anybody attempts to 'get smart' with him, as he calls it, he gives them 'tit for tat' – aye, that he does.

33. He has always some favourite word for the time being; which, for the sake of using often, he commonly abuses,

34. Such as 'vastly' angry, 'vastly' kind, 'vastly' handsome and 'vastly' ugly.

35. He sometimes affects hard words, by way of ornament, which he always mangles.

36. An educated man never has recourse to proverbs and vulgar aphorisms; he uses neither favourite words nor hard words;

37. But takes care to use the instrument of language well.

38. Graces of manner and speech are as necessary to adorn and introduce a person's intrinsic merit, as the polish is to the diamond;

39. Which, without that polish, would never be worn, whatever it might weigh.

Epistle 11

1. I have often asserted, my son, that the profoundest learning and the politest manners were by no means incompatible, though seldom united in the same person.

2. Every rational being, I take it for granted, proposes to himself some object more important than mere respiration and obscure animal existence.

3. He desires to distinguish himself among his fellow-creatures. Pliny leaves mankind only this alternative:

4. Either of doing what deserves to be written about, or of writing what deserves to be read.

5. You have, I am convinced, one or both of these objects in view; but you must know and use the necessary means, or your pursuit will be vain.

6. In either case, knowledge is the principle and basis, but it is by no means all.

7. That knowledge must be adorned, it must have lustre as well as weight, or it will be oftener taken for lead than for gold.

8. Knowledge you have, and will have: I am easy upon that point.

But my business, as your friend, is not to compliment you upon what you have, but to tell you what you lack;

9. And I must tell you plainly that I fear you lack everything other than knowledge.

10. And by this, my dear son, I mean that what you must next acquire is manners.

11. It has been well said that one would be virtuous for one's own sake, though nobody were to know it; as one would be clean for one's own sake, though nobody else were by.

12. I have therefore, since you have had the use of your reason, never written to you upon the subject of vice:

13. It speaks best for itself; and I should now just as soon think of warning you gravely not to fall into the dirt or the fire, as into dishonour.

14. But the requisite next to good morals is good manners, and they are as necessary as they are desirable.

15. Good manners are, to particular societies, what good morals are to society in general: their cement and their security.

16. And, as laws are enacted to enforce good morals, or at least to prevent the ill effects of bad ones,

17. So there are certain rules of civility, universally implied and received, to enforce good manners and punish bad ones.

18. And, indeed, there seems to me less difference between morals and manners, and both the crimes and the punishments involving either, than at first one would imagine.

19. The immoral man, who invades another man's property, is justly punished for it; and the ill-bred man, who, by his ill manners, invades and disturbs the quiet and comforts of private life, is by common consent as justly punished by banishment from society.

20. Mutual complaisances, attentions and sacrifices of little conveniences are as natural an implied compact between civilised people, as protection and obedience are between a state and its citizens;

21. Whoever, in either case, violates that compact, justly forfeits the advantages arising from it.

22. For my own part, I really think that next to the consciousness of doing a good action, that of doing a civil one is the most pleasing;

23. And the description which I should covet the most, next to that of being honest and true, is that of being well-bred.

24. Accordingly one might note these axioms: that the deepest learning, without good breeding, is unwelcome and tiresome pedantry,

25. And as that is of use nowhere but in a man's own study, it is consequently of little or no use at all;

26. That a man who is not well-bred is

unfit for good company and
unwelcome in it;

27. He will consequently dislike it
soon, and afterwards renounce it,
or be renounced by it,

28. And be thus reduced to solitude,
or, what is worse, to low and bad
company.

29. And finally, that a man who is not
well-bred is as unfit for business as
for company.

30. Make good breeding, then, an
object of study. You will negotiate
with very little success, if you do
not previously, by your manners,
conciliate and engage the affections
of those with whom you negotiate.

31. Can you ever get into good
relations with others, if you have
not those pleasing manners, which
alone can establish them?

32. I do not say too much, when I say
that good manners and gentle
address are essential for the good
life.

33. For your knowledge will have very
little influence upon others'
minds, if your manners prejudice
their hearts against you;

34. But, on the other hand, how easily
will you engage the understanding,
where you have first engaged the
heart?

Epistle 12

1. My dear son, those who suppose
that men in general act rationally,
because they are called rational
creatures, know very little of the
world,

2. And if they act themselves upon
that supposition, will nine times
in ten find themselves grossly
mistaken.

3. Thus the speculative, cloistered
pedant, in his solitary cell, forms
systems of things as they should
be, not as they are;

4. And writes as decisively and
absurdly upon war, politics,
manners and characters, as that
pedant talked, who was so kind as
to instruct Hannibal in the art of
war.

5. Such closet politicians never fail to
assign the deepest motives for the
most trifling actions,

6. Instead of often ascribing the
greatest actions to the most trifling
causes, in which they would be
much seldomer mistaken.

7. They read and write of kings,
heroes and statesmen, as never
doing anything but upon the
deepest principles of sound policy.

8. But those who see and observe
kings, heroes and statesmen
discover that they have headaches,
indigestions, humours and
passions, just like other people;

9. Every one of which, in their turn,
determine their wills, in defiance
of their reason.

10. Had we only read in the *Life of
Alexander* that he burned
Persepolis, it would doubtless have
been accounted for from deep
policy:

11. We should have been told that his
new conquest could not have been

secured without the destruction of that capital,

12. Which would have been the constant seat of cabals, conspiracies and revolts.

13. But, luckily, we are informed at the same time that this hero, this paragon, happened to get extremely drunk with a courtesan;

14. And, by way of frolic, destroyed one of the finest cities in the world.

15. Read men, therefore, yourself, not in books but in nature. Adopt no systems, but study them yourself.

16. Observe their weaknesses, their passions, their humours, by all of which their rational minds are duped, nine times in ten.

17. You will then know that they are to be gained, influenced or led much oftener by little things than by great ones;

18. And, consequently, you will no longer think those things little, which tend to such great purposes.

19. The knowledge of mankind is a very useful knowledge for everybody, but a most necessary one for anyone wishing an active, public life.

20. You will have to do with all sorts of characters; you should, therefore, know them thoroughly, in order to manage them ably.

21. This knowledge is not to be got systematically; you must acquire it yourself by your own observation and sagacity,

22. Though you can benefit from the philosophers too, who can give you hints that may be useful.

23. I have often told you that, with regard to mankind, we must not draw general conclusions from certain particular principles, though, in the main, they are true ones.

24. We must not suppose that, because a man is a rational animal, he will therefore always act rationally;

25. Or, because he has such or such a predominant passion, that he will act invariably and consequentially in pursuit of it.

26. No. We are complicated machines: and though we have one mainspring that gives motion to the whole, we have an infinity of little wheels,

27. Which, in their turns, retard, precipitate and sometimes stop that motion.

Epistle 13

1. Let us exemplify. Let us suppose that ambition is, as indeed it commonly is, the dominating passion of a certain politician;

2. And I will suppose that politician to be an able one. Will he, therefore, invariably pursue the aims of his predominant passion?

3. May I be sure that he will do so and so, because he ought? No! Sickness or melancholia may damp that passion;

4. Humour and peevishness may triumph over it; inferior passions

may, at times, surprise it and prevail.

5. Is this ambitious politician amorous? Indiscreet and unguarded confidences, made in tender moments, to his wife or his mistress, may defeat all his schemes.

6. Is he avaricious? Some great lucrative object, suddenly presenting itself, may unravel all the work of his ambition.

7. Does he have strong emotions? Contradiction and provocation, sometimes artfully intended to rouse him, may extort rash and inconsiderate expressions, or actions destructive of his main object.

8. Is he vain, and open to flattery? An artful, flattering favourite may mislead him;

9. And even laziness may, at certain moments, make him neglect or omit the necessary steps to that height he aspires to.

10. Seek first, then, for the predominant passion of the character which you mean to engage and influence, and address yourself to it;

11. But without defying or despising the inferior passions; get them in your interest too, for now and then they will have their turns.

12. In many cases, you may not have it in your power to contribute to the gratification of the prevailing passion;

13. Then take the next best to your aid. There are many avenues to every man,

14. And when you cannot get at him through the great one, try the serpentine ones, and you will arrive at last.

15. There are two inconsistent passions, which frequently accompany each other, like man and wife;

16. And which, like man and wife too, are commonly clogs upon each other. I mean: ambition and avarice.

17. The latter is often the true cause of the former, and then is the predominant passion.

18. Though men are all of one composition, the several ingredients are so differently proportioned in each individual that no two are exactly alike; and no one is at all times like himself.

19. The ablest man will sometimes do weak things; the proudest man, mean things;

20. The most honest man, ill things; and the wickedest man, good ones.

21. Study individuals then, and if you take, as you ought to do, their outlines from their prevailing passion,

22. Suspend your last finishing strokes till you have attended to, and discovered the operations of their inferior passions, appetites and humours.

23. A man's general character may be that of the most honest man of the world: do not dispute it; you

might be thought envious or ill-natured;

24. But, at the same time, do not take this probity upon trust to such a degree as to put your life, fortune or reputation in his power.

25. This honest man may happen to be your rival in power, in interest or in love: three passions that often put honesty to most severe trials, in which it is too often cast;

26. But first analyse this honest man yourself; and then only you will be able to judge how far you may, or may not, with safety trust him.

Epistle 14

1. My son, be on your guard against those who, on very slight acquaintance, obtrude their unasked and unmerited friendship and confidence upon you;

2. For they probably cram you with them only for their own eating;

3. But, at the same time, do not roughly reject them on that mere supposition.

4. Examine further, and see whether those unexpected offers flow from a warm heart and a silly head,

5. Or from a designing head and a cold heart; for knavery and folly have often the same symptoms.

6. In the first case, there is no danger in accepting them; in the latter case, it may be useful to seem to accept them, and artfully to turn the battery upon him who raised it.

7. There is an incontinency of friendship among young fellows who are associated by their mutual pleasures only,

8. Which has, very frequently, bad consequences. A parcel of warm hearts and inexperienced heads, heated by convivial mirth,

9. And possibly a little too much wine, vow, and really mean at the time, eternal friendships to each other,

10. And indiscreetly pour out their whole hearts in common, and without the least reserve.

11. These confidences are as indiscreetly repealed as they were made;

12. For new pleasures and new places soon dissolve this ill-cemented connection; and then very ill uses are made of these rash confidences.

13. Bear your part, however, in young companies; indeed, excel, if you can, in all the social and convivial joy and festivity that become youth.

14. Trust them with your love tales, if you please; but keep your serious views secret.

15. Trust those only to some tried friend, more experienced than yourself,

16. And who, being in a different walk of life from you, is not likely to become your rival;

17. For I would not advise you to depend so much upon the heroic virtue of mankind, as to hope or believe that your competitor will ever be your friend in such matters.

18. These are reserves and cautions very necessary to have, but very imprudent to show.

Epistle 15

1. If you have great talents and great virtues, my son, they will procure you the respect and the admiration of mankind;

2. But it is the lesser talents which must procure you their love and affection.

3. The former, unassisted and unadorned by the latter, will extort praise; but will, at the same time, excite both fear and envy;

4. And these are two sentiments absolutely incompatible with love and affection.

5. Caesar had all the great vices, and Cato all the great virtues, that men could have.

6. But Caesar had the lesser virtues which Cato lacked, and therefore Caesar was beloved by many,

7. Even by his enemies, and he gained the hearts of mankind, in spite of their reason:

8. While Cato was not even beloved by his friends, notwithstanding the esteem and respect which they could not refuse to his virtues.

9. I am inclined to think that if Caesar had lacked, and Cato had possessed, those lesser virtues,

10. The former could not have stolen, and the latter could have protected, the liberties of Rome.

11. As a dramatist says of Caesar, and with truth, 'Curse his virtues, they have undone his country.'

12. By which he means those lesser, but engaging virtues of gentleness, affability, complaisance and good humour.

13. The knowledge of a scholar, the courage of a hero and the virtue of a Stoic will be admired;

14. But if the knowledge be accompanied with arrogance, the courage with ferocity and the virtue with inflexible severity, the man will never be loved.

15. We are all so formed that our understandings are generally the dupes of our hearts, that is, of our emotions;

16. And the surest way to the former is through the latter, which must be engaged by the lesser virtues alone, and the manner of exerting them.

17. The insolent civility of a proud man is, if possible, more shocking than his rudeness could be;

18. Because he shows you by his manner that he thinks it mere condescension in him;

19. And that his goodness alone bestows upon you what you have no pretence to claim.

20. He intimates his protection, instead of his friendship, by a gracious nod, instead of a usual bow;

21. And rather signifies his consent that you may, than his invitation that you should, sit, walk, eat or drink with him.

22. The costive liberality of a purse-proud man insults the distresses it sometimes relieves;

23. He takes care to make you feel your own misfortunes, and the difference between your situation and his,

24. Both of which he insinuates to be justly merited: yours, by your folly; his, by his wisdom.

25. The arrogant pedant does not communicate, but promulgates his knowledge. He does not give it to you, he inflicts it on you;

26. And is if possible more desirous to show you your own ignorance than his own learning.

27. Such manners as these shock and revolt that little pride and vanity which every man has in his heart;

28. And obliterate in us the obligation for the favour conferred, by reminding us of the motive which produced it, and the manner which accompanied it.

29. These faults point out their opposite perfections, and your own good sense, my son, will naturally suggest them to you.

30. But besides these lesser virtues, there are what may be called the lesser talents, or accomplishments, which are of valuable use to adorn and recommend all the greater accomplishments;

31. And the more so, as all people are judges of the lesser, and but few are of the greater.

32. Everybody feels the impression which an engaging address, an agreeable manner of speaking and an easy politeness, makes upon them;

33. And as a result this prepares the way for a favourable reception and friendliness.

Epistle 16

1. No less necessary than either ancient or modern knowledge, therefore, is knowledge of the world, manners, politeness and society.

2. In that view, keeping company and learning well to be sociable is an important part of education.

3. To be well-mannered without ceremony, easy without negligence,

4. Steady and intrepid with modesty, genteel without affectation,

5. Cheerful without noisiness, frank without indiscretion, and able to keep confidences;

6. To know the proper time and place for whatever you say or do, and to do it with an air of condition;

7. All this is not so soon nor so easily learned as people imagine, but requires observation and time.

8. The world is an immense folio, which demands attention to be read and understood as it ought;

9. You have not yet read above four or five pages of it, my son, and you will have barely enough time to dip now and then into other less important books.

10. I would have you not only adopt,

but rival, the best manners and
usages of the place you are at, be
they what they will;

11. That is the versatility of manners
which is so useful in the course of
the world.

12. Choose your models well, then
rival them in their own way.

13. Make yourself master of good and
thoughtful observance;

14. And to such a degree, dear son, as
to make your hosts commend and
welcome you;

15. And when thereafter you shall be
at other places, do the same thing
there, conforming to the manners
and usage of the place.

16. One would desire to please,
wherever one is; and nothing is
more innocently flattering than an
approbation and emulation of the
people one converses with.

17. But be always gentle, in the sense
of the gentleman. This is not so
easily described as felt.

18. It is the compound result of
different things: a quiet friendliness, a flexibility, but not a
servility of manners;

19. An air of agreeableness in the
countenance, gesture and
expression,

20. Equally whether you concur or
differ with the person you
converse with.

21. Observe those carefully who have
that good manner in others that
pleases;

22. And your own good sense will
soon enable you to discover the

different ingredients of which it is
composed.

23. You must be more particularly
attentive to this whenever you are
obliged to refuse what is asked of
you, or to say what in itself cannot
be very agreeable to those to
whom you say it.

24. It is then the necessary gilding of a
disagreeable pill. Amiability
consists in a thousand of these
little things aggregately.

25. It is the appropriateness of manner
which I have so often recommended to you.

Epistle 17

1. As you have not much time to
read, you should employ it in
reading what is the most necessary,

2. And that is, modern historical,
geographical, chronological,
sociological and political knowledge of the world,

3. The science and investigations of
the learned as reported to the
public, and the debates of literature and philosophy.

4. Many who are reckoned good
scholars, though they know pretty
accurately the history and culture
of Athens and Rome,

5. Are totally ignorant of the same in
any one country now in the world,
even of their own.

6. Keep up your classical learning,
which will be an ornament to you
while young, and a comfort to you
when old.

7. But even more keep up the useful

knowledge which is the modern knowledge.

8. It is that which must qualify you both for work and for life, and it is to that, therefore, that you should principally direct your attention.

Epistle 18

1. The consciousness of merit makes a man of sense more modest, though more firm.

2. You will have noticed, my son, that a man who shows off his own merit is a coxcomb, and a man who does not know his own merit is a fool.

3. A man of sense knows it, exerts it, avails himself of it, but never boasts of it;

4. And always seems rather to undervalue than overvalue it, though in truth, he sets the right value upon it.

5. A man who is really diffident, timid and bashful, be his merit what it will, never can push himself in the world;

6. His despondency throws him into inaction; and people who are forward, bustling or petulant will always get the better of him.

7. The manner makes the whole difference. What would be impudence in one, is only a proper and decent assurance in another.

8. A man of sense, and of knowledge in the world, will assert his own rights, and pursue his own objects, as steadily and intrepidly as the most impudent man living, and commonly more so;

9. But then he has sense enough to maintain an outward air of modesty to all he does.

10. This engages and prevails, while the very same things shock and fail, from the overbearing or impudent manner only of doing them.

11. For there are some people who have great qualities whom one cannot, even when praising them, love.

12. How often have I, in the course of my life, found myself in this situation, with regard to many of my acquaintance,

13. Whom I have honoured and respected, without being able to like them.

14. I did not then know why, because, when one is young, one does not take the trouble,

15. Nor allow one's self the time, to analyse one's sentiments and to trace them up to their source.

16. But subsequent observation and reflection have taught me why.

17. There is a man whose moral character, deep learning and superior parts I acknowledge, admire and respect;

18. But whom it is so impossible for me to like that I am almost in a fever whenever I am in his company.

19. His figure, without being deformed, seems made to disgrace or ridicule the common structure of the human body.

20. His legs and arms are never in the position which, according to the situation of his body, they ought to be in,

21. But constantly employed in committing acts of hostility upon the graces.

22. He throws anywhere but down his throat whatever he means to drink, and only mangles what he means to carve.

23. Inattentive to all the regards of social life, he mistimes or misplaces everything.

24. He disputes with heat, and indiscriminately, mindless of the rank, character and situation of those with whom he disputes;

25. Absolutely ignorant of the several gradations of familiarity or respect, he is exactly the same to his superiors, his equals and his inferiors;

26. And therefore, by a necessary consequence, absurd to two of the three.

27. Is it possible to like such a man? No. The utmost I can do for him is to consider him as a respectable savage.

Epistle 19

1. I mentioned to you some time ago a sentence which I would most earnestly wish you always to retain in your thoughts, and observe in your conduct.

2. It is *suaviter in modo, fortiter in re*; 'gentleness of manner, with firmness of mind'.

3. I do not know any one rule so unexceptionably useful and necessary in every part of life.

4. I shall therefore take it for my text today, and as old men love preaching, and I have some right to lecture to you, I here present you with my discourse upon these words.

5. To proceed, then, regularly, I will first show you the necessary connection of the two parts of my text.

6. Next, I shall set forth the advantages and utility resulting from a strict observance of the precept contained in my text;

7. And conclude with an application of the whole. The 'gentleness of manner' alone would degenerate into a mean, timid complaisance and passivity,

8. If not supported and dignified by the 'firmness of mind', which in its turn would run into impetuosity and brutality, if not tempered and softened by the 'gentleness of manner':

9. Yet in the world these two qualities are seldom united.

10. The warm, choleric man, with strong animal appetites, despises the 'gentleness of manner',

11. And thinks to carry all before him by the 'firmness of mind'. He may, possibly, now and then succeed, when he has only weak and timid people to deal with;

12. But his general fate will be to shock, offend, be disliked and fail.

13. On the other hand, the cunning, crafty man thinks to gain all his ends by the 'gentleness of manner' only;

14. He becomes all things to all men; he seems to have no opinion of his own, and servilely adopts the present opinion of the present person;

15. He insinuates himself only into the esteem of fools, but is soon detected, and surely despised by everybody else.

16. The wise man, who differs as much from the cunning as from the choleric man, alone joins the 'gentleness of manner' to the 'firmness of mind'.

17. Now to the advantages arising from the strict observance of this precept.

18. If you are in authority, and have a right to command, your commands delivered in a gentle manner will be willingly, cheerfully, and therefore well obeyed;

19. Whereas, if given only with firmness, they will rather be interrupted than executed.

20. For my own part, if I bid the waiter bring me a glass of wine in a rough insulting manner, I should expect that, in obeying me, he would contrive to spill some of it upon me:

21. And I am sure I should deserve it. A cool, steady resolution should show that where you have a right to command you will be obeyed.

22. But at the same time, a gentleness in the manner of enforcing obedience should make that obedience a cheerful one, and soften as much as possible the mortifying consciousness of inferiority.

23. If you are to ask a favour, or even to solicit your due, you must do it with gentleness,

24. Or you will give those who have a mind to refuse you a pretence to do it by resenting the manner.

25. But, on the other hand, you must, by a steady perseverance and decent tenaciousness, show firmness of mind too.

26. The right motives are seldom the true ones of men's actions, especially of people in positions of authority,

27. Who often give to importunity and fear what they would refuse to justice or to merit. By the gentle manner engage people's hearts, if you can;

28. At least prevent the pretence of offence; but take care to show enough of the firmness of mind to extort from their love of ease, or their fear, what you might in vain hope from their justice or good nature.

29. People in high life are hardened to the wants and distresses of mankind, as surgeons are to their bodily pains;

30. They see and hear of them all day long, and even of so many simulated ones, that they do not know which are real, and which not.

31. Other sentiments are therefore to be applied to than those of mere justice and humanity; their favour must be captivated by the gentle manner;

32. Their love of ease disturbed by unwearied importunity, or their fears wrought upon by a decent intimation of implacable, cool resentment: this is the true firmness of mind.

33. This precept is the only way I know in the world of being loved without being despised, and feared without being hated.

34. It constitutes the dignity of character which every wise man must endeavour to establish.

Epistle 20

1. My son, if you find that you have a hastiness in your temper, which unguardedly breaks out into indiscreet sallies or rough expressions,

2. To either your superiors, your equals or your inferiors,

3. Watch it narrowly, check it carefully, and call the gentleness of manner to your assistance:

4. At the first impulse of passion, be silent till you can be soft.

5. Labour even to get the command of your countenance so well, that those emotions may not be read in it; this is a most unspeakable advantage in business!

6. On the other hand, let no complaisance, no gentleness of temper, no weak desire of pleasing on your part,

7. And no wheedling, coaxing, nor flattery, on other people's part,

8. Make you recede one jot from any point that reason and prudence have bid you pursue;

9. But return to the charge, persist, persevere, and you will find most things attainable that are possible.

10. A yielding, timid meekness is always abused and insulted by the unjust and the unfeeling;

11. But when sustained by firmness of mind, is always respected, and commonly successful.

12. In your friendships and connections, as well as in your enmities, this rule is particularly useful;

13. Let your firmness and vigour preserve and invite attachments to you;

14. But, at the same time, let your manner hinder the enemies of your friends and dependants from becoming yours;

15. Let your enemies be disarmed by the gentleness of your manner, but let them feel, at the same time, the steadiness of your just resentment;

16. For there is a great difference between bearing malice, which is always ungenerous, and a resolute self-defence, which is always prudent and justifiable.

17. In negotiations remember the 'firmness of mind'; give up no point, accept of no expedient, till the utmost necessity reduces you to it,

18. And even then, dispute the ground inch by inch; but then, while you

are contending with firmness of mind,

19. Remember to gain your opponent by the gentleness of your manner.

20. If you engage his heart, you have a fair chance of gaining his mind.

21. Tell him, in a frank, gallant manner, that your wrangles do not lessen your personal regard for his merit;

22. But that, on the contrary, his zeal and ability in the service of his cause increase it;

23. And that, of all things, you desire to make a good friend of so good a person.

24. By these means you may, and very often will, be a gainer: you never can be a loser.

25. Some people cannot prevail upon themselves to be easy and civil to those who are either their rivals, competitors or opposers,

26. Though, independently of those accidental circumstances, they would like and esteem them. They betray a shyness and an awkwardness in company with them,

27. And catch at any little thing to expose them; and so, from temporary and only occasional opponents, make them their personal enemies.

28. This is exceedingly weak and detrimental, as indeed is all humour in business;

29. Which can only be carried on successfully by unadulterated good policy and right reasoning.

30. In such situations I would be more

particularly civil, easy and frank with the man whose designs I traversed:

31. This is generosity and magnanimity, but is also, in truth, good sense and policy.

32. The manner is often as important as the matter, sometimes more so;

33. A favour may make an enemy, and an injury may make a friend, according to the different manner in which they are severally done.

34. The countenance, the address, the words, the enunciation, the graces,

35. All add great efficacy to the gentle manner and great dignity to the firm mind,

36. And consequently they deserve the utmost attention.

37. From what has been said, I conclude with this observation,

38. That gentleness of manners, with firmness of mind, is a short, but full description of human perfection.

Epistle 21

1. My dear son, what a happy period of your life is this!

2. Pleasure is now, and ought to be, your business when you are between school and life.

3. While you were younger, dry rules, facts and examinations were the objects of your labours.

4. When you grow older, the anxiety, vexations and disappointments inseparable from public business will require the greatest share of your time and attention;

5. Your pleasures may, indeed, conduce to your business, and your business will quicken your pleasures; but still your time must, at least, be divided:

6. Whereas now it is wholly your own, and cannot be so well employed as in the pleasures of a gentleman.

7. The world is now your book, a necessary book that can only be read in company, in public places, at dinner, the theatre, at play.

8. You must join in the pleasures of good company, in order to learn the manners of good company.

9. In premeditated or formal business, people conceal, or at least endeavour to conceal, their characters:

10. Whereas pleasures uncover their characters, and the heart breaks out through the guard of the understanding.

11. Those are often propitious moments for forming friendships and connections;

12. And the knowledge of character thus acquired is useful in the windings and labyrinths of the world.

13. Discernment of character, a suppleness, versatility and firmness of mind, with gentleness of manners, are to the mind what neat dress is to the body.

14. Mere plain truth, sense and knowledge are great goods, but in the world of affairs are not yet enough;

15. Art and ornament must come to their assistance, to gain and engage the heart.

16. Mankind, as I have often told you, is more governed by appearances than by realities;

17. And with regard to opinion, people think they had better be really hard, with the appearance of softness, than the reverse.

18. They know that few have penetration enough to discover, attention enough to observe, or even concern enough to examine beyond the exterior;

19. They take their notions from the surface, and go no deeper: they commend, as the gentlest and best-natured man in the world,

20. That man who has the most engaging exterior manner, though possibly they have been but once in his company.

21. An air, a tone of voice, a composure of countenance to mildness and softness, which are all easily acquired, do the business:

22. And without further examination, and possibly with the contrary qualities, that man is reckoned the gentlest, the best-natured man alive.

23. Happy the man who, with a certain fund of parts and knowledge, gets acquainted with the world early enough to make it his property, at an age when most people are the property of the world!

24. For that is the common case of

youth. They grow wiser when it is too late;

25. And, ashamed and vexed at having been owned so long, too often turn knaves at last.

26. Do not therefore trust to appearances and the outside of their behaviour to yourself;

27. You may be sure that nine in ten of mankind try this, and ever will trust to them.

Epistle 22

1. My son, your heart, I know, is good, your sense is sound and your knowledge extensive. What then remains for you to do?

2. Nothing, but to adorn those fundamental qualifications with such engaging manners as will endear you to those who are able to judge your real merit,

3. And which always stand in the stead of merit with those who are not thus able to judge.

4. Let misanthropes declaim as much as they please against the vices, the simulation and dissimulation of the world;

5. Those invectives are always the result of ignorance, ill-humour or envy.

6. Let them show me a cottage where there are not the same vices of which they accuse courts;

7. With this difference only, that in a cottage they appear in their native deformity, and that in courts, manners and good breeding make them less shocking.

8. No, be convinced that manners are a solid good; they prevent a great deal of real mischief;

9. They create, adorn and strengthen friendships; they keep hatred within bounds;

10. They promote good humour and goodwill in families, where the want of good breeding and gentleness of manners is commonly the original cause of discord.

11. Get then, before it is too late, a habit of the little virtues as well as the great ones;

12. Practise them, that they may be easy and familiar to you always; and pass through life with success that makes it possible for you to do more good in the world at large.

Epistle 23

1. It is clear that no man can live a happy life, or even a supportable life, without the study of wisdom.

2. You know also that a happy life is reached when our wisdom is brought to completion,

3. But that life is at least endurable even when our search for wisdom is only begun.

4. This idea, however, clear though it is, must be strengthened and implanted more deeply by daily reflection;

5. It is more important for you to keep the resolutions you have already made than to continue making others.

6. You must persevere, must develop new strength by continuous reflection, until that which is at first only an inclination becomes a settled purpose.

7. I have, my son, great hopes for you, and confidence that you will achieve much; but I do not wish you to slacken your efforts always to improve.

8. Examine yourself; scrutinise and observe yourself in divers ways; but mark, before all else, whether it is in philosophy as well as in life that you have made progress.

9. Philosophy is no trick to catch the public; it is not devised for show. It is a matter, not of words, but of reasonings.

10. It is not pursued in order that the day may yield amusement, or that our leisure may be relieved of tedium. It is far more important:

11. It moulds and constructs the mind; it orders our life, guides our conduct, shows us what we should do and what we should not do;

12. It sits at the helm and directs our course as we waver amid uncertainties.

13. Without it, no one can live fearlessly or in peace of mind.

14. Countless things that happen every hour call for advice; and such advice is to be sought in philosophy.

15. Do not allow your heart to weaken and grow indifferent. Hold fast to your resolve and establish it firmly,

in order that what is now resolve may become a habit of the mind.

16. If I know you well, my son, you have already been trying to find out, from the very beginning of these letters, the essence of what they bring to you.

17. Sift the letters again, and you will find it. Much of it comes from the wisdom of others, for whatever is well said by anyone is our own to take and keep.

Epistle 24

1. You remember that Epicurus wrote: 'If you live according to nature, you will never be poor; if you live according to opinion, you will never be rich.'

2. Nature's wants are slight; the demands of opinion are boundless.

3. Suppose that the property of many millionaires is heaped up in your possession. Suppose that fortune carries you far beyond the limits of a private income,

4. And you accumulate many treasures; you will only learn from such things to crave still more.

5. Natural desires are limited; but those which spring from false opinion typically have no stopping-point.

6. The false has no limits. When you are travelling on a road, there must be an end; but when astray, your wanderings are limitless.

7. Redirect your steps, therefore, from idle things, and when you wish to know whether what you seek is

based on a principled or a misleading desire, consider whether it can stop at any definite point.

8. If you find, after you have travelled far, that there is a more distant goal always in view, you may be right to think that you are on the wrong road.

Epistle 25

1. Make it your business, my son, to know joy. The mind that is happy and confident, able to lift itself above adverse circumstances,

2. Which is as steadfast in itself as it is considerate, just and temperate towards others,

3. Is a cheerful mind; but it is not a superficial cheer, lightly got. Rather, it comes from properly understanding yourself and the world of people.

4. The yield of poor mines is on the surface; the ores of rich mines lie underground, and make more bountiful returns for those who dig deeply.

5. I recommend to you, my son, to do the one thing that will most surely render you happy:

6. Be sceptical about things that glitter outwardly, are cheap and easy to get, and distract you from a clear understanding of what it is right to be and do;

7. Look towards the true good, and rely on what comes from your study and reflection, from your observation of life, and from the best part of yourself.

8. A sense of the good comes from a sound conscience, honourable purposes, right actions, contempt of the gifts of chance, and a rational approach to life's choices.

9. For people who leap from one purpose to another, or do not even leap but are carried over by chance, how can they hope to achieve a fixed and lasting good?

10. Very few control themselves and their affairs by a guiding purpose they have chosen for themselves;

11. The rest do not proceed, they are merely swept along, like flotsam on a river.

12. Of these, some are held back by sluggish waters and drift slowly along;

13. Others are torn along by a more violent current, unable to stop themselves;

14. Some, which are nearest the bank, are left there motionless as the current slackens;

15. And others are carried out to sea by the onrush of the stream, and lost.

16. None of these lives are as good to live as the life considered, chosen, enriched by understanding and shaped by purpose.

17. You remember, my son, another saying by Epicurus: 'They live ill who are always beginning to live.'

18. Some men, indeed, only begin to live when it is time for them to leave off living; some men cease living before they have begun.

19. To live at all is to live well: that is

the burden of all that I have written to you,

20. For we must live not just in the world but in the world of human-kind; that is where we flourish or fail,

21. That is where we can make our contribution to the good not just of ourselves but of our fellows, and well justify our place among them.

22. Gentle in manner, strong in mind, a good proponent of the smaller graces and accomplishments as well as of the greater accomplish-ments they support:

23. Such I would have you, my son, and I commend these lessons to you for your greater benefit and happiness.

THE GOOD

Chapter 1

1. There is a time when nothing is said or thought, but only felt or tasted: the time when the object of happiness is happiness itself.

2. Then one rises with the sun and is happy, one goes walking and is happy, one sees the faces of one's family and is happy.

3. One wanders in the woods and fields and along the hillsides, and is happy; one reads or idles in the sun, and is happy;

4. One picks the fruit or takes water to the flower beds, and is happy; and happiness follows one everywhere.

5. When is this? In the safety of childhood in a country of wealth and peace;

6. With health and leisure, and parents to love one, and quiet nights for sleep;

7. When we have driven away all that troubles or frightens us, there is tranquillity and freedom.

8. Then comes a boundless joy that endures, then comes harmony of mind with nobility and kindliness, for it is only from weakness that evil is born.

9. And yet, the troubled man will see these words and say: 'You speak here only of the idyll of a thoughtless child. Childhood is brief, and few places wholly safe;

10. 'Life is otherwise than such idealism paints it. Its truths are hard, and inevitable:

11. 'And these truths are that we suffer, that our lot is to lose and to grieve, and finally to undergo the pain of dying before the release of death.

12. 'What we must learn is how to endure, how to accept, how to keep our dignity despite the assaults of frailty, of misfortune, and the malice of man.'

13. Alas: there is indeed suffering, frailty and malice; and there are the ill chances that bring or worsen all three. And yet still, the good is possible.

14. The first step of the good life is to seek wisdom and give up fear.

15. Wisdom teaches what is worthwhile and what is illusory.

16. It brings proportion and measure, it dispenses with the false glare cast by human vanity and cupidity, by fashion, falsehood, ignorance and folly.

17. The fear that hampers life is the fear of loss, especially the ultimate loss that is death.

18. Death has two faces: one's own death, and the death of those we

love. Wisdom looks into the eyes of each face and sees there what it must.

19. What is it to die? It is to return to the elements, to continue as part of the whole but in a different way.

20. Now we are a living unity, then we will be changed into something diffuse and organic, part of nature no less than we are now, and no less than we always were before our present form.

21. Thus the components of our substance exist for ever, coeval with the universe, made in the stars and in an endless dance with other elements, constituted and reconstituted throughout time by nature's laws.

22. Though we cease as we now are, what we are never ceases. We are part of the whole, and always so.

23. History cannot shed us from its annals any more than nature can annihilate the particles of our being from its scheme.

24. We are for ever part of what is, indelible, written in the record of nature and the human story, whatever our part or place.

25. For the time we have this shape and this consciousness of its possession, let us be worthy of it.

Chapter 2

1. It is in the death of others that our deepest grief and greatest loss comes.

2. From the viewpoint of our brief and local lives we do not see the loss as change only, or as a returning: rather, it strikes us with the iron of grief.

3. To live is to have a contract with loss. The past eludes us, and carries away what we valued;

4. Some of those we love will surely die before we do, and we will mourn them.

5. For this we must have courage; necessity is hard, so we must accept what is inevitable and unavoidable, and endure.

6. Thus far the troubled man is right, and the truths he insists on are truths indeed.

7. But even grief abates, and those we grieve, if they could speak, would tell us that they do not wish us to grieve for ever,

8. But would wish us to remember the best of them, and to return our thoughts to life and the good. And life is the endeavour of the good.

9. We honour them most, and cherish the memory of them best, by obeying the injunction to live, and to seek the good that endures.

Chapter 3

1. It is this that gives value to remembering the best of our times, so that we know the face of the good always.

2. In youth, before ever we lost sight of it, we were fully alive, and inhabited our hours with inexpressible satisfaction,

3. So that its weariness was as lovely to us as its refreshment.

4. The earth was a glorious orchestra,

and we were its audience, thrilling to the birdsong and the symphony of the breezes;

5. How we remember being astonished by the ecstasies unfolded to us in its music!

6. Sometimes we recapture the joy of savouring our being, not the material pleasure merely of eating and drinking,

7. Of seeing beautiful things or hearing pleasant sounds, of talking or resting;

8. But the different, delicate, larger happiness of being part of the great whole,

9. Of being oneself with one's own life, one's own impressions and thoughts.

10. It is a wonderful and grand thing to be oneself and part of all, and to have the dignity of the capacity for thought.

11. And so it is that when I dance, I dance; when I sleep, I sleep; and yes, when I walk alone in an orchard in the summer light,

12. If my thoughts have been elsewhere, they come back, and dwell on the good of that moment;

13. They come back to the orchard and the light, to the sweetness of the solitude, and to me.

14. To discover and inhabit such experiences is not only the most fundamental but the most illustrious of our occupations; without them we have not lived.

15. Truly, our great and glorious masterpiece is to live appropriately.

Chapter 4

1. The good is two freedoms: freedom from certain hindrances and pains, freedom to choose and to act.

2. The first is freedom from ignorance, fear, loneliness, folly, and the inability to master one's emotions;

3. The second is freedom to develop the best capacities and talents we have, and to use them for the best.

4. The good is what lies within reach of our talents for good, which means that there are as many goods as there are such talents.

5. There is not one single kind of good that suits and fits everyone; there are as many good lives as there are people to live them.

6. It is false that there is only one right way to live and one right way to be,

7. And that to find it we must obey those who claim to have the secret of a 'one right way' and a 'one true good'.

8. If there are guides to the good, one must eventually leave them behind and seek the good of one's choice, and which suits one's own talents.

9. This is the ultimate responsibility: to choose, and to cultivate the talents for one's choice.

10. But though there are many goods and many good kinds of life, the latter will share two notable characteristics:

11. The first is that those seeking them will honour affection, beauty, creativity, peace, patience, fortitude, courage;

12. Will honour self-mastery, wisdom, loyalty, justice, sympathy and kindness;

13. Will honour knowledge, truth, probity and honour itself.

14. And the greatest of what they honour will be affection: of a friend for a friend, a parent for a child, between lovers, between comrades;

15. For affection calls out to the other virtues and teaches them, and is the motive for the continuance of our kind.

16. The second is that lives in which these virtues are honoured will be regarded by those living them, and those touched by them, as good.

17. To seek the good life is an endeavour for a whole life.

18. One can improve, learn, encourage oneself, profit from failure; and still be seeking it on the last day.

Chapter 5

1. Truly, life is short: it must be used well.

2. The flight of time is unstoppably swift, as those see more clearly who are looking backwards.

3. For when we concentrate on the present we do not notice time slipping by, so quick and invisible is its passage.

4. Do you ask the reason for this? All past time is in the same place; it all presents the same aspect to us, it lies together; everything slips into the same abyss.

5. The time we spend in living is merely a point; indeed, even less than a point;

6. But this point of time, infinitesimal as it is, nature has mocked by making it seem outwardly of longer duration.

7. She has taken one portion of it and made it infancy, another portion childhood, another portion youth,

8. Another the gradual incline from youth to old age, and old age itself is still another.

9. How many steps for how short a climb! It was only a moment ago that I saw a friend depart on a journey;

10. And yet this 'moment ago' makes up a large share of my existence, which is so brief.

11. We should reflect, therefore, that it will soon come to an end altogether.

12. In other years time did not seem to go so swiftly; now, it seems fast beyond belief, perhaps, because I feel that the finish-line is moving closer to me,

13. Or it may be that I have begun to notice this at last, and to count my gains and losses.

14. For this reason it amazes me that some people give the major portion of their time to superfluous things,

15. Time which, no matter how carefully it is guarded, cannot suffice even for necessary things.

16. If the number of my days were doubled, I would still not have time to read all the poets.

17. When a soldier is undisturbed and

travelling at his ease, he can hunt
for trifles along his way;

18. But when the enemy is closing in,
and a command is given to quicken
the pace,

19. Necessity makes him throw away
everything that he picked up in
moments of peace and leisure.

Chapter 6

1. Behold, then, the gathering clans,
the fast-shut gates, and weapons
whetted ready for the war!

2. I need a stout heart to hear,
without flinching, the din of time's
battle that sounds round me.

3. And all would rightly think me
mad if, when greybeards and
women were heaping up rocks for
the fortifications,

4. When the armour-clad youths
inside the gates were awaiting, or
even demanding, the order for a
sally,

5. When the spears of the foe were
quivering in our gates and the very
ground was rocking with mines and
subterranean passages,

6. I say, they would rightly think me
mad if I were to sit idle, wasting
time on petty and superfluous
things.

7. And yet I may well seem in your
eyes no less mad, if I spend my
energies on trivialities; for even
now I am in a state of siege.

8. And yet, in the former case it
would be merely a peril from the
outside that threatened me,

9. And a wall that divided me from

the foe; as it is now, death-dealing
perils are in my very presence.

10. I have no time for such nonsense; a
mighty undertaking is on my
hands: the summation of my life,
and its value.

11. This is when men say: 'What am I
to do? Death is on my trail, and life
is fleeting away;

12. 'Teach me something with which
to face these inevitabilities.

13. 'Bring it to pass that I shall cease
trying to escape from death, so that
life may cease to escape from me.

14. 'Give me courage to meet hardships; make me calm in the face of
the unavoidable. Relax the tight
limits of the time which is allotted
me.

15. 'Show me that the good in life does
not depend on life's length, but on
the use we make of it;

16. 'Also, that it is possible, or rather
usual, for a man who has lived long
to have lived too little.

17. 'Say to me that I am mistaken if I
think that only on an ocean voyage
is there a very slight space between
life and death.

18. 'No, the distance between is just as
narrow everywhere. It is not
everywhere that death shows itself
so near at hand; yet everywhere it is
as near at hand.

19. 'Rid me of these shadowy terrors;
then you will more easily deliver to
me the instruction for which I have
prepared myself.

20. 'At our birth nature made us
teachable, and gave us reason, not

perfect, but capable of being perfected.

21. 'Discuss for me justice, duty, thrift and virtue. If you will only refuse to lead me along by-paths, I shall more easily reach the goal at which I aim. For the language of truth is simple.'

Chapter 7

1. If we indulge in nothing but a life of indolence and luxury, the life of the degenerate who thinks that labour is the worst of evils and freedom from toil the height of happiness,

2. Then it will happen that the day will come, and speedily, when we shall be unworthy of ourselves,

3. And with the loss of honour will come the loss of all we hold dear.

4. To have been valiant once is not enough; no man can keep his valour unless he watches over it to the end.

5. As the arts decay through neglect, as the body, once healthy and alert, grows weak through sloth and indolence,

6. Even so the powers of the mind, temperance, self-control and courage, if we grow slack in training, fall back once more to uselessness.

7. We must watch ourselves; we must not surrender to the temptations of laxity that go far beyond rest or pleasure.

8. It is a great work to make a life that is good for ourselves and our fellows, but a far greater to keep it good.

9. To make a good life takes dedication, but to keep it so is impossible without self-restraint, self-command and thoughtfulness.

10. We must not forget this; we must learn the lesson that our enjoyment of good things is in proportion to the pains we undergo for them.

11. Toil is the seasoning of delight; without desire and longing, no dish, however costly, could be sweet.

12. Therefore let us strain every nerve to win and to keep nobility of mind.

13. For what excuse could we offer for becoming unworthy of ourselves, if our very success at attaining the good made us so?

14. Are idleness, thoughtlessness, cowardice, then, the adjuncts of happiness? No: let us watch over ourselves, and maintain the good we have attained;

15. Let us encourage ourselves in the pursuit and keeping of all that is beautiful and brave.

16. And furthermore let us educate our children according to these precepts, if children are born to us,

17. For we cannot but become better ourselves if we strive to set the best example we can to our children,

18. And our children could hardly grow up to be unworthy, even if they wished,

19. When they see nothing base before them, and hear nothing shameful,

20. But live in the practice of all that is beautiful and good.

Chapter 8

1. Shall we ask, by what commandments should we live?
2. Or might we better ask, each of ourselves:
3. What kind of person should I be?
4. The first question assumes that there is one right answer.
5. The second assumes that there are many right answers.
6. If we ask how to answer the second question, we are answered in yet other questions:
7. What should you do when you see another suffering, or in need, afraid, or hungry?
8. What causes are worthy, what world do you dream of where your child plays safely in the street?
9. There are many such questions, some already their own answer, some unanswerable.
10. But when all the answers to all the questions are summed together, no one hears less than this:
11. Love well, seek the good in all things, harm no others, think for yourself, take responsibility, respect nature, do your utmost, be informed, be kind, be courageous: at least, sincerely try.
12. Add to these ten injunctions, this: O friends, let us always be true to ourselves and to the best in things, so that we can always be true to one another.

Chapter 9

1. Seek always for the good that abides. There can be none except as the mind finds it within itself;
2. Wisdom alone affords everlasting and peace-giving joy, for then, even if some obstacle arises,
3. It is only like an intervening cloud, which floats beneath the sun but never prevails against it.
4. When will you attain this joy? It will begin when you think for yourself,
5. When you truly take responsibility for your own life,
6. When you join the fellowship of all who have stood up as free individuals and said,
7. 'We are of the company of those who seek the true and the right, and live accordingly;
8. 'In our human world, in the short time we each have,
9. 'We see our duty to make and find something good for ourselves and our companions in the human predicament.'
10. Let us help one another, therefore; let us build the city together,
11. Where the best future might inhabit, and the true promise of humanity be realised at last.

The Good Book is made from over a thousand texts by several hundred authors and from collections and anonymous traditions, among the most drawn upon being:

Abulfazi, Aeschylus, Anacreontia, Antisthenes, Aristotle, Aurelius, Bacon, Baudelaire, Bayle, Bentham, Beyle, Boyle, Buonarotti, Carvaka, Cato, Catullus, Chaucer, Chesterfield, Cicero, Clemens, Condillac, Condorcet, Confucius, Constant, Cowley, Cowper, Cuihao, d'Alembert, Darwin, Demosthenes, d'Holbach, Diderot, Dryden, Dufu, Emerson, Epictetus, Epicurus, Euripides, folklore, folktales, Gellius, Godwin, Goethe, Grayling, Greek anthology, Hafiz, Harrington, Hazlitt, Herodotus, Herrick, Hobbes, Homer, Horace, Hume, Huxley, Jefferson, Jonson, Juvenal, Kant, Kautilya, Laozi, Libai, Liuyuxi, Locke, Lovelace, Lucretius, Lysias, Machiavelli, Marmontel, Martial, Menander, Mencius, Mill, Milton, Montaigne, Montesquieu, Mozi, Naevius, Nerval, Newton, Nietzsche, Ovid, Paine, Pater, Petrarch, Plato, Pliny, Plutarch, Polybius, Propertius, Rimbaud, Rousseau, Rumi, Sainte-Beuve, Sallust, Sappho, Schiller, Schopenhauer, Seneca, Shaftesbury, Shangguanyi, Shijing, Sophocles, Spinoza, Suetonius, Sully-Prudhomme, Sunzi, Swift, Tacitus, Terence, Thomson, Thucydides, Tibullus, traditional, Turgot, Valery, Vergil, Verlaine, Voltaire, Walpole, Wangbo, Wangwei, Xenophon, Zhuxi.